THE
top10★
OF EVERYTHING
2002

THE
top10
OF EVERYTHING
2002

RUSSELL ASH

A Dorling Kindersley Book

Contents

LONDON, NEW YORK, PARIS, MUNICH,
MELBOURNE, DELHI

A PENGUIN COMPANY

Senior Editor Nicki Lampon
Senior Art Editor Kevin Ryan

DTP Designer Sonia Charbonnier
Production Louise Daly
Picture Research Anna Grapes

Managing Editor Sharon Lucas
Senior Managing Art Editor Derek Coombes

Produced for Dorling Kindersley by
Cooling Brown, 9–11 High Street,
Hampton, Middlesex TW12 2SA

Senior Editor Alison Bolus
Art Editor Tish Mills
Creative Director Arthur Brown

Author's Project Manager Aylla Macphail

Published in Great Britain in 2001 by
Dorling Kindersley Limited,
80 Strand, London WC2R 0RL

2 4 6 8 10 9 7 5 3 1

A CIP catalogue record of this book is available from the British Library.

ISBN 07513 3393 X

Reproduction by Colourscan, Singapore
Printed and bound by Printer Industria Grafica, S.A., Barcelona, Spain

See our complete catalogue at
www.dk.com

Culture & Learning

Word Power 100
Children at School 102
Higher Education 104
Libraries of the World . . . 106
Book Firsts & Records . . 108
Bestsellers &
Literary Awards 110
The Press 112
Toys & Games 114
Art on Show 116
Art on Sale 118
20th-Century Artists 120
Women Artists 122
Objects of Desire 124

Music & Musicians

Popular Songs 128
Chart Hits 130
Record Firsts 132
Chart Toppers 134
Hit Singles of the Decades . . 136
Hit Albums of the Decades 138
Female Singers 140
All-Time Greats 142
Top of the Pops 144
Music Genres 146
Gold & Platinum Disks 148
Classical & Opera 150

Stage & Screen

All the World's a Stage 154
Film Hits 156
Films of the Decades 158
Film Genres 160
Oscar-Winning Films 162
Oscar-Winning Stars 164
And the Winner Is 166
Leading Men 168
Leading Ladies 170
The Directors &
Writers 172
The Studios 174
Film Out-Takes 176
Film Music 178
Animated Action 180
On the Radio 182
Top TV 184
TV Awards 186
Top Videos 188

Commerce & Industry

Wealth of Nations 192
Workers of the World 194
Company Matters 196
Advertising & Brands 198
Retail Therapy 200
That's Rich 202
Natural Resources 204
Energy & Environment 206
Science & Invention 208
Communication Matters 210
The World Wide Web 212
Hazards at Home & Work 214
Industrial & Other Disasters 216
Food for Thought 218
Sweet Dreams 220
Alcoholic & Soft Drinks 222

On the Move

Speed Records 226
Cars & Road Transport 228
Road Accidents 230
Rail Transport 232
Water Transport 234
Air Records 236
Air Transport 238
World Tourism 240

The Sporting World

Summer Olympics 244
Winter Olympics 246
American Football 248
Athletic Achievements 250
Basketball Bests 252
Combat Sports 254
Test Cricket 256
Football Stars 258
International Football 260
Free Wheelers 262
Motor Racing 264
Golfing Greats 266
Horse Racing 268
Rugby Records 270
What a Racquet 272
Water Sports 274
Winter Sports 276
Sporting Miscellany 278

Index 280
Acknowledgments . 287

Introduction

It's a Fact

If you have been buying *The Top 10 of Everything* every year since it was first published, you will now have 13 copies on your book shelf. Fortunately, I do not suffer from triskaidekaphobia (the fear of the number 13), but it is through researching and compiling Top 10 lists that I have discovered a wealth of unusual facts – such as the word triskaidekaphobia. In this year's volume, you too can discover facts, from the 10 places with the heaviest daily downpours to the Top 10 skateboarders, and from the first lie detector to the identity of the originals behind James Bond and Barbie.

A Changing World

During recent years, certain lists have become widely featured in the press, among them lists of school league tables and richest people, while the popularity of general knowledge is exemplified by the increasing number of TV quiz shows. Over the past 13 years, the information that this book presents has changed, and the nature of Top 10 lists has changed too. The Top 10 professions of mobile phone users was once of interest, but now that so many people in Western countries have mobiles, such a list is synonymous with the Top 10 most common professions. Meanwhile, lists containing entries that have been valid for many centuries may alter: while work was in progress on this edition, the 5th tallest statue in the world, the 53-m (173-ft) Buddha at Bamian, Afghanistan, carved in the 3rd–4th centuries AD, was destroyed by the Taliban.

Information Superhighway

In the past, it often took years for data to be processed and disseminated. Today, the use of computers and the Internet means that information is more quickly and more readily available. One of the problems with information is that it piles up. Only a few hundred years ago, an educated person could be well informed about almost every aspect of the arts and sciences, but as each generation adds to the sum total of knowledge, so the task of sifting it for the items you require becomes an occupation in itself. I hope that *The Top 10 of Everything* offers some shortcuts through the information quagmire.

In and Out

To newcomers to *The Top 10 of Everything* it is worth mentioning that there are no "bests", other than bestsellers, and no "worsts" (with the exception of lists about disasters and murders, which are measurable by numbers of victims). The book focuses on superlatives in numerous categories, and also contains a variety of "firsts" or "latests", which recognize the pioneers and most recent achievers in various fields of endeavour. Top 10 lists of films are based on worldwide box office income, and those on such topics as recorded music, videos, DVDs, and books are based on sales, unless otherwise stated.

Thanks for Everything

My ever-expanding network of experts has enabled me to ensure that certain lists are constantly updated as new data become available. As ever, I want to thank the many people who have supplied information, especially private individuals, experts, and enthusiasts, who provide some of the most fascinating and otherwise quite unobtainable information. If you have any list ideas or comments, please write to me c/o the publishers or e-mail me direct at ash@pavilion.co.uk.

Other recent Dorling Kindersley books by Russell Ash:
  The Factastic Book of 1,001 Lists
  The Factastic Book of Comparisons
  Great Wonders of the World

Special Features

- More than 1,000 lists in many new categories make this the **most comprehensive** *Top 10 of Everything* ever.

- **Hundreds of new lists** are included, from the 10 countries with the most teenage brides to the Top 10 baked bean consumers.

- Interesting and unusual **2002 anniversaries** are celebrated throughout with "100 Years Ago" and "50 Years Ago" features.

- Numerous "Who Was…?" entries focus on the people behind **famous names**.

- "Did You Know?" entries offer **offbeat sidelights** on the subjects explored.

- **Quiz questions** with multi-choice answers appear throughout the book.

THE UNIVERSE & THE EARTH

Star Gazing

STARS NEAREST TO THE EARTH*

	STAR	LIGHT YEARS	KM (MILLIONS)	MILES (MILLIONS)
1	Proxima Centauri	4.22	39,923,310	24,792,500
2	Alpha Centauri	4.35	41,153,175	25,556,250
3	Barnard's Star	5.98	56,573,790	35,132,500
4	Wolf 359	7.75	73,318,875	45,531,250
5	Lalande 21185	8.22	77,765,310	48,292,500
6	Luyten 726-8	8.43	79,752,015	49,526,250
7	Sirius	8.65	81,833,325	50,818,750
8	Ross 154	9.45	89,401,725	55,518,750
9	Ross 248	10.40	98,389,200	61,100,000
10	Epsilon Eridani	10.80	102,173,400	63,450,000

Excluding the Sun

A spaceship travelling at 40,237 km/h (25,000 mph) – which is faster than any human has yet reached in space – would take more than 113,200 years to reach the Earth's closest star, Proxima Centauri. While the nearest stars in this list lie just over four light years away from the Earth, others within the Milky Way lie at a distance of 2,500 light years. Our own galaxy may span as much as 100,000 light years from end to end, with the Sun some 25,000 to 30,000 light years from its centre.

NEAR NEIGHBOUR

Proxima Centauri, Earth's closest star beyond the Sun, was discovered in 1913 by Scottish astronomer Robert Thorburn Innes. It has 10 per cent of the Sun's mass but only 0.006 per cent of its luminosity.

BODIES IN THE SOLAR SYSTEM WITH THE GREATEST SURFACE GRAVITY*

	BODY	SURFACE GRAVITY	WEIGHT (KG)#
1	Sun	27.90	1,813.50
2	Jupiter	2.64	171.60
3	Neptune	1.20	78.00
4	Uranus	1.17	76.05
5	Saturn	1.16	75.40
6	Earth	1.00	65.00
7	Venus	0.90	58.50
8 =	Mars	0.38	24.70
=	Mercury	0.38	24.70
10	Pluto	0.06	3.90

*Excluding satellites

Of a 65 kg adult on the body's surface

SMALL WONDER

Pluto is less than a fifth of the size of the Earth. Not only is it the smallest of the Solar System's planets, it also has the lowest gravity. It was discovered in 1930 by American astronomer Clyde Tombaugh.

THIN ICE

Saturn is the furthest planet that can be seen with the naked eye. Its rings, which are composed of ice, are up to 270,000 km (167,770 miles) in diameter, but only a few metres thick.

TOP 10 ★
MOST MASSIVE BODIES IN THE SOLAR SYSTEM*

	BODY	MASS#
1	Sun	332,800.000
2	Jupiter	317.828
3	Saturn	95.161
4	Neptune	17.148
5	Uranus	14.536
6	Earth	1.000
7	Venus	0.815
8	Mars	0.10745
9	Mercury	0.05527
10	Pluto	0.0022

* *Excluding satellites*

Compared with the Earth = 1; the mass of Earth is approximately 73.5 billion tonnes

TOP 10 ★
GALAXIES NEAREST TO THE EARTH

	GALAXY	DISTANCE (LIGHT YEARS)
1	Large Cloud of Magellan	169,000
2	Small Cloud of Magellan	190,000
3	Ursa Minor dwarf	250,000
4	Draco dwarf	260,000
5	Sculptor dwarf	280,000
6	Fornax dwarf	420,000
7 =	Leo I dwarf	750,000
=	Leo II dwarf	750,000
9	Barnard's Galaxy	1,700,000
10	Andromeda Spiral	2,200,000

These, and other galaxies, are members of the so-called "Local Group", although with vast distances such as these, "local" is clearly a relative term.

TOP 10 ★
BODIES IN THE SOLAR SYSTEM WITH THE GREATEST ESCAPE VELOCITY*

	BODY	ESCAPE VELOCITY (KM/SEC)
1	Sun	617.50
2	Jupiter	60.22
3	Saturn	32.26
4	Neptune	23.90
5	Uranus	22.50
6	Earth	11.18
7	Venus	10.36
8	Mars	5.03
9	Mercury	4.25
10	Pluto	1.18

* *Excluding satellites*

Escape velocity is the speed a rocket has to attain upon launching to overcome the gravitational pull of the body it is leaving. The escape velocity of the Moon is 2.38 km/sec.

TOP 10 ★
LONGEST YEARS IN THE SOLAR SYSTEM

	BODY	LENGTH OF YEAR* YEARS	DAYS
1	Pluto	247	256
2	Neptune	164	298
3	Uranus	84	4
4	Saturn	29	168
5	Jupiter	11	314
6	Mars	1	322
7	Earth		365
8	Venus		225
9	Mercury		88
10	Sun		0

* *Period of orbit round the Sun, in Earth years/days (based on a non-leap year of 365 days)*

TOP 10 ★
LARGEST BODIES IN THE SOLAR SYSTEM

	BODY	MAXIMUM DIAMETER KM	MILES
1	Sun	1,392,140	865,036
2	Jupiter	142,984	88,846
3	Saturn	120,536	74,898
4	Uranus	51,118	31,763
5	Neptune	49,532	30,778
6	Earth	12,756	7,926
7	Venus	12,103	7,520
8	Mars	6,794	4,222
9	Ganymede	5,269	3,274
10	Titan	5,150	3,200

Most of the planets are visible from the Earth with the naked eye and have been observed since ancient times. The exceptions are Uranus, discovered on 13 March 1781 by the British astronomer Sir William Herschel; Neptune, found by German astronomer Johann Galle on 23 September 1846 (Galle was led to his discovery by the independent calculations of the French astronomer Urbain Leverrier and the British mathematician John Adams); and, outside the Top 10, Pluto, located using photographic techniques by American astronomer Clyde Tombaugh on 13 March 1930.

Did You Know? The name of the planet Pluto was suggested two days after its discovery by Venetia Burney, an 11-year-old English schoolgirl. Pluto is the Roman god of the underworld, but the name also begins with the initials of Percival Lowell, the astronomer who had suggested its existence.

Asteroids, Meteorites & Comets

MOST FREQUENTLY SEEN COMETS

COMET	YEARS BETWEEN APPEARANCES
1 Encke	3.302
2 Grigg-Skjellerup	4.908
3 Honda-Mrkós-Pajdusáková	5.210
4 Tempel 2	5.259
5 Neujmin 2	5.437
6 Brorsen	5.463
7 Tuttle-Giacobini-Kresák	5.489
8 Tempel-L. Swift	5.681
9 Tempel 1	5.982
10 Pons-Winnecke	6.125

These and several other comets return with regularity (although with some notable variations), while others have such long orbits that they may not be seen again for many thousands, or even millions, of years.

OBJECTS COMING CLOSEST TO THE EARTH

NAME/DESIGNATION	DUE DATE*	DISTANCE# KM	DISTANCE# MILES
1 1999 RQ36	23 Sep 2080	209,440	130,130
2 1998 HH49	17 Oct 2023	374,000	232,393
3 1999 AN10	7 Aug 2027	388,960	241,689
4 1999 RQ36	23 Sep 2060	733,040	455,490
5 1999 MN	3 June 2010	792,880	492,673
6 Hathor (2340)	21 Oct 2086	837,760	520,560
7 1999 RM45	3 Mar 2021	882,640	548,447
8 1997 XF11	26 Oct 2028	912,560	567,038
9 2000 LF3	16 June 2046	972,400	604,221
10 Hathor (2340)	21 Oct 2069	987,360	613,517

* Of closest approach to the Earth

\# Closest distance from Earth

Source: *NASA*

It is believed that there are up to 2,000 "Near-Earth objects" (mostly asteroids and comets) over 1 km (0.6 miles) in diameter that approach Earth's orbit.

COMETS THAT HAVE COME CLOSEST TO THE EARTH

COMET	DATE*	DISTANCE# KM	DISTANCE# MILES
1 Comet of 1491	20 Feb 1491	1,406,220	873,784
2 Lexell	1 July 1770	2,258,928	1,403,633
3 Tempel-Tuttle	26 Oct 1366	3,425,791	2,128,688
4 IRAS-Araki-Alcock	11 May 1983	4,682,413	2,909,516
5 Halley	10 Apr 837	4,996,569	3,104,724
6 Biela	9 Dec 1805	5,475,282	3,402,182
7 Grischow	8 Feb 1743	5,834,317	3,625,276
8 Pons-Winnecke	26 June 1927	5,894,156	3,662,458
9 Comet of 1014	24 Feb 1014	6,088,633	3,783,301
10 La Hire	20 Apr 1702	6,537,427	4,062,168

* Of closest approach to the Earth

\# Closest distance from the Earth

HALLEY'S COMET

The predicted return of Halley's Comet, seen here during its most recent appearance in 1986, proved the theory that comets follow fixed orbits.

LARGEST METEORITES EVER FOUND

	LOCATION	ESTIMATED WEIGHT (TONNES)
1	**Hoba West**, Grootfontein, Namibia	more than 60.0
2	**Ahnighito** ("The Tent"), Cape York, West Greenland	57.3
3	**Campo del Cielo**, Argentina	41.4
4	**Canyon Diablo***, Arizona, USA	30.0
5	**Sikhote-Alin**, Russia	27.0
6	**Chupaderos**, Mexico	24.2
7	**Bacuberito**, Mexico	22.0
8	**Armanty**, Western Mongolia	20.0
9	**Mundrabilla**#, Western Australia	17.0
10	**Mbosi**, Tanzania	16.0

* *Formed Meteor Crater; fragmented; total in public collections is around 11.5 tonnes*

In two parts

SOURCES OF ASTEROID NAMES

	SOURCE	ASTEROIDS*
1	**Astronomers, astrophysicists, and planetary scientists**	1,040
2	**Places and cultures**	822
3	**Scientists other than astronomers**	551
4	**Mythological characters**	439
5	**Astronomers' families and friends**	406
6	**Historical personalities**	360
7	**Writers and editors**	275
8	**Amateur astronomers**	132
9	**Musicians, composers, and film and TV directors**	130
10	**Literary characters**	112

* *Based on an analysis of 4,619 named asteroids within the first 6,000 discovered*

Source: *Jacob Schwartz, Asteroid Name Encyclopedia, 1995*

Asteroid names have also been derived from individuals in fields such as singing and dancing, and art and architecture.

EARTH IMPACT

The Canyon Diablo, or Barringer meteorite crater, in Arizona, one of the largest on the Earth, was caused by the impact of a meteorite weighing 63,000 tonnes, of which some 30 tonnes have been recovered.

LARGEST ASTEROIDS

	NAME	YEAR DISCOVERED	DIAMETER KM	MILES
1	**Ceres**	1801	936	582
2	**Pallas**	1802	607	377
3	**Vesta**	1807	519	322
4	**Hygeia**	1849	450	279
5	**Euphrosyne**	1854	370	229
6	**Interamnia**	1910	349	217
7	**Davida**	1903	322	200
8	**Cybele**	1861	308	192
9	**Europa**	1858	288	179
10	**Patientia**	1899	275	171

Asteroids, sometimes known as "minor planets", are fragments of rock orbiting between Mars and Jupiter. There are perhaps 45,000 of them, but only about 10 per cent have been named. The first and largest to be discovered was Ceres.

LARGEST METEORITES EVER FOUND IN THE UK

	LOCATION	DATE FOUND	WEIGHT KG	LB
1	**Barwell**, Leicestershire	24 Dec 1965	44.0	97.0
2	**Wold Cottage**, Yorkshire	13 Dec 1795	25.4	56.0
3	**Appley Bridge**, Lancashire	13 Oct 1914	15.0	33.0
4	**Strathmore**, Tayside	3 Dec 1917	13.0	28.7
5	**Bovedy**, Co. Londonderry, N. Ireland	25 Apr 1969	5.4	11.9
6	**High Possil**, Strathclyde	5 Apr 1804	4.5	9.9
7	**Crumlin**, Antrim, N. Ireland	13 Sep 1902	4.3	9.5
8	**Rowton**, Shropshire	20 Apr 1876	3.5	7.7
9	**Middlesborough**, Cleveland	14 Mar 1881	1.6	3.5
10	**Ashdon**, Essex	9 Mar 1923	1.3	2.9

In which country is the world's highest waterfall?
see p.18 for the answer
A Norway
B Venezuela
C Nepal

13

Space Discoveries

HUBBLE

American astronomer Edwin Powell Hubble (1889–1953) led a varied career, including heavyweight boxing and studying law at Oxford University, before becoming a professional astronomer. After World War I, he worked at the Mount Wilson Observatory, home of the then most powerful telescope in the world. In 1923 he proved that the Universe extended beyond the Milky Way, and in 1929 that the universe is expanding. This became known as Hubble's Law. Named in his honour, the Hubble Telescope, launched in 1990 by Space Shuttle *Discovery*, has enabled exploration of distant galaxies without the atmospheric interference that is encountered on the Earth.

TOP 10 MOST RECENT PLANETARY MOONS TO BE DISCOVERED

(Moon/planet/year)

❶ **S/1999J1**, Jupiter, 2000
❷ = **Prospero**, Uranus, 1999; = **Setebos**, Uranus, 1999; = **Stephano**, Uranus, 1999
❺ = **Caliban**, Uranus, 1997;
= **Sycorax**, Uranus, 1997 ❼ **Pan**, Saturn, 1990
❽ = **Despina**, Neptune, 1989; = **Naiad**, Neptune, 1989; = **Thalassa**, Neptune, 1989

Space probe *Voyager 2* discovered six moons of Neptune on the same day (25 Aug 1989). Those listed in the Top 10 were the first, followed by Galatea, Larissa, and Proteus.

TOP 10 ★ LARGEST REFLECTING TELESCOPES

TELESCOPE NAME/LOCATION	APERTURE M	FT
1 **Keck I & II Telescopes***, Mauna Kea, Hawaii, USA	10.0	32.8
2 **Hobby-Eberly Telescope**, Mount Fowlkes, Texas, USA	9.2	30.9
3 **Subaru Telescope**, Mauna Kea, Hawaii, USA	8.3	27.2
4 **Gemini North Telescope**, Mauna Kea, Hawaii, USA	8.0	25.6
5 **MMT**#, Mount Hopkins, Arizona, USA	6.5	21.3
6 **Bolshoi Teleskop Azimutalnyi**, Nizhny Arkhyz, Russia	6.0	19.6
7 **Hale Telescope**, Palomar Mountain, California, USA	5.0	16.4
8 **William Herschel Telescope**, La Palma, Canary Islands, Spain	4.2	13.8
9 **Victor Blanco Telescope**, Gerro Tololo, Chile	4.0	13.1
10 **Anglo-Australian Telescope**, Coonabarabran, NSW, Australia	3.9	12.8

* Identical telescopes that work in tandem to produce the largest reflecting surface

 # Formerly the Multiple Mirror Telescope

Antu, Kueyen, and Melipal, three telescopes located in Cerro Paranal, Chile, are soon to be combined to form the appropriately named Very Large Telescope, which will take first place in this list with an aperture of 16.4 m (53.8 ft). The Keck telescopes will combine with several smaller scopes to form the 14.6 m (47.9 ft) Keck Interferometer.

GALILEAN DISCOVERY

Ganymede, largest of Jupiter's satellites, was among the four to be discovered by Galileo, on 7 January 1610, using the newly invented telescope.

THE 10 ★ FIRST PLANETARY MOONS TO BE DISCOVERED

	MOON/DISCOVERER	PLANET	YEAR
1	**Moon**	Earth	Ancient
2	=**Callisto**, Galileo Galilei	Jupiter	1610
	=**Europa**, Galileo Galilei	Jupiter	1610
	=**Ganymede**, Galileo Galilei	Jupiter	1610
	=**Io**, Galileo Galilei	Jupiter	1610
6	**Titan**, Christian Huygens	Saturn	1655
7	**Iapetus**, Giovanni Cassini	Saturn	1671
8	**Rhea**, Giovanni Cassini	Saturn	1672
9	=**Dione**, Giovanni Cassini	Saturn	1684
	=**Tethys**, Giovanni Cassini	Saturn	1684

While the Earth's moon has been observed since ancient times, it was not until the development of the telescope that Italian astronomer Galileo was able to discover (on 7 January 1610) the first moons of another planet. These, which are Jupiter's four largest, were named by German astronomer Simon Marius and are known as the Galileans.

HEAVENLY TWINS

Financed by US philanthropist W. M. Keck, twin telescopes Keck I (1993) and II (1996) on Mauna Kea, Hawaii, are the world's largest optical instruments.

Did You Know? Until 1986, Uranus was believed to have only five moons, but in that year interplanetary probe *Voyager 2* discovered 10 more, all but one of which were named after Shakespearean characters.

THE 10 ★
FIRST PLANETARY PROBES

	PROBE/COUNTRY	PLANET	ARRIVAL*
1	*Venera 4*, USSR	Venus	18 Oct 1967
2	*Venera 5*, USSR	Venus	16 May 1969
3	*Venera 6*, USSR	Venus	17 May 1969
4	*Venera 7*, USSR	Venus	15 Dec 1970
5	*Mariner 9*, USA	Mars	13 Nov 1971
6	*Mars 2*, USSR	Mars	27 Nov 1971
7	*Mars 3*, USSR	Mars	2 Dec 1971
8	*Venera 8*, USSR	Venus	22 July 1972
9	*Venera 9*, USSR	Venus	22 Oct 1975
10	*Venera 10*, USSR	Venus	25 Oct 1975

* Successfully entered orbit or landed

This list excludes "fly-bys" – probes that passed by but did not land on the surface of the planet. The USA's *Pioneer 10*, for example, flew past Jupiter on 3 December 1973, but did not land.

VENUSIAN VOLCANOES

Mapped by the Magellan probe, the volcanoes of Sif Mons (left) and Gula Mons (right) stand out above the lava surface of the Eistla Regio area of Venus.

THE 10 ★
FIRST BODIES TO HAVE BEEN VISITED BY SPACECRAFT

	BODY	SPACECRAFT/COUNTRY	DATE
1	Moon	*Luna 1*, USSR	2 Jan 1959
2	Venus	*Venera 1*, USSR	19 May 1961
3	Sun	*Pioneer 5*, USA	10 Aug 1961
4	Mars	*Mariner 4*, USA	14 July 1965
5	Jupiter	*Pioneer 10*, USA	3 Dec 1973
6	Mercury	*Mariner 10*, USA	29 Mar 1974
7	Saturn	*Pioneer 11*, USA	1 Sep 1979
8	Comet Giacobini-Zinner	*International Sun–Earth Explorer 3 (International Cometary Explorer)* Europe/USA	11 Sep 1985
9	Uranus	*Voyager 2*, USA	30 Jan 1986
10	Halley's Comet	*Vega 1*, USSR	6 Mar 1986

Only the first spacecraft successfully to approach or land on each body is included. Several of the bodies listed have since been visited on subsequent occasions, either by "fly-bys", orbiters, or landers. Other bodies also visited since the first 10 include Neptune (by *Voyager 2*, USA, 1989).

THE 10 ★
FIRST UNMANNED MOON LANDINGS

	NAME	COUNTRY	DATE (LAUNCH/IMPACT)
1	*Lunik 2*	USSR	12/14 Sep 1959
2	*Ranger 4**	USA	23/26 Apr 1962
3	*Ranger 6*	USA	30 Jan/2 Feb 1964
4	*Ranger 7*	USA	28/31 July 1964
5	*Ranger 8*	USA	17/20 Feb 1965
6	*Ranger 9*	USA	21/24 Mar 1965
7	*Luna 5**	USSR	9/12 May 1965
8	*Luna 7**	USSR	4/8 Oct 1965
9	*Luna 8**	USSR	3/7 Dec 1965
10	*Luna 9*	USSR	31 Jan/3 Feb 1966

* Crash-landing

In addition to these 10, debris left on the surface of the Moon includes the remains of several further Luna craft, including unmanned sample-collectors and *Lunakhod 1* and *2* (1966–71; all Soviet), seven *Surveyors* (1966–68; all US), and five *Lunar Orbiters* (1966–67; all US).

Space Explorers

THE 10 ★
FIRST MOONWALKERS

	ASTRONAUT	SPACECRAFT	TOTAL EVA* HR:MIN	MISSION DATES
1	Neil A. Armstrong	Apollo 11	2:32	16–24 July 1969
2	Edwin E. ("Buzz") Aldrin	Apollo 11	2:15	16–24 July 1969
3	Charles Conrad Jr.	Apollo 12	7:45	14–24 Nov 1969
4	Alan L. Bean	Apollo 12	7:45	14–24 Nov 1969
5	Alan B. Shepard	Apollo 14	9:23	31 Jan–9 Feb 1971
6	Edgar D. Mitchell	Apollo 14	9:23	31 Jan–9 Feb 1971
7	David R. Scott	Apollo 15	19:08	26 July–7 Aug 1971
8	James B. Irwin	Apollo 15	18:35	26 July–7 Aug 1971
9	John W. Young	Apollo 16	20:14	16–27 Apr 1972
10	Charles M. Duke	Apollo 16	20:14	16–27 Apr 1972

* Extra Vehicular Activity (i.e. time spent out of the lunar module on the Moon's surface)

Six US Apollo missions resulted in successful Moon landings (Apollo 13, 11–17 April 1970, was aborted after an oxygen tank exploded). During the last of these (Apollo 17, 7–19 December 1972), Eugene A. Cernan and Harrison H. Schmitt became the only other astronauts to date who have walked on the surface of the Moon.

TOP 10 ★
LONGEST SPACE MISSIONS*

	COSMONAUT	MISSION DATES	DAYS
1	Valeri V. Polyakov	8 Jan 1994–22 Mar 1995	437.7
2	Sergei V. Avdeyev	13 Aug 1998–28 Aug 1999	379.6
3 =	Musa K. Manarov	21 Dec 1987–21 Dec 1988	365.9
=	Vladimir G. Titov	21 Dec 1987–21 Dec 1988	365.9
5	Yuri V. Romanenko	5 Feb–5 Dec 1987	326.5
6	Sergei K. Krikalyov	18 May 1991–25 Mar 1992	311.8
7	Valeri V. Polyakov	31 Aug 1988–27 Apr 1989	240.9
8 =	Oleg Y. Atkov	8 Feb–2 Oct 1984	237.0
=	Leonid D. Kizim	8 Feb–2 Oct 1984	237.0
=	Anatoli Y. Solovyov	8 Feb–2 Oct 1984	237.0

* To 1 January 2001

Space medicine specialist Valeri Vladimirovich Polyakov spent his 52nd birthday in space during his record-breaking mission aboard the Mir space station. One of the station's purposes was to study the effects on the human body of long-duration spaceflight.

MAN ON THE MOON
On 21 April 1972, Apollo 16 commander John W. Young (shown here), along with Charles M. Duke (who took this photograph), became the 9th and 10th of the 12 people ever to set foot on the Moon.

TOP 10 ★
YOUNGEST ASTRONAUTS AND COSMONAUTS

ASTRONAUT OR COSMONAUT*	FIRST FLIGHT	AGE#
1 Gherman S. Titov	17 June 1970	25
2 Valentina V. Tereshkova	16 June 1963	26
3 Boris B. Yegorov	15 Oct 1964	26
4 Yuri A. Gagarin	12 Apr 1961	27
5 Helen P. Sharman, UK	18 May 1991	27
6 Dumitru D. Prunatiu, Romania	14 May 1981	28
7 Valery F. Bykovsky	14 June 1963	28
8 Salman Abdel Aziz Al-Saud, Saudi Arabia	17 June 1985	28
9 Vladimir Remek, Czechoslovakia	2 Mar 1978	29
10 Abdul Ahad Mohmand, Afghanistan	29 Aug 1988	29

* All from Russia unless otherwise stated

Those of apparently identical age have been ranked according to their precise age in days

TOP 10 ★
OLDEST ASTRONAUTS AND COSMONAUTS

ASTRONAUT OR COSMONAUT*	LAST FLIGHT	AGE#
1 John H. Glenn	6 Nov 1998	77
2 F. Story Musgrave	7 Dec 1996	61
3 Vance D. Brand	11 Dec 1990	59
4 Jean-Loup Chrétien, France	6 Oct 1997	59
5 Valery V. Ryumin, Russia	12 June 1998	58
6 Karl G. Henize	6 Aug 1985	58
7 Roger K. Crouch	17 July 1997	56
8 William E. Thornton	6 May 1985	56
9 Claude Nicollier, Switzerland	28 Dec 1999	55
10 Don L. Lind	6 May 1985	54

* All from the US unless otherwise stated

Those of apparently identical age have been ranked according to their precise age in days

THE 10 ★
FIRST COUNTRIES TO HAVE ASTRONAUTS OR COSMONAUTS IN ORBIT

COUNTRY/ASTRONAUT OR COSMONAUT	DATE*
1 USSR, Yuri A. Gagarin	12 Apr 1961
2 USA, John H. Glenn	20 Feb 1962
3 Czechoslovakia, Vladimir Remek	2 Mar 1978
4 Poland, Miroslaw Hermaszewski	27 June 1978
5 East Germany, Sigmund Jahn	26 Aug 1978
6 Bulgaria, Georgi I. Ivanov	10 Apr 1979
7 Hungary, Bertalan Farkas	26 May 1980
8 Vietnam, Pham Tuan	23 July 1980
9 Cuba, Arnaldo T. Mendez	18 Sep 1980
10 Mongolia, Jugderdemidiyn Gurragcha	22 Mar 1981

*Of first space entry of a national of that country

THE 10 ★
FIRST WOMEN IN SPACE

ASTRONAUT OR COSMONAUT/ COUNTRY/SPACECRAFT	DATE
1 Valentina V. Tereshkova, USSR, *Vostok 6*	16–19 June 1963
2 Svetlana Savitskaya, USSR, *Soyuz T7*	19 Aug 1982
3 Sally K. Ride, USA, *Challenger STS-7*	18–24 June 1983
4 Judith A. Resnik, USA, *Discovery STS-41-D*	30 Aug–5 Sep 1984
5 Kathryn D. Sullivan, USA, *Challenger STS-41-G*	5–13 Oct 1984
6 Anna L. Fisher, USA, *Discovery STS-51-A*	8–16 Nov 1984
7 Margaret Rhea Seddon, USA, *Discovery STS-51-D*	12–19 Apr 1985
8 Shannon W. Lucid, USA, *Discovery STS-51-G*	17–24 June 1985
9 Bonnie J. Dunbar, USA *Challenger STS-61-A*	30 Oct–6 Nov 1985
10 Mary L. Cleave, USA, *Atlantis STS-61-B*	26 Nov–3 Dec 1985

THE 10 ★
FIRST IN-FLIGHT SPACE FATALITIES

ASTRONAUT OR COSMONAUT(S)/INCIDENT

1 Vladimir M. Komarov
Launched on 24 April 1967, Soviet spaceship Soyuz 1 experienced various technical problems during its 18th orbit. After a successful re-entry, the capsule parachute was deployed at 7,010 m (23,000 ft), but its lines became tangled and it crash-landed near Orsk in the Urals, killing Komarov (the survivor of a previous one-day flight on 12 October 1964), who thus became the first-ever space fatality.

2 =Georgi T. Dobrovolsky
=Viktor I. Patsayev
=Vladislav N. Volkov
After a then record 23 days in space, including a link-up with the Salyut space station, the Soviet Soyuz 9 mission ended in disaster on 29 June 1971, when the capsule depressurized during re-entry. Although it landed intact, all three cosmonauts – who were not wearing spacesuits – were found to be dead. The ashes of the three men were buried, along with those of Yuri Gagarin and Vladimir Komarov, at the Kremlin, Moscow. Spacesuits have been worn during re-entry on all subsequent missions.

5 =Gregory B. Jarvis
=Sharon C. McAuliffe
=Ronald E. McNair
=Ellison S. Onizuka
=Judith A. Resnik
=Francis R. Scobee
=Michael J. Smith
The Challenger STS-51-L, the 25th Space Shuttle mission, exploded on take-off from Cape Canaveral, Florida, on 28 January 1986. The cause was determined to have been leakage of seals in the joint between rocket sections. The disaster, watched by thousands on the ground and millions on worldwide television, halted the US space programme until a comprehensive review of the engineering problems and revision of the safety methods had been undertaken. It was not until 29 September 1988 that the next Space Shuttle, Discovery STS-26, was successfully launched.

The 11 cosmonauts and astronauts in this list are, to date, the only in-flight space fatalities. They are not, however, the only victims of accidents during the space programmes of the former USSR and the US. On 24 October 1960, for example, five months before the first manned flight, Field Marshal Mitrofan Nedelin, the commander of the USSR's Strategic Rocket Forces, and an unknown number of other personnel (165 according to some authorities), were killed in the catastrophic launchpad explosion of an unmanned space rocket at the Baikonur cosmodrome.

What is Manitoulin island's claim to fame?
see p.20 for the answer
A It is the most densely inhabited island
B It is the largest island in a lake
C It has the highest island mountain

17

Waterworld

DEEPEST OCEANS AND SEAS

OCEAN OR SEA	GREATEST DEPTH		AVERAGE DEPTH	
	M	FT	M	FT
1 Pacific Ocean	10,924	35,837	4,028	13,215
2 Indian Ocean	7,455	24,460	3,963	13,002
3 Atlantic Ocean	9,219	30,246	3,926	12,880
4 Caribbean Sea	6,946	22,788	2,647	8,685
5 South China Sea	5,016	16,456	1,652	5,419
6 Bering Sea	4,773	15,659	1,547	5,075
7 Gulf of Mexico	3,787	12,425	1,486	4,874
8 Mediterranean Sea	4,632	15,197	1,429	4,688
9 Japan Sea	3,742	12,276	1,350	4,429
10 Arctic Ocean	5,625	18,456	1,205	3,953

The deepest point in the deepest ocean is the Marianas Trench in the Pacific Ocean, at a depth of 10,924 m (35,837 ft), according to a recent survey. The slightly lesser depth of 10,916 m (35,814 ft) was recorded on 23 January 1960 by Jacques Piccard and Donald Walsh in their 17.7-m (58-ft) long bathyscaphe *Trieste 2* during the deepest-ever ocean descent. Whichever is correct, it is close to 11 km (6.8 miles) down, or almost 29 times the height of the Empire State Building.

HIGHEST WATERFALLS

WATERFALL	RIVER	LOCATION	TOTAL DROP	
			M	FT
1 Angel	Carrao	Venezuela	979	3,212*
2 Tugela	Tugela	South Africa	947	3,107
3 Utigård	Jostedal Glacier	Norway	800	2,625
4 Mongefossen	Monge	Norway	774	2,540
5 Yosemite	Yosemite Creek	USA	739	2,425
6 Østre Mardøla Foss	Mardals	Norway	656	2,152
7 Tyssestrengane	Tysso	Norway	646	2,120
8 Cuquenán	Arabopo	Venezuela	610	2,000
9 Sutherland	Arthur	New Zealand	580	1,904
10 Kjellfossen	Naero	Norway	561	1,841

* *Longest single drop 807 m (2,648 ft)*

FALL AND ANGEL

On 16 November 1933 American adventurer James Angel wrote in his diary, "I found myself a waterfall." He had discovered the world's highest falls, later named Angel Falls.

TOP 10 ★
DEEPEST DEEP-SEA TRENCHES*

	TRENCH	DEEPEST POINT M	FT
1	Marianas	10,924	35,837
2	Tonga#	10,800	35,430
3	Philippine	10,497	34,436
4	Kermadec#	10,047	32,960
5	Bonin	9,994	32,786
6	New Britain	9,940	32,609
7	Kuril	9,750	31,985
8	Izu	9,695	31,805
9	Puerto Rico	8,605	28,229
10	Yap	8,527	27,973

* With the exception of the Puerto Rico (Atlantic), all the trenches are in the Pacific

Some authorities consider these to be parts of the same feature

Each of the eight deepest ocean trenches would be deep enough to submerge Mount Everest, which is 8,850 m (29,035 ft) above sea level.

TOP 10 ★
GREATEST RIVERS*

	RIVER	OUTFLOW/SEA	AV. FLOW CU M/SEC
1	Amazon	Brazil/South Atlantic	175,000
2	Zaïre	Angola–Congo/ South Atlantic	39,000
3	Negro	Brazil/South Atlantic	35,000
4	Yangtze–Kiang	China/Yellow Sea	32,190
5	Orinoco	Venezuela/ South Atlantic	25,200
6	Plata–Paraná– Grande	Uruguay/ South Atlantic	22,900
7	Madeira–Mamoré– Grande	Brazil/ South Atlantic	21,800
8	Brahmaputra	Bangladesh/ Bay of Bengal	19,200
9	Yenisey–Angara– Selenga	Russia/ Kara Sea	17,600
10	Lena–Kirenga	Russia/ Arctic Ocean	16,600

* Based on rate of discharge at mouth

AMAZON v NILE

Although the Amazon is ranked second in length, it is possible to sail from it up the Rio Pará, a total of 6,750 km (4,195 miles), which is a greater distance than the length of the Nile.

TOP 10 ★
LONGEST RIVERS

	RIVER/LOCATION	LENGTH KM	MILES
1	Nile, Tanzania/Uganda/ Sudan/Egypt	6,670	4,145
2	Amazon, Peru/Brazil	6,448	4,007
3	Yangtze–Kiang, China	6,300	3,915
4	Mississippi–Missouri– Red Rock, USA	5,971	3,710
5	Yenisey–Angara– Selenga, Mongolia/Russia	5,540	3,442
6	Huang Ho (Yellow River), China	5,464	3,395
7	Ob'–Irtysh, Mongolia/ Kazakhstan/Russia	5,410	3,362
8	Congo, Angola/ Dem. Rep. of Congo	4,700	2,920
9	Lena–Kirenga, Russia	4,400	2,734
10	Mekong, Tibet/China/ Myanmar (Burma)/ Laos/Cambodia/Vietnam	4,350	2,703

TOP 10 ★
COUNTRIES WITH THE GREATEST AREAS OF INLAND WATER

	COUNTRY	PERCENTAGE OF TOTAL AREA	WATER AREA SQ KM	SQ MILES
1	USA*	4.88	756,600	292,125
2	Canada	7.60	755,170	291,573
3	India	9.56	314,400	121,391
4	China	2.82	270,550	104,460
5	Ethiopia	9.89	120,900	46,680
6	Colombia	8.80	100,210	38,691
7	Indonesia	4.88	93,000	35,908
8	Russia	0.47	79,400	30,657
9	Australia	0.90	68,920	26,610
10	Tanzania	6.25	59,050	22,799

* 50 states and District of Columbia

TOP 10 ★
LAKES WITH THE GREATEST VOLUME OF WATER

	LAKE/LOCATION	VOLUME CU KM	CU MILES
1	Caspian Sea, Azerbaijan/ Iran/Kazakhstan/Russia/ Turkmenistan	89,600	21,497
2	Baikal, Russia	22,995	5,517
3	Tanganyika, Burundi/ Tanzania/Dem. Rep. of Congo/Zambia	18,304	4,391
4	Superior, Canada/USA	12,174	2,921
5	Michigan/Huron, USA/Canada	8,449	2,642
6	Nyasa (Malawi), Malawi/Mozambique/ Tanzania	6,140	1,473
7	Victoria, Kenya/ Tanzania/Uganda	2,518	604
8	Great Bear, Canada	2,258	542
9	Great Slave, Canada	1,771	425
10	Issyk, Kyrgyzstan	1,752	420

Did You Know? Once the world's fourth largest lake, the Aral Sea has shrunk by over a third as a result of feeder rivers being diverted for irrigation, and is in danger of disappearing completely.

Islands of the World

LARGEST VOLCANIC ISLANDS

	ISLAND/LOCATION/TYPE	AREA SQ KM	SQ MILES
1	**Sumatra**, Indonesia, Active volcanic	443,066	171,069
2	**Honshu**, Japan, Volcanic	225,800	87,182
3	**Java**, Indonesia, Volcanic	138,794	53,589
4	**North Island**, New Zealand, Volcanic	111,583	43,082
5	**Luzon**, Philippines, Active volcanic	109,965	42,458
6	**Iceland**, Active volcanic	101,826	39,315
7	**Mindanao**, Philippines, Active volcanic	97,530	37,657
8	**Hokkaido**, Japan, Active volcanic	78,719	30,395
9	**New Britain**, Papua New Guinea, Volcanic	35,145	13,569
10	**Halmahera**, Indonesia, Active volcanic	18,040	6,965

Source: *United Nations*

LARGEST ISLAND COUNTRIES

	COUNTRY	AREA SQ KM	SQ MILES
1	**Indonesia**	1,904,569	735,358
2	**Madagascar**	587,713	226,917
3	**Papua New Guinea**	462,840	178,704
4	**Japan**	372,801	143,939
5	**Malaysia**	329,758	127,320
6	**Philippines**	300,000	115,831
7	**New Zealand***	269,057	103,883
8	**Great Britain**	229,957	88,787
9	**Cuba**	110,861	42,804
10	**Iceland**	103,000	39,769

* Total of all the islands

Greenland is not included in this Top 10 because it is part of Denmark.

LARGEST LAKE ISLANDS

	ISLAND/LAKE/LOCATION	AREA SQ KM	SQ MILES
1	**Manitoulin**, Huron, Ontario, Canada	2,766	1,068
2	**Vozrozhdeniya**, Aral Sea, Uzbekistan/Kazakhstan	2,300	888
3	**René-Lavasseur**, Manicouagan Reservoir, Quebec, Canada	2,020	780
4	**Olkhon**, Baykal, Russia	730	282
5	**Samosir**, Toba, Sumatra, Indonesia	630	243
6	**Isle Royale**, Superior, Michigan, USA	541	209
7	**Ukerewe**, Victoria, Tanzania	530	205
8	**St. Joseph**, Huron, Ontario, Canada	365	141
9	**Drummond**, Huron, Michigan, USA	347	134
10	**Idjwi**, Kivu, Dem. Rep. of Congo	285	110

Not all islands are surrounded by sea: many sizeable islands are situated in lakes. The second largest in this list, Vozrozhdeniya, is growing as the Aral Sea contracts, and is set to link up with the surrounding land to become a peninsula.

LARGEST ISLANDS IN THE US

	ISLAND/LOCATION	AREA SQ KM	SQ MILES
1	**Hawaii**, Hawaii	10,456	4,037
2	**Kodiak**, Alaska	9,510	3,672
3	**Prince of Wales**, Alaska	6,700	2,587
4	**Chicagof**, Alaska	5,400	2,085
5	**Saint Lawrence**, Alaska	4,430	1,710
6	**Admiralty**, Alaska	4,270	1,649
7	**Baranof**, Alaska	4,237	1,636
8	**Nunivak**, Alaska	4,210	1,625
9	**Unimak**, Alaska	4,160	1,606
10	**Long Island**, New York	3,629	1,401

LARGEST ISLANDS IN THE UK

	ISLAND/LOCATION	POPULATION	AREA SQ KM	SQ MILES
1	**Lewis and Harris**, Outer Hebrides	23,390	2,225	859
2	**Skye**, Hebrides	8,139	1,666	643
3	**Mainland**, Shetland	22,184	967	373
4	**Mull**, Inner Hebrides	2,605	899	347
5	**Ynys Môn** (Anglesey), Wales	69,800	714	276
6	**Islay**, Inner Hebrides	3,997	639	247
7	**Isle of Man**, England	69,788	572	221
8	**Mainland**, Orkney	14,299	536	207
9	**Arran**, Inner Hebrides	4,726	435	168
10	**Isle of Wight**, England	126,600	381	147

50TH STATE

Hawaii, the largest US island, is the largest of eight major and 124 smaller volcanic islands that make up the Hawaiian archipelago.

UNDER THE VOLCANO

Indonesia's highest active volcano, Gunung Kerinci, rises to 3,805 m (12,484 ft). It lies in the Barisan Mountains of Sumatra, the world's largest volcanic island.

TOP 10 ★

LARGEST ISLANDS

ISLAND/LOCATION	APPROX. AREA* SQ KM	SQ MILES
1 Greenland (Kalaallit Nunaat)	2,175,600	840,004
2 New Guinea, Papua New Guinea/Indonesia	785,753	303,381
3 Borneo, Indonesia/ Malaysia/Brunei	748,168	288,869
4 Madagascar	587,713	226,917
5 Baffin Island, Canada	503,944	194,574
6 Sumatra, Indonesia	443,066	171,069
7 Great Britain	229,957	88,787
8 Honshu, Japan	225,800	87,182
9 Victoria Island, Canada	220,548	85,154
10 Ellesmere Island, Canada	183,965	71,029

* *Mainlands, including areas of inland water, but excluding offshore islands*

Australia is regarded as a continental land mass rather than an island; otherwise it would rank first at 7,618,493 sq km (2,941,517 sq miles).

TOP 10 ★

LARGEST ISLANDS IN EUROPE

ISLAND/LOCATION	AREA SQ KM	SQ MILES
1 Great Britain, North Atlantic	229,957	88,787
2 Iceland, North Atlantic	103,000	39,769
3 Ireland, North Atlantic	83,766	32,342
4 West Spitsbergen, Arctic Ocean	39,368	15,200
5 Sicily, Mediterranean Sea	25,400	9,807
6 Sardinia, Mediterranean Sea	23,800	9,189
7 North East Land, Barents Sea	15,000	5,792
8 Cyprus, Mediterranean Sea	9,251	3,572
9 Corsica, Mediterranean Sea	8,720	3,367
10 Crete, Mediterranean Sea	8,260	3,189

Great Britain became an island some 8,000 years ago, when the land bridge that had previously existed was inundated and the North Sea became connected with the English Channel.

TOP 10 ★

HIGHEST ISLANDS

ISLAND/LOCATION	HIGHEST ELEVATION M	FT
1 New Guinea, Papua New Guinea/ Indonesia	5,030	16,503
2 Akutan, Alaska, USA	4,275	14,026
3 Hawaii, USA	4,205	13,796
4 Borneo, Indonesia/ Malaysia/Brunei	4,175	13,698
5 Formosa, China	3,997	13,114
6 Sumatra, Indonesia	3,805	12,484
7 Ross, Antarctica	3,794	12,448
8 Honshu, Japan	3,776	12,388
9 South Island, New Zealand	3,764	12,349
10 Lombok, Lesser Sunda Islands, Indonesia	3,726	12,224

Source: *United Nations*

The highest island peak is Puncak Jaya, Indonesia, which soars to 5,030 m (16,503 ft), making it also the highest mountain in the entire Pacific basin.

What is the most common element on Earth?
see p.27 for the answer

A Nitrogen
B Hydrogen
C Oxygen

The Face of the Earth

TOP 10 ★
DEEPEST DEPRESSIONS

	DEPRESSION/LOCATION	MAXIMUM DEPTH BELOW SEA LEVEL	
		M	FT
1	**Dead Sea**, Israel/Jordan	400	1,312
2	**Lake Assal**, Djibouti	156	511
3	**Turfan Depression**, China	154	505
4	**Qattâra Depression**, Egypt	133	436
5	**Mangyshlak Peninsula**, Kazakhstan	132	433
6	**Danakil Depression**, Ethiopia	117	383
7	**Death Valley**, USA	86	282
8	**Salton Sink**, USA	72	235
9	**Zapadny Chink Ustyurta**, Kazakhstan	70	230
10	**Prikaspiyskaya Nizmennost'**, Kazakhstan/Russia	67	220

DEAD DEEP

The Dead Sea is the world's deepest depression, with Ein Bokek alongside it the world's lowest inhabited place at 393.5 m (1,291 ft) below sea level.

TOP 10 ★
HIGHEST ACTIVE VOLCANOES

	VOLCANO/LOCATION	LATEST ACTIVITY	HEIGHT M	HEIGHT FT
1	**Ojos del Salado**, Argentina/Chile	1981	6,895	22,588
2	**San Pedro**, Chile	1960	6,199	20,325
3	**Guallatiri**, Chile	1993	6,071	19,918
4	**Cotopaxi**, Ecuador	1975	5,897	19,347
5	**Tupungatito**, Chile	1986	5,640	18,504
6	**Láscar**, Chile	1995	5,591	18,346
7	**Popocatépetl**, Mexico	1998	5,426	17,802
8	**Nevado del Ruiz**, Colombia	1991	5,321	17,457
9	**Sangay**, Ecuador	1998	5,230	17,159
10	**Guagua Pichincha**, Ecuador	1993	4,784	15,696

This list includes only the volcanoes that were active at some time during the 20th century. The tallest currently active volcano in Europe is Mt. Etna, Sicily (3,311 m/10,855 ft), which has been responsible for numerous deaths.

TOP 10 ★
LARGEST DESERTS

	DESERT/LOCATION	APPROX. AREA SQ KM	APPROX. AREA SQ MILES
1	**Sahara**, Northern Africa	9,100,000	3,500,000
2	**Australian**, Australia*	3,400,000	1,300,000
3	**Arabian Peninsula**, Southwest Asia #	2,600,000	1,000,000
4	**Turkestan**, Central Asia +	1,900,000	750,000
5 =	**Gobi**, Central Asia	1,300,000	500,000
=	**North American Desert**, USA/Mexico ★	1,300,000	500,000
7	**Patagonia**, Southern Argentina	670,000	260,000
8	**Thar**, Northwest India/Pakistan	600,000	230,000
9	**Kalahari**, Southwestern Africa	570,000	220,000
10	**Takla Makan**, Northwestern China	480,000	185,000

* Includes Gibson, Great Sandy, Great Victoria, and Simpson
 # Includes an-Nafud and Rub alKhali   + Includes Kara-Kum and Kyzylkum
★ Includes Great Basin, Mojave, Sonorah, and Chihuahuan

TOP 10 ★
HIGHEST MOUNTAINS

	MOUNTAIN/LOCATION	FIRST ASCENT /TEAM NATIONALITY	HEIGHT* M	FT
1	Everest, Nepal/China	29 May 1953, British/New Zealand	8,850	29,035
2	K2 (Chogori), Pakistan/China	31 July 1954, Italian	8,607	28,238
3	Kangchenjunga, Nepal/India	25 May 1955, British	8,598	28,208
4	Lhotse, Nepal/China	18 May 1956, Swiss	8,511	27,923
5	Makalu I, Nepal/China	15 May 1955, French	8,481	27,824
6	Lhotse Shar (II), Nepal/China	12 May 1970, Austrian	8,383	27,504
7	Dhaulagiri I, Nepal	13 May 1960, Swiss/Austrian	8,172	26,810
8	Manaslu I (Kutang I), Nepal	9 May 1956, Japanese	8,156	26,760
9	Cho Oyu, Nepal	19 Oct 1954, Austrian	8,153	26,750
10	Nanga Parbat (Diamir), Pakistan	3 July 1953, German/Austrian	8,126	26,660

* Height of principal peak; lower peaks of the same mountain are excluded

Dhaulagiri was once believed to be the world's tallest mountain until Kangchenjunga was surveyed and declared to be even higher. When the results of the 19th-century Great Trigonometrical Survey of India were studied, however, it was realized that Everest was the tallest, its height being computed as 8,840 m (29,002 ft). Errors in measurement were corrected in 1955 to 8,848 m (29,029 ft), in April 1993 to 8,847 m (29,028 ft), and finally in November 1999 to its current record-breaking height.

TOP 10 ★
LONGEST CAVES

	CAVE/LOCATION	TOTAL KNOWN LENGTH KM	MILES
1	Mammoth cave system, Kentucky, USA	567	352
2	Optimisticheskaya, Ukraine	208	130
3	Jewel Cave, South Dakota, USA	195	122
4	Hölloch, Switzerland	166	103
5	Lechuguilla Cave, New Mexico, USA	161	100
6	Fisher Ridge cave system, Kentucky, USA	146	91
7	Siebenhengstehohle, Switzerland	140	87
8	Wind Cave, South Dakota, USA	138	86
9	Ozernaya, Ukraine	111	69
10	Gua Air Jernih, Malaysia	109	68

Source: *Tony Waltham, BCRA*

The longest-known cave system in the UK is Ease Gill, West Yorkshire, at 66 km (41 miles).

TOP 10 ★
COUNTRIES WITH THE HIGHEST ELEVATIONS*

	COUNTRY/PEAK	HEIGHT M	FT
1	=China, Everest	8,850	29,035
	=Nepal, Everest	8,850	29,035
3	Pakistan, K2	8,607	28,238
4	India, Kangchenjunga	8,598	28,208
5	Bhutan, Khula Kangri	7,554	24,784
6	Tajikistan, Mt. Garmo (formerly Kommunizma)	7,495	24,590
7	Afghanistan, Noshaq	7,490	24,581
8	Kyrgyzstan, Pik Pobedy	7,439	24,406
9	Kazakhstan, Khan Tengri	6,995	22,949
10	Argentina, Cerro Aconcagua	6,960	22,834

* Based on the tallest peak in each country

An elevation of more than 305 m (1,000 ft) is commonly regarded as a mountain, and using this criterion almost every country in the world can claim to have at least one mountain. There are some 54 countries in the world with elevations of greater than 3,048 m (10,000 ft).

TOP 10 ★
LARGEST METEORITE CRATERS

	CRATER/LOCATION	DIAMETER KM	MILES
1	=Sudbury, Ontario, Canada	140	87
	=Vredefort, South Africa	140	87
3	=Manicouagan, Quebec, Canada	100	62
	=Popigai, Russia	100	62
5	Puchezh-Katunki, Russia	80	50
6	Kara, Russia	60	37
7	Siljan, Sweden	52	32
8	Charlevoix, Quebec, Canada	46	29
9	Araguainha Dome, Brazil	40	25
10	Carswell, Saskatchewan, Canada	37	23

Many astroblemes (collision sites) on Earth have been weathered over time and obscured, unlike those on the Solar System's other planets and moons. As a result of this weathering, one of the ongoing debates in geology is whether or not certain crater-like structures discovered on the Earth's surface are of meteoric origin or are the remnants of long-extinct volcanoes.

TOP 10 ★
DEEPEST CAVES

	CAVE SYSTEM/LOCATION	DEPTH M	FT
1	Lamprechtsofen, Austria	1,632	5,354
2	Gouffre Mirolda, France	1,610	5,282
3	Réseau Jean Bernard, France	1,602	5,256
4	Torca del Cerro, Spain	1,589	5,213
5	Shakta Pantjukhina, Georgia	1,508	4,948
6	Ceki 2, Slovenia	1,480	4,856
7	Sistema Huautla, Mexico	1,475	4,839
8	Sistema de la Trave, Spain	1,444	4,738
9	Boj Bulok, Uzbekistan	1,415	4,642
10	Puerta di Illamina, Spain	1,408	4,619

Source: *Tony Waltham, BCRA*

What was the nationality of Anders Celsius, after whom the Celsius temperature scale is named?
see p.25 for the answer
A Swedish
B Italian
C German

23

World Weather

TOP 10 ★
PLACES WITH THE MOST RAINY DAYS

LOCATION*	RAINY DAYS PER ANNUM#
1 Waialeale, Hawaii, USA	335
2 Marion Island, South Africa	312
3 Pohnpei, Federated States of Micronesia	311
4 Andagoya, Colombia	306
5 Macquarie Island, Australia	299
6 Gough Island, Tristan da Cunha group, South Atlantic	291
7 Palau, Federated States of Micronesia	286
8 Heard Island, Australia	279
9 Camp Jacob, Guadeloupe	274
10 Atu Nau, Alaska, USA	268

* Maximum of two places per country listed
# Averaged over a period of many years
Source: Philip Eden

TOP 10 ★
WETTEST PLACES – AVERAGE

LOCATION*	AVERAGE ANNUAL RAINFALL# MM	IN
1 Cherrapunji, India	12,649	498.0
2 Mawsynram, India	11,872	467.4
3 Waialeale, Hawaii, USA	11,455	451.0
4 Debundscha, Cameroon	10,277	404.6
5 Quibdó, Colombia	8,989	353.9
6 Bellenden Ker Range, Australia	8,636	340.0
7 Andagoya, Colombia	7,137	281.0
8 Henderson Lake, British Columbia, Canada	6,502	256.0
9 Kikori, Papua New Guinea	5,916	232.9
10 Tavoy, Myanmar (Burma)	5,451	214.6

* Maximum of two places per country listed
# Annual rainfall total, averaged over a period of many years
Source: Philip Eden

TOP 10 PLACES WITH THE HEAVIEST DAILY DOWNPOURS*

(Location#/highest rainfall in 24 hours in mm/in)

1. Chilaos, Réunion, 1,870/73.6   2. Baguio, Philippines, 1,168/46.0
3. Alvin, Texas, USA, 1,092/43.0   4. Cherrapunji, India, 1,041/41.0
5. Smithport, Pennsylvania, USA, 1,013/39.9   6. Crohamhurst, Australia, 907/35.7
7. Finch-Hatton, Australia, 879/34.6   8. Suva, Fiji, 673/26.5
9. Cayenne, French Guiana, 597/23.5   10. Aitutaki, Cook Islands, 572/22.5

* Based on limited data   # Maximum of two places per country listed
Source: Philip Eden

TOP 10 ★
PLACES WITH THE FEWEST RAINY DAYS

LOCATION*	NUMBER OF RAINY DAYS#
1 Arica, Chile	1 day every 6 years
2 Asyût, Egypt	1 day every 5 years
3 Dakhla Oasis, Egypt	1 day every 4 years
4 Al'Kufrah, Libya	1 day every 2 years
5= Bender Qaasim, Somalia	1 day per year
= Wadi Halfa, Sudan	1 day per year
7 Iquique, Chile	2 days per year
8= Dongola, Sudan	3 days per year
= Faya-Largeau, Chad	3 days per year
= Masirāh Island, Oman	3 days per year

* Maximum of two places per country listed
# Lowest number of days with rain per year, averaged over a period of many years
Source: Philip Eden

TOP 10 ★
HOTTEST PLACES – EXTREMES*

LOCATION#	HIGHEST TEMPERATURE °C	°F
1 Al'Azīzīyah, Libya	58.0	136.4
2 Greenland Ranch, Death Valley, USA	56.7	134.0
3= Ghudamis, Libya	55.0	131.0
= Kebili, Tunisia	55.0	131.0
5 Tombouctou, Mali	54.5	130.1
6 Araouane, Mali	54.4	130.0
7 Tirat Tavi, Israel	53.9	129.0
8 Ahwāz, Iran	53.5	128.3
9 Agha Jārī, Iran	53.3	128.0
10 Wadi Halfa, Sudan	52.8	127.0

* Highest individual temperatures
# Maximum of two places per country listed
Source: Philip Eden

TOP 10 ★
DRIEST PLACES – AVERAGE

LOCATION*	AVERAGE ANNUAL RAINFALL# MM	IN	LOCATION*	AVERAGE ANNUAL RAINFALL# MM	IN
1 Arica, Chile	0.7	0.03	7 Iquique, Chile	5.0	0.20
2= Al'Kufrah, Libya	0.8	0.03	8 Pelican Point, Namibia	8.0	0.32
= Aswân, Egypt	0.8	0.03	9= Aoulef, Algeria	12.0	0.48
= Luxor, Egypt	0.8	0.03	= Callao, Peru	12.0	0.48
5 Ica, Peru	2.3	0.09			
6 Wadi Halfa, Sudan	2.6	0.10			

* Maximum of two places per country listed
# Annual total averaged over a period of many years
Source: Philip Eden

TOP 10 ★
PLACES WITH THE MOST CONTRASTING SEASONS*

	LOCATION#	WINTER °C	°F	SUMMER °C	°F	DIFFERENCE °C	°F
1	**Verkhoyansk**, Russia	-50.3	-58.5	13.6	56.5	63.9	115.0
2	**Yakutsk**, Russia	-45.0	-49.0	17.5	63.5	62.5	112.5
3	**Manzhouli**, China	-26.1	-15.0	20.6	69.0	46.7	84.0
4	**Fort Yukon**, Alaska, USA	-29.0	-20.2	16.3	61.4	45.3	81.6
5	**Fort Good Hope**, Northwest Territories, Canada	-29.9	-21.8	15.3	59.5	45.2	81.3
6	**Brochet**, Manitoba, Canada	-29.2	-20.5	15.4	59.7	44.6	80.2
7	**Tunka**, Mongolia	-26.7	-16.0	16.1	61.0	42.8	77.0
8	**Fairbanks**, Alaska, USA	-24.0	-11.2	15.6	60.1	39.6	71.3
9	**Semipalatinsk**, Kazakhstan	-17.7	0.5	20.6	69.0	38.3	68.5
10	**Jorgen Bronlund Fjørd**, Greenland	-30.9	-23.6	6.4	43.5	37.3	67.1

* Biggest differences between mean monthly temperatures in summer and winter

Maximum of two places per country listed

Source: Philip Eden

TOP 10 ★
COLDEST PLACES – EXTREMES*

	LOCATION#	LOWEST TEMPERATURE °C	°F
1	**Vostok**+, Antarctica	-89.2	-128.6
2	**Plateau Station**+, Antarctica	-84.0	-119.2
3	**Oymyakon**, Russia	-71.1	-96.0
4	**Verkhoyansk**, Russia	-67.7	-89.8
5	**Northice**+, Greenland	-66.0	-86.8
6	**Eismitte**+, Greenland	-64.9	-84.8
7	**Snag**, Yukon, Canada	-63.0	-81.4
8	**Prospect Creek**, Alaska, USA	-62.1	-79.8
9	**Fort Selkirk**, Yukon, Canada	-58.9	-74.0
10	**Rogers Pass**, Montana, USA	-56.5	-69.7

* Lowest individual temperatures

Maximum of two places per country listed

+ Present or former scientific research base

Source: Philip Eden

TOP 10 ★
CLOUDIEST PLACES*

	LOCATION#	PERCENTAGE OF MAXIMUM POSSIBLE SUNSHINE	AVERAGE ANNUAL HOURS OF SUNSHINE
1	**Ben Nevis**, Scotland	16	736
2	**Hoyvik**, Faeroes, Denmark	19	902
3	**Maam**, Ireland	19	929
4	**Prince Rupert**, British Columbia, Canada	20	955
5	**Riksgransen**, Sweden	20	965
6	**Akureyri**, Iceland	20	973
7	**Raufarhöfn**, Iceland	21	995
8	**Nanortalik**, Greenland	22	1,000
9	**Dalwhinnie**, Scotland	22	1,032
10	**Karasjok**, Norway	23	1,090

* Lowest annual sunshine total, averaged over a period of many years

Maximum of two places per country listed

Source: Philip Eden

TOP 10 ★
SUNNIEST PLACES*

	LOCATION#	PERCENTAGE OF MAXIMUM POSSIBLE SUNSHINE	AVERAGE ANNUAL HOURS OF SUNSHINE
1	**Yuma**, Arizona, USA	91	4,127
2	**Phoenix**, Arizona, USA	90	4,041
3	**Wadi Halfa**, Sudan	89	3,964
4	**Bordj Omar Driss**, Algeria	88	3,899
5	**Keetmanshoop**, Namibia	88	3,876
6	**Aoulef**, Algeria	86	3,784
7	**Upington**, South Africa	86	3,766
8	**Atbara**, Sudan	85	3,739
9	**Mariental**, Namibia	84	3,707
10	**Bilma**, Niger	84	3,699

* Highest yearly sunshine total, averaged over a period of many years

Maximum of two places per country listed

Source: Philip Eden

CELSIUS

Anders Celsius (1701–44) was a Swedish mathematician and, like his father before him, Professor of Astronomy at the University of Uppsala. While Celsius was on an expedition to Lapland, making measurements that proved that the Earth is flattened at the poles, he realized the need for an improved thermometer. In 1742 he devised a new temperature scale, taking two fixed points – 0° as the boiling point of water and 100° as the freezing point of water. It was not until 1750, after Celsius's death, that his pupil Martin Strömer proposed that the two be reversed. This scale became known as Centigrade, but was changed to Celsius in 1948 in honour of its inventor.

WHO WAS · WHO WAS · WHO WAS · WHO WAS ?

What name was given to 1992's most devastating hurricane?
see p.29 for the answer
A Andrew
B George
C Edward

25

Out of This World

HEAVIEST ELEMENTS

ELEMENT	DISCOVERER/COUNTRY	YEAR DISCOVERED	DENSITY*
1 Osmium	Smithson Tennant, UK	1804	22.59
2 Iridium	Smithson Tennant, UK	1804	22.56
3 Platinum	J. C. Scaliger#, Italy/France; Charles Wood+, UK	1557 1741	21.45
4 Rhenium	W. Noddack et al., Germany	1925	21.01
5 Neptunium	Edwin M. McMillan and Philip H. Abelson, USA	1940	20.47
6 Plutonium	Glenn T. Seaborg et al., USA	1940	20.26
7 Gold	–	Prehistoric	19.29
8 Tungsten	Juan José and Fausto de Elhuijar, Spain	1783	19.26
9 Uranium	Martin J. Klaproth, Germany	1789	19.05
10 Tantalum	Anders G. Ekeberg, Sweden	1802	16.67

Grams per cu cm at 20°C #Made earliest reference to* +Discovered by*

The two heaviest elements, the metals osmium and iridium, were discovered at the same time by the British chemist Smithson Tennant (1761–1815), who was also the first to prove that diamonds are made of carbon. 0.028317 cu m (1 cu ft) of osmium weighs 640 kg (1,410 lb) – equivalent to 10 people each weighing 64 kg (141 lb).

LIGHTEST ELEMENTS*

ELEMENT	DISCOVERER/COUNTRY	YEAR DISCOVERED	DENSITY#
1 Lithium	J. A. Arfvedson, Sweden	1817	0.533
2 Potassium	Sir Humphry Davy, UK	1807	0.859
3 Sodium	Sir Humphry Davy, UK	1807	0.969
4 Calcium	Sir Humphry Davy, UK	1808	1.526
5 Rubidium	Robert W. Bunsen and Gustav Kirchoff, Germany	1861	1.534
6 Magnesium	Sir Humphry Davy	1808+	1.737
7 Phosphorus	Hennig Brandt, Germany	1669	1.825
8 Beryllium	Friedrich Wöhler, Germany; A.-A. B. Bussy, France	1828★	1.846
9 Caesium	Robert W. Bunsen and Gustav Kirchoff, Germany	1860	1.896
10 Sulphur	–	Prehistoric	2.070

Solids only #Grams per cu cm at 20°C* +Recognized by Joseph Black, 1755, but not isolated* ★Recognized by Nicholas Vauquelin, 1797, but not isolated*

Osmium, the heaviest element, is over 42 times heavier than lithium, the lightest element. Lithium is not only extremely light, but it is also so soft that it can be easily cut with a knife. It is half as heavy as water, and lighter even than certain types of wood.

TOP 10 PRINCIPAL COMPONENTS OF AIR

(Component/volume per cent)

1 Nitrogen, 78.110 **2** Oxygen, 20.953 **3** Argon, 0.934 **4** Carbon dioxide, 0.01–0.10 **5** Neon, 0.001818 **6** Helium, 0.000524 **7** Methane, 0.0002 **8** Krypton, 0.000114 **9** = Hydrogen, 0.00005; = Nitrous oxide, 0.00005

METALLIC ELEMENTS WITH THE GREATEST RESERVES

ELEMENT	ESTIMATED GLOBAL RESERVES (TONNES)
1 Iron	110,000,000,000
2 Magnesium	20,000,000,000
3 Potassium	10,000,000,000
4 Aluminium	6,000,000,000
5 Manganese	3,600,000,000
6 Zirconium	over 1,000,000,000
7 Chromium	1,000,000,000
8 Barium	450,000,000
9 Titanium	440,000,000
10 Copper	310,000,000

COPPER BOTTOMED

Over 12.7 million tonnes (14 million tons) of copper have been removed from the Bingham Copper Mine, Utah, USA, which is an all-time record for a single mine. This is the world's largest manmade excavation.

TOP 10 MOST COMMON ELEMENTS IN SEAWATER
(Element/tonnes per cu km)

1 Oxygen*, 857,000,000 **2** Hydrogen*, 107,800,000 **3** Chlorine, 19,870,000
4 Sodium, 11,050,000 **5** Magnesium, 1,326,000 **6** Sulphur, 928,000
7 Calcium, 422,000 **8** Potassium, 416,000 **9** Bromine, 67,300 **10** Carbon, 28,000

* Combined as water

TOP 10 ★
MOST COMMON ELEMENTS IN THE EARTH'S CRUST

ELEMENT	PARTS PER MILLION
1 Oxygen	474,000
2 Silicon	277,100
3 Aluminium	82,000
4 =Iron	41,000
=Calcium	41,000
6 =Magnesium	23,000
=Sodium	23,000
8 Potassium	21,000
9 Titanium	5,600
10 Hydrogen	1,520

This Top 10 is based on the average percentages of the elements in igneous rock. At an atomic level, out of every million atoms, some 205,000 are silicon, 62,600 are aluminium, and 29,000 are hydrogen. In the Universe as a whole, however, hydrogen is by far the most common element, comprising some 927,000 out of every million atoms. It is followed in second place by helium at 72,000 per million.

LIGHT FANTASTIC
This computer-generated image shows a nucleus and orbiting electron, which make up a single atom of hydrogen, the lightest, simplest, most abundant, and most extracted of all elements.

TOP 10 ★
MOST COMMON ELEMENTS ON THE MOON

ELEMENT	PERCENTAGE
1 Oxygen	40.0
2 Silicon	19.2
3 Iron	14.3
4 Calcium	8.0
5 Titanium	5.9
6 Aluminium	5.6
7 Magnesium	4.5
8 Sodium	0.33
9 Potassium	0.14
10 Chromium	0.002

This list is based on the chemical analysis of the 20.77 kg (45.8 lb) of rock samples brought back to the Earth by the three-man crew of the 1969 *Apollo 11* lunar mission.

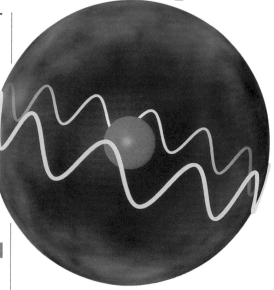

TOP 10 MOST COMMON ELEMENTS IN THE SUN
(Element/parts per million)

1 Hydrogen, 745,000 **2** Helium, 237,000
3 Oxygen, 8,990 **4** Carbon, 3,900
5 Iron, 1,321 **6** Neon, 1,200
7 Nitrogen, 870 **8** Silicon, 830
9 Magnesium, 720 **10** Sulphur, 380

TOP 10 ★
ELEMENTS WITH THE HIGHEST MELTING POINTS

ELEMENT	MELTING POINT °C	°F
1 Carbon	3,527	6,381
2 Tungsten	3,422	6,192
3 Rhenium	3,186	5,767
4 Osmium	3,033	5,491
5 Tantalum	3,017	5,463
6 Molybdenum	2,623	4,753
7 Niobium	2,477	4,491
8 Iridium	2,466	4,471
9 Ruthenium	2,334	4,233
10 Hafnium	2,233	4,051

Other elements that melt at high temperatures include chromium (1,907°C/3,465°F), iron (1,538°C/2,800°F), and gold (1,064°C/1,947°F).

THE DISCOVERY OF RADIUM

In 1898, Polish-born Marie Curie (1867–1934) and her French husband Pierre Curie detected radioactivity (a term Marie invented) in the mineral ore pitchblende, a waste product of mining. It took until 1902 before she had manually refined tons of ore to concentrate the radioactive content, producing about one tenth of a gram of radium chloride, an element that is a million times more radioactive than uranium. The following year, Marie and Pierre shared the Nobel Prize for Physics with Henry Becquerel. Marie eventually obtained pure radium in 1910. Marie was not only the first ever female Nobel winner, but also the first to achieve two Prizes, receiving the Chemistry Prize in 1911. Radium was subsequently used in the treatment of cancer, but, ironically, Marie died in 1934, from leukaemia resulting from her prolonged contact with radium.

• YEARS AGO • YEARS AGO • YEARS AGO • **100**

Did You Know? Following the naming of the element Uranium after the planet Uranus, Neptunium and Plutonium were named after Neptune and Pluto, two more distant planets.

Natural Disasters

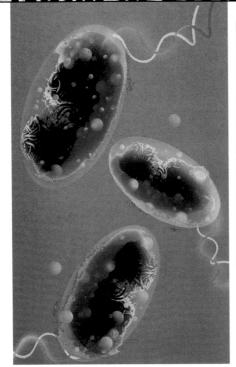

CHOLERA KILLER

One of the scourges of the 19th century, when it killed millions, the cholera bacterium continues to cause illness and death in human communities that lack modern sanitation.

THE 10 ★ WORST EPIDEMICS OF ALL TIME

	EPIDEMIC/LOCATION	DATE	ESTIMATED NO. KILLED
1	Black Death, Europe/Asia	1347–51	75,000,000
2	Influenza, worldwide	1918–20	21,640,000
3	AIDS, worldwide	1981–	16,300,000
4	Bubonic plague, India	1896–1948	12,000,000
5	Typhus, Eastern Europe	1914–15	3,000,000
6 =	"Plague of Justinian", Europe/Asia	541–90	millions*
=	Cholera, worldwide	1846–60	millions*
=	Cholera, Europe	1826–37	millions*
=	Cholera, worldwide	1893–94	millions*
10	Smallpox, Mexico	1530–45	>1,000,000

* No precise figures available

THE 10 WORST YEARS FOR EPIDEMICS IN THE 1990s

(Year/deaths due to epidemics)

1 1991, 28,540 **2** 1996, 13,904 **3** 1998, 11,224 **4** 1997, 9,948 **5** 1992, 5,533 **6** 1999, 4,866 **7** 1995, 4,069 **8** 1990, 2,864 **9** 1994, 2,240 **10** 1993, 859

Source: *International Federation of Red Cross and Red Cross Societies*

Over two-thirds of those killed by epidemics in the 1990s were African. In 1991, 8,000 people died in Peru due to a diarrhoeal/enteric disease, and another 7,000 were killed by an epidemic of cholera in Nigeria.

THE 10 ★ WORST FLOODS OF ALL TIME

	LOCATION	DATE	ESTIMATED NO. KILLED
1	Huang He River, China	Aug 1931	3,700,000
2	Huang He River, China	Spring 1887	1,500,000
3	Holland	1 Nov 1530	400,000
4	Kaifong, China	1642	300,000
5	Henan, China	Sep–Nov 1939	over 200,000
6	Bengal, India	1876	200,000
7	Yangtze River, China	Aug–Sep 1931	140,000
8	Holland	1646	110,000
9	North Vietnam	30 Aug 1971	over 100,000
10 =	Friesland, Holland	1228	100,000
=	Dort, Holland	16 Apr 1421	100,000
=	Canton, China	12 June 1915	100,000
=	Yangtze River, China	Sep 1911	100,000

China's Huang He, or Yellow River, has flooded at least 1,500 times since records began in 2297 BC.

THE 10 ★ COUNTRIES WITH MOST DEATHS DUE TO NATURAL DISASTERS

	COUNTRY	ESTIMATED DEATHS DUE TO NATURAL DISASTERS (1999)
1	Venezuela	30,021
2	Turkey	18,019
3	India	12,074
4	China	2,367
5	Taiwan	2,264
6	Colombia	1,284
7	Nigeria	1,190
8	Mexico	903
9	Vietnam	893
10	USA	792
	UK	39
	World	212,544,647

Source: *International Federation of Red Cross and Red Cross Societies*

Deaths due to natural disasters in 1999 break down by continent to 6,294,514 in Africa, 13,494,780 in the Americas, 187,617,273 in Asia, 4,986,835 in Europe, and 151,245 in Oceania.

THE ERUPTION OF MONT PELÉE

After lying dormant for centuries, Mont Pelée, a 1,350-m (4,430-ft) volcano on the West Indian island of Martinique, began to erupt in April 1902. Assured that the volcano presented no danger to them, the residents of the main city, St. Pierre, stayed in their homes instead of being evacuated. As a result of this catastrophic misreading of the volcano's activity, they were still there when, at 7.30 a.m. on 8 May, the volcano burst apart and showered the port with molten lava, ash, and gas, destroying property, ships in the harbour, and virtually all life. A total of about 40,000 people were killed, which was more than twice as many as when Vesuvius engulfed Pompeii in AD 79. Raoul Sarteret, a prisoner in St. Pierre jail and the town's only survivor, provided a vivid eyewitness account of the event.

100 YEARS AGO · YEARS AGO · YEARS AGO · YEARS

AFTER THE STORM

Hurricane Andrew, one of the costliest hurricanes ever, ravaged Miami, Florida, where it wrecked property and overturned vehicles to a cost of over $35.4 million dollars.

THE 10 ★
MOST COSTLY HURRICANES TO STRIKE THE US

	HURRICANE	YEAR	DAMAGE ($)*
1	Great Miami	1926	77,490,000,000
2	Andrew	1992	35,468,000,000
3	Southwest Florida	1944	18,074,000,000
4	New England	1938	17,821,000,000
5	Southeast Florida/ Lake Okeechobee	1928	14,785,000,000
6	Betsy	1965	13,326,000,000
7	Donna	1960	12,913,000,000
8	Camille	1969	11,572,000,000
9	Agnes	1972	11,472,000,000
10	Diane	1955	10,966,000,000

* Adjusted to 1998 dollars

Source: R. A. Pielke Jr. and C. W. Landsea, Normalized Atlantic Hurricane Damage, 1925–1995

THE 10 ★
MOST COSTLY TYPES OF DISASTER*

	TYPE OF DISASTER	ESTIMATED DAMAGE 1990–99 ($)
1	Floods	243,561,900,000
2	Earthquakes	215,023,211,000
3	Wind storms	179,391,693,000
4	Forest/scrub fires	36,975,436,000
5	Non-natural disasters	28,066,406,000
6	Droughts	21,941,064,000
7	Extreme temperatures	14,362,550,000
8	Avalanches/landslides	929,028,000
9	Volcanoes	672,628,000
10	Other natural disasters (insect infestations, waves, and surges, etc.)	109,467,000
	World total	741,033,383,000

* Includes natural and non-natural

Source: International Federation of Red Cross and Red Cross Societies

THE 10 ★
MOST DEADLY TYPES OF NATURAL DISASTER IN THE 1990s

	TYPE OF DISASTER	REPORTED DEATHS
1	Wind storms	201,790
2	Floods	103,870
3	Earthquakes	98,678
4	Epidemics*	84,047
5	Extreme temperatures	9,055
6	Avalanches/landslides	8,658
7	Droughts	2,790
8	Insect infestations, waves/surges	2,686
9	Volcanoes	1,080
10	Forest/scrub fires	575

* Excluding chronic public health disasters, such as the AIDS pandemic

Source: International Federation of Red Cross and Red Cross Societies

Did You Know? Since 1979, Atlantic hurricanes have been assigned men's and women's names, which alternate alphabetically and from year to year. Hurricane Bob, in July 1979, was the first.

LIFE ON EARTH

Land Animals

HEAVIEST TERRESTRIAL MAMMALS

MAMMAL	LENGTH M	LENGTH FT	WEIGHT KG	WEIGHT LB
1 African elephant	7.3	24	7,000	14,432
2 White rhinoceros	4.2	14	3,600	7,937
3 Hippopotamus	4.0	13	2,500	5,512
4 Giraffe	5.8	19	1,600	3,527
5 American bison	3.9	13	1,000	2,205
6 Arabian camel (dromedary)	3.5	12	690	1,521
7 Polar bear	2.6	8	600	1,323
8 Moose	3.0	10	550	1,213
9 Siberian tiger	3.3	11	300	661
10 Gorilla	2.0	7	220	485

The list excludes domesticated cattle and horses. It also avoids comparing close kin such as the African and Indian elephants, highlighting instead the sumo stars within distinctive large mammal groups, such as the bears, big cats, primates, and bovines (ox-like mammals).

MAMMALS WITH THE SHORTEST GESTATION PERIODS

MAMMAL	AVERAGE GESTATION (DAYS)
1 Short-nosed bandicoot	12
2 Opossum	13
3 Shrew	14
4 Golden hamster	16
5 Lemming	20
6 Mouse	21
7 Rat	22
8 Gerbil	24
9 Rabbit	30
10 Mole	38

The short-nosed bandicoot and the opossum are both marsupial mammals whose new-born young transfer to a pouch to complete their natal development. The babies of marsupials are minute when born.

MOST ENDANGERED MAMMALS

MAMMAL	ESTIMATED NO.
1 = Ghana fat mouse	unknown
= Halcon fruit bat	unknown
= Tasmanian wolf	unknown
4 Javan rhinoceros	50
5 Iriomote cat	60
6 Black lion tamarin	130
7 Pygmy hog	150
8 Kouprey	100–200
9 Tamaraw	200
10 Indus dolphin	400

The first three mammals on the list have not been seen for many years and may well be extinct, but zoologists are hopeful of the possibility of their survival. The Tasmanian wolf, for example, has been technically extinct since the last specimen died in a zoo in 1936, but occasional unconfirmed sightings suggest that there may still be animals in the wild.

HEAVIEST PRIMATES

PRIMATE	LENGTH* CM	LENGTH* IN	WEIGHT KG	WEIGHT LB
1 Gorilla	200	79	220	485
2 Man	177	70	77	170
3 Orang-utan	137	54	75	165
4 Chimpanzee	92	36	50	110
5 = Baboon	100	39	45	99
= Mandrill	95	37	45	99
7 Gelada baboon	75	30	25	55
8 Proboscis monkey	76	30	24	53
9 Hanuman langur	107	42	20	44
10 Siamung gibbon	90	35	13	29

* Excluding tail

ORANG-UTAN

Among the heaviest primates, and noted for its use of tools, the forest-dwelling orang-utan gets its name from the Malay words for "man of the woods".

TOP 10 ★
LONGEST LAND ANIMALS

ANIMAL*	LENGTH M	FT
1 Reticulated python	10.7	35
2 Tapeworm	10.0	33
3 African elephant	7.3	24
4 Estuarine crocodile	5.9	19
5 Giraffe	5.8	19
6 White rhinoceros	4.2	14
7 Hippopotamus	4.0	13
8 American bison	3.9	13
9 Arabian camel (dromedary)	3.5	12
10 Siberian tiger	3.3	11

* Longest representative of each species

NECK AND NECK
The giraffe is the tallest of all living animals. In 1937 a calf giraffe that measured 1.58 m (5 ft 2 in) at birth was found to be growing at an astonishing 1.3 cm (½ in) per hour.

TOP 10 ★
FASTEST MAMMALS

MAMMAL	MAXIMUM RECORDED SPEED KM/H	MPH
1 Cheetah	105	65
2 Pronghorn antelope	89	55
3 =Mongolian gazelle	80	50
=Springbok	80	50
5 =Grant's gazelle	76	47
=Thomson's gazelle	76	47
7 Brown hare	72	45
8 Horse	69	43
9 =Greyhound	68	42
=Red deer	68	42

QUICK OFF THE MARK
The speedy cheetah can accelerate to 96 km/h (60 mph) in just three seconds.

TOP 10 ★
LONGEST SNAKES

SNAKE	MAXIMUM LENGTH M	FT
1 Reticulated python	10.7	35
2 Anaconda	8.5	28
3 Indian python	7.6	25
4 Diamond python	6.4	21
5 King cobra	5.8	19
6 Boa constrictor	4.9	16
7 Bushmaster	3.7	12
8 Giant brown snake	3.4	11
9 Diamondback rattlesnake	2.7	9
10 Indigo or gopher snake	2.4	8

Did You Know? "Old Bet", the first elephant ever seen in the US, arrived from Bengal, India, on 13 April 1796 and was exhibited in New York. She was known for her ability to draw corks from bottles using only her trunk.

Marine Animals

HEAVIEST MARINE MAMMALS

MAMMAL	LENGTH M	FT	WEIGHT (TONNES)
1 Blue whale	33.5	110.0	137.0
2 Bowhead whale (Greenland right)	20.0	65.0	86.0
3 Northern right whale (Black right)	18.6	60.0	77.7
4 Fin whale (Common rorqual)	25.0	82.0	63.4
5 Sperm whale	18.0	59.0	43.7
6 Grey whale	14.0	46.0	34.9
7 Humpback whale	15.0	49.2	34.6
8 Sei whale	18.5	60.0	29.4
9 Bryde's whale	14.6	47.9	20.0
10 Baird's whale	5.5	18.0	12.1

Source: *Lucy T. Verma*

Probably the largest animal that ever lived, the blue whale dwarfs even the other whales listed here, all but one of which far outweigh the biggest land animal, the elephant. The elephant seal, with a weight of 3.5 tonnes, is the heaviest marine mammal that is not a whale.

HEAVIEST TURTLES

TURTLE/TORTOISE	MAX WEIGHT KG	LB
1 Pacific leatherback turtle*	704.4	1,552
2 Atlantic leatherback turtle*	463.0	1,018
3 Green sea turtle	355.3	783
4 Loggerhead turtle	257.8	568
5 Alligator snapping turtle#	100.0	220
6 Flatback (sea) turtle	78.2	171
7 Hawksbill (sea) turtle	62.7	138
8 Kemps ridley turtle	60.5	133
9 Olive ridley turtle	49.9	110
10 Common snapping turtle#	38.5	85

* One species, differing in size according to where they live

\# Freshwater species   Source: *Lucy T. Verma*

MARINE MONSTER

There are several species of right whale, with larger examples of Greenland rights topping 20 m (65 ft) and weighing 86 tonnes. By contrast, the Pygmy right whale, found off New Zealand, rarely exceeds 6 m (20 ft).

TOP 10 LONGEST-LIVED MARINE MAMMALS

(Marine mammal/lifespan in years)

❶ Bowhead whale *(Balaena mysticetus)*, 200
❷ Fin whale, 100 ❸ Orca (Killer whale), 90
❹ Baird's beaked whale, 82
❺ Sperm whale, 65 ❻ = Dugong, 60;
= Sei whale, 60 ❽ Bottlenose dolphin, 48
❾ Grey seal, 46 ❿ Blue whale, 45
Source: *Lucy T. Verma*

TOP 10 ★

SPECIES OF FISH MOST CAUGHT

	SPECIES	TONNES CAUGHT (1998)
1	Anchoveta (Peruvian anchovy)	11,729,064
2	Alaska pollock	4,049,317
3	Japanese anchovy	2,093,888
4	Chilean jack mackerel	2,025,758
5	Chubb mackerel	1,910,254
6	Skipjack tuna	1,850,487
7	Largehead hairtail	1,214,470
8	Atlantic cod	1,191,184
9	Yellowfin tuna	1,152,586
10	Capelin	988,033
	World total all species	86,299,400

Source: *Food and Agriculture Organization of the United Nations*

The Food and Agriculture Organization of the United Nations estimates the volume of the world's fishing catch to be just over 86 million tonnes a year. Of this, about 75 million tonnes is reckoned to be destined for human consumption – equivalent to approximately 13 kg (29 lb) a year for every inhabitant. The foremost species, anchoveta, are small anchovies used principally as bait to catch tuna.

TOP 10 ★

HEAVIEST SPECIES OF FRESHWATER FISH CAUGHT

	SPECIES	ANGLER/LOCATION/DATE	WEIGHT KG	G	LB	OZ
1	White sturgeon	Joey Pallotta III, Benicia, California, USA, 9 July 1983	212	28	468	0
2	Alligator gar	Bill Valverde, Rio Grande, Texas, USA, 2 Dec 1951	126	55	279	0
3	Beluga sturgeon	Merete Lehne, Guryev, Kazakhstan, 3 May 1993	102	00	224	13
4	Nile perch	Adrian Brayshaw, Lake Nasser, Egypt, 18 Dec 1997	96	62	213	0
5	Flathead catfish	Ken Paulie, Withlacoochee River, Florida, USA, 14 May 1998	55	79	123	9
6	Blue catfish	William P. McKinley, Wheeler Reservoir, Tennessee, USA, 5 July 1996	50	35	111	0
7	Redtailed catfish	Gilberto Fernandes, Amazon River, Amazonia, Brazil, 16 July 1988	44	20	97	7
8	Chinook salmon	Les Anderson, Kenai River, Alaska, USA, 17 May 1985	44	11	97	4
9	Giant tigerfish	Raymond Houtmans, Zaïre River, Kinshasa, Zaïre, 9 July 1988	44	00	97	0
10	Guilded catfish	Gilberto Fernandes, Amazon River, Amazonia Brazil, 15 Nov 1986	38	80	85	8

Source: *International Game Fish Association, World Record Game Fishes 2000*

TOP 10 ★

HEAVIEST SHARKS

	SHARK	MAXIMUM WEIGHT KG	LB
1	Whale shark	30,500	67,240
2	Basking shark	9,258	20,410
3	Great white shark	3,507	7,731
4	Greenland shark	1,009	2,224
5	Tiger shark	927	2,043
6	Great hammerhead shark	857	1,889
7	Six-gill shark	602	1,327
8	Grey nurse shark	564	1,243
9	Mako shark	554	1,221
10	Thresher shark	498	1,097

Source: *Lucy T. Verma*

SPEEDY SWIMMER

The highly streamlined sailfish is acknowledged as the fastest over short distances, with anglers reporting them capable of unreeling 91 m (300 ft) of line in three seconds.

TOP 10 FASTEST FISH
(Fish/maximum recorded speed in km/h/mph)

1 Sailfish, 112/69 **2** Marlin, 80/50 **3** Wahoo, 77/48 **4** Bluefin tuna, 76/47 **5** Yellowfin tuna, 74/46 **6** Blue shark, 69/43 **7** = Bonefish, 64/40; = Swordfish, 64/40 **9** Tarpon, 56/35 **10** Tiger shark, 53/33

Source: *Lucy T. Verma*

Did You Know? In a survey of recorded shark attacks from 1580 to 2000, the Great white shark was alone responsible for 348 out of a total of 980, resulting in 67 fatalities.

Flying Animals

TOP 10 ★
FASTEST BIRDS

BIRD	SPEED KM/H	MPH
1 Common eider	76	47
2 Bewick's swan	72	44
3 =Barnacle goose	68	42
=Common crane	68	42
5 Mallard	65	40
6 =Red-throated diver	61	38
=Wood pigeon	61	38
8 Oyster catcher	58	36
9= Pheasant	54	33
=White-fronted goose	54	33

Source: *Chris Mead*

Recent research reveals that, contrary to popular belief, swifts are not fast fliers but very efficient ones, with long, thin wings like gliders and low wing-loading. Fast fliers generally have high wing-loading and fast wing beats.

TOP 10 ★
OLDEST RINGED WILD BIRDS

BIRD	AGE* YEARS	MONTHS
1 Royal albatross	50	0
2 Fulmar	40	11
3 Manx shearwater	37	0
4 Gannet	36	4
5 Oystercatcher	36	0
6 White (Fairy) tern	35	11
7 Common eider	35	0
8 Lesser black-backed gull	34	10
9 Pink-footed goose	34	2
10 Great frigate bird	33	9

* *Elapsed time between marking and report*

Source: *Chris Mead*

Hard rings, likely to last as long as the bird, started to be used about 50 years ago. Land-based songbirds do not live as long as the slow-breeding seabirds. In general, big birds live longer than small ones, so the tiny White (Fairy) tern is especially noteworthy.

TOP 10 ★
FURTHEST BIRD MIGRATIONS

SPECIES	APPROXIMATE DISTANCE KM	MILES
1 Pectoral sandpiper	19,000*	11,806
2 Wheatear	18,000	11,184
3 Slender-billed shearwater	17,500*	10,874
4 Ruff	16,600	10,314
5 Willow warbler	16,300	10,128
6 Arctic tern	16,200	10,066
7 Arctic skua	15,600	9,693
8 Swainson's hawk	15,200	9,445
9 Knot	15,000	9,320
10 Swallow	14,900	9,258

* *Thought to be only half of the path taken during a whole year*

Source: *Chris Mead*

This list is of the likely extremes for a normal migrant, not one that has got lost and wandered into new territory. All migrant birds fly far further than is indicated by the direct route.

TOP 10 ★
LARGEST FLIGHTLESS BIRDS

BIRD*	HEIGHT CM	IN	WEIGHT KG	LB	OZ
1 Ostrich (male)	255.0	100.4	156.0	343	9
2 Northern cassowary	150.0	59.1	58.0	127	9
3 Emu (female)	155.0	61.0	55.0	121	6
4 Emperor penguin (female)	115.0	45.3	46.0	101	4
5 Greater rhea	140.0	55.1	25.0	55	2
6 Flightless steamer# (duck)	84.0	33.1	6.2	13	7
7 Flightless cormorant	100.0	39.4	4.5	9	15
8 Kiwi (female)	65.0	25.6	3.8	8	4
9 Takahe (rail)	50.0	19.7	3.2	7	2
10 Kakapo (parrot)	64.0	25.2	3.2	7	1

* *By species*

The Flightless steamer is 84 cm (33 in) long, but does not stand upright

Source: *Chris Mead*

EMPEROR RULES

The Emperor penguin is the largest of all penguins, with females as much as twice as heavy as males. There are estimated to be 220,000 breeding pairs in the Antarctic.

SMALLEST BATS

BAT/HABITAT	LENGTH CM	IN	WEIGHT GM	OZ
1 Kitti's hognosed bat (*Craseonycteris thonglongyai*), Thailand	2.9	1.10	2.0	0.07
2 Proboscis bat (*Rhynchonycteris naso*), Central and South America	3.8	1.50	2.5	0.09
3 =Banana bat (*Pipistrellus nanus*), Africa	3.8	1.50	3.0	0.11
=Smoky bat (*Furipterus horrens*), Central and South America	3.8	1.50	3.0	0.11
5 =Little yellow bat (*Rhogeessa mira*), Central America	4.0	1.57	3.5	0.12
=Lesser bamboo bat (*Tylonycteris pachypus*), Southeast Asia	4.0	1.57	3.5	0.12
7 Disc-winged bat (*Thyroptera tricolor*), Central and South America	3.6	1.42	4.0	0.14
8 =Lesser horseshoe bat (*Rhinolophus hipposideros*), Europe and Western Asia	3.7	1.46	5.0	0.18
=California myotis (*Myotis californienses*), North America	4.3	1.69	5.0	0.18
10 Northern blossom bat (*Macroglossus minimus*), Southeast Asia to Australia	6.4	2.52	15.0	0.53

This list focuses on the smallest example of 10 different bat families. The weights shown are typical, rather than extreme – and as a bat can eat more than half its own weight, the weights of individual examples may vary considerably. Length is of head and body only, since tail lengths vary from zero (Kitti's hognosed bat and the Northern blossom bat) to long (Proboscis bat and Lesser horseshoe bat).

JUST HANGING AROUND
The Banana bat, the smallest found in Africa, roosts in small groups among the leaves of banana plants, using sucker pads to cling to the slippery leaf surfaces.

LARGEST BIRDS OF PREY (BY LENGTH)

BIRD*	LENGTH CM	IN
1 Himalayan griffon vulture	150	59
2 Californian condor	134	53
3 Andean condor	130	51
4 =Lammergeier	115	45
=Lappet-faced vulture	115	45
6 Eurasian griffon vulture	110	43
7 European black vulture	107	42
8 Harpy eagle	105	41
9 Wedge-tailed eagle	104	41
10 Ruppell's griffon	101	40

* Diurnal only – hence excluding owls

The entrants in this Top 10 all measure more than 1 m (39 in) from beak to tail. In all but the vultures, the female will be larger than the male. All these raptors, or aerial hunters, have remarkable eyesight and can spot their victims from great distances. If they kill animals heavier than themselves, they are generally unable to take wing with them, unless they take advantage of a powerful updraft of air to soar up.

BIRDS WITH THE LARGEST WINGSPANS

BIRD*	MAXIMUM WINGSPAN CM	IN
1 Great white pelican	360	141
2 Wandering albatross#	351	138
3 Andean condor	320	126
4 Himalayan griffon (vulture)	310	122
5 Black vulture (Old World)	295	116
6 Marabou stork	287	113
7 Lammergeier	282	111
8 Sarus crane	280	110
9 Kori bustard	270	106
10 Stellers Sea eagle	265	104

* By species

The royal albatross, a close relative, is the same size

Source: Chris Mead

Very much bigger wingspans have been claimed for many species, but dead specimens of some species may easily be stretched by as much as 15 to 20 per cent. The measurements given are, as far as can be ascertained, for wingtip to wingtip for live birds measured in a natural position.

RAREST BIRDS

BIRD/COUNTRY	ESTIMATED NO.*
1 =Cebu flower pecker, Philippines	1
=Spix's macaw, Brazil	1
3 Hawaiian crow, Hawaii	5
4 Black stilt, New Zealand	12
5 Echo parakeet, Mauritius	13
6 Imperial Amazon parrot, Dominica	15
7 Magpie robin, Seychelles	20
8 Kakapo, New Zealand	24
9 Pink pigeon, Mauritius	70
10 Mauritius kestrel, Mauritius	100

* Of breeding pairs reported since 1986

Several rare bird species are known from old records or from only one specimen, but must be assumed to be extinct in the absence of recent sightings or records of breeding pairs.

Did You Know? On 5 June 1932 near Trondheim, Norway, a white-tailed sea eagle lifted 4-year-old Svanhild Hansen 244 m (800 ft) to its mountain eyrie. She was recovered unharmed.

Popular Pets

PEDIGREE CAT BREEDS IN THE UK

	BREED	NO. REGISTERED BY CAT FANCY (1999)
1	Persian long hair	6,881
2	British short hair	4,683
3	Siamese	4,349
4	Burmese	2,908
5	Birman	2,378
6	Bengal	1,836
7	Maine coon	1,441
8	Ragdoll	1,406
9	Oriental short hair	1,321
10	Exotic short hair	706

This Top 10 is based on a total of 31,950 cats registered with the Governing Council of the Cat Fancy in 1999.

CAT POPULATIONS

	COUNTRY	ESTIMATED CAT POPULATION (1999)
1	USA	72,600,000
2	China	46,800,000
3	Russia	12,500,000
4	Brazil	10,000,000
5	France	8,700,000
6	UK	7,700,000
7	Japan	7,540,000
8	Ukraine	7,150,000
9	Italy	7,000,000
10	Germany	6,500,000

Source: *Euromonitor*

Estimates of the number of domestic cats in the 20 leading countries reveal a total of 221 million, with the greatest increases experienced in China and other Asian countries.

TYPES OF PET IN THE UK

	PET	NUMBER OWNED (2000)
1	Goldfish	15,500,000
2	Cat	8,000,000
3	Tropical fish	7,820,000
4	Dog	6,500,000
5	Birds (excluding budgerigars and canaries)	1,810,000
6	Rabbit	1,300,000
7	Budgerigar	1,000,000
8	Guinea pig	850,000
9	Hamster	800,000
10	Canaries	360,000

Source: *Pet Food Manufacturers' Association*

Half of the households in the UK own a pet of some kind. Changes in lifestyle have affected the relative populations of both cats and dogs. More people are now living alone or as part of a couple of which both members go out to work, which makes dog ownership more difficult. Many people have therefore opted for the more independent cat as their pet.

TOP 10 CATS' NAMES IN THE UK

1 Charlie **2** Oscar **3** Molly **4** Tigger **5** Poppy **6** Sophie **7** Jasper **8** Smudge **9** Lucy **10** Chloe

Source: *PetPlan Pet Insurance*

DOG POPULATIONS

	COUNTRY	ESTIMATED DOG POPULATION (1999)
1	USA	58,500,000
2	Brazil	23,000,000
3	China	19,380,000
4	Japan	9,567,000
5	Russia	9,375,000
6	France	8,100,000
7	South Africa	7,800,000
8	Poland	7,400,000
9	UK	6,700,000
10	Italy	6,300,000

Source: *Euromonitor*

WHAT'S NEW PUSSYCAT?

Although their role as household mouse exterminators is less significant today, cats maintain their place among the world's favourite animals.

TOP 10 DOGS' NAMES IN THE UK

1 Max **2** Ben **3** Holly **4** Charlie **5** Molly **6** Barney **7** Lucy
8 Jake **9** Jack **10** Bonnie

Source: *PetPlan Pet Insurance*

TOP 10 ⭐
DOG BREEDS IN THE UK

BREED	NO. REGISTERED BY KENNEL CLUB (2000)
1 Labrador retriever	34,888
2 German shepherd (Alsatian)	17,852
3 Cocker spaniel	13,445
4 West Highland white terrier	13,051
5 Golden retriever	12,772
6 English springer spaniel	12,599
7 Cavalier King Charles spaniel	11,415
8 Staffordshire bull terrier	11,026
9 Boxer	10,573
10 Yorkshire terrier	6,787

THE 10 ⭐
LATEST WINNERS OF BEST IN SHOW AT CRUFTS

YEAR	BREED	NAME
2000	Kerry blue terrier	Torums Scarf Michael
1999	Irish setter	Caspians Intrepid
1998	Welsh terrier	Saredon Forever Young
1997	Yorkshire terrier	Ozmilion Mystification
1996	Cocker spaniel	Canigou Cambrai
1995	Irish setter	Starchelle Chicago Bear
1994	Welsh terrier	Purston Hit
1993	Irish setter	Danaway Debonair
1992	Whippet	Pencloe Dutch Gold
1991	Clumber spaniel	Raycrofts Socialite

TOP 10 RABBITS' NAMES IN THE UK

1 Thumper **2** Flopsy **3** Smokey
4 Poppy **5** Barney **6** Fudge
7 Charlie **8** Molly **9** Snowy **10** Sooty

Source: *PetPlan Pet Insurance*

JACK RUSSELL

In 1819, according to legend, John "Jack" Russell (1795–1883) spotted a milkman accompanied by a distinctive-looking dog, which he persuaded its owner to sell to him and which he named Trump. He later became Curate of Swimbridge near Barnstaple, Devon, where he devoted himself to breeding a type of fox terrier with short legs and a short white, black, and tan coat, ideally suited for hunting and able to follow animals into burrows. These dogs are today known in his honour as Jack Russell terriers.

WHO WAS · WHO WAS · WHO WAS · WHO WAS · ? ·

TOP 10 ⭐
FILMS STARRING DOGS

FILM	YEAR
1 *101 Dalmatians*	1996
2 *One Hundred and One Dalmatians**	1961
3 *102 Dalmatians*	2000
4 *Lady and the Tramp**	1955
5 *Oliver & Company*	1988
6 *Turner & Hooch*	1989
7 *The Fox and the Hound**	1981
8 *Beethoven*	1992
9 *Homeward Bound II: Lost in San Francisco*	1996
10 *Beethoven's 2nd*	1993

* Animated

Man's best friend has been stealing scenes since the earliest years of film-making, with the 1905 low-budget *Rescued by Rover* outstanding as one of the most successful productions of the pioneer period. The numerous silent-era films starring Rin Tin Tin, an ex-German army dog who emigrated to the US, and his successor Lassie, whose long series of feature and TV films dates from the 1940s onwards, are among the most enduring in cinematic history.

TOP DOGS

Labrador retrievers are the most popular dogs in both the US and the UK, where they were first bred as gundogs in the 19th century.

Creepy Crawlies

FASTEST INSECT FLYERS

INSECT	KM/H	MPH
1 Hawkmoth (*Sphingidaei*)	53.6	33.3
2 =West Indian butterfly (*Nymphalidae prepona*)	48.0	30.0
=Deer bot fly (*Cephenemyia pratti*)	48.0	30.0
4 Deer bot fly (*Chrysops*)	40.0	25.0
5 West Indian butterfly (*Hesperiidae sp.*)	30.0	18.6
6 Dragonfly (*Anax parthenope*)	28.6	17.8
7 Hornet (*Vespa crabro*)	21.4	13.3
8 Bumble bee (*Bombus lapidarius*)	17.9	11.1
9 Horsefly (*Tabanus bovinus*)	14.3	8.9
10 Honey bee (*Apis millefera*)	11.6	7.2

Few accurate assessments of insect flying speeds have ever been attempted, and this Top 10 represents the results of only the handful of scientific studies that are widely recognized by entomologists. Some experts have also suggested that the male *Hybomitra linei wrighti* (*Diptera tabanidae*) is capable of travelling at 145 km/h (90 mph) when in pursuit of a female, while there are exceptional, one-off examples such as that of a dragonfly (*Austophlebia costalis*) allegedly recorded as flying at a speed of 98 km/h (61 mph).

TOP 10 ★

LARGEST BUTTERFLIES

BUTTERFLY	AVERAGE WINGSPAN MM	IN
1 Queen Alexandra's birdwing	280	11.0
2 African giant swallowtail	230	9.1
3 Goliath birdwing	210	8.3
4 =Buru opalescent birdwing	200	7.9
=*Trogonoptera trojana*	200	7.9
=*Troides hypolitus*	200	7.9
7 =Chimaera birdwing	190	7.5
=*Ornithoptera lydius*	190	7.5
=*Troides magellanus*	190	7.5
=*Troides miranda*	190	7.5

TOP 10 ★

CREATURES WITH THE MOST LEGS

CREATURE	AVERAGE LEGS
1 Millipede *Illacme plenipes*	750
2 Centipede *Himantarum gabrielis*	354
3 Centipede *Haplophilus subterraneus*	178
4 Millipedes*	30
5 Symphylans	24
6 Caterpillars*	16
7 Woodlice	14
8 Crabs, shrimps	10
9 Spiders	8
10 Insects	6

* Most species

Despite their names, centipedes, depending on their species, have anything from 28 to 354 legs and millipedes have up to 400 legs, with the record standing at around 750.

TOP 10 ★

LARGEST MOLLUSCS

SPECIES/CLASS	AVERAGE LENGTH* MM	IN
1 Giant squid (*Architeuthis sp.*), Cephalopod	16,764	660#
2 Giant clam (*Tridacna gigas*), Marine bivalve	1,300	51
3 Australian trumpet, Marine snail	770	30
4 *Hexabranchus sanguineus*, Sea slug	520	20
5 *Carinaria cristata*, Heteropod	500	19
6 Steller's coat of mail shell (*Cryptochiton stelleri*), Chiton	470	18
7 Freshwater mussel (*Cristaria plicata*), Freshwater bivalve	300	11
8 Giant African snail (*Achatina achatina*), Land snail	200	7
9 Tusk shell (*Dentalium vernedi*), Scaphopod	138	5
10 Apple snail (*Pila werneri*), Freshwater snail	125	4

* Largest species within each class
 # Estimated; actual length unknown

THE 10 ★

COUNTRIES WITH THE MOST THREATENED INVERTEBRATES

COUNTRY	THREATENED INVERTEBRATE SPECIES
1 USA	594
2 Australia	281
3 South Africa	101
4 Portugal	67
5 France	61
6 Spain	57
7 Tanzania	46
8 =Dem. Rep. of Congo	45
=Japan	45
10 =Austria	41
=Italy	41

Source: *International Union for the Conservation of Nature*

TOP 10 ★

LARGEST MOTHS

MOTH	AVERAGE WINGSPAN MM	IN
1 Atlas moth (*Attacus atlas*)	300	11.8
2 Owlet moth (*Thysania agrippina*)*	290	11.4
3 *Haematopis grataria*	260	10.2
4 Hercules emperor moth (*Coscinocera hercules*)	210	8.3
5 Malagasy silk moth (*Argema mitraei*)	180	7.1
6 *Eacles imperialis*	175	6.9
7 = Common emperor moth (*Bunaea alcinoe*)	160	6.3
=Giant peacock moth (*Saturnia pyri*)	160	6.3
9 Gray moth (*Brahmaea wallichii*)	155	6.1
10 =Black witch (*Ascalapha odorata*)	150	5.9
=Regal moth (*Citheronia regalis*)	150	5.9
=Polyphemus moth (*Antheraea polyphemus*)	150	5.9

* Exceptional specimen measured at 308 mm (12¼ in)

TOP 10 ★
DEADLIEST SPIDERS

SPIDER/LOCATION

1 Banana spider (*Phonenutria nigriventer*), Central and South America

2 Sydney funnel web (*Atrax robustus*), Australia

3 Wolf spider (*Lycosa raptoria/erythrognatha*), Central and South America

4 Black widow (*Latrodectus species*), Widespread

5 Violin spider/Recluse spider, Widespread

6 Sac spider, Southern Europe

7 Tarantula (*Eurypelma rubropilosum*), Neotropics

8 Tarantula (*Acanthoscurria atrox*), Neotropics

9 Tarantula (*Lasiodora klugi*), Neotropics

10 Tarantula (*Pamphobeteus species*), Neotropics

This list ranks spiders according to their "lethal potential" – their venom yield divided by their venom potency. The Banana spider, for example, yields 6 mg of venom, with 1 mg the estimated lethal dose in man.

THE 10 MOST ENDANGERED SPIDERS
(Spider/country)

1 Kauai cave wolf spider, USA **2** Doloff cave spider, USA **3** Empire cave pseudoscorpion, USA **4** Glacier Bay wolf spider, USA **5** Great raft spider, Europe **6** Kocevje subterranean spider (*Troglohyphantes gracilis*), Slovenia **7** Kocevje subterranean spider (*Troglohyphantes similis*), Slovenia **8** Kocevje subterranean spider (*Troglohyphantes spinipes*), Slovenia **9** Lake Placid funnel wolf spider, USA **10** Melones cave harvestman, USA

Source: *International Union for the Conservation of Nature*

THE FLY
The 120,000 known species of flies include houseflies, mosquitoes, midges, and gnats, all of which number among the insects human beings consider the most irritating.

TOP 10 ★
MOST COMMON INSECTS*

SPECIES	APPROX. NO. OF KNOWN SPECIES
1 Beetles (*Coleoptera*)	400,000
2 Butterflies and moths (*Lepidoptera*)	165,000
3 Ants, bees, and wasps (*Hymenoptera*)	140,000
4 True flies (*Diptera*)	120,000
5 Bugs (*Hemiptera*)	90,000
6 Crickets, grasshoppers, and locusts (*Orthoptera*)	20,000
7 Caddisflies (*Trichoptera*)	10,000
8 Lice (*Phthiraptera/Psocoptera*)	7,000
9 Dragonflies and damselflies (*Odonata*)	5,500
10 Lacewings (*Neuroptera*)	4,700

* By number of known species

This list includes only species that have been discovered and named. It is surmised that many thousands of species still await discovery. It takes no account of the truly colossal numbers of each species: there are at least 1 million insects for each of the Earth's 6.1 billion human beings.

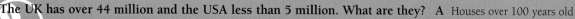

The UK has over 44 million and the USA less than 5 million. What are they? *see p.42 for the answer*

A Houses over 100 years old
B Sheep
C Oak trees

Livestock

CATTLE COUNTRIES

COUNTRY	CATTLE (2000)
1 India	218,800,000
2 Brazil	167,471,000
3 China	104,169,000
4 USA	98,048,000
5 Argentina	55,000,000
6 Sudan	35,300,000
7 Ethiopia	35,100,000
8 Mexico	30,293,000
9 Russian Federation	27,500,000
10 Colombia	26,000,000
UK	*11,423,000*
World	*1,343,794,190*

Source: *Food and Agriculture Organization of the United Nations*

SHEEP COUNTRIES

COUNTRY	SHEEP (2000)
1 China	131,095,000
2 Australia	116,900,000
3 India	57,900,000
4 Iran	55,000,000
5 New Zealand	45,497,000
6 UK	44,656,000
7 Sudan	42,800,000
8 Turkey	30,238,000
9 South Africa	28,700,000
10 Pakistan	24,084,000
World	*1,064,373,000*

Source: *Food and Agriculture Organization of the United Nations*

This is one of the few world lists in which the UK ranks considerably higher than the US, which has only 4,719,000 head of sheep.

CHICKEN COUNTRIES

COUNTRY	CHICKENS (2000)
1 China	3,625,012,000
2 USA	1,720,000,000
3 Indonesia	1,000,000,000
4 Brazil	950,000,000
5 Mexico	476,000,000
6 India	402,000,000
7 Russia	340,000,000
8 Japan	298,000,000
9 France	232,970,000
10 Iran	230,000,000
UK	*154,180,000*
World	*14,525,381,000*

Source: *Food and Agriculture Organization of the United Nations*

The Top 10 countries have 65 per cent of the world's chicken population, with almost half the world total being reared in Asian countries. In the UK, the estimated chicken population of 154,180,000 outnumbers the human population more than twice over.

TOP 10 MILK-PRODUCING COUNTRIES

(Country/production in tonnes*, 2000)

❶ **USA**, 76,294,000 ❷ **Russia**, 31,560,000 ❸ **India**, 30,900,000 ❹ **Germany**, 28,200,000 ❺ **France**, 24,890,000 ❻ **Brazil**, 22,495,000 ❼ **UK**, 14,721,000 ❽ **Ukraine**, 12,400,000 ❾ **New Zealand**, 12,014,000 ❿ **Poland**, 11,845,000

World 484,746,595

* *Fresh cows' milk*   Source: *Food and Agriculture Organization of the United Nations*

GEESE COUNTRIES

COUNTRY	GEESE (2000)
1 China	203,225,000
2 Egypt	9,100,000
3 Romania	4,000,000
4 Russia	3,300,000
5 Madagascar	3,100,000
6 Turkey	1,650,000
7 Hungary	1,226,000
8 Iran	1,200,000
9 Israel	1,100,000
10 France	1,000,000
World	*235,087,000*

Source: *Food and Agriculture Organization of the United Nations*

GOLDEN EGG

Some 86 per cent of the world's geese reside in China, where they play an important part in culture and cuisine. China is also the top producer of goose down.

BUFFALO

More than 95 per cent of the world's buffalo population resides in the Top 10 countries. Only one European country has a significant herd: Italy, with 170,000.

TOP 10 ★ CAMEL COUNTRIES

	COUNTRY	CAMELS (2000)
1	Somalia	5,800,000
2	Sudan	3,180,000
3	Pakistan	1,200,000
4	Mauritania	1,185,000
5	Ethiopia	1,060,000
6	India	1,030,000
7	Kenya	835,000
8	Chad	700,000
9	Saudi Arabia	428,000
10	Niger	400,000
	World	18,970,000

Source: *Food and Agriculture Organization of the United Nations*

TOP 10 ★ PIG COUNTRIES

	COUNTRY	PIGS (2000)
1	China	437,551,000
2	USA	59,337,000
3	Brazil	27,320,000
4	Germany	27,049,000
5	Spain	23,682,000
6	Vietnam	19,584,000
7	Russia	18,300,000
8	Poland	18,200,000
9	India	16,005,000
10	France	14,635,000
	World	909,486,000

Source: *Food and Agriculture Organization of the United Nations*

The distribution of the world's pig population is determined by cultural, religious, and dietary factors, with the result that there are few pigs in African and Islamic countries, and a disproportionate concentration of pigs in those countries that do not have such prohibitions.

TOP 10 ★ DONKEY COUNTRIES

	COUNTRY	DONKEYS (2000)
1	China	9,348,000
2	Ethiopia	5,200,000
3	Pakistan	4,500,000
4	Mexico	3,250,000
5	Egypt	3,050,000
6	Iran	1,600,000
7	Brazil	1,350,000
8	Afghanistan	1,160,000
9 =	India	1,000,000
=	Nigeria	1,000,000
	World	43,564,000

Source: *Food and Agriculture Organization of the United Nations*

DONKEY

The donkey is used extensively throughout the world as a beast of burden. It should not be confused with the mule (the offspring of a horse and a donkey).

TOP 10 ★ BUFFALO COUNTRIES

	COUNTRY	BUFFALOES (2000)
1	India	93,772,000
2	Pakistan	22,670,000
3	China	22,599,000
4	Nepal	3,471,000
5	Egypt	3,200,000
6	Indonesia	3,145,000
7	Philippines	3,018,000
8	Vietnam	3,000,000
9	Myanmar (Burma)	2,400,000
10	Thailand	2,100,000
	World	165,804,000

Source: *Food and Agriculture Organization of the United Nations*

TOP 10 FARM ANIMALS MOST OFTEN TREATED BY VETS IN THE UK

1 Cattle 2 Sheep 3 Goats 4 Pigs 5 Horses 6 Donkeys 7 Deer 8 Poultry 9 Farmed fish 10 = Llamas; = Ostriches

Did You Know? The first pig to fly took to the air on 4 November 1909, the passenger of Claude Moore- (later Lord) Brabazon, in a wicker basket attached to his Voisin biplane.

43

Trees & Forests

RUBBER-PRODUCING COUNTRIES

	COUNTRY	PRODUCTION 1999 (TONNES)
1	Thailand	2,198,410
2	Indonesia	1,564,324
3	Malaysia	885,700
4	India	550,000
5	China	440,000
6	Vietnam	214,827
7	Côte d'Ivoire	118,860
8	Sri Lanka	95,710
9	Nigeria	90,000
10	Philippines	64,000
	World total	6,529,738

Source: *Food and Agriculture Organization of the United Nations*

MOST FORESTED COUNTRIES

	COUNTRY	PERCENTAGE FOREST COVER
1	French Guiana	90.0
2	Solomon Islands	87.8
3	Surinam	86.4
4	Gabon	81.5
5	Guyana	78.5
6	Brunei	76.6
7	Palau	76.1
8	Finland	72.0
9	North Korea	68.1
10	Sweden	66.8
	UK	11.6

Source: *Food and Agriculture Organization of the United Nations*

These are the 10 countries with the greatest area of forest and woodland as a percentage of their total land area. With increasing deforestation, the world average has fallen from about 32 per cent in 1972 to its present 29 per cent. The least forested large countries in the world are the desert lands of the Middle East and North Africa, such as Oman, which has no forests, and Egypt with just 0.1 per cent forested land.

COUNTRIES WITH THE LARGEST AREAS OF FOREST

	COUNTRY	AREA SQ KM	AREA SQ MILES
1	Russia	8,513,920	3,287,243
2	Brazil	5,324,810	2,055,921
3	Canada	2,445,710	944,294
4	USA	2,259,930	872,564
5	China	1,634,800	631,200
6	Australia	1,580,800	610,350
7	Dem. Rep. of Congo	1,352,070	522,037
8	Indonesia	1,049,860	405,353
9	Angola	697,560	269,329
10	Peru	652,150	251,796
	UK	27,940	10,788
	World total	38,561,590	14,888,715

The world's forests occupy some 29 per cent of the total land area of the planet. Just under half of Russia is forested, a total area that is almost the size of the whole of Brazil.

LARGEST FORESTS IN THE UK*

	FOREST	AREA SQ KM	AREA SQ MILES
1	Galloway Forest Park	760	293
2	Kielder Forest Park	720	278
3	New Forest	270	104
4	Dornoch Forest	260	100
5	Argyll Forest Park	220	85
6	Queen Elizabeth Forest Park	210	81
7	Thetford Forest Park	190	73
8 =	Affric Forest (Fort Augustus)	180	69
=	Tay Forest Park	180	69
10	Glengarry (Lochaber Forest District)	165	64

* Forestry Commission forests, including Forest Parks, which can include non-woodland areas

Source: *Forestry Commission*

TAPPING RUBBER

In the 20th century, world demand for natural rubber, especially for the automotive industry, increased from under 50,000 to over 6 million tonnes.

TREE TOPS

The USA leads the world in timber production, supplying the requirements of industries such as construction and paper manufacture.

TOP 10 ★
TIMBER-PRODUCING COUNTRIES

	COUNTRY	CU M	PRODUCTION 1999 CU FT
1	China	582,660,000	20,576,445,622
2	USA	500,745,000	17,683,644,429
3	India	302,793,992	10,693,069,905
4	Brazil	197,897,000	6,988,667,249
5	Indonesia	190,600,508	6,730,994,042
6	Canada	185,658,834	6,556,480,455
7	Russia	111,000,000	3,919,928,370
8	Nigeria	100,637,000	3,553,962,445
9	Sweden	58,700,000	2,072,971,129
10	Finland	53,850,569	1,901,715,074
	World total	3,275,082,160	115,658,445,703

Source: *Food and Agriculture Organization of the United Nations*

TOP 10 ★
MOST COMMON TREES IN THE UK

	TREE	PERCENTAGE OF TOTAL FOREST AREA
1	Sitka spruce	28
2	Scots pine	10
3	Oak	9
4	Birch	7
5 =	Ash	6
=	Lodgepole pine	6
7	Japanese/Hybrid larch	5
8	Beech	4
9 =	Norway spruce	3
=	Sycamore	3

Source: *Forestry Commission*

Six per cent of the UK's forested areas is classified as mixed broadleaves and 1 per cent as mixed conifers.

TOP 10 ★
TALLEST TREES IN THE UK*

	TREE	LOCATION	HEIGHT M	FT
1 =	Douglas fir	Hyslop Arboretum, Dunans, Strathclyde	65	213
=	Douglas fir	Moniac Glen, Highland	65	213
3	Sitka spruce	Private estate, Strathearn, Tayside	61	200
4	Grand fir	Strone house, Strathclyde	60	197
5	Giant sequoia	Castle Leod, Strathpeffer, Highland	53	174
6 =	Japanese larch	Diana's Grove, Blair Castle, Tayside	52	171
=	Noble fir	Ardkinglas Arboretum, Strathclyde	52	171
=	Norway spruce	Moniac Glen, Highland	52	171
9	Western hemlock	Benmore Younger Botanic Gardens, Strathclyde	51	167
10 =	Caucasian fir	Cragside, Northumberland	50	164
=	European silver fir	Thirlmere, Cumbria	50	164

* *The tallest known example of each of the 10 tallest species*

Source: *The Tree Register of the British Isles*

Achatina achatina **is the scientific name for what?**
see p.40 for the answer

A The giant African snail
B The gorilla
C The common toad

THE HUMAN WORLD

The Human Body & Health

TOP 10 ★
LONGEST BONES IN THE HUMAN BODY

BONE	AVERAGE LENGTH CM	IN
1 Femur (thighbone – upper leg)	50.50	19.88
2 Tibia (shinbone – inner lower leg)	43.03	16.94
3 Fibula (outer lower leg)	40.50	15.94
4 Humerus (upper arm)	36.46	14.35
5 Ulna (inner lower arm)	28.20	11.10
6 Radius (outer lower arm)	26.42	10.40
7 7th rib	24.00	9.45
8 8th rib	23.00	9.06
9 Innominate bone (hipbone – half pelvis)	18.50	7.28
10 Sternum (breastbone)	17.00	6.69

These are the average dimensions of the bones of an adult male measured from their extremities (ribs are curved, and the pelvis measurement is taken diagonally). The same bones in the female skeleton are usually 6 to 13 per cent smaller, with the exception of the smallest, the sternum, which is virtually identical in size.

THE 10 MOST COMMON HOSPITAL CASUALTY COMPLAINTS

1 Cuts 2 Bruises 3 Dog bites
4 Sprained ankles 5 Eye injuries
6 Head injuries 7 Minor burns
8 Fractures 9 Upper respiratory tract infections 10 Gastroenteritis

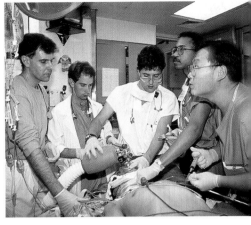

ER, USA
The world's hospital emergency rooms are equipped to treat victims of everything from minor injuries to major traumas from vehicle accidents and disasters.

THE 10 ★
COUNTRIES WITH THE MOST PATIENTS PER DOCTOR

COUNTRY	PATIENTS PER DOCTOR
1 Malawi	49,118
2 Eritrea	46,200
3 Mozambique	36,320
4 Niger	35,141
5 Ethiopia	30,195
6 Chad	27,765
7 Burkina Faso	27,158
8 Rwanda	24,697
9 Liberia	24,600
10 Ghana	22,970

Source: *World Bank*

THE FIRST INJECTABLE ANAESTHETIC

The first anaesthetics – ether, chloroform, and nitrous oxide ("laughing gas") – came into use in the mid-19th century. All were administered by the patient breathing in the vapours or gases, but all had their drawbacks, in particular the difficulty of safely controlling the precise quantity that was being administered. In 1902, German chemist Emil Fischer and pathologist Joseph Freiherr von Mering introduced the hypnotic drugs known as barbiturates, including Veronal, the first injectable anaesthetic. This enabled the anaesthetist to control the patient's breathing. It is said that von Mering proposed that the new substance be called "Veronal", since the most peaceful place he knew was the Italian city of Verona.

100 YEARS AGO · YEARS AGO · YEARS AGO · YEARS

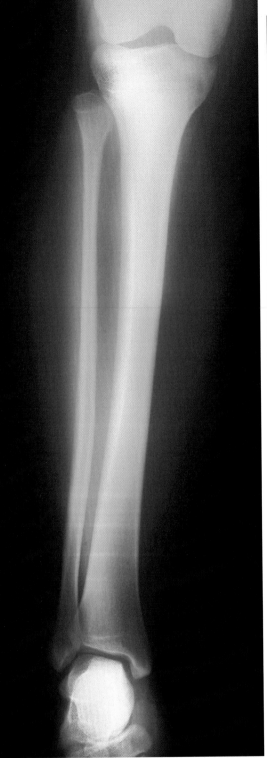

THE WINNING LEG
The second longest bone, the tibia is named after the Latin word for a flute, which it resembles in shape and length. The three longest bones are all in the leg.

How many cigarettes does the average Iraqi smoker consume annually?
see p.50 for the answer

A 3,777
B 5,751
C 18,902

TOP 10 ★
COUNTRIES THAT SPEND THE MOST ON HEALTH CARE

	COUNTRY	HEALTH SPENDING PER CAPITA ($)
1	USA	4,080
2	Switzerland	3,616
3	Germany	2,727
4	Norway	2,616
5	Denmark	2,576
6	Japan	2,379
7	France	2,287
8	Sweden	2,220
9	Austria	2,108
10	Netherlands	1,988
	UK	1,480

Source: *World Bank*, World Development Indicators 2000

THE 10 ★
GLOBAL DISEASES THAT CAUSE THE HIGHEST LEVEL OF DISABILITY

	DISEASE	PERCENTAGE OF TOTAL BURDEN OF DISEASE * #
1	Neuropsychiatric disorders	11.0
2	Cardiovascular diseases	10.9
3	Respiratory infections	7.0
4 =	HIV/AIDS	6.2
=	Perinatal conditions	6.2
6	Malignant neoplasms (cancers)	5.9
7	Diarrhoeal diseases	5.0
8	Respiratory diseases (non-communicable)	4.9
9	Childhood diseases	3.8
10	Malaria	3.1

* *Measured in Disability-Adjusted Life Years (DALYs): a measure of the difference between a population's actual level of health and a normative goal of living in full health*

\# *Total percentage includes injuries at 13.9 per cent*

Source: *World Health Organisation*, World Health Report 2000

TOP 10 ★
LARGEST HUMAN ORGANS

	ORGAN		AVERAGE WEIGHT G	OZ
1	Skin		10,886	384.0
2	Liver		1,560	55.0
3	Brain	male	1,408	49.7
		female	1,263	44.6
4	Lungs	right	580	20.5
		left	510	18.0
		total	1,090	38.5
5	Heart	male	315	11.1
		female	265	9.3
6	Kidneys	right	140	4.9
		left	150	5.3
		total	290	10.2
7	Spleen		170	6.0
8	Pancreas		98	3.5
9	Thyroid		35	1.2
10	Prostate	male only	20	0.7

This list is based on average immediate post-mortem weights, as recorded by St. Bartholemew's Hospital, London, and other sources during a 10-year period.

BRAIN WAVE

The modern technique of Magnetic Resonance Imaging (MRI) enables us to view the human brain, the human body's third-largest organ.

TOP 10 ★
MOST COMMON PHOBIAS

	OBJECT OF PHOBIA	MEDICAL TERM
1	Spiders	Arachnephobia or arachnophobia
2	People and social situations	Anthropophobia or sociophobia
3	Flying	Aerophobia or aviatophobia
4	Open spaces	Agoraphobia, cenophobia, or kenophobia
5	Confined spaces	Claustrophobia, cleisiophobia, cleithrophobia, or clithrophobia
6 =	Vomiting	Emetophobia or emitophobia
=	Heights	Acrophobia, altophobia, hypsophobia, or hypsiphobia
8	Cancer	Carcinomaphobia, carcinophobia, carcinomatophobia, cancerphobia, or cancerophobia
9	Thunderstorms	Brontophobia or keraunophobia
10 =	Death	Necrophobia or thanatophobia
=	Heart disease	Cardiophobia

A phobia is a morbid fear that is out of all proportion to the object of the fear. Many people would admit to being uncomfortable about the objects of these principal phobias, as well as about others, such as snakes (ophiophobia) or ghosts (phasmophobia).

Lifestyle

COUNTRIES WITH THE HEAVIEST SMOKERS

COUNTRY	AVERAGE ANNUAL CIGARETTE CONSUMPTION PER SMOKER (1988–98)*
1 Iraq	5,751
2 Belgium	5,300
3 Australia	4,951
4 Hungary	4,949
5 USA	4,938
6 Greece	4,877
7 Switzerland	4,618
8 Poland	4,544
9 Singapore	4,250
10 Japan	4,126
UK	3,706

* Smokers aged over 15, in those countries for which data available

Source: *World Bank*, World Development Indicators 2000

MOST UNDERNOURISHED COUNTRIES

COUNTRY	APPROXIMATE PERCENTAGE UNDERNOURISHED*, 1995–97
1 Somalia	73
2 Eritrea	67
3 =Burundi	63
=Mozambique	63
5 Afghanistan	62
6 Haiti	61
7 Dem. Rep. of Congo	55
8 Ethiopia	51
9 =Mongolia	49
=North Korea	49

* Food intake that is insufficient to meet dietary requirements continuously

Source: *Food and Agriculture Organization of the United Nations*

FAT CONSUMERS

COUNTRY	DAILY CONSUMPTION PER CAPITA	
	G	OZ
1 France	164.7	5.80
2 Austria	159.9	5.64
3 Belgium and Luxembourg	158.6	5.58
4 Italy	152.3	5.37
5 Greece	151.7	5.35
6 Switzerland	147.3	5.19
7 Germany	147.0	5.18
8 Spain	146.8	5.17
9 USA	146.4	5.16
10 UK	143.7	5.06
World	73.5	2.59

Source: *Food and Agriculture Organization of the United Nations*

CALORIE CONSUMERS

COUNTRY	AVERAGE DAILY CONSUMPTION PER CAPITA
1 USA	3,756.8
2 Portugal	3,691.1
3 Greece	3,629.9
4 Ireland	3,622.0
5 Italy	3,608.3
6 Belgium and Luxembourg	3,606.3
7 Turkey	3,554.1
8 France	3,541.2
9 Austria	3,530.8
10 Cyprus	3,473.8
UK	3,256.7
World	2,791.8

Source: *Food and Agriculture Organization of the United Nations*

The Calorie requirement of the average man is 2,700 and that of a woman 2,500. Inactive people need less, while those engaged in heavy labour might need even to double these figures.

FAT OF THE LAND

The ubiquitous burger and fries contribute to the US's place at the top of the table of high Calorie consumers.

TOP 10 MOST EFFECTIVE KEEP-FIT ACTIVITIES

1 Swimming **2** Cycling **3** Rowing **4** Gymnastics **5** Judo **6** Dancing
7 Football **8** Jogging **9** Walking (briskly!) **10** Squash

These are the sports and activities recommended by keep-fit experts as the best means of acquiring all-round fitness, building stamina and strength, and increasing suppleness.

TOP 10 ★
MULTI-VITAMIN CONSUMERS

COUNTRY	PERCENTAGE OF HEALTH SUPPLEMENT MARKET
1 Mexico	34.8
2 =Brazil	30.9
=Spain	30.9
4 Switzerland	30.5
5 UK	30.4
6 Canada	27.1
7 Italy	24.8
8 USA	24.0
9 Finland	22.0
10 Germany	20.5

Source: *Euromonitor*

TOP 10 ★
CAUSES OF STRESS-RELATED ILLNESS

EVENT	VALUE
1 Death of spouse	100
2 Divorce	73
3 Marital separation	65
4 =Death of close family member	63
=Detention in prison or other institution	63
6 Major personal injury or illness	53
7 Marriage	50
8 Losing one's job	47
9 =Marital reconciliation	45
=Retirement	45

Psychiatrists Dr. Thomas Holmes and Dr. Richard Rahe devised what they called the "Social Readjustment Rating Scale" to place a value on the likelihood of illness occurring as a result of stress caused by various "life events". The cumulative effect of several incidents increases the risk factor.

TOP 10 ★
COUNTRIES SPENDING THE MOST ON WEIGHT MANAGEMENT PRODUCTS

COUNTRY	VALUE OF SALES IN 1999 ($)
1 USA	3,546,300,000
2 Japan	896,000,000
3 France	142,700,000
4 UK	126,800,000
5 Italy	114,400,000
6 China	102,400,000
7 Canada	84,000,000
8 Australia	56,700,000
9 Brazil	56,600,000
10 Germany	44,200,000

Source: *Euromonitor*

TOP 10 ★
SPENDERS ON VITAMINS AND DIETARY SUPPLEMENTS

COUNTRY	VALUE OF SALES IN 1999 ($)
1 USA	11,430,200,000
2 Japan	10,733,400,000
3 Germany	795,500,000
4 UK	630,500,000
5 China	523,300,000
6 France	511,700,000
7 Italy	510,400,000
8 Brazil	465,200,000
9 Canada	430,400,000
10 Russia	230,400,000

Source: *Euromonitor*

TWO WHEELS GOOD

Cycling's popularity has increased since the invention of the mountain bike. It is ranked second only to swimming as one of the most effective keep-fit activities.

TOP 10 ★
COSMETIC SURGERY PROCEDURES

1 Body reshaping by liposuction/liposculpture

2 Nose reshaping (rhinoplasty)

3 Upper or lower eye bag removal (blepharoplasty)

4 Face lift

5 Breast augmentation

6 Breast reduction

7 Ear reshaping (otoplasty)

8 Laser treatment for the removal of lines and wrinkles

9 Laser treatment for snoring problems

10 Varicose veins/thread vein removal

Source: *The Harley Medical Group*

Did You Know? Soon after the press identified 54-year-old Chao Boonchu as Thailand's champion chain-smoker (120 cigarettes a day for 30 years), he collapsed with severe breathing difficulties and heart problems and went into a coma.

Cradle to the Grave

COUNTRIES WITH THE HIGHEST BIRTH RATE

COUNTRY	EST. LIVE BIRTH RATE PER 1,000 POPULATION, 2002
1 Niger	50.5
2 Mali	48.4
3 Chad	47.7
4 Uganda	47.1
5 Somalia	46.8
6 Angola	46.2
7 Liberia	46.0
8 Dem. Rep of Congo	45.5
9 Marshall Islands	45.0
10 Sierre Leone	44.6
UK	11.3

Source: *US Census Bureau, International Data Base*

The countries with the highest birth rates are amongst the poorest countries in the world. In these countries, people often want to have large families so that the children can help earn income for the family when they are older.

CHILDREN FROM MALI

Mali is one of only a handful of countries with a birth rate of more than 45 per 1,000. The country also has the ninth highest fertility rate (the average number of children born to each woman) of 6.6.

TOP 10 COUNTRIES WITH THE LOWEST BIRTH RATE

(Country/est. live birth rate per 1,000 population, 2002)

❶ Bulgaria, 8.1 ❷ Latvia, 8.3 ❸ Italy, 8.9 ❹ = Estonia, 9.0; = Germany, 9.0 ❻ Czech Republic, 9.1 ❼ = Hungary, 9.3; = Slovenia, 9.3; = Spain, 9.3 ❿ = Austria, 9.6; = Monaco, 9.6; = Ukraine, 9.6

Source: *US Census Bureau, International Data Base*

COUNTRIES WITH THE HIGHEST UNDER-5 MORTALITY RATE

COUNTRY	MORTALITY RATE PER 1,000 LIVE BIRTHS (1998)
1 Sierra Leone	316
2 Angola	292
3 Niger	280
4 Afghanistan	257
5 Mali	237
6 Liberia	235
7 Malawi	213
8 Somalia	211
9 Dem. Rep. of Congo	207
10 Mozambique	206
UK	6.2

Source: *UNICEF, The State of the World's Children 2000*

COUNTRIES WITH THE HIGHEST DEATH RATE

COUNTRY	DEATH RATE PER 1,000 POPULATION
1 Angola	25.01
2 Mozambique	23.29
3 Niger	23.17
4 Malawi	22.44
5 Zimbabwe	22.43
6 = Botswana	22.08
= Zambia	22.08
8 Rwanda	20.95
9 Swaziland	20.40
10 Sierra Leone	19.58

Source: *Central Intelligence Agency*

The 15 countries with the highest death rate are all in the African continent; the highest outside Africa is Afghanistan, with a rate of 18.01. Ukraine's 16.48 is the highest of any European country, and Haiti's 15.12 the highest of any in the Western hemisphere.

THE 10 MOST COMMON CAUSES OF DEATH

(Cause/approximate no. of deaths per annum)

❶ Ischaemic heart disease, 7,089,000 ❷ Cancers*, 7,065,000 ❸ Cerebrovascular disease, 5,544,000 ❹ Acute lower respiratory infection, 3,963,000 ❺ HIV/AIDS, 2,673,000 ❻ Chronic obstructive pulmonary disease, 2,660,000 ❼ Diarrhoea, including dysentery, 2,213,000 ❽ Tuberculosis, 1,669,000 ❾ Childhood diseases#, 1,554,000 ❿ Road traffic accidents, 1,230,000

* Lung cancer deaths alone number 1,193,000
 # Childhood diseases include pertussis, polio, diphtheria, measles, and tetanus
Source: *WHO, World Health Report 2000*

GREEK GIFT

The country's traditional Mediterranean diet, high in olive oil, fruits and vegetables, and fish, may partly explain why Greek men enjoy one of the world's highest life expectancies.

TOP 10 ★
COUNTRIES WITH THE HIGHEST MALE LIFE EXPECTANCY

	COUNTRY	LIFE EXPECTANCY AT BIRTH, 2002 (YEARS)
1	Andorra	80.6
2	San Marino	77.8
3	Japan	77.7
4	Iceland	77.4
5	Singapore	77.3
6 =Australia		77.2
=Sweden		77.2
8	Switzerland	77.0
9	Israel	76.8
10	Canada	76.3
	UK	*75.3*

Source: *US Census Bureau, International Data Base*

TOP 10 ★
COUNTRIES WITH THE HIGHEST FEMALE LIFE EXPECTANCY

	COUNTRY	LIFE EXPECTANCY AT BIRTH, 2002 (YEARS)
1	Andorra	86.6
2	San Marino	85.2
3	Japan	84.2
4	Singapore	83.5
5 =Canada		83.2
=Monaco		83.2
7	France	83.1
8	Australia	83.0
9	Switzerland	82.9
10	Spain	82.8
	UK	*80.8*

Source: *US Census Bureau, International Data Base*

THE 10 ★
COUNTRIES WITH THE MOST CASES OF AIDS

	COUNTRY	DEATHS	NO. OF CASES
1	South Africa	250,000	4,200,000
2	India	310,000	3,700,000
3	Ethiopia	280,000	3,000,000
4	Nigeria	250,000	2,700,000
5	Kenya	180,000	2,100,000
6	Zimbabwe	160,000	1,500,000
7	Tanzania	140,000	1,300,000
8	Mozambique	98,000	1,200,000
9	Dem. Rep. of Congo	95,000	1,100,000
10	Zambia	99,000	870,000
	UK	*450*	*31,000*
	World	*2,800,000*	*34,300,000*

Source: *UNAIDS, Report on the Global HIV/AIDS Epidemic, June 2000*

THE 10 ★
MOST COMMON TYPES OF CANCER

	TYPE	ANNUAL DEATHS
1	Trachea, bronchus, and lung	1,193,000
2	Stomach	801,000
3	Liver	589,000
4	Colon and rectum	509,000
5	Breast	467,000
6	Oesophagus	381,000
7	Lymphomas	295,000
8	Mouth and pharynx	282,000
9	Leukaemias	268,000
10	Prostate	255,000

Source: *WHO, World Health Report 2000*

Globally, a clear trend is emerging: the gradual elimination of other fatal diseases, combined with rising life expectancy, means that the risks of developing cancer are steadily growing. One of the most noticeable changes in the ranking compared with 10 years ago is the increase in lung cancer.

THE 10 MOST SUICIDAL COUNTRIES
(Country/suicides per 100,000 population)*

1 Lithuania, 42.0 **2** Russia, 37.4 **3** Belarus, 35.0 **4** Latvia, 34.3 **5** Estonia, 33.2 **6** Hungary, 32.1 **7** Slovenia, 30.9 **8** Ukraine, 29.4 **9** Kazakhstan, 28.7 **10** Finland, 24.3 *UK, 7.5*

* In those countries/latest year for which data available

It is perhaps surprising that the highest suicide rates are not generally recorded in the poorest countries in the world. Source: UN Demographic Yearbook

In what did New Zealand lead the world in 1893?   **A** Granting women the vote
see p.60 for the answer   **B** Abolishing capital punishment
   C Making firearms illegal

Marriage & Divorce

TOP 10 ★
COUNTRIES WITH THE MOST MARRIAGES

COUNTRY	MARRIAGES PER ANNUM*
1 USA	2,384,000
2 Bangladesh	1,181,000
3 Russia	848,306
4 Japan	784,580
5 Brazil	734,045
6 Mexico	707,840
7 Turkey	519,216
8 Egypt	493,787
9 Iran	479,263
10 Thailand	470,751
UK	416,821

In countries/latest year for which data available

Source: *United Nations*

This list, based on United Nations statistics, regrettably excludes certain large countries such as Indonesia, India, and Pakistan, which fail to provide accurate data.

TOP 10 ★
COUNTRIES WITH THE HIGHEST PROPORTION OF TEENAGE BRIDES

COUNTRY	PERCENTAGE OF 15–19-YEAR-OLD GIRLS WHO HAVE EVER BEEN MARRIED*
1 Dem. Rep. of Congo	74.2
2 Congo	55.0
3 Afghanistan	53.7
4 Bangladesh	51.3
5 Uganda	49.8
6 Mali	49.7
7 Guinea	49.0
8 Chad	48.6
9 Mozambique	47.1
10 Senegal	43.8
UK	1.7

In latest year for which data available

Source: *United Nations*

TOP 10 ★
COUNTRIES WITH THE HIGHEST PROPORTION OF TEENAGE HUSBANDS

COUNTRY	PERCENTAGE OF 15–19-YEAR-OLD BOYS WHO HAVE EVER BEEN MARRIED*
1 Iraq	14.9
2 Nepal	13.5
3 Congo	11.8
4 Uganda	11.4
5 India	9.5
6 Afghanistan	9.2
7 Guinea	8.2
8 Central African Republic	8.1
9 Guatemala	7.8
10 Columbia	7.7
UK	0.5

In latest year for which data available

Source: *United Nations*

TOP 10 ★
COUNTRIES WITH THE LOWEST MARRIAGE RATE

COUNTRY	ANNUAL MARRIAGES PER 1,000*
1 United Arab Emirates	2.5
2 =Andorra	2.9
=Bolivia	2.9
4 =Dominica	3.1
=Marshall Islands	3.1
=Qatar	3.1
7 Cape Verde	3.2
8 St. Lucia	3.3
9 =Dominican Republic	3.5
=Sweden	3.5

In countries/latest year for which data available

Source: *United Nations*

Marriage rates around the world vary. At the other end of the scale is Antigua and Barbuda, with an annual rate of 21 marriages per 1,000.

TOP 10 ★
COUNTRIES WHERE MOST WOMEN MARRY

COUNTRY	PERCENTAGE OF WOMEN MARRIED BY AGE 50*
1 =Comoros	100.0
=The Gambia	100.0
=Ghana	100.0
=Nauru	100.0
5 Chad	99.9
6 =China	99.8
=Guinea	99.8
=Mali	99.8
=Papua New Guinea	99.8
10 Benin	99.7
UK	95.1

In latest year for which data available

Source: *United Nations*

Marriage in these countries can be considered the norm, contrasting with others where almost half the female population opts never to marry.

TOP 10 ★
COUNTRIES WHERE MOST MEN MARRY

COUNTRY	PERCENTAGE OF MEN MARRIED BY AGE 50*
1 =Chad	100.0
=The Gambia	100.0
3 Guinea	99.7
4 =Mali	99.6
=Niger	99.6
6 =Bangladesh	99.3
=Mozambique	99.3
8 Cameroon	99.2
9 Nepal	99.1
10 =Central African Republic	99.0
=Eritrea	99.0
=Tajikistan	99.0
UK	91.2

In latest year for which data available

Source: *United Nations*

What invention earned Nobel Prize founder Alfred Nobel his fortune?

see p.64 for the answer

A Dynamite
B The typewriter
C Aspirin

TOP 10 ★
COUNTRIES WHERE WOMEN MARRY THE LATEST

	COUNTRY	AVERAGE AGE AT FIRST MARRIAGE
1	Jamaica	33.1
2 =	Barbados	31.8
=	Sweden	31.8
4	Iceland	31.7
5 =	Antigua and Barbuda	31.5
=	Dominica	31.5
=	Greenland	31.5
8	St. Kitts and Nevis	31.3
9	Martinique	31.0
10 =	Grenada	30.9
=	St. Vincent and the Grenadines	30.9

Source: *United Nations*

This list is based on the "Singulate Mean Age of Marriage" (SMAM), or average age for first marriage among those who ever marry by the age of 50, after which first marriages are so rare as to be statistically insignificant.

TOP 10 ★
COUNTRIES WITH THE HIGHEST DIVORCE RATES

	COUNTRY	DIVORCE RATE PER 1,000*
1	Maldives	10.97
2	Belarus	4.63
3	USA	4.34
4	Cuba	3.72
5	Estonia	3.65
6 =	Panama	3.61
=	Puerto Rico	3.61
8	Ukraine	3.56
9	Russia	3.42
10	Antigua and Barbuda	3.40
	UK	2.91

* In countries/latest year for which data available

Source: *United Nations*

The UK has the highest divorce rate in Europe (excluding republics of the former Soviet Union). According to the UN, the Isle of Man, if it were an independent country, would appear seventh, with a divorce rate of 4.04 per 1,000 population.

TOP 10 ★
COUNTRIES WITH THE LOWEST DIVORCE RATES

	COUNTRY	DIVORCE RATE PER 1,000*
1	Colombia	0.11
2	Libya	0.24
3	Mongolia	0.38
4	Georgia	0.42
5 =	Mexico	0.43
=	Chile	0.43
7	Italy	0.47
8	El Salvador	0.49
9	Macedonia	0.51
10	Turkey	0.52

* In countries/latest year for which data available

Source: *United Nations*

The UN data on divorce rates omit a number of large countries and ones that we might expect to have a low divorce rate, such as Ireland. The data are very difficult to collect, given the different divorce laws in each country. In some countries, no legal document has to be signed. In others, divorce rates are rarely accurately recorded.

TOP 10 ★
COUNTRIES WHERE MEN MARRY THE LATEST

	COUNTRY	AVERAGE AGE AT FIRST MARRIAGE
1	Dominica	35.4
2	Jamaica	34.6
3	St. Vincent and the Grenadines	34.5
4	Grenada	34.4
5	Barbados	34.3
6	Sweden	34.0
7	Greenland	33.7
8	Iceland	33.3
9	Antigua and Barbuda	33.2
10	Martinique	33.0
	UK	28.4

Source: *United Nations*

TOP 10 ★
COUNTRIES WHERE THE FEWEST WOMEN MARRY

	COUNTRY	PERCENTAGE OF WOMEN MARRIED BY AGE 50*
1 =	French Guiana	54.2
=	Jamaica	54.2
3	Grenada	57.4
4	St. Vincent and the Grenadines	58.3
5	Dominica	59.7
6	Barbados	59.8
7	St. Kitts and Nevis	62.1
8	Antigua and Barbuda	62.6
9	Martinique	67.1
10	Netherlands Antilles	72.4

* In latest year for which data available

Source: *United Nations*

TOP 10 ★
COUNTRIES WHERE THE FEWEST MEN MARRY

	COUNTRY	PERCENTAGE OF MEN MARRIED BY AGE 50*
1	St. Kitts and Nevis	51.1
2	Jamaica	51.8
3	French Guiana	53.9
4	Grenada	59.8
5 =	Montserrat	60.7
=	St. Vincent and the Grenadines	60.7
7	Barbados	62.8
8 =	Dominica	63.4
=	Greenland	63.4
10	Antigua and Barbuda	68.1

* In latest year for which data available

Source: *United Nations*

People on the Move

COUNTRIES RECEIVING THE MOST REFUGEES AND ASYLUM SEEKERS

COUNTRY OR TERRITORY	REFUGEES/ASYLUM SEEKERS, 1999
1 Iran	1,980,000
2 Jordan	1,518,000
3 Pakistan	1,125,000
4 Gaza Strip	798,000
5 West Bank	570,000
6 USA	505,000
7 Yugoslavia	480,000
8 Guinea	450,000
9 Tanzania	400,000
10 Syria	379,200

Source: *US Committee for Refugees*

SEEKING REFUGE

Refugees displaced during the 1990 Iraq–Kuwait War are among the millions who fled from the many conflicts that beset the 1990s.

COUNTRIES WITH THE MOST INTERNALLY DISPLACED PEOPLE

COUNTRY	INTERNALLY DISPLACED PEOPLE, 1999
1 Sudan	4,000,000
2 Colombia	1,800,000
3 Angola	1,500,000
4 Russia	1,000,000
5 Iraq	900,000
6 Bosnia and Herzegovina	830,000
7 Dem. Rep. of Congo	800,000
8 Afghanistan	750,000
9 Yugoslavia	640,000
10 =Burundi	600,000
=Myanmar (Burma)	600,000
=Rwanda	600,000
=Turkey	600,000

Source: *US Committee for Refugees*

COUNTRIES OF ORIGIN OF US IMMIGRANTS, 1820–1998

COUNTRY OF LAST RESIDENCE	IMMIGRANTS
1 Germany	7,156,257
2 Mexico*	5,819,966
3 Italy	5,431,454
4 UK	5,247,821
5 Ireland	4,779,998
6 Canada	4,453,149
7 USSR#	3,830,033
8 Austria+	1,842,722
9 Hungary+	1,675,324
10 Philippines	1,460,421

* *Unreported 1886–93*

\# *Russia before 1917*

\+ *Unreported before 1861; combined 1862–1904; separately 1905; Austria included with Germany 1938–45*

TOP 10 ★
ANCESTRIES OF THE US POPULATION

	ANCESTRY GROUP	NUMBER
1	German	57,947,873
2	Irish	38,735,539
3	English	32,651,788
4	Afro-American	23,777,098
5	Italian	14,664,550
6	American	12,395,999
7	Mexican	11,586,983
8	French	10,320,935
9	Polish	9,366,106
10	American Indian	8,708,220

The 1990 US Census asked people to identify the ancestry group to which they believed themselves to belong. Five per cent were unable to define their family origin more precisely than "American", while many claimed multiple ancestry.

TOP 10 ★
COUNTRIES OF ORIGIN OF UK ASYLUM SEEKERS

	COUNTRY	ASYLUM SEEKERS, 1999*
1	Yugoslavia	11,465
2	Somalia	7,495
3	Sri Lanka	5,130
4	Afghanistan	3,975
5	Turkey	2,850
6	China	2,625
7	Pakistan	2,615
8	Romania	1,985
9	Poland	1,860
10	Iraq	1,800

* Excluding dependants and overseas applications

Source: Home Office

In 1999, a total of 71,160 people applied for asylum in the UK. These comprised 28,280 from Europe, 18,435 from Africa, 17,465 from Asia, 4,165 from the Middle East, and 2,025 from the Americas, together with various others whose nationality was unknown.

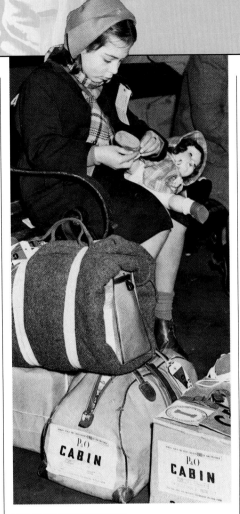

HEADING DOWN UNDER
A young British emigrant waits to embark for Australia in 1950. The two countries' long-standing links have been maintained over the decades.

TOP 10 ★
COUNTRIES OF ORIGIN OF UK IMMIGRANTS

	COUNTRY	IMMIGRANTS, 1999
1	Pakistan	11,860
2	Former Yugoslavia	6,650
3	India	6,290
4	Sri Lanka	5,370
5	Turkey	5,220
6	USA	3,760
7	Ghana	3,480
8	Bangladesh	3,280
9 =	Nigeria	3,180
=	Somalia	3,180

Source: Home Office

TOP 10 ★
COUNTRIES OF ORIGIN OF IMMIGRANTS TO AUSTRALIA

	COUNTRY OF BIRTH	IMMIGRANTS, 1999
1	UK	8,876
2	China*	5,982
3	South Africa	5,558
4	Philippines	3,409
5	Indonesia	3,313
6	India	3,156
7	Iraq	2,307
8	Former Yugoslavia	1,998
9	Vietnam	1,889
10	Fiji	1,554

* Excluding Taiwan and Special Administrative Regions

Source: Australian Department of Immigration and Multicultural Affairs

Since the era of the first settlement of Australia the UK has always been the principal country of origin of immigrants, and it still provides 13.5 per cent of the total. In 1999, a further 27,911 immigrants were recorded as having arrived from other countries not listed in the Top 10, together with 1,272 whose birthplace was unknown, making an overall total of 67,215.

TOP 10 ★
FOREIGN BIRTHPLACES OF THE US POPULATION

	BIRTHPLACE	NUMBER*
1	Mexico	4,298,014
2	Philippines	912,674
3	Canada	744,830
4	Cuba	736,971
5	Germany	711,929
6	UK	640,145
7	Italy	580,592
8	Korea	568,397
9	Vietnam	543,262
10	China	529,837

* US Census figures, 1990

Did You Know? The top single year for immigration to the US was 1907, with 1,285,349 arrivals; Italy was the leading country of origin, with 285,731 emigrants.

What's in a Name?

MOST COMMON FEMALE NAMES IN ENGLAND AND WALES

	NAME	NUMBER
1	Margaret Smith	7,640
2	Margaret Jones	7,068
3	Susan Smith	6,531
4	Susan Jones	5,108
5	Mary Smith	5,049
6	Patricia Smith	4,743
7	Margaret Williams	4,636
8	Elizabeth Jones	4,604
9	Mary Jones	4,522
10	Sarah Jones	4,359

Source: *Office for National Statistics*

The Office for National Statistics conducted a survey of the most common combinations of first names and surnames based on the NHS Register, which accounts for everyone currently registered with a GP or who has been registered since 1991. The survey revealed a number of differences between the male and female lists: there are 24 different surnames in the male top 100, but only 11 different female surnames, with Smith appearing 44 times in the male list, but only 22 times in the female version.

MOST COMMON MALE NAMES IN ENGLAND AND WALES

	NAME	NUMBER
1	David Jones	15,763
2	David Smith	14,341
3	John Smith	12,793
4	David Williams	11,392
5	Michael Smith	10,516
6	John Jones	10,021
7	John Williams	8,738
8 =	Paul Smith	8,348
=	Peter Smith	8,348
10	David Evans	8,103

Source: *Office for National Statistics*

FIRST NAMES IN ENGLAND AND WALES, 2000

GIRLS/RISE OR FALL		BOYS/RISE OR FALL
Chloe	1	Jack
Emily	2	Thomas
Megan	3	James
Charlotte (+2)	4	Joshua
Jessica (+3)	5	Daniel
Lauren (+1)	6	Harry (+8)
Sophie (−2)	7	Samuel
Olivia (−4)	8	Joseph
Hannah (+1)	9	Matthew (−3)
Lucy (+2)	10	Callum (−1)

+ *Indicates rise in popularity since previous year*

− *Represents decline in popularity since previous year*

The abrupt rise in the popularity of the name Harry may be attributed partly to the birth of Prince Harry in 1984, and since 1997 to the phenomenal success of the Harry Potter books. Harry was ranked in 50th place in both 1700 and 1800, but steadily rose during the second half of the 19th century to be ranked in 14th position in 1875. It progressively declined in popularity to hit 100th place in 1954, since when it has experienced a steady rise: to 30 in 1994, 22 in 1995, 18 in 1996, 17 in 1997, 15 in 1998, 14 in 1999, and 6 in 2000.

MOST COMMON SURNAMES IN THE UK

	SURNAME	NUMBER
1	Smith	538,369
2	Jones	402,489
3	Williams	279,150
4	Brown	260,652
5	Taylor	251,058
6	Davies/Davis	209,584
7	Wilson	191,006
8	Evans	170,391
9	Thomas	152,945
10	Johnson	146,535

TOP 10 SURNAMES IN SCOTLAND*

1 Smith 2 Brown 3 Wilson
4 Thomson 5 Robertson 6 Campbell
7 Stewart 8 Anderson
9 Macdonald 10 Scott

* *Based on a survey of names appearing on birth and death registers, and both names on marriage registers*

FIRST NAMES IN SCOTLAND, 2000

GIRLS/RISE OR FALL		BOYS/RISE OR FALL
Chloe	1	Jack
Amy (+3)	=2/2	Lewis
Lauren (+2)	=/3	Ryan
Emma (−1)	4	Cameron
Rebecca (−3)	5	James (+2)
Megan	6	Andrew
Caitlin	7	Matthew (+6)
Rachel	8	Liam
Erin	9	Callum (+3)
Hannah (+2)	10	Jamie (+6)

+ *Indicates rise in popularity since previous year*

− *Represents decline in popularity since previous year*

FIRST NAMES IN AUSTRALIA*

GIRLS		BOYS
Jessica	1	Joshua
Emily	2	Jack
Sarah	3	Thomas
Georgia	4	Lachlan
Olivia	5	Matthew
Chloe	6	James
Emma	7	Daniel
Sophie	8	Benjamin
Hannah	9	Nicholas
Isabella	10	William

* *Based on births registered in New South Wales*

TOP 10 ★
FIRST NAMES IN IRELAND

GIRLS		BOYS
Chloe	1	Conor
Aoife	2	Sean
Sarah	3	Jack
Ciara	4	James
Niamh	5	Adam
Emma	6	Michael
Rachel	7	David
Rebecca	8	Aaron
Lauren	9	Daniel
Megan	10	Dylan

While these were the Top 10 girls' and boys' names among the total of 53,354 births registered in Ireland in 1999, there are certain regional variations: Rachel was the most popular girls' name in the West, and Sean was the most popular boy's name in the West and Dublin. As with other first name lists, boys' names remain more static than girls': the top five are identical to the previous year.

TOP 10 ★
FIRST NAMES IN CANADA*

GIRLS		BOYS
Emily	1	Matthew
Sarah	2	Joshua
Emma	3	Jacob
Hannah	4	Nicholas
Taylor	5	Ryan
Jessica	6	Brandon
Megan	7	Michael
Samantha	8	Jordan
Ashley	9	Alexander
Madison	10	Liam

* Based on births in British Columbia

TOP 10 ★
FIRST NAMES IN WALES, 2000

GIRLS/RISE OR FALL		BOYS/RISE OR FALL
Chloe	1	Thomas
Megan	2	Jack
Emily	3	Joshua
Sophie	4	Callum (+1)
Lauren	5	Rhys (+8)
Hannah (+3)	6	Daniel (−2)
Jessica (−1)	7	Jordan (+5)
Georgina (−1)	8	Ryan (+1)
Ffion (−1)	9	Liam (−2)
Olivia (+1)	10	James (−4)

+ *Indicates rise in popularity since previous year*

− *Represents decline in popularity since previous year*

Among girls' names, all those in the Top 10 also appear, though in different order of popularity, in the combined England and Wales Top 10, with the exception of Georgina (No. 11 in England and Wales) and Ffion, which does not even appear in the Top 50.

TOP 10 ★
NAMES IN THE UK 100 YEARS AGO

GIRLS		BOYS
Florence	1	William
Mary	2	John
Alice	3	George
Annie	4	Thomas
Elsie	5	Charles
Edith	6	Frederick
Elizabeth	7	Arthur
Doris	8	James
Dorothy	9	Albert
Ethel	10	Ernest

THE JONESES

San Diego-born artist Arthur R. "Pop" Momand (1886–1987) settled in Cedarhurst, New York, where he rubbed shoulders with a group of wealthy people, each of whom he noticed was competing with those with even more money. After moving to Manhattan, he devised a comic strip featuring the exploits of such people, which he called "Keeping up with the Joneses" – perhaps named after American novelist Edith Wharton's wealthy aunt Elizabeth Schermerhorn Jones, the owner of a large New York estate. The strip ran for many years, and the phrase entered the language.

WHO WAS • WHO WAS • WHO WAS • WHO WAS ?

TOP 10 ★
MOST COMMON SURNAMES IN THE US

	NAME	PERCENTAGE OF ALL US NAMES
1	Smith	1.006
2	Johnson	0.810
3	Williams	0.699
4	=Brown	0.621
	=Jones	0.621
6	Davis	0.480
7	Miller	0.424
8	Wilson	0.339
9	Moore	0.312
10	=Anderson	0.311
	=Taylor	0.311
	=Thomas	0.311

The Top 10 (or, in view of those in equal 10th place, 12) US surnames together make up over 6 per cent of the entire US population – in other words, one American in every 16 bears one of these names. Extending the list, some 28 different names comprise 10 per cent of the entire population, 115 names 20 per cent, 315 names 30 per cent, 755 names 40 per cent, 1,712 names 50 per cent, and 3,820 names 60 per cent. Beyond this, large numbers of less common – and in some instances, unique – names make up the remainder.

TOP 10 SURNAMES IN CHINA

1 Zhang **2** Whang **3** Li **4** Zhao **5** Chen **6** Yang **7** Wu **8** Liu **9** Huang **10** Zhou

It has been estimated that there are more than 100 million people with the surname Zhang in China.

Did You Know? Although it is often claimed that J. M. Barrie invented the name Wendy in his 1904 play *Peter Pan*, researchers have uncovered a record of a 21-year-old woman and two girls with this name in the 1851 British census.

World Leaders & Politics

FIRST COUNTRIES TO GIVE WOMEN THE VOTE

	COUNTRY	YEAR
1	New Zealand	1893
2	Australia (South Australia 1894; Western Australia 1898)	1902
3	Finland (then a Grand Duchy under the Russian Crown)	1906
4	Norway (restricted franchise; all women over 25 in 1913)	1907
5	Denmark and Iceland (a Danish dependency until 1918)	1915
6	= Netherlands	1917
	= USSR	1917
8	= Austria	1918
	= Canada	1918
	= Germany	1918
	= Great Britain and Ireland (Ireland part of the United Kingdom until 1921; women over 30 only – lowered to 21 in 1928)	1918
	= Poland	1918

Until 1920, the only other European countries to enfranchise women were Sweden in 1919 and Czechoslovakia in 1920.

TOP 10 BEST-PAID MEMBERS OF THE ROYAL FAMILY

(Member/annual payment in £)

❶ The Queen, 7,900,000
❷ The Queen Mother, 643,000
❸ The Duke of Edinburgh, 359,000
❹ The Duke of York, 249,000 ❺ The Duke of Kent, 236,000 ❻ The Princess Royal, 228,000 ❼ Princess Alexandra, 225,000 ❽ Princess Margaret, 219,000
❾ The Duke of Gloucester, 175,500
❿ Prince Edward, 96,000

The Civil List is not technically the Royal Family's "pay" but is the allowance made by the Government for their staff and costs incurred while performing their public duties. The Prince of Wales receives nothing from the Civil List, his income deriving from the Duchy of Cornwall.

VOTES FOR WOMEN
The women of New Zealand, granted suffrage on 19 September 1893, were able to cast their votes at the country's General Election on 28 November.

PARLIAMENTS WITH THE HIGHEST PERCENTAGE OF WOMEN MEMBERS*

	PARLIAMENT/ ELECTION DATE	WOMEN MEMBERS	TOTAL MEMBERS	% WOMEN		PARLIAMENT/ ELECTION DATE	WOMEN MEMBERS	TOTAL MEMBERS	% WOMEN
1	Sweden, 1998	149	349	42.7	7	Germany, 1998	207	669	30.9
2	Denmark, 1998	67	179	37.4	8	New Zealand, 1999	37	120	30.8
3	Finland, 1999	73	200	36.5	9	Mozambique, 1999	75	250	30.0
4	Norway, 1997	60	165	36.4	10	South Africa, 1999	119	399	29.8
5	Netherlands, 1998	54	150	36.0					
6	Iceland, 1999	22	63	34.9					

* As at 25 April 2001
Source: Inter-Parliamentary Union

AUSTRALIAN WOMEN GET THE VOTE

Following pressure exerted by the Womanhood Suffrage League, Australia followed the lead of New Zealand (the first country to grant women suffrage) when, on 12 June 1902, Melbourne Governor-General Lord Hopetoun signed the Uniform Franchise Act. Although a major advance, it still imposed a number of limitations: it was restricted to Federal elections and was granted only to British subjects aged over 21 and with a minimum of six months' residence; "Aboriginal natives of Australia, Asia, Africa or the Islands of the Pacific" were excluded. Over the next few years, all women aged over 21 were progressively granted the vote, though it was not until 1962 that aboriginal women (and men) were given the vote.

100 YEARS AGO · YEARS AGO · YEARS AGO · YEARS

TOP 10 ★
LONGEST-SERVING PRESIDENTS TODAY

	PRESIDENT/COUNTRY	TOOK OFFICE
1	**General Gnassingbé Eyadéma**, Togo	14 Apr 1967
2	**El Hadj Omar Bongo**, Gabon	2 Dec 1967
3	**Colonel Mu'ammar Gadhafi**, Libya*	1 Sep 1969
4	**Zayid ibn Sultan al-Nuhayyan**, United Arab Emirates	2 Dec 1971
5	**Fidel Castro**, Cuba	2 Nov 1976
6	**France-Albert René**, Seychelles	5 June 1977
7	**Ali Abdullah Saleh**, Yemen	17 July 1978
8	**Daniel Teroitich arap Moi**, Kenya	14 Oct 1978
9	**Maumoon Abdul Gayoom**, Maldives	11 Nov 1978
10	**Saddam Hussein**, Iraq	16 July 1979

* Since a reorganization in 1979, Colonel Gadhafi has held no formal position, but continues to rule under the ceremonial title of "Leader of the Revolution"

All the presidents in this list have been in power for more than 20 years, some for over 30. Fidel Castro was Prime Minister of Cuba from February 1959. As he was also chief of the army, and there was no opposition party, he effectively ruled as dictator from then, but he was not technically President until the Cuban constitution was revised in 1976. Among those no longer in office, Abu Sulayman Hafiz al-Assad, President of Syria, died on 10 June 2000 after serving as leader of his country since 22 February 1971.

TOP 10 ★
LONGEST-REIGNING LIVING MONARCHS*

	MONARCH/COUNTRY	DATE OF BIRTH	ACCESSION
1	**Bhumibol Adulyadej**, Thailand	5 Dec 1927	9 June 1946
2	**Prince Rainier III**, Monaco	31 May 1923	9 May 1949
3	**Elizabeth II**, UK	21 Apr 1926	6 Feb 1952
4	**Malietoa Tanumafili II**, Western Samoa	4 Jan 1913	1 Jan 1962#
5	**Taufa'ahau Tupou IV**, Tonga	4 July 1918	16 Dec 1965+
6	**Haji Hassanal Bolkiah**, Brunei	15 July 1946	5 Oct 1967
7	**Sayyid Qaboos ibn Said al-Said**, Oman	18 Nov 1942	23 July 1970
8	**Margrethe II**, Denmark	16 Apr 1940	14 Jan 1972
9	**Birendra Bir Bikram Shah Dev**, Nepal	28 Dec 1945	31 Jan 1972
10	**Jigme Singye Wangchuk**, Bhutan	11 Nov 1955	24 July 1972

* Including hereditary rulers of principalities, dukedoms, etc.

 # Sole ruler since 15 April 1963

+ Full sovereignty from 5 June 1970 when British protectorate ended

There are 28 countries that have emperors, kings, queens, princes, dukes, sultans, or other hereditary rulers as their heads of state. Earlier lists included Grand Duke Jean of Luxembourg, who abdicated on 28 September 2000.

THE 10 ★
FIRST COUNTRIES TO RATIFY THE UN CHARTER

	COUNTRY	DATE
1	**Nicaragua**	6 July 1945
2	**USA**	8 Aug 1945
3	**France**	31 Aug 1945
4	**Dominican Republic**	4 Sep 1945
5	**New Zealand**	19 Sep 1945
6	**Brazil**	21 Sep 1945
7	**Argentina**	24 Sep 1945
8	**China**	28 Sep 1945
9	**Denmark**	9 Oct 1945
10	**Chile**	11 Oct 1945

In New York on 26 June 1945, 50 nations signed the World Security Charter, thus establishing the UN as an international peace-keeping organization.

WORLD PEACE
While World War II still raged in the Far East, delegates signed the charter that inaugurated the United Nations as the world's peace-keepers.

What was unusual about the transatlantic balloon crossing reported in 1844?
see p.63 for the answer

A It was kept secret for over 100 years
B It was the first
C It was a hoax

Human Achievements

FIRST MOUNTAINEERS TO CLIMB EVEREST

	MOUNTAINEER/NATIONALITY	DATE
1	**Edmund Hillary**, New Zealander	29 May 1953
2	**Tenzing Norgay**, Nepalese	29 May 1953
3	**Jürg Marmet**, Swiss	23 May 1956
4	**Ernst Schmied**, Swiss	23 May 1956
5	**Hans-Rudolf von Gunten**, Swiss	24 May 1956
6	**Adolf Reist**, Swiss	24 May 1956
7	**Wang Fu-chou**, Chinese	25 May 1960
8	**Chu Ying-hua**, Chinese	25 May 1960
9	**Konbu**, Tibetan	25 May 1960
10	=**Nawang Gombu**, Indian	1 May 1963
	=**James Whittaker**, American	1 May 1963

Nawang Gombu and James Whittaker are 10th equal because, neither wishing to deny the other the privilege of being first, they ascended the last feet to the summit side by side.

FIRST PEOPLE TO REACH THE SOUTH POLE

	NAME/NATIONALITY	DATE
1	=**Roald Amundsen***, Norwegian	14 Dec 1911
	=**Olav Olavsen Bjaaland**, Norwegian	14 Dec 1911
	=**Helmer Julius Hanssen**, Norwegian	14 Dec 1911
	=**Helge Sverre Hassel**, Norwegian	14 Dec 1911
	=**Oscar Wisting**, Norwegian	14 Dec 1911
6	=**Robert Falcon Scott***, British	17 Jan 1912
	=**Henry Robertson Bowers**, British	17 Jan 1912
	=**Edgar Evans**, British	17 Jan 1912
	=**Lawrence Edward Grace Oates**, British	17 Jan 1912
	=**Edward Adrian Wilson**, British	17 Jan 1912

* Expedition leader

FIRST EXPEDITIONS TO REACH THE NORTH POLE OVERLAND

	NAME*/NATIONALITY	DATE
1	**Ralph S. Plaisted**, American	19 Apr 1968
2	**Wally W. Herbert**, British	5 Apr 1969
3	**Naomi Uemura**, Japanese	1 May 1978
4	**Dmitri Shparo**, Soviet	31 May 1979
5	**Sir Ranulph Fiennes/ Charles Burton**, British	11 Apr 1982
6	**Will Steger/Paul Schurke**, American	1 May 1986
7	**Jean-Louis Etienne**, French	11 May 1986
8	**Fukashi Kazami**, Japanese	20 Apr 1987
9	**Helen Thayer**, American	20 Apr 1988
10	**Robert Swan**, British	14 May 1989

* Expedition leader or co-leader

FASTEST CROSS-CHANNEL SWIMMERS

	SWIMMER/NATIONALITY	YEAR	TIME HR:MIN		SWIMMER/NATIONALITY	YEAR	TIME HR:MIN
1	**Chad Hundeby**, American	1994	7:17	6	**Richard Davey**, British	1988	8:05
2	**Penny Lee Dean**, American	1978	7:40	7	**Irene van der Laan**, Dutch	1982	8:06
3	**Tamara Bruce**, Australian	1994	7:53	8	=**Paul Asmuth**, American	1985	8:12
4	**Philip Rush**, New Zealander	1987	7:55		=**Gail Rice**, American	1999	8:12
5	**Hans Van Goor**, Dutch	1995	8:02	10	**Anita Sood**, Indian	1987	8:15

Source: *Channel Swimming Association*

FIRST US LANDING AT THE NORTH POLE

The first US landing at the Pole was that of Lt.-Col. William Pershing Benedict, with a team of 10 US Air Force scientists. They flew in a C-47 fitted with skis, landing on 3 May 1952. Co-pilot Lt.-Col. Joseph Otis Fletcher became the first American undisputedly to set foot on the North Pole. (This achievement had previously been claimed by American Robert Peary and his companions, who were reported to have reached the Pole in 1909. This claim has since been widely discredited.) Dr. Albert Paddock Crary, one of the scientists on the American expedition, later trekked to the South Pole, arriving there on 12 February 1961, thus becoming the first man to set foot on both North and South Poles.

50 YEARS AGO · YEARS AGO · YEARS AGO · YEARS AGO

LATEST WINNERS OF *TIME MAGAZINE'S* "PERSON OF THE YEAR" AWARD

	RECIPIENT	YEAR
1	**George W. Bush** (1946–), 43rd US President	2000
2	**Jeffrey T. Bezos** (1964–), entrepreneur, founder of Amazon.com	1999
3	**Bill Clinton** (1946–), US President, **Kenneth Starr** (1946–), Independent Counsel	1998
4	**Andrew S. Grove** (1936–), CEO of Intel microchip company	1997
5	**David Ho** (1952–), AIDS researcher	1996
6	**Newt Gingrich** (1943–), US politician	1995
7	**Pope John Paul II** (1920–)	1994
8	**Yasser Arafat** (1929–), **F. W. de Klerk** (1936–), **Nelson Mandela** (1918–), **Yitzhak Rabin** (1922–95), "Peacemakers"	1993
9	**Bill Clinton** (1946–), US President	1992
10	**George Bush** (1924–), US President	1991

TOP 10 ★
CIRCUMNAVIGATION FIRSTS

	CIRCUMNAVIGATION	CRAFT	CAPTAIN(S)	RETURN DATE
1	First voyage	*Vittoria*	Juan Sebastian de Elcano	6 Sep 1522
2	First in less than 80 days	Various	"Nellie Bly" (Elizabeth Cochrane)	25 Jan 1890
3	First solo voyage	*Spray*	Capt. Joshua Slocum	3 July 1898
4	First by air	*Chicago* and *New Orleans*	Lt. Lowell Smith and Lt. Leslie P. Arnold	28 Sep 1924
5	First non-stop by air	*Lucky Lady I*	Capt. James Gallagher	2 Mar 1949
6	First underwater voyage	*Triton*	Capt. Edward Latimer Beach	25 Apr 1960
7	First non-stop solo voyage	*Suhaili*	Robin Knox-Johnston	22 Apr 1969
8	First helicopter	*Spirit of Texas*	H. Ross Perot Jr. and Jay Coburn	30 Sep 1982
9	First air without refuelling	*Voyager*	Richard Rutan and Jeana Yeager	23 Dec 1986
10	First by balloon	*Breitling Orbiter 3*	Brian Jones and Bertrand Piccard	21 Mar 1999

The first ever circumnavigation, by Juan Sebastian de Elcano and his crew of 17, sailed from Spain, returning to Italy. US journalist "Nellie Bly" (Elizabeth Cochrane) set out to beat the fictitious "record" established in Jules Verne's novel *Around the World in 80 Days*, travelling from New York and returning on 25 January 1890 – a record circumnavigation of 72 days, 6 hours, 11 minutes, and 14 seconds.

AROUND THE WORLD IN 19 DAYS
In 1999, travelling from Switzerland to Egypt, the 55-m (180-ft) tall Breitling Orbiter 3 achieved the first balloon circumnavigation of the Earth.

THE 10 ★
FIRST SUCCESSFUL HUMAN DESCENTS OVER NIAGARA FALLS

	NAME/METHOD	DATE
1	**Annie Edson Taylor**, Wooden barrel	24 Oct 1901
2	**Bobby Leach**, Steel barrel	25 July 1911
3	**Jean Lussier**, Steel and rubber ball fitted with oxygen cylinders	4 July 1928
4	**William Fitzgerald** (aka Nathan Boya), Steel and rubber ball fitted with oxygen cylinders	15 July 1961
5	**Karel Soucek**, Barrel	3 July 1984
6	**Steven Trotter**, Barrel	18 Aug 1985
7	**Dave Mundy**, Barrel	5 Oct 1985
8 =	**Peter deBernardi**, Metal container	28 Sep 1989
=	**Jeffrey Petkovich**, Metal container	28 Sep 1989
10	**Dave Mundy**, Diving bell	26 Sep 1993

Source: *Niagara Falls Museum*

WITH KIND AUTHORIZATION OF BREITLING SA

Did You Know? The first transatlantic crossing by balloon, reported in the *New York Sun* of 13 April 1844, was a hoax perpetrated by novelist Edgar Allan Poe. It was another 134 years before balloonists truly achieved the feat.

The Nobel Prize

THE 10 ★
LATEST WINNERS OF THE NOBEL PRIZE FOR ECONOMIC SCIENCES

	WINNER	COUNTRY	YEAR
1 =	James J. Heckman	USA	2000
=	Daniel L. McFadden	USA	2000
3	Robert A. Mundell	Canada	1999
4	Amartya Sen	India	1998
5 =	Robert C. Merton	USA	1997
=	Myron S. Scholes	USA	1997
7 =	James A. Mirrlees	UK	1996
=	William Vickrey	Canada	1996
9	Robert E. Lucas	USA	1995
10 =	John C. Harsanyi	Hungary/USA	1994
=	Reinhard Selten	Germany	1994
=	John F. Nash	USA	1994

Correctly called the Bank of Sweden Prize in Economic Sciences in Memory of Alfred Nobel, this is a recent addition to the Nobel Prizes. It is presented annually by the Royal Swedish Academy of Sciences and consists of a gold medal, a diploma, and a sum of money. The presentation of this and the other Prizes is made on 10 December, the anniversary of Alfred Nobel's death.

NOBEL

Swedish scientist Alfred Bernhard Nobel (1833–96) studied widely in Europe and the US. He perfected a way of stabilizing nitroglycerine, a dangerous explosive. The result was dynamite, which Nobel patented in 1866. It was used extensively in quarrying and railway construction. At his death in 1896, the unmarried Nobel left a will establishing a trust fund, which is now estimated to be worth over £280 million ($420 million). Interest earned from this has enabled annual prizes to be awarded to those who have achieved the greatest common good in the fields of Physics, Chemistry, Literature, Physiology or Medicine, Peace, and, since 1969, Economic Sciences.

WHO WAS · WHO WAS · WHO WAS · WHO WAS

TOP 10 ★
NOBEL LITERATURE PRIZE-WINNING COUNTRIES

	COUNTRY	LITERATURE PRIZES
1	France	12
2	USA	10
3	UK	8
4 =	Germany	7
=	Sweden	7
6	Italy	6
7	Spain	5
8 =	Denmark	3
=	Ireland	3
=	Norway	3
=	Poland	3
=	USSR	3

TOP 10 ★
NOBEL PHYSIOLOGY OR MEDICINE PRIZE-WINNING COUNTRIES

	COUNTRY	PHYSIOLOGY OR MEDICINE PRIZES
1	USA	80
2	UK	24
3	Germany	16
4	Sweden	8
5	France	7
6	Switzerland	6
7	Denmark	5
8 =	Austria	4
=	Belgium	4
10 =	Italy	3
=	Australia	3

THE 10 ★
LATEST WINNERS OF THE NOBEL PRIZE FOR LITERATURE

	WINNER	COUNTRY	YEAR
1	Gao Xingjian	China	2000
2	Günter Grass	Germany	1999
3	José Saramago	Portugal	1998
4	Dario Fo	Italy	1997
5	Wislawa Szymborska	Poland	1996
6	Seamus Heaney	Ireland	1995
7	Kenzaburo Oe	Japan	1994
8	Toni Morrison	USA	1993
9	Derek Walcott	Saint Lucia	1992
10	Nadine Gordimer	South Africa	1991

THE 10 ★
LATEST WINNERS OF THE NOBEL PRIZE FOR PHYSICS

	WINNER	COUNTRY	YEAR
1 =	Zhores I. Alferov	Russia	2000
=	Herbert Kroemer	USA	2000
=	Jack S. Kilby	USA	2000
4 =	Gerardus 't Hooft	Netherlands	1999
=	Martinus J.G. Veltman	Netherlands	1999
6 =	Robert B. Laughlin	USA	1998
=	Horst L. Störmer	Germany	1998
=	Daniel C. Tsui	USA	1998
9 =	Steven Chu	USA	1997
=	William D. Phillips	USA	1997
=	Claude Cohen-Tannoudji	France	1997

TOP 10 NOBEL PHYSICS PRIZE-WINNING COUNTRIES
(Country/physics prizes)

❶ USA, 69 ❷ UK, 21 ❸ Germany, 20 ❹ France, 12 ❺ Netherlands, 8 ❻ USSR, 7 ❼ Sweden, 4 ❽ = Austria, 3; = Denmark, 3; = Italy, 3; = Japan, 3

Which country does not appear among the Top 10 largest armed forces? *see p.72 for the answer*

A Israel
B Turkey
C India

NOBEL PRIZE-WINNING COUNTRIES

	COUNTRY	PHY	CHE	PH/MED	LIT	PCE	ECO	TOTAL
1	USA	69	45	80	10	18	27	249
2	UK	21	25	24	8	13	7	98
3	Germany*	20	27	16	7	4	1	75
4	France	12	7	7	12	9	1	48
5	Sweden	4	4	8	7	5	2	30
6	Switzerland	2	5	6	2	3	–	18
7 =	USSR	7	1	2	3	2	1	16
=	Institutions	–	–	–	–	16	–	16
9	Netherlands	8	3	2	–	1	1	15
10	Italy	3	1	3	6	1	–	14

Phy – Physics; Che – Chemistry; Ph/Med – Physiology or Medicine; Lit – Literature; Pce – Peace; Eco – Economic Sciences.

* Includes the united country before 1948, West Germany to 1990, and the united country since 1990

PEACE OF MIND
Selected from a record 150 nominees, South Korean president Kim Dae Jung was awarded the first Nobel Peace Prize of the 21st century for his work in forging ties with North Korea.

TOP 10 NOBEL PEACE PRIZE-WINNING COUNTRIES

(Country/peace prizes)

❶ USA, 18 ❷ International institutions, 16 ❸ UK, 13 ❹ France, 9 ❺ Sweden, 5
❻ = Belgium, 4; = Germany, 4; = South Africa, 4 ❾ = Israel, 3; = Switzerland, 3

LATEST WINNERS OF THE NOBEL PRIZE FOR CHEMISTRY

	WINNER	COUNTRY	YEAR
1 =	Alan J. Heeger	USA	2000
=	Alan G. MacDiarmid	USA	2000
=	Hideki Shirakawa	Japan	2000
4	Ahmed Zewail	Egypt	1999
5 =	Walter Kohn	USA	1998
=	John A. Pople	UK	1998
7 =	Paul D. Boyer	USA	1997
=	Jens C. Skou	Denmark	1997
=	John E. Walker	UK	1997
10 =	Sir Harold W. Kroto	UK	1996
=	Richard E. Smalley	USA	1996

LATEST WINNERS OF THE NOBEL PRIZE FOR PHYSIOLOGY OR MEDICINE

	WINNER	COUNTRY	YEAR
1 =	Arvid Carlsson	Sweden	2000
=	Paul Greengard	USA	2000
=	Eric Kandel	USA	2000
4	Günter Blobel	Germany	1999
5 =	Robert F. Furchgott	USA	1998
=	Louis J. Ignarro	USA	1998
=	Ferid Murad	USA	1998
8	Stanley B. Prusiner	USA	1997
9 =	Peter C. Doherty	Australia	1996
=	Rolf M. Zinkernagel	Switzerland	1996

LATEST WINNERS OF THE NOBEL PEACE PRIZE

	WINNER	COUNTRY	YEAR
1	Kim Dae Jung	South Korea	2000
2	Médecins Sans Frontières	Belgium	1999
3 =	John Hume	UK	1998
=	David Trimble	UK	1998
5 =	International Campaign to Ban Landmines	–	1997
=	Jody Williams	USA	1997
7 =	Carlos Filipe Ximenes Belo	East Timor	1996
=	José Ramos-Horta	East Timor	1996
9	Joseph Rotblat	UK	1995
10 =	Yasir Arafat	Palestine	1994
=	Shimon Peres	Israel	1994
=	Itzhak Rabin	Israel	1994

Criminal Records

THE 10 ★
COUNTRIES WITH THE HIGHEST PRISON POPULATION RATES

	COUNTRY	TOTAL PRISON POPULATION*	PRISONERS PER 100,000#
1	Russia	1,060,085	730
2	USA	1,860,520	680
3	Belarus	58,879	575
4	Kazakhstan	82,945	495
5	Bahamas	1,401	485
6	Belize	1,097	460
7	Kyrgyzstan	19,857	440
8	Surinam	1,933	435
9	Ukraine	217,400	430
10	Dominica	298	420
	UK	73,195	125

* Including pre-trial detainees

In latest year for which figures are available

Source: *Home Office*

THE 10 ★
COUNTRIES WITH THE MOST PRISONERS

	COUNTRY	PRISONERS*
1	USA	1,860,520
2	China	1,408,860
3	Russia	1,060,085
4	India	381,147
5	Ukraine	217,400
6	Thailand	197,214
7	Brazil	194,074
8	South Africa	161,163
9	Rwanda	143,021#
10	Mexico	139,707
	UK	73,195

* In latest year for which figures are available

Includes 135,000 held on suspicion of participation in genocide

Source: *Home Office*

TOP 10 ★
LARGEST WOMEN'S PRISONS IN THE UK

	PRISON/LOCATION	INMATES*
1	Holloway, London	469
2	Styal, Wilmslow, Cheshire	431
3	New Hall, Flockton, Wakefield	360
4	Eastwood Park, Wotton-under-Edge, Gloucestershire	274
5	Low Newton, Durham	233
6	Send, Woking, Surrey	214
7	Cornton Vale, Stirling	194
8	Highpoint, Newmarket, Suffolk	193
9	Drake Hall, Eccleshall, Staffordshire	188
10=	Bullwood Hall, Hockley, Essex	168
=	Foston Hall, Foston, Derbyshire	168

* As at 30 September 2000

THE 10 ★
MOST COMMON OFFENCES IN ENGLAND AND WALES

	OFFENCE	OFFENDERS FOUND GUILTY (1999)
1	Motoring offences	632,900
2	Summary offences (other than motoring)	433,600
3	Theft and handling stolen goods	131,200
4	Drug offences	48,700
5	Other indictable offences	47,900
6	Violence against the person	35,700
7	Burglary	29,300
8	Fraud and forgery	20,300
9	Criminal damage	10,900
10	Robbery	5,600
	Total (indictable 342,000/ summary 1,066,500)	1,408,500

This list includes both indictable offences (those normally calling for a trial before a jury) and summary offences (usually tried before a magistrates' court). In the latter category, motoring offences comprise the largest proportion, but other offences are less precisely itemized and hence appear in official statistics under a general heading.

THE 10 COUNTRIES WITH THE HIGHEST CRIME RATES
(Country/crime rate)*

❶ Gibraltar, 18,316 ❷ Surinam, 17,819 ❸ St. Kitts and Nevis, 15,468
❹ Finland, 14,799 ❺ Rwanda, 14,550 ❻ New Zealand, 13,854 ❼ Sweden, 12,982
❽ Denmark, 10,525 ❾ Canada, 10,451 ❿ US Virgin Islands, 10,441

England and Wales, 9,980
* Reported crime per 100,000 population

THE FIRST MECHANICAL LIE DETECTOR

Italian criminologist Cesare Lombroso first described using blood pressure changes to measure the reactions of suspects during questioning in 1895, but it was not until 1902 that this proposal was put into practice. Working in Burnley, UK, Scottish doctor James MacKenzie (1853–1925) published a book, *The Study of the Pulse*, and, with the aid of a local watchmaker, invented the polygraph, a machine to record the rhythms of the heart. Although MacKenzie's instrument, which was later produced commercially, was primarily designed for medical purposes, its principles were used by subsequent researchers to develop increasingly sophisticated devices to relate such phenomena as blood pressure, respiratory changes, and even voice frequencies to lying, and thus to create lie detectors. However, since the results of tests using such devices can be literally a matter of life or death, to this day few jurisdictions accept their results.

100 YEARS AGO · YEARS AGO · YEARS AGO · YEARS AGO

TOP 10 ★
LARGEST PRISONS IN THE UK

PRISON	INMATES*
1 Wandsworth, London	1,290
2 Armley, Leeds	1,248
3 Walton, Liverpool	1,245
4 Strangeways, Manchester	1,114
5 Pentonville, London	1,107
6 Winson Green, Birmingham	1,065
7 Doncaster	1,024
8 Barlinnie, Glasgow	978
9 Elmley, Isle of Sheppey	898
10 Holme House, Stockton	850

* As at 30 September 2000

TOP 10 ★
CRIMES WITH THE FASTEST REDUCTION RATE IN REPORTED INCIDENTS IN THE UK

TYPE OF CRIME	INCIDENTS 1999	% DECREASE 1997–99
1 Snatch theft from person	53,000	36
2 Bicycle theft	397,000	27
3 Attempted burglary/burglary without loss	746,000	23
4 Violence committed by an acquaintance	1,178,000	19
5 Burglary with loss	538,000	18
6 Theft from vehicle	1,811,000	16
7 =Attempted theft of/from vehicle	812,000	13
=Burglary with entry	760,000	13
9 =Theft of vehicle	333,000	11
=Wounding	634,000	11

Source: British Crime Survey, 2000

At the other end of the scale, the incidence of violence committed by a stranger has increased by 29 per cent over the same period.

THE 10 ★
TYPES OF OFFENCE FOR WHICH MOST PEOPLE ARE IMPRISONED IN ENGLAND AND WALES

OFFENCE	FEMALE PRISONERS	TOTAL PRISONERS*
1 Violence against the person	460	11,440
2 Burglary	140	8,930
3 Drugs offences	990	8,580
4 Robbery	210	6,310
5 Sexual offences	20	5,050
6 Theft and handling	480	4,920
7 Other offences	170	3,280
8 Motoring offences	40	2,340
9 Offence not recorded	90	1,300
10 Fraud and forgery	120	1,000

* As at 30 September 2000, male and female sentenced prisoners

Source: Home Office Prison Population Brief

The number of women serving jail sentences increased by 6 per cent over the period September 1999–September 2000.

THE 10 ★
MOST FREQUENTLY BURGLED ITEMS IN THE UK

ITEM	PERCENTAGE OF BURGLARIES INVOLVING THEFT OF ITEM (2000)
1 Cash	36
2 =Jewellery	28
=Video	28
4 Stereo/hi-fi equipment	20
5 Computer equipment	14
6 Television	12
7 =Camera	11
=Purse/wallet	11
9 Clothes	10
10 Credit cards/cheque books	9

Source: British Crime Survey, 2000

THE 10 ★
MOST COMMON CRIMES IN ENGLAND AND WALES 100 YEARS AGO

OFFENCE	NO. REPORTED
1 Larcenies	60,715
2 Burglary and housebreaking	8,038
3 Frauds	2,954
4 Attempted suicide	2,061
5 Crimes of violence (not murder)	1,890
6 Crimes against morals	1,615
7 Receiving	998
8 Forgery	395
9 Robbery and extortion	308
10 Arson	285

These are the annual averages of indictable crimes reported to the police in England and Wales during 1898–1902. Falling just outside is the now virtually defunct crime of "coining" – the forgery of coins – with 155 cases, followed by murder (143). In the same period, various non-indictable offences also resulted in large numbers of trials.

THE 10 ★
MOST COMMON METHODS OF ENTRY FOR BURGLARS IN THE UK

METHOD OF ENTRY	PERCENTAGE OF BURGLARIES (2000)
1 Door lock forced	28
2 Window lock/catch forced	17
3 =Door panel broken/cut	14
=Door was not locked	14
5 Window glass broken/cut	10
6 Door, other method	9
7 False pretences	6
8 =Had a door key	5
=Window open/could be pushed open	5
10 Pushed past person who opened the door	4

Source: British Crime Survey, 2000

Did You Know? Although regarded as "priceless", Leonardo da Vinci's *Mona Lisa* is believed to be the most valuable single object ever stolen. It was taken from the Louvre Museum on 21 August 1911, and returned on 4 January 1914.

Capital Punishment

LAST PUBLIC HANGINGS IN THE UK

HANGED/CRIME	DATE
1 Michael Barrett	26 May 1868
Murder of Sarah Ann Hodgkinson, one of 12 victims of bombing in Clerkenwell, London	
2 Robert Smith	12 May 1868
Murder of a girl (the last public hanging in Scotland)	
3 Richard Bishop	30 Apr 1868
Stabbing of Alfred Cartwright	
4 John Mapp	9 Apr 1868
Murder of a girl	
5 Frederick Parker	4 Apr 1868
Murder of Daniel Driscoll	
6 Timothy Faherty	4 Apr 1868
Murder of Mary Hanmer	
7 Miles Wetherill or Weatherill	4 Apr 1868
Murder of Rev. Plow and his maid	
8 Frances Kidder	2 Apr 1868
Murder of 12-year-old Louise Kidder-Staple (the last public hanging of a woman)	
9 William Worsley	31 Mar 1868
Murder of William Bradbury	
10 Frederick Baker	24 Dec 1867
Murder and mutilation of 8-year-old Fanny Adams	

FIRST COUNTRIES TO ABOLISH CAPITAL PUNISHMENT

COUNTRY	ABOLISHED
1 Russia	1826
2 Venezuela	1863
3 Portugal	1867
4 = Brazil	1882
= Costa Rica	1882
6 Ecuador	1897
7 Panama	1903
8 Norway	1905
9 Uruguay	1907
10 Colombia	1910
UK	1965

PRISONS WITH THE MOST HANGINGS IN ENGLAND AND WALES, 1868–1964

PRISON	HANGINGS 1868–99	1900–64	TOTAL
1 Wandsworth, London	18	98	116
2 Pentonville, London	–	105	105
3 Manchester (Strangeways)	28	71	99
4 Liverpool (Walton)	39	52	91
5 Leeds (Armley)	23	66	89
6 Durham	21	54	75
7 Newgate, London	50	9	59
8 Birmingham (Winson Green)	6	34	40
9 Lincoln	12	18	30
10 = Maidstone	17	11	28
= Winchester	14	14	28

WORST YEARS FOR LYNCHINGS IN THE US*

YEAR	LYNCHING VICTIMS WHITE	BLACK	TOTAL
1 1892	69	161	230
2 1884	160	51	211
3 1894	58	134	192
4 = 1885	110	74	184
= 1891	71	113	184
6 1895	66	113	179
7 1889	76	94	170
8 1897	35	123	158
9 1893	34	118	152
10 1886	64	74	138

* Since 1882

Lynching is the "rough justice" of a mob seizing a crime suspect and hanging him or her (92 women were lynched between 1882 and 1927) without trial. Although lynching progressively became a racial crime, in its early years white victims actually outnumbered black.

FIRST EXECUTIONS BY LETHAL INJECTION IN THE US

NAME	EXECUTION
1 Charles Brooks	7 Dec 1982
2 James Autry	14 Mar 1984
3 Ronald O'Bryan	31 Mar 1984
4 Thomas Barefoot	30 Oct 1984
5 Dovle Skillem	16 Jan 1985
6 Stephen Morin	13 Mar 1985
7 Jesse de la Rosa	15 May 1985
8 Charles Milton	25 June 1985
9 Henry M. Porter	9 July 1985
10 Charles Rumbaugh	11 Sep 1985

Source: *Death Penalty Information Center*

Although Oklahoma was the first State to legalize execution by lethal injection, the option was not taken there until 1990. All of the above were executed in Texas (where, curiously, death row inmates with the first name of Charles figure prominently). It is now the most commonly used form of execution in the US.

COUNTRIES WITH THE MOST EXECUTIONS

COUNTRY	EXECUTIONS (1998)
1 China	1,067
2 Dem. Rep. of Congo	100
3 USA	68
4 Iran	66
5 Egypt	48
6 Belarus	33
7 Taiwan	32
8 Saudi Arabia	29
9 Singapore	28
10 = Rwanda	24
= Sierra Leone	24

Source: *Amnesty International*

Although unconfirmed, Amnesty International also received reports of many hundreds of executions in Iraq.

THE 10 ★
US STATES WITH THE MOST PRISONERS ON DEATH ROW

STATE	PRISONERS UNDER DEATH SENTENCE*
1 California	582
2 Texas	448
3 Florida	385
4 Pennsylvania	238
5 North Carolina	237
6 Ohio	202
7 Alabama	185
8 Illinois	172
9 Oklahoma	137
10 Georgia	136

* As at 1 October 2000

Source: *Death Penalty Information Center*

A total of 3,703 prisoners were on death row at the end of 2000. Some were sentenced in more than one state, causing a higher total to be achieved than by adding individual state figures together.

THE 10 ★
US STATES WITH THE MOST EXECUTIONS, 1977–2000*

STATE	EXECUTIONS
1 Texas	239
2 Virginia	81
3 Florida	50
4 Missouri	46
5 Oklahoma	30
6 Louisiana	26
7 South Carolina	25
8 =Alabama	23
=Arkansas	23
=Georgia	23

* To 19 December 2000

Source: *Death Penalty Information Center*

A total of 557 people have been executed since 1977, when the death penalty was re-introduced after a 10-year moratorium. During this period, 20 states have not carried out any executions.

THE 10 ★
FIRST ELECTROCUTIONS AT SING SING

PERSON ELECTROCUTED	AGE	ELECTROCUTED		PERSON ELECTROCUTED	AGE	ELECTROCUTED
1 Harris A. Smiler	32	7 July 1891		8 Fred McGuire	24	19 Dec 1892
2 James Slocum	22	7 July 1891		9 James L. Hamilton	40	3 Apr 1893
3 Joseph Wood	21	7 July 1891		10 Carlyle Harris	23	8 May 1893
4 Schihick Judigo	35	7 July 1891				
5 Martin D. Loppy	51	7 Dec 1891				
6 Charles McElvaine	20	8 Feb 1892				
7 Jeremiah Cotte	40	28 Mar 1892				

The electric chair was installed in Sing Sing Prison, Ossining, New York, in 1891, just a year after it was first used to execute William Kemmler at Auburn Prison, also in New York State. By the end of the 19th century, 29 inmates had been executed by this means.

THE 10 ★
US STATES WITH THE MOST WOMEN ON DEATH ROW

STATE	WOMEN UNDER DEATH SENTENCE*
1 California	12
2 Texas	7
3 North Carolina	6
4 =Illinois	4
=Pennsylvania	4
6 =Alabama	3
=Florida	3
8 =Arizona	2
=Tennessee	2
10 =Georgia	1
=Idaho	1
=Indiana	1
=Kentucky	1
=Louisiana	1
=Mississipi	1
=Nevada	1
=Oklahoma	1

* As at 2 May 2001, when a total of 51 women were on death row

Source: *Death Penalty Information Center*

At the beginning of 2001, women represented only 1.4 per cent of death row prisoners. Since 1973, California, Florida, North Carolina, and Texas have accounted for more than 40 per cent of the death sentences passed on women.

THE 10 ★
US STATES WITH THE MOST WOMEN SENTENCED TO DEATH, 1973–2000

STATE	WOMEN SENTENCED TO DEATH*
1 North Carolina	16
2 Florida	15
3 California	14
4 Texas	13
5 Ohio	9
6 Alabama	8
7 =Illinois	7
=Mississippi	7
=Oklahoma	7
10 Georgia	6

* As at 30 June 2000

Source: *Death Penalty Information Center*

In the US, the sentencing of women to death is comparatively rare, and occasions when the sentence is actually carried are even rarer. In fact, there are only 561 known instances since 1632 out of a massive total of some 19,200 executions. A total of 45 executions of women have been carried out since 1900. Of these, seven have been executed since 2 May 1962, when Elizabeth Ann Duncan was executed. The most recent was of Wanda Jean Allen in Oklahoma on 11 Jan 2001.

Which country lost most ships during World War II? A Germany
see p.75 for the answer B Japan
C UK

Murder File

WORST GUN MASSACRES*

PERPETRATOR/LOCATION/DATE/CIRCUMSTANCES   VICTIMS

1 Woo Bum Kong, Sang-Namdo, South Korea, 28 Apr 1982   57
Off-duty policeman Woo Bum Kong (or Wou Bom-Kon), 27, went on a drunken rampage with rifles and hand grenades, killing 57 and injuring 38 before blowing himself up with a grenade.

2 Martin Bryant, Port Arthur, Tasmania, Australia, 28 Apr 1996   35
Bryant, a 28-year-old Hobart resident, used a rifle in a horrific spree that began in a restaurant and ended with a siege in a guesthouse in which he held hostages. He set the building on fire before being captured by police.

3 Baruch Goldstein, Hebron, occupied West Bank, Israel, 25 Feb 1994   29
Goldstein, a 42-year-old US immigrant doctor, carried out a gun massacre of Palestinians at prayer at the Tomb of the Patriarchs before being beaten to death by the crowd.

4 Campo Elias Delgado, Bogota, Colombia, 4 Dec 1986   28
Delgado, a Vietnamese war veteran and electronics engineer, stabbed two and shot a further 26 people before being killed by police.

5 =James Oliver Huberty, San Ysidro, California, USA, 18 July 1984   22
Huberty, aged 41, opened fire in a McDonald's restaurant, killing 21 before being shot dead by a SWAT marksman. A further 19 were wounded, including a victim who died the following day.

=George Jo Hennard, Killeen, Texas, USA, 16 Oct 1991   22
Hennard drove his pick-up truck through the window of Luby's Cafeteria and, in 11 minutes, killed 22 with semi-automatic pistols before shooting himself.

7 Thomas Hamilton, Dunblane, Stirling, UK, 13 Mar 1996   17
Hamilton, 43, shot 16 children and a teacher in Dunblane Primary School before killing himself in the UK's worst-ever shooting incident.

8 =Charles Joseph Whitman, Austin, Texas, USA, 31 July–1 Aug 1966   16
25-year-old ex-Marine marksman Whitman killed his mother and wife; the following day he shot 14 and wounded 34 from the observation deck at the University of Texas at Austin, before being shot dead by police.

=Michael Ryan, Hungerford, Berkshire, UK, 19 Aug 1987   16
Ryan, 26, shot 14 dead and wounded 16 others (two of whom died later) before shooting himself.

=Ronald Gene Simmons, Russellville, Arkansas, USA, 28 Dec 1987   16
47-year-old Simmons killed 16, including 14 members of his own family, by shooting or strangling. He was caught and then sentenced to death on 10 Feb 1989.

* By individuals, excluding terrorist and military actions; totals exclude perpetrator

Gun massacres at workplaces in the US have attracted considerable attention in recent years, with post offices being especially notable: on 20 August 1986 in Edmond, Oklahoma, 44-year-old postal worker Patrick Henry Sherrill shot 14 dead and wounded six others at the post office where he worked, before killing himself. Since then, there have been some 15 such incidents perpetrated by postal workers, in which 40 victims have been killed. Equally distressing have been a number of shootings at schools and other educational establishments, among the worst of which – and Canada's worst gun massacre – was that committed by Marc Lépine, a student at the Université de Montreal, Quebec, Canada. On 6 December 1989 he went on an armed rampage, shooting 14 women before killing himself.

MOST PROLIFIC SERIAL KILLERS OF THE 20TH CENTURY

KILLER/COUNTRY/CRIME   VICTIMS*

1 Pedro Alonso López, Colombia   300
Captured in 1980, López, nicknamed the "Monster of the Andes", led police to 53 graves, but probably murdered at least 300 in Colombia, Ecuador, and Peru. He was sentenced to life imprisonment.

2 Dr. Harold Shipman, UK   236
In January 2000, Manchester doctor Shipman was found guilty of the murder of 15 women patients, but an official report published in January 2001 suggested that the potential figure could be at least 236 and perhaps as high as 345.

3 Henry Lee Lucas, USA   200
Lucas confessed in 1983 to 360 murders, although the number of murder sites to which he led police was "only" 200. He committed many crimes with his partner-in-crime Ottis Toole, who died in jail in 1996. He remains on Death Row in Huntsville Prison, Texas.

4 Hu Wanlin, China   196
Posing as a doctor specializing in ancient Chinese medicine, Hu Wanlin was sentenced on 1 October 2000 to 15 years imprisonment for three deaths, but authorities believe he was responsible for considerably more, an estimated 20 in Taiyuan, 146 in Shanxi, and 30 in Shangqiu.

5 Luis Alfredo Gavarito, Colombia   140
Gavarito confessed in 1999 to a spate of murders that are still the subject of investigation.

6 Dr. Jack Kevorkian, USA   130
In 1999 Kevorkian, who admitted to assisting in 130 suicides since 1990, was convicted of second-degree murder. His 10- to 25-year prison sentence is subject to appeal.

7 =Donald Henry "Pee Wee" Gaskins, USA   100
Gaskins was executed in 1991 for a series of murders that may have reached 200.

=Javed Iqbal, Pakistan   100
Iqbal and two accomplices were found guilty in March 2000 of murdering boys in Lahore. Iqbal was sentenced to be publicly strangled, dismembered, and his body dissolved in acid.

9 Delfina and Maria de Jesús Gonzales, Mexico   91
In 1964 the Gonzales sisters were sentenced to 40 years imprisonment after the remains of 80 women and 11 men were discovered on their property.

10 Bruno Lüdke, Germany   86
Lüdke confessed to murdering 86 women between 1928 and 1943. He died in hospital in 1944 after a lethal injection.

* Estimated minimum; includes only individual and partnership murderers; excludes "mercy killings" by doctors, murders by bandits, those carried out by groups, such as political and military atrocities, and gangland slayings

Serial killers are mass murderers who kill repeatedly, often over long periods, in contrast to the so-called "spree killers" who have been responsible for single occasion massacres, usually with guns, and other perpetrators of single outrages, often by means of bombs, resulting in multiple deaths. Because of the secrecy surrounding their horrific crimes, and the time-spans involved, it is almost impossible to calculate the precise numbers of their victims.

THE 10 ★
MOST COMMON MURDER WEAPONS AND METHODS IN ENGLAND AND WALES

	WEAPON/METHOD	VICTIMS (1999/2000)
1	Sharp instrument	219
2	Hitting and kicking	106
3	Blunt instrument	70
4	Poison or drugs	64
5	Shooting	62
6	Strangulation and asphyxiation	57
7	Motor vehicle	13
8	Burning	12
9	Drowning	7
10	Explosion	4

Source: *Home Office Criminal Statistics England and Wales 1999*

THE 10 ★
MOST COMMON RELATIONSHIPS OF MURDER VICTIMS TO PRINCIPAL SUSPECTS IN ENGLAND AND WALES

	RELATIONSHIP	VICTIMS (1999/2000)
1	Stranger	182
2	Friend or acquaintance	169
3	Current or former spouse, cohabitant, or lover	119
4	Son or daughter	56
5	Other person in course of employment	39
6	Other family member	22
7	Parent	15
8	Other associate	5
9	Act of terrorism	3
10	Police or prison officer on duty	2

Source: *Home Office Criminal Statistics England and Wales 1999*

FIREPOWER
While handguns are the most common murder weapons in the US and certain other countries, restrictions on their use elsewhere relegates them to a less significant position.

TOP 10 ★
COUNTRIES WITH THE LOWEST MURDER RATES

	COUNTRY	MURDERS PER ANNUM PER 100,000 POPULATION
1 =	Argentina	0.1
=	Brunei	0.1
3 =	Burkina Faso	0.2
=	Niger	0.2
5 =	Guinea	0.5
=	Guinea-Bissau	0.5
=	Iran	0.5
8 =	Finland	0.6
=	Saudi Arabia	0.6
10 =	Cameroon	0.7
=	Ireland	0.7
=	Mongolia	0.7

THE 10 ★
COUNTRIES WITH THE HIGHEST MURDER RATES

	COUNTRY	MURDERS PER ANNUM PER 100,000 POPULATION
1	Swaziland	88.1
2	Colombia	81.9
3	Namibia	72.4
4	South Africa	56.9
5	Lesotho	33.9
6	Belize	33.2
7	Philippines	30.1
8	Jamaica	27.6
9	Guatemala	27.4
10	French Guiana	27.2
	England and Wales	1.4

Did You Know? The peak year for murder in the US was 1994, when 22,084 cases were recorded, 14,463 of them, or 65 per cent, involving firearms.

Military Matters

CHINESE ARMED FORCES

Members of the Chinese army, the largest military force in the world, parade in the now infamous Tiananmen Square, Beijing.

THE 10 YEARS WITH THE MOST NUCLEAR EXPLOSIONS

(Year/explosions)

1 1962, 178 **2** 1958, 116 **3** 1968, 79 **4** 1966, 76 **5** 1961, 71 **6** 1969, 67 **7** 1978, 66 **8** = 1967, 64; = 1970, 64 **10** 1964, 60

TOP 10 ★
COUNTRIES WITH THE LARGEST DEFENCE BUDGETS

	COUNTRY	BUDGET ($)
1	USA	291,200,000,000
2	Japan	45,600,000,000
3	UK	34,500,000,000
4	Russia	29,000,000,000
5	France	27,000,000,000
6	Germany	23,300,000,000
7	Saudi Arabia	18,700,000,000
8	Italy	16,000,000,000
9	India	15,900,000,000
10	China	14,500,000,000

The savings made as a consequence of the end of the Cold War between the West and the former Soviet Union mean that both the numbers of personnel and the defence budgets of many countries have been cut.

TOP 10 ★
LARGEST ARMED FORCES

	COUNTRY	ESTIMATED ACTIVE FORCES			
		ARMY	NAVY	AIR	TOTAL
1	China	1,700,000	220,000	420,000	2,340,000
2	USA	471,700	370,700	353,600	1,365,800*
3	India	1,100,000	53,000	150,000	1,303,000
4	North Korea	950,000	46,000	86,000	1,082,000
5	Russia	348,000	171,500	184,600	1,004,100#
6	South Korea	560,000	60,000	63,000	683,000
7	Pakistan	550,000	22,000	40,000	612,000
8	Turkey	495,000	54,600	60,100	609,700
9	Iran	325,000	18,000	45,000	513,000+
10	Vietnam	412,000	42,000	30,000	484,000
	UK	113,950	43,770	54,730	212,450

* *Includes 169,800 Marine Corps*
# *Includes Strategic Deterrent Forces, Paramilitary, National Guard, etc.*
+ *Includes 125,000 Revolutionary Guards*

TOP 10 COUNTRIES WITH THE HIGHEST MILITARY/CIVILIAN RATIO

(Country/ratio* in 2000)

❶ North Korea, 503 **❷** Israel, 278 **❸** United Arab Emirates, 240 **❹** Jordan, 201
❺ Iraq, 192 **❻** Oman, 189 **❼** Syria, 187 **❽** Qatar, 178
❾ Bahrain, 172 **❿** Taiwan, 168   *UK, 36*

* Military personnel per 10,000 population

TOP 10 ★
COUNTRIES WITH THE HIGHEST PER CAPITA DEFENCE EXPENDITURE

	COUNTRY	EXPENDITURE PER CAPITA, 1999 ($)
1	Qatar	2,026
2	Israel	1,435
3	Kuwait	1,407
4	Brunei	1,211
5	United Arab Emirates	1,185
6	Singapore	1,138
7	Saudi Arabia	1,006
8	USA	1,000
9	Norway	743
10	Oman	696

THOMPSON OF THE TOMMY GUN

The "Tommy gun", or Thompson sub-machine gun, was originally produced as a military weapon. It takes its name from US Army ordnance officer John Taliaferro Thompson (1860–1940), but the operating mechanism of the .45-calibre weapon was the brainchild of naval officer John N. Blish, from whom John Thompson acquired the patent. The gun was manufactured by Thompson's Auto-Ordnance Company from 1919, but was not widely used until World War II, when over 2 million were made. Unusually, the nickname "Tommy Gun" was registered as a trademark.

TOP 10 ★
COUNTRIES WITH THE LARGEST NAVIES

	COUNTRY	MANPOWER, 2000*
1	USA	370,700
2	China	220,000
3	Russia	171,500
4	Taiwan	62,000
5	South Korea	60,000
6	Turkey	54,600
7	India	53,000
8	France	49,490
9	North Korea	46,000
10	UK	43,770

* Including naval air forces and marines

TOP 10 ★
ARMS IMPORTERS

	COUNTRY	ANNUAL IMPORTS ($)
1	Saudi Arabia	6,103,000,000
2	Taiwan	2,604,000,000
3	Japan	1,866,000,000
4	South Korea	1,847,000,000
5	Israel	1,504,000,000
6	Egypt	800,000,000
7	Indonesia	767,000,000
8	China	500,000,000
9	Thailand	410,000,000
10	Kuwait	314,000,000
	UK	undisclosed

CRUISE SHIP
The US Navy is the world's largest. Here, the destroyer USS Merrill *launches a Tomahawk cruise missile.*

TOP 10 ★
COUNTRIES WITH THE MOST COMBAT AIRCRAFT*

	COUNTRY	COMBAT AIRCRAFT
1	China	3,000
2	Russia	2,733
3	USA	2,529
4	Ukraine	911
5	India	774
6	North Korea	621
7	Egypt	580
8	Taiwan	570
9	South Korea	555
10	France	517
	UK	429

* Air force only, excluding long-range strike/attack aircraft

---

Which country has the largest Muslim population? *see p.77 for the answer*

A India
B Egypt
C Indonesia

The World at War

LARGEST ARMED FORCES OF WORLD WAR I

COUNTRY	PERSONNEL*
1 Russia	12,000,000
2 Germany	11,000,000
3 British Empire#	8,904,000
4 France	8,410,000
5 Austria–Hungary	7,800,000
6 Italy	5,615,000
7 USA	4,355,000
8 Turkey	2,850,000
9 Bulgaria	1,200,000
10 Japan	800,000

*Total at peak strength
Inc. Australia, Canada, India, New Zealand, etc.

Russia's armed forces were relatively small in relation to the country's population – some 6 per cent, compared with 17 per cent in Germany. Several other European nations had forces that were similarly sized in relation to their populations: Serbia's army was equivalent to 4 per cent of its population. In total, more than 65 million combatants were involved in fighting some of the costliest battles, in terms of numbers killed, that the world has ever known.

SMALLEST ARMED FORCES OF WORLD WAR I

COUNTRY	PERSONNEL*
1 Montenegro	50,000
2 Portugal	100,000
3 Greece	230,000
4 Belgium	267,000
5 Serbia	707,000
6 Romania	750,000
7 Japan	800,000
8 Bulgaria	1,200,000
9 Turkey	2,850,000
10 USA	4,355,000

* Total at peak strength

THE 10 COUNTRIES WITH THE MOST PRISONERS OF WAR, 1914–18

(Country/captured)

① Russia, 2,500,000 ② Austria–Hungary, 2,200,000 ③ Germany, 1,152,800 ④ Italy, 600,000 ⑤ France, 537,000 ⑥ Turkey, 250,000 ⑦ British Empire, 191,652 ⑧ Serbia, 152,958 ⑨ Romania, 80,000 ⑩ Belgium, 34,659

COUNTRIES SUFFERING THE GREATEST MILITARY LOSSES IN WORLD WAR I

COUNTRY	KILLED
1 Germany	1,773,700
2 Russia	1,700,000
3 France	1,357,800
4 Austria–Hungary	1,200,000
5 British Empire*	908,371
6 Italy	650,000
7 Romania	335,706
8 Turkey	325,000
9 USA	116,516
10 Bulgaria	87,500

* Inc. Australia, Canada, India, New Zealand, etc.

The number of battle fatalities and deaths from other causes among military personnel varied enormously from country to country. Romania's death rate was highest, at 45 per cent of its total mobilized forces; Germany's was 16 per cent, Austria–Hungary's and Russia's 15 per cent, and the British Empire's 10 per cent, with the US's 2 per cent and Japan's 0.04 per cent among the lowest. Japan's forces totalled only 800,000, of which an estimated 300 were killed, 907 wounded, and just three taken prisoner or reported missing.

WAR GRAVES
The first Battle of the Somme (1 July to 18 November 1916) resulted in some 1,265,000 casualties, with no significant territorial gain.

THE 10 ★
COUNTRIES SUFFERING THE GREATEST MILITARY LOSSES IN WORLD WAR II

	COUNTRY	KILLED
1	USSR	13,600,000*
2	Germany	3,300,000
3	China	1,324,516
4	Japan	1,140,429
5	British Empire#	357,116
6	Romania	350,000
7	Poland	320,000
8	Yugoslavia	305,000
9	USA	292,131
10	Italy	279,800
	Total	21,268,992

* Total, of which 7,800,000 battlefield deaths

Inc. Australia, Canada, India, New Zealand, etc.; UK figure 264,000

The actual numbers killed in World War II have been the subject of intense argument for over 50 years. Most authorities now agree that of the 30 million Soviets who bore arms, there were 13.6 million military deaths.

TOP 10 ★
LARGEST ARMED FORCES OF WORLD WAR II

	COUNTRY	PERSONNEL*
1	USSR	12,500,000
2	USA	12,364,000
3	Germany	10,000,000
4	Japan	6,095,000
5	France	5,700,000
6	UK	4,683,000
7	Italy	4,500,000
8	China	3,800,000
9	India	2,150,000
10	Poland	1,000,000

* Total at peak strength

THE 10 ★
COUNTRIES SUFFERING THE GREATEST CIVILIAN LOSSES IN WORLD WAR II

	COUNTRY	KILLED
1	China	8,000,000
2	USSR	6,500,000
3	Poland	5,300,000
4	Germany	2,350,000
5	Yugoslavia	1,500,000
6	France	470,000
7	Greece	415,000
8	Japan	393,400
9	Romania	340,000
10	Hungary	300,000

Deaths among civilians during this war – many resulting from famine and internal purges, such as those in China and the USSR – were colossal, but they were less well documented than those among fighting forces. Although the figures are the best available from authoritative sources, and present a broad picture of the scale of civilian losses, the precise numbers will never be known.

TOP 10 ★
LARGEST SUBMARINE FLEETS OF WORLD WAR II

	COUNTRY	SUBMARINES
1	Japan*	163
2	USA*	112
3	France	77
4	USSR	75
5	Germany	57
6	UK	38
7	Netherlands	21
8	Italy	15
9	Denmark	12
10	Greece	6

* Strength at December 1941

These show submarine strengths at the outbreak of the war. During hostilities, production rose sharply.

THE 10 ★
COUNTRIES SUFFERING THE GREATEST NUMBER OF WARSHIP LOSSES IN WORLD WAR II

	COUNTRY	WARSHIPS SUNK
1	UK	213
2	Japan	198
3	USA	105
4	Italy	97
5	Germany	60
6	USSR	37
7	Canada	17
8	France	11
9	Australia	9
10	Norway	2

TOP 10 ★
TANKS OF WORLD WAR II

	TANK	COUNTRY	WEIGHT (TONS)	NO. PRODUCED
1	M4A3 Sherman	USA	31.0	41,530
2	T34 Model 42	USSR	28.5	35,120
3	T34/85	USSR	32.0	29,430
4	M3 General Stuart	USA	12.2	14,000
5	Valentine II	UK	17.5	8,280
6	M3A1 Lee/Grant	USA	26.8	7,400
7	Churchill VII	UK	40.0	5,640
8 =	Panzer IVD	Germany	20.0	5,500
=	Panzer VG	Germany	44.8	5,500
10	Crusader I	UK	19.0	4,750

The tank named after US Civil War General William Tecumseh Sherman was used in large numbers by both US and British troops during World War II. It carried a crew of five and could cruise over a distance of 230 km (143 miles) at up to 40 km/h (25 mph). Its weaponry comprised two machine guns and, originally, a 75-mm cannon, but after 1944 about half the Shermans in operation had their cannons replaced by one capable of firing a powerful 7.7-kg shell or a 5.5-kg armour-piercing shell.

World Religions

TOP 10 ★
RELIGIONS IN THE UK

	RELIGION	MEMBERS (2000)
1	Anglican	25,600,000
2	Roman Catholic	5,800,000
3	Presbyterian	2,600,000
4	Muslim	1,400,000
5	Methodist	1,300,000
6	Sikh	600,000
7=	Baptist	500,000
=	Orthodox	500,000
=	Church of Scientology	500,000
10	Hindu	400,000

Membership of Christian churches in the UK has fallen since the 1970s, while membership of other religions, particularly Sikhism and Islam, has risen. This list represents the number of people belonging to a religion – not necessarily practising members, but according to whether they stated that they belonged to a particular religion or denomination. Of the 25.6 million Anglicans in the UK in 2000, it is estimated that less than 1 million regularly attended church services on Sundays, although twice that number attended at least once a year, often for celebrations of traditional church calendar events, such as Easter or Christmas, or for weddings and baptisms.

TOP 10 ★
COUNTRIES WITH THE HIGHEST PROPORTION OF HINDUS

	COUNTRY	HINDU PERCENTAGE OF POPULATION
1	Nepal	89
2	India	79
3	Mauritius	52
4	Guyana	40
5	Fiji	38
6	Suriname	30
7	Bhutan	25
8	Trinidad and Tobago	24
9	Sri Lanka	15
10	Bangladesh	11

Source: Adherents.com

THE 10 LATEST DALAI LAMAS
(Dalai Lama/lifespan)

❶ Tenzin Gyatso, 1935– ❷ Thupten Gyatso, 1876–1933
❸ Trinley Gyatso, 1856–1875 ❹ Khendrup Gyatso, 1838–1856
❺ Tsultrim Gyatso, 1816–1837 ❻ Luntok Gyatso, 1806–1815 ❼ Jampel Gyatso, 1758–1804 ❽ Kesang Gyatso, 1708–1757 ❾ Tsangyang Gyatso, 1683–1706
❿ Ngawang Lobsang Gyatso, 1617–1682

The current Dalai Lama is the fourteenth in line since the first head of the "Yellow Hat Order" of Tibetan Buddhists (1391–1475).

TOP 10 ★
LARGEST CHRISTIAN POPULATIONS

	COUNTRY	CHRISTIAN POPULATION (2000)
1	USA	189,983,000
2	Brazil	170,405,000
3	Mexico	96,614,000
4	China	86,801,000
5	Philippines	72,255,000
6	Germany	60,712,000
7	Nigeria	54,012,000
8	Italy	47,704,000
9	France	45,505,000
10	Dem. Rep. of Congo	42,283,000
	World total	2,094,371,000

Source: *Christian Research*

TOP 10 ★
CHRISTIAN DENOMINATIONS

	DENOMINATION	MEMBERS
1	Roman Catholic	936,192,000
2	Orthodox	139,469,000
3	Pentecostal	122,096,000
4	Lutheran	82,943,000
5	Anglican	78,395,000
6	Baptist	71,590,000
7	Presbyterian	49,286,000
8	Methodist	26,374,000
9	Seventh Day Adventist	11,589,000
10	Churches of Christ	6,759,000

Source: *Christian Research*

TOP 10 ★
RELIGIOUS BELIEFS

	RELIGION	FOLLOWERS (2000)
1	Christianity	2,094,371,000
2	Islam	1,188,242,000
3	Hinduism	811,337,000
4	Non-religions	768,158,000
5	Buddhism	359,981,000
6	Ethnic religions	228,366,000
7	Atheism	150,089,000
8	New religions	102,356,000
9	Sikhism	23,259,000
10	Judaism	13,191,500

TOP 10 ★
LARGEST JEWISH POPULATIONS

	COUNTRY	JEWISH POPULATION (2000)
1	USA	5,700,000
2	Israel	4,882,000
3	France	521,000
4	Canada	362,000
5	Russia	290,000
6	UK	276,000
7	Argentina	200,000
8	Ukraine	100,000
9	Brazil	98,000
10	Australia	97,000
	World total	13,191,500

Source: American Jewish Year Book, *Vol.100*

Jewish communities are found in virtually every country in the world.

Did You Know? Completed in 1989, the world's largest church, Our Lady of Peace Basilica in Yamoussoukro, Côte d'Ivoire, is taller than and has double the floor area of St. Peter's, Rome, the previous record holder.

TOP 10 ★
LARGEST MUSLIM POPULATIONS

	COUNTRY	MUSLIM POPULATION (2000)
1	Indonesia	182,570,000
2	Pakistan	134,480,000
3	India	121,000,000
4	Bangladesh	114,080,000
5	Turkey	65,510,000
6	Iran	62,430,000
7	Egypt	58,630,000
8	Nigeria	53,000,000
9	Algeria	30,530,000
10	Morocco	28,780,000
	World total	1,188,242,000

There are at least 15 countries where the population is 95 per cent Muslim, including Bahrain, Kuwait, Somalia, and the Yemen. Historically, Islam spread both as a result of missionary activity and through contacts with Muslim traders.

BOWING TO MECCA

Islam places many strictures on its female members but is nonetheless the world's fastest-growing religion. Here, hundreds of Muslim women unite in prayers.

TOP 10 ★
COUNTRIES WITH THE HIGHEST PROPORTION OF BUDDHISTS

	COUNTRY	BUDDHIST PERCENTAGE OF POPULATION
1	Thailand	95
2	Cambodia	90
3	Myanmar (Burma)	88
4	Bhutan	75
5	Sri Lanka	70
6	Tibet*	65
7	Laos	60
8	Vietnam	55
9	Japan*	50
10	Macau	45

* No accurate figures available
Source: Adherents.com

HEAD OF THE FAITH

Buddhism originated in India in the 6th century BC, since when it has flourished throughout Asia, becoming the dominant religion in several countries.

TOWN & COUNTRY

Country Matters

TOP 10 ★

LARGEST COUNTRIES IN EUROPE

	COUNTRY	AREA SQ KM	AREA SQ MILES
1	Russia (in Europe)	4,710,227	1,818,629
2	Ukraine	603,700	233,090
3	France	551,500	212,935
4	Spain*	504,781	194,897
5	Sweden	449,964	173,732
6	Germany	356,733	137,735
7	Finland	338,145	130,559
8	Norway	323,877	125,050
9	Poland	323,250	124,808
10	Italy	301,268	116,320

* Including offshore islands

The UK falls just outside the Top 10 at 244,101 sq km (94,247 sq miles). Excluding the Isle of Man and Channel Islands, its area comprises: England (130,410 sq km/50,351 sq miles), Scotland (78,789 sq km/30,420 sq miles), Wales (20,758 sq km/8,015 sq miles), and Northern Ireland (14,144 sq km/5,461 sq miles).

SPANISH MAIN STREET

Spain covers most of the Iberian Peninsula in southwestern Europe. At its centre lies Madrid, which has been Spain's capital city since 1561.

TOP 10 ★

LARGEST COUNTRIES

	COUNTRY	AREA SQ KM	AREA SQ MILES	PERCENTAGE OF WORLD TOTAL
1	Russia	17,070,289	6,590,876	11.46
2	Canada	9,970,599	3,849,670	6.69
3	USA	9,629,091	3,717,813	6.46
4	China	9,596,961	3,705,408	6.44
5	Brazil	8,511,965	3,286,488	5.71
6	Australia	7,686,848	2,967,909	5.16
7	India	3,287,590	1,269,346	2.20
8	Argentina	2,766,890	1,068,302	1.85
9	Kazakhstan	2,717,300	1,049,156	1.82
10	Sudan	2,505,813	967,500	1.68
	UK	244,101	94,247	0.16
	World total	148,940,000	57,506,061	100.00

The world's largest countries, the Top 10 of which comprise more than 50 per cent of the Earth's land, have undergone substantial revision of late. The break-up of the former Soviet Union has effectively introduced two new countries into the list, with Russia taking pre-eminent position (since it occupies a vast 76 per cent of the area of the old USSR, which it replaces, and, for comparison, is 70 times the size of the UK), while Kazakhstan, which enters in 9th position, ousts Algeria from the bottom of the former list.

WESTWARD EXPANSION

The land area of the United States 200 years ago, at 2,239,682 sq km (864,746 sq miles), was less than a quarter of its present extent.

TOP 10 ★

COUNTRIES WITH THE LONGEST COASTLINES

	COUNTRY	TOTAL COASTLINE LENGTH KM	MILES
1	Canada	243,791	151,485
2	Indonesia	54,716	33,999
3	Russia	37,653	23,396
4	Philippines	36,289	22,559
5	Japan	29,751	18,486
6	Australia	25,760	16,007
7	Norway	21,925	13,624
8	USA	19,924	12,380
9	New Zealand	15,134	9,404
10	China	14,500	9,010

Including all its islands, the coastline of Canada is more than six times as long as the distance round the Earth at the Equator (40,076 km/24,902 miles). The coastline of the UK (12,429 km/ 7,723 miles – greater than the distance from London to Honolulu) puts it in 13th place after Greece (13,676 km/8,498 miles). Were it included as a country, Greenland (44,087 km/27,394 miles) would be in 3rd place.

TOP 10 ★
COUNTRIES WITH THE MOST NEIGHBOURS

COUNTRY/NEIGHBOURS	NO.

1 China — 15
Afghanistan, Bhutan, India, Kazakhstan, Kyrgyzstan, Laos, Mongolia, Myanmar (Burma), Nepal, North Korea, Pakistan, Russia, Tajikistan, Thailand, North Vietnam

2 Russia — 14
Azerbaijan, Belarus, China, Estonia, Finland, Georgia, Kazakhstan, Latvia, Lithuania, Mongolia, North Korea, Norway, Poland, Ukraine

3 Brazil — 10
Argentina, Bolivia, Colombia, French Guiana, Guyana, Paraguay, Peru, Surinam, Uruguay, Venezuela

4 Dem. Rep. of Congo — 9
Angola, Burundi, Central African Republic, Congo, Rwanda, Sudan, Tanzania, Uganda, Zambia

=Germany — 9
Austria, Belgium, Czech Republic, Denmark, France, Luxembourg, Netherlands, Poland, Switzerland

=Sudan — 9
Central African Republic, Chad, Dem. Rep. of Congo, Egypt, Eritrea, Ethiopia, Kenya, Libya, Uganda

7 =Austria — 8
Czech Republic, Germany, Hungary, Italy, Liechtenstein, Slovac Republic, Slovenia, Switzerland

=France — 8
Andorra, Belgium, Germany, Italy, Luxembourg, Monaco, Spain, Switzerland

=Saudi Arabia — 8
Iraq, Jordan, Kuwait, Oman, People's Democratic Republic of Yemen, Qatar, United Arab Emirates, Yemen Arab Republic

=Tanzania — 8
Burundi, Dem. Rep. of Congo, Kenya, Malawi, Mozambique, Rwanda, Uganda, Zambia

=Turkey — 8
Armenia, Azerbaijan, Bulgaria, Georgia, Greece, Iran, Iraq, Syria

Some countries have more than one discontinuous border with the same country; this has been counted only once. Outside the Top 10, five countries – Mali, Niger, the Ukraine, Zambia, and Yugoslavia – each have seven neighbours. Political changes make this a volatile list: the former Soviet Union had 12 neighbours, but since its break-up Russia has 14, while Eritrea's separation from Ethiopia in 1993 increased Sudan's total.

TOP 10 ★
LARGEST LANDLOCKED COUNTRIES

COUNTRY	SQ KM	AREA SQ MILES
1 Kazakhstan	2,717,300	1,049,156
2 Mongolia	1,566,500	604,829
3 Chad	1,284,000	495,755
4 Niger	1,267,000	489,191
5 Mali	1,240,192	478,841
6 Ethiopia	1,104,300	426,373
7 Bolivia	1,098,581	424,165
8 Zambia	752,618	290,587
9 Afghanistan	652,090	251,773
10 Central African Republic	622,984	240,535

There are more than 40 landlocked countries, although the largest, Kazakhstan, and the 12th largest, Turkmenistan, both have coasts on the Caspian Sea – which is itself landlocked. The largest landlocked state in Europe is Hungary (93,030 sq km/35,919 sq miles). Europe contains the world's smallest landlocked states: Andorra, Liechtenstein, San Marino, and Vatican City.

MONACO GRAND PRIX

An enclave within France, Monaco's wealth, from tourism, gambling, and other sources, is out of proportion to its status as one of the world's smallest sovereign states.

TOP 10 SMALLEST COUNTRIES
(Country/area in sq km/sq miles)

1 Vatican City, 0.44/0.17 **2** Monaco, 1.00/0.38 **3** Gibraltar, 6.47/2.49
4 Nauru, 21.23/8.19 **5** Tuvalu, 25.90/10.00 **6** Bermuda, 53.35/20.59
7 San Marino, 59.57/23.00 **8** Liechtenstein, 157.99/61.00
9 Marshall Islands, 181.00/70.00 **10** Antigua, 279.72/108.00

The "country" status of several of these micro-states is questionable, since their government, defence, currency, and other features are often intricately linked with those of larger countries – the Vatican City with Italy, and Monaco with France, for example, while Gibraltar and Bermuda are dependent territories of the UK.

THE FOUNDATION OF SAUDI ARABIA

Today one of the largest and, through its oil wealth, richest countries in the world, Saudi Arabia has a history that dates back just 100 years. The territory had long been subject to rule by Egypt, the Ottoman Empire, and competing Arab families, with the head of one, Abdul Aziz Bin Abdul Rahman Al-Saud (known in the West as Ibn Saud), living in exile in Kuwait. At the age of just 21, he became the leader of a small group that in 1902 captured the city of Riyadh from the rival Al-Rashid family. This conquest marks the beginning of the formation of the modern state, but it took 30 years to incorporate all the regions into one kingdom, which, in honour of its founder, was named Saudi Arabia. Oil was discovered in 1938, and Ibn Saud ruled until 1953, fathering 45 sons and over 200 daughters.

100 YEARS AGO · YEARS AGO · YEARS AGO ·

Did You Know? Greenland is part of Danish territory, but if regarded as a country, its 2,175,600 sq km (840,004 sq miles) would make it the 12th largest in the world.

81

World & Country Populations

TOP 10 ★

FASTEST GROWING COUNTRIES

COUNTRY	ANNUAL GROWTH RATE, 1998–2015 (%)
1 Yemen	3.4
2 Oman	3.2
3 Niger	3.0
4 =Angola	2.9
=Dem. Rep. of Congo	2.9
=Saudi Arabia	2.9
7 =Burkina Faso	2.8
=Rwanda	2.8
=Solomon Islands	2.8
10 Congo	2.7
=Iraq	2.7
=Jordan	2.7
UK	0.1

Source: *UN, Human Development Report 2000*

TOP 10 ★

FASTEST SHRINKING COUNTRIES

COUNTRY	ANNUAL GROWTH RATE, 1998–2015 (%)
1 =Estonia	-0.9
=Latvia	-0.9
3 Bulgaria	-0.6
4 St. Kitts and Nevis	-0.5
5 =Hungary	-0.4
=Romania	-0.4
=Ukraine	-0.4
8 =Belarus	-0.3
=Italy	-0.3
=Lithuania	-0.3

Source: *UN, Human Development Report 2000*

Many of the countries in the Top 10 are in the former Soviet Union or Eastern Europe. They have a negative population growth rate, which means that their populations are actually shrinking, in some cases at a rate of almost 1 per cent a year. This is probably related to the rapid social and economic changes that these countries experienced in the final years of the 20th century.

TOP 10 ★

COUNTRIES WITH THE YOUNGEST POPULATIONS

COUNTRY	PERCENTAGE UNDER 15, 2002
1 Uganda	50.9
2 Marshall Islands	49.1
3 Dem. Rep. of Congo	48.2
4 Niger	47.9
5 Chad	47.8
6 São Tomé and Principe	47.7
7 Burkina Faso	47.4
8 Ethiopia	47.3
9 Benin	47.2
10 =Zambia	47.1
=Mali	47.1
UK	18.7

Source: *US Census Bureau International Data Base*

Countries with a high proportion of their population under the age of 15 are usually characterized by high birth and high death rates.

TOP 10 ★

COUNTRIES WITH THE OLDEST POPULATIONS

COUNTRY	PERCENTAGE OVER 65, 2002
1 Monaco	22.4
2 Italy	18.6
3 =Greece	18.0
=Japan	18.0
5 Spain	17,4
6 Sweden	17.3
7 Belgium	17.1
8 Germany	17.0
9 Bulgaria	16.9
10 San Marino	16.4

Source: *US Census Bureau International Data Base*

Nine of the 10 countries with the oldest populations are in Europe, implying that this region has lower death rates and a higher life expectancy than the rest of the world. On average, one in every 6.6 people (15.2 per cent) in Europe is over the age of 65.

TOP 10 ★

COUNTRIES IN WHICH MEN MOST OUTNUMBER WOMEN

COUNTRY	MEN PER 100 WOMEN (2000)
1 Qatar	187
2 United Arab Emirates	172
3 Bahrain	132
4 Saudi Arabia	123
5 Oman	113
6 =Cook Islands	111
=Guam	111
=Kuwait	111
9 =Brunei	110
=Northern Mariana Islands	110

Source: *United Nations*

The world male/female ratio is balanced virtually 50:50, although in many Western countries male births slightly outnumber female by a very small percentage. There are certain countries, however, where one sex dominates more obviously. No one knows why these imbalances occur, or even if such apparent differentials represent a true picture.

TOP 10 ★

COUNTRIES IN WHICH WOMEN MOST OUTNUMBER MEN

COUNTRY	WOMEN PER 100 MEN (2000)
1 Latvia	120
2 Ukraine	115
3 =Cape Verde	114
=Russia	114
5 =Belarus	112
=Estonia	112
=Lithuania	112
8 =Georgia	109
=Hungary	109
=Moldova	109
UK	104

Source: *United Nations*

TOP 10 ⭐
MOST DENSELY POPULATED COUNTRIES

	COUNTRY	AREA (SQ KM)	ESTIMATED POPULATION (2002)	POPULATION PER SQ KM
1	Monaco	1.95	31,987	15,993.5
2	Singapore	624	4,452,732	7,135.8
3	Malta	321	397,499	1,238.3
4	Maldives	300	320,165	1,067.2
5	Bahrain	619	656,397	1,060.4
6	Bangladesh	133,911	133,376,684	996.0
7	Taiwan	32,261	22,548,009	698.9
8	Mauritius	1,849	1,196,172	649.1
9	Barbados	430	276,607	643.3
10	Nauru	21	12,329	587.1
	UK	241,590	59,778,002	247.4
	World	131,003,055	6,234,250,387	47.6

Source: *US Census Bureau International Data Base*

TOP 10 ⭐
MOST HIGHLY POPULATED COUNTRIES

	COUNTRY	1980	POPULATION 1990	2000*
1	China	984,736,000	1,138,895,000	1,256,168,000
2	India	690,462,000	850,558,000	1,017,645,000
3	USA	227,726,000	249,949,000	274,943,000
4	Indonesia	154,936,000	187,728,000	219,267,000
5	Brazil	122,936,000	151,040,000	173,791,000
6	Russia	139,045,000	148,088,000	145,905,000
7	Pakistan	85,219,000	113,914,000	141,145,000
8	Bangladesh	88,077,000	110,118,000	129,147,000
9	Japan	116,807,000	123,537,000	126,434,000
10	Nigeria	65,699,000	86,530,000	117,171,000
	UK	56,314,000	57,507,000	59,247,000
	World	4,453,778,000	5,276,992,000	6,073,099,000

* Estimated

Source: *US Census Bureau*

According to estimates prepared by the US Bureau of the Census, the world entered the 21st century with a total population topping 6 billion. In 1999, India joined China as the second country to achieve a population in excess of 1 billion, while Mexico ascended to the 100-million-plus club in 11th place, with a population of 102,027,000. In contrast, the populations of certain countries, such as Russia and (in 22nd place in the world) Italy, actually declined during the 1990s as their birth rates fell.

TOP 10 ⭐
MOST POPULOUS ISLAND COUNTRIES

	ISLAND COUNTRY	POPULATION PER SQ KM	SQ MILE	POPULATION
1	Indonesia	118.0	305.6	224,784,210
2	Japan	339.4	879.1	126,549,976
3	Philippines	270.5	700.6	81,159,644
4	UK	243.7	631.4	59,508,382
5	Taiwan	620.8	1,608.0	22,191,087
6	Sri Lanka	293.2	759.4	19,238,575
7	Madagascar	26.4	68.4	15,506,472
8	Cuba	100.5	260.3	11,141,997
9	Dominican Republic	173.2	448.6	8,442,533
10	Haiti	247.4	641.0	6,867,995

TOP 10 ⭐
LEAST DENSELY POPULATED COUNTRIES

	COUNTRY	AREA (SQ KM)	ESTIMATED POPULATION (2002)	POPULATION PER SQ KM
1	Mongolia	1,565,000	2,694,432	1.7
2	Namibia	823,291	1,820,916	2.2
3	Australia	7,617,931	19,546,792	2.6
4 =Botswana	585,371	1,591,232	2.7
=Mauritania	1,030,400	2,828,858	2.7
=Surinam	161,471	436,494	2.7
7	Iceland	100,251	279,384	2.8
8	Libya	1,759,540	5,368,585	3.2
9 =Canada	9,220,970	31,902,268	3.5
=Guyana	196,850	698,209	3.5

Source: *US Census Bureau International Data Base*

TOP 10 MOST HIGHLY POPULATED COUNTRIES 100 YEARS AGO
(Country/population)

❶ China, 372,563,000 ❷ India, 287,223,431 ❸ Russia, 147,277,000 ❹ USA, 76,356,000 ❺ Germany, 56,345,014 ❻ Austro-Hungarian Empire, 47,013,835 ❼ Japan, 43,759,577 ❽ UK, 41,605,220 ❾ France, 38,641,333 ❿ Italy, 32,100,000

The extensive Austro-Hungarian Empire included all its territories in its census, the largest being Austria, with a population of 26,150,708.

Did You Know? China has led the world as the most highly populated country since ancient times: as early as 1393 a figure of 60 million was recorded.

Future Shock

MOST POPULATED COUNTRIES IN EUROPE IN 2050

	COUNTRY	EST. POPULATION IN 2050
1	Russia (including in Asia)	118,233,243
2	Germany	79,702,511
3	France	58,967,418
4	UK	58,210,627
5	Italy	45,016,465
6	Ukraine	37,726,401
7	Poland	33,779,568
8	Spain	32,562,163
9	Romania	18,340,400
10	Netherlands	16,721,036

Source: *US Census Bureau, International Data Base*

DECADES OF WORLD POPULATION, 1960–2050

YEAR	WORLD POPULATION
1960	3,039,332,401
1970	3,707,610,112
1980	4,456,705,217
1990	5,283,755,345
2000	6,080,141,683
2010	6,823,634,553
2020	7,518,010,600
2030	8,140,344,240
2040	8,668,391,454
2050	9,104,205,830

Source: *US Census Bureau, International Data Base*

MOST POPULATED METROPOLITAN AREAS IN THE US IN 2010

	METRO AREA*/STATE	ESTIMATED POPULATION IN 2010
1	New York, New York	8,635,700
2	Chicago, Illinois	8,626,300
3	Philadelphia, Pennsylvania	5,396,200
4	Houston, Texas	4,491,500
5	Detroit, Michigan	4,408,000
6	Atlanta, Georgia	4,231,300
7	Riverside–San Bernardino, California	4,130,200
8	Los Angeles–Long Beach, California	3,597,556
9	Dallas, Texas	3,538,100
10	San Diego, California	3,434,900

* Primary and Metropolitan Statistical Areas only, hence not comparable to city populations

Source: *US Bureau of Economic Analysis*

The greatest population increases in the coming decade – in some instances approaching a million new inhabitants – are focused in the "sun belt", with major northern centres of population experiencing relatively slower growth.

TOP 10 MOST POPULATED US STATES IN 2025

(State/estimated population in 2025)

❶ **California**, 49,285,000 ❷ **Texas**, 27,183,000 ❸ **Florida**, 20,710,000 ❹ **New York**, 19,830,000 ❺ **Illinois**, 13,440,000 ❻ **Pennsylvania**, 12,683,000 ❼ **Ohio**, 11,744,000 ❽ **Michigan**, 10,078,000 ❾ **Georgia**, 9,869,000 ❿ **New Jersey**, 9,558,000

Source: *US Census Bureau*

MOST POPULATED WORLD CITIES IN 2015

	CITY	COUNTRY	% GROWTH 2000–15	ESTIMATED POPULATION IN 2015
1	Tokyo	Japan	0.0	26,400,000
2	Bombay	India	2.4	26,100,000
3	Lagos	Nigeria	3.7	23,200,000
4	Dhaka	Bangladesh	3.6	21,100,000
5	São Paulo	Brazil	0.9	20,400,000
6 =	Karachi	Pakistan	3.2	19,200,000
=	Mexico City	Mexico	0.4	19,200,000
8	New York	USA	0.3	17,400,000
9 =	Calcutta	India	1.9	17,300,000
=	Jakarta	Indonesia	3.0	17,300,000

Source: *United Nations*, World Urbanization Prospects: The 1999 Revision

FASTEST-GROWING CITIES*

	CITY	COUNTRY	INCREASE (%) 1975–95	ESTIMATED INCREASE (%) 1995–2010
1	Hangzhou	China	283.5	171.1
2	Addis Ababa	Ethiopia	161.6	170.7
3	Kabul	Afghanistan	200.9	156.3
4	Handan	China	245.9	141.6
5	Isfahan	Iran	150.9	141.3
6	Maputo	Mozambique	318.6	139.9
7	Lagos	Nigeria	211.7	139.5
8	Luanda	Angola	210.9	138.8
9	Nairobi	Kenya	167.4	133.6
10	Qingdao	China	183.8	132.4

* Urban agglomerations of over 1 million population only

Source: *United Nations*

TEEMING MILLIONS

*China began the 20th century with a population of
some 400 million and ended it with 1.2 billion —
about one-fifth of the world's population.*

TOP 10 ★

MOST POPULATED COUNTRIES IN 2005

	COUNTRY	ESTIMATED POPULATION IN 2005
1	China	1,315,507,068
2	India	1,092,502,123
3	USA	287,972,263
4	Indonesia	242,799,696
5	Brazil	180,395,927
6	Pakistan	156,689,148
7	Russia	143,736,793
8	Bangladesh	139,794,159
9	Nigeria	139,779,647
10	Japan	127,404,212
	UK	*60,129,050*

Source: *US Census Bureau, International Data Base*
China and India entered the 21st century as the
first countries ever with billion-plus populations.

TOP 10 ★

MOST POPULATED COUNTRIES IN 2025

	COUNTRY	ESTIMATED POPULATION IN 2025
1	China	1,464,028,860
2	India	1,377,264,176
3	USA	338,070,951
4	Indonesia	301,461,556
5	Pakistan	213,338,252
6	Nigeria	204,453,333
7	Brazil	200,606,553
8	Bangladesh	177,499,122
9	Russia	135,951,626
10	Mexico	133,834,712
	UK	*60,613,482*

Source: *US Census Bureau, International Data Base*
In a single generation (2000–25), Nigeria's
population is set to increase by almost 75 per cent.

TOP 10 ★

MOST POPULATED COUNTRIES IN 2050

	COUNTRY	ESTIMATED POPULATION IN 2050
1	India	1,619,582,271
2	China	1,470,468,924
3	USA	403,943,147
4	Indonesia	337,807,011
5	Nigeria	303,586,770
6	Pakistan	267,813,495
7	Brazil	206,751,477
8	Bangladesh	205,093,861
9	Ethiopia	187,892,174
10	Dem. Rep. of Congo	181,922,656
	UK	*58,210,627*

Source: *US Census Bureau, International Data Base*
Estimates of populations in 2050 present a striking
change: China should be eclipsed by India in 2036.

What is the world's highest capital city?
see p.89 for the answer

A La Paz, Bolivia
B Brasilia, Brazil
C Quito, Ecuador

Parks & Reserves

TOP 10 MOST VISITED NATIONAL PARKS IN THE UK

(National Park/annual visitors)

1 Lake District, 13,925,000   **2** Peak District, 12,400,000   **3** Yorkshire Dales, 8,303,000   **4** North York Moors, 7,790,000   **5** New Forest, 6,624,000   **6** Snowdonia, 6,568,000   **7** The Broads, 5,361,000   **8** Pembrokeshire Coast, 4,662,000   **9** Dartmoor, 3,825,000   **10** Brecon Beacons, 3,622,000

TOP 10 ★ LARGEST NATURE RESERVES IN SCOTLAND

NATURE RESERVE/ LOCATION	AREA HECTARES	ACRES
1 **Cairngorms**, Grampian and Highland Regions	25,949	64,121
2 **Inverpolly**, Highland Region	10,857	26,828
3 **Rum**, Highland Region	10,684	26,401
4 **Caerlaverock**, Dumfries and Galloway Region	7,706	19,042
5 **Ben Wyvis**, Highland Region	5,673	14,026
6 **Beinn Eighe**, Highland Region	4,758	11,757
7 **Glen Tanar**, Grampian Region	4,185	10,341
8 **Ben Lawers**, Tayside and Central Regions	4,035	9,970
9 **Creag Meagaidh**, Highland Region	3,948	9,756
10 **Gualin**, Sutherland	2,522	6,232

Source: *Scottish Natural Heritage*

TOP 10 ★ LARGEST NATURE RESERVES IN ENGLAND

NATURE RESERVE/ LOCATION	AREA HECTARES	ACRES
1 **The Wash**, Lincolnshire	9,899	24,461
2 **Moor House–Upper Teesdale**, Cumbria/ North Yorkshire	7,387	18,254
3 **Ribble Marshes**, Lancashire/Merseyside	4,520	11,169
4 **Holkham**, Norfolk	3,851	9,516
5 **Kielderhead**, Northumberland	3,795	9,377
6 **Lindisfarne**, Northumberland	3,300	8,154
7 **Dengie**, Essex	2,544	6,286
8 **Bridgwater Bay**, Somerset	2,411	5,827
9 **Lizard**, Cornwall	1,662	4,107
10 **Dunkery and Horner Wood**, Somerset	1,604	3,964

Source: *English Nature*

TOP 10 ★ LARGEST NATURE RESERVES IN WALES

NATURE RESERVE/ LOCATION	AREA HECTARES	ACRES
1 **Berwyn**, Gwynedd/ Denbighshire/Powys	3,238.80	8,003.24
2 **Dyfi**, Ceredigion	2,262.96	5,591.89
3 **Yr Wyddfa–Snowdon**, Gwynedd	1,677.40	4,144.94
4 **Newborough Warren**, Anglesey	1,452.90	3,590.19
5 **Morfa Harlech**, Gwynedd	883.86	2,184.06
6 **Cors Caron**, Ceredigion	816.02	2,016.43
7 **Claerwen**, Ceredigion/Powys	788.50	1,948.42
8 **Whiteford**, Swansea	782.00	1,932.36
9 **Rhinog**, Gwynedd	598.10	1,477.94
10 **Kenfig Pool and Dunes**, Bridgend	518.30	1,280.75

Source: *Cyngor Cefn Gwlad Cymru/Countryside Council for Wales*

THE 10 ★ FIRST NATIONAL PARKS IN THE US

NATIONAL PARK/LOCATION	ESTABLISHED
1 **Yellowstone**, Wyoming/ Montana/Idaho	1 Mar 1872
2 **Sequoia**, California	25 Sep 1890
3 = **Yosemite**, California	1 Oct 1890
= **General Grant**, California*	1 Oct 1890
5 **Mount Rainier**, Washington	2 Mar 1899
6 **Crater Lake**, Oregon	22 May 1902
7 **Wind Cave**, South Dakota	9 Jan 1903
8 **Mesa Verde**, Colorado	29 June 1906
9 **Glacier**, Montana	11 May 1910
10 **Rocky Mountain**, Colorado	26 Jan 1915

* *Name changed to Kings Canyon National Park on 4 Mar 1940*

Several other National Parks may claim a place in this list by virtue of having been founded under different appellations (such as a public park or a National Monument) at earlier dates.

CRATER LAKE BECOMES A NATIONAL PARK

According to Native American legend, the collapse of Mount Mazama and the creation of Crater Lake, Oregon, resulted from a battle between rival chiefs: Llao of the Below World and Skell of the Above World. Revered as a sacred place, it lay undiscovered by outsiders until 1853, when three gold prospectors, John Wesley Hillman, Henry Klippel, and Isaac Skeeters, stumbled upon it, naming it Deep Blue Lake. In 1886, it was explored by Captain Clarence Dutton, who carried the survey ship *Cleetwood* overland and took soundings that established the lake to be the world's sixth deepest. Crater Lake became a popular tourist attraction and, following the efforts of William Gladstone Steel, who named many of its features, achieved National Park status on 22 May 1902.

· YEARS AGO · YEARS AGO · YEARS AGO · **100**

TOP 10 ★
LARGEST AREAS OF OUTSTANDING NATURAL BEAUTY IN ENGLAND AND WALES

	AREA	ESTABLISHED	AREA SQ KM	SQ MILES
1	Cotswolds	Aug 1966/Dec 1990	2,038	787
2	North Pennines	June 1988	1,983	766
3	North Wessex Downs	Dec 1972	1,730	668
4	High Weald	Oct 1983	1,460	564
5	Dorset	July 1959	1,129	436
6	=Sussex Downs	Apr 1966	983	380
	=Cranborne Chase and West Wiltshire Downs	Oct 1983	983	380
8	Cornwall	Nov 1959/Oct 1983	958	370
9	Kent Downs	July 1968	878	339
10	Chilterns	Dec 1965/Mar 1990	833	322

Source: *Countryside Agency*

Between them, England and Wales have 42 Areas of Outstanding Natural Beauty, comprising a total of 21,237 sq km (8,200 sq miles): 20,393 sq km (7,874 sq miles) in England and 844 sq km (326 sq miles) in Wales, representing some 14 per cent of the total area of the two countries. There are also nine Areas of Outstanding Natural Beauty in Northern Ireland, and 40 National Scenic Areas designated in Scotland, occupying some 10,018 sq km (3,867 sq miles).

TOP 10 ★
COUNTRIES WITH THE LARGEST PROTECTED AREAS

	COUNTRY	PERCENTAGE OF TOTAL AREA	DESIGNATED AREA SQ KM	SQ MILES
1	USA	24.9	2,336,406	902,091
2	Australia	13.4	1,025,405	395,911
3	Greenland	45.2	982,500	379,345
4	Canada	9.3	925,226	357,231
5	Saudi Arabia	34.4	825,717	318,811
6	China	7.1	682,410	263,480
7	Venezuela	61.7	563,056	217,397
8	Brazil	6.6	557,656	215,312
9	Russia	3.1	529,067	204,273
10	Indonesia	18.6	357,425	138,002

"Protected areas" encompass national parks, nature reserves, national monuments, and other sites. There are at least 44,300 Protected Areas around the world, covering more than 10 per cent of the total land area. In the case of some islands, such as Easter Island, almost 100 per cent of the land is designated a Protected Area.

JOSHUA TREE NATIONAL PARK
Over 20 per cent of the US land area is protected. National Parks, such as that of the Biosphere Reserve of Joshua Tree National Monument in the Californian desert, comprise some 80 per cent of the total.

What is the name of the legendary character associated with two of the world's longest place names?
see p.93 for the answer

A Tannhäuser
B Tamberlane
C Tamatea

World Cities

RUSH HOUR, NIGERIAN STYLE

Former capital Lagos, one of the world's largest, most densely populated, and fastest growing cities, suffers from massive traffic congestion, overcrowding, and slum dwellings.

TOP 10 ★
LARGEST NON-CAPITAL CITIES

	CITY/COUNTRY/CAPITAL CITY	POPULATIONS*
1	**Bombay**, India	15,138,000
	New Delhi	*8,419,000*
2	**Shanghai**, China	13,584,000
	Beijing	*11,299,000*
3	**Calcutta**#, India	11,923,000
	New Delhi	*8,419,000*
4	**Lagos**#, Nigeria	10,287,000
	Abuja	*378,671*
5	**São Paulo**, Brazil	10,017,821
	Brasília	*1,864,000*
6	**Karachi**#, Pakistan	9,733,000
	Islamabad	*350,000*
7	**Tianjin**, China	9,415,000
	Beijing	*11,299,000*
8	**Istanbul**#, Turkey	8,274,921
	Ankara	*2,937,524*
9	**New York**, USA	7,420,166
	Washington, DC	*523,124*
10	**Madras**, India	6,002,000
	New Delhi	*8,419,000*

* Based on comparison of population within administrative boundaries

\# Former capital

TOP 10 ★
MOST CROWDED CITIES

	CITY/COUNTRY	AVERAGE FLOOR SPACE PER PERSON*	
		SQ M	SQ FT
1	=**Lahore**, Pakistan	1.2	12.9
	=**Tangail**, Bangladesh	1.2	12.9
3	**Bhiwandi**, India	2.4	25.8
4	**Dhaka**, Bangladesh	2.7	29.1
5	**Kano**, Nigeria	2.8	30.1
6	**Bamako**, Mali	3.2	34.4
7	**Bombay**, India	3.5	37.7
8	=**Mwanza**, Tanzania	4.0	43.1
	=**Kampala**, Uganda	4.0	43.1
	=**Sana'a**, Yemen	4.0	43.1

* In those countries for which data available

Source: *World Bank*, World Development Indicators 2000

TOP 10 ★
FASTEST DECLINING CITIES

	CITY/COUNTRY	PEAK	LATEST	% DECLINE FROM PEAK
1	**St. Louis**, USA	875,000	334,000	-61.0
2	**Pittsburgh**, USA	677,000	341,000	-49.6
3	**Buffalo**, USA	580,000	301,000	-48.1
4	**Detroit**, USA	1,850,000	970,000	-47.6
5	**Manchester**, UK	766,000	403,000	-47.4
6	**Cleveland**, USA	915,000	496,000	-45.8
7	**Liverpool**, UK	857,000	479,000	-44.1
8	**Copenhagen**, Denmark	768,000	456,000	-39.5
9	**Newark**, USA	442,000	268,000	-39.4
10	**Glasgow**, UK	1,088,000	681,000	-37.4

THE 10 FIRST CITIES WITH POPULATIONS OF MORE THAN ONE MILLION

(City/country)

❶ **Rome**, Italy ❷ **Alexandria**, Egypt
❸ **Angkor**, Cambodia ❹ **Hangchow**, China
❺ **London**, UK ❻ **Paris**, France
❼ **Peking**, China ❽ **Canton**, China
❾ **Berlin**, Prussia ❿ **New York**, USA

Rome's population was reckoned to have exceeded 1 million some time in the 2nd century BC. Alexandria was soon after.

In its first 10 years, how many times was the Empire State Building struck by lightning?
see p.95 for the answer

A None
B 68
C 1,002

TOP 10 ★
HIGHEST CITIES

CITY/COUNTRY	HEIGHT	
---	M	FT
1 **Wenchuan**, China	5,099	16,730
2 **Potosí**, Bolivia	3,976	13,045
3 **Oruro**, Bolivia	3,702	12,146
4 **Lhasa**, Tibet	3,684	12,087
5 **La Paz**, Bolivia	3,632	11,916
6 **Cuzco**, Peru	3,399	11,152
7 **Huancayo**, Peru	3,249	10,660
8 **Sucre**, Bolivia	2,835	9,301
9 **Tunja**, Colombia	2,820	9,252
10 **Quito**, Ecuador	2,819	9,249

Lhasa was formerly the highest capital city in the world, a role now occupied by La Paz, the capital of Bolivia. Wenchuan is situated at more than half the elevation of Everest, and even the cities at the bottom of this list are more than one-third as high as Everest.

THE 10 ★
LATEST CITIES IN THE UK

CITY	CHARTER GRANTED
1 = Brighton & Hove	2000
= Inverness	2000
= Wolverhampton	2000
4 = St. David's	1995
= Armagh	1995
6 Sunderland	1992
7 Derby	1977
8 Ely	1974
9 Swansea	1969
10 Westminster	1965

There are 64 places in the UK that are entitled to call themselves "cities". Some are so-called traditionally, others by statute or by royal charter and Letters Patent. The later system has provided city status to all those in this list (even though some already had charters dating back as early as the 11th century). The three latest cities (making a total of 19 since the turn of the 20th century) commemorate the Millennium, while others celebrate such events as Queen Elizabeth II's Silver Jubilee (1977) and the 40th anniversary of her accession (1992).

TOP 10 ★
MOST URBANIZED COUNTRIES

COUNTRY	% OF POPULATION LIVING IN URBAN AREAS, 1998
1 Singapore	100.0
2 Kuwait	97.4
3 Belgium	97.2
4 Qatar	92.1
5 Iceland	92.0
6 Uruguay	90.9
7 Luxembourg	90.4
8 Malta	90.1
9 = Argentina	88.9
= Lebanon	88.9
UK	89.4

Source: *UN, Human Development Report 2000*

The last few decades have brought about a world that is far more urbanized, with a much higher proportion of the world's population living in large cities and metropolitan areas. There are also tens of millions of "rural-urban dwellers", who live in rural settlements but work in urban areas.

TOP 10 ★
LEAST URBANIZED COUNTRIES

COUNTRY	% OF POPULATION LIVING IN URBAN AREAS, 1998
1 Rwanda	5.9
2 Bhutan	6.7
3 Burundi	8.4
4 Nepal	11.2
5 Uganda	13.5
6 Malawi	14.6
7 Ethiopia	16.7
8 Papua New Guinea	16.8
9 Burkino Faso	17.4
10 Eritrea	18.0

Source: *United Nations*

TOP 10 ★
LARGEST CITIES IN EUROPE, 2000

CITY/COUNTRY	EST. POPULATION, 2000*
1 **Moscow**, Russia	13,200,000
2 **London**, UK	11,800,000
3 **Paris**, France	10,150,000
4 **Essen**, Germany	6,050,000
5 **St. Petersburg**, Russia	5,550,000
6 **Madrid**, Spain	5,050,000
7 **Barcelona**, Spain	4,200,000
8 **Berlin**, Germany	4,150,000
9 **Milan**, Italy	3,800,000
10 **Athens**, Greece	3,500,000

* Of urban agglomeration

Source: *Th. Brinkhoff: Principal Agglomerations and Cities of the World, www.citypopulation.de, 4.6.00*

CAPITAL CITY

Paris grew from 2.7 million at the turn of the 20th century to just over 10 million in 2000, making it Europe's third largest city.

The British Isles

MOST HIGHLY POPULATED COUNTIES IN THE UK*

COUNTY	POPULATION
1 Kent	1,332,000
2 Essex	1,295,000
3 Hampshire	1,238,000
4 Lancashire	1,136,000
5 Tyne and Wear	1,116,000
6 Surrey	1,061,000
7 Hertfordshire	1,034,000
8 Staffordshire	810,000
9 Norfolk	790,000
10 West Sussex	752,000

* Excluding metropolitan counties and city regions

The shifting of county boundaries and the creation of new Unitary Authorities make it difficult to provide comparative figures across the UK. The metropolitan counties and city regions have been excluded here in order to avoid a list dominated by cities; nevertheless, all the most populated counties in the UK are in England.

SMALLEST REGIONS IN THE UK*

REGION	AREA SQ KM	SQ MILES
1 Dundee City, Scotland	65	25
2 =Carrickfergus, N. Ireland	81	31
=North Down, N. Ireland	81	31
4 Castlereagh, N. Ireland	85	33
5 Blaenau Gwent, Wales	109	42
6 Belfast, N. Ireland	110	42
7 Merthyr Tydfil, Wales	111	43
8 Torfaen, Wales	126	49
9 Cardiff, Wales	140	54
10 Newtownabbey, N. Ireland	151	58

* Excluding English Unitary Authorities

Following local government reorganization in 1996, counties have been replaced by considerably smaller Council Areas, of which there are 32 in Scotland, and by Unitary Authorities, of which there are 22 in Wales, and 26 in Northern Ireland. Unitary Authorities in England (which usually cover small city areas) have been excluded in order to avoid a list consisting solely of English cities.

LEAST POPULATED COUNTIES IN ENGLAND

COUNTY	POPULATION
1 Isle of Wight	127,000*
2 Shropshire	280,000
3 Northumberland	310,000
4 Bedfordshire	373,000
5 Dorset	387,000
6 Wiltshire	426,000
7 Buckinghamshire	479,000
8 Somerset	489,000
9 Cornwall and the Isles of Scilly	490,000
10 East Sussex	491,000
England total population	49,495,000
UK total population	59,237,000

* Unitary Authority with County Council status

LEAST POPULATED REGIONS IN THE UK

REGION/LOCATION	POPULATION
1 Moyle, Northern Ireland	15,000
2 Orkney Islands, Scotland	20,000
3 Shetland Islands, Scotland	23,000
4 Ballymoney, Northern Ireland	26,000
5 Eilean Siar (Western Isles), Scotland	28,000
6 Larne, Northern Ireland	31,000
7 = Cookstown, Northern Ireland	32,000
= Limavady, Northern Ireland	32,000
9 Rutland, England	36,000
10 Strabane, Northern Ireland	37,000

The six traditional counties of Northern Ireland no longer have administrative functions. These have been replaced by Unitary Authorities, which are considerably smaller than most regions in the rest of Britain and hence feature prominently in this list.

LARGEST REGIONS IN THE UK

REGION/LOCATION	AREA SQ KM	SQ MILES
1 Highland, Scotland	25,784	9,952
2 North Yorkshire, England	8,038	3,208
3 Argyll and Bute, Scotland	6,930	2,676
4 Cumbria, England	6,824	2,635
5 Devon, England	6,562	2,533
6 Dumfries and Galloway, Scotland	6,439	2,486
7 Aberdeenshire, Scotland	6,318	2,439
8 Lincolnshire, England	5,921	2,286
9 Norfolk, England	5,372	2,074
10 Perth and Kinross, Scotland	5,311	2,051

The largest region in Wales is the Unitary Authority of Powys, covering 5,196 sq km (2,006 sq miles), and in Northern Ireland it is Fermanagh, which covers 1,699 sq km (644 sq miles).

MOST DENSELY POPULATED COUNTIES IN ENGLAND

COUNTY	POPULATION PER SQ KM	SQ MILE
1 Greater London	4,549	11,781
2 Bristol	3,657	9,471
3 West Midlands	2,923	7,570
4 Merseyside	2,152	5,573
5 Tyne and Wear	2,066	5,350
6 Greater Manchester	2,004	5,190
7 West Yorkshire	1,039	2,691
8 South Yorkshire	837	2,167
9 Surrey	632	1,636
10 Hertfordshire	631	1,634

The most overcrowded piece of land in England is Kensington and Chelsea in London, where each 12 sq km accommodates the incredible figure of 14,161 people. Outside London, the 40 sq km area covered by the Unitary Authority of Portsmouth is the most densely populated, with 4,749 people per sq km.

TOP 10 ★
LEAST DENSELY POPULATED REGIONS IN WALES

UNITARY AUTHORITY	POPULATION PER SQ KM	SQ MILE
1 Powys	24	62
2 Ceredigion	39	101
3 Gwynedd	46	119
4 Carmarthenshire	71	184
5 Pembrokeshire	72	186
6 Isle of Anglesey	92	238
7 Conwy	99	256
8 Monmouthshire	101	261
9 Denbighshire	107	277
10 Wrexham	251	650

TOP 10 ★
LEAST DENSELY POPULATED REGIONS IN NORTHERN IRELAND

UNITARY AUTHORITY	POPULATION PER SQ KM	SQ MILE
1 Moyle	31	80
2 Fermanagh	34	88
3 Omagh	42	109
4 Strabane	43	111
5 Limavady	55	142
6 Ballymoney	61	158
7 = Cookstown	62	161
= Dungannon	62	161
9 Magherafelt	68	176
10 Armagh	82	212

TOP 10 ★
LEAST DENSELY POPULATED REGIONS IN SCOTLAND

COUNCIL AREA	POPULATION PER SQ KM	SQ MILE
1 Highland	8	21
2 Eilean Siar (Western Isles)	9	23
3 Argyll and Bute	13	34
4 Shetland Islands	16	41
5 Orkney Islands	20	52
6 The Scottish Borders	22	57
7 Dumfries and Galloway	23	60
8 Perth and Kinross	25	65
9 Aberdeenshire	36	93
10 = Moray	38	98
= Stirling	38	98

TOP 10 ★
MOST DENSELY POPULATED REGIONS IN WALES

UNITARY AUTHORITY	POPULATION PER SQ KM	SQ MILE
1 Cardiff	2,292	5,936
2 Newport	733	1,898
3 Torfaen	716	1,854
4 Blaenau Gwent	661	1,711
5 Caerphilly	610	1,579
6 Swansea	607	1,572
7 Rhondda, Cynon, Taff	567	1,468
8 Bridgend	534	1,383
9 Merthyr Tydfil	513	1,328
10 The Vale of Glamorgan	362	937

While following a pattern of population decline similar to those that occurred in Northern Ireland and Scotland, a number of densely populated regions of Wales underwent expansion in the period from 1981 to 1998. Cardiff increased its population by 11.9 per cent, making it the highest among those in the Top 10. Outside this list, Ceredigion experienced the greatest population increase at 15.6 per cent, followed by Conwy with 13.1 per cent.

TOP 10 ★
MOST DENSELY POPULATED REGIONS IN NORTHERN IRELAND

UNITARY AUTHORITY	POPULATION PER SQ KM	SQ MILE
1 Belfast	2,623	6,793
2 North Down	938	2,429
3 Castlereagh	784	2,030
4 Newtownabbey	537	1,390
5 Carrickfergus	466	1,206
6 Craigavon	281	727
7 Derry	278	720
8 Lisburn	250	647
9 Ards	186	481
10 Antrim	119	308

Although heading this list, Belfast is the only region of Northern Ireland to experience a population decrease in the late 20th century. In the period from 1981 to 1998, it went down by 9.1 per cent. By contrast, Carrickfergus went up by 31.2 per cent, the greatest increase in the province, closely followed by Lisburn (30.9 per cent) and, outside the Top 10, by Banbridge (30.8 per cent), Limavady (18.5 per cent), and Coleraine (18.4 per cent).

TOP 10 ★
MOST DENSELY POPULATED REGIONS IN SCOTLAND

COUNCIL AREA	POPULATION PER SQ KM	SQ MILE
1 Glasgow City	3,540	9,168
2 Dundee City	2,252	5,832
3 City of Edinburgh	1,716	4,444
4 Aberdeen City	1,147	2,970
5 North Lanarkshire	690	1,787
6 Renfrewshire	680	1,761
7 East Dunbartonshire	638	1,652
8 West Dunbartonshire	585	1,515
9 Inverclyde	528	1,367
10 East Renfrewshire	509	1,318

Despite being the most densely populated, most of the regions listed actually declined in population during the period 1981 to 1998. Inverclyde suffered the greatest decrease, with a 15.6 per cent drop. Although heading the list, Glasgow City's population similarly declined, by 13 per cent. East Renfrewshire was the only region in the Top 10 to show a noticeable increase, with a population rise of 9.6 per cent.

Where is the world's longest cantilever bridge?
see p.96 for the answer

A Quebec, Canada
B San Francisco, USA
C The Firth of Forth, Scotland

Place Names

TOP 10 MOST COMMON PLACE NAMES IN GREAT BRITAIN

(Name/occurrences)

1 Newton, 150 **2** Blackhill/Black Hill, 136 **3** Castlehill/Castle Hill, 128 **4** Mountpleasant/Mount Pleasant, 126 **5** Woodside/Wood Side, 112 **6** Newtown/New Town, 110 **7** Burnside, 107 **8** Greenhill/Green Hill, 105 **9** Woodend/Wood End, 101 **10** Beacon Hill, 95

These entries include the names of towns and villages, as well as woods, hills, and other named locations, but exclude combinations of these names with others (Newton Abbot and Newton-le-Willows, for example, are not counted with the Newtons).

TOP 10 ★ COUNTRIES WITH THE LONGEST OFFICIAL NAMES

	OFFICIAL NAME*	COMMON ENGLISH NAME	LETTERS
1	al-Jamāhīrīyah al-'Arabīyah al-Lībīyah ash-Sha'bīyah al-Ishtirākīyah	Libya	59
2	al-Jumhūrīyah al-Jazā'irīyah ad-Dīmuqrātīyah ash-Sha'bīyah	Algeria	51
3	United Kingdom of Great Britain and Northern Ireland	United Kingdom	45
4 =	Śrī Lankā Prajātāntrika Samājavādī Janarajaya	Sri Lanka	41
=	Jumhurīyat al-Qumur al-Ittihādīyah al-Islāmīyah	The Comoros	41
6	República Democrática de São Tomé e Príncipe	São Tomé and Príncipe	38
7	al-Jūmhurīyah al-Islāmīyah al-Mūrītānīyah	Mauritania	36
8 =	al-Mamlakah al-Urdunnīyah al-Hāshimīyah	Jordan	34
=	Sathalanalat Paxathipatai Paxaxôn Lao	Laos	34
10	Federation of St. Christopher and Nevis	St. Kitts and Nevis	33

* Some official names have been transliterated from languages that do not use the Roman alphabet; their length may vary according to the method used

There is no connection between the length of names and the longevity of the nation states that bear them, for since this list was first published in 1991, three have ceased to exist: Socijalisticka Federativna Republika Jugoslavija (Yugoslavia, 45 letters), Soyuz Sovetskikh Sotsialisticheskikh Respublik (USSR, 43), and Ceskoslovenská Socialistická Republika (Czechoslovakia, 36).

TOP 10 MOST COMMON STREET NAMES IN THE UK

1 High Street **2** Station Road **3** Church Road **4** Park Road **5** The Drive **6** Station Approach **7** Green Lane **8** The Avenue **9** London Road **10** Church Lane

TOP 10 ★ LARGEST COUNTRIES THAT CHANGED THEIR NAMES IN THE 20TH CENTURY

	FORMER NAME	CURRENT NAME	YEAR CHANGED	AREA SQ KM	AREA SQ MILES
1	Zaïre	Dem. Rep. of Congo	1997	2,345,409	905,567
2	Persia	Iran	1935	1,633,188	630,577
3	Tanganyika/Zanzibar	Tanzania	1964	945,087	364,900
4	South West Africa	Namibia	1990	824,292	318,261
5	Northern Rhodesia	Zambia	1964	752,614	290,586
6	Burma	Myanmar	1989	676,552	261,218
7	Ubanghi Shari	Central African Republic	1960	622,984	240,535
8	Bechuanaland	Botswana	1966	581,730	224,607
9	Siam	Thailand	1939	513,115	198,115
10	Mesopotamia	Iraq	1921	438,317	169,235

Although not a country, Greenland (2,175,600 sq km/840,004 sq miles) has been officially known as Kalaallit Nunaat since 1979. Some old names die hard: it is still common for Myanmar to be written as "Myanmar (Burma)".

TOP 10 ★ LARGEST COUNTRIES NAMED AFTER REAL PEOPLE

	COUNTRY	NAMED AFTER	AREA SQ KM	AREA SQ MILES
1	United States of America	Amerigo Vespucci (Italy; 1451–1512)	9,629,091	3,717,8138
2	Saudi Arabia	Abdul Aziz Ibn Saud (Nejd; 1882–1953)	2,149,690	830,000
3	Colombia	Christopher Columbus (Italy; 1451–1506)	1,138,914	439,737
4	Bolivia	Simon Bolivar (Venezuela; 1783–1830)	1,098,581	424,165
5	Philippines	Philip II (Spain; 1527–98)	300,000	115,831
6	Falkland Islands	Lucius Cary, 2nd Viscount Falkland (UK; c.1610–43)	12,173	4,700
7	Northern Mariana	Maria Theresa (Austria; 1717–80)	464	179
8	Cook Islands	Capt. James Cook (UK; 1728–79)	236	91
9	Wallis & Futuna	Samuel Wallis (UK; 1728–95)	200	77
10	Marshall Islands	Capt. John Marshall (UK; 1748–after 1818)	181	70

TOP 10 ★
LONGEST PLACE NAMES*

NAME	LETTERS

1 Krung thep mahanakhon bovorn ratanakosin mahintharayutthaya mahadilok pop noparatratchathani burirom udomratchanivetmahasathan amornpiman avatarnsathit sakkathattiyavisnukarmprasit — 167

When the poetic name of Bangkok, capital of Thailand, is used, it is usually abbreviated to "Krung Thep" (city of angels).

2 Taumatawhakatangihangakoauauotamateaturipukakapiki-maungahoronukupokaiwhenuakitanatahu — 85

This is the longer version (the other has a mere 83 letters) of the Māori name of a hill in New Zealand. It translates as "The place where Tamatea, the man with the big knees, who slid, climbed and swallowed mountains, known as land-eater, played on the flute to his loved one".

3 Gorsafawddachaidraigddanheddogleddollônpenrhynareurdraethceredigion — 67

A name contrived by the Fairbourne Steam Railway, Gwynedd, North Wales, for publicity purposes and in order to outdo its rival, No. 4. It means "The Mawddach station and its dragon teeth at the Northern Penrhyn Road on the golden beach of Cardigan Bay".

4 Llanfairpwllgwyngyllgogerychwyrndrobwllllantysiliogogogoch — 58

This is the place in Gwynedd famed especially for the length of its railway tickets. It means "St Mary's Church in the hollow of the white hazel near to the rapid whirlpool of the church of St Tysilo near the Red Cave". Questions have been raised about its authenticity, since its official name comprises only the first 20 letters and the full name appears to have been invented as a hoax in the 19th century by a local tailor.

5 El Pueblo de Nuestra Señora la Reina de los Ángeles de la Porciúncula — 57

The site of a Franciscan mission and the full Spanish name of Los Angeles; it means "The town of Our Lady the Queen of the Angels of the Little Portion". Nowadays it is customarily known by its initial letters, "LA", making it also one of the shortest-named cities in the world.

6 Chargoggagoggmanchaugagoggchaubunagungamaug — 43

America's second longest place name is that of a lake near Webster, Massachusetts. Its Indian name, loosely translated, means "You fish on your side, I'll fish on mine, and no one fishes in the middle". It is said to be pronounced "Char-gogg-a-gogg (pause) man-chaugg-a-gog (pause) chau-bun-a-gung-a-maug". It is, however, an invented extension of its real name (Chabunagungamaug, or "boundary fishing place"), devised in the 1920s by Larry Daly, the editor of the Webster Times.

7 =Lower North Branch Little Southwest Miramichi — 40

Canada's longest place name – a short river in New Brunswick.

= Villa Real de la Santa Fé de San Francisco de Asis — 40

The full Spanish name of Santa Fe, New Mexico, translates as "Royal city of the holy faith of St. Francis of Assisi".

9 Te Whakatakanga-o-te-ngarehu-o-te-ahi-a-Tamatea — 38

The Māori name of Hammer Springs, New Zealand; like the second name in this list, it refers to a legend of Tamatea, explaining how the springs were warmed by "the falling of the cinders of the fire of Tamatea". Its name is variously written either hyphenated or as a single word.

10 Meallan Liath Coire Mhic Dhubhghaill — 32

The longest multiple name in Scotland, a place near Aultanrynie, Highland, alternatively spelled Meallan Liath Coire Mhic Dhughaill (30 letters).

* Including single-word, hyphenated, and multiple names

THE LONG AND THE SHORT OF IT

The original 57-letter Spanish name of Los Angeles contrasts with its more common designation as "LA".

What is special about the Rôve tunnel?
see p.97 for the answer

A It is the world's longest canal tunnel
B It is the first undersea tunnel
C It is the highest rail tunnel

The Tallest Buildings

TALLEST APARTMENT BUILDINGS

BUILDING/LOCATION/ YEAR COMPLETED	STOREYS	HEIGHT M	FT
1 **Trump World Tower**, New York City, USA, 2000	72	263	863
2 **Tregunter Tower III**, Hong Kong, China, 1994	70	200	656
3 **Lake Point Tower**, Chicago, USA, 1968	70	197	645
4 **Central Park Place**, New York City, USA, 1988	56	191	628
5 **Huron Plaza Apartments**, Chicago, USA, 1983	61	183	599
6 **3 Lincoln Centre**, New York City, USA, 1993	60	181	593
7 =**May Road Apartments**, Hong Kong, China, 1993	58	180	590
=**1000 Lake Shore Plaza**, Chicago, USA, 1964	55	180	590
9 **Marina City Apartments**, Chicago, USA, 1968	61	179	588
10 **North Pier Apartments**, Chicago, USA, 1990	61	177	581

These towers are all purely residential, rather than office buildings with a proportion given over to residential use. Above its 50 levels of office suites, the 343-m (1,127-ft) John Hancock Center, Chicago, built in 1968, has 48 levels of apartments (floors 44 through to 92 at 155 m/509 ft to 315 m/1,033 ft above street level), which are thus the "highest" apartments in the world.

TALLEST BUILDINGS ERECTED MORE THAN 100 YEARS AGO

BUILDING/LOCATION/ YEAR COMPLETED	HEIGHT M	FT
1 **Eiffel Tower**, Paris, France, 1889	300	984
2 **Washington Monument**, Washington, DC, USA, 1885	169	555
3 **Ulm Cathedral**, Ulm, Germany, 1890	161	528
4 **Lincoln Cathedral**, Lincoln, England, c.1307 (destroyed 1548)	160	525
5 **Cologne Cathedral**, Cologne, Germany, 1880	156	513
6 **Rouen Cathedral I**, Rouen, France, 1530 (destroyed 1822)	156	512
7 **St. Pierre Church**, Beauvais, France, 1568 (collapsed 1573)	153	502
8 **St. Paul's Cathedral**, London, England, 1315 (destroyed 1561)	149	489
9 **Rouen Cathedral II**, Rouen, France, 1876	148	485
10 **Great Pyramid**, Giza, Egypt, c.2580 BC	146	480

The height of the Washington Monument is less than it was when it was erected because it has steadily sunk into the ground.

TALLEST HABITABLE* BUILDINGS IN THE UK

BUILDING/LOCATION/ YEAR COMPLETED	HEIGHT M	FT
1 **One Canada Square**, Canary Wharf, London, 1991	244	800
2 **HSBC Tower**, Canary Wharf, London, 2002#	213	699
3 **Citigroup Tower**, Canary Wharf, London, 2002#	199	653
4 **National Westminster Tower**, London, 1979	183	600
5 **Post Office Tower**, London, 1966	177	580
6 **Blackpool Tower**, Blackpool, 1894	158	519
7 **City Point Tower**, London, 2001	140	459
8 **St. John's Beacon**, Liverpool, 1967	138	452
9 **Barbican, London:** Shakespeare Tower, 1971	128	419
Cromwell Tower, 1973	128	419
Lauderdale Tower, 1974	128	419
10 **Euston Centre**, London, 1969	124	408

* Excluding radio masts, chimneys, and church spires
# Under construction; scheduled completion date

WORLD CITIES WITH MOST SKYSCRAPERS

CITY/LOCATION	SKYSCRAPERS*
1 **New York City**, USA	162
2 **Chicago**, USA	75
3 **Hong Kong**, China	42
4 **Shanghai**, China	38
5 =**Houston**, USA	30
=**Tokyo**, Japan	30
7 **Singapore City**, Singapore	26
8 **Los Angeles**, USA	22
9 **Dallas**, USA	20
10 =**Melbourne**, Australia	18
=**Sydney**, Australia	18

* Habitable buildings of more than 152 m (500 ft)

SKY HIGH
Despite the ever-attendant earthquake threat to tall buildings, Tokyo boasts one of the world's highest city skylines.

EIFFEL

French engineer Alexandre Gustave Eiffel (1832–1923) is one of the few people after whom a world famous structure has been named. Drawing on his experience as a bridge designer, Eiffel built the Eiffel Tower as a temporary structure for the 1889 Universal Exhibition. It proved so popular that it was decided to retain it. It remained the world's tallest structure until 1930, when it was overtaken by New York's Chrysler Building. Eiffel also designed the iron framework that supports the Statue of Liberty. In 1893, when a project to build a Panama Canal collapsed, Eiffel was implicated in a scandal and was sent to prison for two years.

TOP 10 ★
TALLEST HOTELS

BUILDING/LOCATION/ YEAR COMPLETED	STOREYS	HEIGHT M	FT
1 Baiyoke II Tower, Bangkok, Thailand, 1997	89	319	1,046
2 Yu Kyong, Pyong Yang, North Korea, 1993	105	300	985
3 Emirates Tower 2, Dubai, United Arab Emirates, 1999 *with spire*	50	262 308	858 1,010
4 Shangri-la, Hong Kong, China, 1990	60	228	748
5 Raffles Western Hotel, Singapore, 1986	73	226	742
6 Westin Peachtree Hotel, Atlanta, USA, 1973	71	220	723
7 Westin Hotel, Detroit, USA, 1973	71	219	720
8 Four Seasons Hotel, New York City, USA, 1993	52	208	682
9 Trump International Hotel, New York City, USA, 1995	45	207	679
10 Trump Tower, New York City, USA, 1983	68	202	664

TOP 10 ★
TALLEST HABITABLE BUILDINGS

BUILDING/LOCATION/ YEAR COMPLETED	STOREYS	HEIGHT M	FT
1 Petronas Towers, Kuala Lumpur, Malaysia, 1996	96	452	1,482
2 Taipei Financial Centre, Taipei, China, 2003* *with spire*	101	445 508	1,460 1,666
3 Sears Tower, Chicago, USA, 1974 *with spires*	110	443 527	1,454 1,730
4 World Trade Center#, New York, USA, 1972	110	417	1,368
5 Jin Mao Building, Shanghai, China, 1997 *with spire*	93	382 420	1,255 1,378
6 Empire State Building, New York, USA, 1931 *with spire*	102	381 449	1,250 1,472
7 T & C Tower, Kao-hsiung, Taiwan, 1997	85	348	1,142
8 Amoco Building, Chicago, USA, 1973	80	346	1,136
9 John Hancock Center, Chicago, USA, 1969 *with spires*	100	343 449	1,127 1,470
10 Shun Hing Square, Shenzen, China, 1996 *with spires*	80	330 384	1,082 1,260

* *Under construction; scheduled completion date*

Twin towers; the second tower, completed in 1973, has the same number of storeys but is slightly smaller at 415 m (1,362 ft) – although its spire takes it up to 521 m (1,710 ft)

Heights do not include television and radio antennae and uninhabited extensions. Although the twin Petronas Towers are now officially accepted as the world's tallest, their completion generated a controversy when it became clear that their overall measurement includes their spires, and that their roof height (at the point where the two towers are connected) is "only" 379 m (1,244 ft).

EMPIRE BUILDING

Over 70 years old and still going strong, the majestic 102-storey Empire State Building has become a symbol of New York, dominating its skyline.

Did You Know? Lightning does strike (at least) twice: the lightning conductor on the Empire State Building was struck 68 times in the structure's first 10 years.

Bridges & Other Structures

TOP 10 ★

LONGEST SUSPENSION BRIDGES

	BRIDGE/LOCATION	YEAR COMPLETED	LENGTH OF MAIN SPAN M	FT
1	**Akashi-Kaiko**, Kobe–Naruto, Japan	1998	1,991	6,532
2	**Great Belt**, Denmark	1997	1,624	5,328
3	**Humber Estuary**, UK	1980	1,410	4,626
4	**Jiangyin**, China	1998	1,385	4,544
5	**Tsing Ma**, Hong Kong, China	1997	1,377	4,518
6	**Verrazano Narrows**, New York, NY, USA	1964	1,298	4,260
7	**Golden Gate**, San Francisco, CA, USA	1937	1,280	4,200
8	**Höga Kusten** (High Coast), Veda, Sweden	1997	1,210	3,970
9	**Mackinac Straits**, Michigan, USA	1957	1,158	3,800
10	**Minami Bisan-seto**, Kojima–Sakaide, Japan	1988	1,100	3,609

The Messina Strait Bridge between Sicily and Calabria, Italy, remains a speculative project but, if constructed according to plan, it will have by far the longest centre span of any bridge at 3,300 m (10,827 ft).

TOP 10 ★

LONGEST CANTILEVER BRIDGES

	BRIDGE/LOCATION	YEAR COMPLETED	LONGEST SPAN M	FT
1	**Pont de Quebec**, Quebec, Canada	1917	549	1,800
2	**Firth of Forth**, Scotland	1890	521	1,710
3	**Minato**, Osaka, Japan	1974	510	1,673
4	**Commodore John Barry**, New Jersey/Pennsylvania, USA	1974	494	1,622
5 =	**Greater New Orleans 1**, Louisiana, USA	1958	480	1,575
=	**Greater New Orleans 2**, Louisiana, USA	1988	480	1,575
7	**Howrah**, Calcutta, India	1943	457	1,500
8	**Gramercy**, Louisiana, USA	1995	445	1,460
9	**Transbay**, San Francisco, CA, USA	1936	427	1,400
10	**Baton Rouge**, Louisiana, USA	1969	376	1,235

SHANGHAI SURPRISE

One of the world's longest cable-stayed bridges, Shanghai's Yang Pu was built to ease traffic congestion on the city's busy inner ring road.

TOP 10 ★

LONGEST BRIDGES IN THE UK

	BRIDGE/LOCATION	TYPE*	YEAR COMPLETED	LENGTH OF MAIN SPAN M	FT
1	**Humber Estuary**, Hessle–Barton-on-Humber	S	1980	1,410	4,626
2	**Forth Road**, North Queensferry–South Queensferry	S	1964	1,006	3,300
3	**Severn Bridge**, Bristol	S	1966	988	3,240
4	**Firth of Forth**, North Queensferry–South Queensferry	CT	1890	521	1,710
5	**Second Severn Crossing**, Bristol	CSG	1996	456	1,496
6	**Queen Elizabeth II**, Dartford	CSG	1991	450	1,476
7	**Tamar**, Saltash–Plymouth	S	1961	335	1,100
8	**Runcorn–Widnes**	SA	1961	330	1,082
9	**Erskine**, Glasgow	CSG	1971	305	1,000
10	**Skye**, Kyleakin–Kyle of Lochalsh	PCG	1995	250	820

* *S = Suspension; CT = Cantilever Truss; CSG = Cable-stayed Steel Girder and Truss; SA = Steel Arch; PCG = Pre-stressed Concrete Girder*

TOP 10 ★

LONGEST CABLE-STAYED BRIDGES

	BRIDGE/LOCATION	YEAR COMPLETED	LENGTH OF MAIN SPAN M	FT
1	**Tatara**, Onomichi–Imabari, Japan	1999	890	2,920
2	**Pont de Normandie**, Le Havre, France	1994	856	2,808
3	**Qinghzhou Minjiang**, Fozhou, China	1996	605	1,985
4	**Yang Pu**, Shanghai, China	1993	602	1,975
5 =	**Meiko-chuo**, Nagoya, Japan	1997	590	1,936
=	**Xu Pu**, Shanghai, China	1997	590	1,936
7	**Skarnsundet**, Trondheim Fjord, Norway	1991	530	1,739
8	**Tsurumi Tsubasa**, Yokohama, Japan	1994	510	1,673
9 =	**Ikuchi**, Onomichi–Imabari, Japan	1994	490	1,608
=	**Öresund**, Copenhagen–Malmö, Denmark/Sweden	2000	490	1,608

TOP 10 ★
LONGEST CANAL TUNNELS

	TUNNEL/CANAL/LOCATION	LENGTH M	FT
1	**Rôve**, Canal de Marseille au Rhône, France	7,120	23,360
2	**Bony** ("Le Grand Souterrain"), Canal de St. Quentin, France	5,677	18,625
3	**Standedge**, Huddersfield Narrow, UK	5,210	17,093
4	**Mauvages**, Canal de la Marne et Rhin, France	4,970	16,306
5	**Balesmes**, Canal Marne à la Saône, France	4,800	15,748
6	**Ruyaulcourt**, Canal du Nord, France	4,500	14,764
7	**Strood***, Thames and Medway, UK	3,608	11,837
8	**Lapal**, Birmingham, UK	3,570	11,713
9	**Sapperton**, Thames and Severn, UK	3,488	11,444
10	**Pouilly-en-Auxois**, Canal de Bourgogne, France	3,333	10,935

* Later converted to a rail tunnel

TOP 10 ★
LONGEST RAIL TUNNELS

	TUNNEL/LOCATION/ YEAR COMPLETED*	LENGTH KM	MILES
1	**Seikan**, Japan, 1988	53.90	33.49
2	**Channel Tunnel**, France–England, 1994	49.94	31.03
3	**Moscow Metro** (Medvedkovo/Belyaevo section), Russia, 1979	30.70	19.07
4	**London Underground** (East Finchley–Morden, Northern Line), UK, 1939	27.84	17.30
5	**Hakkoda**, Japan, U/C	26.46	16.44
6	**Iwate**, Japan, U/C	25.81	16.04
7	**Iiyama**, Japan, U/C	22.50	13.98
8	**Dai-Shimizu**, Japan, 1982	22.17	13.78
9	**Simplon II**, Italy–Switzerland, 1922	19.82	12.31
10	**Simplon I**, Italy–Switzerland, 1906	19.80	12.30

* U/C = under construction

In the UK, the first purpose-built passenger rail tunnel was the 766-m (2,514-ft) Tyler Hill Tunnel, Kent, opened on 4 May 1830.

TOP 10 ★
LARGEST SPORTS STADIUMS

	STADIUM/LOCATION	CAPACITY
1	**Strahov Stadium**, Prague, Czech Republic	240,000
2	**Maracaña Municipal Stadium**, Rio de Janeiro, Brazil	220,000
3	**Rungnado Stadium**, Pyongyang, North Korea	150,000
4	**Mineiro Stadium**, Belo Horizonte, Brazil	130,000
5	**National Stadium of Iran**, Azadi, Iran	128,000
6	**Estádio Maghalaes Pinto**, Belo Horizonte, Brazil	125,000
7=	**Estádio da Luz**, Lisbon, Portugal	120,000
=	**Estádio Morumbi**, São Paulo, Brazil	120,000
=	**Saltlake Stadium**, Calcutta, India	120,000
=	**Senayan Main Stadium**, Jakarta, Indonesia	120,000
=	**Yuba Bharati Krirangan**, Nr. Calcutta, India	120,000

TOP 10 ★
HIGHEST DAMS

	DAM/RIVER/LOCATION	YEAR COMPLETED*	HEIGHT M	FT
1	**Rogun**, Vakhsh, Tajikistan	U/C	335	1,099
2	**Nurek**, Vakhsh, Tajikistan	1980	300	984
3	**Grande Dixence**, Dixence, Switzerland	1961	285	935
4	**Inguri**, Inguri, Georgia	1980	272	892
5	**Vajont**, Vajont, Italy	1960	262	860
6=	**Manuel M. Torres**, Chicoasén, Grijalva, Mexico	1980	261	856
=	**Tehri**, Bhagirathi, India	U/C	261	856
8	**Alvaro Obregon**, El Gallinero, Tenasco, Mexico	1946	260	853
9	**Mauvoisin**, Drance de Bagnes, Switzerland	1957	250	820
10	**Alberto Lleras C.**, Guavio, Colombia	1989	243	797

* U/C = under construction

Source: International Commission on Large Dams (ICOLD)

DAM RECORD BUSTER
An incongruous mural depicting Lenin celebrates this Soviet engineering accomplishment, the building of the world's second highest dam, the Nurek in Tajikistan.

Did You Know? So vast is the 2,484,800 cu m (3,250,000 cu yd) volume of concrete in the Hoover Dam (1936), Colorado River, on the Arizona/Nevada border, that it will take until the year 2030 for it to set completely.

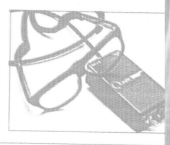

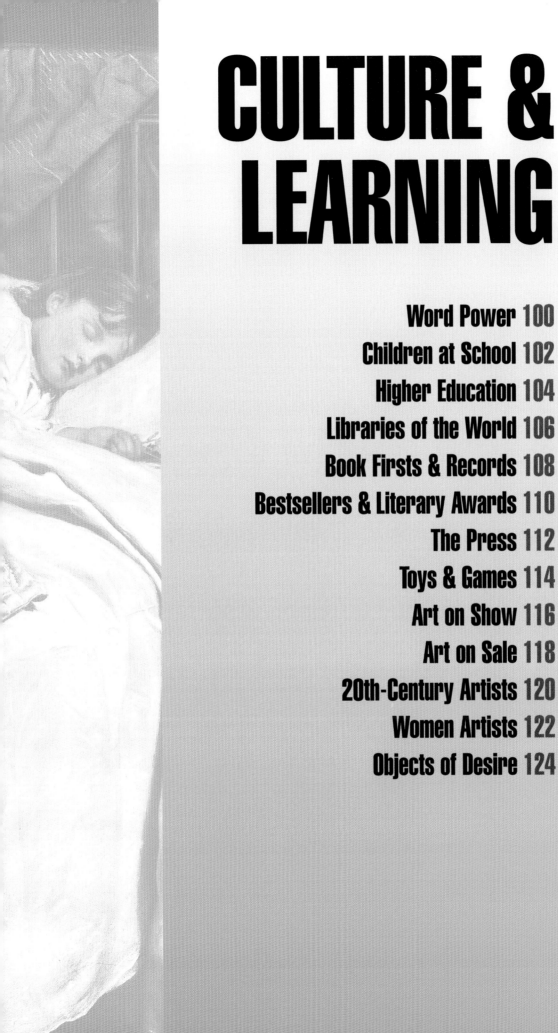

CULTURE & LEARNING

Word Power

TOP 10 ★
MOST WIDELY SPOKEN LANGUAGES

LANGUAGE	APPROXIMATE NO. OF SPEAKERS
1 Chinese (Mandarin)	1,075,000,000
2 Hindustani*	602,000,000
3 English	514,000,000
4 Spanish	425,000,000
5 Russian	275,000,000
6 Arabic	256,000,000
7 Bengali	215,000,000
8 Portuguese	194,000,000
9 Malay-Indonesian	176,000,000
10 French	129,000,000

* Hindi and Urdu are essentially the same language, Hindustani. As the official language of Pakistan, it is written in modified Arabic script and called Urdu. As the official language of India, it is written in the Devanagari script and called Hindi

According to mid-1999 estimates by Emeritus Professor Sidney S. Culbert of the University of Washington, Seattle, in addition to those languages appearing in the Top 10, there are two further languages that are spoken by more than 100 million individuals: German and Japanese.

TOP 10 ★
MOTHER TONGUES MOST SPOKEN BY LONDON SCHOOL CHILDREN

LANGUAGE	SPEAKERS
1 English	608,500
2 Bengali and Silheti	40,400
3 Punjabi	29,800
4 Gujarati	28,600
5 Hindi/Urdu	26,000
6 Turkish	15,600
7 Arabic	11,000
8 English-based Creole	10,700
9 Yoruba	10,400
10 Somali	8,300

Source: University of Westminster

TOP 10 ★
LANGUAGES OFFICIALLY SPOKEN IN THE MOST COUNTRIES

LANGUAGE	COUNTRIES
1 English	57
2 French	33
3 Arabic	23
4 Spanish	21
5 Portuguese	7
6 =Dutch	5
=German	5
8 =Chinese (Mandarin)	3
=Danish	3
=Italian	3
=Malay	3

TOP 10 ★
COUNTRIES WITH THE MOST ENGLISH-LANGUAGE SPEAKERS*

COUNTRY	APPROX. NO. OF SPEAKERS
1 USA	237,320,000
2 UK	58,090,000
3 Canada	18,218,000
4 Australia	15,561,000
5 Ireland	3,720,000
6 South Africa	3,700,000
7 New Zealand	3,338,000
8 Jamaica	2,460,000
9 Trinidad and Tobago	1,245,000
10 Guyana	764,000

* Inhabitants for whom English is their mother tongue

TOP 10 ★
MOST COMMON WORDS IN ENGLISH

SPOKEN ENGLISH		WRITTEN ENGLISH
the	1	the
and	2	of
I	3	to
to	4	in
of	5	and
a	6	a
you	7	for
that	8	was
in	9	is
it	10	that

Various surveys have been conducted to establish the most common words in spoken English, from telephone conversations to broadcast commentaries.

THE 10 ★
EARLIEST DATED WORDS IN THE *OXFORD ENGLISH DICTIONARY*

WORD	SOURCE	DATE
1 =priest	Laws of Ethelbert	601–4
=town	Laws of Ethelbert	601–4
3 earl	Laws of Ethelbert	616
4 this	Bewcastle Column	c.670
5 streale	Ruthwell Cross	c.680
6 ward	Caedmon, *Hymn*	680
7 thing	Laws of Hlothaer and Eadric	685–6
8 theft	Laws of Ine	688–95
9 worth	Laws of Ine	695
10 then	Laws of King Wihtraed	695–6

TOP 10 MOST COMMONLY MISSPELLED ENGLISH WORDS

1 consensus **2** innovate **3** practice/practise **4** facsimile **5** instalment **6** supersede **7** fulfil **8** withhold **9** occurred **10** possession

This list is based on the mistakes most frequently made by entrants for the Royal Society of Arts Examinations Board's Spelltest for Officeworkers.

TOP 10 ★
FOREIGN LANGUAGES STUDIED IN THE UK AT GCSE

	LANGUAGE	NO. OF STUDENTS
1	French	335,816
2	German	135,158
3	Spanish	47,969
4	Welsh*	7,877
5	Urdu	6,348
6	Italian	5,313
7	Irish	2,464
8	Chinese	2,133
9	Bengali	1,706
10	Russian	1,583

* Studied as a second language; does not include the Welsh GCSE studied in Wales as a first language

Source: CiLT (Centre for information on Language Teaching and Research)

TOP 10 ★
MOST USED LETTERS IN WRITTEN ENGLISH

SURVEY*		MORSE #
e	1	e
t	2	t
a	3	a
o	4	i
i	5	n
n	6	o
s	7	s
r	8	h
h	9	r
l	10	d

* The order as indicated by a survey across approximately 1 million words appearing in a wide variety of printed texts, ranging from newspapers to novels

 # The order estimated by Samuel Morse, the inventor in the 1830s of Morse Code, based on his calculations of the respective quantities of type used by a printer. The number of letters in the printer's type trays ranged from 12,000 for "e" to 4,400 for "d", with only 200 for "z"

TOP 10 ★
LONGEST WORDS IN THE ENGLISH LANGUAGE*

WORD/MEANING	LETTERS

1 Ornicopytheobibliopsychocrystarroscioaerogenethliometeoroaustrohiero-anthropoichthyopyrosiderochpnomyoalectryoophiobotanopegohydrorhab-docrithoaleuroalphitohalomolybdocleroheloaxinocoscinodactyliogeolitho-pessopsephocatoptrotephraoneirochiroonychodactyloarithstichooxogelo-scogastrogyrocerobletonooenoscapulinaniac — **310**

Medieval scribes used this word to refer to "A deluded human who practises divination or forecasting by means of phenomena, interpretation of acts, or other manifestations related to the following animate or inanimate objects and appearances: birds, oracles, Bible, ghosts, crystal gazing, shadows, air appearances, birth stars, meteors, winds, sacrificial appearances, entrails of humans and fishes, fire, red-hot irons, altar smoke, mice, grain picking by rooster, snakes, herbs, fountains, water, wands, dough, meal, barley, salt, lead, dice, arrows, hatchet balance, sieve, ring suspension, random dots, precious stones, pebbles, pebble heaps, mirrors, ash writing, dreams, palmistry, nail rays, finger rings, numbers, book passages, name letterings, laughing manners, ventriloquism, circle walking, wax, susceptibility to hidden springs, wine, and shoulder blades."

2 Lopadotemachoselachogaleokranioleipsanodrimhypotrimmatosilphioparao-melitokatakechymenokichlepikossyphophattoperisteralektryonoptekephall-iokigklopeleiolagoiosiraiobaphetraganopterygon — **182**

The English transliteration of a 170-letter Greek word that appears in The Ecclesiazusae (a comedy by the Greek playwright Aristophanes, c.448–380 BC). It is used as a description of a 17-ingredient dish.

3 Aequeosalinocalcalinosetaceoaluminosocupreovitriolic — **52**

Invented by a medical writer, Dr. Edward Strother (1675–1737), to describe the spa waters at Bath.

4 Osseocarnisanguineovisceri cartilaginonervomedullary — **51**

Coined by writer and East India Company official Thomas Love Peacock (1785–1866), and used in his satire Headlong Hall (1816) as a description of the structure of the human body.

5 Pneumonoultramicroscopicsilicovolcanoconiosis — **45**

It first appeared in print (though ending in "-koniosis") in F. Scully's Bedside Manna [sic] (1936), then found its way into Webster's Dictionary and is now in the Oxford English Dictionary. It is said to mean a lung disease caused by breathing fine dust.

6 Hepaticocholecystostcholecystenterostomies — **42**

Surgical operations to create channels of communication between gall bladders and hepatic ducts or intestines.

7 Praetertranssubstantiationalistically — **37**

The adverb describing the act of surpassing the act of transubstantiation; the word is found in Mark McShane's novel Untimely Ripped (1963).

8= Pseudoantidisestablishmentarianism — **34**

A word meaning "false opposition to the withdrawal of state support from a Church", derived from that perennial favourite long word, antidisestablishmentarianism (a mere 28 letters).

= Supercalifragilisticexpialidocious — **34**

An invented word, but perhaps now eligible since it has appeared in the Oxford English Dictionary. It was popularized by the song of this title in the film Mary Poppins (1964), where it is used to mean "wonderful", but it was originally written in 1949 in an unpublished song by Parker and Young who spelt it "supercalafajalistickespialadojus" (32 letters).

10= Encephalomyeloradiculoneuritis — **30**

Inflammation of the whole nervous system.

= Hippopotomonstrosesquipedalian — **30**

Appropriately, the word that means "pertaining to an extremely long word".

= Pseudopseudohypoparathyroidism — **30**

First used (hyphenated) in the US in 1952 and (unhyphenated) in Great Britain in The Lancet in 1962 to describe a medical case in which a patient appeared to have symptoms of pseudohypoparathyroidism, but with "no manifestations suggesting hypoparathyroidism".

* Excluding names of chemical compounds

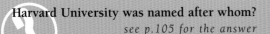

Harvard University was named after whom?
see p.105 for the answer

A John Harvard, a British preacher
B Johannes Harvard, a Dutch trader
C Harvard Hawkins, an American actor

Children at School

EASTERN PROMISE

China has the most children at school and the world's longest school year, but spends just 2 per cent of its GNP on education – less than half that of Western countries.

TOP 10 ★
COUNTRIES WITH THE HIGHEST NUMBER OF PRIMARY SCHOOL PUPILS PER TEACHER

COUNTRY	NO. OF PUPILS PER TEACHER IN PRIMARY SCHOOLS*
1 Central African Republic	77
2 Congo	70
3 Chad	67
4 Bangladesh	63
5 Malawi	59
6 =Afghanistan	58
=Mozambique	58
=Rwanda	58
9 =Benin	56
=Senegal	56
UK	19

* In latest year for which figures are available
Source: *UNESCO*

TOP 10 ★
COUNTRIES SPENDING THE MOST ON EDUCATION

COUNTRY	EXPENDITURE AS PERCENTAGE OF GNP*
1 Kiribati	11.4
2 Moldova	10.3
3 Namibia	8.5
4 Denmark	7.7
5 Sweden	7.6
6 =South Africa	7.5
=Zimbabwe	7.5
8 Uzbekistan	7.4
9 Barbados	7.3
10 Saudi Arabia	7.2
UK	4.9

* GNP in latest year for which data available
Source: *UNESCO*

TOP 10 ★
COUNTRIES WITH THE MOST PRIMARY SCHOOLS

COUNTRY	PRIMARY SCHOOLS
1 China	628,840
2 India	598,354
3 Brazil	196,479
4 Indonesia	173,893
5 Mexico	95,855
6 Pakistan	77,207
7 USA	72,000
8 Russia	66,235
9 Iran	63,101
10 Colombia	48,933
UK	23,306

Source: *UNESCO*

TOP 10 ★
OLDEST SCHOOLS IN THE UK

SCHOOL	YEAR FOUNDED
1 King's School, Canterbury	600
2 King's School, Rochester, Kent	604
3 St. Peter's School, York	627
4 Warwick School	914
5 King's School, Ely	970
6 Thetford Grammer School, Norfolk	1119
7 Bristol Cathedral School	1140
8 Norwich School	1250
9 Abingdon School	1256
10 Royal Grammar School, Worcester	1291

TOP 10 COUNTRIES WITH THE LONGEST SCHOOL YEARS

(Country/school year in days)

❶ China, 251 ❷ Japan, 243 ❸ South Korea, 220 ❹ Israel, 215 ❺ = Germany, 210;
= Russia, 210 ❼ Switzerland, 207 ❽ = Netherlands, 200;
= Scotland, 200; = Thailand, 200
England, 192

EDUCATING THE MASSES

Indian culture places a high value on education, and consequently some 7 per cent of the country's entire population attends secondary school.

TOP 10 ★
COUNTRIES WITH THE MOST SECONDARY SCHOOL PUPILS

	COUNTRY	PERCENTAGE FEMALE	SECONDARY SCHOOL PUPILS
1	China	45	71,883,000
2	India	38	68,872,393
3	USA	49	21,473,692
4	Indonesia	46	14,209,974
5	Russia	50	13,732,000
6	Japan	49	9,878,568
7	Iran	46	8,776,792
8	Germany	48	8,382,335
9	Mexico	49	7,914,165
10	UK	52	6,548,786

Source: *UNESCO*

The number of pupils enrolled at secondary schools as a percentage of the total population in those countries in this Top 10 list varies from 6 per cent in China to 14 per cent in both Iran and Germany. The figures for the US and UK are 8 per cent and 11 per cent respectively.

TOP 10 ★
MOST EXPENSIVE INDEPENDENT SCHOOLS IN THE UK*

	SCHOOL	BOARDING FEES PER ANNUM (£)
1	Winchester College, Hampshire	17,319
2	Harrow School, Middlesex	16,860
3	Millfield, Somerset	16,770
4	Tonbridge School, Kent	16,767
5	Bryanston School, Dorset	16,755
6	Bedales School, Hampshire	16,587
7	Stowe, Buckinghamshire	16,545
8 =	Marlborough College, Wiltshire	16,410
=	Radley College, Berkshire	16,410
10 =	Rugby School, Warwickshire	16,380
=	Wellington College, Somerset	16,380

* *Excluding schools for the disabled, and music and religious schools, which can be more expensive*

TOP 10 ★
'A' LEVEL SUBJECTS

	SUBJECT	TOTAL TAKING EXAM IN 2000
1	General Studies	89,805
2	English	86,428
3	Mathematics	67,036
4	Biology	54,814
5	Chemistry	40,856
6	History	38,779
7	Business Studies	38,226
8	Art*	37,609
9	Geography	37,112
10	Physics	32,059

* *Includes a range of related subjects*

Source: *Associated Examining Board*

The relative popularity of the principal 'A' level subjects varies slightly from year to year. Between 1999 and 2000, General Studies overtook English to take the No. 1 position.

TOP 10 ★
COUNTRIES WITH THE HIGHEST ILLITERACY RATES

	COUNTRY	PERCENTAGE ADULT ILLITERACY RATE*
1	Niger	84.3
2	Burkina Faso	77.0
3 =	Afghanistan	63.7
=	Sierra Leone	63.7
5	Gambia	63.5
6	Guinea-Bissau	63.2
7	Senegal	62.7
8	Benin	62.5
9	Ethiopia	61.3
10	Mauritania	60.1

* *Age over 15; estimates for the year 2000*

Source: *UNESCO*

Did You Know? The first blackboards used in schools were invented in Skippack, Pennsylvania, in 1714 by Christopher Dock (1698–1771), a German immigrant schoolmaster who also wrote the first teaching manual published in America.

Higher Education

CRÈME DE LA CRÈME

Between the late 1960s and 1970, the University of Paris was split into 13 separate establishments, which comprise the world's largest higher education body.

TOP 10 ★
LARGEST UNIVERSITIES

	UNIVERSITY	STUDENTS
1	University of Paris, France	311,163
2	University of Calcutta, India	300,000
3	University of Mexico, Mexico	269,000
4	University of Bombay, India	262,350
5	University of Guadalajara, Mexico	214,986
6	University of Rome, Italy	189,000
7	University of Buenos Aires, Argentina	183,397
8	University of Rajasthan, India	175,000
9	University of California, USA	157,331
10	University of Wisconsin, USA	155,298

Several other universities in India, Egypt, Italy, and the US have more than 100,000 students. It should be noted, however, that certain universities listed are divided into numerous separate centres – the University of Wisconsin, for example, comprises some 14 campuses, with Madison's enrolment of over 40,000 the largest.

TOP 10 ★
COUNTRIES WITH THE HIGHEST PERCENTAGE OF FEMALE UNIVERSITY STUDENTS

	COUNTRY	% OF FEMALE STUDENTS*
1	Cyprus	75
2	US Virgin Islands	74
3	Qatar	73
4=	St. Lucia	72
=	United Arab Emirates	72
6	Kuwait	67
7	Myanmar (Burma)	64
8	Barbados	62
9	Namibia	61
10=	Bulgaria	60
=	Cuba	60
=	Latvia	60
=	Lesotho	60
=	Mongolia	60
=	Panama	60
	UK	50

* In latest year for which data available
Source: *UNESCO*

TOP 10 ★
COUNTRIES WITH THE LOWEST PERCENTAGE OF FEMALE UNIVERSITY STUDENTS

	COUNTRY	% OF FEMALE STUDENTS*
1	Samoa	3
2	Equatorial Guinea	4
3	Central African Republic	9
4	Somalia	10
5	Guinea	11
6	Chad	12
7	Yemen	13
8	Eritrea	14
9	Rwanda	15
10	Cambodia	16

* In latest year for which data available
Source: *UNESCO*

WOMAN'S WORK

Women study separately but in large numbers at the United Arab Emirates University in Al-Ain, which was founded in 1976.

HARVARD

Harvard, the first college founded in America, takes its name from John Harvard (1607–38). Born in Southwark, London, he graduated from Emmanuel College, Cambridge, in 1631, and in 1637 married Ann Sadler, a clergyman's daughter, in Lewes, England. He later emigrated to Charlestown, Massachusetts, where he worked as a preacher. Barely a year after his arrival, he died of consumption. In his will he bequeathed his library of 300 books and a sum of £779 to Cambridge College, which had been founded in 1636. Two years later, it was renamed as Harvard College in honour of its benefactor.

TOP 10 ★
COUNTRIES WITH THE HIGHEST PROPORTION OF ADULTS IN HIGHER EDUCATION

	COUNTRY	TOTAL	STUDENTS PER 100,000*
1	Canada	1,763,105	5,997
2	South Korea	2,541,659	5,609
3	Australia	1,002,476	5,552
4	USA	14,261,778	5,339
5	New Zealand	162,350	4,508
6	Finland	213,995	4,190
7	Norway	180,383	4,164
8	Spain	1,591,863	4,017
9	Ireland	47,955	3,618
10	France	2,091,688	3,600
	UK	1,820,489	3,135

In latest year for which data available
Source: *UNESCO*

GRADUATION DAY

Decked in their traditional tasselled mortar boards and gowns, more students graduate from US universities than from those of any other country.

TOP 10 ★
COUNTRIES WITH THE MOST UNIVERSITY STUDENTS

	COUNTRY	PERCENTAGE FEMALE	UNIVERSITY STUDENTS*
1	USA	56	14,261,778
2	India	36	6,060,418
3	Japan	44	3,917,709
4	China	36	3,350,715
5	Russia	53	2,587,510
6	France	55	2,091,688
7	Philippines	57	2,017,972
8	Italy	54	1,892,542
9	Indonesia	31	1,889,408
10	Brazil	52	1,868,529
	UK	50	1,820,489

In latest year for which data available
Source: *UNESCO*

TOP 10 ★
COUNTRIES WITH THE MOST UNIVERSITIES

	COUNTRY	UNIVERSITIES
1	India	8,407
2	USA	5,758
3	Argentina	1,705
4	Spain	1,415
5	Mexico	1,341
6	Bangladesh	1,268
7	Indonesia	1,236
8	Japan	1,223
9	France	1,062
10	China	1,054

As a result of the 1992 Further and Higher Education Acts, the UK has increased its tally of universities from 48 to 88 by reclassifying former polytechnics and colleges of further education as universities. Of the total, 71 are in England, 13 in Scotland, two in Wales, and two in Northern Ireland.

Libraries of the World

THE 10 FIRST PUBLIC LIBRARIES IN THE UK

(Library/founded)

1 Canterbury, 1847 **2** Warrington, 1848
3 Salford, 1850 **4** Winchester, 1851
5 = Manchester Free, 1852; = Liverpool, 1852 **7** = Bolton, 1853; = Ipswich, 1853
9 Oxford, 1854 **10** = Cambridge, 1855; = Kidderminster, 1855

MOST BORROWED ADULT AUTHORS IN THE UK, 1999–2000

1	Catherine Cookson
2	Danielle Steel
3	Josephine Cox
4	Dick Francis
5	Jack Higgins
6	Ruth Rendell
7	Agatha Christie
8	Patricia Cornwell
9	Emma Blair
10	Audrey Howard

Source: *Public Lending Right*

DEWEY

Any visitor to a library will have noticed the system by which books are organized into 10 subject groups and a series of sub-groups, each bearing a decimal number. This was the brainchild of Melville Louis Kossuth Dewey (1851–1931). At the age of 21, Dewey devised the system that bears his name. Published in 1876, it became adopted throughout the world and still remains the most widely used classification system. Dewey also helped to establish the American Library Association (ALA).

WHO WAS • WHO WAS • WHO WAS • WHO WAS

OLDEST NATIONAL LIBRARIES

	LIBRARY	LOCATION	FOUNDED
1	National Library of the Czech Republic	Prague, Czech Republic	1366
2	National Library of Austria	Vienna, Austria	1368
3	Biblioteca Nazionale Marciana	Venice, Italy	1468
4	Bibliothèque Nationale de France	Paris, France	1480
5	National Library of Malta	Valetta, Malta	1555
6	Bayericsche Staatsbibliothek	Munich, Germany	1558
7	National Library of Belgium	Brussels, Belgium	1559
8	Zagreb National and University Library	Zagreb, Croatia	1606
9	National Library of Finland	Helsinki, Finland	1640
10	National Library of Denmark	Copenhagen, Denmark	1653

What may claim to be the world's first national library was that in Alexandria, Egypt, founded in about 307 BC by King Ptolemy I Soter. The library assembled the world's largest collection of scrolls, which were partly destroyed during Julius Caesar's invasion of 47 BC, and totally by Arab invaders in 642 AD, an event that is considered one of the greatest ever losses to scholarship. Among national libraries in the English-speaking world, Scotland's dates from 1682 (thus pre-dating the British Library, part of the British Museum, established in 1753). The US Library of Congress was founded in 1800.

LARGEST REFERENCE LIBRARIES IN THE UK

	LIBRARY	LOCATION	FOUNDED	BOOKS
1	British Library	London	1753	15,000,000
2 =	Bodleian Library	Oxford	1602	6,500,000
=	National Library of Scotland	Edinburgh	1682	6,500,000
4	University Library	Cambridge	c.1400	6,050,000
5	National Library of Wales	Aberystwyth	1907	5,000,000
6	British Library of Political and Economic Science	London School of Economics	1894	4,000,000
7	John Rylands University Library	Manchester	1972*	3,500,000
8	University of Edinburgh Library	Edinburgh	1580	2,700,000
9	University of Leeds Library	Leeds	1874	2,500,000
10	University of Birmingham Library	Birmingham	1880	2,100,000

* In 1972 the John Rylands Library (founded in 1900) was amalgamated with Manchester University Library (founded 1851)

TOP 10 COUNTRIES WITH THE MOST PUBLIC LIBRARIES

(Country/public libraries)

1 Russia, 33,200 **2** UK, 23,678 **3** Germany, 20,448 **4** USA, 9,097
5 Czech Republic, 8,398 **6** Romania, 7,181 **7** Bulgaria, 5,591 **8** Hungary, 4,765
9 Brazil, 3,600 **10** China, 2,406

TOP 10 ★
LARGEST LIBRARIES

	LIBRARY	LOCATION	FOUNDED	BOOKS
1	Library of Congress	Washington DC, USA	1800	24,616,867
2	National Library of China	Beijing, China	1909	20,000,000
3	National Library of Canada	Ottawa, Canada	1953	16,000,000
4	Deutsche Bibliothek*	Frankfurt, Germany	1990	15,997,000
5	British Library#	London, UK	1753	15,000,000
6	Harvard University Library	Cambridge, Massachusetts, USA	1638	14,190,704
7	Vernadsky Central Scientific Library of the National Academy of Sciences	Kiev, Ukraine	1919	13,000,000
8	Russian State Library+	Moscow, Russia	1862	11,750,000
9	Bibliothèque Nationale de Paris	Paris, France	1400	11,000,000
10	New York Public Library★	New York, USA	1895	10,421,691

* *Formed in 1990 through the unification of the Deutsche Bibliothek, Frankfurt (founded 1947) and the Deutsche Bucherei, Leipzig*

Founded as part of the British Museum, 1753; became an independent body in 1973

+ *Founded 1862 as Rumyantsev Library, formerly State V. I. Lenin Library*

★ *Astor Library founded 1848, consolidated with Lenox Library and Tilden Trust to form New York Public Library in 1895*

The figures for books in such vast collections as held by these libraries represent only a fraction of the total collections, which include manuscripts, microfilms, maps, prints, and records. The Library of Congress has perhaps more than 100 million catalogued items.

DEUTSCHE BIBLIOTHEK

Formed in October 1990 through the merging of West and East German libraries, the Deutsche Bibliothek contains unified Germany's largest collection of books and other printed and recorded material.

TOP 10 ★
LARGEST PUBLIC LIBRARIES IN THE UK

	LIBRARY	FOUNDED	BOOKS
1	Hampshire	1974	3,500,000
2	Kent	1921	3,300,000
3	Lancashire	1924	3,189,800
4	Essex	1926	3,006,349
5	Glasgow	1877	2,557,554
6	Manchester	1852	2,430,000
7 =	Devon	1974	2,000,000
=	Leeds	1870	2,000,000
=	Liverpool	1852	2,000,000
10	Hertfordshire	1925	1,932,393

These figures are for the number of books held by each county in its public libraries. No figures are available for the number of books held by individual public libraries in the UK.

Whose valuable notebooks are known as the Codex Hammer?
see p.109 for the answer

A Leonardo da Vinci
B William Shakespeare
C Albert Einstein

Book Firsts & Records

TOP 10 ★
MOST-PUBLISHED AUTHORS OF ALL TIME
AUTHOR/NATIONALITY

1 **William Shakespeare** (British; 1564–1616)
2 **Charles Dickens** (British; 1812–70)
3 **Sir Walter Scott** (British; 1771–1832)
4 **Johann Goethe** (German; 1749–1832)
5 **Aristotle** (Greek; 384–322 BC)
6 **Alexandre Dumas** (père) (French; 1802–70)
7 **Robert Louis Stevenson** (British; 1850–94)
8 **Mark Twain** (American; 1835–1910)
9 **Marcus Tullius Cicero** (Roman; 106–43 BC)
10 **Honoré de Balzac** (French; 1799–1850)

TOP 10 ★
BOOK PRODUCING COUNTRIES

COUNTRY	TITLES PUBLISHED*
1 UK	101,504
2 China	73,923
3 Germany	62,277
4 USA	49,276
5 France	45,379
6 Japan	42,245
7 Spain	37,325
8 Italy	26,620
9 South Korea	25,017
10 Russia	22,028

* Total of new titles, new editions, and reprints in latest year for which figures are available

TOP 10 ★
BOOK MARKETS

COUNTRY	EST. BOOK SALES, 2001 ($)
1 USA	28,379,200,000
2 Japan	10,872,400,000
3 Germany	9,764,400,000
4 UK	4,870,100,000
5 China	2,771,400,000
6 Italy	2,760,400,000
7 Brazil	2,735,500,000
8 Spain	2,733,300,000
9 France	2,733,000,000
10 South Korea	1,805,200,000

Source: *Euromonitor*

TOP 10 ★
TYPES OF BOOK PUBLISHED IN THE UK

SUBJECT	NEW TITLES PUBLISHED, 1999
1 Fiction	9,800
2 Children's	9,099
3 History	5,193
4 Economics	4,670
5 Religion	4,595
6 Social sciences	4,495
7 Computers/computer games	4,100
8 Medicine	4,093
9 School textbooks	3,963
10 Art	3,842
Total (including new editions and categories not in Top 10)	110,155

Source: The Bookseller

TOP 10 ★
BESTSELLING PAPERBACKS PUBLISHED OVER 50 YEARS AGO

BOOK/AUTHOR/YEAR	US SALES ($)*
1 *The Common Sense Book of Baby and Child Care*, Benjamin Spock, 1946	23,285,000
2 *The Merriam-Webster Pocket Dictionary*, 1947	15,500,000
3 *English–Spanish, Spanish–English Dictionary*, Carlos Castillo and Otto F. Bond, 1948	10,187,000
4 *Gone With the Wind*, Margaret Mitchell, 1936	8,630,000
5 *God's Little Acre*, Erskine Caldwell, 1946	8,258,400
6 *1984*, George Orwell, 1949	8,147,629
7 *Animal Farm*, George Orwell, 1946	7,070,892
8 *Roget's Pocket Thesaurus*, 1946	7,020,000
9 *How to Win Friends and Influence People*, Dale Carnegie, 1940	6,578,314
10 *Lady Chatterley's Lover*, D. H. Lawrence, 1932	6,326,470

* Includes hardback sales where relevant, estimated to 1975

DR. SPOCK
Dr. Benjamin McLane Spock (1903–98) was the eldest of six children. He became a paediatric specialist and studied psychoanalysis, but his chief celebrity came from his *The Common Sense Book of Baby and Child Care*, which was published in 1946. Originally sold for 25 cents, this manual became the bestselling paperback of all time in the US. Translated into some 40 languages, it also sold more than 50 million copies worldwide, making Dr. Spock the most famous of all childcare experts.

WHO WAS · WHO WAS · WHO WAS · WHO WAS · WHO WAS **?**

UNDER THE HAMMER
The Codex Hammer, *a collection of Leonardo da Vinci's scientific writings, was compiled c.1508–10. It contains over 350 drawings illustrating the artist's scientific theories. In 1994 it achieved a record price at auction when bought by Bill Gates.*

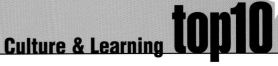

BEST RED BOOK

During the Cultural Revolution, Chinese Communist leader Mao Tse-tung (Zedong) became the subject of a personality cult, with his bestselling Quotations ... *(Little Red Book) its most potent symbol.*

THE 10 ★
FIRST PENGUIN PAPERBACKS

BOOK/AUTHOR

1 *Ariel*, André Maurois

2 *A Farewell to Arms*, Ernest Hemingway

3 *Poet's Pub*, Eric Linklater

4 *Madame Claire*, Susan Ertz

5 *The Unpleasantness at the Bellona Club*, Dorothy L. Sayers

6 *The Mysterious Affair at Styles*, Agatha Christie

7 *Twenty-five*, Beverley Nichols

8 *William*, E. H. Young

9 *Gone to Earth*, Mary Webb

10 *Carnival*, Compton Mackenzie

It was the British publisher Allen Lane who, remarking "I would be the first to admit that there is no fortune in this series for anyone concerned", launched his first "Penguin" titles in Great Britain on 30 July 1935. Originally Penguins were paperback reprints of books that had been previously published as hardbacks; their quality, range of subjects, and low price established them as the pioneering books in the "paperback revolution".

TOP 10 ★
BESTSELLING BOOKS OF ALL TIME

BOOK/AUTHOR	FIRST PUBLISHED	APPROX. SALES
1 *The Bible*	c.1451–55	more than 6,000,000,000
2 *Quotations from the Works of Mao Tse-tung* (dubbed *Little Red Book* by the Western press)	1966	900,000,000
3 *American Spelling Book*, Noah Webster	1783	up to 100,000,000
4 *The Guinness Book of Records* (now *Guinness World Records*)	1955	more than 90,000,000*
5 *World Almanac*	1868	73,500,000*
6 *The McGuffey Readers*, William Holmes McGuffey	1836	60,000,000
7 *The Common Sense Book of Baby and Child Care*, Benjamin Spock	1946	more than 50,000,000
8 *A Message to Garcia*, Elbert Hubbard	1899	up to 40,000,000
9 =*In His Steps: "What Would Jesus Do?"*, Rev. Charles Monroe Sheldon	1896	more than 30,000,000
=*Valley of the Dolls*, Jacqueline Susann	1966	more than 30,000,000

* Aggregate sales of annual publication

TOP 10 ★
MOST EXPENSIVE BOOKS AND MANUSCRIPTS EVER SOLD AT AUCTION

BOOK OR MANUSCRIPT/SALE	PRICE (£)*
1 *The Codex Hammer*, c.1508–10, Christie's, New York, 11 Nov 1994 ($28,800,000)	18,643,190

Leonardo da Vinci notebook purchased by Bill Gates, the billionaire founder of Microsoft.

2 *The Rothschild Prayerbook*, c.1505, Christie's, London, 8 July 1999	7,800,000

The world record price for an illuminated manuscript.

3 *The Gospels of Henry the Lion*, c.1173–75, Sotheby's, London, 6 Dec 1983	7,400,000

At the time of sale, the most expensive manuscript or book ever sold.

4 *The Birds of America*, **John James Audubon**, 1827–38, Christie's, New York, 10 Mar 2000 ($8,000,000)	5,187,731

The record for any natural history book.

5 *The Canterbury Tales*, **Geoffrey Chaucer**, c.1476–77, Christie's, London, 8 July 1998	4,200,000

Printed by William Caxton and bought by Paul Getty.

6 **The Gutenberg Bible**, 1455, Christie's, New York, 22 Oct 1987 ($4,900,000)	2,996,026

One of the first books ever printed, by Johann Gutenberg and Johann Fust in 1455.

7 *The Northumberland Bestiary*, c.1250–60, Sotheby's, London, 29 Nov 1990	2,700,000

The highest price ever paid for an English manuscript.

8 *The Cornaro Missal*, c.1503, Christie's, London, 8 July 1999	2,600,000

The world record price for an Italian manuscript.

9 **The Burdett Psalter and Hours**, 1282–86, Sotheby's, London, 23 June 1998	2,500,000

The third most expensive illuminated manuscript.

10 **Autographed manuscript of nine symphonies by Wolfgang Amadeus Mozart**, c.1773–74, Sotheby's, London, 22 May 1987	2,350,000

The record for a music manuscript.

* Excluding premiums

Did You Know? Audubon's *The Birds of America* is not only one of the most expensive books ever published, but it is also one of the largest: its pages measure 63.5 x 96.5 cm (25 x 38 in).

Bestsellers & Literary Awards

PULITZER

Joseph Pulitzer (1847–1911) was born in Makó, Hungary. He settled in St. Louis, USA, where he became a journalist and within a few years publisher of the *St. Louis Post-Dispatch*. He then purchased the *New York World*, which became America's largest circulation newspaper. In his publications, he had waged war against corruption in business and government and promoted freedom of the press and journalistic professionalism. He left a $2 million endowment to establish the Columbia School of Journalism, which since 1917 has administered the Pulitzer Prizes in a range of categories for journalism, literature, music, and drama.

TOP 10 ★
HISTORY TITLES OF 2000 IN THE UK

TITLE/AUTHOR	SALES
1 *History of Britain: At the Edge of the World? 3000BC–AD1603*, Simon Schama	110,427
2 *Daughters of Britannia: The Lives and Times of Diplomatic Wives*, Katie Hickman	69,997
3 *London: The Biography*, Peter Ackroyd	56,094
4 *The Africa House*, Christina Lamb	49,376
5 *Stalingrad*, Antony Beevor	49,170
6 *The Year 1000*, Robert Lacey and Danny Danziger	38,685
7 *My East End*, Gilda O'Neill	27,188
8 *Encyclopaedia of British History*	24,847
9 *Finest Hour*, Phil Craig and Tim Clayton	24,827
10 *Conquistadors*, Michael Wood	22,499

Source: *Whitaker BookTrack General Retail Market*

The year's No. 1 bestseller was the book of an equally popular television series, but history as a genre has experienced a notable recent upsurge.

TOP 10 ★
NON-FICTION TITLES OF 2000 IN THE UK

TITLE/AUTHOR	SALES
1 *The Return of the Naked Chef*, Jamie Oliver	474,394
2 *Angela's Ashes: A Memoir of a Childhood* (film tie-in), Frank McCourt	394,580
3 *Delia's How to Cook Book Two*, Delia Smith	325,373
4 *Guinness World Records 2001*	280,186
5 *'Tis*, Frank McCourt	222,599
6 *Down Under*, Bill Bryson	194,900
7 *Angela's Ashes: A Memoir of a Childhood*, Frank McCourt	172,404
8 *The Naked Chef*, Jamie Oliver	166,546
9 *Wan2tlk?: Ltle Bk of Txt Msgs*	142,943
10 *"Who Wants to be a Millionaire?": The Bumper Quiz Book*, Question Masters	135,574

Source: *Whitaker BookTrack General Retail Market*

In addition to such perennials as TV-linked cookery books, the fashion for "little books" and text messaging was exemplified in the success of a title that combined the two genres.

TOP 10 ★
ADULT FICTION TITLES OF 2000 IN THE UK

TITLE/AUTHOR	SALES
1 *Hannibal*, Thomas Harris	423,241
2 *The Testament*, John Grisham	357,085
3 *Bridget Jones: Edge of Reason*, Helen Fielding	330,640
4 *Man and Boy*, Tony Parsons	310,336
5 *Black Notice*, Patricia Cornwell	263,170
6 *Monsoon*, Wilbur Smith	209,053
7 *Chocolat*, Joanne Harris	201,055
8 *Score!*, Jilly Cooper	193,668
9 *Inconceivable*, Ben Elton	187,976
10 *The Beach*, Alex Garland	183,368

Source: *Whitaker BookTrack General Retail Market*

TOP 10 ★
CHILDREN'S TITLES OF 2000 IN THE UK

TITLE/AUTHOR	SALES
1 *Harry Potter and the Goblet of Fire*, J. K. Rowling	1,036,494
2 *Harry Potter and the Philosopher's Stone*, J. K. Rowling	780,379
3 *Harry Potter and the Prisoner of Azkaban*, J. K. Rowling	716,508
4 *Harry Potter and the Chamber of Secrets*, J. K. Rowling	643,755
5 *Children's Book of Books 2000*	256,428
6 *The Official Pokémon Handbook*, Maria S. Barbo	240,654
7 *The Official Pokémon Collector's Sticker Book*, Maria S. Barbo	168,262
8 *The Beano Book 2001*	159,282
9 *The Illustrated Mum*, Jacqueline Wilson	148,955
10 *Pokémon "I Choose You"*, (tabbed colouring book)	116,980

Source: *Whitaker BookTrack General Retail Market*

THE 10 ★
LATEST WINNERS OF THE NATIONAL BOOK AWARD FOR FICTION

YEAR	AUTHOR/TITLE
2000	Susan Sontag, *In America*
1999	Ha Jin, *Waiting*
1998	Alice McDermott, *Charming Billy*
1997	Charles Frazier, *Cold Mountain*
1996	Andrea Barrett, *Ship Fever and Other Stories*
1995	Philip Roth, *Sabbath's Theater*
1994	William Gaddis, *A Frolic of His Own*
1993	E. Annie Proulx, *The Shipping News*
1992	Cormac McCarthy, *All the Pretty Horses*
1991	Norman Rush, *Mating*

The National Book Award is presented by the National Book Foundation as part of its programme to foster reading in the US through author events and literacy campaigns.

With what product is the German company Steiff associated?
see p.114 for the answer

A Guns
B Camera lenses
C Teddy bears

THE 10 ★
LATEST WINNERS OF THE PULITZER PRIZE FOR FICTION

YEAR	AUTHOR/TITLE
2001	Michael Chabon, *The Amazing Adventures of Kavalier & Clay*
2000	Jhumpa Lhiri, *Interpreter of Maladies*
1999	Michael Cunningham, *The Hours*
1998	Philip Roth, *American Pastoral*
1997	Steven Millhauser, *Martin Dressler: The Tale of an American Dreamer*
1996	Richard Ford, *Independence Day*
1995	Carol Shields, *The Stone Diaries*
1994	E. Annie Proulx, *The Shipping News*
1993	Robert Olen Butler, *A Good Scent From a Strange Mountain: Stories*
1992	Jane Smiley, *A Thousand Acres*

THE 10 ★
LATEST BOOKER PRIZE WINNERS

YEAR	AUTHOR/TITLE
2000	Margaret Atwood, *The Blind Assassin*
1999	J. M. Coetzee, *Disgrace*
1998	Ian McEwan, *Amsterdam*
1997	Arundhati Roy, *The God of Small Things*
1996	Graham Swift, *Last Orders*
1995	Pat Barker, *The Ghost Road*
1994	James Kelman, *How Late It Was, How Late*
1993	Roddy Doyle, *Paddy Clarke Ha Ha Ha*
1992	= Michael Ondaatje, *The English Patient* = Barry Unsworth, *Sacred Hunger*

The South African writer J. M. Coetzee is the only person to have won the Booker prize twice, in 1999 with *Disgrace* and in 1983 with *Life and Times of Michael K.*

MARGARET ATWOOD
Canadian poet and novelist Margaret Atwood joins the list of Booker Prize winners for her tenth novel, The Blind Assassin. *Two of her previous books,* The Handmaid's Tale *and* Cat's Eye, *were shortlisted.*

THE 10 ★
LATEST WINNERS OF THE WHITBREAD "BOOK OF THE YEAR" AWARD

YEAR	AUTHOR/TITLE
2000	Matthew Kneale, *English Passengers*
1999	Seamus Heaney, *Beowulf*
1998	Ted Hughes, *Birthday Letters*
1997	Ted Hughes, *Tales From Ovid*
1996	Seamus Heaney, *The Spirit Level*
1995	Kate Atkinson, *Behind the Scenes at the Museum*
1994	William Trevor, *Felicia's Journey*
1993	Joan Brady, *Theory of War*
1992	Jeff Torrington, *Swing Hammer Swing!*
1991	John Richardson, *A Life of Picasso*

THE 10 ★
LATEST WINNERS OF THE WHITBREAD "CHILDREN'S BOOK OF THE YEAR" AWARD

YEAR	AUTHOR/TITLE
2000	Jamila Gavin, *Coram Boy*
1999	J. K. Rowling, *Harry Potter and the Prisoner of Azkaban*
1998	David Almond, *Skellig*
1997	Andrew Norris, *Aquila*
1996	Anne Fine, *The Tulip Touch*
1995	Michael Morpurgo, *The Wreck of the Zanzibar*
1994	Geraldine McCaughrean, *Gold Dust*
1993	Anne Fine, *Flour Babies*
1992	Gillian Cross, *The Great Elephant Chase*
1991	Diana Hendry, *Harvey Angell*

The Press

TOP 10 ★
NON-ENGLISH-LANGUAGE DAILY NEWSPAPERS

	NEWSPAPER	COUNTRY	AVERAGE DAILY CIRCULATION
1	Yomiuri Shimbun	Japan	14,476,000
2	Asahi Shimbun	Japan	12,475,000
3	Mainichi Shimbun	Japan	5,785,000
4	Nihon Keizai Shimbun	Japan	4,674,000
5	Chunichi Shimbun	Japan	4,667,000
6	Bild-Zeitung	Germany	4,256,000
7	Sankei Shimbun	Japan	2,890,000
8	Reference News	China	2,800,000
9	Chosen Ilbo	South Korea	2,348,000
10	People's Daily	China	2,300,000

Source: *World Association of Newspapers*

TOP 10 ★
ENGLISH-LANGUAGE DAILY NEWSPAPERS

	NEWSPAPER	COUNTRY	AVERAGE DAILY CIRCULATION
1	The Sun	UK	3,554,000
2	Daily Mail	UK	2,367,000
3	The Mirror	UK	2,262,000
4	Wall Street Journal	USA	1,753,000
5	USA Today	USA	1,672,000
6	Times of India	India	1,479,000
7	The New York Times	USA	1,086,000
8	Los Angeles Times	USA	1,078,000
9	Daily Express	UK	1,044,000
10	The Daily Telegraph	UK	1,033,000

Source: *World Association of Newspapers*

TOP 10 ★
MAGAZINE GENRES IN THE UK

	GENRE	AVERAGE NET CIRCULATION PER ISSUE
1	Women's lifestyle/fashion	7,939,202
2	Women's weeklies	7,475,174
3	General motoring	7,349,535
4	Radio and TV guides	5,644,468
5	Cookery and kitchen	5,449,758
6	Electronics and radio	4,960,413
7	Satellite/cable TV listings	4,083,615
8	Men's lifestyle	2,843,799
9	Home interests	2,461,071
10	Teenage	2,054,586

Source: *Audit Bureau of Circulations Ltd.*

TOP 10 ★
NEWSPAPER-READING COUNTRIES

	COUNTRY	DAILY COPIES PER 1,000 PEOPLE		COUNTRY	DAILY COPIES PER 1,000 PEOPLE
1	Norway	583	6	Austria	356
2	Japan	574	7	Iceland	341
3	Finland	452	8	Singapore	334
4	Sweden	420	9	UK	321
5	Switzerland	376	10	Germany	300

Source: *World Association of Newspapers*

TOP 10 COUNTRIES WITH THE HIGHEST NEWSPAPER CIRCULATIONS
(Country/average daily circulation)

❶ Japan, 72,218,000 ❷ USA, 55,979,000 ❸ China, 50,000,000
❹ India, 25,587,000 ❺ Germany, 24,565,000 ❻ Russia, 23,800,000
❼ UK, 18,939,000 ❽ France, 8,799,000 ❾ Brazil, 7,245,000
❿ Italy, 5,937,000

Source: *World Association of Newspapers*

HOLD THE FRONT PAGE

The USA is well served by its local press, but few US newspapers can claim national readership. The circulations of the three major publications shown here tend to be as regionally based as their titles imply.

TOP 10 ★
MOST SUBSCRIBED TO MAGAZINES IN THE UK

MAGAZINE	SUBSCRIPTIONS
1 Reader's Digest	981,277
2 Saga Magazine	518,093
3 National Geographic Magazine	299,024
4 Good Housekeeping	122,751
5 BBC Gardener's World	112,581
6 Computeractive	100,611
7 Choice	79,020
8 PC Pro	77,870
9 Moneywise	77,162
10 Woman & Home	67,826

Source: Audit Bureau of Circulations Ltd.

Several of the UK's most subscribed-to magazines are also among its oldest established. *Reader's Digest* dates back to 1922 in the US and 1939 in the UK, while *National Geographic Magazine* was founded in the US in 1888. If global subscriptions were included, *The Economist* would rank at No. 10 with 69,846, excluding the US. Its UK subscriptions rank it at No. 11 with 66,112.

TOP 10 ★
COUNTRIES WITH THE MOST NEWSPAPER TITLES PER CAPITA

COUNTRY	DAILY TITLES PER 1,000,000 PEOPLE
1 Uruguay	24.79
2 Norway	18.67
3 Russia	18.00
4 Switzerland	14.74
5 Cyprus	12.27
6 Estonia	11.76
7 Luxembourg	11.48
8 =Iceland	10.87
=Sweden	10.87
10 Finland	10.85
UK	1.80

Source: World Association of Newspapers

TOP 10 TEEN MAGAZINES IN THE UK

(Magazine/average circulation per issue)

1 *Sugar*, 422,179 **2** *Top of the Pops*, 305,122 **3** *More!*, 302,825
4 *It's Bliss*, 300,191 **5** *Smash Hits*, 221,622 **6** *TV Hits*, 201,855 **7** *J17*, 200,330
8 *Mizz*, 163,672 **9** *19*, 130,198 **10** *Live & Kicking*, 123,360

Source: *Audit Bureau of Circulations Ltd.*

TOP 10 ★
DAILY NEWSPAPERS IN THE UK, 2000

NEWSPAPER	AVERAGE DAILY CIRCULATION*
1 The Sun	3,488,965
2 Daily Mail	2,426,487
3 The Mirror	2,038,264
4 The Daily Telegraph	994,845
5 Daily Express	943,199
6 The Times	697,462
7 Daily Record	591,990
8 Daily Star	538,183
9 The Guardian	371,043
10 The Independent	195,339

* For the six month period August 2000–January 2001
Source: Audit Bureau of Circulations Ltd.

TOP 10 ★
CONSUMER MAGAZINES IN THE UK

MAGAZINE	AVERAGE CIRCULATION PER ISSUE*
1 What's on TV	1,699,833
2 Radio Times	1,229,062
3 Take a Break	1,125,707
4 Reader's Digest	1,005,003
5 TV Choice	732,259
6 TV Times	686,156
7 FHM	684,548
8 Woman	602,842
9 That's Life	564,313
10 TV Quick	553,148

* Actively purchased
Source: Audit Bureau of Circulations Ltd.

TOP 10 ★
SUNDAY NEWSPAPERS IN THE UK, 2000

NEWSPAPER	AVERAGE CIRCULATION*
1 News of the World	3,829,689
2 The Mail on Sunday	2,314,008
3 Sunday Mirror	1,751,190
4 Sunday People	1,402,076
5 The Sunday Times	1,267,430
6 Sunday Express	841,870
7 The Sunday Telegraph	773,887
8 Sunday Mail	696,065
9 The Observer	396,833
10 Independent on Sunday	216,604

* For the six month period August 2000–January 2001
Source: Audit Bureau of Circulations Ltd.

TOP 10 ★
WOMEN'S MONTHLY MAGAZINES IN THE UK

MAGAZINE	AVERAGE CIRCULATION PER ISSUE*
1 Cosmopolitan	460,086
2 Candis	448,331
3 Good Housekeeping	404,476
4 Marie Claire	400,543
5 Prima	395,164
6 New Woman	281,828
7 Woman & Home	269,401
8 Company	260,646
9 Essentials	234,727
10 Know Your Destiny	228,511

* Actively purchased
Source: Audit Bureau of Circulations Ltd.

Did You Know? British writer Rudyard Kipling was fired as a reporter on the *San Francisco Examiner*, which told him "You just don't know how to use the English language." In 1907, he won the Nobel Prize for Literature.

Toys & Games

TOP 10 FACTORS PEOPLE CONSIDER MOST IMPORTANT WHEN BUYING A TOY

1 Safety **2** Educational **3** Price **4** Durability **5** Well designed **6** Toy the child specifically wants **7** Brand/manufacturer's name is well known **8** Unlikely to go out of fashion in the near future **9** Possible to add to or buy accessories **10** Suitable for various age groups

Source: *BRMB/Mintel*

TOP 10 ★ TOY-BUYING COUNTRIES

	COUNTRY*	SPENDING ON TOYS, 2000 ($)
1	USA	34,554,900,000
2	Japan	9,190,600,000
3	UK	5,348,100,000
4	France	3,397,200,000
5	Germany	3,117,900,000
6	Canada	2,689,500,000
7	Italy	1,941,000,000
8	Australia	937,100,000
9	Spain	933,600,000
10	Belgium	754,700,000

* Of those covered by survey
Source: *Euromonitor*

TOP 10 MOST POPULAR TYPES OF TOY

(Type of toy/market share percentage, 1998)

1 Video games, 21.5 **2** Activity toys, 13.0 **3** Infant/pre-school toys, 11.0 **4** = Dolls, 10.5; = Games/puzzles, 10.5; = Other toys, 10.5 **7** Toy vehicles, 9.0 **8** = Action figures, 5.0; = Soft toys, 5.0 **10** Ride-on toys, 4.0

Source: *Eurotoys/The NPD Group Worldwide*
This list is based on a survey of toy consumption in the European Union, and can be taken as a reliable guide to the most popular types of toy in the developed world.

TOP 10 ★ TOYS AND GAMES OF 2000 IN THE UK

TOY/MANUFACTURER

1 **Pokémon Booster pack**, Wizards of the Coast

2 **Pokémon Fossil Booster ENI-7**, Wizards of the Coast

3 **Pokémon Jungle Booster**, Wizards of the Coast

4 **Pokémon Team Rocket Booster**, Wizards of the Coast

5 **Pokémon Battle Figures** (2 pack), Hasbro

6 **Pokémon Beanie assistant**, Hasbro

7 **Pokémon Theme Decks**, Wizards of the Coast

8 **Who Wants to be a Millionaire?**, Upstarts

9 **Pokémon Sliders**, Oddz On (Vivid)

10 **Poo-Chi**, Tiger Electronics

Source: *NPD Group Worldwide*

TOP 10 ★ MOST LANDED-ON SQUARES IN MONOPOLY®*

UK GAME		US GAME
Trafalgar Square	1	Illinois Avenue
Go	2	Go
Fenchurch Street Station	3	B. & O. Railroad
Free Parking	4	Free Parking
Marlborough Street	5	Tennessee Avenue
Vine Street	6	New York Avenue
King's Cross Station	7	Reading Railroad
Bow Street	8	St. James Place
Water Works	9	Water Works
Marylebone Station	10	Pennsylvania Railroad

Monopoly® is a registered trade mark of Parker Brothers division of Tonka Corporation, USA, under licence to Waddington Games Ltd.

* Based on a computer analysis of the probability of landing on each square

TOP 10 ★ MOST EXPENSIVE TEDDY BEARS SOLD AT AUCTION IN THE UK

BEAR/SALE	PRICE (£)*
1 "Teddy Girl", Steiff cinnamon teddy bear, 1904, Christie's, London, 5 Dec 1994	110,000

Formerly owned by Lt.-Col. Bob Henderson, this sale precisely doubled the previous world record for a teddy bear when it was acquired by Yoshiro Sekiguchi for display at his teddy bear museum near Tokyo.

2 Black mohair Steiff teddy bear, c.1912, Christie's, London, 4 Dec 2000	91,750

One of a number of black Steiff teddy bears brought out in the UK after of the sinking of the Titanic; these have since become known as "mourning" teddies.

3 "Happy", dual-plush Steiff teddy bear, 1926, Sotheby's, London, 19 Sep 1989	55,000

Although estimated at £700–900, competitive bidding pushed the price up to the then world record, when it was acquired by collector Paul Volpp.

4 "Elliot", blue Steiff bear, 1908, Christie's, London, 6 Dec 1993	49,500

Produced as a sample for Harrods but never manufactured commercially.

5 "Teddy Edward", golden mohair teddy bear, Christie's, London, 9 Dec 1996	38,500
6 Black mohair Steiff teddy bear, c.1912, Sotheby's, London, 18 May 1990	24,200

See entry no. 2.

7 Blank button, brown Steiff teddy bear, c.1905, Christie's, London, 8 Dec 1997	23,000
8 Black mohair Steiff teddy bear, c.1912, Christie's, London, 5 Dec 1994	22,000

See entry no. 2.

9 "Albert", Steiff teddy bear, c.1910, Christie's, London, 9 Dec 1996	18,400
10 Steiff teddy bear, Christie's, London, 9 Dec 1996	17,250

* Prices include buyer's premium where appropriate

It is said that, while on a hunting trip, US President Theodore ("Teddy") Roosevelt refused to shoot a young bear. A New York shopkeeper made some stuffed bears and sold them as "Teddy's Bears".

TOP 10 ★
MOST EXPENSIVE TOYS EVER SOLD AT AUCTION IN THE UK*

TOY/SALE	PRICE (£)
1 **Roullet et Decamps musical automaton of a snake charmer**, Sotheby's, London, 17 Oct 1996	155,500
2 *Titania's Palace*, a doll's house with 2,000 items of furniture, Christie's, London, 10 Jan 1978	135,000
3 **Roullet et Decamps musical automaton of a mask seller**, Sotheby's, London, 17 Oct 1996	122,500
4 **Silver mounted set of carved boxwood chessmen**, Sotheby's, London, 23 May 1996	96,100
5 **Gustave Vichy bird trainer automaton**, Sotheby's, London, 20 Nov 1996	84,000
6 **Hornby 00-gauge train set**, Christies, London, 27 Nov 1992 *The largest ever sold at auction.*	80,178
7 **Russian carousel** (tinplate Ferris wheel), c.1904, Sotheby's, London, 10 Feb 1993	62,500
8 = **Tinplate carousel by Märklin**, c.1910, Sotheby's, London, 23 Jan 1992	47,300
= **Set of Märklin horse-drawn fire appliances**, c.1902, Sotheby's, London, 23 Jan 1992	47,300
10 **Machine Man**, Sotheby's, London, 7 Nov 1996	42,500

* Excluding dolls and teddy bears

TOP 10 BESTSELLING COMPUTER GAMES AT W.H. SMITH, 2000

(Game/publisher)

1 **Who Wants to be a Millionaire?**, Eidos **2** **Pokémon Yellow**, Nintendo
3 **WWF Smackdown**, THQ **4** **Babyz**, The Learning Company **5** **Pokémon Red**, Nintendo
6 **Pokémon Blue**, Nintendo **7** **Gran Turismo 2**, Sony
8 **The Sims**, Electronic Arts **9** **Driver 2**, Infogrames UK **10** **Championship Manager**, Eidos

TOP 10 BESTSELLING BOARD GAMES AT W.H. SMITH, 2000

1 Jenga **2** Junior Who Wants to be a Millionaire? **3** Scrabble **4** Monopoly
5 Cluedo **6** Disney Trivial Pursuit **7** Friends **8** Rummikub Numbers
9 Absolute Balderdash **10** Who's in the Bag?

TOP 10 ★
MOST EXPENSIVE DOLLS SOLD AT AUCTION IN THE UK

DOLL/SALE	PRICE (£)
1 **Kämmer and Reinhardt doll**, Sotheby's, London, 8 Feb 1994	188,500
2 **Kämmer and Reinhardt bisque character doll**, c.1909, Sotheby's, London, 17 Oct 1996	108,200
3 **Kämmer and Reinhardt bisque character doll**, c.1909, Sotheby's, London, 17 Oct 1996	91,700
4 **Albert Marque bisque character doll**, Sotheby's, London, 17 Oct 1996	71,900
5 = **William and Mary wooden doll**, English, c.1690, Sotheby's, London, 24 Mar 1987	67,000
= **Wooden doll, Charles II**, 17th century, Christie's, London, 18 May 1989	67,000
7 **Albert Marque bisque character doll**, Sotheby's, London, 17 Oct 1996	58,700
8 = **Albert Marque bisque character doll**, Christie's, London, 23 May 1997	56,500
= **Mulatto pressed bisque swivel-head Madagascar doll**, Sotheby's, London, 17 Oct 1996	56,500
10 **Shellacked pressed bisque swivel-head doll**, Sotheby's, London, 17 Oct 1996	45,500

THE 10 ★
LATEST TOYS OF THE YEAR

YEAR	TOY
2000	Teksta
1999	Furby Babies
1998	Furby
1997	Teletubbies
1996	Barbie
1995	POGS
1994	Power Rangers
1993	Thunderbird's Tracey Island
1992	WWF Wrestlers
1991	Nintendo Game Boy

The British Association of Toy Retailers' Toy of the Year Award was started in 1965, when it was awarded to the James Bond Aston Martin die-cast car. At the end of the 20th century, the Association awarded Lego the title of Toy of the Century, after votes had been cast by a group of retailers and the public, who voted over the Internet.

BARBIE

Ruth and Elliot Handler, co-founders of American toy manufacturers Mattel, introduced the first Barbie doll in February 1959. Previously, most dolls were babies, but Ruth Handler had seen her daughter Barbara – who provided the doll's name – playing with paper dolls with adult attributes and realized that there would be a market for a grown-up doll, complete with an extensive wardrobe of clothes and accessories. The first Barbie was dressed in a striped swimsuit, with high heels, sunglasses, and gold hoop earrings. Sold at $3.00 each, 351,000 Barbies were sold in the first year.

Which native American is depicted in the world's largest statue?
see p.117 for the answer

A Crazy Horse
B Geronimo
C Pocahontas

Art on Show

BEST-ATTENDED ART EXHIBITIONS, 2000

EXHIBITION/ART GALLERY/LOCATION	DATES	ATTENDANCE TOTAL	DAILY
1 *Earthly Art – Heavenly Beauty*, State Hermitage, St. Petersburg, Russia	13 June–17 Sep	570,000*	5,876
2 *Sinai: Byzantium, Russia*, State Hermitage, St. Petersburg, Russia	20 June–18 Sep	500,000*	5,495
3 *Seeing Salvation: Image of Christ*, National Gallery, London, UK	26 Feb–7 May	355,175	5,002
4 *Picasso's World of Children*, National Museum of Western Art, Tokyo, Japan	14 Mar–18 June	386,086	4,290
5 *Dutch Art: Rembrandt and Vermeer*, National Museum of Western Art, Tokyo, Japan	4 July–24 Sep	280,259	3,892
6 *Amazons of the Avant-Garde*, Guggenheim Museum, Bilbao, Spain	13 June–27 Aug	283,181	3,879
7 *The Glory of the Golden Age*, Rijksmuseum, Amsterdam, Netherlands	15 Apr–17 Sep	594,122	3,808
8 *Van Gogh: Face to Face*, Museum of Fine Arts, Boston, USA	2 July–24 Sep	316,049	3,762
9 *Van Gogh: Face to Face*, Detroit Institute of Arts, Detroit, USA	12 Mar–4 June	315,000*	3,706
10 *Triumph of the Baroque*, National Gallery of Art, Washington, D.C., USA	21 May–9 Oct	526,050	3,705

* Approximate total provided by museum

Source: The Art Newspaper

OLDEST MUSEUMS AND ART GALLERIES IN THE UK

MUSEUM OR ART GALLERY/LOCATION	FOUNDED
1 **Ashmolean Museum**, Oxford	1683
2 **British Museum**, London	1753
3 **National Museum of Antiquities**, Edinburgh	1780
4 **Hunterian Museum**, Glasgow	1807
5 =**Museum of Antiquities**, Newcastle upon Tyne	1813
=**Royal College of Surgeons Museum**, London	1813
7 **Dulwich Picture Gallery**, London	1814
8 **Fitzwilliam Museum**, Cambridge	1816
9 **Leeds City Museum**	1820
10 **Manchester Museum**	1821

BEST-ATTENDED EXHIBITIONS AT THE ROYAL ACADEMY, LONDON*

EXHIBITION	YEAR	TOTAL ATTENDANCE
1 *The Genius of China*	1974	771,466
2 *Monet in the 20th Century*	1999	739,324
3 *Monet: The Series Paintings*	1990	658,289
4 *Pompeii AD 79*	1977	633,347
5 *Post-Impressionism*	1980	558,573
6 *The Great Japan Exhibition*	1982	523,005
7 *The Genius of Venice*	1983	452,885
8 *J.M.W. Turner*	1975	424,629
9 *The Great Age of Chivalry*	1987–88	349,750
10 *The Gold of El Dorado*	1979	319,006

* During the past 25 years, the only period for which detailed comparative figures exist

BEST-ATTENDED EXHIBITIONS AT THE VICTORIA AND ALBERT MUSEUM, LONDON

EXHIBITION	YEAR	TOTAL ATTENDANCE
1 *Britain Can Make It*	1946	1,500,000
2 *Spanish Art Treasures*	1881	1,022,000
3 *Scientific Apparatus*	1876	275,813
4 *Art Nouveau 1890–1914*	2000	231,393
5 *The Cutting Edge*	1997	230,836
6 *Wedding Presents* (Prince and Princess of Wales)	1863	229,425
7 *William Morris*	1996	218,134
8 *Power of the Poster*	1998	186,961
9 *Six Wives of Henry VIII* (BBC drama costumes)	1970	182,825
10 *Visions of Japan*	1991	177,669

The V&A is unusual in having records of exhibitions held as early as 1863, when the display of the wedding presents of the Prince and Princess of Wales (later King Edward VII and Queen Alexandra) attracted an average of 13,496 visitors a day during its 17-day run. *Britain Can Make It*, an exhibit devoted to British industry, was the second best-attended of all time in the UK, after the British Museum's *Treasures of Tutankhamun*. However, other major exhibitions, in which art shows were only one element, were often visited by colossal numbers: more than 6 million saw the 1851 Great Exhibition, while 8.5 million attended the 1951 Festival of Britain.

In which year was Dr. Spock's baby and child care book published?   A 1952
see p.108 for the answer   B 1946
C 1943

TOP 10 ★
TALLEST FREE-STANDING STATUES

STATUE/LOCATION	HEIGHT	
	M	FT

1 Chief Crazy Horse, Thunderhead Mountain, South Dakota, USA — 172 / 563

Started in 1948 by Polish–American sculptor Korczak Ziolkowski, and continued after his death in 1982 by his widow and eight of his children, this gigantic equestrian statue is even longer (195 m/641 ft) than it is high. It is being carved out of the granite mountain by dynamiting and drilling, and is not expected to be completed for several years.

2 Buddha, Tokyo, Japan — 120 / 394

This Japanese–Taiwanese project, unveiled in 1993, took seven years to complete and weighs 1,000 tonnes.

3 The Indian Rope Trick, Riddersberg Säteri, Jönköping, Sweden — 103 / 337

Sculptor Calle Örnemark's 144-tonne wooden sculpture depicts a long strand of "rope" held by a fakir, while another figure ascends.

4 Motherland, Volgograd, Russia — 82 / 270

This concrete statue of a woman with a raised sword, designed by Yevgeniy Vuchetich, commemorates the Soviet victory at the Battle of Stalingrad (1942–43).

5 Kannon, Otsubo-yama, near Tokyo, Japan — 52 / 170

The immense statue of the goddess of mercy was unveiled in 1961 in honour of the dead of World War II.

6 Statue of Liberty, New York, USA — 46 / 151

Designed by Auguste Bartholdi and presented to the US by the people of France, the statue was shipped in sections to Liberty (formerly Bedloes) Island, where it was assembled before being unveiled on 28 October 1886.

7 Christ, Rio de Janeiro, Brazil — 38 / 125

The work of sculptor Paul Landowski and engineer Heitor da Silva Costa, the figure of Christ was unveiled in 1931.

8 Tian Tan (Temple of Heaven) Buddha, Po Lin Monastery, Lantau Island, Hong Kong, China — 34 / 112

This was completed after 20 years' work and was unveiled on 29 December 1993.

9 Quantum Cloud, Greenwich, London, UK — 29 / 95

A gigantic steel human figure surrounded by a matrix of steel struts, it was created in 1999 by Antony Gormley, the sculptor of the similarly gigantic 20-m (66-ft) Angel of the North, Gateshead, UK.

10 Colossi of Memnon, Karnak, Egypt — 21 / 70

This statue portrays two seated sandstone figures of Pharaoh Amenhotep III.

Various projects are in the planning stages, including a 169-m (555-ft) statue of a woman, the Spirit of Houston, and even taller statues of Buddha. If realized, these will enter this Top 10 in the future.

STATUE OF LIBERTY

Originally called "Liberty Enlightening the World", the Statue of Liberty was a gift to the people of the United States of America from the French nation.

Art on Sale

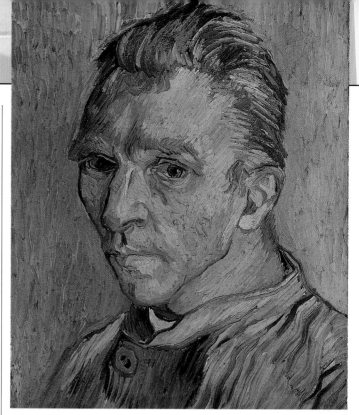

TOP 10 ⭐

MOST EXPENSIVE PAINTINGS EVER SOLD AT AUCTION

PAINTING/ARTIST/SALE	PRICE (£)
1 *Portrait of Dr. Gachet*, **Vincent van Gogh** (Dutch; 1853–90), Christie's, New York, 15 May 1990	44,378,696 ($75,000,000)
2 *Au Moulin de la Galette*, **Pierre-Auguste Renoir** (French; 1841–1919), Sotheby's, New York, 17 May 1990	42,011,832 ($71,000,000)
3 *Portrait de l'Artiste sans Barbe*, **Vincent van Gogh**, Christie's, New York, 19 Nov 1998	39,393,940 ($65,000,000)
4 *Femme aux Bras Croisés*, **Pablo Picasso** (Spanish; 1881–1973), Christie's Rockefeller, New York, 8 Nov 2000	34,965,036 ($50,000,000)
5 *Rideau, Cruchon et Compotier*, **Paul Cézanne** (French; 1839–1906), Sotheby's, New York, 10 May 1999	33,950,616 ($55,000,000)
6 *Les Noces de Pierrette, 1905*, **Pablo Picasso**, Binoche et Godeau, Paris, 30 Nov 1989	33,123,028 (F.Fr315,000,000)
7 *Irises*, **Vincent van Gogh**, Sotheby's, New York, 11 Nov 1987	28,000,000 ($49,000,000)
8 *Femme Assise dans un Jardin*, **Pablo Picasso**, Sotheby's, New York, 10 Nov 1999	27,950,310 ($45,000,000)
9 *Self Portrait: Yo Picasso*, **Pablo Picasso**, Sotheby's, New York, 9 May 1989	26,687,116 ($43,500,000)
10 *Le Rêve*, **Pablo Picasso**, Christie's, New York, 10 Nov 1997	26,035,502 ($44,000,000)

RAGS TO RICHES

The impoverished van Gogh painted this self-portrait, Portrait de l'Artiste sans Barbe, *at Arles in September 1888. Just over a century later, it realized $65 million, making it the third most expensive painting ever sold at auction.*

TOP 10 ⭐

ARTISTS WITH THE MOST WORKS SOLD AT AUCTION FOR MORE THAN £1 MILLION

ARTIST	TOTAL VALUE OF WORKS SOLD (£)	NO. OF WORKS SOLD
1 Pablo Picasso (Spanish; 1881–1973)	746,493,190	190
2 Claude Monet (French; 1840–1926)	643,542,465	164
3 Pierre Auguste Renoir (French; 1841–1919)	317,773,737	109
4 Edgar Degas (French; 1834–1917)	153,078,886	59
5 Paul Cézanne (French; 1839–1906)	237,412,086	56
6 Amedeo Modigliani (Italian; 1884–1920)	164,671,253	52
7 Vincent van Gogh (Dutch; 1853–90)	319,930,295	45
8 Henri Matisse (French; 1869–1954)	138,809,240	44
9 Camille Pissaro (French; 1830–1903)	52,410,284	35
10 Paul Gauguin (French; 1848–1903)	88,246,022	30

TOP 10 ⭐

MOST EXPENSIVE PIECES OF SCULPTURE EVER SOLD AT AUCTION

SCULPTURE/ARTIST/SALE	PRICE (£)
1 *Grande Femme Debout I*, **Alberto Giacometti** (Swiss; 1901–66), Christie's Rockefeller, New York, 8 Nov 2000	9,090,910 ($13,000,000)
2 *La Serpentine Femme à la Stèle – l'Araignée*, **Henri Matisse** (French; 1869–1954), Sotheby's, New York, 10 May 2000	8,443,709 ($12,750,000)
3 *Petite Danseuse de Quatorze Ans*, **Edgar Degas**, (French; 1834–1917), Sotheby's, London, 27 June 2000	7,000,000
4 *Petite Danseuse de Quatorze Ans*, **Edgar Degas**, Sotheby's, New York, 11 Nov 1999	6,987,578 ($11,250,000)
5 *Petite Danseuse de Quatorze Ans*, **Edgar Degas**, Sotheby's, New York, 12 Nov 1996	6,506,024 ($10,800,000)
6 *The Dancing Faun*, **Adriaen de Vries**, (Dutch; c.1550–1626), Sotheby's, London, 7 Dec 1989	6,200,000
7 *Nu Couché, Aurore*, **Henri Matisse**, Christie's Rockefeller, New York, 9 Nov 1999	5,217,392 ($8,400,000)
8 *Petite Danseuse de Quatorze Ans*, **Edgar Degas**, Christie's, New York, 14 November 1988	5,082,418 ($9,250,000)
9 *Petite Danseuse de Quatorze Ans*, **Edgar Degas**, Sotheby's, New York, 10 May 1988	4,893,617 ($9,200,000)
10 *La Muse Endormie III*, **Constantin Brancusi** (Romanian; 1876–1957), Christie's, New York, 14 Nov 1989	4,838,710 ($7,500,000)

What is the most expensive item of pop memorabilia ever sold at auction?
see p.125 for the answer

A A guitar
B A dress
C A car

TOP 10 ★

MOST EXPENSIVE OLD MASTER PAINTINGS EVER SOLD AT AUCTION

PAINTING/ARTIST/SALE	PRICE (£)

1 *Portrait of Duke Cosimo I de Medici*, **Jacopo da Carucci (Pontormo)** (Italian; 1493–1558), Christie's, New York, 31 May 1989 — 20,253,164 ($32,000,000)

2 *The Old Horse Guards, London, from St. James's Park*, **Canaletto** (Italian; 1697–1768), Christie's, London, 15 Apr 1992 — 9,200,000

3 *Vue de la Giudecca et du Zattere à Venise*, **Francesco Guardi** (Italian; 1712–93), Sotheby's, Monaco, 1 Dec 1989 — 8,937,960 (F.Fr85,000,000)

4 *Le Retour du Bucentaure le Jour de l'Ascension*, **Canaletto**, Ader Tajan, Paris, 15 Dec 1993 — 7,594,937 (F.Fr66,000,000)

5 = *Tieleman Roosterman in Black Doublet, White Ruff*, **Frans Hals the Elder** (Dutch; c.1580–1666), Christie's, London, 8 July 1999 — 7,500,000

= *Adoration of the Magi*, **Andrea Mantegna** (Italian; 1431–1506), Christie's, London, 18 Apr 1985 — 7,500,000

7 *The Risen Christ*, **Michelangelo** (Italian; 1475–1564), Christie's, London, 4 July 2000 — 7,400,000

8 *Venus and Adonis*, **Titian** (Italian; c.1488–1576), Christie's, London, 13 Dec 1991 — 6,800,000

9 *Portrait of a Girl Wearing a Gold-trimmed Cloak*, **Rembrandt** (Dutch; 1606–69), Sotheby's, London, 10 Dec 1986 — 6,600,000

10 *View of Molo from Bacino di San Marco, Venice* and *View of the Grand Canal Facing East from Campo di Santi, Venice* (pair), **Canaletto**, Sotheby's, New York, 1 June 1990 — 5,988,024 ($10,000,000)

PRICEY PRE-RAPHAELITE

Although popular in their day, the Pre-Raphaelites fell out of favour until the late 20th century, when works such as Sleeping *by Sir John Everett Millais began to command record prices.*

TOP 10 ★

MOST EXPENSIVE PRE-RAPHAELITE PAINTINGS EVER SOLD AT AUCTION

PAINTING/ARTIST*/SALE	PRICE (£)

1 *St. Cecilia*, **John William Waterhouse** (1849–1917), Christie's, London, 14 June 2000 — 6,000,000

2 *Pandora*, **Dante Gabriel Rossetti** (1828–82), Christie's, London, 14 June 2000 — 2,400,000

3 *Sleeping*, **Sir John Everett Millais** (1829–96), Christie's, London, 10 June 1999 — 1,900,000

4 *The Shadow of Death*, **William Holman Hunt**, (1827–1910), Sotheby's, London, 2 Nov 1994 — 1,700,000

5 *Ophelia*, **John William Waterhouse**, Phillips, London, 14 June 2000 — 1,500,000

6 *Proserpine*, **Dante Gabriel Rossetti**, Christie's, London, 27 Nov 1987 — 1,300,000

7 *The Awakening of Adonis*, **John William Waterhouse**, Sotheby's, New York, 10 Nov 1998 — 1,280,121 ($2,125,000)

8= *Val d'Aosta*, **John Brett** (1830–1902), Sotheby's, London, 20 June 1989 — 1,200,000

= *Joan of Arc*, **Sir John Everett Millais**, Sotheby's, London, 10 Nov 1999 — 1,200,000

10 *Master Hilary – The Tracer*, **William Holman Hunt**, Christie's, London, 3 June 1994 — 880,000

* All British

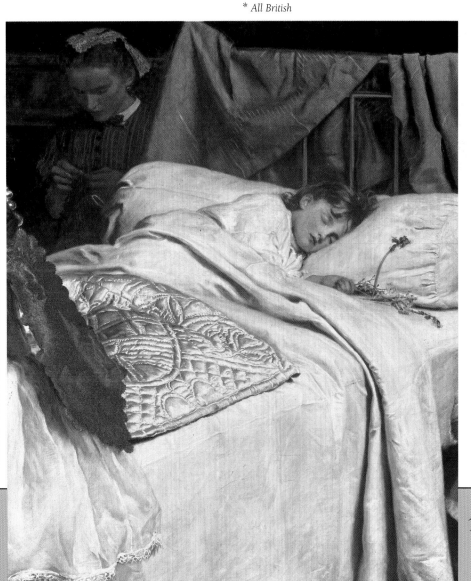

20th-Century Artists

MOST EXPENSIVE WORKS
BY ALEXANDER CALDER

MOBILE OR SCULPTURE/SALE	PRICE (£)
1 **Brazilian Fish**, Sotheby's, New York, 17 Nov 1999	2,204,969 ($3,550,000)
2 **The Tree**, Selkirks, St. Louis, 22 May 1989	1,202,532 ($1,900,000)
3 **Constellation**, Sotheby's, New York, 10 Nov 1993	1,114,865 ($1,650,000)
4 **Constellation**, Sotheby's, New York, 18 May 1999	1,111,111 ($1,800,000)
5 **Trépied**, Sotheby's, New York, 18 May 1999	864,198 ($1,400,000)
6 **Mobile au Plomb**, Christie's, London, 28 June 2000	720,000
7 **Eighteen Numbered Black**, Sotheby's, New York, 17 Nov 1998	696,970 ($1,150,000)
8 **Haverford Monster**, Sotheby's, New York, 4 May 1994	657,718 ($980,000)
9 **Laocoon**, Christie's, New York, 14 Nov 1995	580,645 ($900,000)
10 **Hanging Apricot**, Christie's Rockefeller, New York, 13 May 1999	555,556 ($900,000)

MOST EXPENSIVE PAINTINGS
BY PABLO PICASSO

PAINTING/SALE	PRICE (£)
1 **Femme aux Bras Croisés**, Christie's Rockefeller, New York, 8 Nov 2000	34,965,036 ($50,000,000)
2 **Les Noces de Pierrette, 1905**, Binoche et Godeau, Paris, 30 Nov 1989	33,123,028 (F.Fr315,000,000)
3 **Femme Assise dans un Jardin**, Sotheby's, New York, 10 Nov 1999	27,950,310 ($45,000,000)
4 **Self Portrait: Yo Picasso**, Sotheby's, New York, 9 May 1989	26,687,116 ($43,500,000)
5 **Le Rêve**, Christie's, New York, 10 Nov 1997	26,035,502 ($44,000,000)
6 **Nu au Fauteuil Noir**, Christie's Rockefeller, New York, 9 Nov 1999	25,465,838 ($41,000,000)
7 **Au Lapin Agile**, Sotheby's, New York, 15 Nov 1989	23,870,968 ($37,000,000)
8 **Acrobate et Jeune Arlequin**, Christie's, London, 28 Nov 1988	19,000,000
9 **Nature Morte aux Tulipes**, Christie's Rockefeller, New York, 9 May 2000	17,218,544 ($26,000,000)
10 **Les Femmes d'Alger, Version O**, Christie's, New York, 10 Nov 1997	17,159,762 ($29,000,000)

MOST EXPENSIVE PAINTINGS
BY LUCIAN FREUD

PAINTING/SALE	PRICE (£)
1 **Large Interior, W11**, Sotheby's, New York, 14 May 1998	3,271,605 ($5,300,000)
2 **Naked Portrait with Reflection**, Sotheby's, London, 9 Dec 1998	2,550,000
3 **Painter's Mother**, Sotheby's, New York, 18 May 1999	1,851,852 ($3,000,000)
4 **Evening in the Studio**, Sotheby's, New York, 17 Nov 1999	1,366,460 ($2,200,000)
5 **Man in Headscarf**, Christie's, London, 30 June 1999	1,050,000
6 **Portrait of Frank Auerbach**, Sotheby's, London, 3 Dec 1998	830,000
7 **John Deakin**, Christie's, London, 25 June 1997	810,000
8 **Man Smoking**, Sotheby's, London 28 June 1990	600,000
9 **The Painter's Room**, Sotheby's, London, 29 June 1994	460,000
10 **Naked Man on Bed**, Sotheby's, New York, 17 Nov 1998	363,636 ($600,000)

MOST EXPENSIVE PAINTINGS
BY MARC CHAGALL

PAINTING/SALE	PRICE (£)
1 **Anniversaire**, Sotheby's, New York, 17 May 1990	7,988,166 ($13,500,000)
2 **Au Dessus de la Ville**, Christie's, New York, 15 May 1990	5,325,444 ($9,000,000)
3 **Le Village Russe de la Lune**, Sotheby's, New York, 11 Nov 1999	4,658,385 ($7,500,000)
4 **La Mariée sous le Baldaquin**, Sotheby's, London, 3 Apr 1990	3,400,000
5 **La Chambre Jaune**, Christie's Rockefeller, New York, 9 Nov 1999	3,105,590 ($5,000,000)
6 **Le Bouquet des Fermiers**, Sotheby's, London, 3 April 1990	2,800,000
7 **Two Bouquets**, Sotheby's, New York, 17 May 1990	2,603,550 ($4,400,000)
8 **Le Violoniste au Monde Renversé**, Habsburg, New York, 8 May 1989	2,576,687 ($4,200,000)
9 **Le Buveur – Le Saoul**, Christie's, New York, 14 Nov 1990	2,538,070 ($5,000,000)
10 **Les Amoureux**, Sotheby's, London, 24 June 1996	2,500,000

Did You Know? Alexander Calder's *White Cascade* mobile, installed in Philadelphia, Pennsylvania, in 1976, is one of the biggest works of art ever constructed: it is 30.5 m (100 ft) tall and weighs 8 tonnes.

TOP 10 ★
MOST EXPENSIVE PAINTINGS BY FRANCIS BACON

PAINTING/SALE	PRICE (£)
1 *Triptych May–June*, Sotheby's, New York, 2 May 1989	3,433,735 ($5,700,000)
2 *Study for Pope*, Christie's, New York, 7 Nov 1989	3,291,139 ($5,200,000)
3 *Study for Portrait of van Gogh II*, Sotheby's, New York, 2 May 1989	3,192,770 ($5,300,000)
4 *Study for Portrait*, Sotheby's, New York, 8 May 1990	2,976,190 ($5,000,000)
5 *Study for a Portrait – Man Screaming*, Christie's, London, 28 June 2000	2,700,000
6 *Portrait of Lucian Freud*, Sotheby's, New York, 8 Nov 1989	1,964,286 ($3,300,000)
7 *Turning Figure*, Sotheby's, New York, 8 Nov 1989	1,898,734 ($3,000,000)
8 *Study for Portrait VIII, 1953*, Sotheby's, London, 5 Dec 1991	1,800,000
9 *Portrait of George Dyer Staring into Mirror*, Christie's, New York, 7 Nov 1990	1,785,714 ($3,500,000)
10 *Studies for Self-Portrait*, Christie's, London, 30 June 1999	1,700,000

TOP 10 ★
MOST EXPENSIVE WORKS BY JASPER JOHNS

WORK/SALE	PRICE (£)
1 *False Start*, Sotheby's, New York, 10 Nov 1988	8,611,112 ($15,500,000)
2 *Two Flags*, Christie's Rockefeller, New York, 13 May 1999	4,012,346 ($6,500,000)
3 *Jubilee*, Sotheby's, New York, 13 Nov 1991	2,513,967 ($4,500,000)
4 *Device Circle*, Christie's, New York, 12 Nov 1991	2,234,637 ($4,000,000)
5 *Alphabets*, Sotheby's, New York, 2 May 1989	1,566,265 ($2,600,000)
6 *0 Through 9*, Christie's, New York, 18 Nov 1992	1,390,729 ($2,100,000)
7 *Double Flag*, Sotheby's, New York, 11 Dec 1986	1,118,880 ($1,600,000)
8 *Screen Piece II*, Sotheby's, New York, 10 Nov 1988	694,444 ($1,250,000)
9 *Screen Piece No. 3, The Sonnets*, Sotheby's, New York, 1 Nov 1994	375,000 ($600,000)
10 *Untitled*, Christie's, New York, 4 May 1993	359,477 ($550,000)

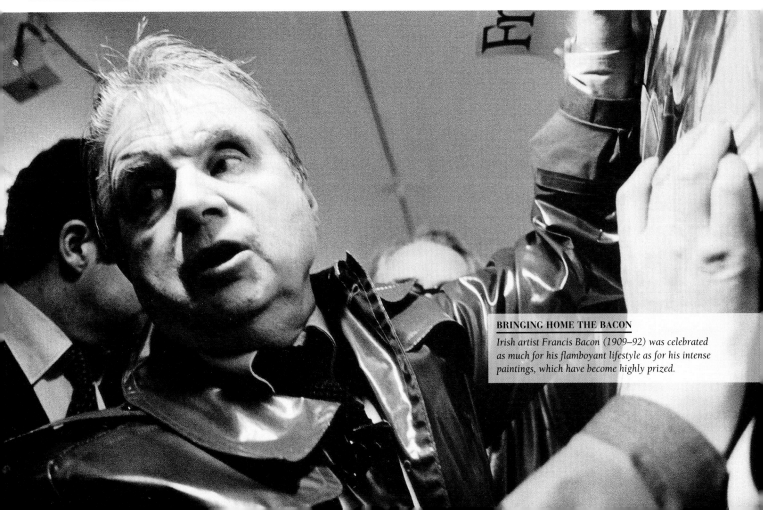

BRINGING HOME THE BACON

Irish artist Francis Bacon (1909–92) was celebrated as much for his flamboyant lifestyle as for his intense paintings, which have become highly prized.

Women Artists

GEORGIA ON MY MIND

Georgia O'Keeffe (1887–1986), who specialized in richly coloured paintings of plants and natural forms, is ranked high in the pantheon of 20th-century American painters.

TOP 10 ★
MOST EXPENSIVE PAINTINGS BY FRIDA KAHLO

	PAINTING/SALE	PRICE (£)
1	*Autoretrato con Chango y Loro*, Sotheby's, New York, 17 May 1995	1,847,134 ($2,900,000)
2	*Autorretrato con Pelo Suelto*, Christie's, New York, 15 May 1991	872,093 ($1,500,000)
3	*Diego and I*, Sotheby's, New York, 2 May 1990	783,133 ($1,300,000)
4	*Los Cuatro Habitantes de Mexico*, Sotheby's, New York, 14 May 1996	529,801 ($800,000)
5	*Recuerdo*, Christie's, New York, 18 May 1992	469,613 ($850,000)
6	*Parade in a Street in Detroit*, Gary Nader, Miami, 23 Jan 2000	460,123 ($750,000)
7	*La Tierra Misma o Dos Desnudos en la Jungla*, Christie's, New York, 21 Nov 1989	294,872 ($460,000)
8	*What the Water Gave Me*, Sotheby's, New York, 29 Nov 1983	160,959 ($235,000)
9	*Moses*, Sotheby's, New York, 26 Nov 1985	143,835 ($210,000)
10	*Ella Juega Sola o Nina con Mascara de la Muerte*, Christie's, New York, 21 Nov 1989	141,026 ($220,000)

Mexican painter Frida Kahlo (1907–54) overcame disabilities resulting from childhood polio and a road accident to become a talented artist whose work was much revered by the Surrealists. She was married to the artist Diego Rivera, and their turbulent life together (they divorced in 1939 and married again the following year) and Kahlo's personal joys and suffering are revealed in her vivid, often autobiographical paintings.

TOP 10 ★
MOST EXPENSIVE PAINTINGS BY GEORGIA O'KEEFFE

	PAINTING/SALE	PRICE (£)
1	*From the Plains*, Sotheby's, New York, 3 Dec 1997	2,000,000 ($3,300,000)
2	*Calla Lily with Red Roses*, Sotheby's, New York, 20 May 1998	1,472,393 ($2,400,000)
3	*Black Hollyhocks with Blue Larkspur*, Sotheby's, New York, 3 Dec 1987	1,046,512 ($1,800,000)
4	*Dark Iris, No. 2*, Sotheby's, New York, 24 May 1989	949,367 ($1,500,000)
5	*At the Rodeo, New Mexico*, Sotheby's, New York, 3 Dec 1987	831,395 ($1,430,000)
6	*White Rose, New Mexico*, Sotheby's, New York, 5 Dec 1985	771,812 ($1,150,000)
7	*Yellow Cactus Flowers*, Sotheby's, New York, 24 May 1989	759,494 ($1,200,000)
8	*Ritz Tower, Night*, Christie's, New York, 4 Dec 1992	696,203 ($1,100,000)
9	*Cow's Skull on Red*, Christie's, New York, 30 Nov 1994	645,161 ($1,000,000)
10	*Two Jimson Weeds*, Sotheby's, New York, 3 Dec 1987	639,535 ($1,100,000)

TOP 10 ★
MOST EXPENSIVE SCULPTURES BY DAME BARBARA HEPWORTH

	SCULPTURE/SALE	PRICE (£)
1	*Family of Man, Ultimate Form*, Sotheby's, New York, 11 May 2000	278,146 ($420,000)
2	*Concoid, Sphere and Hollow II*, Sotheby's, London, 25 June 1997	205,000
3	*Musician*, Christie's, London, 23 Oct 1996	185,000
4	*Two Segments and Sphere*, Sotheby's, New York, 11 Nov 1999	161,491 ($260,000)
5 =	*Sculpture with Colour, Oval Form, Pale Blue and Red*, Christie's, London, 1 July 1998	160,000
=	*Sunlon*, Christie's, London, 1 July 1998	160,000
7	*Sea Form, Atlantic*, Christie's, New York, 13 May 1998	141,975 ($230,000)
8	*The Family of Man, Figure 1, Ancestor 1*, Sotheby's, New York, 14 May 1992	136,612 ($250,000)
9	*Rock Form – Porthcurno*, Sotheby's, New York, 12 May 1993	120,915 ($185,000)
10	*Three Part Vertical*, Sotheby's, London, 31 Mar 1987	95,000

Did You Know? In 1947, Madame Claude Latour was convicted of producing forgeries of paintings by Pablo Picasso and Maurice Utrillo that were so skilful that Utrillo himself could not tell which were his and which she had painted.

TOP 10 ★

MOST EXPENSIVE PAINTINGS BY BERTHE MORISOT

PAINTING/SALE	PRICE (£)
1 *Cache-cache*, Sotheby's, New York, 9 Nov 2000	2,797,203 ($4,000,000)
2 *Cache-cache*, Sotheby's, New York, 10 May 1999	2,160,494 ($3,500,000)
3 *Après le Déjeuner*, Christie's, New York, 14 May 1997	1,993,865 ($3,250,000)
4 *La Femme au Gant, ou La Parisienne*, Sotheby's, New York, 16 Nov 1998	909,091 ($1,500,000)
5 *Derrière la Jalousie*, Sotheby's, New York, 10 May 2000	794,702 ($1,200,000)
6 *Le Thé*, Sotheby's, New York, 9 May 1995	732,484 ($1,150,000)
7 *Derrière la Jalousie*, Christie's, New York, 5 May 1998	674,847 ($1,100,000)
8 *Fillettes à la Fenêtre, Jeanne et Edma Bodeau*, Christie's, New York, 11 Nov 1997	650,888 ($1,100,000)
9 *Julie Manet à la Perruche*, Sotheby's, New York, 17 May 1990	562,130 ($950,000)
10 *La Leçon au Jardin*, Christie's, New York, 10 May 1989	552,147 ($900,000)

Berthe Morisot (1841–95) was a French Impressionist painter who was closely associated with the leading figures in the movement (and married to Manet's brother). Landscapes and women and children chiefly feature in her work, which has commanded escalating prices in the world's salerooms.

THERE'S SOMETHING ABOUT MARY

Five paintings by Mary Cassatt, including her Mother, Sara and the Baby, *are numbered among the 10 highest priced paintings by a woman.*

TOP 10 ★

MOST EXPENSIVE PAINTINGS BY WOMEN ARTISTS EVER SOLD AT AUCTION

PAINTING/ARTIST/SALE	PRICE (£)
1 *Cache-cache*, Berthe Morisot (French; 1841–95), Sotheby's, New York, 9 Nov 2000	2,797,203 ($4,000,000)
2 *In the Box*, Mary Cassatt (American; 1844–1926), Christie's, New York, 23 May 1996	2,450,331 ($3,700,000)
3 *The Conversation*, Mary Cassatt, Christie's, New York, 11 May 1988	2,180,850 ($4,100,000)
4 *Cache-cache*, Berthe Morisot, Sotheby's, New York, 10 May 1999	2,160,494 ($3,500,000)
5 *Mother, Sara and the Baby*, Mary Cassatt, Christie's, New York, 10 May 1989	2,147,239 ($3,500,000)
6 *From the Plains*, Georgia O'Keeffe (American; 1887–1986), Sotheby's, New York, 3 Dec 1997	2,000,000 ($3,300,000)
7 *Après le Déjeuner*, Berthe Morisot, Christie's, New York, 14 May 1997	1,993,865 ($3,250,000)
8 *Autoretrato con Chango y Loro*, Frida Kahlo (Mexican; 1907–54), Sotheby's, New York, 17 May 1995	1,847,134 ($2,900,000)
9 *Augusta Reading to Her Daughter*, Mary Cassatt, Sotheby's, New York, 9 May 1989	1,717,790 ($2,800,000)
10 *Children Playing with Cat*, Mary Cassatt, Sotheby's, New York, 3 Dec 1998	1,626,506 ($2,700,000)

Objects of Desire

TOP 10 ★
MOST EXPENSIVE ITEMS OF ENGLISH FURNITURE

ITEM/SALE	PRICE (£)
1 *The Anglesey Desk*, Regency bronze-mounted and brass-inlaid ebony and mahogany library desk, attributed to Marsh & Tatbam, Christie's, London, 8 July 1993	1,761,500
2 *The Dundas Armchairs*, pair of George III giltwood armchairs, designed by Robert Adam and made by Thomas Chippendale, Christie's, London, 3 July 1997	1,706,500
3 *The Warwick Tables*, supplied to Queen Anne for St. James's Palace in 1704–5, by Gerrit Jensen, probably in association with Thomas Pelletier, Sotheby's, London, 10 July 1998	1,651,500
4 *The Dundas Sofas*, pair of George III giltwood sofas designed by Robert Adam and made by Thomas Chippendale, Christie's, London, 3 July 1997	1,541,500
5 *The Lonsdale Langlois Commode*, a George III ormolu-mounted rosewood, fruitwood, and marquetry bombe commode, Christie's, New York, 24 Nov 1998	1,519,500 ($2,532,500)
6 *The St. Giles's Dining-Chairs*, set of seventeen George II mahogany dining chairs, attributed to William Hallett Senior, Christie's, London, 8 July 1999	1,211,500
7 A George II ormolu-mounted mahogany dressing and writing commode, attributed to John Channon, Christie's, London, 6 July 1989	1,100,000
8 A pair of George II mahogany commodes, attributed to Vile and Cobb, Sotheby's, London, 18 Nov 1993	991,500
9 *The Stowe Apollo Tables*, pair of George II gilt-gesso side tables, attributed to Benjamin Goodison, Christie's, London, 9 July 1998	936,500
10 A George III mahogany commode, attributed to Thomas Chippendale, Christie's, London, 5 Dec 1991	936,000

TOP 10 ★
MOST EXPENSIVE PRINTS

PRINT/ARTIST/SALE	PRICE (£)
1 *Diehard*, **Robert Rauschenberg** (American; 1925–), Sotheby's, New York, 2 May 1989	963,855 ($1,600,000)
2 *Mao*, **Andy Warhol** (American; 1928–87), Sotheby's, London, 26 June 1996	610,000
3 *Elles**, **Henri de Toulouse-Lautrec** (French; 1864–1901), Sotheby's, New York, 10 May 1999	493,097 ($800,000)
4 *Famille Tahitienne*, **Paul Gauguin** (French; 1848–1903), Francis Briest, Paris, 4 Dec 1998	486,097 (F.Fr4,545,010)
5 *Glider*, **Robert Rauschenberg**, Christie's, New York, 14 Nov 1995	483,871 ($750,000)
6 *The Kiss – Bela Lugosi*, **Andy Warhol**, Christies Rockefeller, New York, 9 May 2000	476,821 ($720,000)
7 *Elles**, **Henri de Toulouse-Lautrec**, Sotheby's, New York, 7 Nov 1997	411,243 ($695,000)
8= *La Suite Vollard*, **Pablo Picasso** (Spanish; 1881–1973), Christie's, New York, 2 Nov 1999	401,235 ($650,000)
= *Suicide*, **Andy Warhol**, Sotheby's, New York, 18 May 1999	401,235 ($650,000)
10 *Les Saltimbanques*, **Pablo Picasso**, Sotheby's, New York, 3 May 1996	400,000 ($600,000)

* A collection of 10 lithographs

Included within the classification of prints are silkscreens, lithographs, monotypes, aquatints, woodcuts, engravings, and etchings.

TOP 10 ★
MOST EXPENSIVE PHOTOGRAPHS

PHOTOGRAPH/PHOTOGRAPHER/SALE	PRICE (£)
1 *The North American Indian** (1907–30), **Edward S. Curtis** (American; 1868–1952), Sotheby's, New York, 7 Oct 1993	441,519 ($662,500)
2 *Egypte et Nubie: Sites et monuments les plus intéressants pour l'étude de l'art et de l'histoire** (1858), **Félix Teynard** (French; 1817–92), Laurin Guilloux Buffetaud Tailleur, Paris, 21 Dec 1990	377,469 (F.Fr3,700,000)
3 *Noire et Blanche* (1926), **Man Ray** (American; 1890–1976), Christie's, New York, 4 Oct 1998	363,076 ($607,500)
4 *Light Trap for Henry Moore No. 1*, **Bruce Nauman** (American; 1941–), Sotheby's, New York, 17 May 2000	324,324 ($480,000)
5 *The North American Indian** (1907–30), **Edward S. Curtis**, Christie's, New York, 6 Apr 1995	299,194 ($464,500)
6 *Georgia O'Keeffe: A Portrait – Hands with Thimble* (1930), **Alfred Stieglitz** (American; 1864–1946), Christie's, New York, 8 Oct 1993	265,578 ($398,500)
7 *Equivalents (21)** (1920s), **Alfred Stieglitz**, Christie's, New York, 30 Oct 1989	254,826 ($396,000)
8 *Arrival of the Body of Admiral Bruat and Flagship Montebello at Toulon* (1855), **Gustave le Gray** (French; 1820–82), Bearnes, Exeter, 6 May 2000	250,000
9 *Mondrian's Pipe and Glasses* (1926), **André Kertész** (Hungarian–American; 1894–1985), Christie's, New York, 17 April 1997	237,464 ($376,500)
10 *Noire et Blanche* (1926), **Man Ray**, Christie's, New York, 21 Apr 1994	229,479 ($354,500)

* Collections; all others are single prints

LENNON'S LIMO
Repainted in 1967, John Lennon's Rolls-Royce was eventually donated to Queen Elizabeth and is preserved by the Royal British Columbia Museum in Victoria, British Columbia.

TOP 10 ★
MOST EXPENSIVE MUSICAL INSTRUMENTS

INSTRUMENT*/SALE	PRICE (£)
1 John Lennon's Steinway Model Z upright piano (on which he composed *Imagine*), teak veneered, complete with cigarette burns, Fleetwood-Owen online auction, Hard Rock Café, London and New York, 17 Oct 2000	1,450,000
2 "Kreutzer" violin by Antonio Stradivari, Christie's, London, 1 April 1998	946,000
3 "Cholmondeley" violincello by Antonio Stradivari, Sotheby's, London, 22 June 1998	682,000
4 "Brownie", one of Eric Clapton's favourite guitars, Christie's, New York, 24 June 1999	313,425 ($497,500)

Clapton used the 1956 sunburst Fender to record his definitive guitar track, Layla. It was sold to an anonymous telephone bidder for double the expected price, making it the most expensive guitar ever bought at auction.

5 Jimi Hendrix's Fender *Stratocaster* electric guitar, Sotheby's, London, 25 April 1990	198,000
6 Double bass by Domenico Montagnana, Sotheby's, London, 16 Mar 1999	155,500
7 Viola by Giovanni Paolo Maggini, Christie's, London, 20 Nov 1984	129,000
8 Verne Powell's platinum flute, Christie's, New York, 18 Oct 1986	126,200 ($187,000)
9 English double-manual harpsichord by Burkat Shudi and John Broadwood, Sotheby's, London, 27 Oct 1999	106,000
10 Bundfrei clavichord by Marcus Gabriel Sondermann, late 18th/early 19th century, Sotheby's, London, 16 Nov 2000	20,625

* *Most expensive example only for each category of instrument*

TOP 10 ★
MOST EXPENSIVE ITEMS OF POP MEMORABILIA

ITEM/SALE	PRICE (£)*
1 John Lennon's 1965 Rolls-Royce Phantom V touring limousine, finished in psychedelic paintwork, Sotheby's, New York, 29 June 1985	1,768,462 ($2,299,000)
2 John Lennon's Steinway Model Z upright piano (on which he composed *Imagine*), teak veneered, complete with cigarette burns, Fleetwood-Owen online auction, Hard Rock Café, London and New York, 17 Oct 2000	1,450,000
3 "Brownie", one of Eric Clapton's favourite guitars (on which he recorded *Layla*), Christie's, New York, 24 June 1999	313,425 ($497,500)
4 Bernie Taupin's handwritten lyrics for the rewritten *Candle in the Wind*, Christie's, Los Angeles, 11 Feb 1998	278,512 ($400,000)
5 Jimi Hendrix's Fender *Stratocaster* electric guitar, which he played at Woodstock in 1969, Sotheby's, London, 25 Apr 1990	198,000
6 Paul McCartney's handwritten lyrics for *Getting Better*, 1967, Sotheby's, London, 14 Sep 1995	161,000
7 Buddy Holly's Gibson acoustic guitar, *c*.1945, in a tooled leather case made by Holly, Sotheby's, New York, 23 June 1990	139,658 ($242,000)
8 John Lennon's 1970 Mercedes-Benz 600 Pullman four-door limousine, Christie's, London, 27 Apr 1989	137,500
9 John Lennon's 1965 Ferrari 330 GT 2+2 two-door coupé, right-hand drive, Fleetwood-Owen online auction, Hard Rock Café, London and New York, 17 Oct 2000	130,000
10 Mal Evan's notebook, compiled 1967–68, which includes a draft by Paul McCartney of the lyrics for *Hey Jude*, Sotheby's, London, 15 Sep 1998	111,500

* *Including 10 per cent buyer's premium, where appropriate*

What was the nationality of the painter Frida Kahlo?
see p.122 for the answer
A Russian
B Mexican
C Swedish

MUSIC & MUSICIANS

Popular Songs

TOP 10 ⭐
UK HITS COMPOSED BY BOB DYLAN

TITLE	CHARTING ARTIST(S)
1 Knockin' on Heaven's Door	Eric Clapton, Bob Dylan, Guns N' Roses
2 Mr. Tambourine Man	Byrds
3 Mighty Quinn (Quinn the Eskimo)	Manfred Mann
4 If You Gotta Go, Go Now	Manfred Mann*
5 All I Really Want to Do	Byrds, Cher
6 All Along the Watchtower	Jimi Hendrix Experience (twice)
7 Like a Rolling Stone	Bob Dylan
8 Blowin' in the Wind	Peter, Paul & Mary, Stevie Wonder
9 Lay Lady Lay	Bob Dylan
10 I'll Be Your Baby Tonight	Robert Palmer & UB40

* Fairport Convention also had a hit in 1969 with a French version of the song, Si Tu Dois Partir

The strength of Dylan's songs is demonstrated by the wide variety of acts that have succeeded with cover versions from his catalogue.

TOP 10 ⭐
UK HITS COMPOSED BY BRUCE SPRINGSTEEN

TITLE	CHARTING ARTIST(S)
1 Dancing in the Dark	Big Daddy, Bruce Springsteen
2 Streets of Philadelphia	Bruce Springsteen
3 Because the Night	Patti Smith Group
4 Pink Cadillac	Natalie Cole
5 I'm on Fire/ Born in the USA	Bruce Springsteen
6 Blinded by the Light	Manfred Mann's Earth Band
7 Cover Me	Bruce Springsteen (twice)
8 My Hometown	Bruce Springsteen
9 Tougher Than the Rest	Bruce Springsteen
10 Human Touch	Bruce Springsteen

TOP 10 KARAOKE TUNES

1. You've Lost That Lovin' Feelin' 2. I Will Survive 3. Like a Virgin 4. Summer Nights 5. Love Shack 6. New York, New York 7. Pretty Woman 8. Should I Stay or Should I Go 9. It's Not Unusual 10. My Way

TOP 10 ⭐
UK HITS COMPOSED BY PRINCE

TITLE	CHARTING ARTIST(S)
1 Nothing Compares 2 U	Sinead O'Connor
2 I Feel For You	Chaka Khan (twice)
3 Kiss	Age of Chance, Art of Noise featuring Tom Jones, Prince & the Revolution
4 1999	Prince (three times)
5 Little Red Corvette	Prince (three times)
6 When Doves Cry/Pray*	MC Hammer, Prince
7 The Most Beautiful Girl in the World	Prince
8 Manic Monday	Bangles
9 Batdance	Prince
10 Purple Rain	Prince & the Revolution

* MC Hammer's hit Pray used the rhythm track from When Doves Cry

TOP 10 ⭐
UK HITS COMPOSED BY GEORGE MICHAEL

TITLE	CHARTING ARTIST(S)
1 Last Christmas	Wham! (three times)
2 Careless Whisper	George Michael
3 Wake Me up Before You Go-Go	Wham!
4 Fastlove	George Michael
5 Freedom	Wham!
6 Jesus to a Child	George Michael
7 I'm Your Man	Wham!
8 Bad Boys	Wham!
9 A Different Corner	George Michael
10 Outside	George Michael

The million-plus selling Last Christmas was held off the top spot in December 1984 only by the unique sales of Band Aid's Do They Know It's Christmas?.

TOP 10 ⭐
UK HITS COMPOSED BY JOHN LENNON AND PAUL McCARTNEY

TITLE	CHARTING ARTIST(S)
1 She Loves You	The Beatles
2 I Want to Hold Your Hand	The Beatles
3 Can't Buy Me Love	The Beatles, Blackstreet, Ella Fitzgerald
4 I Feel Fine	The Beatles
5 We Can Work It Out	The Beatles, Stevie Wonder
6 Help!	Bananarama & La Nee Nee Noo Noo, The Beatles, Tina Turner
7 Day Tripper	The Beatles, Otis Redding
8 Hey Jude	The Beatles, Wilson Pickett
9 Let It Be	The Beatles, Ferry Aid
10 A Hard Day's Night	The Beatles, Peter Sellers

Yesterday, the most widely recorded Lennon and McCartney song of all, is missing from this list because virtually all of its hundreds of cover versions were album tracks not hit singles.

TOP 10 SINGER-SONGWRITERS IN THE UK

1. Elton John 2. Madonna 3. David Bowie 4. Stevie Wonder 5. Paul McCartney 6. Bryan Adams 7. Prince 8. George Michael 9. Kate Bush 10. John Lennon

These are the 10 artists who have had the highest UK singles sales with their own material. Most are self-contained singer-songwriters, although Elton John has used a variety of lyricists (most notably Bernie Taupin), and Madonna has collaborated on most of her hits. Paul McCartney's and John Lennon's joint compositions for the Beatles are not counted towards their rankings here.

TOP 10 ⭐
COUNTRIES WITH THE MOST WINS AT THE EUROVISION SONG CONTEST

COUNTRY	YEARS	WINS
1 Ireland	1970, 1980, 1987, 1992, 1993, 1994, 1996	7
2 =France	1958, 1960, 1962, 1969*, 1977	5
=Luxembourg	1961, 1965, 1972, 1973, 1983	5
=UK	1967, 1969*, 1976, 1981, 1997	5
5 =Netherlands	1957, 1959, 1969*, 1975	4
=Sweden	1974, 1984, 1991, 1999	4
7 Israel	1978, 1979, 1998	3
8 =Denmark	1963, 2000	2
=Italy	1964, 1990	2
=Norway	1984, 1995	2
=Spain	1968, 1969*	2
=Switzerland	1956, 1988	2

* All four countries tied as winners in 1969

The Eurovision Song Contest has been an annual event since its 24 May 1956 debut at Lugarno, Switzerland, which was won by Switzerland.

THE 10 ⭐
LATEST WINNERS OF THE Q MAGAZINE AWARD FOR CLASSIC SONGWRITER

YEAR	SONGWRITER(S)
2000	Guy Chambers and Robbie Williams
1999	Ian Dury and Chas Jankel
1998	Paul Weller
1997	Paul McCartney
1996	Elvis Costello
1995	Van Morrison
1994	Morissey
1993	Neil Finn
1992	U2
1991	Richard Thompson

TOP 10 ⭐
SONGWRITERS WITH THE MOST IVOR NOVELLO AWARDS

SONGWRITER	AWARDS
1 Paul McCartney	19
2 =John Lennon	14
=Andrew Lloyd Webber	14
4 Tim Rice	12
5 Elton John	11
6 =Barry Gibb	9
=Robin Gibb	9
8 =Matt Aitken	8
=Maurice Gibb	8
=Tony Macauley	8
=Mike Stock	8
=Bernie Taupin	8
=Pete Waterman	8

Source: *British Academy of Composers & Songwriters*

TOP 10 ⭐
MOST COVERED BEATLES SONGS

SONG	YEAR WRITTEN
1 Yesterday	1965
2 Eleanor Rigby	1966
3 Something	1969
4 Hey Jude	1968
5 Let It Be	1969
6 Michelle	1965
7 With a Little Help from My Friends	1967
8 Day Tripper	1965
9 Come Together	1969
10 The Long and Winding Road	1969

Yesterday is one of the most-covered songs of all time, with the number of recorded versions now in four figures. Although most of these songs are Lennon and McCartney compositions, the No. 3 song, *Something*, was written by George Harrison. *Hey Jude* and *Day Tripper* were both No. 1 hits.

TOP 10 ⭐
ROCK SONGS OF ALL TIME*

TITLE	ARTIST OR GROUP
1 (I Can't Get No) Satisfaction	The Rolling Stones
2 Respect	Aretha Franklin
3 Stairway to Heaven	Led Zeppelin
4 Like a Rolling Stone	Bob Dylan
5 Born to Run	Bruce Springsteen
6 Hotel California	The Eagles
7 Light My Fire	The Doors
8 Good Vibrations	The Beach Boys
9 Hey Jude	The Beatles
10 Imagine	John Lennon

* Determined by a panel of 700 voters assembled by the music network VH1

The all-time Top 100 list, from which this Top 10 is taken, is dominated by songs dating from the 1960s. Within it, there are no fewer than nine Beatles songs, as well as five by the Rolling Stones and three by Bob Dylan.

TOP 10 ⭐
SONGS REQUESTED AT FUNERALS

TITLE/ARTIST OR GROUP	YEAR RELEASED
1 My Heart Will Go On, Celine Dion	1998
2 Candle in the Wind, Elton John	1997
3 Wind Beneath My Wings, Bette Midler	1989
4 Search for the Hero, M People	1995
5 My Way, Frank Sinatra	1969
6 You'll Never Walk Alone, Gerry and the Pacemakers	1963
7 Release Me, Engelbert Humperdinck	1967
8 Memory, Elaine Paige	1981
9 Strangers in the Night, Frank Sinatra	1966
10 Bright Eyes, Art Garfunkel	1979

Who recorded the two "greatest hits" albums that are among the bestselling of all time in the UK?
see p.130 for the answer

A The Beatles and the Rolling Stones
B Michael Jackson and Elvis Presley
C Queen and Abba

Chart Hits

TOP 10 ★
ALBUMS OF 2000 IN THE UK

	ALBUM/ARTIST OR GROUP
1	*1*, The Beatles
2	*Sing When You're Winning*, Robbie Williams
3	*The Marshall Mathers LP*, Eminem
4	*Coast to Coast*, Westlife
5	*Play*, Moby
6	*Born to Do It*, Craig David
7	*The Greatest Hits*, Texas
8	*Parachutes*, Coldplay
9	*The Greatest Hits*, Whitney Houston
10	*Music*, Madonna

Source: *CIN*

TOP 10 ★
SINGLES THAT STAYED LONGEST IN THE UK CHARTS

	SINGLE/ARTIST OR GROUP/ FIRST CHART ENTRY	WEEKS IN CHARTS
1	*Release Me*, Engelbert Humperdinck, 1967	56
2	*Stranger on the Shore*, Mr. Acker Bilk, 1961	55
3	*Relax*, Frankie Goes to Hollywood, 1983	48
4	*My Way*, Frank Sinatra, 1969	47
5	*Rivers of Babylon/Brown Girl in the Ring*, Boney M, 1978	40
6 =	*I Love You Because*, Jim Reeves, 1964	39
=	*Tie a Yellow Ribbon Round the Old Oak Tree*, Dawn featuring Tony Orlando, 1973	39
8 =	*A Scottish Soldier*, Andy Stewart, 1961	38
=	*White Lines (Don't Don't Do It)*, Grandmaster Flash and Melle Mel, 1983	38
10	*Love is All Around*, Wet Wet Wet, 1994	37

Source: *The Popular Music Database*

BEAT ALL

Although disbanded over 30 years ago, the Beatles remain prominent in many all-time Top 10 lists and continue to achieve chart success in the 21st century.

TOP 10 ★
ALBUMS OF ALL TIME IN THE UK

	ALBUM/ARTIST OR GROUP	YEAR
1	*Sgt Pepper's Lonely Hearts Club Band*, The Beatles	1967
2	*(What's the Story) Morning Glory*, Oasis	1995
3	*Bad*, Michael Jackson	1987
4	*Brothers in Arms*, Dire Straits	1985
5	*Stars*, Simply Red	1991
6	*Thriller*, Michael Jackson	1982
7	*Greatest Hits (Volume One)*, Queen	1981
8	*Spice*, Spice Girls	1996
9	*Abba Gold Greatest Hits*, Abba	1990
10	*Come On Over*, Shania Twain	1998

Source: *BPI*

TOP 10 ★
ARTISTS WITH THE MOST CONSECUTIVE UK TOP 10 ALBUMS

	ARTIST OR GROUP	PERIOD	ALBUMS
1	Elvis Presley	Nov 1958–July 1964	17
2	Queen	Nov 1974–June 1989	14
3 =	David Bowie	May 1973–Jan 1981	13
=	The Rolling Stones	Apr 1964–May 1971	13
=	Madonna	Feb 1984–Oct 2000	13
6 =	Bob Dylan	May 1965–Nov 1970	12
=	Bob Dylan	Feb 1974–Nov 1983	12
=	Depeche Mode	Nov 1981–Oct 1998	12
9 =	Cliff Richard	Apr 1959–July 1964	11
=	Elton John	June 1972–Nov 1978	11
=	Led Zeppelin	Apr 1969–Oct 1990	11

Source: *The Popular Music Database*

TOP 10 ARTISTS WITH THE MOST WEEKS ON THE UK SINGLES CHART*

(Artist or group/total weeks)

1 Elvis Presley, 1,155 **2** Cliff Richard, 1,140 **3** Elton John, 566
4 Madonna, 546 **5** Michael Jackson, 479 **6** Rod Stewart, 466 **7** The Beatles, 456
8 David Bowie, 445 **9** Frank Sinatra, 440 **10** Diana Ross, 434

* As at 1 January 2001
Source: *The Popular Music Database*

CANDLE POWER

Elton John's Candle in the Wind 1997 *tribute to Princess Diana overtook* White Christmas, *the world's bestselling single for over 50 years.*

TOP 10 ★
SINGLES OF 2000 IN THE UK

SINGLE/ARTIST OR GROUP

1	*Can We Fix It*, Bob The Builder
2	*Pure Shores*, All Saints
3	*It Feels So Good*, Sonique
4	*Who Let the Dogs Out*, Baha Men
5	*Rock DJ*, Robbie Williams
6	*Stan*, Eminem
7	*Toca's Miracle*, Fragma
8	*Groove Jet (If This Ain't Love)*, Spiller
9	*Never Had a Dream Come True*, S Club 7
10	*Fill Me In*, Craig David

Source: *CIN*

An eclectic mix of singles in a variety of genres, from ballads to rap and the pervasive Ibiza sound, and performed by both established artists and newcomers, achieved chart success in the first year of the new millennium.

TOP 10 ★
YOUNGEST SINGERS OF ALL TIME IN THE UK SINGLES CHARTS

		HIGHEST CHART POSITION	AGE YRS	MTHS
ARTIST/SINGLE/YEAR				
1	Microbe (Ian Doody), *Groovy Baby*, 1969	29	3	0
2	Natalie Casey, *Chick Chick Chicken*, 1984	72	3	0
3	Little Jimmy Osmond, *Long Haired Lover from Liverpool*, 1974	1	9	7
4	Lena Zavaroni, *Ma He's Making Eyes at Me*, 1974	10	10	4
5	Neil Reid, *Mother of Mine*, 1972	2	11	0
6	Michael Jackson, *Got to Be There*, 1972	5	13	5
7	Laurie London, *He's Got the Whole World in His Hands*, 1957	12	13	9
8	Jimmy Boyd, *I Saw Mommy Kissing Santa Claus*, 1953	3	13	10
9	Marie Osmond, *Paper Roses*, 1973	2	14	1
10	Helen Shapiro, *Don't Treat Me Like a Child*, 1961	3	14	5

TOP 10 ★
SINGLES OF ALL TIME

	SINGLE/ARTIST OR GROUP/YEAR	SALES EXCEED
1	*Candle in the Wind (1997)/ Something About the Way You Look Tonight*, Elton John, 1997	37,000,000
2	*White Christmas*, Bing Crosby, 1945	30,000,000
3	*Rock Around the Clock*, Bill Haley and His Comets, 1954	17,000,000
4	*I Want to Hold Your Hand*, The Beatles, 1963	12,000,000
5=	*Hey Jude*, The Beatles, 1968	10,000,000
=	*It's Now or Never*, Elvis Presley, 1960	10,000,000
=	*I Will Always Love You*, Whitney Houston, 1993	10,000,000
8=	*Hound Dog/Don't Be Cruel*, Elvis Presley, 1956	9,000,000
=	*Diana*, Paul Anka, 1957	9,000,000
10=	*I'm a Believer*, The Monkees, 1966	8,000,000
=	*(Everything I Do) I Do it for You*, Bryan Adams, 1991	8,000,000

FENDER

Californian-born Leo Fender (1909–91) set up the Fender Electrical Instrument Company in 1946, launching the Broadcaster (later Telecaster) electric guitar in 1948. He then developed the solid-bodied, contoured, double cutaway *Stratocaster* (the "Strat"), with his patented tremolo, which first went on sale in 1954. It was immediately and enduringly popular with rock musicians from Buddy Holly to Eric Clapton and Jimi Hendrix. The Fender Company was sold for $13 million to CBS in 1965, but Fender continued designing guitars until his death.

WHO WAS • WHO WAS • WHO WAS • WHO WAS

After Elvis Presley, who has achieved the most weeks at UK No. 1?   A Madonna
see p.135 for the answer   B The Beatles
   C Cliff Richard

131

Record Firsts

THE 10 ★
FIRST UK CHART ALBUMS

THE KING

Elvis Presley's first two UK album successes featured in the earliest British album chart, which was published in 1958, the year he joined the army.

	ALBUM	ARTIST OR GROUP
1	South Pacific	Soundtrack
2	Come Fly With Me	Frank Sinatra
3	Elvis' Golden Records	Elvis Presley
4	King Creole	Elvis Presley
5	My Fair Lady	Broadway Cast
6	Warm	Johnny Mathis
7	The King and I	Soundtrack
8	Dear Perry	Perry Como
9	Oklahoma!	Soundtrack
10	Songs by Tom Lehrer	Tom Lehrer

Source: Melody Maker (8 November 1958)

THE 10 ★
FIRST UK CHART SINGLES

	SINGLE	ARTIST OR GROUP
1	Here in My Heart	Al Martino
2	You Belong to Me	Jo Stafford
3	Somewhere Along the Way	Nat "King" Cole
4	Isle of Innisfree	Bing Crosby
5	Feet Up	Guy Mitchell
6	Half as Much	Rosemary Clooney
7 =	Forget Me Not	Vera Lynn
=	High Noon	Frankie Lane
9 =	Blue Tango	Ray Martin
=	Sugarbush	Doris Day & Frankie Lane

Source: New Musical Express (15 November 1952)

Curiously, the first Top 10 singles chart contained 12 entries because those of equal rank shared the same placing. *High Noon* and *Forget Me Not* shared the No. 7 slot, and *Sugarbush* and *Blue Tango* shared the No. 8 slot. No. 9, by the original numbering system, was *Homing Waltz* and No. 10 was *Auf Wiedersehen (Sweetheart)*, both of which were by Vera Lynn.

THE 10 ★
FIRST EUROPEAN CHART SINGLES

	SINGLE	ARTIST OR GROUP
1	Let's Dance	David Bowie
2	Billie Jean	Michael Jackson
3	99 Luftballons	Nena
4	Too Shy	Kajagoogoo
5	Major Tom	Peter Schilling
6	You Can't Hurry Love	Phil Collins
7	Electric Avenue	Eddy Grant
8	Together We Are Strong	Mireille Mathieu and Patrick Duffy
9	Words	F. R. David
10	Just an Illusion	BZM

Long before MTV Europe, BBC's *Top of the Pops* featured a shortlived weekly European singles chart. This first Top 10, compiled by MRIB, was broadcast on 19 April 1983, and includes singles that were hits in up to seven European countries.

THE 10 ★
FIRST FEMALE SINGERS TO HAVE A NO. 1 SINGLE IN THE UK

	ARTIST/SINGLE	DATE AT NO. 1
1	Jo Stafford, *You Belong to Me*	16 Jan 1953
2	Kay Starr, *Comes A-Long A-Love*	23 Jan 1953
3	Lita Roza, *(How Much Is That) Doggie in the Window?*	17 Apr 1953
4	Doris Day, *Secret Love*	16 Apr 1954
5	Kitty Kallen, *Little Things Mean a Lot*	10 Sep 1954
6	Vera Lynn, *My Son, My Son*	5 Nov 1954
7	Rosemary Clooney, *This Ole House*	26 Nov 1954
8	Ruby Murray, *Softly Softly*	18 Feb 1955
9	Alma Cogan, *Dreamboat*	15 July 1955
10	Anne Shelton, *Lay Down Your Arms*	21 Sep 1956

Before his solo career, in what group did Lionel Richie perform?
see p.138 for the answer

A The Temptations
B The Commodores
C The Four Tops

THE 10 ★
FIRST UK "INDIE" CHART SINGLES

	SINGLE/ARTIST OR GROUP	LABEL
1	*Where's Captain Kirk?*, Spizzenergi	Rough Trade
2	*Daytrip to Bangor*, Fiddler's Dram	Dingles
3	*Mind Your Own Business*, Delta Five	Rough Trade
4	*White Mice*, Mo-Dettes	Mode
5	*California Uber Alles*, Dead Kennedys	Fast
6	*Transmission*, Joy Division	Factory
7	*Earcom Three* (EP), Various	Fast
8	*We Are All Prostitutes*, Pop Group	Rough Trade
9	*Kamikaze*, Boys	Safari
10	*Silent Command*, Cabaret Voltaire	Rough Trade

The independent chart by MRIB made its first appearance in February 1980. It was initiated as a post-Punk reaction that saw hundreds of small independent record companies emerge.

THE 10 ★
FIRST UK RAP CHART SINGLES

	SINGLE	ARTIST OR GROUP
1	*The Boomin' System*	L. L. Cool J featuring Uncle J
2	*Gangsta Gangsta*	N.W.A.
3	*Simba Groove/ Cult of Snap*	Hi Power
4	*Bonita Applebum*	A Tribe Called Quest
5	*Raise (63 Steps to Heaven)*	Bocca Juniors
6	*Superfly 1990*	Curtis Mayfield & Ice T
7	*Amerikkka's Most Wanted*	Ice Cube
8	*Steppin' to the A.M.*	3rd Bass
9	*100 Miles and Runnin'*	N.W.A.
10	*U Can't Touch This*	MC Hammer

Regarded by most as a specialist, almost novelty, musical fad until the late 1980s, rap simply refused to go away and has become a fully fledged and highly profitable market force. The first chart was compiled by MRIB for London's Kiss FM radio station on 8 September 1990.

THE 10 ★
FIRST UK DISCO CHART SINGLES

	SINGLE	ARTIST OR GROUP
1	*Three Times a Lady*	Commodores
2	*Galaxy of Love*	Crown Heights Affair
3	*British Hustle*	Hi-Tension
4	*Let the Music Play*	Charles Earland
5	*You Make Me Feel (Mighty Real)*	Sylvester
6	*Let's Start the Dance*	Bohannon
7	*Supernature*	Cerrone
8	*I Thought It Was You*	Herbie Hancock
9	*Hot Shot*	Karen Young
10	*Stuff Like That*	Quincy Jones

A necessary by-product of the disco boom in the record industry in the mid-1970s, the first-ever UK disco chart appeared on 28 August 1978. It is still compiled today by MRIB, though the now-dated monicker "disco" has been replaced with "dance". It is somewhat ironic that the only soul ballad in this Top 10 should debut at No. 1.

THE 10 ★
FIRST BRITISH SOLO ARTISTS TO HAVE A NO. 1 HIT IN THE US

	ARTIST	SINGLE	DATE AT NO. 1
1	Mr. Acker Bilk	*Stranger on the Shore*	26 May 1962
2	Petula Clark	*Downtown*	23 Jan 1965
3	Donovan	*Sunshine Superman*	3 Sep 1966
4	Lulu	*To Sir With Love*	21 Oct 1967
5	George Harrison	*My Sweet Lord*	26 Dec 1970
6	Rod Stewart	*Maggie May*	2 Oct 1971
7	Gilbert O'Sullivan	*Alone Again Naturally*	29 July 1972
8	Elton John	*Crocodile Rock*	3 Feb 1973
9	Ringo Starr	*Photograph*	24 Nov 1973
10	Eric Clapton	*I Shot the Sheriff*	14 Sep 1974

Source: *The Popular Music Database*

ROD THE MOD

Only the sixth British solo artist to crack the US No. 1 spot, Rod Stewart has continued to notch up hits on both sides of the Atlantic over three decades.

Chart Toppers

TOP 10 ARTISTS WITH THE MOST NO. 1 SINGLES IN THE UK

(Artist or group/no. 1 singles*)

1 = The Beatles, 17; = Elvis Presley, 17 **3** Cliff Richard, 14
4 Madonna, 10 **5** = Abba, 9; = Spice Girls, 9
7 = The Rolling Stones, 8; = Take That, 8 **9** = Michael Jackson, 7;
= George Michael, 7; = Westlife#, 7

* As at 1 January 2001   # Including one with Mariah Carey
Source: *The Popular Music Database*

TOP 10 ★
SINGLES WITH THE MOST WEEKS AT NO. 1 IN THE UK

SINGLE/ARTIST OR GROUP/YEAR	WEEKS AT NO. 1
1 *I Believe*, Frankie Laine, 1953	18
2 *(Everything I Do) I Do It For You*, Bryan Adams, 1991	16
3 *Love Is all Around*, Wet Wet Wet, 1994	15
4 *Bohemian Rhapsody*, Queen, 1975/1991	14
5 *Rose Marie*, Slim Whitman, 1955	11
6 =*Cara Mia*, David Whitfield, 1954	10
=*I Will Always Love You*, Whitney Houston, 1992	10
8 =*Diana*, Paul Anka, 1957	9
=*Here in My Heart*, Al Martino, 1952	9
=*Mull of Kintyre*, Wings, 1977	9
=*Oh Mein Papa*, Eddie Calvert, 1954	9
=*Secret Love*, Doris Day, 1954	9
=*Two Tribes*, Frankie Goes To Hollywood, 1984	9
=*You're the One that I Want*, John Travolta and Olivia Newton-John, 1978	9

Source: *The Popular Music Database*

HOUSTON LIFTS OFF
Whitney Houston's long-running No. 1 single I Will Always Love You, *from the film* The Bodyguard, *in which she also starred, was written by Dolly Parton.*

TOP 10 ARTISTS WITH THE MOST WEEKS AT NO. 1 IN THE UK

(Artist or group/weeks at No. 1)

❶ Elvis Presley, 73 ❷ The Beatles, 69
❸ Cliff Richard, 44* ❹ Frankie Laine, 32
❺ Abba, 31 ❻ Wet Wet Wet, 23
❼ = Spice Girls, 21; = Take That, 21
❾ = Madonna, 20; = Queen#, 20;
= Slade, 20

* Including three weeks with the Young Ones
 # Including two weeks with David Bowie and three
with George Michael and Lisa Stansfield
Source: *The Popular Music Database*

TOP 10 ★

OLDEST ARTISTS TO HAVE A NO. 1 SINGLE IN THE UK*

	ARTIST OR GROUP/TITLE/YEAR	AGE# YRS	MTHS
1	Louis Armstrong, *What a Wonderful World*, 1968	67	10
2	Cliff Richard, *The Millennium Prayer*, 1999	59	1
3	Isaac Hayes+, *Chocolate Salty Balls*, 1998	56	4
4	Cher, *Believe*, 1999	52	7
5	Elton John, *Candle in the Wind* (1997)/*Something About the Way You Look Tonight*, 1997	51	7
6	Frank Sinatra, *Somethin' Stupid*, 1967	51	4
7	Telly Savalas, *If*, 1975	51	1
8	Righteous Brothers, *Unchained Melody*, 1990	50 and 50	2 1
9	Charles Aznavour, *She*, 1974	50	1
10	Clive Dunn, *Grandad*, 1970	49	0

* Up to 1 January 2001

 # Those of apparently identical age have been ranked according to their precise age in days

+ Credited as "Chef"

Source: *The Popular Music Database*

The ages listed are those of the artists during the final week of their last No. 1 hit. Many are still alive, so there is room for further improvement.

TOP 10 ★

LONGEST GAPS BETWEEN NO. 1 HIT SINGLES IN THE UK

	ARTIST OR GROUP/PERIOD	GAP YRS	MTHS
1	Righteous Brothers, 11 Feb 1965–28 Oct 1990	25	8
2	Hollies, 15 July 1965–18 Sep 1988	23	2
3	Blondie, 22 Nov 1980–13 Feb 1999	18	3
4	Queen, 24 Jan 1976–20 Jan 1991	15	0
5	Diana Ross, 11 Sep 1971–2 Mar 1986	14	6
6	Frank Sinatra, 1 Oct 1954–27 May 1966	11	7
7	Cliff Richard, 17 Apr 1968–19 Aug 1979	11	4
8	Bee Gees, 4 Sep 1968–23 Apr 1978	9	7
9	Cliff Richard, 15 Sep 1979–4 Dec 1988	9	3
10	Cliff Richard, 29 Dec 1990–4 Dec 1999	8	11

Source: *The Popular Music Database*

TOP 10 ★

ALBUMS LONGEST AT NO. 1 IN THE UK

	ALBUM/ARTIST OR GROUP	WEEKS AT NO. 1
1	*South Pacific*, Soundtrack	115
2	*The Sound of Music*, Soundtrack	70
3	*Bridge Over Troubled Water*, Simon & Garfunkel	41
4	*Please Please Me*, The Beatles	30
5	*Sgt. Pepper's Lonely Hearts Club Band*, The Beatles	27
6	*G.I. Blues*, Elvis Presley/Soundtrack	22
7	= *With the Beatles*, The Beatles	21
	= *A Hard Day's Night*, The Beatles/Soundtrack	21
9	= *Blue Hawaii*, Elvis Presley/Soundtrack	18
	= *Saturday Night Fever*, Soundtrack	18

Source: *The Popular Music Database*

TOP 10 ★

SLOWEST UK ALBUM CHART RISES TO NO. 1

	ALBUM/ARTIST OR GROUP	WEEKS TO REACH NO. 1
1	*My People Were Fair and Had Sky in Their Hair, But Now They're Content to Wear Stars on Their Brows*, Tyrannosaurus Rex	199
2	*Abba Gold*, Abba	117
3	*40 Greatest Hits*, Elvis Presley	114
4	*Fame*, Soundtrack	98
5	*Come On Over*, Shania Twain	88
6	*Everybody Else is Doing It, So Why Can't We?*, Cranberries	67
7	*Tubular Bells*, Mike Oldfield	65
8	*Happy Nation*, Ace of Base	54
9	*Rumours*, Fleetwood Mac	49
10	*The Freewheelin' Bob Dylan*, Bob Dylan	48

Source: *The Popular Music Database*

The T. Rex album also holds the distinction of being the album with the longest title ever to chart.

TOP 10 ★

ALBUMS WITH THE MOST CONSECUTIVE WEEKS AT NO. 1 IN THE UK

	ALBUM/ARTIST OR GROUP	WEEKS AT NO. 1
1	*South Pacific*, Soundtrack	70
2	*Please Please Me*, The Beatles	30
3	*Sgt. Pepper's Lonely Hearts Club Band*, The Beatles	23
4	= *With The Beatles*, The Beatles	21
	= *A Hard Day's Night*, The Beatles/Soundtrack	21
6	*South Pacific*, Soundtrack	19
7	= *The Sound of Music*, Soundtrack	18
	= *Saturday Night Fever*, Soundtrack	18
9	*Blue Hawaii*, Elvis Presley/Soundtrack	17
10	*Summer Holiday*, Cliff Richard and The Shadows	14

Source: *The Popular Music Database*

Did You Know? In addition to their impressive reigns at the UK No. 1 spot, *South Pacific* spent a total of 306 weeks in the charts and *The Sound of Music* 362 weeks – almost 7 years.

Hit Singles of the Decades

SINGLES OF THE 1960s IN THE UK

	SINGLE/ARTIST OR GROUP	YEAR RELEASED
1	*She Loves You*, The Beatles	1963
2	*I Want to Hold Your Hand*, The Beatles	1963
3	*Tears*, Ken Dodd	1965
4	*Can't Buy Me Love*, The Beatles	1964
5	*I Feel Fine*, The Beatles	1964
6	*We Can Work It Out/Day Tripper*, The Beatles	1965
7	*The Carnival Is Over*, Seekers	1965
8	*Release Me*, Engelbert Humperdinck	1967
9	*It's Now or Never*, Elvis Presley	1960
10	*Green Green Grass of Home*, Tom Jones	1966

The Beatles' domination of the 1960s is clear, with five of the decade's top six singles being by the group. Intriguingly, all the other five in this Top 10 are ballads of varying degrees of what, in those days, would have been termed squareness.

TOP 10 ★

SINGLES OF THE 1970s IN THE UK

	SINGLE/ARTIST OR GROUP	YEAR RELEASED
1	*Mull of Kintyre*, Wings	1977
2	*Rivers of Babylon/ Brown Girl in the Ring*, Boney M	1978
3	*You're the One That I Want*, John Travolta and Olivia Newton-John	1978
4	*Mary's Boy Child/Oh My Lord*, Boney M	1978
5	*Summer Nights*, John Travolta and Olivia Newton-John	1978
6	*Y.M.C.A.*, Village People	1979
7	*Bohemian Rhapsody*, Queen	1975
8	*Heart of Glass*, Blondie	1979
9	*Merry Xmas Everybody*, Slade	1973
10	*Don't Give Up on Us*, David Soul	1977

Most of the biggest sellers of the 1970s in the UK occurred between December 1977 and May 1979. The single that started this golden (or, rather, platinum) era, *Mull of Kintyre*, was the first-ever in Britain to top 2 million copies.

TOP 10 ★

SINGLES OF THE 1980s IN THE UK

	SINGLE/ARTIST OR GROUP	YEAR RELEASED
1	*Do They Know It's Christmas?*, Band Aid	1984
2	*Relax*, Frankie Goes to Hollywood	1984
3	*I Just Called to Say I Love You*, Stevie Wonder	1984
4	*Two Tribes*, Frankie Goes to Hollywood	1984
5	*Don't You Want Me*, Human League	1981
6	*Last Christmas*, Wham!	1984
7	*Karma Chameleon*, Culture Club	1983
8	*Careless Whisper*, George Michael	1984
9	*The Power of Love*, Jennifer Rush	1985
10	*Come on Eileen*, Dexy's Midnight Runners	1982

Singles from the boom year of 1984 dominate the UK 1980s' Top 10, two of them by newcomers Frankie Goes to Hollywood, and two by Wham!/ George Michael (who also sang one of the Band Aid leads – as did Boy George from Culture Club). Stevie Wonder and Jennifer Rush are the sole US entrants. In fact, they were the only two Americans to have UK million-sellers during this decade.

OUT OF PUFF

I'll Be Missing You, *by Sean Combs, aka Puff Daddy, is the world's most successful rap single. It was written as a tribute to Notorious B.I.G.*

TOP 10 ★

SINGLES OF EACH YEAR IN THE 1980s IN THE UK

YEAR	SINGLE/ARTIST OR GROUP
1980	*Don't Stand So Close to Me*, Police
1981	*Don't You Want Me*, Human League
1982	*Come on Eileen*, Dexy's Midnight Runners
1983	*Karma Chameleon*, Culture Club
1984	*Do They Know It's Christmas?*, Band Aid
1985	*The Power of Love*, Jennifer Rush
1986	*Every Loser Wins*, Nick Berry
1987	*Never Gonna Give You Up*, Rick Astley
1988	*Mistletoe and Wine*, Cliff Richard
1989	*Ride on Time*, Black Box

TOP 10 ★
SINGLES OF THE 1990s IN THE UK

	SINGLE/ARTIST OR GROUP	YEAR RELEASED
1	*Candle in the Wind (1997)/ Something About the Way You Look Tonight*, Elton John	1997
2	*Unchained Melody/The White Cliffs of Dover*, Robson and Jerome	1995
3	*Love Is All Around*, Wet Wet Wet	1994
4	*Barbie Girl*, Aqua	1997
5	*Believe*, Cher	1998
6	*Perfect Day*, Various Artists	1997
7	*(Everything I Do) I Do It for You*, Bryan Adams	1991
8	*...Baby One More Time*, Britney Spears	1999
9	*I'll Be Missing You*, Puff Daddy & Faith Evans	1997
10	*I Will Always Love You*, Whitney Houston	1992

TOP 10 ★
SINGLES OF EACH YEAR IN THE 1990s IN THE UK

YEAR	SINGLE/ARTIST OR GROUP
1990	*Unchained Melody*, Righteous Brothers
1991	*(Everything I Do) I Do It for You*, Bryan Adams
1992	*I Will Always Love You*, Whitney Houston
1993	*I'd Do Anything for Love, (But I Won't Do That)*, Meat Loaf
1994	*Love Is All Around*, Wet Wet Wet
1995	*Unchained Melody/ The White Cliffs of Dover*, Robson and Jerome
1996	*Killing Me Softly*, The Fugees
1997	*Candle in the Wind (1997)/ Something About the Way You Look Tonight*, Elton John
1998	*Believe*, Cher
1999	*...Baby One More Time*, Britney Spears

TOP 10 ★
SINGLES OF THE 1990s IN THE UK (MALE)

	SINGLE/ARTIST	YEAR RELEASED
1	*Candle in the Wind (1997)/ Something About the Way You Look Tonight*, Elton John	1997
2	*(Everything I Do) I Do It for You*, Bryan Adams	1991
3	*Angels*, Robbie Williams	1998
4	*I'd Do Anything for Love (But I Won't Do That)*, Meat Loaf	1991
5	*Earth Song*, Michael Jackson	1996
6	*Ice Ice Baby*, Vanilla Ice	1990
7	*Sacrifice/Healing Hands*, Elton John	1990
8	*Baby Come Back*, Pato Banton	1994
9	*Men in Black*, Will Smith	1997
10	*The One and Only*, Chesney Hawkes	1991

TOP 10 ★
SINGLES OF THE 1990s IN THE UK (FEMALE)

	SINGLE/ARTIST	YEAR RELEASED
1	*Believe*, Cher	1998
2	*My Heart Will Go On*, Celine Dion	1998
3	*...Baby One More Time*, Britney Spears	1999
4	*I Will Always Love You*, Whitney Houston	1992
5	*How Do I Live*, LeAnn Rimes	1998
6	*Think Twice*, Celine Dion	1995
7	*Saturday Night*, Whigfield	1994
8	*Shoop Shoop Song (It's in His Kiss)*, Cher	1990
9	*Without You*, Mariah Carey	1994
10	*Vogue*, Madonna	1990

CHER SUCCESS

Now into her fifth decade of chart successes, both in partnership with Sonny Bono and solo, Cher has also carved out an Oscar-winning film career.

What is unusual about John Lennon's single *Imagine*?

see p.143 for the answer

A It was a posthumous hit
B It has the shortest title of a No. 1 single
C It was the first-ever CD single

Hit Albums of the Decades

TOP 10 ★
ALBUMS OF THE 1960s IN THE UK

	ALBUM/ARTIST OR GROUP	YEAR RELEASED
1	*Sgt. Pepper's Lonely Hearts Club Band*, The Beatles	1967
2	*The Sound of Music*, Soundtrack	1965
3	*With The Beatles*, The Beatles	1963
4	*Abbey Road*, The Beatles	1969
5	*South Pacific*, Soundtrack	1958
6	*Beatles for Sale*, The Beatles	1964
7	*A Hard Day's Night*, The Beatles	1964
8	*Rubber Soul*, The Beatles	1965
9	*The Beatles ("White Album")*, The Beatles	1968
10	*West Side Story*, Soundtrack	1962

Three further albums by The Beatles, *Revolver*, *Please Please Me*, and *Help!*, were also the 11th, 12th, and 13th bestselling albums of the decade.

TOP 10 ★
ALBUMS OF THE 1970s IN THE UK

	ALBUM/ARTIST OR GROUP	YEAR RELEASED
1	*Bridge over Troubled Water*, Simon and Garfunkel	1970
2	*Simon and Garfunkel's Greatest Hits*, Simon and Garfunkel	1972
3	*Rumours*, Fleetwood Mac	1977
4	*Dark Side of the Moon*, Pink Floyd	1973
5	*Tubular Bells*, Mike Oldfield	1973
6	*Greatest Hits*, Abba	1976
7	*Bat Out of Hell*, Meat Loaf	1978
8	*Saturday Night Fever*, Soundtrack	1978
9	*And I Love You So*, Perry Como	1973
10	*The Singles, 1969–1973*, The Carpenters	1974

Each of the top five albums of the 1970s clocked up over 250 weeks on the British chart.

TOP 10 ★
ALBUMS OF EACH YEAR OF THE 1980s IN THE UK

YEAR	ALBUM/ARTIST OR GROUP
1980	*Super Trouper*, Abba
1981	*Kings of the Wild Frontier*, Adam and the Ants
1982	*Love Songs*, Barbra Streisand
1983	*Thriller*, Michael Jackson
1984	*Can't Slow Down*, Lionel Richie
1985	*Brothers in Arms*, Dire Straits
1986	*True Blue*, Madonna
1987	*Bad*, Michael Jackson
1988	*Kylie*, Kylie Minogue
1989	*Ten Good Reasons*, Jason Donovan

RICH REWARDS

Formerly a member of the Commodores, Lionel Richie began a successful solo career in the 1980s, with Can't Slow Down *selling 8 million copies in the US alone within a year of its release.*

TOP 10 ★
ALBUMS OF EACH YEAR OF THE 1970s IN THE UK

YEAR	ALBUM/ARTIST OR GROUP
1970	*Bridge over Troubled Water*, Simon and Garfunkel
1971	*Bridge over Troubled Water*, Simon and Garfunkel
1972	*20 Dynamic Hits*, Various Artists
1973	*Don't Shoot Me, I'm Only the Piano Player*, Elton John
1974	*The Singles, 1969–1973*, The Carpenters
1975	*The Best of The Stylistics*, The Stylistics
1976	*Greatest Hits*, Abba
1977	*Arrival*, Abba
1978	*Saturday Night Fever*, Soundtrack
1979	*Breakfast in America*, Supertramp

TOP 10 ★
ALBUMS OF THE 1980s IN THE UK

	ALBUM/ARTIST OR GROUP	YEAR RELEASED
1	*Brothers in Arms*, Dire Straits	1985
2	*Bad*, Michael Jackson	1987
3	*Thriller*, Michael Jackson	1982
4	*Greatest Hits*, Queen	1981
5	*Kylie*, Kylie Minogue	1988
6	*Whitney*, Whitney Houston	1987
7	*Tango in the Night*, Fleetwood Mac	1987
8	*No Jacket Required*, Phil Collins	1985
9	*True Blue*, Madonna	1986
10	*The Joshua Tree*, U2	1987

Brothers in Arms stayed in the chart for nearly four years during the 1980s, becoming the UK's third bestselling album ever. While Michael Jackson's *Thriller* was his bestselling album in most countries around the world (and, of course, the bestselling global album of all time), British buyers eventually preferred *Bad*.

TOP 10 ★
ALBUMS OF EACH YEAR IN THE 1990s IN THE UK

YEAR	ALBUM/ARTIST OR GROUP
1990	*The Immaculate Collection*, Madonna
1991	*Stars*, Simply Red
1992	*The Bodyguard*, Soundtrack
1993	*Bat Out of Hell II – Back into Hell*, Meat Loaf
1994	*Cross Road – The Best of Bon Jovi*, Bon Jovi
1995	*(What's the Story) Morning Glory?*, Oasis
1996	*Spice*, Spice Girls
1997	*Urban Hymns*, The Verve
1998	*Falling into You*, Celine Dion
1999	*Come on Over*, Shania Twain

Source: *BPI*

TOP 10 ★
ALBUMS OF THE 1990s IN THE UK

	ALBUM/ARTIST OR GROUP	YEAR RELEASED
1	*(What's the Story) Morning Glory?*, Oasis	1995
2	*Stars*, Simply Red	1991
3	*Spice*, Spice Girls	1996
4	*Talk on Corners*, The Corrs	1997
5	*Jagged Little Pill*, Alanis Morissette	1996
6	*Robson and Jerome*, Robson and Jerome	1995
7	*The Immaculate Collection*, Madonna	1990
8	*Urban Hymns*, The Verve	1997
9	*Gold – Greatest Hits*, Abba	1992
10	*Falling into You*, Celine Dion	1996

Source: *CIN*

The bestselling albums of the 1990s present an end-of-century summary of the musical tastes of the buying public, pitting 1990s' newcomer groups The Corrs, Spice Girls, and Oasis *et al.* alongside such long-established chart stars as Madonna, and even Abba, who experienced a surprising revival despite being defunct as a group for almost 10 years.

TWAIN MAKES HER MARK
After achieving her first chart success in 1993, Canadian-born country singer Shania Twain has rapidly become one of the bestselling female artistes of all time.

Did You Know? Shania Twain was born Eileen Regina Edwards. Her new name, adopted in 1990, comes from the Native North American Chippewa (Ojibway) phrase for "I'm on my way".

Female Singers

TOP 10 ★
FEMALE GROUPS OF ALL TIME IN THE UK*

GROUP	NO. 1	TOP 10	TOP 20
1 Supremes	1	13	31
2 Bananarama	–	10	16
3 Eternal	1	12	15
4 =Sister Sledge	1	5	10
=Spice Girls	9	10	10
6 =B*Witched	5	6	8
=Salt-n-Pepa	–	5	8
8 =Three Degrees	1	5	7
=Nolans	–	3	7
=TLC	–	4	7
=All Saints	5	7	7

* To 1 January 2001; ranked according to total number of Top 20 singles

Source: *The Popular Music Database*

The Supremes also had three other Top 20 hits, not included here, in partnership with Motown male groups the Four Tops and Temptations. However, Bananarama's charity revival of *Help!*, shared with comediennes Dawn French and Jennifer Saunders, has been included since all the participants are female.

TOP 10 ★
SINGLES BY FEMALE GROUPS IN THE UK

SINGLE/GROUP		YEAR
1 *Wannabe*, Spice Girls		1996
2 *Say You'll Be There*, Spice Girls		1996
3 *2 Become 1*, Spice Girls		1996
4 *Never Ever*, All Saints		1997
5 *C'Est La Vie*, B*Witched		1998
6 *Goodbye*, Spice Girls		1998
7 *Viva Forever*, Spice Girls		1998
8 *Spice up Your Life*, Spice Girls		1997
9 *Too Much*, Spice Girls		1997
10 *Pure Shores*, All Saints		2000

Such has been the Spice Girls' impact on popular music that they have totally re-written the record book as far as successful girl-group singles are concerned, taking seven of the all-time biggest sellers.

GIRL POWER

In a relatively short period, the Spice Girls set new records for bestsellers and single and album chart entries on both sides of the Atlantic.

TOP 10 ★
ALBUMS BY FEMALE GROUPS IN THE UK

ALBUM/GROUP	YEAR
1 *Spice*, Spice Girls	1996
2 *Spiceworld*, Spice Girls	1997
3 *All Saints*, All Saints	1997
4 *Always and Forever*, Eternal	1993
5 *Greatest Hits*, Eternal	1997
6 *The Greatest Hits Collection*, Bananarama	1988
7 *Power of a Woman*, Eternal	1995
8 *B*Witched*, B*Witched	1998
9 *Different Light*, Bangles	1986
10 *Greatest Hits*, Bangles	1990

All of these albums were released within the last two decades, and the three biggest sellers of all within the last six years. All of the groups are British, except B*Witched, who are Irish, and the Bangles, who are American.

TOP 10 ★
FEMALE SINGERS WITH THE MOST TOP 10 HITS IN THE UK*

SINGER	TOP 10 HITS
1 Madonna	50
2 Kylie Minogue (including duets with Keith Washington and Robbie Williams)	20
3 =Mariah Carey (including duets with Boyz II Men, Luther Vandross, Whitney Houston, and Westlife)	18
=Diana Ross (including duets with Marvin Gaye and Lionel Richie)	18
5 =Janet Jackson (including duets with Michael Jackson, Luther Vandross, Busta Rhymes, and Q-Tip & Joni Mitchell)	15
=Whitney Houston (including duets with Mariah Carey and George Michael)	15
7 Celine Dion (including duets with Peabo Bryson, the Bee Gees, Barbra Streisand, and R. Kelly)	14
8 Petula Clark	12
9 =Cher	11
=Olivia Newton-John (including duets with John Travolta and Electric Light Orchestra)	11

* To 1 January 2001

What was the name of Cher's 1998 smash hit?
see p.137 for the answer

A Strong Enough
B Believe
C Walking in Memphis

TOP 10 ★
SINGLES BY FEMALE SINGERS IN THE UK

	SINGLE/ARTIST	YEAR
1	*Believe*, Cher	1998
2	*I Will Always Love You*, Whitney Houston	1992
3	*...Baby One More Time*, Britney Spears	1999
4	*My Heart Will Go On*, Celine Dion	1998
5	*The Power of Love*, Jennifer Rush	1985
6	*How Do I Live*, LeAnn Rimes	1998
7	*Perfect Moment*, Martine McCutcheon	1999
8	*Think Twice*, Celine Dion	1994
9	*That Don't Impress Me Much*, Shania Twain	1999
10	*Don't Cry for Me Argentina*, Julie Covington	1977

Perhaps the most significant aspect of this list is how comparatively recent most of its entries are. Only two of these singles were released before 1990. Statistically, therefore, a female artist has stood a better chance of major chart success since the 1980s than in any of pop music's earlier eras.

TOP 10 ★
ALBUMS BY FEMALE SINGERS IN THE UK

	ALBUM/ARTIST	YEAR
1	*Come On Over*, Shania Twain	1997
2	*Jagged Little Pill*, Alanis Morissette	1995
3	*Simply the Best*, Tina Turner	1991
4	*The Immaculate Collection*, Madonna	1990
5	*Falling into You*, Celine Dion	1996
6	*True Blue*, Madonna	1986
7	*Whitney*, Whitney Houston	1987
8	*Let's Talk About Love*, Celine Dion	1997
9	*Colour of My Love*, Celine Dion	1995
10	*Ray of Light*, Madonna	1998

TOP 10 ★
YOUNGEST FEMALE SINGERS TO HAVE A NO. 1 SINGLE IN THE UK

	SINGER/SINGLE	YEAR	YEARS	AGE MTHS	DAYS
1	Helen Shapiro, *You Don't Know*	1961	14	10	13
2	Billie, *Because We Want To*	1998	15	9	20
3	Tiffany, *I Think We're Alone Now*	1988	16	3	28
4	Nicole, *A Little Peace*	1982	17	0	0
5	Britney Spears, *...Baby One More Time*	1999	17	2	25
6	Sandie Shaw, *(There's) Always Something There to Remind Me*	1964	17	7	26
7	Mary Hopkin, *Those Were the Days*	1968	18	4	22
8	Sonia, *You'll Never Stop Me Loving You*	1989	18	5	9
9	Christina Aguilera, *Genie in a Bottle*	1999	18	9	29
10	Connie Francis, *Who's Sorry Now*	1958	19	5	4

The ages shown are those of each artist on the publication date of the chart in which she achieved her first No. 1 single. All ten of these girls were still in their teens when they had their first taste of chart-topping glory.

CHRISTINA AGUILERA
Within a year of her professional debut, Christina Aguilera became one of only a handful of teenage girls to achieve a No. 1 single. She also sold over 8 million copies of her first album and won a Grammy award.

All-Time Greats

ARTISTS WITH THE MOST BRIT AWARDS

ARTIST	AWARDS
1 Annie Lennox	8
2 =Phil Collins	6*
=Prince	6#
4 =Michael Jackson	5
=George Michael	5+
6 =Blur	4
=Bjork	4
=Oasis	4
=Dave Stewart	4
=Spice Girls	4
=Take That	4
=U2	4
=Robbie Williams	4

* Includes award for Best Film Soundtrack (1989, for Buster Original Soundtrack)

Includes award for Best Film Soundtrack (1990, for Batman Original Soundtrack)

+ Includes two awards with Wham! (1985 and 1986)

BEATLES SINGLES IN THE UK

SINGLE	YEAR RELEASED
1 She Loves You	1963
2 I Want to Hold Your Hand	1963
3 Can't Buy Me Love	1964
4 I Feel Fine	1964
5 We Can Work It Out/Day Tripper	1965
6 Help!	1965
7 Hey Jude	1968
8 A Hard Day's Night	1964
9 From Me to You	1963
10 Hello Goodbye	1967

The Beatles' two bestselling UK singles remain among the UK's all-time Top 15 almost 40 years on.

DAVID BOWIE ALBUMS IN THE UK

ALBUM	YEAR RELEASED
1 The Rise and Fall of Ziggy Stardust and the Spiders from Mars	1972
2 Hunky Dory	1972
3 Let's Dance	1983
4 Pinups	1973
5 Scary Monsters and Super Creeps	1980
6 Changesbowie	1990
7 The Ultimate Singles Collection	1994
8 Aladdin Sane	1973
9 Changesonebowie	1976
10 The Very Best of David Bowie	1981

TOP 10 SOLO SINGERS OF THE 1980s IN THE UK*

❶ Madonna ❷ Michael Jackson ❸ Phil Collins ❹ Cliff Richard
❺ Shakin' Stevens ❻ Paul McCartney ❼ Kylie Minogue ❽ Whitney Houston
❾ Prince ❿ David Bowie

*Based on estimated UK record sales   Source: MRIB

PRINCE, CHARMING

Although he achieved a string of hit singles and albums throughout the 1980s, and picked up six BRIT awards, Prince did not gain a UK No. 1 – his only chart-topper to date – until 1994.

TOP 10 ★
JOHN LENNON SINGLES IN THE UK

	SINGLE	YEAR RELEASED
1	*Imagine*	1975/81
2	*Woman*	1981
3	*(Just Like) Starting Over*	1980
4	*Happy Xmas (War Is Over)*	1972
5	*Give Peace a Chance*	1969
6	*Instant Karma*	1970
7	*Power to the People*	1971
8	*Nobody Told Me*	1984
9	*Cold Turkey*	1969
10	*Mind Games*	1973

Source: *MRIB*

KEY PLAYER
The most charismatic of the Beatles, John Lennon achieved a run of hits before and after his 1980 murder, including the all-time posthumous hit Imagine.

TOP 10 ★
POSTHUMOUS SINGLES IN THE UK

	SINGLE/ARTIST	DIED	HIT YEAR
1	*Imagine*, John Lennon	1980	1981
2	*Reet Petite*, Jackie Wilson	1984	1986
3	*It Doesn't Matter Anymore*, Buddy Holly	1959	1959
4	*Woman*, John Lennon	1980	1981
5	*Way Down*, Elvis Presley	1977	1977
6	*I Won't Forget You*, Jim Reeves	1964	1964
7	*Distant Drums*, Jim Reeves	1964	1966
8	*Three Steps to Heaven*, Eddie Cochran	1960	1960
9	*Voodoo Chile*, Jimi Hendrix	1970	1970
10	*The Trail of the Lonesome Pine*, Laurel & Hardy	1965/75	1975

Jackie Wilson's *Reet Petite* had originally been a chart hit during the 1950s, but it was the 1986 UK reissue that saw by far the greater success. The same applied to *Imagine*, which had been a more moderate hit for John Lennon in 1975. The 1991 reissue of Queen's *Bohemian Rhapsody* is excluded, since Queen continued to exist as a group after the death of singer Freddie Mercury.

TOP 10 ★
BOB DYLAN ALBUMS IN THE UK

	SINGLE	YEAR RELEASED
1	*Blonde on Blonde*	1966
2	*Bringing It All Back Home*	1965
3	*Bob Dylan's Greatest Hits*	1967
4	*Nashville Skyline*	1969
5	*John Wesley Harding*	1968
6	*Highway 61 Revisited*	1965
7	*Street Legal*	1978
8	*The Freewheelin' Bob Dylan*	1963
9	*Desire*	1976
10	*New Morning*	1970

Bob Dylan's sales heyday in Britain was in the mid- and late 1960s, when he was one of the first artists to sell large quantities of albums rather than singles. Titles such as *Blonde on Blonde* and *Bringing It All Back Home* continue to sell healthily as catalogue CDs, with a lot of original fans replacing their worn-out vinyl copies.

TOP 10 ★
ARTISTS WITH THE MOST GRAMMY AWARDS

	ARTIST	AWARDS
1	Sir Georg Solti	31
2	Quincy Jones	26
3	Vladimir Horowitz	25
4	Pierre Boulez	23
5	Stevie Wonder	21
6	Henry Mancini	20
7 =	John T. Williams	17
=	Leonard Bernstein	17
9 =	Aretha Franklin	15
=	Itzhak Perlman	15

The Grammy Awards ceremony has been held annually in the US since its inauguration on 4 May 1959, and the awards are considered to be the most prestigious in the music industry. The proliferation of classical artists in this Top 10 (not least, conductor Sir George Solti) is largely attributable to the large number of classical award categories at the Grammys, which have been latterly overshadowed by the rise of pop and rock. Grammy winners are selected annually by the voting membership of NARAS (the National Academy of Recording Arts & Sciences).

TOP 10 GROUPS OF THE 1970s IN THE UK*
❶ Abba ❷ Slade ❸ T. Rex ❹ Bay City Rollers ❺ Sweet ❻ Showaddywaddy
❼ Mud ❽ Wings ❾ Electric Light Orchestra ❿ The Osmonds
* Based on comparative UK singles chart performance Source: *MRIB*

Did You Know? John Lennon's single *Imagine* was released in the US in 1971. Its UK release was delayed until 1975, and it made No. 1 only after his death in 1980.

Top of the Pops

TOP 10 ⭐ BOYZONE SINGLES IN THE UK

SINGLE	YEAR
1 When the Going Gets Tough the Tough Get Going	1999
2 No Matter What	1998
3 I Love the Way You Love Me	1998
4 You Needed Me	1999
5 Words	1996
6 All That I Need	1998
7 A Different Beat	1996
8 Father and Son	1995
9 Every Day I Love You	1999
10 Picture of You	1999

TOP 10 ⭐ SPICE GIRLS SINGLES IN THE UK

SINGLE	YEAR
1 Wannabe	1996
2 2 Become 1	1996
3 Too Much	1997
4 Goodbye	1998
5 Say You'll Be There	1996
6 Spice Up Your Life	1997
7 Viva Forever	1998
8 Mama/Who Do You Think You Are	1997
9 Stop	1998
10 Holler/Let Love Lead the Way	2000

THE 10 LATEST GRAMMY NEW ARTISTS OF THE YEAR

(Year/artist or group)

① 2000, Shelby Lynne
② 1999, Christina Aguilera ③ 1998, Lauryn Hill ④ 1997, Paula Cole
⑤ 1996, LeeAnn Rimes ⑥ 1995, Hootie & The Blowfish ⑦ 1994, Sheryl Crow
⑧ 1993, Toni Braxton ⑨ 1992, Arrested Development ⑩ 1991, Mark Cohn

TOP 10 BACKSTREET BOYS SINGLES IN THE UK

(Single/year)

① I Want It That Way, 1999 ② Show Me the Meaning of Being Lonely, 2000
③ As Long as You Love Me, 1997 ④ All I Have to Give, 1998
⑤ Quit Playing Games (With My Heart), 1997 ⑥ Everybody (Backstreet's Back), 1997
⑦ Larger Than Life, 1999 ⑧ I'll Never Break Your Heart, 1996
⑨ Anywhere for You, 1997 ⑩ We've Got It Goin' On, 1996

THE 10 ⭐ LATEST WINNERS OF THE BRIT AWARD FOR BEST SINGLE BY A BRITISH ARTIST

YEAR	SINGLE/ARTIST OR GROUP
2001	Rock DJ, Robbie Williams
2000	She's the One, Robbie Williams
1999	Angels, Robbie Williams
1998	Never Ever, All Saints
1997	Wannabe, The Spice Girls
1996	Back for Good, Take That
1995	Parklife, Blur
1994	Pray, Take That
1993	Could It Be Magic, Take That
1992	These Are the Days of Our Lives, Queen

TOP 10 ⭐ MANIC STREET PREACHERS SINGLES IN THE UK

SINGLE	YEAR
1 If You Tolerate This Your Children Will Be Next	1998
2 A Design for Life	1996
3 The Masses Against the Classes	2000
4 Everything Must Go	1996
5 Australia	1996
6 You Stole the Sun from My Heart	1999
7 Theme from M*A*S*H (Suicide is Painless)	1992
8 Kevin Carter	1996
9 The Everlasting	1998
10 Motorcycle Emptiness	1992

THE 10 ⭐ LATEST WINNERS OF THE Q MAGAZINE AWARD FOR THE BEST NEW ACT

YEAR	ARTIST OR GROUP
2000	Badly Drawn Boy
1999	Basement Jaxx
1998	Gomez
1997	Fun Lovin' Criminals
1996	Alanis Morissette
1995	Supergrass
1994	Oasis
1993	Suede
1992	Tori Amos
1991	Seal

THE 10 ⭐ LATEST WINNERS OF THE Q MAGAZINE AWARD FOR THE BEST ALBUM

YEAR	ALBUM/ARTIST OR GROUP
2000	Parachutes, Coldplay
1999	Surrender, Chemical Brothers
1998	Mezzanine, Massive Attack
1997	OK Computer, Radiohead
1996	Everything Must Go, Manic Street Preachers
1995	The Great Escape, Blur
1994	Parklife, Blur
1993	Ten Summoner's Tales, Sting
1992	Automatic for the People, R.E.M.
1991	Out of Time, R.E.M.

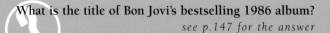

What is the title of Bon Jovi's bestselling 1986 album?
see p.147 for the answer

A *Slippery When Wet*
B *Slipping and Sliding*
C *Many a Slip...*

TOP 10 ★
ROBBIE WILLIAMS SINGLES IN THE UK

	SINGLE	YEAR
1	*Angels*	1997
2	*Rock DJ*	2000
3	*She's the One/It's Only Us*	1999
4	*Millennium*	1998
5	*Freedom*	1996
6	*Old Before I Die*	1997
7	*Let Me Entertain You*	1998
8	*No Regrets*	1998
9	*Strong*	1999
10	*Lazy Days*	1997

TOP 10 ★
MADONNA SINGLES IN THE UK

	SINGLE	YEAR
1	*Like a Virgin*	1984
2	*Into the Groove*	1985
3	*Papa Don't Preach*	1986
4	*Crazy for You*	1985
5	*Holiday*	1984
6	*True Blue*	1986
7	*Vogue*	1990
8	*La Isla Bonita*	1987
9	*American Pie*	2000
10	*Music*	2000

Source: *MRIB*

The most successful chart artist of the 1980s, Madonna had scored 25 UK Top 10 hits, including seven No. 1s, by the end of the decade, despite the fact that she did not first make the charts until the beginning of 1984. Interestingly, her biggest seller, *Like a Virgin*, failed to make No. 1, being held at No. 3 over Christmas 1984 by the gigantic sales of the Band Aid single *Do They Know It's Christmas?* and Wham!'s *Last Christmas*.

MATERIAL GIRL

Madonna's hit singles span three decades. Her marriage in 2000 to British film director Guy Ritchie generated media frenzy, despite being an unusually private celebrity event.

Music Genres

TOP 10 ★ R&B/HIP-HOP ALBUMS IN THE US, 2000

ALBUM/ARTIST OR GROUP

1	*Dr. Dre – 2001*, Dr. Dre
2	*The Marshall Mathers LP*, Eminem
3	*…And Then There Was X*, DMX
4	*Unleash the Dragon*, Sisqo
5	*Vol. 3 … Life and Times of S. Carter*, Jay-Z
6	*Country Grammar*, Nelly
7	*Voodoo*, D'Angelo
8	*My Name Is Joe*, Joe
9	*Born Again*, Notorious B.I.G.
10	*J.E. Heartbreak*, Jagged Edge

Source: Billboard

TOP 10 DANCE SINGLES IN THE UK, 2000

(Single/artist or group)

1 *Toca's Miracle*, Fragma **2** *Groovejet (If This Ain't Love)*, Spiller **3** *Killer 2000*, ATB **4** *Move Your Body*, Eiffel 65 **5** *Blow Ya Mind*, Lock 'n' Load **6** *Deeper Shade of Blue*, Steps **7** *Bag It Up*, Geri Halliwell **8** *Adelante*, Sash! **9** *It Feels So Good*, Sonique **10** *Don't Give Up*, Chicane

Source: *CIN*

TOP 10 ★ RAP SINGLES IN THE UK

	SINGLE/ARTIST OR GROUP	YEAR
1	*I'll Be Missing You*, Puff Daddy featuring Faith Evans	1997
2	*Killing Me Softly*, The Fugees	1996
3	*Stan*, Eminem	2000
4	*Ghetto Supastar (That Is What You Are)*, Pras featuring ODB & Maya	1998
5	*The Bad Touch*, Bloodhound Gang	2000
6	*Wild Wild West*, Will Smith	2000
7	*Gangsta's Paradise*, Coolio featuring LV	1995
8	*It's Like That*, Run DMC vs. Jason Nevins	1998
9	*Men in Black*, Will Smith	1997
10	*Ice Ice Baby*, Vanilla Ice	1990

Grandmaster Flash's hit single *White Lines (Don't Don't Do It)*, next on this list, spent 43 weeks in the charts between 1983 and 1985, making it the longest-charting rap single ever.

TOP 10 ★ REGGAE ALBUMS IN THE UK

	ALBUM/ARTIST OR GROUP	YEAR
1	*Legend*, Bob Marley and the Wailers	1984
2	*The Best of UB40 Vol. 1*, UB40	1987
3	*Labour of Love II*, UB40	1989
4	*Labour of Love*, UB40	1983
5	*Promises and Lies*, UB40	1993
6	*Present Arms*, UB40	1981
7	*Signing Off*, UB40	1980
8	*The Very Best of UB40*, UB40	2000
9	*Tease Me*, Chaka Demus and Pliers	1993
10	*The Best of UB40 Vol. 2*, UB40	1998

Source: *The Popular Music Database*

TOP 10 ★ IRISH ALBUMS IN THE UK

	ALBUM/ARTIST OR GROUP	YEAR
1	*Talk on Corners*, Corrs	1997
2	*By Request*, Boyzone	1999
3	*The Joshua Tree*, U2	1987
4	*Where We Belong*, Boyzone	1998
5	*Coast to Coast*, Westlife	2000
6	*Watermark*, Enya	1988
7	*Shepherd Moons*, Enya	1991
8	*Westlife*, Westlife	1999
9	*Rattle and Hum*, U2	1988
10	*Achtung Baby!*, U2	1991

Source: *The Popular Music Database*

TOP 10 ★
JAZZ ALBUMS IN THE UK

	ALBUM/ARTIST OR GROUP	YEAR
1	*We Are in Love*, Harry Connick Jr.	1990
2	*Blue Light, Red Light*, Harry Connick Jr.	1991
3	*Jazz on a Summer's Day*, Various	1992
4	*Morning Dance*, Spyro Gyra	1979
5	*In Flight*, George Benson	1977
6	*Duotones*, Kenny G	1987
7	*Best of Ball, Barber and Bilk*, Kenny Ball, Chris Barber, and Acker Bilk	1962
8	*Sinatra/Basie*, Frank Sinatra and Count Basie	1963
9	*Kenny Ball's Golden Hits*, Kenny Ball	1963
10	*Time Out Featuring Take Five*, Dave Brubeck Quartet	1960

Source: *MRIB*

Despite a solid base of afficionados, jazz has always been a comparatively poor-selling musical genre in the UK, and the jazz albums that have made the Top 10 through the years can be counted on little more than two hands. The only jazz album ever to top the UK chart was the Ball, Barber, and Bilk compilation, long ago in 1962.

TOP 10 LATIN POP ALBUMS IN THE US, 2000
(Album/artist or group)

❶ *Mi Reflejo*, Christina Aguilera ❷ *Amor, Familia y Respeto ...*, A. B. Quintanilla y Los Kumbia Kings ❸ *MTV Unplugged*, Shakira ❹ *Donde Estan los Ladrones?*, Shakira ❺ *MTV Unplugged*, Maná ❻ *The Best Hits*, Enrique Iglesias ❼ *Amarte es un Placer*, Luis Miguel ❽ *Trovos de mi Alma*, Marco Antonio Solis ❾ *Llegar a Ti*, Jaci Velasquez ❿ *Entre tus Brazos*, Alejandro Fernandez

Source: Billboard

TOP 10 ★
HEAVY METAL ALBUMS IN THE UK

	ALBUM/ARTIST OR GROUP	YEAR
1	*Bat Out of Hell*, Meat Loaf	1978
2	*Bat Out of Hell II – Back to Hell*, Meat Loaf	1993
3	*Led Zeppelin II*, Led Zeppelin	1969
4	*Hysteria*, Def Leppard	1987
5	*Led Zeppelin IV*, Led Zeppelin	1971
6	*Cross Road – The Best of Bon Jovi*, Bon Jovi	1994
7	*So Far So Good*, Bryan Adams	1993
8	*Eliminator*, ZZ Top	1983
9	*Appetite for Destruction*, Guns N' Roses	1987
10	*Slippery When Wet*, Bon Jovi	1986

Source: *MRIB*

TOP 10 ★
COUNTRY ALBUMS IN THE UK

	ALBUM/ARTIST OR GROUP	YEAR
1	*Come on Over*, Shania Twain	1998
2	*20 Golden Greats*, Glen Campbell	1976
3	*40 Golden Greats*, Jim Reeves	1975
4	*Images*, Don Williams	1978
5	*Trampoline*, Mavericks	1998
6	*The Woman in Me*, Shania Twain	2000
7	*Johnny Cash at San Quentin*, Johnny Cash	1969
8	*Greatest Hits*, Glen Campbell	1971
9	*The Very Best of Slim Whitman*, Slim Whitman	1976
10	*Johnny Cash Live at Folsom Prison*, Johnny Cash	1968

Source: *The Popular Music Database*

BON JOVI
Born John Francis Bongiovi, Jon Bon Jovi and his band Bon Jovi have won chart success and global acclaim since their first recordings in 1984, with Slippery When Wet *one of the best-selling albums of the 1980s.*

Gold & Platinum Disks

FEMALE ARTISTS WITH THE MOST GOLD ALBUMS IN THE UK

ARTIST	GOLD ALBUM AWARDS
1 Diana Ross	17
2 =Madonna	12
=Barbra Streisand	12
4 =Mariah Carey	9
=Donna Summer	9
6 Tina Turner	8
7 =Kate Bush	7
=Cher	7
=Celine Dion	7
10 =Joan Armatrading	6
=Janet Jackson	6

Source: *BPI*

Gold discs have been awarded since 1 April 1973 in the UK. They are presented for sales of 400,000 singles or 100,000 albums, cassettes, or CDs (200,000 for budget-priced products).

MALE ARTISTS WITH THE MOST GOLD ALBUMS IN THE UK

ARTIST	GOLD ALBUM AWARDS
1 Rod Stewart	21
2 =Elton John	20
=Cliff Richard	20
4 Paul McCartney*	18
5 =Neil Diamond	17
=James Last	17
7 Mike Oldfield	16
8 =David Bowie	15
=Elvis Presley	15
10 Prince	13

* *Including gold albums with Wings*

Source: *BPI*

FEMALE ARTISTS WITH THE MOST PLATINUM AND MULTI-PLATINUM ALBUMS IN THE UK

ARTIST	PLATINUM AND MULTI-PLATINUM ALBUM AWARDS
1 Madonna	38
2 =Celine Dion	21
=Tina Turner	21
4 Whitney Houston*	16
5 =Enya	12
=Gloria Estefan	12
7 =Kylie Minogue	10
=Mariah Carey	10
=Alanis Morissette	10
=Kate Bush	10

* *Not including the album* The Bodyguard

Source: *BPI*

MARIAH CAREY

Mariah Carey has sold over 100 million albums since 1990, and her singles success ranks her third for most weeks at US No. 1.

GROUPS WITH THE MOST PLATINUM AND MULTI-PLATINUM ALBUMS IN THE UK

GROUP	PLATINUM AND MULTI-PLATINUM ALBUM AWARDS
1 Simply Red	38
2 Queen	33
3 Oasis	28
4 Dire Straits	27
5 U2	25
6 Fleetwood Mac	23
7 Abba	21
8 =R.E.M.	17
=UB40	17
=Wet Wet Wet	17

Source: *BPI*

MALE ARTISTS WITH THE MOST PLATINUM AND MULTI-PLATINUM ALBUMS IN THE UK

ARTIST	PLATINUM AND MULTI-PLATINUM ALBUM AWARDS
1 Michael Jackson	38
2 Phil Collins	31
3 George Michael	23
4 Elton John	20
5 Robbie Williams	19
6 Meat Loaf	17
7 =Chris Rea	14
=Rod Stewart	14
9 =Michael Bolton	13
=Cliff Richard	13

Source: *BPI*

In the UK, platinum disks are awarded for sales of 300,000 albums. Relative to the population of the UK, this represents approximately one sale per 195 inhabitants. Multi-platinum awards are earned through even higher sales (600,000 earn a double platinum award, 900,000 earn a triple platinum award, and so on).

TWO OF U2
Formed in Ireland in 1976, supergroup U2 has enjoyed two decades of chart hits and sell-out international tours. The band still retains its original line-up.

TOP 10 ★

FEMALE ARTISTS WITH THE MOST PLATINUM AND MULTI-PLATINUM ALBUMS IN THE US

ARTIST	PLATINUM AND MULTI-PLATINUM ALBUM AWARDS
1 Barbra Streisand	55
2 = Madonna	51
= Whitney Houston	51
= Mariah Carey	51
5 Celine Dion	39
6 Reba McEntire	32
7 Shania Twain	29
8 Linda Ronstadt	24
9 Janet Jackson	20
10 = Sade	19
= Gloria Estefan	19

Source: *RIAA*

TOP 10 ★

GROUPS WITH THE MOST GOLD ALBUMS IN THE UK

GROUP	GOLD ALBUM AWARDS
1 Queen	22
2 = The Rolling Stones	19
= Status Quo	19
4 = Abba	15
= The Beatles	15
= Genesis	15
7 = Roxy Music	13
= UB40	13
9 Pink Floyd	11
10 10cc	9

Source: *BPI*

Longevity is clearly a factor here: several of the groups earned their first golds in the 1960s.

TOP 10 ★

GROUPS WITH THE MOST PLATINUM AND MULTI-PLATINUM ALBUMS IN THE US

GROUP	PLATINUM AND MULTI-PLATINUM ALBUM AWARDS
1 Beatles	118
2 Led Zeppelin	97
3 Pink Floyd	66
4 Eagles	63
5 Aerosmith	53
6 Van Halen	50
7 Fleetwood Mac	43
8 = Alabama	42
= AC/DC	42
= U2	42

Source: *RIAA*

Who composed Sinead O'Connor's hit *Nothing Compares 2 U*?
see p.128 for the answer

A George Michael
B Dolly Parton
C Prince

Classical & Opera

TOP 10 CITIES WITH THE MOST OPERAS
(City/performances*)

1 **Vienna**, Austria, 32 **2** **Berlin**, Germany, 21 **3** **Prague**, Czech Republic, 20 **4** **Paris**, France, 16 **5** **Hamburg**, Germany, 13 **6** = **London**, UK, 12; = **Zurich**, Switzerland, 12 **8** = **New York**, USA, 11; = **Munich**, Germany, 11 **10** **Hanover**, Germany, 10

* Sample during a 12-month period

TOP 10 ★
LONGEST OPERAS PERFORMED AT THE ROYAL OPERA HOUSE, COVENT GARDEN

OPERA/COMPOSER	RUNNING TIME* HR:MIN
1 *Götterdämmerung*, Richard Wagner	6:00
2 *Die Meistersinger von Nürnberg*, Richard Wagner	5:40
3 *Siegfried*, Richard Wagner	5:25
4 *Tristan und Isolde*, Richard Wagner	5:19
5 *Die Walküre*, Richard Wagner	5:15
6 *Parsifal*, Richard Wagner	5:09
7 *Donnerstag aus Licht*, Karlheinz Stockhausen	4:42
8 *Palestrina*, Hans Pfitzner	4:30
9 *Lohengrin*, Richard Wagner	4:26
10 *Der Rosenkavalier*, Richard Strauss	4:25

* Including intervals

ENRICO CARUSO'S FIRST MILLION-SELLING RECORDINGS

Opera singer Enrico Caruso (1873–1921) was born in Naples, Italy, and made his first public appearance in 1895, playing the role of Faust. Performing in opera houses as far afield as Russia and Argentina, he rapidly established an international reputation. On 12 November 1902 he recorded the aria "Vesti la Giubba" ("On with the Motley") from *I Pagliacci* for the Gramophone Co. By now regarded as the world's greatest operatic tenor, Caruso appeared in this year at the Royal Opera House, Covent Garden, London, and then at the Metropolitan Opera House, New York. "Vesti la Giubba" was later re-recorded with orchestral accompaniment for recording company Victor. The cumulative sales of the two versions easily passed the million mark, perhaps the first record ever to do so.

· YEARS AGO · 100 · YEARS AGO · YEARS AGO ·

ANDREA BOCELLI
Despite his blindness, Italian opera singer Andrea Bocelli has achieved remarkable success both in performance and through his internationally best-selling albums.

TOP 10 ★
MOST PROLIFIC CLASSICAL COMPOSERS

COMPOSER	HOURS OF MUSIC
1 Joseph Haydn (1732–1809, Austrian)	340
2 George Handel (1685–1759, German–English)	303
3 Wolfgang Amadeus Mozart (1756–91, Austrian)	202
4 Johann Sebastian Bach (1685–1750, German)	175
5 Franz Schubert (1797–1828, German)	134
6 Ludwig van Beethoven (1770–1827, German)	120
7 Henry Purcell (1659–95, English)	116
8 Giuseppe Verdi (1813–1901, Italian)	87
9 Anton Dvorák (1841–1904, Czech)	79
10 = Franz Liszt (1811–86, Hungarian)	76
= Peter Tchaikovsky (1840–93, Russian)	76

This list is based on a survey conducted by *Classical Music* magazine, which ranked classical composers by the total number of hours of music each composed. If the length of the composer's working life is brought into the calculation, Schubert wins: his 134 hours were composed in a career of 18 years, giving an average of 7 hours 27 minutes per annum.

TOP 10 ★
CLASSICAL ALBUMS IN THE UK

ALBUM/PERFORMER(S)/ORCHESTRA	YEAR
1 *The Three Tenors Concert*, Carreras, Domingo, Pavarotti	1990
2 *The Essential Pavarotti*, Luciano Pavarotti	1990
3 *Vivaldi: The Four Seasons*, Nigel Kennedy/English Chamber Orchestra	1989
4 *The Three Tenors – In Concert 1994*, Carreras, Domingo, Pavarotti	1994
5 *Voice of an Angel*, Charlotte Church	1998
6 *The Essential Pavarotti, 2*, Luciano Pavarotti	1991
7 *The Pavarotti Collection*, Luciano Pavarotti	1986
8 *Sogno*, Andrea Bocelli	1999
9 *The Voice*, Russell Watson	2000
10 *Charlotte Church*, Charlotte Church	1999

Source: *The Popular Music Database*

THE 10 ★

LATEST WINNERS OF THE "BEST SOLOIST PERFORMANCE"* GRAMMY AWARD

YEAR	SOLOIST/INSTRUMENT#	COMPOSER/WORK
2000	Sharon Isbin, guitar	Lauro, Ruiz-Pipo, Duarte, etc., *Dreams of a World*
1999	Vladimir Ashkenazy	Shostakovich, *24 Preludes and Fugues, Op. 87*
1998	Murray Perahia	Bach, *English Suites Nos. 1, 3, and 6*
1997	Janos Starker, cello	Bach, *Suites for Solo Cello Nos. 1–6*
1996	Earl Wild	Saint-Saens, Handel, etc., *The Romantic Master*
1995	Radu Lupu	Schubert, *Piano Sonatas (B Flat Maj. and A Maj.)*
1994	Emanuel Ax	Haydn, *Piano Sonatas Nos. 32, 47, 53, and 59*
1993	John Browning	Barber, *The Complete Solo Piano Music*
1992	Vladimir Horowitz	Chopin, Liszt, Scarlatti, Scriabin, Clementi, *Discovered Treasures*
1991	Alicia de Larrocha	Granados, *Goyescas; Allegro de Concierto; Danza Lenta*

Without orchestra   #Piano unless otherwise stated

TOP 10 ★

LARGEST OPERA THEATRES

	THEATRE	LOCATION	CAPACITY*
1	**Arena di Verona**#	Verona, Italy	16,663
2	**Municipal Opera Theatre**#	St. Louis, USA	11,745
3	**Teatro alla Scala**	Milan, Italy	3,600
4	**Civic Opera House**	Chicago, USA	3,563
5 =	**The Metropolitan**	New York, USA	3,500
=	**Teatro San Carlo**	Naples, Italy	3,500
7	**Music Hall**	Cincinnati, USA	3,417
8 =	**Teatro Massimo**	Palermo, Italy	3,200
=	**The Hummingbird Centre**	Toronto, Canada	3,200
10	**Halle aux Grains**	Toulouse, France	3,000

* For indoor venues seating capacity only is given, although capacity is often larger when standing capacity is included

 # Open-air venue

Although there are many more venues in the world where opera is regularly performed, the above list is limited to those venues where the principal performances are opera.

THE 10 ★

LATEST WINNERS OF THE "BEST CLASSICAL ALBUM" GRAMMY AWARD

YEAR	COMPOSER/WORK	CONDUCTOR/SOLOIST/ORCHESTRA
2000	Shostakovich, *The String Quartets*	Emerson String Quartet
1999	Stravinsky, *Firebird; The Right of Spring; Perséphone*	Michael Tilson Thomas, Stuart Neill, San Francisco Symphony Orchestra
1998	Barber, *Prayers of Kierkegaard*/ Vaughan Williams, *Dona Nobis Pacem*/ Bartok, *Cantata Profana*	Robert Shaw, Richard Clement, Nathan Gunn, Atlanta Symphony Orchestra and Chorus
1997	Danielpour, Kirchner, Rouse, *Premieres – Cello Concertos*	Yo-Yo Ma, David Zinman, Philadelphia Orchestra
1996	Corigliano, *Of Rage and Remembrance*	Leonard Slatkin, National Symphony Orchestra
1995	Claude Debussy, *La Mer*	Pierre Boulez, Cleveland Orchestra
1994	Béla Bartók, *Concerto for Orchestra; Four Orchestral Pieces, Op. 12*	Pierre Boulez, Chicago Symphony Orchestra
1993	Béla Bartók, *The Wooden Prince*	Pierre Boulez, Chicago Symphony Orchestra and Chorus
1992	Gustav Mahler, *Symphony No. 9*	Leonard Bernstein, Berlin Philharmonic Orchestra
1991	Leonard Bernstein, *Candide*	Leonard Bernstein, London Symphony Orchestra

CLASSIC CONDUCTOR

Leonard Bernstein's posthumous Grammy Award for Candide was one of the 16 Grammys he won, including a Lifetime Achievement Award.

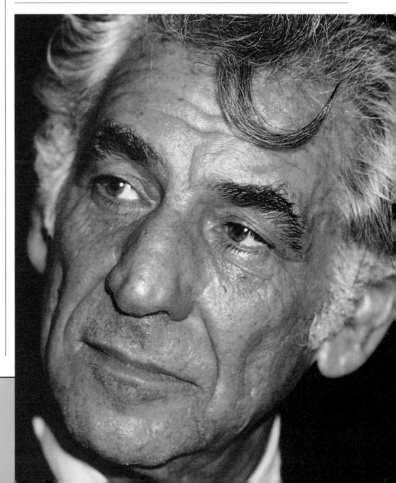

STAGE & SCREEN

All the World's a Stage

MONEY FOR NOTHING

Much Ado About Nothing, *starring Emma Thompson and Kenneth Branagh (who also directed it), achieved both critical and commercial success.*

THE 10 ★
LATEST WINNERS OF THE LAURENCE OLIVIER AWARD FOR BEST ACTOR

YEAR	ACTOR/PLAY
2001	Conleth Hill, *Stones in His Pockets*
2000	Henry Goodman, *The Merchant of Venice*
1999	Kevin Spacey, *The Iceman Cometh*
1998	Ian Holm, *King Lear*
1997	Anthony Sher, *Stanley*
1996	Alex Jennings, *Peer Gynt*
1995	David Bamber, *My Night with Reg*
1994	Mark Rylance, *Much Ado About Nothing*
1993	Robert Stephens, *Henry IV, Parts 1 and 2*
1992	Nigel Hawthorne, *The Madness of George III*

THE 10 ★
LATEST WINNERS OF THE LAURENCE OLIVIER AWARD FOR BEST ACTRESS

YEAR	ACTOR/PLAY
2001	Julie Walters, *All My Sons*
2000	Janie Dee, *Comic Potential*
1999	Eileen Atkins, *The Unexpected Man*
1998	Zoë Wanamaker, *Electra*
1997	Janet McTeer, *A Doll's House*
1996	Judi Dench, *Absolute Hell*
1995	Clare Higgins, *Sweet Bird of Youth*
1994	Fiona Shaw, *Machinal*
1993	Alison Steadman, *The Rise and Fall of Little Voice*
1992	Juliet Stevenson, *Death and the Maiden*

TOP 10 ★
FILMS OF SHAKESPEARE PLAYS

	FILM	YEAR
1	*William Shakespeare's Romeo + Juliet*	1996
2	*Romeo and Juliet*	1968
3	*Much Ado About Nothing*	1993
4	*Hamlet*	1990
5	*Henry V*	1989
6	*Hamlet*	1996
7	*Richard III*	1995
8	*Othello*	1995
9	*The Taming of the Shrew*	1967
10	*Hamlet*	1948

The romantic appeal of *Romeo and Juliet* has ensured its place in first and second positions.

THE 10 ★
FIRST PLAYS WRITTEN BY SHAKESPEARE

	PLAY	YEAR WRITTEN (APPROX.)
1	*Titus Andronicus*	1588–90
2	*Love's Labour's Lost*	1590
3	*Henry VI, Parts I–III*	1590–91
4 =	*The Comedy of Errors*	1591
=	*Richard III*	1591
=	*Romeo and Juliet*	1591
7	*The Two Gentlemen of Verona*	1592–93
8	*A Midsummer Night's Dream*	1593–94
9	*Richard II*	1594
10	*King John*	1595

There are only scant contemporary records of Shakespeare's plays' early performances, and only half of them appeared in print in his lifetime.

THE 10 LATEST WINNERS OF THE AMERICAN EXPRESS AWARD FOR BEST NEW MUSICAL
(Year/musical)

1 2001 *Merrily We Roll Along* **2** 2000 *Honk! The Ugly Duckling* **3** 1999 *Kat and the Kings* **4** 1998 *Beauty and the Beast* **5** 1997 *Martin Guerre* **6** 1996 *Jolson* **7** 1995 *Once on This Island* **8** 1994 *City of Angels* **9** 1993 *Crazy for You* **10** 1992 *Carmen Jones*

TOP 10 ★
LONGEST-RUNNING MUSICALS IN THE UK

MUSICAL/YEARS	PERFORMANCES
1 *Cats* (1981–)	8,419*
2 *Starlight Express* (1984–)	7,026*
3 *Les Misérables* (1985–)	6,290*
4 *The Phantom of the Opera* (1986–)	5,947*
5 *Miss Saigon* (1989–99)	4,263
6 *Oliver!* (1960–69)	4,125
7 *Jesus Christ, Superstar* (1972–80)	3,357
8 *Evita* (1978–86)	2,900
9 *The Sound of Music* (1961–67)	2,386
10 *Salad Days* (1954–60)	2,283

* *Still running; total as at 1 February 2001*

On 12 May 1989, *Cats* became the longest continuously running musical in British theatre history, and on 26 January 1996, with its 6,138th performance, it became the longest-running musical of all time either in the West End or on Broadway.

THE 10 ★
LATEST WINNERS OF THE *EVENING STANDARD* AWARD FOR BEST COMEDY

YEAR*	PLAY/PLAYWRIGHT
2000	*Stones in His Pocket*, Marie Jones
1997	*Closer*, Patrick Marber
1996	*Art*, Yasmina Reza
1995	*Dealer's Choice*, Patrick Marber
1994	*My Night With Reg*, Kevin Elyot
1993	*Jamais Vu*, Ken Campbell
1992	*The Rise and Fall of Little Voice*, Jim Cartwright
1991	*Kvetch*, Steven Berkoff
1990 =	*Man of the Moment*, Alan Ayckbourn
=	*Jeffrey Bernard Is Unwell*, Keith Waterhouse
1989	*Henceforward*, Alan Ayckbourn

* *No awards in 1999 or 1998*

TOP 10 ★
LONGEST-RUNNING SHOWS IN THE UK

SHOW/YEARS	PERFORMANCES
1 *The Mousetrap* (1952–)	20,069*
2 *Cats* (1981–)	8,419*
3 *Starlight Express* (1984–)	7,026*
4 *No Sex, Please – We're British* (1971–81; 1982–86; 1986–87)	6,761
5 *Les Misérables* (1985–)	6,290*
6 *The Phantom of the Opera* (1986–)	5,947*
7 *Miss Saigon* (1989–99)	4,263
8 *Oliver!* (1960–69)	4,125
9 *Oh! Calcutta!* (1970–80)	3,918
10 *Jesus Christ, Superstar* (1972–80)	3,357

* *Still running; total as at 1 February 2001*

All the longest-running shows in the UK have been London productions. *The Mousetrap* opened on 25 November 1952 at the Ambassadors Theatre. After 8,862 performances, it transferred to St. Martin's Theatre, where it re-opened on 25 March 1974. It is not the only play in the world to have run continuously since the 1950s – Eugène Ionesco's *La Cantatrice Chauve* was first performed in Paris on 11 May 1950 and ran on a double bill with *La Leçon* (which had its debut on 20 February 1951) after 16 February 1957, clocking up 13,365 performances to 31 December 1998. The two plays were seen by over 1 million people – despite being staged in la Huchette, a theatre with just 90 seats.

OUT OF THEIR MISERY
Les Misérables has achieved the dual feat of being one of the longest-running musicals both in London and on Broadway.

TOP 10 ★
LONGEST-RUNNING COMEDIES OF ALL TIME IN THE UK

COMEDY/YEARS	PERFORMANCES
1 *No Sex, Please – We're British* (1971–81; 1982–86; 1986–87)	6,761
2 *Run for Your Wife* (1983–91)	2,638
3 *There's a Girl in My Soup* (1966–69; 1969–72)	2,547
4 *The Complete Works of William Shakespeare (abridged)* (1996–)	2,512*
5 *Pyjama Tops* (1969–75)	2,498
6 *Worm's Eye View* (1945–51)	2,245
7 *Boeing Boeing* (1962–65; 1965–67)	2,035
8 *Blithe Spirit* (1941–42; 1942; 1942–46)	1,997
9 *Dirty Linen* (1976–80)	1,667
10 *Reluctant Heroes* (1950–54)	1,610

* *Still running; total as at 1 February 2001*

No Sex, Please – We're British opened at the Strand Theatre, London, on 3 June 1971.

Film Hits

FILMS SHOWN AT THE MOST CINEMAS IN THE US

	FILM	OPENING WEEKEND	CINEMAS
1	Mission: Impossible 2	24 May 2000	3,653
2	Scream 3	4 Feb 2000	3,467
3	The Perfect Storm	30 June 2000	3,407
4	Wild Wild West	30 June 1999	3,342
5	Book of Shadows: Blair Witch 2	27 Oct 2000	3,317
6	Austin Powers: The Spy Who Shagged Me	11 June 1999	3,312
7	Godzilla	20 May 1998	3,310
8	Battlefield Earth	12 May 2000	3,307
9	Lost in Space	3 Apr 1998	3,306
10	The Lost World: Jurassic Park	23 May 1997	3,281

FILMS BY ATTENDANCE

	FILM	YEAR	ATTENDANCE
1	Gone With the Wind	1939	208,100,000
2	Star Wars	1977	198,600,000
3	The Sound of Music	1965	170,600,000
4	E.T.: The Extra-Terrestrial	1982	151,600,000
5	The Ten Commandments	1956	132,800,000
6	The Jungle Book	1967	126,300,000
7	Titanic	1997	124,300,000
8	Jaws	1975	123,300,000
9	Doctor Zhivago	1965	122,700,000
10	101 Dalmatians	1961	119,600,000

This list is based on the actual number of people buying tickets at the US box office. Because it takes account of the large numbers of tickets sold to children and other discounted sales, it differs both from lists that present total box office receipts and those that are adjusted for inflation.

FILM SERIES OF ALL TIME

	FILM SERIES	DATES
1	Star Wars / The Empire Strikes Back / Return of the Jedi / Episode I – The Phantom Menace	1977–99
2	Jurassic Park / The Lost World: Jurassic Park	1993–97
3	Batman / Batman Returns / Batman Forever / Batman & Robin	1989–97
4	Raiders of the Lost Ark / Indiana Jones and the Temple of Doom / Indiana Jones and the Last Crusade	1981–89
5	Mission: Impossible / Mission: Impossible II	1996–2000
6	Star Trek: The Motion Picture / II / III / IV / V / VI / Generations / First Contact / Insurrection	1979–98
7	Back to the Future / II / III	1985–90
8	Lethal Weapon / 2 / 3 / 4	1987–98
9	Toy Story / Toy Story 2	1995–99
10	Home Alone / 2: Lost in NY	1990–92

HIGHEST-GROSSING FILMS OF ALL TIME

	FILM	YEAR	GROSS INCOME ($) USA	WORLD TOTAL
1	Titanic	1997	600,800,000	1,835,400,000
2	Star Wars: Episode I – The Phantom Menace	1999	431,100,000	922,600,000
3	Jurassic Park	1993	357,100,000	920,100,000
4	Independence Day	1996	306,200,000	811,200,000
5	Star Wars	1977/97	461,000,000	798,000,000
6	The Lion King	1994	312,900,000	771,900,000
7	E.T.: The Extra-Terrestrial	1982	399,800,000	704,800,000
8	Forrest Gump	1994	329,700,000	679,700,000
9	The Sixth Sense	1999	293,500,000	660,700,000
10	The Lost World: Jurassic Park	1997	229,100,000	614,400,000

HIGHEST GROSSING FILMS OF ALL TIME IN THE UK

	FILM	YEAR	UK GROSS (£)
1	Titanic	1998	68,532,000
2	The Full Monty	1997	51,992,000
3	Star Wars: Episode I – The Phantom Menace	1999	50,734,000
4	Jurassic Park	1993	47,140,000
5	Toy Story 2	2000	43,491,000
6	Independence Day	1996	36,800,000
7	Men in Black	1997	35,400,000
8	Gladiator	2000	30,908,000
9	Notting Hill	1999	30,403,000
10	Chicken Run	2000	29,428,000

TITANIC RISES

All-time highest grossing film Titanic has earned almost twice as much at the global box office as its closest rival, Star Wars: Episode I.

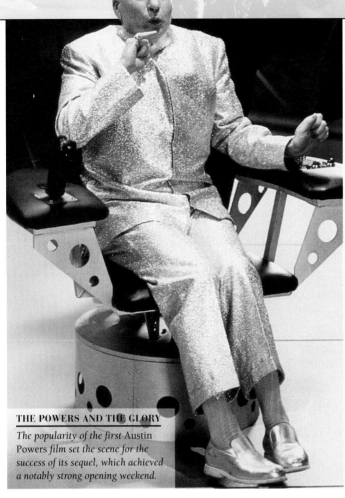

THE POWERS AND THE GLORY

The popularity of the first Austin Powers film set the scene for the success of its sequel, which achieved a notably strong opening weekend.

TOP 10 ★
FILMS OF 2000

	FILM	GROSS INCOME ($) USA	WORLD TOTAL
1	Mission: Impossible II	215,400,000	545,400,000
2	Gladiator	186,700,000	445,000,000
3	The Perfect Storm	182,600,000	325,800,000
4	How the Grinch Stole Christmas	254,900,000	320,400,000
5	Dinosaur	137,700,000	317,800,000
6	X-Men	157,300,000	291,300,000
7	Scary Movie	157,000,000	277,000,000
8	What Lies Beneath	154,800,000	269,400,000
9	Erin Brockovich	125,600,000	253,900,000
10	Charlie's Angels	122,800,000	235,800,000

GLAD TO SEE YOU

One of the most successful films of 2000, Gladiator echoes the epics of the past, a genre that many believed had been consigned to cinema history.

TOP 10 ★
OPENING WEEKENDS
OF ALL TIME IN THE US

	FILM	RELEASE DATE	OPENING WEEKEND GROSS INCOME ($)
1	The Lost World: Jurassic Park	23 May 1997	72,132,785
2	Star Wars: Episode I – The Phantom Menace	21 May 1999	64,820,970
3	Mission: Impossible 2	24 May 2000	57,845,297
4	Toy Story 2	24 Nov 1999	57,388,839
5	Austin Powers: The Spy Who Shagged Me	11 June 1999	54,917,604
6	X-Men	14 July 2000	54,471,475
7	Batman Forever	16 June 1995	52,784,433
8	Men in Black	2 July 1997	51,068,455
9	Independence Day	3 July 1996	50,228,264
10	Jurassic Park	11 June 1993	47,059,560

A high-earning opening weekend (generally three days, Friday to Sunday, but sometimes a four-day holiday weekend) in the US is usually a pointer to the ongoing success of a film, but does not guarantee it.

TOP 10 ★
FILMS OF 2000 IN THE UK

	FILM	GROSS INCOME (£)
1	Toy Story 2	43,491,000
2	Gladiator	30,908,000
3	Chicken Run	29,428,000
4	American Beauty	21,341,000
5	Stuart Little	17,829,000
6	Mission: Impossible II	17,292,000
7	Billy Elliot	16,792,000
8	X-Men	14,976,000
9	The Beach	13,332,000
10	What Lies Beneath	13,230,000

Films of the Decades

FILMS OF THE 1930s

1	Gone With the Wind*	1939
2	Snow White and the Seven Dwarfs	1937
3	The Wizard of Oz	1939
4	The Woman in Red	1935
5	King Kong	1933
6	San Francisco	1936
7=	Hell's Angels	1930
=	Lost Horizon	1937
=	Mr. Smith Goes to Washington	1939
10	Maytime	1937

* Winner of "Best Picture" Academy Award

Gone With the Wind and Snow White and the Seven Dwarfs have generated more income than any other pre-war film. If the income of Gone With the Wind is adjusted to allow for inflation in the period since its release, it could also be regarded as the most successful film ever, earning some $885 million in the US alone.

FILMS OF THE 1940s

1	Bambi	1942
2	Pinocchio	1940
3	Fantasia	1940
4	Cinderella	1949
5	Song of the South	1946
6	The Best Years of Our Lives*	1946
7	The Bells of St. Mary's	1945
8	Duel in the Sun	1946
9	Mom and Dad	1948
10	Samson and Delilah	1949

* Winner of "Best Picture" Academy Award

With the top four films of the decade classic Disney cartoons, the 1940s may be regarded as the "golden age" of the animated film. This colourful genre was especially appealing during and after the drabness of the war years.

MONKEY BUSINESS

In an iconic scene from King Kong, one of the 1930s' highest-earning films, the giant ape fights off his attackers while perched atop the newly opened Empire State Building.

FILMS OF THE 1950s

1	Lady and the Tramp	1955
2	Peter Pan	1953
3	Ben-Hur*	1959
4	The Ten Commandments	1956
5	Sleeping Beauty	1959
6	Around the World in 80 Days*	1956
7=	The Greatest Show on Earth*	1952
=	The Robe	1953
9	The Bridge on the River Kwai*	1957
10	Peyton Place	1957

* Winner of "Best Picture" Academy Award

While the popularity of animated films continued, the 1950s was outstanding as the decade of the "big" picture (in cast and scale).

TOP 10 FILMS OF THE 1960s

❶ *101 Dalmatians*, 1961 ❷ *The Jungle Book*, 1967 ❸ *The Sound of Music**, 1965 ❹ *Thunderball*, 1965 ❺ *Goldfinger*, 1964 ❻ *Doctor Zhivago*, 1965 ❼ *You Only Live Twice*, 1967 ❽ *The Graduate*, 1968 ❾ *Mary Poppins*, 1964 ❿ *Butch Cassidy and the Sundance Kid*, 1969

* Winner of "Best Picture" Academy Award

TOP 10 ★
FILMS OF THE LAST 10 YEARS

1	Titanic*	1997
2	Star Wars: Episode I – The Phantom Menace	1999
3	Jurassic Park	1993
4	Independence Day	1996
5	The Lion King	1994
6	Forrest Gump*	1994
7	The Sixth Sense	1999
8	The Lost World: Jurassic Park	1997
9	Men in Black	1997
10	Armageddon	1998

* Winner of "Best Picture" Academy Award

BRINGING THE HOUSE DOWN

The White House sustains a direct hit from an invading spacecraft in a scene from Independence Day, *one of the top films of the last 10 years.*

TOP 10 ★
FILMS OF THE 1970s

1	Star Wars	1977/97*
2	Jaws	1975
3	Close Encounters of the Third Kind	1977/80*
4	The Exorcist	1973/98*
5	Moonraker	1979
6	The Spy Who Loved Me	1977
7	The Sting#	1973
8	Grease	1978
9	The Godfather#	1972
10	Saturday Night Fever	1977

* Date of re-release

\# Winner of "Best Picture" Academy Award

In the 1970s the arrival of two prodigies, Steven Spielberg and George Lucas, set the scene for the high-adventure blockbusters whose domination has continued ever since.

JAWS OF DEATH

After holding the record as the world's highest-earning film, Jaws *was overtaken before the decade was out by* Star Wars.

TOP 10 FILMS OF THE 1980s

1 *E.T.: The Extra-Terrestrial*, 1982 **2** *Indiana Jones and the Last Crusade*, 1989 **3** *Batman*, 1989 **4** *Rain Man*, 1988 **5** *Return of the Jedi*, 1983 **6** *Raiders of the Lost Ark*, 1981 **7** *The Empire Strikes Back*, 1980 **8** *Who Framed Roger Rabbit?*, 1988 **9** *Back to the Future*, 1985 **10** *Top Gun*, 1986

Did You Know? In *Independence Day*, the American flag left on the Moon in 1969 by *Apollo 11* astronauts is seen standing proudly on the surface. In reality, the flag fell over when Neil Armstrong and "Buzz" Aldrin blasted off from the surface.

Film Genres

TOP 10 ★
WESTERNS

1	*Dances With Wolves*	1990
2	*Wild Wild West*	1999
3	*Maverick*	1994
4	*Unforgiven*	1992
5	*Butch Cassidy and the Sundance Kid*	1969
6	*Jeremiah Johnson*	1972
7	*How the West Was Won*	1962
8	*Young Guns*	1988
9	*Young Guns II*	1990
10	*Pale Rider*	1985

TOP 10 ★
GHOST FILMS

1	*The Sixth Sense*	1999
2	*Ghost*	1990
3	*Ghostbusters*	1984
4	*Casper*	1995
5	*What Lies Beneath*	2000
6	*Ghostbusters II*	1989
7	*Sleepy Hollow*	1999
8	*The Haunting*	1999
9	*Beetlejuice*	1988
10	*The Nightmare Before Christmas*	1993

TOP 10 ★
WEDDING FILMS

1	*My Best Friend's Wedding*	1997
2	*Runaway Bride*	1999
3	*Four Weddings and a Funeral*	1994
4	*The Wedding Singer*	1998
5	*Father of the Bride*	1991
6	*Father of the Bride Part II*	1995
7	*Muriel's Wedding*	1994
8	*The Princess Bride*	1987
9	*Betsy's Wedding*	1990
10	*A Wedding*	1978

TOP 10 ★
HORROR FILMS

1	*Jurassic Park*	1993
2	*The Sixth Sense*	1999
3	*The Lost World: Jurassic Park*	1997
4	*Jaws*	1975
5	*The Mummy*	1999
6	*Godzilla*	1998
7	*The Exorcist*	1973
8	*Scary Movie*	2000
9	*The Blair Witch Project*	1999
10	*Interview With the Vampire*	1994

TOP 10 ★
JAMES BOND FILMS

	FILM/YEAR	BOND ACTOR
1	*The World Is Not Enough*, 1999	Pierce Brosnan
2	*GoldenEye*, 1995	Pierce Brosnan
3	*Tomorrow Never Dies*, 1997	Pierce Brosnan
4	*Moonraker*, 1979	Roger Moore
5	*For Your Eyes Only*, 1981	Roger Moore
6	*The Living Daylights*, 1987	Timothy Dalton
7	*The Spy Who Loved Me*, 1977	Roger Moore
8	*Octopussy*, 1983	Roger Moore
9	*Licence to Kill*, 1990	Timothy Dalton
10	*A View to a Kill*, 1985	Roger Moore

TOP 10 ★
FILMS FEATURING DINOSAURS

1	*Jurassic Park*	1993
2	*The Lost World: Jurassic Park*	1997
3	*Godzilla*	1998
4	*Dinosaur**	2000
5	*Mission to Mars*	2000
6	*Fantasia**	1940
7	*T-Rex: Back to the Cretaceous*	1998
8	*The Flintstones in Viva Rock Vegas*	2000
9	*The Land Before Time**	1988
10	*Super Mario Bros.*	1993

* Animated; others live-action with mechanical or computer-generated sequences

BLOCKBUSTERS

Ghostbusters *starred Bill Murray alongside Dan Aykroyd and Harold Ramis, both of whom also co-wrote the first film and its sequel.*

FUTURE PERFECT

Schoolkid Marty McFly (Michael J. Fox) and scientist Dr. Emmett "Doc" L. Brown (Christopher Lloyd) test the Doc's time machine DeLorean.

TOP 10 ★
TIME TRAVEL FILMS

1	Terminator II: Judgment Day	1991
2	Back to the Future	1985
3	Austin Powers: The Spy Who Shagged Me	2000
4	Back to the Future III	1990
5	Back to the Future II	1989
6	Twelve Monkeys	1995
7	Timecop	1994
8	The Terminator	1984
9	Austin Powers: International Man of Mystery	1997
10	Pleasantville	1998

JAMES BOND

In 1952, at his Jamaican house, Goldeneye, former Royal Navy intelligence officer-turned-journalist Ian Fleming (1908–64) was working on a spy story and searching for a suitable name for his hero, when his eye fell on a book, *Field Guide of Birds of the West Indies* by American ornithologist James Bond (1900–89). As Fleming later commented, "It struck me that this name, brief, unromantic, and yet very masculine, was just what I needed", and thus an internationally popular fictitious character and, later, a huge cinema industry, was born. The fictional James Bond's first appearance in print was in *Casino Royale*, published in Britain in 1953 and in the US a year later.

TOP 10 MAFIA FILMS

❶ *The Untouchables*, 1987 ❷ *Analyze This*, 1999
❸ *The Godfather, Part III*, 1990 ❹ *The Godfather*, 1972
❺ *L.A. Confidential*, 1997 ❻ *Donnie Brasco*, 1997
❼ *The Client*, 1994 ❽ *The Godfather, Part II*, 1974
❾ *The Firm*, 1993 ❿ *The Whole Nine Yards*, 2000

TOP 10 ★
COP FILMS

1	The Fugitive	1993
2	Die Hard: With a Vengeance	1995
3	Basic Instinct	1992
4	Se7en	1995
5	Lethal Weapon 3	1993
6	Beverly Hills Cop	1984
7	Beverly Hills Cop II	1987
8	Lethal Weapon 4	1998
9	Speed	1994
10	Die Hard 2	1990

Although films in which one of the central characters is a policeman have never been among the most successful films of all time, many have earned respectable amounts at the box office. Both within and outside the Top 10, they are divided between those with a comic slant, such as the two *Beverly Hills Cop* films, and darker police thrillers, such as *Basic Instinct*. Films featuring FBI and CIA agents have been excluded from the reckoning, hence eliminating blockbusters such as *Mission: Impossible* and *The Silence of the Lambs*.

TOP 10 ★
COMEDY FILMS

1	Forrest Gump	1994
2	Home Alone	1990
3	Ghost	1990
4	Pretty Woman	1990
5	Mrs. Doubtfire	1993
6	There's Something About Mary	1998
7	The Flintstones	1994
8	Notting Hill	1999
9	Who Framed Roger Rabbit	1988
10	How the Grinch Stole Christmas	1999

"LIFE IS LIKE A BOX OF CHOCOLATES ..."

As Forrest Gump, Tom Hanks plays a man whose simple, homespun philosophy enables him to succeed against all odds.

From what 1968 film did the Oscar-winning song *The Windmills of Your Mind* come?

A *The Graduate*
B *Funny Girl*
C *The Thomas Crown Affair*

see p.179 for the answer

Oscar-Winning Films

FILMS NOMINATED FOR THE MOST OSCARS

FILM/YEAR	AWARDS	NOMINATIONS
1 =All About Eve, 1950	6	14
=Titanic, 1997	11	14
3 =Gone With the Wind, 1939	8*	13
=From Here to Eternity, 1953	8	13
=Mary Poppins, 1964	5	13
=Who's Afraid of Virginia Woolf?, 1966	5	13
=Forrest Gump, 1994	6	13
=Shakespeare in Love, 1998	7	13
9 =Mrs. Miniver, 1942	6	12
=The Song of Bernadette, 1943	4	12
=Johnny Belinda, 1948	1	12
=A Streetcar Named Desire, 1951	4	12
=On the Waterfront, 1954	8	12
=Ben-Hur, 1959	11	12
=Becket, 1964	1	12
=My Fair Lady, 1964	8	12
=Reds, 1981	3	12
=Dances With Wolves, 1990	7	12
=Schindler's List, 1993	7	12
=The English Patient, 1996	9	12
=Gladiator, 2000	5	12

* Plus two special awards

While Johnny Belinda and Becket at least had the consolation of winning once out of their 12 nominations each, both The Turning Point (1977) and The Color Purple (1985) suffered the ignominy of receiving 11 nominations without a single win.

FILMS TO WIN THE MOST OSCARS

FILM/YEAR	NOMINATIONS	AWARDS
1 =Ben-Hur, 1959	12	11
=Titanic, 1997	14	11
3 West Side Story, 1961	11	10
4 =Gigi, 1958	9	9
=The Last Emperor, 1987	9	9
=The English Patient, 1996	12	9
7 =Gone With the Wind, 1939	13	8*
=From Here to Eternity, 1953	13	8
=On the Waterfront, 1954	12	8
=My Fair Lady, 1964	12	8
=Cabaret, 1972	10	8
=Gandhi, 1982	11	8
=Amadeus, 1984	11	8

* Plus two special awards

FIRST "BEST PICTURE" OSCAR-WINNING FILMS

YEAR	FILM
1927/28	Wings
1928/29	Broadway Melody
1930	All Quiet on the Western Front
1931	Cimarron
1932	Grand Hotel
1933	Cavalcade
1934	It Happened One Night*
1935	Mutiny on the Bounty
1936	The Great Ziegfeld
1937	The Life of Emile Zola

* Winner of Oscars for "Best Director", "Best Actor", "Best Actress", and "Best Screenplay"

The first Academy Awards, popularly known as Oscars, were presented at a ceremony at the Hollywood Roosevelt Hotel on 16 May 1929, and were for films released in the period 1927–28. Wings, the first film to be honoured as "Best Picture", was silent. A second ceremony, held at the Ambassador Hotel on 31 October of the same year, was for films released in 1928–29, and was won by Broadway Melody.

HIGHEST-EARNING "BEST PICTURE" OSCAR WINNERS

FILM	YEAR
1 Titanic	1997
2 Forrest Gump	1994
3 Gladiator	2000
4 Dances With Wolves	1990
5 Rain Man	1988
6 Schindler's List	1993
7 Shakespeare in Love	1998
8 The English Patient	1996
9 American Beauty	1999
10 Braveheart	1995

Winning the Academy Award for "Best Picture" is no guarantee of box-office success: the award is given for a picture released the previous year, and by the time the Oscar ceremony takes place, the film-going public has already effectively decided on the winning picture's fate. Receiving the Oscar may enhance a successful picture's continuing earnings, but it is generally too late to revive a film that may already have been judged mediocre.

"BEST PICTURE" OSCAR WINNERS OF THE 1950s

YEAR	FILM
1950	All About Eve
1951	An American in Paris
1952	The Greatest Show on Earth
1953	From Here to Eternity
1954	On the Waterfront
1955	Marty
1956	Around the World in 80 Days
1957	The Bridge on the River Kwai
1958	Gigi
1959	Ben-Hur

The first winning film of the 1950s, All About Eve, received the most Oscar nominations (14), while the last, Ben-Hur, won the most (11).

SWORD PLAY

Michelle Yeoh stars in Crouching Tiger, Hidden Dragon, which crowned its international success and host of awards with the "Best Foreign Language Film" Oscar.

THE 10 ★
LATEST "BEST FOREIGN LANGUAGE FILM" OSCAR WINNERS

YEAR	ENGLISH TITLE/LANGUAGE
2000	*Crouching Tiger, Hidden Dragon*, Mandarin
1999	*All About My Mother*, Spanish
1998	*Life is Beautiful*, Italian
1997	*Character*, Dutch/English/German/French
1996	*Kolya*, Czech/Russsian
1995	*Antonia's Line*, Dutch
1994	*Burnt by the Sun*, Russian
1993	*The Age of Beauty*, Spanish
1992	*Indochine*, French/Vietnamese
1991	*Mediterraneo*, Italian

THE 10 ★
"BEST PICTURE" OSCAR WINNERS OF THE 1960s

YEAR	FILM
1960	*The Apartment*
1961	*West Side Story*
1962	*Lawrence of Arabia*
1963	*Tom Jones*
1964	*My Fair Lady*
1965	*The Sound of Music*
1966	*A Man for All Seasons*
1967	*In the Heat of the Night*
1968	*Oliver!*
1969	*Midnight Cowboy*

The 1960 winner, *The Apartment*, was the last black-and-white winner until *Schindler's List*, which was released in 1993.

THE 10 "BEST PICTURE" OSCAR WINNERS OF THE 1970s
(Year/film)

① 1970 *Patton* ② 1971 *The French Connection* ③ 1972 *The Godfather*
④ 1973 *The Sting* ⑤ 1974 *The Godfather Part II* ⑥ 1975 *One Flew Over the Cuckoo's Nest*
⑦ 1976 *Rocky* ⑧ 1977 *Annie Hall* ⑨ 1978 *The Deer Hunter*
⑩ 1979 *Kramer vs. Kramer*

THE 10 ★
"BEST PICTURE" OSCAR WINNERS OF THE 1980s

YEAR	FILM
1980	*Ordinary People*
1981	*Chariots of Fire*
1982	*Gandhi*
1983	*Terms of Endearment*
1984	*Amadeus*
1985	*Out of Africa*
1986	*Platoon*
1987	*The Last Emperor*
1988	*Rain Man*
1989	*Driving Miss Daisy*

THE 10 ★
LATEST "BEST PICTURE" OSCAR WINNERS

YEAR	FILM
2000	*Gladiator*
1999	*American Beauty*
1998	*Shakespeare in Love*
1997	*Titanic*
1996	*The English Patient*
1995	*Braveheart*
1994	*Forrest Gump*
1993	*Schindler's List*
1992	*Unforgiven*
1991	*The Silence of the Lambs*

Which actor supplied the voice of Mushu in the animated film *Mulan*?
see p.169 for the answer

A Bruce Willis
B Eddie Murphy
C Jim Carrey

Oscar-Winning Stars

YOUNGEST OSCAR-WINNING ACTORS AND ACTRESSES

	ACTOR OR ACTRESS	AWARD/FILM (WHERE SPECIFIED)	YEAR	AGE*
1	Shirley Temple	Special Award – outstanding contribution during 1934	1934	6
2	Margaret O' Brien	Special Award (*Meet Me in St Louis*)	1944	8
3	Vincent Winter	Special Award (*The Little Kidnappers*)	1954	8
4	Ivan Jandl	Special Award (*The Search*)	1948	9
5	Jon Whiteley	Special Award (*The Little Kidnappers*)	1954	10
6	Tatum O'Neal	"Best Supporting Actress" (*Paper Moon*)	1973	10
7	Anna Paquin	"Best Supporting Actress" (*The Piano*)	1993	11
8	Claude Jarman, Jr.	Special Award (*The Yearling*)	1946	12
9	Bobby Driscoll	Special Award (*The Window*)	1949	13
10	Hayley Mills	Special Award (*Pollyanna*)	1960	13

* At the time of the Award ceremony; those of apparently identical age have been ranked according to their precise age in days at the time of the ceremony

The Academy Awards ceremony usually takes place at the end of March in the year following that in which the film was released in the US, so the winners are generally at least a year older when they receive their Oscars than when they acted in their award-winning films.

THE 10 "BEST ACTRESS" OSCAR WINNERS OF THE 1970s

(Year/actress/film)

1 1970 Glenda Jackson, *Women in Love* **2** 1971 Jane Fonda, *Klute*
3 1972 Liza Minnelli, *Cabaret* **4** 1973 Glenda Jackson, *A Touch of Class*
5 1974 Ellen Burstyn, *Alice Doesn't Live Here Any More* **6** 1975 Louise Fletcher, *One Flew Over the Cuckoo's Nest**# **7** 1976 Faye Dunaway, *Network* **8** 1977 Diane Keaton, *Annie Hall**
9 1978 Jane Fonda, *Coming Home* **10** 1979 Sally Field, *Norma Rae*

* Winner of "Best Picture" Oscar
 # Winner of "Best Director", "Best Actor", and "Best Screenplay" Oscars

OSCAR

Founded on 4 May 1927, the Hollywood-based Academy of Motion Picture Arts and Sciences proposed improving the image of the film industry by issuing "awards for merit or distinction" in various categories. The award itself, a statuette designed by Cedric Gibbons, was modelled by a young artist, George Stanley. The gold-plated naked male figure holds a sword and stands on a reel of film. It was simply called "the statuette" up until 1931, when Academy librarian Mrs Margaret Herrick said, "It looks like my Uncle Oscar!" – and the name stuck until this day.

WHO WAS · WHO WAS · WHO WAS · WHO WAS · ?

"BEST ACTOR" OSCAR WINNERS OF THE 1970s

YEAR	ACTOR/FILM
1970	George C. Scott, *Patton**
1971	Gene Hackman, *The French Connection**
1972	Marlon Brando, *The Godfather**
1973	Jack Lemmon, *Save the Tiger*
1974	Art Carney, *Harry and Tonto*
1975	Jack Nicholson, *One Flew Over the Cuckoo's Nest**#
1976	Peter Finch, *Network*
1977	Richard Dreyfuss, *The Goodbye Girl*
1978	John Voight, *Coming Home*
1979	Dustin Hoffman, *Kramer vs. Kramer**

* Winner of "Best Picture" Oscar

 # Winner of "Best Director", "Best Actress", and "Best Screenplay" Oscars

FIRST CUCKOO

Winner of five Oscars, One Flew Over the Cuckoo's Nest *established the movie careers of both its star, Jack Nicholson, and producer, Michael Douglas.*

THE 10 ★
"BEST ACTOR" OSCAR WINNERS OF THE 1980s

YEAR	ACTOR/FILM
1980	Robert De Niro, *Raging Bull*
1981	Henry Fonda, *On Golden Pond**
1982	Ben Kingsley, *Gandhi*#
1983	Robert Duvall, *Tender Mercies*
1984	F. Murray Abraham, *Amadeus*#
1985	William Hurt, *Kiss of the Spider Woman*
1986	Paul Newman, *The Color of Money*
1987	Michael Douglas, *Wall Street*
1988	Dustin Hoffman, *Rain Man*#
1989	Daniel Day-Lewis, *My Left Foot*

* *Winner of "Best Actress" Oscar*

Winner of "Best Picture" Oscar

THE 10 ★
"BEST ACTRESS" OSCAR WINNERS OF THE 1980s

YEAR	ACTRESS/FILM
1980	Sissy Spacek, *Coal Miner's Daughter*
1981	Katharine Hepburn, *On Golden Pond**
1982	Meryl Streep, *Sophie's Choice*
1983	Shirley MacLaine, *Terms of Endearment*#
1984	Sally Field, *Places in the Heart*
1985	Geraldine Page, *The Trip to Bountiful*
1986	Marlee Matlin, *Children of a Lesser God*
1987	Cher, *Moonstruck*
1988	Jodie Foster, *The Accused*
1989	Jessica Tandy, *Driving Miss Daisy*#

* *Winner of "Best Actor" Oscar*

Winner of "Best Picture" Oscar

THE 10 ★
LATEST "BEST ACTOR" OSCAR WINNERS

YEAR	ACTOR/FILM
2000	Russell Crowe, *Gladiator**
1999	Kevin Spacey, *American Beauty**
1998	Roberto Benigni, *La vita é bella* (*Life Is Beautiful*)
1997	Jack Nicholson, *As Good as It Gets*#
1996	Geoffrey Rush, *Shine*
1995	Nicolas Cage, *Leaving Las Vegas*
1994	Tom Hanks, *Forrest Gump**
1993	Tom Hanks, *Philadelphia*
1992	Al Pacino, *Scent of a Woman*
1991	Anthony Hopkins, *The Silence of the Lambs**#

* *Winner of "Best Picture" Oscar*

Winner of "Best Actress" Oscar

Tom Hanks shares the honour of two consecutive wins with Spencer Tracy (1937: *Captains Courageous* and 1938: *Boys Town*). Only four other actors have won twice: Marlon Brando (1954; 1972), Gary Cooper (1941; 1952), Dustin Hoffman (1977; 1988), and Jack Nicholson (1975; 1997).

THE 10 ★
LATEST "BEST ACTRESS" OSCAR WINNERS

YEAR	ACTRESS/FILM
2000	Julia Roberts, *Erin Brockovich*
1999	Hilary Swank, *Boys Don't Cry*
1998	Gwyneth Paltrow, *Shakespeare in Love**
1997	Helen Hunt, *As Good as It Gets*#
1996	Frances McDormand, *Fargo*
1995	Susan Sarandon, *Dead Man Walking*
1994	Jessica Lange, *Blue Sky*
1993	Holly Hunter, *The Piano*
1992	Emma Thompson, *Howard's End*
1991	Jodie Foster, *The Silence of the Lambs**#

* *Winner of "Best Picture" Oscar*

Winner of "Best Actor" Oscar

FARGO

Frances McDormand's performance as policewoman Marge Gunderson in Fargo, *directed by her husband Joel Cohen, gained her the 1996 "Best Actress" Oscar.*

And the Winner Is . . .

THE 10 ★
LATEST WINNERS OF THE CANNES PALME D'OR FOR "BEST FILM"

YEAR	FILM/COUNTRY
2000	*Dancer in the Dark*, Denmark
1999	*Rosetta*, France
1998	*Eternity and a Day*, Greece
1997	*The Eel*, Japan/ *The Taste of Cherries*, Iran
1996	*Secrets and Lies*, UK
1995	*Underground*, Yugoslavia
1994	*Pulp Fiction*, USA
1993	*Farewell My Concubine*, China/ *The Piano*, Australia
1992	*Best Intentions*, Denmark
1991	*Barton Fink*, USA

In its early years, there was no single "Best Film" award at the Cannes Film Festival, several films being honoured jointly. A "Grand Prize", first awarded in 1949, has been known since 1955 as the "Palme d'Or".

THE 10 ★
LATEST ENGLISH-LANGUAGE FILMS TO WIN THE CANNES PALME D'OR

	FILM/DIRECTOR/COUNTRY	YEAR
1	*Secrets and Lies*, Mike Leigh, UK	1996
2	*Pulp Fiction*, Quentin Tarantino, USA	1994
3	*The Piano**, Jane Campion, Australia	1993
4	*Barton Fink*, Joel Coen, USA	1991
5	*Wild at Heart*, David Lynch, USA	1990
6	*sex, lies, and videotape*, Steven Soderbergh, USA	1989
7	*The Mission*, Roland Joffé, UK	1986
8	*Paris, Texas*, Wim Wenders, USA	1984
9	*Missing*#, Constantin Costa-Gavras, USA	1982
10	*All that Jazz*+, Bob Fosse, USA	1980

* *Shared with* Farewell My Concubine *(Chen Kaige, China)*

Shared with Yol *(Serif Goren, Turkey)*

+ *Shared with* Kagemusha *(Akira Kurosawa, Japan)*

THE 10 ★
FIRST WINNERS OF THE BAFTA "BEST FILM" AWARD

YEAR	FILM/COUNTRY
1947	*The Best Years of Our Lives*, USA
1948	*Hamlet*, UK
1949	*Bicycle Thieves*, Italy
1950	*All About Eve*, USA
1951	*La Ronde*, France
1952	*The Sound Barrier*, UK
1953	*Jeux Interdits*, France
1954	*Le Salaire de la Peur*, France
1955	*Richard III*, UK
1956	*Gervaise*, France

THE 10 ★
FIRST WINNERS OF THE BAFTA "BEST DIRECTOR" AWARD

YEAR	DIRECTOR/FILM/COUNTRY
1968	Mike Nichols, *The Graduate*, USA
1969	John Schlesinger, *Midnight Cowboy*, USA
1970	George Roy Hill, *Butch Cassidy and the Sundance Kid*, USA
1971	John Schlesinger, *Sunday, Bloody Sunday*, UK
1972	Bob Fosse, *Cabaret*, USA
1973	François Truffault, *Day for Night*, France
1974	Roman Polanski, *Chinatown*, USA
1975	Stanley Kubrick, *Barry Lyndon*, UK
1976	Milos Forman, *One Flew Over the Cuckoo's Nest*, USA
1977	Woody Allen, *Annie Hall*, USA

SONG AND DANCE

Winner of the 2000 Palme d'Or, Dancer in the Dark *also won the "Best Actress" award for Icelandic singer Björk. She had previously appeared in* Juniper Tree *(1987) and in a cameo role in* Prêt-à-Porter *(1994).*

THE 10 ★
LATEST WINNERS OF THE BAFTA "BEST DIRECTOR" AWARD

YEAR	DIRECTOR/FILM/COUNTRY
2000	Ang Lee, *Crouching Tiger, Hidden Dragon*, China, Taiwan/USA
1999	Pedro Almodovar, *All About My Mother*, Spain
1998	Peter Weir, *The Truman Show*, USA
1997	Baz Luhrmann, *William Shakespeare's Romeo + Juliet*, USA
1996	Joel Cohen, *Fargo*, USA
1995	Michael Radford, *Il Postino*, Italy
1994	Mike Newell, *Four Weddings and a Funeral*, UK
1993	Steven Spielberg, *Schindler's List*, USA
1992	Robert Altman, *The Player*, USA
1991	Alan Parker, *The Commitments*, USA/UK

Although the winner of BAFTA "Best Film" often corresponds with the Oscar equivalent, only one recent "Best Director" coincides: Steven Spielberg for *Schindler's List*.

THE 10 ★
LATEST WINNERS OF THE BAFTA "BEST ACTOR" AWARD

YEAR	ACTOR/FILM/COUNTRY
2000	Jamie Bell, *Billy Elliot*, UK
1999	Kevin Spacey, *American Beauty*, USA
1998	Roberto Benigni, *Life is Beautiful*, Italy
1997	Robert Carlyle, *The Full Monty*, UK
1996	Geoffrey Rush, *Shine*, Australia
1995	Nigel Hawthorne, *The Madness of King George*, UK
1994	Hugh Grant, *Four Weddings and a Funeral*, UK
1993	Anthony Hopkins, *The Remains of the Day*, UK
1992	Robert Downey Jr, *Chaplin*, UK
1991	Anthony Hopkins, *The Silence of the Lambs*, USA

THE 10 ★
LATEST WINNERS OF THE BAFTA "BEST FILM" AWARD

YEAR	FILM/COUNTRY
2000	*Gladiator*, USA
1999	*American Beauty*, USA
1998	*Shakespeare in Love*, USA
1997	*The Full Monty*, UK
1996	*The English Patient*, UK
1995	*Sense and Sensibility*, UK
1994	*Four Weddings and a Funeral*, UK
1993	*Schindler's List*, USA
1992	*Howards End*, UK
1991	*The Commitments*, USA/UK

THE 10 ★
LATEST WINNERS OF THE BAFTA "BEST ACTRESS" AWARD

YEAR	ACTRESS/FILM/COUNTRY
2000	Julia Roberts, *Erin Brockovich*, USA
1999	Annette Bening, *American Beauty*, USA
1998	Cate Blanchett, *Elizabeth*, UK
1997	Judi Dench, *Mrs. Brown*, UK
1996	Brenda Blethyn, *Secrets and Lies*, UK
1995	Emma Thompson, *Sense and Sensibility*, UK
1994	Susan Sarandon, *The Client*, USA
1993	Holly Hunter, *The Piano*, Australia
1992	Emma Thompson, *Howards End*, UK
1991	Jodie Foster, *The Silence of the Lambs*, USA

ERIN BROCKOVICH
Julia Roberts's BAFTA and Golden Globe Award for her eponymous role in Erin Brockovich foreshadowed her "Best Actress" Oscar. The real Erin Brockovich appears in the film as a waitress called Julia.

Whose debut screen role was billed as "Pretty girl on train"?
see p.171 for the answer
A Glenn Close
B Marilyn Monroe
C Sharon Stone

Leading Men

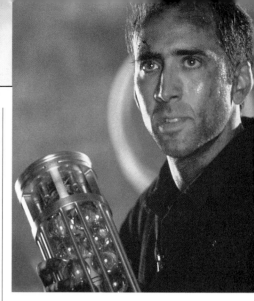

TOP 10 ★
JIM CARREY FILMS

1	Batman Forever	1995
2	The Mask	1994
3	How the Grinch Stole Christmas	2000
4	Liar Liar	1997
5	The Truman Show	1998
6	Dumb and Dumber	1994
7	Ace Ventura: When Nature Calls	1995
8	Me, Myself & Irene	2000
9	The Cable Guy	1996
10	Ace Ventura: Pet Detective	1994

TOP 10 ★
NICOLAS CAGE FILMS

1	The Rock	1996
2	Face/Off	1997
3	Gone in Sixty Seconds	2000
4	Con Air	1997
5	City of Angels	1998
6	Snake Eyes	1998
7	8MM	1999
8	Moonstruck	1987
9	Leaving Las Vegas	1995
10	Peggy Sue Got Married	1986

RATTLING THE CAGE

Nicolas Cage stars as FBI biochemist Dr. Stanley Goodspeed in the 1996 film The Rock, *which is his highest-earning film to date.*

TOP 10 ★
PIERCE BROSNAN FILMS

1	Mrs. Doubtfire	1993
2	The World Is Not Enough	1999
3	GoldenEye	1995
4	Tomorrow Never Dies	1997
5	Dante's Peak	1997
6	The Thomas Crown Affair	1999
7	Mars Attacks!	1996
8	The Mirror Has Two Faces	1996
9	The Lawnmower Man	1992
10	Love Affair	1994

Pierce Brosnan, now best known as James Bond, provided the voice of King Arthur in the animated film *Quest for Camelot* (1998). If included, it would be ranked ninth.

PIERCING LOOK

Irish-born Pierce Brosnan took over the role of James Bond with GoldenEye. This, along with Tomorrow Never Dies and The World Is Not Enough, are the highest earning of all the Bond series.

TOP 10 ★
TOM CRUISE FILMS

1	Mission: Impossible 2	2000
2	Mission: Impossible	1996
3	Rain Man	1988
4	Top Gun	1986
5	Jerry Maguire	1996
6	The Firm	1993
7	A Few Good Men	1992
8	Interview With the Vampire	1994
9	Days of Thunder	1990
10	Eyes Wide Shut	1999

TOP 10 ★
KEVIN SPACEY FILMS

1	American Beauty	1999
2	Se7en	1995
3	Outbreak	1995
4	A Time to Kill	1996
5	L.A. Confidential	1997
6	The Negotiator	1998
7	The Usual Suspects	1995
8	Pay it Forward	2000
9	See No Evil, Hear No Evil	1989
10	Heartburn	1986

Kevin Spacey provided the voice of Hopper in the animated film *A Bug's Life* (1998). If included, this would be his No. 1 film.

TOP 10 ★
$100 MILLION FILM ACTORS

	ACTOR*	FILMS#	TOTAL ($)+
1	Harrison Ford	16	5,090,800,000
2	Samuel L. Jackson	10	3,426,000,000
3	Bruce Willis	13	3,420,100,000
4	Tom Cruise	10	3,055,300,000
5	James Earl Jones	9	3,001,200,000
6	Robin Williams	11	2,749,800,000
7	Mel Gibson	14	2,595,700,000
8	Tommy Lee Jones	11	2,405,800,000
9	Eddie Murphy	10	2,366,000,000
10	Leonardo DiCaprio	4	2,293,500,000

* Appeared in or provided voice in film

Earning over $100 million worldwide to end of 2000

+ Of all $100-million-plus films

TOP 10 ★
BRAD PITT FILMS

1	Se7en	1995
2	Interview With the Vampire	1994
3	Sleepers	1996
4	Legends of the Fall	1994
5	Twelve Monkeys	1995
6	The Devil's Own	1997
7	Meet Joe Black	1998
8	Seven Years in Tibet	1997
9	Fight Club	1999
10	Thelma & Louise	1991

PITT STOPPER

Brad (William Bradley) Pitt plays Detective David Mills in Se7en, his most successful film to date. Pitt appeared in more than 20 films during the 1990s.

TOP 10 EDDIE MURPHY FILMS

❶ *Beverly Hills Cop*, 1984 ❷ *Beverly Hills Cop II*, 1987 ❸ *Doctor Dolittle*, 1998
❹ *Coming to America*, 1988 ❺ *The Nutty Professor*, 1996
❻ *Nutty Professor II: The Klumps*, 2000 ❼ *Another 48 Hrs.*, 1990
❽ *The Golden Child*, 1986 ❾ *Boomerang*, 1992 ❿ *Harlem Nights**, 1989

* Also director

Eddie Murphy also provided the voice of Mushu in the animated film *Mulan* (1998), which, if included, would rank second in his Top 10.

TOP 10 ★
SAMUEL L. JACKSON FILMS

1	Star Wars: Episode I – The Phantom Menace	1999
2	Jurassic Park	1993
3	Die Hard: With a Vengeance	1995
4	Coming to America	1988
5	Pulp Fiction	1994
6	Patriot Games	1992
7	Deep Blue Sea	1999
8	A Time to Kill	1996
9	Unbreakable	2000
10	Sea of Love	1989

TOP 10 ★
JOHN CUSACK FILMS

1	Con Air	1997
2	The Thin Red Line	1998
3	Stand by Me	1986
4	Broadcast News	1987
5	Being John Malkovich	1999
6	High Fidelity	2000
7	City Hall	1996
8	Grosse Pointe Blank	1997
9	Midnight in the Garden of Good and Evil	1997
10	The Player	1992

John Cusack supplied the voice of Dimitri in the animated film *Anastasia* (1997). Were it included here, it would rank in second place.

TOP 10 ★
BRUCE WILLIS FILMS

1	The Sixth Sense	1999
2	Armageddon	1998
3	Die Hard: With a Vengeance	1995
4	The Fifth Element	1997
5	Die Hard 2	1990
6	Pulp Fiction	1994
7	Twelve Monkeys	1995
8	The Jackal	1997
9	Death Becomes Her	1992
10	Die Hard	1988

Look Who's Talking (1989), in which typically tough-guy Willis took the role of a baby, is discounted here because the role consisted only of Willis's dubbed voice.

TOP 10 KEANU REEVES FILMS

❶ *The Matrix*, 1999 ❷ *Speed*, 1994
❸ *Bram Stoker's Dracula*, 1992 ❹ *The Devil's Advocate*, 1997 ❺ *Parenthood*, 1989 ❻ *A Walk in the Clouds*, 1995
❼ *Chain Reaction*, 1996 ❽ *Johnny Mnemonic*, 1995 ❾ *The Replacements*, 2000 ❿ *Point Break*, 1991

Did You Know? The first actor to receive a movie contract was prizefighter James John Corbett. In August 1894, he signed with the Kinetoscope Exhibition Company to appear in a film of a six-round fight against Pete Courtney.

Leading Ladies

RYAN'S DAUGHTER

Born Margaret Mary Emily Anne Hyra, Meg Ryan took her mother's maiden name before her film debut in 1981. She has gone on to enjoy huge success in a range of romantic comedies.

TOP 10

MICHELLE PFEIFFER FILMS

1	Batman Returns	1992
2	What Lies Beneath	2000
3	Dangerous Minds	1995
4	Wolf	1994
5	Up Close and Personal	1996
6	One Fine Day	1996
7	The Witches of Eastwick	1987
8	The Story of Us	1999
9	Tequila Sunrise	1988
10	Scarface	1983

Michelle Pfeiffer also provided the voice of Tzipporah in the animated film *The Prince of Egypt* (1998). If included in her Top 10, this would feature in third place.

CATWOMAN

Batman Returns is Michelle Pfeiffer's most successful film to date, but half the films in her Top 10 have earned a healthy $100 million-plus.

TOP 10 ★ MEG RYAN FILMS

1	Top Gun	1986
2	You've Got M@il	1998
3	Sleepless in Seattle	1993
4	City of Angels	1998
5	French Kiss	1995
6	Courage under Fire	1996
7	When Harry Met Sally	1989
8	Addicted to Love	1997
9	When a Man Loves a Woman	1994
10	Hanging Up	2000

Meg Ryan provided the voice of Anastasia in the 1997 film of that title. If included, it would appear in ninth place.

TOP 10 ★ BETTE MIDLER FILMS

1	The First Wives Club	1996
2	What Women Want	2000
3	Get Shorty	1995
4	Ruthless People	1986
5	Down and Out in Beverly Hills	1986
6	Beaches*	1988
7	Outrageous Fortune	1987
8	The Rose	1979
9	Big Business	1988
10	Hocus Pocus	1993

* Also producer

Bette Midler's role in *Get Shorty* is no more than a cameo. If this was excluded, *Hawaii* (1966) would join the list in 10th place.

TOP 10 JUDI DENCH FILMS

❶ *The World is Not Enough*, 1999 ❷ *GoldenEye*, 1995 ❸ *Tomorrow Never Dies*, 1997 ❹ *Shakespeare in Love*, 1998 ❺ *Tea with Mussolini*, 1999 ❻ *A Room with a View*, 1986 ❼ *Mrs. Brown*, 1997 ❽ *Henry V*, 1989 ❾ *Chocolat*, 2000 ❿ *Hamlet*, 1996

TOP 10 ★ MINNIE DRIVER FILMS

1	GoldenEye	1995
2	Good Will Hunting	1997
3	Sleepers	1996
4	Circle of Friends	1995
5	Return to Me	2000
6	Grosse Pointe Blank	1997
7	Hard Rain	1998
8	An Ideal Husband	1999
9	Big Night	1996
10	The Governess	1998

Minnie Driver has also had three successful voice-only roles: Jane Porter in *Tarzan* (1999), Lady Eboshi in *Mononoke Hime* (1997), and Brooke Shields in *South Park: Bigger, Longer and Uncut* (1999).

PRETTY WOMAN

Julia Roberts became the first Hollywood actress to be paid $10 million (for her role in the 1996 film Mary Reilly). She now commands almost $20 million.

TOP 10
JULIA ROBERTS FILMS

1	*Pretty Woman**	1990
2	*Notting Hill*	1999
3	*Hook*	1991
4	*My Best Friend's Wedding*	1997
5	*Runaway Bride*	1999
6	*Erin Brockovich*#	2000
7	*The Pelican Brief*	1993
8	*Sleeping with the Enemy*	1991
9	*Stepmom*	1998
10	*Conspiracy Theory*	1997

* *Academy Award nomination for "Best Actress"*

Winner of "Best Actress" Oscar

TOP 10
$100 MILLION FILM ACTRESSES

	ACTRESS*	FILMS#	TOTAL ($)+
1	Julia Roberts	10	2,602,300,000
2	Carrie Fisher	4	2,047,700,000
3	Whoopi Goldberg	7	2,027,200,000
4	Glenn Close	6	1,777,700,000
5	Demi Moore	6	1,672,200,000
6	Bonnie Hunt	5	1,577,800,000
7	Drew Barrymore	5	1,561,800,000
8	Rene Russo	7	1,524,900,000
9	Annie Potts	4	1,351,600,000
10	Minnie Driver	5	1,337,400,000

* *Appeared in or provided voice in film*

Earning over $100 million worldwide to end of 2000

+ *Of all $100-million-plus films*

Among well-known high-earning stars, this list contains several surprising names of less familiar or prolific artists who have appeared in or provided voices for some of the most successful films of all time. One such is Annie Potts, who appeared in both *Ghostbusters* films and supplied the voice of Bo Peep for both *Toy Story* films.

TOP 10
SHARON STONE FILMS

1	*Basic Instinct*	1992
2	*Total Recall*	1990
3	*The Specialist*	1995
4	*Last Action Hero*	1993
5	*Sliver*	1993
6	*Casino**	1995
7	*Sphere*	1998
8	*Diabolique*	1996
9	*Police Academy 4: Citizens on Patrol*	1987
10	*Gloria*	1999

* *Academy Award nomination for "Best Actress"*

Sharon Stone's first film role was a fleeting appearance in Woody Allen's *Stardust Memories* (1980), where she appears credited only as "Pretty girl on train".

TOP 10
DREW BARRYMORE FILMS

1	*E.T.: The Extra-Terrestrial*	1982
2	*Batman Forever*	1995
3	*Charlie's Angels*	2000
4	*Scream*	1996
5	*The Wedding Singer*	1998
6	*Never Been Kissed*	1999
7	*Ever After*	1998
8	*Wayne's World 2*	1993
9	*Everyone Says I Love You*	1996
10	*Boys on the Side*	1995

Drew Barrymore also provided the voice of Akima in the animated *Titan A.E.* (2000), which would be in 10th place in her Top 10.

TOP 10
GWYNETH PALTROW FILMS

1	*Se7en*	1995
2	*Hook*	1991
3	*Shakespeare in Love**	1998
4	*A Perfect Murder*	1998
5	*The Talented Mr. Ripley*	1999
6	*Sliding Doors*	1998
7	*Great Expectations*	1998
8	*Malice*	1993
9	*Emma*	1996
10	*Bounce*	2000

* *Winner of "Best Actress" Oscar*

TOP 10 UMA THURMAN FILMS

❶ *Batman & Robin*, 1997 ❷ *Pulp Fiction*, 1994 ❸ *The Truth About Cats and Dogs*, 1996 ❹ *The Avengers*, 1998 ❺ *Dangerous Liaisons*, 1988 ❻ *Final Analysis*, 1992 ❼ *Beautiful Girls*, 1996 ❽ *Les Misérables*, 1998 ❾ *Johnny Be Good*, 1988 ❿ *Gattaca*, 1997

Did You Know? One of the most prolific actresses in movie history was Bess Flowers (1898–1984). In the period from 1923 to 1964, she appeared, often uncredited, in at least 371 films.

The Directors & Writers

FILMS DIRECTED BY ACTORS

FILM/YEAR	DIRECTOR
1 *Pretty Woman*, 1990	Garry Marshall
2 *Dances With Wolves*, 1990	Kevin Costner
3 *The Bodyguard*, 1992	Kevin Costner
4 *How the Grinch Stole Christmas*, 2000	Ron Howard
5 *Apollo 13*, 1995	Ron Howard
6 *Ransom*, 1996	Ron Howard
7 *Rocky IV*, 1985	Sylvester Stallone
8 *Doctor Dolittle*, 1998	Betty Thomas
9 *Runaway Bride*, 1999	Garry Marshall
10 *Waterworld*, 1995	Kevin Costner

FILMS DIRECTED BY WOMEN

FILM/YEAR	DIRECTOR
1 *Look Who's Talking*, 1989	Amy Heckerling
2 *Doctor Dolittle*, 1998	Betty Thomas
3 *Sleepless in Seattle*, 1993	Nora Ephron
4 *What Women Want*, 2000	Nancy Meyers
5 *The Birdcage*, 1996	Elaine May
6 *You've Got M@il*, 1998	Nora Ephron
7 *Wayne's World*, 1992	Penelope Spheeris
8 *Big*, 1988	Penny Marshall
9 *Michael*, 1996	Nora Ephron
10 *A League of Their Own*, 1992	Penny Marshall

DIRECTORS, 2000

DIRECTOR*	FILM(S)#
1 Ron Howard	*How the Grinch Stole Christmas*
2 John Woo	*Mission: Impossible 2*
3 Robert Zemeckis	*What Lies Beneath*, *Cast Away*
4 Ridley Scott	*Gladiator*
5 Wolfgang Petersen	*The Perfect Storm*
6 Jay Roach	*Meet the Parents*
7 Bryan Singer	*X-Men*
8 Keenan Ivory Wayans	*Scary Movie*
9 Eric Leighton, Ralph Zondag	*Dinosaur*
10 Steven Soderbergh	*Erin Brockovich*, *The Limey*

* *Including co-directors*

Ranking based on total domestic (US) gross of all films released in 2000

WOOING THE AUDIENCES

Mission: Impossible 2 *director John Woo moved from Hong Kong to Hollywood to become a thriller specialist. He was the first Asian director to make a mainstream Hollywood film, Hard Target in 1993.*

FILMS DIRECTED BY RON HOWARD

1	*How the Grinch Stole Christmas*	2000
2	*Apollo 13*	1995
3	*Ransom*	1996
4	*Backdraft*	1991
5	*Parenthood*	1989
6	*Cocoon*	1985
7	*Splash*	1984
8	*Far and Away*	1992
9	*Willow*	1988
10	*The Paper*	1994

FILMS DIRECTED BY STEVEN SPIELBERG

1	*Jurassic Park*	1993
2	*E.T.: The Extra-Terrestrial*	1982
3	*The Lost World: Jurassic Park*	1997
4	*Indiana Jones and the Last Crusade*	1989
5	*Saving Private Ryan*	1998
6	*Jaws*	1975
7	*Raiders of the Lost Ark*	1981
8	*Indiana Jones and the Temple of Doom*	1984
9	*Schindler's List*	1993
10	*Hook*	1991

TOP 10 FILMS DIRECTED BY STANLEY KUBRICK

❶ *Eyes Wide Shut*, 1999 ❷ *The Shining*, 1980 ❸ *2001: A Space Odyssey*, 1968 ❹ *Full Metal Jacket*, 1987 ❺ *A Clockwork Orange*, 1971 ❻ *Spartacus*, 1960 ❼ *Barry Lyndon*, 1975 ❽ *Dr. Strangelove*, 1964 ❾ *Lolita*, 1962 ❿ *Paths of Glory*, 1957

TOP 10 FILMS WRITTEN BY STEPHEN KING

1 *The Green Mile*, 1999 **2** *The Shining*, 1980 **3** *Misery*, 1990 **4** *The Shawshank Redemption*, 1994 **5** *Pet Sematary*, 1989 **6** *Stand by Me*, 1986 **7** *Dolores Claiborne*, 1995 **8** *The Running Man*, 1987 **9** *Carrie*, 1976 **10** *Sleepwalkers*, 1992

TOP 10 ★
FILMS BASED ON CLASSIC ENGLISH NOVELS

FILM/YEAR	NOVELIST/PUBLISHED
1 *Bram Stoker's Dracula*, 1992	Bram Stoker, 1897
2 *Sense and Sensibility*, 1995	Jane Austen, 1811
3 *Mary Shelley's Frankenstein*, 1994	Mary Shelley, 1818
4 *Emma*, 1996	Jane Austen, 1816
5 *The Age of Innocence*, 1993	Edith Wharton, 1920
6 *A Passage to India*, 1984	E. M. Forster, 1924
7 *Howard's End*, 1992	E. M. Forster, 1910
8 *A Room with a View*, 1986	E. M. Forster, 1908
9 *The Portrait of a Lady*, 1996	Henry James, 1881
10 *The Wings of the Dove*, 1997	Henry James, 1902

This Top 10 excludes films inspired by novels but not following the text and storyline.

TOP 10 FILMS WRITTEN BY RON BASS

1 *Rain Man*, 1988 **2** *My Best Friend's Wedding*, 1997 **3** *Entrapment*, 1999 **4** *Dangerous Minds*, 1995 **5** *Sleeping With the Enemy*, 1991 **6** *Stepmom*, 1998 **7** *What Dreams May Come*, 1998 **8** *Waiting to Exhale*, 1995 **9** *How Stella Got Her Groove Back*, 1998 **10** *When a Man Loves a Woman*, 1994

TOP 10 ★
WRITERS, 2000

WRITER*	FILM(S)#
1 William Goldman	*Mission: Impossible 2, Hollow Man*
2 Ed Solomon	*X-Men, Charlie's Angels*
3 Zak Penn	*Nutty Professor II: The Klumps, Charlie's Angels*
4 John Logan	*Gladiator, Any Given Sunday*
5 Jeffrey Price, Peter S. Seaman, Dr. Seuss	*How the Grinch Stole Christmas*
6 Brannon Braga, David Marconi, Ronald D. Moore, Michael Tolkin, Robert Towne	*Mission: Impossible 2*
7 David H. Franzoni, William Nicholson	*Gladiator*
8 Bo Goldman, Sebastian Junger, William D. Wittliff	*The Perfect Storm*
9 Joss Whedon	*X-Men, Titan A.E.*
10 Susannah Grant	*Erin Brockovich, 28 Days, Center Stage*

* Including writing teams

\# Ranking based on total domestic (US) gross of all films by these writers released in 2000

MILES AHEAD

The Green Mile *is by far the highest-earning film based on a Stephen King story. To date, some 40 film adaptations of his work have been released.*

TOP 10 ★
PRODUCERS, 2000

PRODUCER*	HIGHEST-EARNING FILM#
1 Steven Spielberg	*Gladiator*
2 Bob Weinstein	*Scary Movie*
3 Harvey Weinstein	*Scary Movie*
4 Douglas Wick	*Gladiator*
5 Jerry Bruckheimer, Chad Oman, Pat Sandston, Mike Stenson	*Remember the Titans*
6 Brian Grazer	*How the Grinch Stole Christmas*
7 Cary Granat	*Scary Movie*
8 Mark Johnson	*What Lies Beneath*
9 Terence Chang	*Mission: Impossible 2*
10 Todd Hallowell, Aldric L'Auli Porter, Louisa Velis, David Womark	*How the Grinch Stole Christmas*

* Including producer teams

\# Ranking based on total domestic (US) gross of all films released in 2000

How many extras are estimated to have appeared in the 1982 film *Gandhi*?
see p.176 for the answer
A 1 million
B 100,000
C 300,000

The Studios

TOP 10 NEW LINE FILMS

1 *Se7en*, 1995 **2** *The Mask*, 1994 **3** *Austin Powers: The Spy Who Shagged Me*, 1999
4 *Dumb and Dumber*, 1994 **5** *Rush Hour*, 1998 **6** *Teenage Mutant Ninja Turtles*, 1990
7 *Lost in Space*, 1998 **8** *Blade*, 1998 **9** *Mortal Kombat*, 1995
10 *The Wedding Singer*, 1998

TOP 10 ★ PARAMOUNT FILMS

1	Titanic*	1997
2	Forrest Gump	1994
3	Mission: Impossible 2	2000
4	Ghost	1990
5	Indiana Jones and the Last Crusade	1989
6	Mission: Impossible	1996
7	Grease	1978
8	Raiders of the Lost Ark	1981
9	Deep Impact	1998
10	Top Gun	1986

* Co-production with Fox, who had overseas rights

TOP 10 ★ MCA/UNIVERSAL FILMS

1	Jurassic Park	1993
2	E.T.: The Extra-Terrestrial	1982
3	The Lost World: Jurassic Park	1997
4	Jaws	1975
5	The Mummy	1999
6	The Flintstones	1994
7	Notting Hill	1999
8	Back to the Future	1985
9	How the Grinch Stole Christmas	2000
10	Apollo 13	1995

TOP 10 MIRAMAX FILMS

1 *Shakespeare in Love*, 1998 **2** *Scary Movie*, 2000 **3** *The English Patient*, 1996
4 *Good Will Hunting*, 1997 **5** *Life is Beautiful (La Vita è Bella)*, 1998
6 *Pulp Fiction*, 1994 **7** *Scream*, 1996 **8** *Scream 2*, 1997 **9** *Scream 3*, 2000
10 *The Talented Mr. Ripley*, 1999

TOP 10 ★ DREAMWORKS FILMS

1	Saving Private Ryan*	1998
2	Gladiator*	2000
3	Deep Impact*	1998
4	American Beauty	1999
5	What Lies Beneath*	2000
6	The Prince of Egypt	1998
7	The Haunting	1990
8	Chicken Run	2000
9	Antz	1998
10	Mouse Hunt	1997

* Co-production with another studio

TOP 10 ★ WARNER BROS. FILMS

1	Twister	1996
2	The Matrix	1999
3	Batman	1989
4	The Bodyguard	1992
5	Robin Hood: Prince of Thieves	1991
6	The Fugitive	1993
7	Batman Forever	1995
8	The Perfect Storm	2000
9	Lethal Weapon 3	1992
10	The Exorcist	1973

It was the coming of sound that launched the newly formed Warner Bros. into its important place in cinema history, with *The Jazz Singer* (1927) its best-known early sound production. The Depression years were not easy for the company, but in the 1940s it produced a number of films that received acclaim from both critics and public. Meanwhile, it came to be acknowledged as one of the major forces in the field of animation with its *Bugs Bunny* and other cartoons.

STORMING AHEAD

Each of the top four films produced by Warner Bros. has earned more than $400 million at the world box office, while earnings from Twister *approach half a billion dollars.*

From the Producers of "JURASSIC PARK" and the Director of "SPEED"

Don't breathe. Don't look back.

TWISTER

The Dark Side of Nature.

TOP 10 TWENTIETH CENTURY-FOX FILMS

❶ *Titanic**, 1997 **❷** *Star Wars: Episode I – The Phantom Menace*, 1999 **❸** *Independence Day*, 1996 **❹** *Star Wars*, 1977 **❺** *The Empire Strikes Back*, 1980 **❻** *Home Alone*, 1990 **❼** *Return of the Jedi*, 1983 **❽** *Mrs. Doubtfire*, 1993 **❾** *True Lies*, 1994 **❿** *Die Hard: With a Vengeance*, 1995

* *Co-produced with Paramount; Twentieth Century-Fox controlled overseas rights*

TOP 10 ★
WALT DISNEY/ BUENA VISTA FILMS

1	The Lion King	1994
2	The Sixth Sense	1999
3	Armageddon	1998
4	Toy Story 2	1999
5	Aladdin	1992
6	Pretty Woman	1990
7	Tarzan	1999
8	A Bug's Life	1998
9	Toy Story	1995
10	Beauty and the Beast	1991

TOP 10 ★
STUDIOS WITH THE MOST "BEST PICTURE" OSCARS

	STUDIO	AWARDS
1	United Artists	13
2	Columbia	12
3	Paramount	11
4	MGM	9
5	Twentieth Century-Fox	7
6	Warner Bros.	6
7	Universal	5
8	Orion	4
9	=Dreamworks	2
	=Miramax	2
	=RKO	2

TOP 10 ★
SONY (COLUMBIA/ TRI-STAR) FILMS

1	Men in Black	1997
2	Terminator 2: Judgment Day	1991
3	Godzilla	1998
4	Basic Instinct	1992
5	Close Encounters of the Third Kind	1977/80
6	As Good as It Gets	1997
7	Air Force One	1997
8	Hook	1991
9	Rambo: First Blood Part II	1985
10	Look Who's Talking	1989

Founded in 1924 by Harry Cohn and his brother Jack, Columbia was built up into a studio to rival the established giants MGM and Paramount. In 1934, Frank Capra's *It Happened One Night*, starring Clark Gable and Claudette Colbert, swept the board, unprecedentedly winning "Best Picture", "Best Director", "Best Actor", and "Best Actress" Oscars. In subsequent years, films such as *Lost Horizon* (1937) and *The Jolson Story* (1946) consolidated Columbia's commercial success.

SENSE OF ACHIEVEMENT

Disney's The Lion King *remains its most successful film so far, but* The Sixth Sense *comes an honourable second, with world earnings of nearly $700 million.*

TOP 10 ★
STUDIOS, 2000

	STUDIO	EARNINGS ($)*	MARKET SHARE (%)
1	Buena Vista	1,174,000,000	15.78
2	Universal	1,053,600,000	14.16
3	Warner Bros.	903,400,000	12.14
4	DreamWorks	789,800,000	10.62
5	Paramount	781,000,000	10.50
6	Sony	688,200,000	9.25
7	Twentieth Century-Fox	659,300,000	8.86
8	New Line	372,500,000	5.01
9	Dimension	322,500,000	4.44
10	Miramax	128,400,000	1.73

* *Domestic (US) box office gross in 2000*

Total US box office gross for 2000 was estimated as $7,439,400,655, of which the Top 10 studios earned $6,872,700,000, or 92 per cent.

Did You Know? Although United Artists has won the most "Best Picture" Oscars, MGM has received the most wins in all categories, with a total of 190.

Film Out-Takes

MOST EXPENSIVE ITEMS OF FILM MEMORABILIA EVER SOLD AT AUCTION

ITEM/SALE	PRICE (£)
1 Judy Garland's ruby slippers from *The Wizard of Oz*, Christie's, New York, 26 May 2000	410,874 ($666,000)
2 Vivien Leigh's Oscar for *Gone With the Wind*, Sotheby's, New York, 15 Dec 1993	380,743 ($562,500)
3 Clark Gable's Oscar for *It Happened One Night*, Christie's, Los Angeles, 15 Dec 1996	364,500 ($607,500)
4 Poster for *The Mummy*, 1932, Sotheby's, New York, 1 Mar 1997	252,109 ($453,500)
5 James Bond's Aston Martin DB5 from *Goldfinger*, Sotheby's, New York, 28 June 1986	179,793 ($275,000)
6 Clark Gable's personal script for *Gone With the Wind*, Christie's, Los Angeles, 15 Dec 1996	146,700 ($244,500)
7 "Rosebud" sled from *Citizen Kane*, Christie's, Los Angeles, 15 Dec 1996	140,000 ($233,500)
8 Herman J. Mankiewicz's scripts for *Citizen Kane* and *The American*, Christie's, New York, 21 June 1989	139,157 ($231,000)
9 Mel Gibson's 5ft broadsword from *Braveheart*, Sotheby's, New York, 6 Mar 2001	116,000 ($170,000)
10 Judy Garland's ruby slippers from *The Wizard of Oz*, Christie's, New York, 21 June 1988	104,430 ($165,000)

FILMS WITH THE MOST EXTRAS

FILM/COUNTRY/YEAR	EXTRAS
1 *Gandhi*, UK, 1982	300,000
2 *Kolberg*, Germany, 1945	187,000
3 *Monster Wang-magwi*, South Korea, 1967	157,000
4 *War and Peace*, USSR, 1967	120,000
5 *Ilya Muromets*, USSR, 1956	106,000
6 *Tonko*, Japan, 1988	100,000
7 *The War of Independence*, Romania, 1912	80,000
8 *Around the World in 80 Days*, USA, 1956	68,894
9 = *Dny Zrady*, Czechoslovakia, 1972	60,000
= *Intolerance*, USA, 1916	60,000

COUNTRIES WITH THE BIGGEST INCREASES IN CINEMA VISITS

COUNTRY	TOTAL ATTENDANCE 1998	1999	INCREASE
1 Mexico	104,000,000	120,000,000	16,000,000
2 Australia	80,000,000	88,000,000	8,000,000
3 Poland	19,900,000	26,620,000	6,720,000
4 UK	136,500,000	140,260,000	3,760,000
5 Finland	6,320,000	7,040,000	720,000
6 New Zealand	16,270,000	16,760,000	490,000
7 Germany	148,880,000	149,000,000	120,000
8 Sweden	15,890,000	15,980,000	90,000
9 Iceland	1,510,000	1,570,000	60,000
10 Spain	112,140,000	131,350,000	19,210

Source: Screen Digest

TOP 10 MOST PROLIFIC FILM-PRODUCING COUNTRIES

(Country/films produced, 1999)

❶ India, 764 ❷ USA, 628 ❸ Japan, 270 ❹ Philippines, 220 ❺ France, 181 ❻ Hong Kong, 146 ❼ Italy, 108 ❽ Spain, 97 ❾ UK, 92 ❿ China, 85

Source: Screen Digest

JUDY'S RUBY SLIPPERS

One of several pairs made for her most famous role, the ruby slippers worn by Judy Garland in The Wizard of Oz *top the list of expensive film memorabilia.*

TOP 10 ★
COUNTRIES IN WHICH THE TOP FILM TAKES THE LARGEST SHARE OF THE BOX OFFICE

COUNTRY	TOP FILM'S PERCENTAGE OF BOX OFFICE, 1998
1 Poland	24.2
2 Japan	18.3
3 Denmark	16.9
4 Sweden	16.5
5 Czech Republic	15.5
6 Norway	14.7
7 Argentina	14.1
8 France	12.2
9 =Germany	12.1
=UK	12.1

Source: Screen Digest

TOP 10 ★
CINEMA-GOING COUNTRIES

COUNTRY	TOTAL ATTENDANCE, 1999
1 India	2,860,000,000
2 USA	1,465,200,000
3 Indonesia	222,200,000
4 France	155,500,000
5 Germany	149,000,000
6 Japan	144,760,000
7 UK	140,260,000
8 Spain	131,350,000
9 China	121,000,000
10 Mexico	120,000,000

Source: Screen Digest

Countries such as the former Soviet Union and China have long reported massive cinema attendance figures – the latter once claiming a figure of over 20 billion. However, such inflated statistics include local screenings of propaganda films in mobile cinemas as well as the commercial feature films on which this list is based. Ranked on a per capita basis, Iceland edges ahead of the US with 5.71 annual cinema visits per person compared with the US's 5.45, while India drops out of the Top 10 with 2.99.

TOP 10 ★
COUNTRIES WITH THE MOST CINEMAS

COUNTRY	CINEMA SCREENS
1 China	65,000
2 USA	37,185
3 India	12,900
4 France	5,000
5 Germany	4,651
6 Spain	3,343
7 UK	2,825
8 Italy	2,740
9 Canada	2,685
10 Indonesia	2,100

Source: Screen Digest

TOP 10 ★
COUNTRIES WITH THE MOST BOX OFFICE REVENUE

COUNTRY	BOX OFFICE REVENUE, 1999 ($)
1 USA	7,490,000,000
2 UK	1,037,800,000
3 France	891,100,000
4 Germany	860,900,000
5 Italy	566,700,000
6 Spain	528,200,000
7 Canada	399,000,000
8 Switzerland	135,100,000
9 Belgium	113,700,000
10 Netherlands	111,400,000

Source: Screen Digest

TOP 10 ★
FILM-RELEASING COUNTRIES

COUNTRY*	NEW RELEASES, 1999
1 Japan	568
2 Spain	505
3 Belgium	500
4 France#	448
5 USA	442
6 Taiwan#	441
7 Hong Kong	439
8 Italy	423
9 UK	387
10 South Korea	370

* No reliable figures available for India
# 1998 figure

Source: Screen Digest

TOP 10 ★
COUNTRIES SPENDING THE MOST ON FILM PRODUCTION

COUNTRY	INVESTMENT, 1999 ($)
1 USA	8,699,000,000
2 Japan	1,053,160,000
3 UK	817,850,000
4 France	732,580,000
5 Bulgaria	544,020,000
6 Germany	380,450,000
7 Canada	225,950,000
8 Italy	171,100,000
9 Spain	168,460,000
10 Argentina	133,330,000

Source: Screen Digest

TOP 10 COUNTRIES WITH THE BIGGEST INCREASE IN FILM PRODUCTION
(Country/percentage increase in production, 1989–98)

❶ Ireland, 400.0 ❷ Luxembourg, 200.0 ❸ UK, 117.5 ❹ Iceland, 100.0
❺ New Zealand, 75.0 ❻ Australia, 72.7 ❼ Norway, 55.6 ❽ Venezuela, 42.9
❾ France, 33.6 ❿ = Austria, 33.3; = Brazil, 33.3

Source: Screen Digest

Did You Know? The longest non-stop film screening ran for 250 hours in Montreal, Canada, from midnight on Thursday, 11 June to dawn on Monday 22 June 1992. Only one person sat through all the 136 films that were shown.

Film Music

TOP 10 ★ MUSICAL FILMS

FILM	YEAR
1 Grease	1978
2 Saturday Night Fever	1977
3 The Sound of Music	1965
4 Evita	1996
5 The Rocky Horror Picture Show	1975
6 Staying Alive	1983
7 American Graffiti	1973
8 Mary Poppins	1964
9 Flashdance	1983
10 Fantasia 2000	2000

TOP 10 ★ POP MUSIC FILMS

FILM	YEAR
1 Spice World	1997
2 Purple Rain	1984
3 The Blues Brothers	1980
4 La Bamba	1987
5 What's Love Got to Do With It?	1993
6 The Doors	1991
7 Blues Brothers 2000	1998
8 The Wall	1982
9 The Commitments	1991
10 Sgt. Pepper's Lonely Hearts Club Band	1978

TOP 10 ★ JAMES BOND FILM THEMES IN THE UK

THEME/ARTIST OR GROUP	YEAR
1 A View to a Kill, Duran Duran	1985
2 We Have All the Time in the World (from On Her Majesty's Secret Service), Louis Armstrong	1994
3 The Living Daylights, a-ha	1987
4 Licence to Kill, Gladys Knight	1989
5 Nobody Does It Better (from The Spy Who Loved Me), Carly Simon	1977
6 For Your Eyes Only, Sheena Easton	1981
7 Live and Let Die, Paul McCartney and Wings	1973
8 GoldenEye, Tina Turner	1995
9 You Only Live Twice, Nancy Sinatra	1967
10 Tomorrow Never Dies, Sheryl Crow	1997

Not all the James Bond themes have been major hits. Although all 10 in this list reached the Top 20, there has never been a Bond-associated UK song that has hit the No. 1 spot.

TOP 10 SOUNDTRACK ALBUMS IN THE UK

(Album/year)

1 The Bodyguard, 1992 **2** Titanic, 1997 **3** Trainspotting, 1996 **4** The Commitments, 1991 **5** The Full Monty, 1997 **6** Top Gun, 1986 **7** Evita, 1996 **8** The Blues Brothers, 1980 **9** The Sound of Music, 1965 **10** Saturday Night Fever, 1978

Source: *MRIB*

TOP 10 ★ "BEST SONG" OSCAR-WINNING SINGLES IN THE UK

SINGLE/ARTIST OR GROUP	YEAR
1 I Just Called to Say I Love You, Stevie Wonder	1984
2 Fame, Irene Cara	1980
3 Take My Breath Away, Berlin	1986
4 My Heart Will Go On, Celine Dion	1998
5 Flashdance...What a Feeling, Irene Cara	1983
6 Evergreen, Barbra Streisand	1976
7 Streets of Philadelphia, Bruce Springsteen	1994
8 Moon River, Danny Williams	1961
9 Whatever Will Be, Will Be, Doris Day	1956
10 Raindrops Keep Falling on My Head, Sacha Distel	1969

Source: *The Popular Music Database*

ON AND ON

Featured in the world's most successful film, Titanic, *Celine Dion's* My Heart Will Go On *became one of the bestselling Oscar-winning singles of all time.*

BREAKFAST AT TIFFANY'S

Sung by Audrey Hepburn in the film Breakfast at Tiffany's, *Oscar-winning song* Moon River *became a chart hit for Andy Williams in the US and for Danny Williams in the UK.*

THE 10 ★
LATEST "BEST SONG" OSCAR WINNERS

YEAR	SONG/FILM
2000	*Things Have Changed*, Wonder Boys
1999	*You'll Be in My Heart*, Tarzan
1998	*When You Believe*, The Prince of Egypt
1997	*My Heart Will Go On*, Titanic
1996	*You Must Love Me*, Evita
1995	*Colors of the Wind*, Pocahontas
1994	*Can You Feel the Love Tonight*, The Lion King
1993	*Streets of Philadelphia*, Philadelphia
1992	*Whole New World*, Aladdin
1991	*Beauty and the Beast*, Beauty and the Beast

TOP 10 ★
"BEST SONG" OSCAR WINNERS OF THE 1980s

YEAR	SONG/FILM
1980	*Fame*, Fame
1981	*Up Where We Belong*, An Officer and a Gentleman
1982	*Arthur's Theme (Best That You Can Do)*, Arthur
1983	*Flashdance*, Flashdance
1984	*I Just Called to Say I Love You*, The Woman in Red
1985	*Say You, Say Me*, White Nights
1986	*Take My Breath Away*, Top Gun
1987	*(I've Had) The Time of My Life*, Dirty Dancing
1988	*Let the River Run*, Working Girl
1989	*Under the Sea*, The Little Mermaid

TOP 10 ★
"BEST SONG" OSCAR WINNERS OF THE 1970s

YEAR	SONG/FILM
1970	*For All We Know*, Lovers and Other Strangers
1971	*Theme from Shaft*, Shaft
1972	*The Morning After*, The Poseidon Adventure
1973	*The Way We Were*, The Way We Were
1974	*We May Never Love Like This Again*, The Towering Inferno
1975	*I'm Easy*, Nashville
1976	*Evergreen*, A Star Is Born
1977	*You Light up My Life*, You Light up My Life
1978	*Last Dance*, Thank God It's Friday
1979	*It Goes Like It Goes*, Norma Rae

TOP 10 ★
"BEST SONG" OSCAR WINNERS OF THE 1960s

YEAR	SONG/FILM
1960	*Never on Sunday*, Never on Sunday
1961	*Moon River*, Breakfast at Tiffany's
1962	*Days of Wine and Roses*, Days of Wine and Roses
1963	*Call Me Irresponsible*, Papa's Delicate Condition
1964	*Chim Chim Cheree*, Mary Poppins
1965	*The Shadow of Your Smile*, The Sandpiper
1966	*Born Free*, Born Free
1967	*Talk to the Animals*, Dr. Doolittle
1968	*The Windmills of Your Mind*, The Thomas Crown Affair
1969	*Raindrops Keep Falling on My Head*, Butch Cassidy and the Sundance Kid

Did You Know? The first "Best Song" Oscar winner *The Continental*, from the 1934 film *The Gay Divorcee*, entered the charts 42 years later when it was released by Maureen McGovern.

Animated Action

ANIMATED FILMS

1	*The Lion King*	1994
2	*Toy Story 2*	1999
3	*Aladdin*	1992
4	*Tarzan*	1999
5	*A Bug's Life*	1998
6	*Toy Story*	1995
7	*Beauty and the Beast*	1991
8	*Who Framed Roger Rabbit**	1988
9	*Pocahontas*	1995
10	*The Hunchback of Notre Dame*	1996

* Part animated, part live action

The 1990s provided nine of the 10 most successful animated films of all time, which in turn ejected a number of their high-earning predecessors from this Top 10. Animated films stand out among the leading money-makers of each decade: *Snow White* was the second highest earning film of the 1930s (after *Gone With the Wind*), while *Bambi, Fantasia, Cinderella,* and, through additional earnings from its re-release, *Pinocchio* were the four most successful films of the 1940s.

TOP 10 ★

PART ANIMATION/PART LIVE-ACTION FILMS

1	*Who Framed Roger Rabbit*	1988	6	*Small Soldiers*	1999
2	*Casper*	1995	7	*Song of the South*	1946
3	*Space Jam*	1996	8	*Fantasia 2000*	2000
4	*9 to 5*	1980	9	*James and the Giant Peach*	1996
5	*Mary Poppins*	1964	10	*Pete's Dragon*	1977

THE 10 ★

FIRST TOM AND JERRY CARTOONS

	CARTOON	RELEASE DATE
1	*Puss Gets The Boot**	20 Feb 1940
2	*The Midnight Snack*	19 July 1941
3	*The Night Before Christmas**	6 Dec 1941
4	*Fraidy Cat*	17 Jan 1942
5	*Dog Trouble*	18 Apr 1942
6	*Puss 'N' Toots*	30 May 1942
7	*The Bowling Alley-Cat*	18 July 1942
8	*Fine Feathered Friend*	10 Oct 1942
9	*Sufferin' Cats!*	16 Jan 1943
10	*The Lonesome Mouse*	22 May 1943

* Academy Award nomination; although in their debut Tom is called Jasper and the mouse is unnamed

Created by William Hanna and Joseph Barbera, Tom and Jerry have been perennially popular during six decades. Hannah and Barbera directed 114 cartoons featuring them from 1940 to 1958, when MGM closed its animation department.

THE 10 ★

FIRST FULL-LENGTH SIMPSONS EPISODES

	EPISODE	FIRST SCREENED
1	*Simpsons Roasting on an Open Fire*	17 Dec 1989
2	*Bart the Genius*	14 Jan 1990
3	*Homer's Odyssey*	21 Jan 1990
4	*There's No Disgrace Like Homer*	28 Jan 1990
5	*Bart the General*	4 Feb 1990
6	*Moaning Lisa*	11 Feb 1990
7	*The Call of the Simpsons*	18 Feb 1990
8	*The Telltale Head*	25 Feb 1990
9	*Life in the Fast Lane*	18 Mar 1990
10	*Homer's Night Out*	25 Mar 1990

Matt Groening's enormously successful animated series originally appeared in 1987 as short episodes screened on the Tracey Ullman Show.

THE 10 ★

FIRST DISNEY ANIMATED FEATURES

1	*Snow White and the Seven Dwarfs*	1937
2	*Pinocchio*	1940
3	*Fantasia*	1940
4	*Dumbo*	1941
5	*Bambi*	1942
6	*Victory Through Air Power*	1943
7	*The Three Caballeros*	1945
8	*Make Mine Music*	1946
9	*Fun and Fancy Free*	1947
10	*Melody Time*	1948

Excluding part-animated films such as *Song of the South* and *Mary Poppins*, and films made specially for television serialization, Disney has made a total of 42 full-length animated feature films up to the end of 2000.

SMALL SOLDIERS, BIG SUCCESS

Part animation/part live-action films are comparatively rare, but Small Soldiers stands out as the highest earner of the last year of the 20th century.

MONSTER MOVIE

Riding high on 1999's pre-eminent marketing phenomenon, Pokémon The First Movie *earned over $150 million worldwide.*

TOP 10 ★
NON-DISNEY ANIMATED FEATURE FILMS

1	*The Prince of Egypt*	1998
2	*Chicken Run*	2000
3	*Antz*	1998
4	*Pokémon The First Movie: Mewtwo Strikes Back*	1999
5	*Pocket Monsters Revelation Lugia*	1999
6	*The Rugrats Movie*	1998
7	*South Park: Bigger, Longer and Uncut*	1999
8	*The Land Before Time*	1988
9	*Pokémon: The Movie 2000*	2000
10	*An American Tail*	1986

Such was the success of *Pocket Monsters Revelation Lugia* in Japan that it earned a place in this list even before being released internationally.

THE 10 ★
FIRST BUGS BUNNY CARTOONS

	TITLE	RELEASED
1	*Porky's Hare Hunt*	30 Apr 1938
2	*Hare-um Scare-um*	12 Aug 1939
3	*Elmer's Candid Camera*	2 Mar 1940
4	*A Wild Hare*	27 July 1940
5	*Elmer's Pet Rabbit*	4 Jan 1941
6	*Tortoise Beats Hare*	15 Mar 1941
7	*Hiawatha's Rabbit Hunt*	7 June 1941
8	*The Heckling Hare*	5 July 1941
9	*All This and Rabbit Stew*	13 Sep 1941
10	*Wabbit Twouble*	20 Dec 1941

Bugs Bunny's debut was as a co-star alongside Porky Pig in *Porky's Hare Hunt*, but he was not named until the release of *Elmer's Pet Rabbit*. *A Wild Hare* was the first in which he said the line that became his trademark: "Eh, what's up, Doc?"

THE 10 ★
FIRST OSCAR-WINNING ANIMATED FILMS*

	FILM	YEAR
1	*Flowers and Trees*	1931/32
2	*The Three Little Pigs*	1932/33
3	*The Tortoise and the Hare*	1934
4	*Three Orphan Kittens*	1935
5	*The Country Cousin*	1936
6	*The Old Mill*	1937
7	*Ferdinand the Bull*	1938
8	*The Ugly Duckling*	1939
9	*The Milky Way*	1940
10	*Lend a Paw*	1941

* *In the category "Short Subjects (Cartoons)"*

With the exception of *The Milky Way*, which was directed by Rudolf Ising, all were directed by Walt Disney. Oscars were awarded in the category "Short Subjects (Cartoons)" until 1971, when it was altered to "Short Subjects (Animated Films)"; in 1974 it changed again, to "Short Films (Animated)".

THE 10 ★
LATEST OSCAR-WINNING ANIMATED FILMS*

YEAR	FILM/DIRECTOR/COUNTRY
2000	*Father and Daughter*, Michel Dudok de Wit, Netherlands
1999	*The Old Man and the Sea*, Aleksandr Petrov, USA
1998	*Bunny*, Chris Wedge, USA
1997	*Geri's Game*, Jan Pinkava, USA
1996	*Quest*, Tyron Montgomery, UK
1995	*A Close Shave*, Nick Park, UK
1994	*Bob's Birthday*, David Fine and Alison Snowden, UK
1993	*The Wrong Trousers*, Nick Park, UK
1992	*Mona Lisa Descending a Staircase*, Joan C. Gratz, USA
1991	*Manipulation*, Daniel Greaves, UK

* *In the category "Short Films (Animated)"*

What is the name of the character played by Michael J. Fox in the *Back to the Future* films?
see p.161 for the answer

A Minty Maclean
B Marty McFly
C Mickey McQueen

On the Radio

RADIO-OWNING COUNTRIES

	COUNTRY	RADIO SETS PER 1,000 POPULATION*
1	USA	2,116
2	Finland	1,498
3	UK	1,443
4	Gibraltar	1,429
5	Guam	1,400
6	Australia	1,391
7	Denmark	1,145
8	Canada	1,067
9	Monaco	1,039
10	New Zealand	997

* In latest year for which data available

Source: UNESCO

BBC RADIO 1 PROGRAMMES

	SHOW	LISTENERS
1	Breakfast Show with Sarah Cox	7,040,000
2	Simon Mayo	6,280,000
3	Chris Moyles (Mon–Fri)	5,610,000
4	Mark Radcliffe	5,310,000
5	Jo Whiley	5,230,000
6	Dave Pearce (Mon–Thurs)	3,910,000
7	UK Top 40 with Mark Goodier	3,290,000
8	Chris Moyles (Sat)	2,660,000
9	Nemone (Sat breakfast)	2,120,000
10	Evening Session with Steve Lamacq (Tue–Thurs)	2,070,000

RADIO STATIONS IN THE UK, 2000

	STATION	LISTENER HOURS*
1	BBC Radio 2	136,464,000
2	BBC Radio 4	117,293,000
3	BBC Radio 1	114,749,000
4	Classic FM	43,578,000
5	BBC Radio 5 Live	40,020,000
6	Capital Radio London (excl. xFM)	31,686,000
7	95.8 Capital FM	25,037,000
8	Virgin Radio (AM)	17,426,000
9	talkSPORT (Talk Radio)	14,384,000
10	BBC Radio 3	13,557,000

* Total number of hours spent by all adults (over 15) listening to the station in an average week, July to Sep 2000

Source: RAJAR

BBC RADIO 4 PROGRAMMES

	SHOW
1	Today
2	The Archers
3	PM
4	Six o'clock News
5	You and Yours
6	The World at One
7	Woman's Hour
8	Daily Service
9	Afternoon Play
10	Front Row

Source: RAJAR/BBC

LATEST WINNERS OF THE SONY PUBLIC SERVICE/ COMMUNITY AWARD

YEAR	PROGRAMME	PRODUCERS
2001	Floodwatch 2000	BBC Radio York
2000	Out of the Red, Chemical Beats, Sunday Surgery	BBC Music Entertainment for Radio 1
1999	Omagh	BBC Radio Ulster for BBC Northern Ireland
1998	Breast Cancer Awareness Week	BBC Radio Ulster
1997	Dunblane	BBC Radio Scotland
1996	Affairs of the Heart	BBC Radio 2
1995	Man Matters	BBC Radio 2
1994	Shout It Out	BBC Radio Devon
1993	Year of Action	BBC Radio Nottingham
1992	In Touch	BBC Radio 4

FIRST YEARS OF THE SONY RADIO PERSONALITY/ BROADCASTER OF THE YEAR AWARD

YEAR	PERSONALITY OR BROADCASTER OF THE YEAR
1983	Brian Johnston Sue MacGregor
1984	Brian Matthew Margaret Howard
1985	Jimmy Young
1986	Douglas Cameron
1987	Derek Jameson
1988	Alan Freeman
1989	Sue Lawley
1990	Chris Tarrant
1991	James Naughtie
1992	Danny Baker

TOP 10 LUXURIES MOST CHOSEN BY CASTAWAYS ON *DESERT ISLAND DISCS*

❶ Piano ❷ Writing materials ❸ Bed ❹ Guitar ❺ Typewriter ❻ Radio receiver ❼ Golf club and balls ❽ Painting materials ❾ Wine ❿ Perfume

"An inanimate object, purely for the senses, which is not going to help you live", was how the programme's creator Roy Plomley described what is now known more simply as the "luxury object" that "castaways" are permitted to take to their mythical desert island.

THE 10 ⭐
FIRST WINNERS OF THE SONY RADIO GOLD AWARD

YEAR	PRESENTER OR PROGRAMME
1983	Frank Muir / Dennis Norden
1984	David Jacobs
1985	British Forces Broadcasting Service
1986	John Timpson
1987	*The Archers*
1988	Gerald Mansell
1989	Tony Blackburn
1990	Roy Hudd
1991	Charlie Gillett
1992	Sir James Saville

The electronics company Sony has sponsored the British radio awards that bear its name since 1983. They are presented to "celebrate the quality, creativity and excellence of those whose work brings enjoyment to millions of listeners".

THE 10 ⭐
LATEST WINNERS OF THE SONY RADIO COMEDY AWARD

YEAR	PROGRAMME/PRODUCERS
2001	*Dead Ringers*, BBC Radio Entertainment for Radio 4
2000	*Blue Jam*, TalkBack Productions for BBC Radio 1
1999	*Old Harry's Game*, BBC Radio 4
1998	*Blue Jam*, TalkBack Productions for BBC Radio 1
1997	*Goodness Gracious Me!*, BBC Radio 4
1996	*People Like Us*, BBC Radio 4
1995	*I'm Sorry I Haven't a Clue*, BBC Radio 4
1994	*A Look Back at the Nineties*, BBC Radio 4
1993	*Knowing Me, Knowing You*, BBC Radio 4
1992	*Perforated Ulster*, BBC Radio Ulster

THE 10 ⭐
LATEST WINNERS OF THE SONY RADIO GOLD AWARD

YEAR	PRESENTER
2001	Chris Tarrant
2000	Ralph Bernard
1999	Zoë Ball
1998	Chris Evans
1997	Jimmy Young
1996	Richard Baker
1995	Alistair Cooke
1994	Kenny Everett
1993	Humphrey Lyttleton
1992	Sir James Saville

The Gold Award is presented for "Outstanding Contribution to Radio Over the Years".

TOP 10 ⭐
LONGEST-RUNNING PROGRAMMES ON BBC RADIO

	PROGRAMME	FIRST BROADCAST
1	The Week's Good Cause	24 January 1926
2	The Shipping Forecast	26 January 1926
3	Choral Evensong	7 October 1926
4	Daily Service	2 January 1928*
5	The Week in Westminster	6 November 1929
6	Sunday Half Hour	14 July 1940
7	Desert Island Discs	29 January 1942
8	Saturday Night Theatre	3 April 1943
9	Composer of the Week#	2 August 1943
10	Letter From America+	24 March 1946

* *Experimental broadcast; national transmission began December 1929*

\# *Formerly* This Week's Composer

\+ *Formerly* American Letter

In addition to these 10 long-runners, a further seven that started in the 1940s are still on the air.

THE 10 ⭐
LATEST WINNERS OF THE SONY RADIO DRAMA AWARD

YEAR	PROGRAMME/PRODUCERS
2001	*Alpha*, BBC World Service Drama for BBC World Service
2000	*Plum's War*, The Fiction Factory for BBC Radio 4
1999	*Bleak House*, Goldhawk Universal Productions for BBC Radio 4
1998	*The Trick Is to Keep Breathing*, BBC Scotland for BBC Radio 4
1997	*The Voluptuous Tango*, BBC Radio 3
1996	*Albion Tower*, BBC Radio 3
1995	*Mr. McNamara*, BBC World Service
1994	*Blue*, Basilisk Productions in association with Channel 4 and BBC Radio 3
1993	*The Master and Margarita*, BBC World Service/BBC Radio 4
1992	*Lavender Song*, BBC Radio 4

THE 10 ⭐
LATEST WINNERS OF THE SONY RADIO NEWS AWARD

YEAR*	PROGRAMME/PRODUCERS
2001	*The Jon Gaunt Breakfast Show*, BBC Three Counties Radio
2000	*Late Night Live: Soho Bomb*, BBC Current Affairs News for BBC Radio 5 Live
1999	*Farming Today*, BBC Radio 4
1998	*The Death of the Princess of Wales*, BBC Radio 4 and BBC Radio 5 Live
1997	*Drumcree*, BBC Radio Ulster
1996	*Dallyn on Saturday*, BBC Radio 5 Live
1995	*The Magazine: IRA Ceasefire*, BBC Radio 5 Live
1994	*Today – The Moscow White House Siege*, BBC Radio 4
1993	*Ayodhya*, BBC Radio Leicester
1991	*Nelson Mandela Release*, BBC World Service for Africa

* *No award made in 1992*

Top TV

TV REVENUE-EARNING COMPANIES

COMPANY/COUNTRY	TV REVENUE IN 1999 ($)
1 Time Warner, USA	18,802,000,000
2 Viacom, USA	7,663,600,000
3 Walt Disney, USA	7,512,000,000
4 GE/NBC, USA	5,790,000,000
5 NHK, Japan	5,275,700,000
6 CBS, USA	4,915,000,000
7 AT&T, USA	4,871,000,000
8 News Corporation, Australia	4,004,700,000
9 Cablevision, USA	3,943,000,000
10 DirecTV, USA	3,785,000,000

Source: Television Business International

BBC 1 AUDIENCES, 2000

PROGRAMME*	DATE	AUDIENCE
1 EastEnders	3 Jan	18,353,000
2 Match of the Day: Euro 2000	20 June	14,556,000
3 EastEnders' 15th Birthday Special	20 Feb	12,902,000
4 One Foot in the Grave	20 Nov	12,843,000
5 The Vicar of Dibley	1 Jan	12,488,000
6 Casualty	12 Feb	12,343,000
7 I Don't Believe It	20 Nov	11,247,000
8 The Antiques Roadshow	20 Feb	10,780,000
9 Men in Black (film)	17 Oct	10,690,000
10 Airport	21 Mar	10,664,000

* The highest-rated episode only of series shown
Source: BARB/SPC

Many of BBC1's most-watched programmes are also among the longest-running. *EastEnders* has attracted a loyal following since it was first broadcast on 19 February 1985, and *Casualty* has been a favourite since its launch on 6 September 1986. Long-runner *Match of the Day* was first screened on 22 August 1964.

TELEVISION-WATCHING COUNTRIES*

COUNTRY	AVERAGE DAILY VIEWING TIME	
	HRS	MINS
1 USA	3	58
2 Greece	3	39
3 = Italy	3	36
= UK	3	36
5 Spain	3	31
6 = Canada	3	14
= Ireland	3	14
8 Germany	3	8
9 France	3	7
10 Belgium	2	57

* In Western Europe and North America
Source: Screen Digest

A survey of TV-viewing habits in Western Europe and North America showed that the number of channels, including new digital channels, is proliferating at a much faster rate than the time spent actually watching them, thus creating, in the jargon of the industry, "audience fragmentation".

ITV AUDIENCES, 2000

PROGRAMME*	DATE	AUDIENCE
1 Coronation Street	3 Jan	18,952,000
2 Who Wants to Be a Millionaire?	19 Jan	15,873,000
3 Heartbeat	6 Feb	15,159,000
4 Euro 2000: Portugal v England	12 June	14,944,000
5 Who Wants to Be a Millionaire?: Celebrity Special	1 May	13,903,000
6 Inspector Morse	15 Nov	13,659,000
7 Emmerdale	22 Mar	13,249,000
8 Seeing Red	19 Mar	12,338,000
9 Stars in Their Eyes: Results	2 Dec	12,090,000
10 National Television Awards	10 Oct	12,048,000

* The highest-rated episode only of series shown
Source: BARB/SPC

CHILDREN'S PROGRAMMES ON UK TELEVISION, 2000

PROGRAMME*	CHANNEL	DATE	AUDIENCE
1 LA 7	BBC1	22 June	1,334,000
2 The Ghost Hunter	BBC1	11 Jan	1,256,000
3 Blue Peter	BBC1	19 Jan	1,211,000
4 Rugrats	BBC1	26 May	1,206,000
5 Pokémon	ITV	5 Apr	1,191,000
6 SM:tv Live	ITV	15 Apr	1,171,000
7 Sabrina the Teenage Witch	ITV	9 Oct	1,160,000
8 Steps to the Stars	BBC1	11 Feb	1,156,000
9 Byker Grove	BBC1	30 Nov	1,150,000
10 The Worst Witch	ITV	6 Jan	1,126,000

* The highest-rated episode only of series shown
Source: BARB/SPC

CHANNEL 4 AUDIENCES, 2000

PROGRAMME*	DATE	AUDIENCE
1 Big Brother	15 Sep	9,454,000
2 Friends	15 Sep	5,371,000
3 Heroes of Comedy	28 Dec	4,855,000
4 Victoria's Secrets	11 Jan	4,598,000
5 The Real Queen Mother	10 July	4,549,000
6 Brookside	8 Nov	4,446,000
7 Countdown	21 Jan	4,433,000
8 Jerry Maguire (film)	30 July	4,190,000
9 Escape From Colditz	14 Feb	4,156,000
10 100 Great TV Moments	24 Apr	4,086,000

* The highest-rated episode only of series shown
Source: BARB/SPC

TOP 10 ★
TV PROGRAMMES
OF THE LAST DECADE IN THE UK

	PROGRAMME	CHANNEL	DATE	AUDIENCE
1	Funeral of Diana, Princess of Wales	BBC1	6 Sep 1997	31,000,000
2	*Only Fools and Horses*	BBC1	29 Dec 1996	24,350,000
3	*Panorama* (Diana, Princess of Wales interview)	BBC1	20 Nov 1995	22,750,000
4	*Only Fools and Horses*	BBC1	27 Dec 1996	21,350,000
5	*Only Fools and Horses*	BBC1	25 Dec 1996	21,300,000
6	*Coronation Street*	Granada	22 Mar 1993	20,750,000
7	*Olympic Ice Dancing* (Torvill & Dean)	BBC1	21 Feb 1994	20,650,000
8	*Coronation Street*	Granada	6 Jan 1993	20,500,000
9 =	*Coronation Street*	Granada	25 Nov 1991	20,450,000
=	*Coronation Street*	Granada	22 Jan 1992	20,450,000

Source: *Royal Television Society*

TOP 10 ★
CARTOONS ON UK TELEVISION
MOST WATCHED BY CHILDREN, 2000

	PROGRAMME	CHANNEL	DATE	AUDIENCE*
1	*Rugrats*	BBC1	26 May	1,206,000
2	*Pokémon*	BBC1	5 Apr	1,191,000
3	*Hercules*	ITV	13 May	1,094,000
4	*Woody Woodpecker*	BBC1	17 Jan	1,016,000
5	*Digimon*	ITV	21 June	990,000
6	*Pocket Dragon*	BBC1	21 Mar	979,000
7	*Dexter's Laboratory*	ITV	26 May	967,000
8	*Hey Arnold*	ITV	14 Dec	958,000
9	*Mona the Vampire*	BBC1	3 Apr	948,000
10	*Pepper Anne*	ITV	19 Feb	925,000

* *Children only*   Source: *BARB/SPC*

TOP 10 CABLE TELEVISION COUNTRIES
(Country/subscribers)

❶ USA, 67,011,180 ❷ Germany, 18,740,260 ❸ Netherlands, 6,227,472 ❹ Russia, 5,784,432 ❺ Belgium, 3,945,342 ❻ Poland, 3,830,788 ❼ Romania, 3,000,000 ❽ UK, 2,666,783 ❾ France, 2,478,630 ❿ Switzerland, 2,156,120

Source: *The Phillips Group*

TOP 10 ★
TELEVISION AUDIENCES
OF ALL TIME IN THE UK

	PROGRAMME	DATE	AUDIENCE
1	Royal Wedding of HRH Prince Charles to Lady Diana Spencer	29 July 1981	39,000,000
2	1970 World Cup: Brazil v England	10 June 1970	32,500,000
3 =	1966 World Cup Final: England v West Germany	30 July 1966	32,000,000
=	Cup Final Replay: Chelsea v Leeds	28 Apr 1970	32,000,000
5	Funeral of Diana, Princess of Wales	6 Sep 1997	31,000,000
6	*EastEnders* Christmas episode	26 Dec 1987	30,000,000
7	*Morecambe and Wise Christmas Show*	25 Dec 1977	28,000,000
8 =	World Heavyweight Boxing Championship: Joe Frazier v Muhammad Ali	8 Mar 1971	27,000,000
=	*Dallas*	22 Nov 1980	27,000,000
10	*Only Fools and Horses*	29 Dec 1996	24,350,000

The funeral of Diana, Princess of Wales, is thought to have been seen by 2.5 billion people worldwide, which is the largest audience in television history. The most-watched film of all time on British television is *Live and Let Die*. Although already seven years old when it was first broadcast on 20 January 1980, it attracted an audience of 23,500,000.

TOP 10 ★
FASTEST-GROWING CABLE AND SATELLITE TV COMPANIES

	COMPANY/COUNTRY	CABLE AND SATELLITE SUBSCRIBERS 1998	1999	GROWTH (%)
1	**BSkyB**, UK	244,000	2,600,000	965.6
2	**Premiere World**, Germany	145,000	1,300,000	796.6
3	**Cyfra Plus**, Poland	60,000	295,000	391.7
4	**Foxtel**, Australia	40,000	131,800	229.5
5	**Wizja TV**, Poland	94,000	300,000	219.1
6	**Canal Digitaal** (Flemish), Belgium	11,900	25,400	113.4
7	**Bell ExpressVu**, Canada	180,000	370,000	105.6
8	**Tele+**, Italy	502,300	962,000	91.5
9	**Star Choice**, Canada	175,000	320,000	82.9
10	**Echostar (DISH)**, USA	1,940,000	3,410,000	75.8

Source: *Screen Digest*

The arrival of digital broadcasting and attractive incentives offered by many service providers have attracted large numbers of first-time subscribers.

TV Awards

LATEST DOCUMENTARY FILMS TO RECEIVE THE GRIERSON AWARD

YEAR*	DOCUMENTARY/ PRODUCER/COMMISSIONING COMPANY
1999	*Gulag: Enemy of the People*, Angus Macqueen, BBC
1998	*Inside Story – Tongue Tied*, Olivia Lichtenstein, BBC
1997	*The System – The Nature of the Beast*, Peter Dale, BBC
1996	*Man and Animal*, Antony Thomas, Carlton
1995	*Tripping with Zhirinovsky*, Paul Pawlikowski, BBC
1994	*Beyond the Clouds*, Philip Agland, Channel 4
1993	*Aileen Wuornos: The Selling of a Serial Killer*, Nick Broomfield, Lafayette Films
1992	*Children of Chernobyl*, Clive Gordon, Yorkshire Television
1991	*Absurdistan*, John Whiston, BBC
1990	*Four Hours in Mai Lai*, Kevin Sim, Yorkshire Television

* 2000 award delayed due to changes in funding

LATEST WINNERS OF THE BAFTA BEST ACTOR AWARD

YEAR	ACTOR/SHOW
2001	Michael Gambon, *Longitude*
2000	Michael Gambon, *Wives and Daughters*
1999	Tom Courtenay, *A Rather English Marriage*
1998	Simon Russell-Beale, *A Dance to the Music of Time*
1997	Nigel Hawthorne, *The Fragile Heart*
1996	Robbie Coltrane, *Cracker*
1995	Robbie Coltrane, *Cracker*
1994	Robbie Coltrane, *Cracker*
1993	John Thaw, *Inspector Morse*
1992	Robert Lindsay, *G.B.H.*

FIRST GOLDEN ROSE OF MONTREUX AWARDS WON BY BRITISH TV

YEAR	SHOW/COMMISSIONING COMPANY
1961	*The Black and White Minstrel Show*, BBC
1967	*Frost Over England*, BBC
1972	*Marty: The Best of the Comedy Machine*, ATV
1977	*The Muppet Show*, ATV
1982	*Dizzy Feet*, Central Television
1985	*The Paul Daniels Magic Easter Show*, BBC
1988	*The Comic Strip Presents*, Channel 4
1989	*Hale and Pace*, London Weekend Television
1990	*Mr. Bean*, Thames Television
1995	*Don't Forget Your Toothbrush*, Channel 4

The Montreux international competition for light entertainment programmes was first held in 1961. A Silver Rose is awarded to the best programme in each of three categories, and the Golden Rose award is presented to the best of these winners.

WINNERS OF THE BAFTA BEST ACTOR AWARD, 1980s

YEAR	ACTOR/SHOW(S)
1980	Denholm Elliott, *Gentle Folk*, *In Hiding*, *Blade on the Feather*, and *The Stinker*
1981	Anthony Andrews, *Brideshead Revisited*
1982	Alec Guinness, *Smiley's People*
1983	Alan Bates, *An Englishman Abroad*
1984	Tim Piggott-Smith, *The Jewel in the Crown*
1985	Bob Peck, *Edge of Darkness*
1986	Michael Gambon, *The Singing Detective*
1987	David Jason, *Porterhouse Blue*
1988	Ray McAnally, *A Very British Coup*
1989	John Thaw, *Inspector Morse*

LATEST WINNERS OF THE BAFTA TV DRAMA SERIES/SERIAL AWARD

YEAR	SHOW
2001	Series: *Clocking Off* Serial: *Longitude*
2000	Series: *The Cops* Serial: *Warriors*
1999	Series: *The Cops* Serial: *Our Mutual Friend*
1998	Series: *Jonathan Creek* Serial: *London, Holding on*
1997	Series: *EastEnders* Serial: *Our Friends in the North*
1996	Series: *Cracker* Serial: *The Politician's Wife*
1995	Series: *Cracker* Serial: *Takin' Over the Asylum*
1994	Series: no award Serial: *Prime Suspect 3*
1993	Series: *Inspector Morse* Serial: *Anglo-Saxon Attitudes*
1992	Series: *Inspector Morse* Serial: *Prime Suspect*

WINNERS OF THE BAFTA TV DRAMA SERIES/SERIAL AWARD, 1980s

YEAR	SHOW
1980	*Oppenheimer*
1981	*Brideshead Revisited*
1982	*Boys from the Blackstuff*
1983	*Kennedy*
1984	*The Jewel in the Crown*
1985	*Edge of Darkness*
1986	*The Life and Loves of a She Devil*
1987	*Tutti Frutti*
1988	*A Very British Coup*
1989	*Traffik*

THE 10 ★
LATEST WINNERS OF THE BAFTA BEST ACTRESS AWARD

YEAR	ACTOR/SHOW
2001	Judi Dench, *Last of the Blonde Bombshells*
2000	Thora Hird, *Lost for Words*
1999	Thora Hird, *Talking Heads: Waiting for the Telegram*
1998	Daniela Nardini, *This Life*
1997	Gina McKee, *Our Friends in the North*
1996	Jennifer Ehle, *Pride and Prejudice*
1995	Juliet Aubrey, *Middlemarch*
1994	Helen Mirren, *Prime Suspect 3*
1993	Helen Mirren, *Prime Suspect 2*
1992	Helen Mirren, *Prime Suspect*

In 1959, the Society of Film and Television Arts was formed by the amalgamation of the British Film Academy and the Guild of Television Producers and Directors. It changed its name to BAFTA (the British Academy of Film and Television Arts) in 1975. Past winners of the "Best Actress" award have included stars such as Vanessa Redgrave.

THE 10 ★
LATEST WINNERS OF THE BAFTA COMEDY SERIES AWARD

YEAR	SHOW
2001	*Da Ali G Show*
2000	*The League of Gentlemen*
1999	*Father Ted*
1998	*I'm Alan Partridge*
1997	*Only Fools and Horses*
1996	*Father Ted*
1995	*Three Fights, Two Weddings and a Funeral*
1994	*Drop the Dead Donkey*
1993	*Absolutely Fabulous*
1992	*One Foot in the Grave*

Among earlier winners of the award are series that have become regarded as British television comedy classics, such as *Porridge* (which won twice), *Rising Damp*, and *Fawlty Towers*. Both long-running and short-lived series have received this accolade, some more than once, but programmes broadcast by the BBC have won it considerably more frequently than those on ITV.

THE 10 ★
LATEST WINNERS OF THE BAFTA TV LIGHT ENTERTAINMENT AWARD

YEAR	SHOW
2001	*So Graham Norton*
2000	*Robbie the Reindeer: Hooves of Fire*
1999	*Who Wants to be a Millionaire?*
1998	*The Fast Show*
1997	*The Mrs. Merton Show*
1996	*The Fast Show*
1995	*Shooting Stars*
1994	*The Mrs. Merton Show*
1993	*Don't Forget Your Toothbrush*
1992	*Rory Bremner – Who Else?*

Past winners of this award have included a diverse range of programmes, from *Monty Python's Flying Circus* (1972) to *The Muppet Show* (1976). As the list of the winners of this award during the 1980s (below) indicates, shows starring Victoria Wood scooped the prize on a record four consecutive occasions.

THE 10 ★
WINNERS OF THE BAFTA BEST ACTRESS AWARD, 1980s

YEAR	ACTOR/SHOW(S)
1980	Peggy Ashcroft, *Cream in My Coffee* and *Caught on a Train*
1981	Judi Dench, *Going Gently, A Fine Romance,* and *The Cherry Orchard*
1982	Beryl Reid, *Smiley's People*
1983	Coral Browne, *An Englishman Abroad*
1984	Peggy Ashcroft, *The Jewel in the Crown*
1985	Claire Bloom, *Shadowlands*
1986	Anna Massey, *Hôtel du Lac*
1987	Emma Thompson, *Fortunes of War* and *Tutti Frutti*
1988	Thora Hird, *A Cream Cracker Under the Settee*
1989	Diana Rigg, *Mother Love*

THE 10 ★
WINNERS OF THE BAFTA COMEDY SERIES AWARD, 1980s

YEAR	SHOW
1980	*Yes Minister*
1981	*Yes Minister*
1982	*Yes Minister*
1983	*Hi-De-Hi*
1984	*The Young Ones*
1985	*Only Fools and Horses*
1986	*Just Good Friends*
1987	*Blackadder the Third*
1988	*Only Fools and Horses*
1989	*The New Statesman*

Yes Minister achieved the unique feat of winning the award in three consecutive years, while a 12-year gap separates the first (1985) and latest (1997) of the hat trick of wins by *Only Fools and Horses*.

THE 10 ★
WINNERS OF THE BAFTA TV LIGHT ENTERTAINMENT AWARD, 1980s

YEAR	SHOW
1980	*Not the Nine O'Clock News*
1981	*The Stanley Baxter Series*
1982	*Three of a Kind*
1983	*Carrott's Lib*
1984	*Another Audience with Dame Edna Everage*
1985	*Victoria Wood as Seen on TV*
1986	*Victoria Wood as Seen on TV*
1987	*Victoria Wood TV Special*
1988	*An Audience with Victoria Wood*
1989	*Clive James on the 80s*

Top Videos

TOP 10 ★
COUNTRIES WITH THE MOST VCRS

	COUNTRY	VIDEO-OWNING HOUSEHOLDS
1	USA	91,602,000
2	Japan	38,982,000
3	Germany	31,425,000
4	China	23,956,000
5	Brazil	21,330,000
6	UK	21,306,000
7	France	18,903,000
8	Russia	14,555,000
9	Italy	12,706,000
10	South Korea	11,616,000

Source: Screen Digest

TOP 10 ★
BESTSELLING VIDEOS IN THE UK*

1	Titanic
2	The Jungle Book
3	The Lion King
4	Toy Story
5	Snow White and the Seven Dwarfs
6	Fantasia
7	101 Dalmatians
8	The Full Monty
9	Star Wars
10	Lady and the Tramp

* To 1 January 2001
Source: BVA/CIN

TOP 10 MOST RENTED VIDEOS OF 2000 IN THE UK

❶ The Sixth Sense ❷ Gladiator ❸ The Green Mile ❹ East is East ❺ Deep Blue Sea ❻ American Pie ❼ American Beauty ❽ Fight Club ❾ The Mummy ❿ End of Days

Source: MRIB

TOP 10 CHILDREN'S VIDEOS IN THE UK, 2000

❶ Toy Story 2 ❷ Chicken Run ❸ Tarzan ❹ The Tigger Movie ❺ Pokémon – The First Movie ❻ The Jungle Book ❼ Toy Story ❽ The Iron Giant ❾ Thomas and the Magic Railroad ❿ Tweenies – Song Time

Source: BVA/CIN

TOP 10 ★
VIDEOS THAT SPENT LONGEST AT NO. 1 IN THE UK RENTAL CHART

	TITLE/YEAR OF RELEASE	WEEKS AT NO.1
1	Raiders of the Lost Ark, 1983	14
2	First Blood, 1983	11
3	Police Academy, 1985	13
4 =	An Officer and a Gentleman, 1984	9
=	Tightrope, 1985*	9
=	Se7en, 1996	9
7 =	Trading Places, 1984–85	8
=	The Goonies, 1986	8
=	Aliens, 1987	8
=	Big Trouble in Little China, 1987	8

* Split into two runs of six weeks and three weeks

TOP 10 ★
MOST-PURCHASED VIDEO CATEGORIES IN THE UK

	CATEGORY	% OF TOTAL SALES
1	Feature films	51.9
2	TV programmes	16.6
3	Children's animated films	8.9
4	Children's pre-school	7.3
5	Children's school age	4.6
6	Music	4.3
7	Sport	2.8
8	Live comedy	1.8
9	Special interest	1.0
10	Fitness	0.8

Source: British Video Association

TOP 10 ★
BESTSELLING CHILDREN'S VIDEOS IN THE UK*

1	The Jungle Book
2	The Lion King
3	Toy Story
4	Snow White and the Seven Dwarfs
5	Fantasia
6	101 Dalmatians
7	Lady and The Tramp
8	Beauty and the Beast
9	Cinderella
10	Aladdin

* To 1 January 2001

TOP 10 ★
MUSIC VIDEOS IN THE UK, 2000

	TITLE/ARTIST OR GROUP
1	Steps – Live at Wembley, Steps
2	Coast to Coast, Westlife
3	Gold, Michael Flatley
4	Jesus Christ Superstar, Original cast
5	Rock DJ, Robbie Williams
6	Countdown Concert, Cliff Richard
7	Ronan Keating – Live, Ronan Keating
8	Joseph and the Amazing Technicolour Dreamcoat, Original cast
9	Platinum, Shania Twain
10	The Next Step Live, Steps

Source: BVA/CIN

Did You Know? By 2002 it is estimated that 58 per cent of homes in the USA and 34 per cent in Europe will own a DVD player, and that in 2003 DVD sales will overtake those of VHS tapes.

THE NUMBER ONE...

The Matrix *was the fastest-selling DVD of all time, as well as the bestselling, until it was finally overtaken by Gladiator.*

TOP 10 ⭐

DVD TITLES PURCHASED IN THE UK, 2000

1	*Gladiator*
2	*The Matrix*
3	*The Sixth Sense*
4	*Mission: Impossible II*
5	*The Mummy*
6	*The World Is Not Enough*
7	*Toy Story 2*
8	*Deep Blue Sea*
9	*Chicken Run*
10	*The Perfect Storm*

Source: *BVA/CIN*

TOP 10 ⭐

MOST RENTED VIDEOS IN THE UK*

1	*Four Weddings and a Funeral*
2	*Dirty Dancing*
3	*Basic Instinct*
4	*Crocodile Dundee*
5	*Sister Act*
6	*Forrest Gump*
7	*Home Alone*
8	*Ghost*
9	*Pretty Woman*
10	*Speed*

* To 1 January 2001

Following its international box office success, the British comedy *Four Weddings and a Funeral* was a consistently huge UK renter on video at the tail-end of 1994 and through much of the following year, when it wrested the all-time champion slot from the long-resident *Dirty Dancing*.

COMMERCE & INDUSTRY

Wealth of Nations

POOREST COUNTRIES

COUNTRY	1998 GDP PER CAPITA ($)
1 Ethiopia	100
2 Dem. Rep. of Congo	110
3 =Burundi	140
=Sierra Leone	140
5 Guinea-Bissau	160
6 Niger	190
7 =Eritrea	200
=Malawi	200
9 =Mozambique	210
=Nepal	210
=Tanzania	210

Source: *World Bank*, World Development Indicators

TOP 10 ★

COUNTRIES WITH THE HIGHEST ANNUAL PER CAPITA EXPENDITURE

COUNTRY	EXPENDITURE PER CAPITA ($)
1 Switzerland	26,060
2 Japan	24,670
3 USA	18,840
4 Denmark	17,730
5 Germany	16,850
6 Norway	16,570
7 Belgium	16,550
8 Austria	16,020
9 Iceland	15,850
10 France	15,810
UK	*12,020*

Average per capita expenditure varies enormously from country to country, from the levels encountered in the Top 10 to those in the low hundreds of dollars, or less. In Western industrial economies, the proportion of expenditure that is devoted to food is often about 20 per cent, but this rises to 50 and even as much as 70 per cent in less developed countries. Depending on levels of taxation, the more disposable expenditure that is not allocated to such essential items, the more may be spent on consumer goods, on education, and on leisure activities.

TOP 10 ★

RICHEST COUNTRIES

COUNTRY	1998 GDP PER CAPITA ($)
1 Liechtenstein	50,000*
2 Luxembourg	43,570
3 Switzerland	40,080
4 Norway	34,330
5 Denmark	33,260
6 Japan	32,380
7 Singapore	30,060
8 USA	29,340
9 Iceland	28,010
10 Austria	26,850
UK	*21,400*
World average	*4,890*

* *World Bank estimate for the purpose of ranking*

Source: *World Bank*, World Development Indicators

GDP (Gross Domestic Product) is the total value of all the goods and services provided annually within a country. Gross National Product, or GNP, also includes income from overseas. Dividing GDP by the country's population produces the GDP per capita, often used as a measure of how "rich" a country is.

THE 10 ★

COUNTRIES WITH THE FASTEST-SHRINKING INCOME PER CAPITA

COUNTRY	AVERAGE ANNUAL GROWTH IN GNP PER CAPITA, 1997–98 (%)
1 Guinea-Bissau	-30.4
2 Indonesia	-18.0
3 United Arab Emirates	-10.6
4 Moldova	-9.2
5 Thailand	-8.6
6 Romania	-8.1
7 Malaysia	-8.0
8 South Korea	-7.5
9 Eritrea	-6.7
10 Russia	-6.4

Source: *World Bank*, World Development Indicators 2000

TOP 10 ★

FASTEST-GROWING ECONOMIES

COUNTRY	AVERAGE ANNUAL GROWTH IN GNP PER CAPITA, 1997–98 (%)
1 Angola	16.3
2 Tajikistan	13.3
3 Belarus	10.8
4 Mozambique	9.7
5 Azerbaijan	8.9
6 Republic of Congo	8.4
7 Ireland	7.4
8 Chile	7.2
9 Rwanda	7.1
10 Albania	6.8
UK	*2.0*

Source: *World Bank*, World Development Indicators 2000

THE 10 ★

COUNTRIES WITH THE LOWEST ANNUAL PER CAPITA EXPENDITURE

COUNTRY	ANNUAL EXPENDITURE PER CAPITA ($)
1 Somalia	17
2 Mozambique	57
3 Ethiopia	87
4 Malawi	109
5 Laos	140
6 Tanzania	150
7 =Bangladesh	170
=Bhutan	170
=Chad	170
=Eritrea	170
=Nepal	170

It is hard for those brought up in Western consumer cultures to comprehend the poverty of the countries appearing in this Top – or Bottom – 10, where the total average annual expenditure of an individual would barely cover the cost of a few meals in the West. Such economies inevitably rely on a greater degee of self-sufficiency in food production.

THE 10 ★ COUNTRIES MOST IN DEBT

	COUNTRY	TOTAL EXTERNAL DEBT ($)
1	Brazil	232,004,000,000
2	Russia	183,601,000,000
3	Mexico	159,959,000,000
4	China	154,599,000,000
5	Indonesia	150,875,000,000
6	Argentina	144,050,000,000
7	South Korea	139,097,000,000
8	Turkey	102,074,000,000
9	India	98,232,000,000
10	Thailand	86,172,000,000

Source: *World Bank*, World Development Indicators 2000

TOP 10 ★ COINS AND NOTES IN CIRCULATION IN THE UK BY VALUE

	UNIT	VALUE IN CIRCULATION (£)
1	£20 note	13,198,000,000
2	£10 note	5,683,000,000
3	£50 note	4,195,000,000
4	£1 coin	1,089,000,000
5	£5 note	1,045,000,000
6	20p coin	359,400,000
7	50p coin	270,500,000
8	£2 coin	264,000,000
9	5p coin	176,500,000
10	10p coin	149,800,000

The 660 million £20 notes in circulation weigh 66 tonnes and, stacked on top of each other, would form a pile 66 m (216 ft) tall, about as high as a 20-storey building. All the £1 coins weigh 10,215 tonnes and would make a pile 3,376 km (2,098 miles) high. Outside the Top 10, there are 8,459 million 1p coins in circulation, along with 5,102 million 2p coins. £1 notes were last issued in England on 31 December 1984 and ceased to be legal tender on 11 March 1988. Despite this, a decade later there were believed to be over £50 million-worth still in circulation.

TOP 10 ★ EXPORT MARKETS FOR GOODS FROM THE UK

	MARKET	TOTAL VALUE OF EXPORTS, 1999 (£)
1	USA	24,927,000,000
2	Germany	20,350,000,000
3	France	16,809,000,000
4	Netherlands	13,544,000,000
5	Ireland	10,716,000,000
6	Belgium and Luxembourg	9,188,000,000
7	Italy	7,781,000,000
8	Spain	7,484,000,000
9	Sweden	4,012,000,000
10	Japan	3,303,000,000

TOP 10 ★ AID DONORS

	COUNTRY	ANNUAL CONTRIBUTION ($)
1	Japan	9,358,000,000
2	USA	6,878,000,000
3	France	6,307,000,000
4	Germany	5,857,000,000
5	UK	3,433,000,000
6	Netherlands	2,947,000,000
7	Canada	2,045,000,000
8	Sweden	1,731,000,000
9	Denmark	1,637,000,000
10	Norway	1,306,000,000

TOP 10 AID RECIPIENTS

(Country/annual amount received in $)

1 China, 2,040,000,000 **2** Egypt, 1,947,000,000 **3** India, 1,678,000,000 **4** Israel, 1,191,000,000 **5** Bangladesh, 1,009,000,000 **6** Vietnam, 997,000,000 **7** = Mozambique, 963,000,000; = Tanzania, 963,000,000 **9** Bosnia, 863,000,000 **10** Uganda, 840,000,000

TOP 10 ★ GOODS IMPORTED TO THE UK

	PRODUCT	TOTAL VALUE OF IMPORTS, 1999 (£)
1	Electrical machinery	40,843,000,000
2	Road vehicles	24,080,000,000
3	Mechanical machinery	17,289,000,000
4	Clothing and footwear	9,511,000,000
5	Transport equipment	6,338,000,000
6	Scientific and photographic equipment	6,177,000,000
7	Petroleum and petroleum products	4,842,000,000
8	Organic chemicals	4,803,000,000
9	Textile manufactures	4,385,000,000
10	Paper and paperboard manufactures	4,323,000,000
	Total (including goods not in Top 10)	192,434,000,000

Source: *Office for National Statistics*

In 1999, the UK imported machinery and transport equipment totalling £88,550 million, manufactured goods worth £26,815 million, and chemicals totalling £18,145 million. Food and live animal imports amounted to £13,343 million, and beverages to £2,786 million.

TOP 10 ★ SOURCES OF UK GOVERNMENT INCOME

	SOURCE	ESTIMATED INCOME, 1999–2000 (£)
1	Income Tax	90,800,000,000
2	Social Security contributions	55,700,000,000
3	Value Added Tax	54,000,000,000
4	Corporation Tax	29,900,000,000
5	Fuel duties	23,100,000,000
6	Business rates	15,600,000,000
7	Council Tax	12,800,000,000
8	Tobacco duties	7,000,000,000
9	Alcohol duties	6,100,000,000
10	Stamp duties	5,700,000,000

Did You Know? Inflation in Hungary in June 1946 reached such a record level that the pre-war gold pengő coin was valued at 130 million trillion paper pengős, and notes with a face value of 1,000 trillion pengős were printed.

Workers of the World

COUNTRIES WITH THE MOST WORKERS

COUNTRY	WORKERS*
1 China	743,000,000
2 India	431,000,000
3 USA	138,000,000
4 Indonesia	98,000,000
5 Russia	78,000,000
6 Brazil	76,000,000
7 Japan	68,000,000
8 Bangladesh	64,000,000
9 Pakistan	49,000,000
10 Nigeria	48,000,000

* Based on people aged 15–64 who are currently employed; unpaid groups are not included

Source: *World Bank*, World Development Indicators 2000

COUNTRIES WITH THE HIGHEST PROPORTION OF CHILD WORKERS

COUNTRY	PERCENTAGE OF CHILDREN WORKING*
1 Mali	52
2 Burundi	49
3 Burkina Faso	47
4 =Niger	44
=Uganda	44
6 Nepal	43
7 Ethiopia	42
8 Rwanda	41
9 Kenya	40
10 Tanzania	38

* Aged 10–14 years

Source: *World Bank*, World Development Indicators 2000

COUNTRIES WITH THE HIGHEST PROPORTION OF WORKERS IN SERVICE INDUSTRIES*

COUNTRY	LABOUR FORCE PERCENTAGE
1 Puerto Rico	77.0
2 =Argentina	76.5
=Jordan	76.5
4 Canada	74.5
5 =Australia	74.0
=USA	74.0
7 =Ecuador	73.5
=Netherlands	73.5
9 =Peru	73.0
=Norway	73.0
UK	72.5

* Service industries include wholesale and retail trade, restaurants, and hotels; transport, storage, and communications; financing, insurance, real estate, and business services; and community, social, and personal services

Source: *World Bank*, World Development Indicators 2000

TOP 10 COUNTRIES IN THE EC WORKING THE LONGEST HOURS

(Country/average hours per week)

1 UK, 43.6 **2** Portugal, 42.3 **3** Spain, 40.9 **4** = Germany, 40.5; = Ireland, 40.5 **6** Greece, 40.4 **7** France, 39.9 **8** = Denmark, 39.8; = Luxembourg, 39.8 **10** Netherlands, 39.2

These are average working weeks for full-time employees of both sexes in agriculture, industry, and services in the 12 member countries of the European Community (EC). The two countries working the shortest hours are Italy (38.6) and Belgium (38.0).

HARD LABOUR

India's huge work force relies on traditional manual labour, but the country is increasingly becoming a major centre for computer technology.

TOP 10 BRITISH COMPANIES WITH MOST EMPLOYEES

(Company/employees)*

1 Compass Group, 191,407 **2** HSBC Holdings, 144,521 **3** Tesco, 131,031 **4** Invensys, 130,626 **5** Rentokil Initial, 129,357 **6** British Telecommunications, 124,900 **7** J. Sainsbury, 109,245 **8** British American Tobacco, 101,081 **9** BP Amoco, 98,900 **10** The Boots Company, 87,394

* As at 4 May 2000 Source: The Financial Times Ltd 2000
This list includes only publicly-quoted companies (companies whose shares are on the Stock Exchange).

TOP 10 ★
OCCUPATIONS IN THE UK, 1901

	OCCUPATION	EMPLOYEES
1	Farmers and gardeners	2,262,454
2	Domestic service	2,199,517
3	Conveyance (road, rail, canal, etc.)	1,497,629
4	Textile manufacturing	1,462,001
5	Clothing makers and dealers	1,395,795
6	Builders	1,335,820
7	Metal workers	1,175,715
8	Miners and quarry workers	943,880
9	Food trade	865,777
10	Professional (clergymen, teachers, lawyers, etc.)	733,582

At the turn of the century, there were 18.3 million in the UK labour force. Mining and transport industries' workforces have halved since then, while office workers have increased from 18 per cent of the workforce to 40 per cent.

TOP 10 ★
OCCUPATIONS IN THE UK 2000

	OCCUPATION	EMPLOYEES
1	Manufacturing	3,855,000
2	Real estate, renting, and business activities	3,475,000
3	Retail (except motor and repair of personal/ household goods)	2,365,000
4	Transport, storage, and communication	1,425,000
5	Hotels and restaurants	1,378,000
6	=Wholesale and commission trade (excluding motor)	1,092,000
	=Construction	1,092,000
8	Financial intermediation	1,156,000
9	Motor vehicles (including retail of automotive fuel)	538,000
10	Agriculture, hunting, forestry, and fishing	327,000

FACTORY-MADE
Despite the growth of the service sector, manufacturing remains a vital component of most developed economies, providing employment for countless workers in factories across the world.

TOP 10 ★
LARGEST TRADE UNIONS IN THE UK

	TRADE UNION	MEMBERS
1	UNISON	1,272,330
2	Transport & General Workers' Union (TGWU)	881,625
3	Amalgamated Engineering and Electrical Union (AEEU)	727,977
4	GMB (formerly General, Municipal Boilermakers and Allied Trades Union)	712,010
5	Manufacturing, Science & Finance Union (MSF)	416,000
6	Royal College of Nursing (RCN)	320,206
7	Union of Shop, Distributive & Allied Workers (USDAW)	303,060
8	Communications Workers Union (CWU)	287,732
9	National Union of Teachers (NUT)	286,503
10	National Association of Schoolmasters and Union of Women Teachers	250,783

Source: *Certification Office, Annual Report 1999–2000*

TOP 10 COUNTRIES WITH THE HIGHEST PROPORTION OF FARMERS

(Country/percentage in agriculture, 1999)

1 Bhutan, 93.8 **2** Nepal, 93.1 **3** Burkina Faso, 92.2 **4** Rwanda, 90.5 **5** Burundi, 90.4 **6** Niger, 88.1 **7** Guinea Bissau, 83.1 **8** Ethiopia, 82.8 **9** Mali, 81.5 **10** Uganda, 79.5

Source: *Food and Agriculture Organization of the United Nations*
This is based on a study of the number of people who depend on agriculture for their livelihood as a proportion of the total population of the country.

Which is the only South American country to appear among the world's Top 10 gold producers?
see p.204 for the answer
A Brazil
B Bolivia
C Peru

Company Matters

LARGEST BANKS (BY ASSETS)

BANK/COUNTRY	ASSETS ($)
1 Deutsche Bank, Germany	841,796,920,000
2 Bank of Tokyo-Mitsubishi, Japan	729,249,600,000
3 BNP Paribas, France	700,232,030,000
4 Bank of America Corp., USA	632,574,000,000
5 UBS, Switzerland	613,198,370,000
6 Fuji Bank, Japan	567,899,800,000
7 HSBC Holdings, UK	567,793,290,000
8 Sumitomo Bank, Japan	524,227,780,000
9 Dai-Ichi Kangyo Bank, Japan	506,980,440,000
10 HypoVereinsbank, Germany	504,412,630,000

LARGEST BANKS (BY REVENUE)

BANK/COUNTRY	REVENUE ($)
1 J. P. Morgan Chase, USA	60,065,000,000
2 Deutsche Bank, Germany	58,585,150,000
3 Bank of America Corp., USA	57,757,000,000
4 Credit Suisse, Switzerland	49,361,980,000
5 Fortis, Belgium	43,660,190,000
6 BNP Paribas, France	40,098,550,000
7 HSBC Holdings, UK	39,348,150,000
8 ABN AMRO Holdings, Netherlands	38,820,670,000
9 Crédit Agricole, France	32,923,500,000
10 Bank of Tokyo-Mitsubishi, Japan	32,624,000,000

Source: Fortune 5000/Fortune Global 500

INTERNATIONAL INDUSTRIAL COMPANIES

COMPANY/SECTOR/LOCATION	ANNUAL SALES ($)
1 Exxon Mobil, Oil, gas, fuel, USA	210,392,000,000
2 Wal-Mart Stores, Inc, Retailing, USA	193,295,000,000
3 General Motors Corp., Transport, USA	184,632,000,000
4 Ford Motor Co., Transport, USA	180,598,000,000
5 DaimlerChrysler, Transport, Germany	159,986,000,000
6 General Electric, Electronics, electrical equipment, USA	129,853,000,000
7 Mitsui and Co. Ltd., Trading, Japan	118,555,000,000
8 Mitsubishi Corp., Trading, Japan	117,766,000,000
9 Toyota Motor, Transport, Japan	115,671,000,000
10 Itochu Corp., Trading, Japan	109,069,000,000

Source: Fortune Global 500

Fortune magazine's authoritative Global 500 list contains 500 companies each with annual sales in excess of $9.7 billion. All those in the Top 100 achieve sales of more than $32.7 billion, but only those in the Top 10 (plus one other – the Royal Dutch/Shell Group) make the stratospheric $100-billion-plus league.

AS LONG AS IT'S BLACK...

Long the world's bestselling car, the Model T Ford established the company's place among the foremost global manufacturers.

TOP 10 ★
BANKS WITH THE MOST BRANCHES IN THE UK

BANK	BRANCHES*
1 National Westminster Bank/ Royal Bank of Scotland	2,360
2 Lloyds TSB	2,122
3 Barclays Bank	1,899
4 HSBC	1,662
5 Halifax	909
6 Abbey National	765
7 Woolwich	405
8 Bank of Scotland	350
9 Alliance & Leicester	319
10 Cheltenham & Gloucester	221

As at 1 January 2000

TOP 10 ★
CORPORATIONS IN THE US

CORPORATION	REVENUE* ($)
1 Exxon Mobil	210,392,000,000
2 Wal-Mart Stores	193,295,000,000
3 General Motors	184,632,000,000
4 Ford Motor Company	180,598,000,000
5 General Electric	129,853,000,000
6 Citigroup	111,826,000,000
7 Enron	100,789,000,000
8 IBM	88,396,000,000
9 AT&T	65,981,000,000
10 Verizon Communications	64,707,000,000

In latest year for which data available

Source: Fortune Global 500

Despite their involvement in new technologies, several of the corporations listed here have a history dating back to the late 19th century: AT&T – originally the American Telephone and Telegraph Company – dates from 1885, while General Electric was established in 1892, when the Edison General Electric Company and Thomson Houston Company were merged. Even portions of IBM have their roots back in the 1880s.

TOP 10 ★
US COMPANIES MAKING THE GREATEST PROFIT PER SECOND

COMPANY	PROFIT PER SECOND ($)
1 Exxon Mobil	561
2 Citigroup	428
3 General Electric	403
4 Verizon Communications	374
5 Intel Corp.	334
6 Microsoft	298
7 Philip Morris	269
8 IBM	256
9 SBC Communications	252
10 Bank of America Corporation	238

TOP 10 ★
BRITISH COMPANIES*

COMPANY/SECTOR	ANNUAL SALES (£)
1 Shell Transport & Trading Company, Petroleum refining	57,234,000,000
2 BP Amoco, Petroleum products, oil and gas exploration	41,725,100,000
3 Unilever, Food	27,094,000,000
4 Tesco, Supermarkets	17,158,000,000
5 British Telecommunications, Telecommunications	16,953,000,000
6 J. Sainsbury, Supermarkets	16,433,000,000
7 Diageo, Beverages	11,795,000,000
8 Invensys, Industrial and farm equipment	9,414,000,000
9 Imperial Chemical Industries, Chemicals	9,286,000,000
10 British Airways, Airlines	8,915,000,000

In latest year for which figures are available; excluding banks and insurance companies

Source: Financial Times

TOP 10 ★
OLDEST-ESTABLISHED BUSINESSES IN THE UK

BUSINESS/LOCATION	FOUNDED
1 The Royal Mint, Cardiff (formerly London)	886
2 Kirkstall Forge, Kirkstall, Leeds	1200
3 The Shore Porters Society of Aberdeen, Aberdeen	1498
4 Cambridge University Press, Cambridge	1534
5 John Brooke and Sons, Huddersfield	1541
6 Child's Bank (now part of Royal Bank of Scotland), London	1559
7 Whitechapel Bell Foundry, London	1570
8 Oxford University Press, Oxford	1585
9 Richard Durtnell and Sons, Brasted, nr. Westerham, Kent	1591
10 Hays at Guildford, Guildford (formerly London)	1651

TOP 10 ★
OLDEST-ESTABLISHED BRITISH INSURANCE COMPANIES

COMPANY	ESTABLISHED
1 Sun	1710
2 Union Assurance	1714
3 Westminster Fire	1717
4 =London Assurance	1720
=Royal Exchange	1720
6 Equitable Life	1762
7 Phoenix	1782
8 Norwich Union	1797
9 Essex & Suffolk	1802
10 =Law Union & Rock	1806
=London Life	1806

The Great Fire of London in 1666 led to the establishment of the first fire insurance companies. The Sun Fire Office, at No. 1 on this list, has original deeds dating from 7 April 1710.

Did You Know? General Motors, the world's biggest car makers, became the first company in the world to assemble 100 million vehicles when, on 16 March 1966, an Oldsmobile Toronado rolled off the production line.

Advertising & Brands

TOP 10 ★
MOST ADVERTISED GROCERY BRANDS IN THE UK, 2000

BRAND/BRAND OWNER	AD SPEND (£)*
1 Coca-Cola, Coca-Cola GB	25,676,436
2 Nescafé, Nestlé	23,967,924
3 Persil, Unilever (Lever Brothers)	21,175,215
4 Weetabix, Weetabix	16,776,496
5 Brooke Bond PG Tips, Unilever (Van den Bergh Foods)	12,571,557
6 Pepsi, PepsiCo International	12,165,921
7 Colgate, Colgate Palmolive	11,308,684
8 Kenco, Kraft Foods International,	11,124,800
9 Comfort, Unilever (Lever Brothers)	10,533,420
10 Huggies, Kimberly-Clark Corporation (KCC)	10,285,292

* In year to 12 August 2000

Source: Checkout/ACNielsen MMS

TOP 10 ★
GLOBAL MARKETERS

COMPANY/BASE	MEDIA SPENDING, 1998 ($)
1 Procter & Gamble Company, USA	4,747,600,000
2 Unilever, Netherlands/UK	3,428,500,000
3 General Motors Corporation, USA	3,193,500,000
4 Ford Motor Company, USA	2,229,500,000
5 Philip Morris Companies, USA	1,980,300,000
6 DaimlerChrysler, Germany/USA	1,922,200,000
7 Nestlé, Switzerland	1,833,000,000
8 Toyota Motor Corporation, Japan	1,692,400,000
9 Sony Corporation, Japan	1,337,700,000
10 Coca-Cola Company, USA	1,327,300,000

Source: Competitive Media Reporting/ACNielsen MMS/Advertising Age

TOP 10 ★
ADVERTISERS ON THE WEB

WEBSITE	IMPRESSIONS*
1 TRUSTe	504,182,490
2 Microsoft	370,575,192
3 Yahoo!	228,032,781
4 America Online	128,433,841
5 AllAdvantage	120,408,883
6 Amazon	110,318,224
7 eBay	95,391,668
8 Casino On Net	90,831,841
9 Next Card	71,844,247
10 Barnes and Noble	67,581,608

* Number of times the advertising banner has been loaded within a browser, week ending 23 July 2000

TOP 10 ★
BESTSELLING BRANDS IN THE UK, 2000*

BRAND/BRAND OWNER	SALES (£)
1 Coca-Cola, Coca-Cola GB	451,700,000
2 Walkers crisps, PepsiCo (Walkers Snack Foods)	356,700,000
3 Nescafé, Nestlé	332,000,000
4 Müller pot desserts, Müller Dairy (UK)	252,600,000
5 Persil, Unilever (Lever Brothers)	243,300,000
6 Andrex toilet tissue, Kimberly-Clark Corporation	221,100,000
7 Kingsmill bread, Allied Bakeries	180,600,000
8 Ariel, Procter & Gamble	180,000,000
9 Pampers nappies, Procter & Gamble	166,900,000
10 Robinsons, Britvic Soft Drinks	163,000,000

* In year to 12 August 2000

Source: Checkout/ACNielsen MMS

BIG MAC

Global fast food company McDonald's is ranked second only to Coca-Cola as one of the world's most valuable food and drink brands.

Crowd cheers! Coke nears!
Game goes better refreshed.
Coca-Cola, never too sweet,
gives that special zing...refreshes best.

things go
**better
with
Coke**
Drink
Coca-Cola

THE REAL THING

Bestselling, most advertised, and most valuable are only three of the many superlatives applied to Coca-Cola's world-beating status.

TOP 10 ⭐
MOST VALUABLE GLOBAL BRANDS

	BRAND*	INDUSTRY	BRAND VALUE ($)
1	Coca-Cola	Beverages	72,537,000,000
2	Microsoft-Windows	Technology	70,197,000,000
3	IBM	Technology	53,184,000,000
4	Intel	Technology	39,049,000,000
5	Nokia, Finland	Technology	38,528,000,000
6	General Electric	Diversified	38,128,000,000
7	Ford	Automobiles	36,368,000,000
8	Disney	Leisure	33,553,000,000
9	McDonald's	Food retail	27,859,000,000
10	AT&T	Telecommunications	25,548,000,000

* All US-owned unless otherwise stated

Source: *Interbrand*

Brand consultants Interbrand use a method of estimating value that takes account of the profitability of individual brands within a business (rather than the companies that own them), as well as such factors as their potential for growth. Well over half of the 75 most valuable global brands surveyed by Interbrand are US-owned, with Europe accounting for another 30 per cent.

TOP 10 ⭐
BESTSELLING GLOBAL BRANDS*

	BRAND/COUNTRY	INDUSTRY	SALES, 1999 ($)
1	**Ford**, USA	Automobiles	121,603,000,000
2	**General Electric**, USA	Diversified	105,840,000,000
3	**Shell**, UK	Oil	105,366,000,000
4	**Toyota**, Japan	Automobiles	100,704,000,000
5	**IBM**, USA	Technology	87,548,000,000
6	**Mercedes**, Germany	Automobiles	65,249,000,000
7	**AT&T**, USA	Telecommunications	62,391,000,000
8	**Honda**, Japan	Automobiles	60,902,000,000
9	**Panasonic**, Japan	Electronics	60,314,000,000
10	**BP**, UK	Oil	56,464,000,000

* By value of sales

Source: *Interbrand*

Most of the companies appearing in this list have in common not only their impressive size and status but also a long history. Ford, Mercedes, and Shell, for example, date back over 100 years.

TOP 10 ⭐
MOST VALUABLE
FOOD AND DRINK BRANDS

	BRAND*	INDUSTRY	BRAND VALUE ($)
1	Coca-Cola	Food/beverages	72,537,000,000
2	McDonald's	Food retail	27,859,000,000
3	Marlboro	Tobacco	22,111,000,000
4	Nescafé, Switzerland	Beverages	13,681,000,000
5	Heinz	Food/beverages	11,742,000,000
6	Budweiser	Alcohol	10,685,000,000
7	Kelloggs	Food/beverages	7,357,000,000
8	Pepsi-Cola	Beverages	6,637,000,000
9	Wrigley's	Food	4,324,000,000
10	Bacardi	Alcohol	3,187,000,000

* All US-owned unless otherwise stated

Source: *Interbrand*

Nearly half of these companies (McDonald's, Heinz, Kelloggs, Wrigley's, and Bacardi) are eponymous, deriving their names from those of their founders.

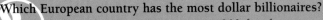

Which European country has the most dollar billionaires?

see p.202 for the answer

A Germany
B France
C Luxembourg

Retail Therapy

TOP 10 ★ RETAILERS IN THE UK*

	GROUP/SECTOR#	SALES, 1998/99 (£)
1	Marks & Spencer	6,601,100,000
2	Kingfisher plc	5,412,729,000
3	The Boots Company	4,474,700,000
4	Great Universal Stores	3,639,600,000
5	John Lewis Partnership	3,168,000,000
6	Dixons Group plc, electricals	3,028,400,000
7	Arcadia Group plc	1,875,100,000
8	Littlewoods Org.	1,853,000,000
9	First Quench, off-licences	1,383,670,000
10	Debenhams, department stores	1,349,200,000

* Excluding retailers whose main business is groceries

All multi-sector unless otherwise stated

Based on The Retail Rankings (2000) published by The Corporate Intelligence Group Ltd.

TOP 10 ★ RETAILERS WITH THE MOST OUTLETS IN THE UK

	RETAILER	OUTLETS*
1	First Quench	3,000
2	Spar	2,676
3	Boots	2,113
4	Kingfisher (including Woolworths, Comet, Superdrug, B & Q, etc.)	2,100
5	BP Amoco	1,878
6	Arcadia	1,872
7	Londis	1,830
8	Esso	1,754
9	Somerfield	1,422
10	Shell	1,411

* Includes concessions (shops within stores, etc.)

Based on The Retail Rankings (2000) published by The Corporate Intelligence Group Ltd.

TOP 10 ★ BOOKSELLERS AND STATIONERS IN THE UK

	RETAILER	SALES, 1998/99 (£)*
1	W.H. Smith	1,067,000,000
2	Waterstone's	390,628,000
3	Clinton Cards	208,460,000
4	Staples	148,851,000
5	Birthdays	123,473,000
6	Globus Office World	106,940,000
7	Blackwell	62,423,000
8	Borders	58,341,000
9	Ottakar's	57,316,000
10	Remainders	52,000,000

* Excluding VAT

Based on The Retail Rankings (2000) published by The Corporate Intelligence Group Ltd.

TOP 10 ★ MUSIC AND VIDEO RETAILERS IN THE UK

	RETAILER	SALES, 1998/99 (£)*
1	Virgin	498,200,000
2	HMV	444,105,000
3	Blockbuster	199,004,000
4	MVC Entertainment	80,107,000
5	Home Entertainment	49,954,000
6	Tower Records	47,000,000
7	Global Video	31,285,000
8	Andy's Records	28,451,000
9	A&R	11,243,000
10	Dawsons Music	8,442,000

* Excluding VAT

Based on The Retail Rankings (2000) published by The Corporate Intelligence Group Ltd.

SHOPPING SPREE

Despite the growth of online retailing, traditional shopping continues to be an activity enjoyed by many, and is both a yardstick and a mainstay of Western economies.

TOP 10 ★
WORLD RETAIL SECTORS

	SECTOR	COMPANIES*
1	Supermarket	108
2	Speciality	94
3	Department	62
4	Hypermarket	53
5=	Convenience	40
=	Discount	40
7	Mail order	22
8	Restaurant	21
9	Drug	16
10	DIY	15

* Of those listed in Stores' Top 200 Global Retailers; stores can operate in more than one area

Source: Stores

A survey of the global retail industry in 1999 revealed that the overall sales of the 200 largest retailers reached $2 trillion. Of the 200, 39 per cent are in the US, followed by Japan with 14 per cent, and the UK with 9 per cent. The 77 US companies in the full list are even more dominant in terms of total sales, achieving some $922 billion, or 47 per cent of the combined revenue of the global 200.

TOP 10 ★
PRODUCTS SOLD IN DEPARTMENT STORES IN THE UK

	PRODUCT	% TOTAL DEPT STORE SALES
1	Clothing	29.2
2	Food	13.1
3	Cosmetics and perfumery	8.6
4	Toys, games, and sports goods*	7.1
5	Domestic electrical appliances	6.0
6	Soft furnishings	5.7
7	Hardware and glassware	4.6
8	Footwear	3.9
9	Alcoholic drinks	3.5
10	Jewellery	1.7

* Including video and audio software

Source: Euromonitor

TOP 10 ★
CLOTHING RETAILERS IN THE UK

	RETAILER	CLOTHING SALES, 1998/99 (£)*
1	Marks & Spencer (non-food)	3,996,000,000
2	Arcadia Group	1,837,374,000
3	Storehouse plc (including BHS, Mothercare)	1,238,300,000
4	Next Retail	821,600,000
5	C&A	650,000,000
6	New Look Group plc	355,400,000
7	Littlewoods Stores	286,000,000
8	Matalan plc	278,200,000
9	River Island Clothing Co.	270,090,000
10	Dunnes Stores	211,087,000

* Excluding VAT

Based on The Retail Rankings (2000) published by The Corporate Intelligence Group Ltd.

TOP 10 ★
SUPERMARKET GROUPS IN THE UK

	GROUP*	SALES, 1998/99 (£)#
1	Tesco (UK) plc	15,835,000,000
2	J. Sainsbury	12,103,000,000
3	ASDA Group plc	8,198,300,000
4	Safeway Stores plc+	7,510,700,000
5	Somerfield Stores Ltd.★	5,897,900,000
6	William Morrison Supermarkets	2,533,781,000
7	Iceland Group plc	1,741,600,000
8	Waitrose Ltd.	1,635,800,000
9	Aldi Stores Ltd.	798,594,000
10	Budgens plc	411,200,000

* Excluding Co-ops and "mixed goods" retailers, such as Marks & Spencer

 # Excluding VAT

+ Including Presto

★ Merged with Kwik Save in 1998

Based on The Retail Rankings (2000) published by The Corporate Intelligence Group Ltd.

TOP 10 ★
COMPLAINTS TO THE CONSUMERS' ASSOCIATION

	CATEGORY	NUMBER OF COMPLAINTS*
1	Home maintenance, repairs, and improvements	18,670
2	Secondhand motor vehicles	17,969
3	Radio, TV, and audiovisual equipment	10,116
4	Personal computers and related hardware	9,164
5	Clothing and clothing fabrics	8,840
6	Large white goods and major fixed appliances	8,228
7	Upholstered furniture	8,100
8	Double glazing products and installation	7,822
9	Food and drink	7,682
10	Mobile phones and services	6,840

* Figures for last quarter of 1999

Source: Office of Fair Trading

TOP 10 ★
RETAILERS

	COMPANY/COUNTRY	RETAIL SALES, 1999 ($)
1	Wal-Mart, USA	163,217,000,000
2	Kroger, USA	45,352,000,000
3	Sears, USA	41,071,000,000
4	METRO AG, Germany	40,357,000,000
5	Carrefour, France	39,780,000,000
6	Home Depot, USA	38,434,000,000
7	Intermarché, France	38,390,000,000
8	Albertson's, USA	37,478,000,000
9	Kmart, USA	35,925,000,000
10	Ahold, Netherlands	33,811,000,000

Source: National Retail Federation, Top 200 Global Retailers

Britain's top supermarket, Tesco, features at No. 14 in this list with sales of 30,350,000,000.

How many patents did Thomas A. Edison register?
see p.208 for the answer
A 87
B 302
C 1,093

That's Rich

TOP 10 ★
RICHEST PEOPLE IN THE UK

NAME/SOURCE OF WEALTH	ASSETS (£)
1 **Duke of Westminster**, Land and property	4,400,000,000
2 **Hans Rausing**, Packaging	4,200,000,000
3 **Bernie and Slavica Ecclestone**, Formula One motor racing	3,000,000,000
4 **Lord Sainsbury and family**, Retailing	2,900,000,000
5 **Joseph Lewis**, Finance	2,200,000,000
6 **Bruno Schroder and family**, Banking	1,750,000,000
7 = **Nadhmi Auchi**, Finance	1,700,000,000
= **Terry Matthews**, Electronics	1,700,000,000
9 **Philippe Foriel-Destezet**, Recruitment services	1,600,000,000
10 = **Mark Dixon**, Business services	1,400,000,000
= **Sir Adrian and John Swire**, Shipping and aviation	1,400,000,000

Based on data published in The Sunday Times

TOP 10 ★
HIGHEST-EARNING ENTERTAINERS*

ENTERTAINER(S)/PROFESSION	2000 INCOME ($)
1 **George Lucas**, Film producer/director	250,000,000
2 **Oprah Winfrey**, TV host/producer	150,000,000
3 **The Beatles**, Rock band	70,000,000
4 **David Copperfield**, Illusionist	60,000,000
5 **Steven Spielberg**, Film producer/director	51,000,000
6 **Siegfried & Roy**, Illusionists	50,000,000
7 **Brian Grazer/Ron Howard**, Film producers	45,000,000
8 **Stephen King**, Writer	44,000,000
9 **'N Sync**, Male vocal group	42,000,000
10 **Britney Spears**, Pop singer	38,500,000

* Excluding actors, actresses, and sports stars
Used by permission of Forbes *magazine*

TOP 10 ★
RICHEST PEOPLE

NAME/COUNTRY	NET WORTH ($)
1 **William H. Gates III**, USA	63,000,000,000
2 **Lawrence Joseph Ellison**, USA	58,000,000,000
3 **Paul Gardner Allen**, USA	36,000,000,000
4 **Warren Edward Buffett**, USA	28,000,000,000
5 **Gordon Earle Moore**, USA	26,000,000,000
6 = **Prince Alwaleed Bin Talal Alsaud**, Saudi Arabia	20,000,000,000
= **Theo & Karl Albrecht and family**, Germany	20,000,000,000
8 **Masayoshi Son**, Japan	19,400,000,000
9 **Philip F. Anschutz**, USA	18,000,000,000
10 = **Steven Anthony Ballmer**, USA	17,000,000,000
= **S. Robson Walton***, USA	17,000,000,000

* Other members of the Walton family have equal wealth

Based on data published in Forbes *magazine*

TOP 10 ★
HIGHEST-EARNING ACTORS AND ACTRESSES

ACTOR OR ACTRESS	2000 INCOME ($)
1 **Bruce Willis**	70,000,000
2 **Tom Cruise**	43,200,000
3 **Eddie Murphy**	39,500,000
4 **Mel Gibson**	31,800,000
5 **Nicolas Cage**	28,400,000
6 **Keanu Reeves**	25,500,000
7 **Brad Pitt**	23,800,000
8 **Julia Roberts**	18,900,000
9 **Ben Affleck**	18,300,000
10 **Robin Williams**	17,100,000

Used by permission of Forbes *magazine*

Actors such as Bruce Willis and Tom Cruise can routinely command $20 million or more per film.

CLOSING ON GATES

The fortune of Oracle software magnate Larry Ellison has risen sharply, placing him a close second to the world's richest person, Bill Gates.

TOP 10 ★
COUNTRIES WITH THE MOST DOLLAR BILLIONAIRES

COUNTRY	$ BILLIONAIRES*
1 **USA**	55
2 **Japan**	43
3 **Germany**	42
4 = **Canada**	15
= **UK**	15
6 = **France**	14
= **Switzerland**	14
8 = **China (Hong Kong)**	13
= **Mexico**	13
10 = **Brazil**	9
= **India**	9

* Individuals/families with a net worth of $1 billion or more Source: Forbes *magazine*

MOST EXPENSIVE SINGLE PRECIOUS STONES EVER SOLD AT AUCTION*

STONE/SALE	PRICE (£)
1 *The Patino*, cushion-cut Burmese ruby of 32.08 carats, Chaumet (from the Patiño collection), Sotheby's, New York, 26 Oct 1989	2,924,050 ($4,620,000)
2 Cushion-cut Burmese ruby of 27.37 carats, Sotheby's, Geneva, 17 May 1995	2,562,698 (SF4,843,500)
3 Cushion-cut Burmese ruby of 15.97 carats, Sotheby's, New York, 18 Oct 1988	2,074,285 ($3,630,000)
4 Oval-cut Burmese ruby of 16.51 carats, Sotheby's, Geneva, 26 May 1993	1,957,111 (SF4,403,500)
5 *The Rockefeller Sapphire*, step-cut Burmese sapphire of 62.02 carats, Sotheby's, St. Moritz, 20 Feb 1988	1,616,326 (SF3,960,000)
6 Jadeite cabochon ring, 33.08 x 18.78 x 14.83 mm (1.3 x 0.74 x 0.58 in), Christie's, Hong Kong, 1 Nov 1999	1,480,000 (HK$18,500,000)
7 Cushion-cut Burmese ruby of 16.20 carats, Christie's, New York, 23 Oct 1990	1,470,588 ($2,750,000)
8 Cushion-cut sapphire of 337.66 carats in a diamond pendant, Christie's, Geneva, 16 May 1991	1,320,000 (SF3,300,000)
9 Cushion-cut Burmese ruby of 12.10 carats, Christie's, Geneva, 19 November 1992	1,317,972 (SF2,860,000)
10 Rectangular step-cut emerald of 19.77 carats, Cartier (from the Duchess of Windsor collection), Sotheby's, Geneva, 2 April 1987	1,312,757 (SF3,190,000)

* Excluding diamonds

COUNTRIES MAKING GOLD JEWELLERY

COUNTRY	GOLD USED IN 1999 (TONNES)
1 India	644.0
2 Italy	511.0
3 USA	178.2
4 China	166.0
5 Saudi Arabia and Yemen	149.2
6 Indonesia	126.0
7 Turkey	115.0
8 Egypt	114.3
9 Malaysia	68.0
10 Taiwan	63.0
UK	43.9
World	3,128.0

Source: *Gold Fields Mineral Services Ltd.*, Gold Survey 2000

GOLD MANUFACTURERS

COUNTRY	GOLD USED IN FABRICATION, 1999 (TONNES)
1 India	685.2
2 Italy	522.8
3 USA	323.1
4 China	181.5
5 Japan	158.7
6 Saudi Arabia and Yemen	149.2
7 Turkey	139.3
8 Indonesia	126.0
9 Egypt	114.3
10 South Korea	93.5
UK	53.8
World	3,722.3

Source: *Gold Fields Mineral Services Ltd.*, Gold Survey 2000

PIECES OF JEWELLERY AUCTIONED BY CHRISTIE'S

JEWELLERY/SALE	PRICE (£)
1 Single strand jadeite necklace of 27 beads, 15.09 to 15.84 mm (0.59 to 0.62 in), Christie's, Hong Kong, 6 Nov 1997	5,809,600 (HK$72,620,000)
2 *The Begum Blue* (from the collection of Princess Salimah Aga Khan), Christie's, Geneva, 13 Nov 1995	5,001,989 (SF8,803,500)

Fancy, deep blue, heart-shaped diamond of 13.78 carats and a heart-shaped diamond of 16.03 carats, D colour, internally flawless.

3 *The Mouna Diamond*, Christie's, Geneva, 15 May 1996	1,984,055 (SF3,743,500)

Fancy, intense yellow diamond brooch of 102.07 carats by Cartier, 1953.

4 *The Allnat*, Christie's, Geneva, 16 Nov 1998	1,939,868 (SF4,403,500)

Fancy, intense yellow cushion-shaped diamond pendant of 112.53 carats (VS1), mounted by Bulgari.

5 *The Harcourt Emeralds*, Christie's, London, 21 June 1989	1,870,000

Necklace set with diamonds and 13 emeralds weighing 16.219 carats.

6 Single strand jadeite and diamond lavalière of 29 jadeite beads, 4.78 to 16.22 mm (0.19 to 0.64 in), Christie's, Hong Kong, 1 Nov 1999	1,761,600 (HK$22,020,000)
7 Jadeite bangle, Christie's, Hong Kong, 1 Nov 1999	1,585,600 (HK$19,820,000)
8 A diamond necklace suspending a 17.57-carat heart-shaped diamond, with matching diamond ear-pendants, Christie's, Geneva, 15 Nov 1995	1,506,795 (SF2,643,500)
9 *The Indore Pears*, Christie's, Geneva, 12 Nov 1987	1,488,300 (SF3,630,000)
10 Jadeite ring, 33.08 x 18.78 x 14.83 mm (1.30 x 0.74 x 0.58 in), Christie's, Hong Kong, 1 Nov 1999	1,480,000 (HK$18,500,000)

WORTH ITS WEIGHT IN GOLD

International trade in gold is customarily carried out with either 1-kg (32.15-troy ounce) or 12.5-kg (400-troy ounce) gold bars.

Natural Resources

TOP 10 ★
MOST PRODUCED NON-FUEL MINERALS

	MINERAL	1998 PRODUCTION (TONNES)
1	Iron ore*	1,020,000,000
2	Bauxite	122,000,000
3	Clay, kaolin	115,000,000
4	Aluminium	22,100,000
5	Manganese ore	18,700,000
6	Chromite	12,700,000
7	Copper	12,200,000
8	Clay, bentonite	9,330,000
9	Feldspar	8,080,000
10	Zinc	7,540,000

From which iron and steel are produced

Source: *U.S. Geological Survey*, Minerals Yearbook

TOP 10 ★
SALT PRODUCERS

	COUNTRY	1999 PRODUCTION (TONNES)*
1	USA	45,000,000
2	China	28,100,000
3	Germany	15,700,000
4	India	14,400,000
5	Canada	12,500,000
6	Australia	10,000,000
7	Mexico	8,500,000
8	France	7,000,000
9	Brazil	6,900,000
10	UK	5,800,000
	World	209,000,000

Includes salt in brine

Source: *U.S. Geological Survey*, Minerals Yearbook

TOP 10 ★
DIAMOND PRODUCERS, BY VALUE

	COUNTRY	1999 VALUE ($)
1	Botswana	1,600,000,000
2	Russia	1,500,000,000
3	South Africa	900,000,000
4	Dem. Rep. of Congo	700,000,000
5	Angola	500,000,000
6	=Australia	400,000,000
	=Canada	400,000,000
	=Namibia	400,000,000
9	=Guinea	100,000,000
	=Sierra Leone	100,000,000

Source: *De Beers*

TOP 10 ★
GOLD PRODUCERS

	COUNTRY	1999 PRODUCTION (TONNES)
1	South Africa	449.5
2	USA	341.9
3	Australia	302.8
4	Canada	157.9
5	China	156.3
6	Indonesia	154.5
7	Russia	138.2
8	Peru	127.4
9	Uzbekistan	85.7
10	Ghana	78.2

Source: *Gold Fields Mineral Services Ltd.*

World-dominating gold producer South Africa saw its output fall yet again for the seventh consecutive year. Australia's output also fell in 1999, after having increased dramatically over recent years: the country's record annual production had stood at 119 tonnes since 1903, but in 1988 it rocketed to 152 tonnes, a total it doubled in 1998. During the 1990s, several other countries increased their mine output dramatically, most notably Indonesia and Peru, each of which escalated production by a factor of almost nine, while Papua New Guinea's production falls only just outside the Top 10.

TOP 10 ★
SILVER PRODUCERS

	COUNTRY	1998 PRODUCTION (TONNES)
1	Mexico	2,686
2	USA	2,060
3	Peru	1,934
4	Australia	1,469
5	China	1,400
6	Chile	1,340
7	Canada	1,179
8	Poland	1,000
9	Kazakhstan	470
10	Bolivia	380
	World	16,400

Source: *U.S. Geological Survey*, Minerals Yearbook

TOP 10 ★
IRON PRODUCERS

	COUNTRY	1999 PRODUCTION (TONNES)*
1	China	125,390,000
2	Japan	74,520,000
3	USA	46,300,000
4	Russia	40,033,000
5	Germany	27,931,000
6	Brazil	25,060,000
7	South Korea	23,329,000
8	Ukraine	21,937,000
9	India	20,139,000
10	France	13,854,000
	UK	12,399,000
	World	541,000,000

Pig iron

Source: *U.S. Geological Survey*, Minerals Yearbook

TOP 10 ALUMINIUM PRODUCERS
(Country/1999 production in tonnes)

❶ USA, 3,779,000 ❷ Russia, 3,146,000 ❸ China, 2,450,000 ❹ Canada, 2,390,000 ❺ Australia, 1,718,000 ❻ Brazil, 1,250,000 ❼ Norway, 1,034,000 ❽ South Africa, 687,000 ❾ Germany, 600,000 ❿ Venezuela, 570,000

UK, 272,000   World, 23,100,000
Source: *U.S. Geological Survey*, Minerals Yearbook

Did You Know? Estimates indicate that if current production levels are maintained, US oil reserves will be exhausted in 2009, while those of the Middle East will last until 2086.

TOP 10 ★
COAL PRODUCERS

	COUNTRY	1999 PRODUCTION (TONNES OIL EQUIVALENT*)
1	USA	580,500,000
2	China	512,100,000
3	Australia	149,800,000
4	India	144,100,000
5	South Africa	116,700,000
6	Russia	112,600,000
7	Poland	73,100,000
8	Germany	59,600,000
9	Ukraine	42,300,000
10	Indonesia	40,100,000
	UK	22,800,000

* Commercial solid fuels only, i.e. bituminous coal and anthracite (hard coal), lignite, and brown (sub-bituminous) coal

Source: BP Amoco Statistical Review of World Energy 2000

TOP 10 ★
COUNTRIES WITH THE GREATEST COAL RESERVES

	COUNTRY	RESERVES AT END OF 1999 (TONNES)
1	USA	246,643,000,000
2	Russia	157,010,000,000
3	China	114,500,000,000
4	Australia	90,400,000,000
5	India	74,733,000,000
6	Germany	67,000,000,000
7	South Africa	55,333,000,000
8	Ukraine	34,356,000,000
9	Kazakhstan	34,000,000,000
10	Poland	14,309,000,000
	UK	1,500,000,000

Source: BP Amoco Statistical Review of World Energy 2000

Coal reserves are quantities of coal that can be recovered from known deposits, based on existing engineering and economic conditions, which, of course, may change over time.

TOP 10 ★
NATURAL GAS PRODUCERS

	COUNTRY	1999 PRODUCTION (TONNES OIL EQUIVALENT*)
1	Russia	495,900,000
2	USA	486,400,000
3	Canada	146,100,000
4	UK	89,700,000
5	Algeria	74,000,000
6	Indonesia	59,800,000
7	Netherlands	54,100,000
8	Uzbekistan	46,700,000
9	Norway	45,900,000
10	Saudi Arabia	41,600,000

* The amount of oil that would be required to produce the same energy output

Source: BP Amoco Statistical Review of World Energy 2000

TOP 10 ★
COUNTRIES WITH THE GREATEST NATURAL GAS RESERVES

	COUNTRY	1999 RESERVES TRILLION M³	TRILLION FT³
1	Russia	48.14	1,700.0
2	Iran	23.00	812.3
3	Qatar	8.49	300.0
4	United Arab Emirates	6.00	212.0
5	Saudi Arabia	5.79	204.5
6	USA	4.65	164.0
7	Algeria	4.52	159.7
8	Venezuela	4.04	142.5
9	Nigeria	3.51	124.0
10	Iraq	3.11	109.8
	UK	0.76	26.7

Source: BP Amoco Statistical Review of World Energy 2000

Total world reserves in 1999 were put at 146.43 trillion cubic metres (5,171.8 trillion cubic feet), more than double the 1979 estimate.

TOP 10 ★
OIL PRODUCERS

	COUNTRY	1999 PRODUCTION (TONNES)
1	Saudi Arabia	411,800,000
2	USA	354,700,000
3	Russia	304,800,000
4	Iran	175,200,000
5	Mexico	166,100,000
6	Venezuela	160,500,000
7	China	159,300,000
8	Norway	149,100,000
9	UK	137,100,000
10	Iraq	125,500,000
	World	3,452,000,000

Source: BP Amoco Statistical Review of World Energy 2000

While most leading countries have increased their oil production, Russia has fallen from the No. 1 slot in the global ranking it occupied 10 years ago.

TOP 10 ★
COUNTRIES WITH THE GREATEST CRUDE OIL RESERVES

	COUNTRY	RESERVES AT END OF 1999 (TONNES)
1	Saudi Arabia	36,000,000,000
2	Iraq	15,100,000,000
3	Kuwait	13,300,000,000
4	United Arab Emirates	12,600,000,000
5	Iran	12,300,000,000
6	Venezuela	10,500,000,000
7	Russia	6,700,000,000
8	Mexico	4,100,000,000
9	Libya	3,900,000,000
10	USA	3,500,000,000
	UK	700,000,000

Source: BP Amoco Statistical Review of World Energy 2000

The discovery of new oil means that total world reserves at the end of 1999 stood at 140.4 billion tonnes, 63 per cent more than the 1979 estimate.

Background image: COPPER, NICKEL, AND IRON ORES

205

Energy & Environment

NUCLEAR ELECTRICITY-PRODUCING COUNTRIES

	COUNTRY	1999 PRODUCTION (KW/HR)
1	USA	728,200,000,000
2	France	375,100,000,000
3	Japan	308,700,000,000
4	Germany	161,000,000,000
5	Russia	110,900,000,000
6	South Korea	97,900,000,000
7	UK	91,500,000,000
8	Canada	69,800,000,000
9	Ukraine	67,300,000,000
10	Sweden	66,600,000,000
	World	2,395,900,000,000

Source: *Energy Information Administration*

PAPER-RECYCLING COUNTRIES

	COUNTRY	1999 RECYCLING (TONNES)
1	USA	41,167,828
2	Japan	14,841,000
3	China	12,014,000
4	Germany	10,292,000
5	France	5,000,000
6	South Korea	3,869,000
7	UK	3,675,000
8	Italy	3,628,800
9	Netherlands	2,417,000
10	Canada	1,478,000
	World	115,331,303

Source: *Food and Agriculture Organization of the United Nations*

WATT

James Watt (1736–1819) is remembered as the inventor of the modern steam engine, and the man after whom the unit of power is named. He introduced great improvements to the steam engine invented by Thomas Newcomen, patented many other inventions, and undertook experiments relating to power, introducing the concept of "horsepower". The use of the term "watt" was proposed in 1882, and is equivalent to an amp multiplied by a volt (each named after other electrical pioneers, André Marie Ampère and Allessandro Volta), or one joule per second. It is most commonly used as a measure of the intensity of light bulbs, and in terms of electrical consumption in kilowatt/hours.

WHO WAS • WHO WAS • WHO OHM • WHO WAS ?

TOP 10 COUNTRIES WITH THE MOST RELIANCE ON NUCLEAR POWER

(Country/nuclear electricity as percentage of total electricity)

1 France, 75.00 **2** Lithuania, 73.11 **3** Belgium, 57.74 **4** Bulgaria, 47.12 **5** Slovak Republic, 47.02 **6** Sweden, 46.80 **7** Ukraine, 43.77 **8** South Korea, 42.84 **9** Hungary, 38.30 **10** Slovenia, 37.18 *UK, 28.87*

Source: *International Atomic Energy Agency*

ALTERNATIVE POWER-CONSUMING COUNTRIES*

	COUNTRY	1999 CONSUMPTION (KW/HR)
1	USA	83,000,000,000
2	Japan	24,700,000,000
3	Germany	15,000,000,000
4	Brazil	9,900,000,000
5	Finland	9,500,000,000
6	Philippines	8,300,000,000
7	UK	8,200,000,000
8	Canada	7,500,000,000
9	Italy	7,000,000,000
10	Mexico	5,300,000,000
	World	227,400,000,000

* *Includes geothermal, solar, wind, wood, and waste electric power*

Source: *Energy Information Administration*

NUCLEAR REACTOR

Opened in 1985–86, Pacific Gas and Electric's Diablo Canyon Nuclear Power Station in California is one of the US's 104 nuclear reactors.

206

TOP 10 ★
CARBON DIOXIDE-EMITTING COUNTRIES

	COUNTRY	CO₂ EMISSIONS PER HEAD (1997) TONNES OF CARBON
1	Qatar	18.19
2	United Arab Emirates	9.40
3	Kuwait	7.88
4	Guam	7.04
5	Bahrain	6.95
6	Singapore	6.39
7	USA	5.48
8	Luxembourg	5.16
9	Brunei	4.79
10	Australia	4.71

Source: *Gregg Marland and Tom Boden (Oak Ridge National Laboratory) and Bob Andres (University of North Dakota)*

CO_2 emissions derive from three principal sources: fossil fuel burning, cement manufacturing, and gas flaring. Since World War II, increasing industrialization in many countries has resulted in huge increases in carbon output, a trend that most countries are now actively attempting to reverse. There has been some degree of success among the former leaders in this Top 10, although the USA remains the worst offender in total, with 1,500 million tonnes released in 1997.

TOP 10 ★
DEFORESTING COUNTRIES

	COUNTRY	AVERAGE ANNUAL FOREST LOSS, 1990-95 SQ KM	SQ MILES
1	Brazil	25,544	9,863
2	Indonesia	10,844	4,187
3	Dem. Rep. of Congo	7,400	2,857
4	Bolivia	5,814	2,245
5	Mexico	5,080	1,961
6	Venezuela	5,034	1,944
7	Malaysia	4,002	1,545
8	Myanmar (Burma)	3,874	1,496
9	Sudan	3,526	1,361
10	Thailand	3,294	1,271

Source: *Food and Agriculture Organization of the United Nations*

Some 47,740 sq km (18,433 sq miles) of tropical forest was lost in South America each year between 1990 and 1995, plus a further 37,480 sq km (14,471 sq miles) in Africa, and 33,280 sq km (12,849 sq miles) in Asia. The total global loss during that five-year period was 563,460 sq km (217,553 sq miles), an area equivalent to twice the size of the UK. However, while Brazil tops the list of countries with the highest amount of forest loss, the rate of deforestation is only 0.5 per cent.

POWER TO THE PEOPLE

In the 20th century the creation of national grids for the transmission of electricity brought power to even the most remote communities.

TOP 10 ★
ENERGY-CONSUMING COUNTRIES

	COUNTRY	OIL	GAS	1999 ENERGY CONSUMPTION* COAL	NUCLEAR	HEP#	TOTAL
1	USA	882.8	555.3	543.3	197.7	25.8	2,204.9
2	China	200.0	19.3	511.0	4.1	18.2	752.6
3	Russia	126.2	327.3	109.3	31.2	13.8	607.8
4	Japan	258.8	67.1	91.5	82.0	8.0	507.4
5	Germany	132.4	72.1	80.6	43.8	2.0	330.9
6	India	94.8	21.4	150.0	3.3	6.9	276.4
7	France	96.4	33.9	14.1	101.5	6.6	252.4
8	Canada	83.0	64.3	31.9	19.0	29.6	227.8
9	UK	78.7	82.5	35.8	24.8	0.6	222.4
10	South Korea	99.9	16.9	38.1	26.6	0.5	182.0
	World	3,462.4	2,063.9	2,129.5	650.8	226.8	8,533.6

* *Millions of tonnes of oil equivalent* # *Hydroelectric power*

Source: *BP Amoco Statistical Review of World Energy 2000*

TOP 10 ★
ELECTRICITY-CONSUMING COUNTRIES

	COUNTRY	1999 CONSUMPTION (KW/HR)
1	USA	3,254,900,000,000
2	China	1,084,100,000,000
3	Japan	947,000,000,000
4	Russia	728,200,000,000
5	Canada	497,500,000,000
6	Germany	495,200,000,000
7	India	424,000,000,000
8	France	398,800,000,000
9	Brazil	353,700,000,000
10	UK	333,000,000,000
	World	12,832,700,000,000

Source: *Energy Information Administration*

Did You Know? While other countries have steadily increased their energy consumption, in the 15 years from 1984 to 1999 India more than doubled its requirements.

Science & Invention

TOP 10 ★

CATEGORIES OF PATENTS IN THE UK IN 1900

CATEGORY	PATENTS GRANTED (1900)
1 Metals, cutting, etc.	614
2 Mechanism etc.	475
3 Electricity, regulating	471
4 Furnaces etc.	431
5 Furniture etc.	430
6 Railways, vehicles	426
7 Steam engines	370
8 Velocipedes (early bicycles)	354
9 Lamps etc.	353
10 Locomotives etc.	345

Source: *Patent Office*

THE 10 ★

FIRST PATENTEES IN THE UK

PATENTEE/PATENT	DATE
1 **Nicholas Hillyard**, Engraving and printing the king's head on documents	5 May 1617
2 **John Gason**, Locks, mills, and other river and canal improvements	1 July 1617
3 **John Miller and John Jasper Wolfen**, Oil for suits of armour	3 Nov 1617
4 **Robert Crumpe**, Tunnels and pumps	9 Jan 1618
5 **Aaron Rathburne and Roger Burges**, Making maps of English cities	11 Mar 1618
6 **John Gilbert**, River dredger	16 July 1618
7 **Clement Dawbeney**, Water-powered engine for making nails	11 Dec 1618
8 **Thomas Murray**, Sword blades	11 Jan 1619
9 **Thomas Wildgoose and David Ramsey**, Ploughs, pumps, and ships' engines	17 Jan 1619
10 **Abram Baker**, Smalt (glass) manufacture	16 Feb 1619

TOP 10 ★

CATEGORIES OF PATENTS IN THE UK IN 1999

CATEGORY	PATENTS GRANTED (1999)
1 Telecommunications	865
2 Machine elements	633
3 Measuring and testing	476
4 Civil engineering and building	462
5 Electric circuit elements and magnets	429
6 Conveyancing, packing, load handling, hoisting, and storing	397
7 Calculating, counting, checking, signalling, and data-handling	359
8 Furniture and household articles	294
9 Transport	291
10 Electric power	282

Source: *Patent Office*

TOP 10 ★

MOST PROLIFIC PATENTEES IN THE US

PATENTEE	PATENTS*
1 Thomas A. Edison	1,093
2 Donald E. Weder	934
3 Shunpei Yamazaki	679
4 Francis H. Richards	619
5 Edwin Herbert Land	533
6 = Marvin Camras	500
= Jerome H. Lemelson	500
8 Elihu Thomson	444
9 George Westinghouse	400
10 Charles E. Scribner	374

* Minimum number credited to each inventor

Such is the complexity of the whole subject of patent registration (patents may be registered to individuals or to the companies that employ them) that this list can only be a tentative attempt to rank the 10 leading US inventors. Electricity, radio, and television feature prominently among the many patents credited to these individuals, but their inventions also encompass Land's Polaroid camera and Lemelson's tape drive, used in the Sony Walkman, and his Velcro dart-board.

TOP 10 ★

COUNTRIES TO REGISTER THE MOST PATENTS

COUNTRY	PATENTS REGISTERED (1998)
1 USA	147,520
2 Japan	141,448
3 Germany	51,685
4 France	46,213
5 UK	43,181
6 Italy	38,988
7 Russia	23,368
8 Netherlands	22,411
9 Spain	20,128
10 Sweden	18,482

Source: *World Intellectual Property Organization*

A patent is an exclusive licence to manufacture and exploit a unique product or process for a fixed period. The figures refer to the number of patents actually granted during 1998 – which, in most instances, represents only a fraction of the patents applied for. For example, a total of 262,787 applications were registered in the US, but the process of obtaining a patent can be tortuous, and many are refused after investigations show that the product is too similar to one already patented.

TOP 10 ★

COMPANIES REGISTERING THE MOST PATENTS IN THE UK

COMPANY	PATENTS GRANTED (1999)
1 Samsung Electronics	237
2 Nec	146
3 Bosch	125
4 Motorola	101
5 Daimler-Benz	93
6 Mitsubishi Denki	82
7 Honda	80
8 Fujitsu	76
9 Hyundai Electronics	68
10 Daewoo Electronics	66

TOP 10 ★
COUNTRIES TO REGISTER THE MOST TRADEMARKS

	COUNTRY	TRADEMARKS REGISTERED (1998)
1	Japan	132,066
2	USA	129,871
3	China	98,961
4	Argentina	61,671
5	Spain	59,810
6	Germany	57,919
7	UK	48,600
8	Italy	46,707
9	Benelux	32,093
10	Mexico	28,362

Source: *World Intellectual Property Organization*

TOP 10 ★
US ACADEMIC INSTITUTIONS FOR RESEARCH AND DEVELOPMENT FUNDING

	INSTITUTION	TOTAL R&D FUNDING (1997)
1	University of Michigan	483,000,000
2	Johns Hopkins University	421,000,000
3	University of Wisconsin-Madison	420,000,000
4	Massachusetts Institute of Technology	411,000,000
5	University of Washington-Seattle	410,000,000
6	Johns Hopkins University Applied Physics Laboratory	408,000,000
7	Stanford University	395,000,000
8	University of California-San Diego	378,000,000
9	University of California-Los Angeles	375,000,000
10	Texas A&M University	367,000,000
	Total (all institutions)	24,348,000,000

Source: *US National Science Foundation*

TOP 10 ★
COUNTRIES FOR RESEARCH AND DEVELOPMENT EXPENDITURE

	COUNTRY	R&D EXPENDITURE AS PERCENTAGE OF GNP*
1	Sweden	3.76
2	South Korea	2.82
3	Japan	2.80
4	Finland	2.78
5	USA	2.63
6	Switzerland	2.60
7	Germany	2.41
8	Israel	2.35
9	France	2.25
10	Italy	2.21
	UK	1.95

* In latest year for which statistics available

Source: *World Bank*, World Development Indicators 2000

TOP 10 ★
COUNTRIES FOR SCIENTIFIC AND TECHNICAL JOURNAL ARTICLES

	COUNTRY	AVERAGE NUMBER PUBLISHED PER ANNUM (1995–97)
1	USA	173,233
2	Japan	43,655
3	UK	39,670
4	Germany	35,294
5	France	26,455
6	Canada	20,989
7	Russia	17,589
8	Italy	16,256
9	Australia	11,830
10	Netherlands	10,914
	World total	515,708

Source: *US National Science Foundation*

TOP 10 ★
COUNTRIES FOR RESEARCH AND DEVELOPMENT SCIENTISTS AND ENGINEERS

	COUNTRY	R&D SCIENTISTS AND ENGINEERS PER MILLION*
1	Japan	4,909
2	Sweden	3,826
3	USA	3,676
4	Norway	3,664
5	Russia	3,587
6	Australia	3,357
7	Denmark	3,259
8	Switzerland	3,006
9	Germany	2,831
10	Finland	2,799
	UK	2,448

* In latest year for which statistics available

Source: *World Bank*, World Development Indicators 2000

TOP 10 ★
COUNTRIES FOR HIGH-TECHNOLOGY EXPORTS

	COUNTRY	HIGH-TECHNOLOGY EXPORTS ($)*
1	USA	170,681,000,000
2	Japan	94,777,000,000
3	UK	64,461,000,000
4	Germany	63,698,000,000
5	Singapore	54,783,000,000
6	France	54,183,000,000
7	Netherlands	35,377,000,000
8	Malaysia	31,419,000,000
9	South Korea	30,582,000,000
10	Ireland	23,944,000,000

* In latest year for which statistics available

Source: *World Bank*, World Development Indicators 2000

Did You Know? On the first day that Britain's trademark law came into force in 1876, an employee of the Bass brewery queued all night outside the registrar's office to ensure that his company's red triangle design was the first to be registered.

Communication Matters

COUNTRIES WITH THE MOST TELEPHONES

	COUNTRY	TOTAL TELEPHONE LINES	TELEPHONE LINES PER 100 INHABITANTS		COUNTRY	TOTAL TELEPHONE LINES	TELEPHONE LINES PER 100 INHABITANTS
1	Luxembourg	308,000	73.33	7	Iceland	183,000	65.36
2	Norway	3,155,000	71.19	8	Canada	19,630,000	63.67
3	USA	193,862,000	70.98	9	Netherlands	9,878,000	62.60
4	Switzerland	5,023,000	70.11	10	Australia	11,609,000	61.04
5	Sweden	6,160,000	69.45				
6	Denmark	3,555,000	67.08				

Source: *Siemens AG,* International Telecom Statistics 2000

COUNTRIES WITH THE HIGHEST RATIO OF CELLULAR MOBILE PHONE USERS

	COUNTRY	SUBSCRIBERS	MOBILES PER 100 INHABITANTS
1	Finland	3,499,000	67.8
2	Norway	2,779,000	62.7
3	Sweden	5,234,000	59.0
4	Italy	30,068,000	52.2
5	Austria	4,147,000	51.3
6	Denmark	2,682,000	50.6
7	South Korea	23,493,000	49.9
8	Taiwan	10,835,000	49.4
9	Portugal	4,720,000	47.4
10	Switzerland	3,164,000	44.2
	UK	23,944,000	40.9

Source: *Siemens AG,* International Telecom Statistics 2000

COUNTRIES MAKING THE MOST INTERNATIONAL PHONE CALLS

	COUNTRY	MINUTES PER HEAD, 1999	TOTAL MINUTES OUTGOING CALLS, 1999
1	USA	102.7	28,363,000,000
2	Germany	89.9	7,385,000,000
3	UK	101.9	6,066,000,000
4	Canada	174.1	5,310,000,000
5	France	74.9	4,386,000,000
6	Italy	54.0	3,100,000,000
7	Switzerland	335.9	2,400,000,000
8	Netherlands	135.7	2,150,000,000
9	Japan	15.5	1,957,000,000
10	China	1.5	1,950,000,000

Source: *International Telecommunication Union*

THE FIRST TRANSPACIFIC TELEGRAPH CABLE

In 1858, the first transatlantic cable was laid, and, following this, the idea of a transpacific cable between Canada and Australia was proposed in 1887. It was not until 1902, however, that the dream became a reality. In that year, a specially built ship, the *Colonia*, laid an undersea cable from Bamfield, Vancouver Island, in Canada, to the Fanning, Fiji, and Norfolk islands. From here it branched to Brisbane, Australia, and Doubtless Bay on the north island of New Zealand. Despite the technical difficulties of laying some 12,875 km (8,000 miles) of cable, often at great depths, the project was completed on schedule. On 31 October, Canadian engineer Sir Sandford Fleming sent the first telegram from Canada to Australia, and the whole system was opened on 8 December, remaining in service until 1964.

100 YEARS AGO · YEARS AGO · YEARS AGO · YEARS

KEY DEVELOPMENT

The inexorable rise of the cellular mobile phone is one of the most significant changes in world communications. Scandinavian countries have the world's highest ratio of phones to population.

END OF THE LINE

In many countries, the recent expansion of mobile phone networks has resulted in a decline in the popularity of public telephones.

TOP 10 ★
LETTER-POSTING COUNTRIES

	COUNTRY	AVERAGE NO. OF LETTER POST ITEMS POSTED PER INHABITANT*
1	Vatican City	5,740.0
2	USA	734.4
3	Sweden	502.8
4	France	442.8
5	Finland	396.5
6	Austria	371.6
7	Belgium	344.1
8	Norway	338.0
9	Luxembourg	336.1
10	Denmark	334.7
	UK	324.8

* In 1999 or latest year for which data available
Source: *Universal Postal Union*

The Vatican's population seldom exceeds 750. The above statistical anomaly results in part from the large numbers of official missives dispatched via the Holy See's post office and postboxes, but mainly because Rome's inhabitants have discovered that mail posted in the Vatican City and bearing Vatican stamps is treated as priority.

TOP 10 ★
COUNTRIES WITH THE MOST POST OFFICES

	COUNTRY	POST OFFICES*
1	India	154,149
2	China	117,052
3	Russia	41,556
4	USA	38,169
5	Japan	24,755
6	Indonesia	20,139
7	UK	18,341
8	France	16,930
9	Italy	15,079
10	Ukraine	14,931

* 1999 or latest year for which data available
Source: *Universal Postal Union*

There are some 770,000 post offices around the world. These range from major city post offices offering a wide range of services, to small establishments providing only basic facilities, such as the sale of postage stamps. The average number of inhabitants served by each post office also varies considerably, from fewer than 2,000 people in countries such as Cyprus and Belize to as many as 230,000 people in Burundi.

THE 10 COUNTRIES RECEIVING THE MOST LETTERS FROM ABROAD

(Country/items of mail handled, 1999*)

❶ Germany, 702,000,000 ❷ India, 561,640,000
❸ UK, 535,812,069 ❹ France, 476,000,000
❺ USA, 474,347,500 ❻ Saudi Arabia, 340,105,000
❼ Netherlands, 299,000,000 ❽ Japan, 289,593,000
❾ Algeria, 217,600,000 ❿ Italy, 217,446,283

* Or latest year for which data available
Source: *Universal Postal Union*

THE 10 COUNTRIES SENDING THE MOST LETTERS ABROAD

(Country/items of mail handled, 1999*)

❶ UK, 986,786,244 ❷ USA, 904,600,000 ❸ France, 576,200,000
❹ Germany, 402,600,000 ❺ Saudi Arabia, 347,696,000
❻ Finland, 306,300,000 ❼ Russia, 221,800,000 ❽ Algeria,
201,000,000 ❾ Belgium, 193,793,831 ❿ India, 177,300,000

* Or latest year for which data available
Source: *Universal Postal Union*

INDIAN STAMPS

India has more post offices and more postal workers than any other country in the world. Its system handles over 16 billion letters and 285 million parcels a year.

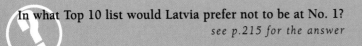

In what Top 10 list would Latvia prefer not to be at No. 1?
see p.215 for the answer

A Most accident-prone country
B Country with the most bank robberies
C Country with the highest suicide rate

The World Wide Web

TOP 10 ★
ONLINE LANGUAGES

	LANGUAGE	INTERNET ACCESS*
1	English	230,000,000
2	Chinese	160,000,000
3	Spanish	60,000,000
4	Japanese	58,000,000
5	German	46,000,000
6	Korean	35,000,000
7	Portuguese	32,000,000
8	French	30,000,000
9	Italian	23,000,000
10	Russian	15,000,000
	World total	774,000,000

* Online population estimate for 2003

Source: *Global Reach*

TOP 10 ★
BUSIEST INTERNET SITES

	SITE	HITS*
1	yahoo.com	65,910,000
2	aol.com	53,373,000
3	msn.com	47,330,000
4	microsoft.com	39,905,000
5	passport.com	37,807,000
6	geocities.com	36,294,000
7	AOLProprietary.aol	32,879,000
8	amazon.com	28,534,000
9	lycos.com	25,898,000
10	ebay.com	25,031,000

* Number of accesses during December 2000

Source: *PC Data Online*

TOP 10 ★
INTERNET DOMAINS

	DOMAIN	COUNTRY	REGISTRATIONS
1	.com	USA/International	21,151,560
2	.net	International	3,986,781
3	.org	International	2,503,682
4	.co.uk	UK	2,317,009
5	.de	Germany	1,032,618
6	.nl	Netherlands	544,594
7	.it	Italy	404,893
8	.co.kr	South Korea	332,801
9	.com.ar	Argentina	301,394
10	.org.uk	UK	154,838
	World total		34,995,298

TOP 10 ★
ITEMS MOST PURCHASED ONLINE IN THE UK

	ITEM	PERCENTAGE*
1	Books	66
2	CDs, recorded music	58
3	Computers and computer products	38
4	Air travel reservations	26
5	Videos, filmed entertainment	19
6	Flowers	18
7	Event tickets (concert, theatre, etc.)	17
8	Food, drink	13
9=	Clothing and accessories (men's)	12
=	Clothing and accessories (women's)	12
=	Hotel reservations	12

* Percentage of purchasers who have bought item online

Source: *Stores/Ernst & Young*, Global Online Retailing, 2000

E-SHOPPING

The ability to locate and purchase both new and used books online has been heralded as among the most popular of the Internet's many benefits.

TOP 10 ★
COUNTRIES WITH THE HIGHEST DENSITY OF INTERNET HOSTS

COUNTRY	INTERNET HOSTS PER 1,000 PEOPLE
1 Finland	108.00
2 USA	88.90
3 Iceland	78.70
4 Norway	71.80
5 Canada	53.50
6 New Zealand	49.70
7 Australia	42.70
8 Sweden	35.10
9 Netherlands	34.60
10 Switzerland	27.90
UK	23.30

Source: *United Nations,* Human Development Report, 1999

An Internet host is a computer system connected to the Internet – either a single terminal directly connected, or a computer that allows multiple users to access network services through it. The ratio of hosts to population is a crude measure of how "wired" a country is.

TOP 10 ★
COMPUTER COMPANIES

COMPANY/COUNTRY	ANNUAL SALES ($)*
1 **IBM**, USA	88,396,000,000
2 **Hewlett-Packard**, USA	48,782,000,000
3 **Fujitsu**, Japan	47,196,000,000
4 **Compaq Computer**, USA	42,383,000,000
5 **Dell Computer**, USA	31,888,000,000
6 **Canon**, Japan	23,062,000,000
7 **Xerox**, USA	18,632,000,000
8 **Sun Microsystems**, USA	15,721,000,000
9 **Ricoh**, Japan	12,997,000,000
10 **Gateway**, USA	9,601,000,000

* *In latest year for which figures are available*
Source: Fortune *Global 500*

TOP 10 ★
COUNTRIES WITH THE MOST INTERNET USERS

COUNTRY	PERCENTAGE OF POPULATION	INTERNET USERS*	COUNTRY	PERCENTAGE OF POPULATION	INTERNET USERS*
1 USA	54.7	153,840,000	7 Italy	23.4	13,420,000
2 Japan	30.5	38,640,000	8 Canada	42.6	13,280,000
3 Germany	24.4	20,100,000	9 Brazil	5.8	9,840,000
4 UK	33.9	19,940,000	10 Russia	6.3	9,200,000
5 China	1.3	16,900,000	*World total*	6.7	407,100,000
6 South Korea	35.0	16,400,000			

* *Estimates for weekly usage as at end of 2000*
Source: *Computer Industry Almanac, Inc.*

TOP 10 ★
COUNTRIES WITH THE MOST COMPUTERS

COUNTRY	PERCENTAGE OF WORLD TOTAL	COMPUTERS
1 USA	28.32	164,100,000
2 Japan	8.62	49,900,000
3 Germany	5.28	30,600,000
4 UK	4.49	26,000,000
5 France	3.77	21,800,000
6 Italy	3.02	17,500,000
7 Canada	2.76	16,000,000
8 China	2.75	15,900,000
9 =Australia	1.82	10,600,000
=South Korea	1.82	10,600,000

Source: *Computer Industry Almanac, Inc.*

Computer industry estimates put the number of computers in the world at 98 million in 1990, 222 million in 1995, and 579 million in 2000 – a sixfold increase over the decade – with the Top 10 countries owning over 62 per cent of the total.

TOP 10 ★
USES OF THE INTERNET

ACTVITY	PERCENTAGE OF INTERNET USERS*
1 E-mail	90
2 General information	77
3 Surfing	69
4 Reading	67
5 Hobbies	63
6 Product information	62
7 Travel information	54
8 Work/business	46
9 =Entertainment/games	36
=Buying	36

* *Based on US sample survey, 2000*
Source: *Stanford Institute for the Quantitative Study of Society*

In addition, those polled also identified stock quotations (27%), job search (26%), chat rooms (24%), homework (21%), auctions (13%), banking (12%), and trading stocks (7%).

COMPUTER POWER FIRST DEMONSTRATED

Automatic programming of computers is credited to Grace Hopper, an employee of US manufacturers Remington-Rand. In 1951, her company had created the Univac I (UNIVersal Automatic Computer), an expensive and gigantic machine weighing some 32 tonnes (35 tons). It was slow (its clock speed was 2.25 MHz, while 500 MHz or more is now commonplace), and it required the operator to write programmes on to punched cards and then transfer them on to magnetic tape. Despite these drawbacks, the Univac I proved its accuracy when it was used by the CBS television network to correctly predict a landslide victory for Eisenhower at the 1952 US election. In 1954, General Electric purchased a Univac, thus becoming the first commercial organization to use a computer.

50 YEARS AGO · YEARS AGO · YEARS AGO · YEARS AGO

Did You Know? In 1943 Thomas Watson, chairman of IBM, stated "I think there is a world market for maybe five computers." Six years later, *Popular Mechanics* magazine predicted that "Computers in the future may weigh no more than 1.5 tons."

Hazards at Home & Work

MOST DANGEROUS PLACES IN UK HOMES

LOCATION/ MOST COMMON ACCIDENT	ACCIDENTS PER ANNUM (1999)*
1 **Garden/grassed area**, Tripping up	337,470
2 **Living/dining area**, Tripping up	315,391
3 **Kitchen/utility room**, Cut/tear	266,432
4 **Bedroom**, Falling	223,817
5 **Stairs inside**, Falling down	213,355
6 **Yard/driveway/path**, Tripping up	107,068
7 **Bathroom/toilet**, Tripping up	91,560
8 **Hallway/lobby**, Tripping up	63,284
9 **Porch/threshold**, Falling on steps	47,074
10 **Garage**, Cut/tear	28,168
Total	2,861,214

* National estimates based on actual Home Accident Surveillance System figures for sample population

According to HASS figures, the safest places in the home are cupboards, and the places where people suffer most from overexertion are the garden, living and dining rooms, and bedroom.

DANGER ON DECK

Exposure to extreme weather conditions and other hazards places fishing among the world's most dangerous industries.

THE 10 MOST COMMON ACCIDENTS IN UK HOMES

(Accident/no. per annum, 1999)*

❶ **Tripping over**, 419,372 ❷ **Struck by static object**, 292,823 ❸ **Falls on or from stairs**, 290,536 ❹ **Cut or tear from sharp object**, 273,161 ❺ **Struck by moving object**, 156,947 ❻ **Foreign body**, 134,377 ❼ **Thermal effect**, 100,010 ❽ **Pinched or crushed by blunt object**, 95,565 ❾ **Acute overexertion**, 88,633 ❿ **Bite/sting**, 74,806

* National estimates based on actual Home Accident Surveillance System figures for sample population

BODY PARTS MOST INJURED AT WORK*

BODY PART	FATAL	MAJOR	TOTAL#
1 Back	-	664	31,288
2 One or more finger/thumb	–	1,904	17,884
3 Lower limb, excluding ankle and foot	3	2,310	15,180
4 Upper limb, excluding hand and wrist	–	4,401	15,041
5 Several locations	38	1,325	11,987
6 Ankle	1	2,468	11,284
7 Hand	–	2,325	10,206
8 Wrist	–	4,073	7,316
9 Foot	–	2,802	7,192
10 Trunk	13	1,824	6,271

* 1999/2000 provisional figures

\# Includes all injuries resulting in over 3 days away from work

Source: Health and Safety Executive

INDUSTRIES IN WHICH MOST MEMBERS OF THE PUBLIC ARE INJURED IN GREAT BRITAIN

INDUSTRY	INJURIES TO THE PUBLIC*
1 Education	8,260
2 Transport, storage, and communication	3,223
3 Wholesale and retail trade, and repairs	3,117
4 Health and social work	2,422
5 Hotels and restaurants	1,168
6 Public administration and defence	1,057
7 Construction	401
8 Real estate, renting, and business activities	338
9 Agriculture, hunting, forestry, and fishing	198
10 Manufacturing	163
Total all industries	24,104

* 1999/2000 provisional figures

Source: Health and Safety Executive

THE 10 MOST DANGEROUS JOBS IN THE UK*

❶ **Bomb disposal officer** ❷ **Deep-sea diver** ❸ **Deep-sea fisherman** ❹ **Demolition worker** ❺ **Fast jet pilot** ❻ **Oil platform worker** ❼ **Professional motor/motorcycle racer** ❽ **Professional stuntman** ❾ **Steeplejack** ❿ **Tunneller (face worker)**

* In alphabetical order

MOST COMMON TYPES OF INJURY AT WORK*

	INJURY	FATAL	MAJOR	TOTAL#
1	Sprain/strain	–	313	59,195
2	Contusion	8	551	26,863
3	Fracture	25	20,231	26,207
4	Laceration/open wound	3	1,332	15,535
5	Superficial injury	–	298	10,827
6	Burn	6	651	4,568
7	Injury of more than one type	44	503	4,145
8	Dislocation	–	1,163	1,604
9	Concussion/internal injury	11	594	1,343
10	Poisoning/gassing	16	189	597

* 1999/2000 provisional figures

Includes all injuries resulting in over 3 days away from work

Source: Health and Safety Executive

MOST COMMON CAUSES OF DOMESTIC FIRES IN THE UK

	CAUSE	APPROX. NO OF FIRES PER ANNUM
1	Misuse of equipment or appliances	20,000
2	Malicious (or suspected malicious)	13,800
3	Chip/fat pan fires	11,600
4	Faulty appliances and leads	7,900
5	Careless handling of fire or hot substances	5,600
6	Placing articles too close to heat	5,300
7	Other accidental	4,500
8	Faulty fuel supplies	1,800
9	Playing with fire	900
10	Unspecified	700
	UK total	72,100

DOMESTIC INFERNO

A combination of deliberate and accidental fires, many of which result from avoidable causes, contribute to losses of life and property.

MOST ACCIDENT-PRONE COUNTRIES

	COUNTRIES	ACCIDENT DEATH RATE PER 100,000*
1	Latvia	104.2
2	Estonia	103.0
3	Belarus	99.6
4	Russia	98.8
5	Lithuania	88.0
6	Ukraine	76.4
7	Moldova	63.2
8	Kazakhstan	59.6
9	Romania	56.0
10	South Korea	53.9

* In those countries/latest year for which data available

Source: UN Demographic Yearbook

What gaseous phenomenon did safety lamp inventor Sir Humphrey Davy also discover?
see p.216 for the answer

A Hydrogen can be used in balloons
B The effects of laughing gas
C Inhaling helium makes human voices squeaky

Industrial & Other Disasters

THE 10 ★
WORST FIRES*

LOCATION/DATE/TYPE	ESTIMATED NO. KILLED
1 **Moscow**, Russia, 1570#, City	200,000
2 **Constantinople**, Turkey, 1729#, City	7,000
3 **London**, UK, 11 July 1212, London Bridge	3,000+
4 **Peshtigo**, Wisconsin, USA, 8 Oct 1871, Forest	2,682
5 **Santiago**, Chile, 8 Dec 1863, Church of La Compañía	2,500
6 **Chungking**, China, 2 Sep 1949, Docks	1,700
7 **Hakodate**, Japan, 22 Mar 1934, City	1,500
8 **Constantinople**, Turkey, 5 June 1870, City	900
9 **Cloquet**, Minnesota, USA, 12 Oct 1918, Forest	559
10=**Lagunillas**, Venezuela, 14 Nov 1939, Oil refinery and city	over 500
=**Mandi Dabwali**, India, 23 Dec 1995, School tent	over 500

* Excluding sports and entertainment venues, mining disasters, the results of military action, and fires associated with earthquakes

\# Precise date unknown

\+ Burned, crushed, and drowned in ensuing panic; some chroniclers give the year as 1213

THE 10 ★
WORST DISASTERS AT SPORTS VENUES

LOCATION/DATE/TYPE	NO. KILLED
1 **Hong Kong Jockey Club**, Hong Kong, 26 Feb 1918, Stand collapse and fire	604
2 **Lenin Stadium**, Moscow, USSR, 20 Oct 1982, Crush in football stadium	340
3 **Lima**, Peru, 24 May 1964, Riot in football stadium	320
4 **Sinceljo**, Colombia, 20 Jan 1980, Bullring stand collapse	222
5 **Hillsborough**, Sheffield, UK, 15 Apr 1989, Crush in football stadium	96
6 **Guatemala City**, Guatemala, 16 Oct 1996, Stampede in Mateo Flores National Stadium during World Cup soccer qualifying match, Guatemala v Costa Rica, with 127 injured	83
7 **Le Mans**, France, 11 June 1955, Racing car crash	82
8 **Katmandu**, Nepal, 12 Mar 1988, Stampede in football stadium	80
9 **Buenos Aires**, Argentina, 23 May 1968, Riot in football stadium	74
10 **Ibrox Park**, Glasgow, Scotland, 2 Jan 1971, Barrier collapse in football stadium	66

THE 10 ★
WORST MINING DISASTERS

LOCATION/DATE	NO. KILLED
1 **Honkeiko**, China, 26 Apr 1942	1,549
2 **Courrières**, France, 10 Mar 1906	1,060
3 **Omuta**, Japan, 9 Nov 1963	447
4 **Senghenydd**, UK, 14 Oct 1913	439
5=**Hokkaido**, Japan, 1 Dec 1914	437
=**Coalbrook**, South Africa, 21 Jan 1960	437
7 **Wankie**, Rhodesia, 6 June 1972	427
8 **Tsinan**, China, 13 May 1935	400
9 **Dhanbad**, India, 28 May 1965	375
10 **Chasnala**, India, 27 Dec 1975	372

A mine disaster at the Fushun mines, Manchuria, on 12 February 1931, may have resulted in up to 3,000 deaths, but information was suppressed by the Chinese government. Soviet security was also responsible for obscuring details of an explosion at the East German Johanngeorgendstadt uranium mine on 29 November 1949, when as many as 3,700 may have died. The two worst disasters in the Top 10 both resulted from underground explosions, and the large numbers of deaths among mine workers resulted from that cause and from asphyxiation by poisonous gases. Among the most tragic disasters of the last century was the collapse of a slag heap at Aberfan, Wales, which killed 144, most of them children.

THE 10 ★
WORST FIRES AT THEATRE AND ENTERTAINMENT VENUES*

LOCATION/DATE/TYPE	NO. KILLED
1 **Canton**, China, 25 May 1845, Theatre	1,670
2 **Shanghai**, China, June 1871, Theatre	900
3 **Vienna**, Austria, 8 Dec 1881, Ring Theatre	640–850
4 **St. Petersburg**, Russia, 14 Feb 1836, Lehmann Circus	800
5 **Antoung**, China, 13 Feb 1937, Cinema	658
6 **Chicago**, IL, USA, 30 Dec 1903, Iroquois Theatre	602
7 **Boston**, MA, USA, 28 Nov 1942, Cocoanut Grove Night Club	491
8 **Berditschoft**, Poland, 13 Jan 1883, Circus Ferroni	430
9 **Abadan**, Iran, 20 Aug 1978, Theatre	422
10 **Niterói**, Brazil, 17 Dec 1961, Circus	323

* 19th and 20th centuries, excluding sports stadiums and race tracks

TROUBLE IN STORE

Some 1,500 people were inside the Sampoong Department Store, Seoul, when it collapsed, leaving over a third of them dead and as many as 900 injured.

THE 10 ★
WORST EXPLOSIONS*

	LOCATION/DATE	TYPE	ESTIMATED NO. KILLED
1	**Rhodes**, Greece, 1856[#]	Lightning strike of gunpowder store	4,000
2	**St. Nazaiere**, Breschia, Italy, 1769[#]	Arsenal	over 3,000
3	**Salang Tunnel**, Afghanistan, 3 Nov 1982	Petrol tanker colision	over 2,000
4	**Lanchow**, China, 26 Oct 1935	Arsenal	2,000
5	**Halifax**, Canada, 6 Dec 1917	Ammunition ship *Mont Blanc*	1,963
6	**Hamont Station**, Belgium, 3 Aug 1918	Ammunition trains	1,750
7	**Memphis**, USA, 27 Apr 1865	*Sultana* boiler explosion	1,547
8=	**Archangel**, Russia, 20 Feb 1917	Munitions ship	1,500
=	**Ft. Smederovo**, Yugoslavia, 9 June 1941	Ammunition dump	1,500
10	**Bombay**, India, 14 Apr 1944	Ammunition ship *Fort Stikine*	1,376

* Excluding mining disasters, terrorist and military bombs, and natural explosions, such as volcanoes # Precise date unknown

THE 10 ★
WORST COMMERCIAL AND INDUSTRIAL DISASTERS*

	LOCATION/DATE	TYPE	NO. KILLED
1	**Bhopal**, India, 3 Dec 1984	Methylisocyante gas escape at Union Carbide plant	up to 3,000
2	**Seoul**, S. Korea, 29 June 1995	Collapse of Sampoong Department Store	640
3	**Oppau**, Germany, 21 Sep 1921	Chemical plant explosion	561
4	**Mexico City**, Mexico, 20 Nov 1984	Explosion at a PEMEX liquified petroleum gas plant	540
5	**Brussels**, Belgium, 22 May 1967	Fire in l'Innovation department store	322
6	**Novosibirsk**, USSR, Apr 1979 (precise date unknown)	Anthrax infection following accident at biological and chemical warfare plant	up to 300
7	**Guadalajara**, Mexico, 22 Apr 1992	Explosions caused by gas leak into sewers	230
8	**São Paulo**, Brazil, 1 Feb 1974	Fire in Joelma bank and office building	227
9	**Oakdale**, Pennsylvania, USA, 18 May 1918	Chemical plant explosion	193
10	**Bangkok**, Thailand, 10 May 1993	Fire at a 4-storey doll factory	187

* Including industrial sites, factories, offices, and stores; excluding military, mining, marine, and other transport disasters, and mass poisonings

In the per capita consumption of what food does the UK lead the world?
see p.218 for the answer

A Avocados
B Baked beans
C Hamburgers

Food for Thought

TOP 10 ★

FROZEN FOOD CONSUMERS

COUNTRY	ANNUAL CONSUMPTION PER CAPITA		
	KG	LB	OZ
1 Norway	35.6	78	8
2 Denmark	32.5	71	10
3 UK	30.9	68	2
4 Israel	28.8	63	8
5 Czech Republic	21.3	46	15
6 Sweden	20.3	44	12
7 Ireland	18.9	41	11
8 Belgium	17.8	39	4
9 Finland	16.6	36	10
10 USA	16.3	35	15

Source: *Euromonitor*

CRISP CONSUMERS

COUNTRY	ANNUAL CONSUMPTION PER CAPITA		
	KG	LB	OZ
1 =UK	3.1	6	13
=USA	3.1	6	13
3 =Ireland	2.7	5	15
=New Zealand	2.7	5	15
5 Norway	2.6	5	12
6 Portugal	2.4	5	5
7 Netherlands	2.3	5	1
8 Australia	2.0	4	7
9 =Israel	1.6	3	8
=Sweden	1.6	3	8

Source: *Euromonitor*

BIRDSEYE

In 1915, while conducting a survey for the US Government in Labrador, Brooklyn-born Clarence "Bob" Birdseye (1886–1956) experimented with the Eskimo method of preserving food in the winter by freezing it in barrels. After returning to the US in 1917, he became interested in the possibility of preserving food commercially by the same method. In Gloucester, Mass., he opened General Seafoods and began preserving fish by rapid freezing. In 1929 he sold the company for $22 million. Birdseye himself became a millionaire, devoting his life to inventing.

WHO WAS · WHO WAS · WHO WAS · WHO WAS ·

BAKED BEAN CONSUMERS

COUNTRY	ANNUAL CONSUMPTION PER CAPITA		
	KG	LB	OZ
1 UK	5.3	11	11
2 Ireland	5.1	11	4
3 Mexico	4.2	9	4
4 New Zealand	2.2	4	14
5 =Australia	1.8	4	0
=France	1.8	4	0
7 Switzerland	1.5	3	5
8 Saudi Arabia	1.4	3	1
9 =Canada	1.3	2	14
=USA	1.3	2	14

Source: *Euromonitor*

BREAD CONSUMERS

COUNTRY	ANNUAL CONSUMPTION PER CAPITA		
	KG	LB	OZ
1 Slovak Republic	129.9	286	6
2 Turkey	129.7	285	15
3 Bulgaria	129.6	285	12
4 Saudi Arabia	112.1	247	2
5 Egypt	106.2	234	2
6 Romania	96.1	211	14
7 Chile	80.2	176	13
8 Poland	79.4	175	1
9 =Denmark	74.7	164	11
=Hungary	74.7	164	11
UK	34.8	76	12

Source: *Euromonitor*

MEAT CONSUMERS

COUNTRY	ANNUAL CONSUMPTION PER CAPITA		
	KG	LB	OZ
1 USA	122.5	270	1
2 Cyprus	113.6	250	7
3 New Zealand	110.1	242	11
4 Australia	108.2	238	8
5 Spain	107.3	236	9
6 Austria	104.8	231	0
7 Denmark	103.2	227	8
8 Netherlands	101.4	223	9
9 Bahamas	100.9	222	7
10 France	99.6	219	9
UK	76.8	169	5

Figures from the Meat and Livestock Commission show a huge range of meat consumption in countries around the world, ranging from the No. 1 meat consumer, the USA, at 122.5 kg (270 lb 1 oz) per person per year, to very poor countries such as India, where meat consumption may be as little as 4.6 kg (10 lb 2 oz) per person per year. In general, meat is an expensive food and in poor countries is saved for special occasions, so the richer the country, the more likely it is to have a high meat consumption. In recent years, however, health scares relating to meat, and the rise in the number of vegetarians, have contributed to deliberate declines in consumption.

TOP 10 HOTTEST CHILLIES

(Chilli*/Scoville units#)

❶ **Datil, Habanero, Scotch Bonnet**, 100,000–350,000 ❷ **Chiltepin, Santaka, Thai**, 50,000–100,000 ❸ **Aji, Cayenne, Piquin, Tabasco**, 30,000–50,000 ❹ **de Arbol**, 15,000–30,000 ❺ **Serrano, Yellow Wax**, 5,000–15,000 ❻ **Chipotle, Jalapeno, Mirasol**, 2,500–5,000 ❼ **Cascabel, Sandia, Rocotillo**, 1,500–2,500 ❽ **Ancho, Espanola, Pasilla, Poblano**, 1,000–1,500 ❾ **Anaheim, New Mexico**, 500–1,000 ❿ **Cherry, Peperoncini**, 100–500

* Examples – there are others in most categories
 # One part of capsaicin (the principal substance that determines how "hot" a chilli is) per million equals 15,000 Scoville units; the test was pioneered by pharmacist Wilbur Scoville.

TOP 10 ⭐
SPICE CONSUMERS

COUNTRY	ANNUAL CONSUMPTION PER CAPITA		
	KG	LB	OZ
1 United Arab Emirates	6.3	13	1
2 Hungary	5.9	13	0
3 Jamaica	4.5	9	14
4 Brunei	4.1	9	0
5 =Slovenia	3.7	8	3
=Sri Lanka	3.7	8	3
7 Seychelles	3.3	7	4
8 Cape Verdi	3.1	6	13
9 Kuwait	3.0	6	10
10 Bermuda	2.8	6	3
UK	0.5	1	2
World	0.8	1	12

Source: *Food and Agriculture Organization of the United Nations*

This list inevitably features those countries where spices play an important part in national cuisine. India just fails to find a place in the list, its per capita consumption being estimated at 2 kg (4 lb 6 oz).

TOP 10 ⭐
VEGETABLE CONSUMERS

COUNTRY	ANNUAL CONSUMPTION PER CAPITA		
	KG	LB	OZ
1 Lebanon	347.9	766	1
2 United Arab Emirates	271.9	599	0
3 Greece	262.8	579	0
4 Israel	224.7	495	0
5 Libya	222.8	491	0
6 Turkey	213.9	471	1
7 South Korea	207.5	457	0
8 Kuwait	196.1	432	5
9 Iran	188.8	416	4
10 Portugal	186.2	410	0
UK	86.2	190	0
World	94.6	208	0

Source: *Food and Agriculture Organization of the United Nations*

TOP 10 ⭐
FOOD ITEMS CONSUMED IN THE UK BY WEIGHT

PRODUCT	ANNUAL CONSUMPTION PER CAPITA		
	KG	LB	OZ
1 Milk and cream	107.4	236	9
2 Meat and meat products	47.4	104	8
3 Fresh vegetables (except potatoes)	38.7	85	6
4 Bread	37.2	82	3
5 Fresh fruit	36.9	81	8
6 Fresh potatoes	34.9	77	15
7 Processed vegetables (including processed potatoes)	28.4	62	13
8 Flour and other cereals or cereal products	25.3	55	15
9 Processed fruit and nuts	18.3	40	5
10 Cakes and biscuits	13.4	29	11

Source: *Ministry of Agriculture, Fisheries and Food, National Food Survey*

TOP 10 ⭐
POTATO CONSUMERS

COUNTRY	ANNUAL CONSUMPTION PER CAPITA		
	KG	LB	OZ
1 Belarus	168.5	411	0
2 Ukraine	137.7	303	9
3 Latvia	136.8	301	9
4 Poland	134.3	296	1
5 Lithuania	131.5	289	14
6 Ireland	129.8	286	3
7 Portugal	127.4	280	1
8 Russia	123.4	272	2
9 Croatia	113.9	251	2
10 Malawi	113.4	250	0
UK	110.1	242	1
World	30.0	66	0

Source: *Food and Agriculture Organization of the United Nations*

The potato has long been a staple part of the national diet for the countries at the top of the list.

TOP 10 ⭐
BUTTER CONSUMERS

COUNTRY	ANNUAL CONSUMPTION PER CAPITA		
	KG	LB	OZ
1 New Zealand	9.5	20	15
2 France	9.0	19	13
3 Estonia	8.0	17	5
4 Germany	7.0	15	6
5 Switzerland	6.2	13	10
6 =Belgium–Luxembourg	5.8	12	12
=Fiji Islands	5.8	12	12
8 Iceland	5.7	12	9
9 Belarus	5.5	12	2
10 Macedonia	5.0	11	0
UK	3.1	6	13
World	1.1	2	6

Source: *Food and Agriculture Organization of the United Nations*

TOP 10 ⭐
FISH CONSUMERS

COUNTRY	ANNUAL CONSUMPTION PER CAPITA*		
	KG	LB	OZ
1 Maldives	160.2	353	2
2 Iceland	91.7	202	2
3 Kiribati	77.2	170	3
4 Japan	72.2	159	2
5 Seychelles	64.8	142	13
6 Portugal	58.7	129	7
7 Norway	54.6	120	6
8 Malaysia	54.1	119	4
9 French Polynesia	51.8	114	3
10 South Korea	51.6	113	12
UK	24.7	54	7
World	20.4	44	14

* Combines sea and freshwater fish totals

Source: *Food and Agriculture Organization of the United Nations*

The majority of the fish consumed in the world comes from the sea, the average annual consumption of freshwater fish being 4.4 kg (9 lb 11 oz). The largest consumers are Norwegians, who each consume 11.8 kg (26 lb) per annum.

Did You Know? The cultivation of potatoes was banned in Scotland in 1728 because they were considered an "unholy nightshade" and were not mentioned in the Bible.

Sweet Dreams

TOP 10 ★
SUGAR PRODUCERS

	COUNTRY	TOTAL ANNUAL SUGAR PRODUCTION (TONNES)*
1	India	18,935,000
2	Brazil	14,500,000
3	China	8,379,000
4	USA	7,937,000
5	Australia	5,778,000
6	Thailand	5,630,000
7	Mexico	4,984,000
8	France	4,380,000
9	Cuba	4,134,000
10	Germany	4,100,000
	UK	1,434,000
	World	128,810,000

* Raw centrifugal sugar

Source: *Food and Agriculture Organization of the United Nations*

TOP 10 ★
CHEWING GUM CONSUMERS

	COUNTRY	ANNUAL CONSUMPTION PER CAPITA		
		KG	LB	OZ
1	Denmark	1.2	2	10
2	Norway	1.0	2	3
3 =	Switzerland	0.7	1	9
=	USA	0.7	1	9
5 =	Israel	0.6	1	5
=	Spain	0.6	1	5
7 =	Argentina	0.5	1	2
=	France	0.5	1	2
=	Germany	0.5	1	2
10 =	Canada	0.4	0	14
=	Ireland	0.4	0	14
=	Japan	0.4	0	14
=	Mexico	0.4	0	14
=	Morocco	0.4	0	14
=	UK	0.4	0	14

Source: *Euromonitor*

Worldwide chewing gum consumption in 1999 was estimated as 761,293.3 tonnes.

TOP 10 ★
SUGAR CONSUMERS

	COUNTRY	ANNUAL CONSUMPTION PER CAPITA*		
		KG	LB	OZ
1	Belize	62.0	136	10
2	Cape Verde	59.2	130	8
3	Cuba	59.0	130	1
4	Ecuador	55.0	121	4
5	Barbados	52.2	115	11
6 =	Brazil	51.5	113	8
=	Trinidad and Tobago	51.5	113	8
8	Iceland	50.6	111	8
9	Macedonia	50.4	111	1
10	Swaziland	49.4	108	14
	UK	31.2	68	12
	World	19.0	41	14

* Refined equivalent

Source: *Food and Agriculture Organization of the United Nations*

Each citizen of Belize, the current world leader in the sweet-tooth stakes, would appear to consume more than 1 kg (2.2 lb) of sugar every week.

TOP 10 ★
SWEETENER CONSUMERS*

	COUNTRY	ANNUAL CONSUMPTION PER CAPITA		
		KG	LB	OZ
1	USA	40.1	88	6
2	South Korea	14.0	30	13
3	Brunei	12.2	26	14
4	Bermuda	11.6	25	9
5 =	Hungary	11.4	25	2
=	Iceland	11.4	25	2
7	Japan	10.6	23	5
8	Bahamas	8.5	18	11
9	Canada	8.3	18	4
10	Estonia	6.8	14	15
	UK	0.6	1	5
	World	2.8	6	2

* Excluding sugar

Source: *Food and Agriculture Organization of the United Nations*

TOP 10 ★
FRUIT CONSUMERS

	COUNTRY	ANNUAL CONSUMPTION PER CAPITA		
		KG	LB	OZ
1	Dominica	401.7	885	9
2	Belize	321.8	709	0
3	Lebanon	241.7	532	14
4	Uganda	237.1	522	11
5	Saint Lucia	220.8	486	12
6	São Tomé and Principe	217.0	478	6
7	Rwanda	216.6	477	8
8	Bermuda	207.2	456	13
9	Papua New Guinea	204.6	451	1
10	Bahamas	193.0	425	8
	UK	89.3	196	14
	World	57.0	125	10

Source: *Food and Agriculture Organization of the United Nations*

World fruit consumption varies from those in the list – where some people devour more than five times their own body weight every year – to Eritrea, with just 1.4 kg (3 lb) per capita.

TOP 10 ★
HONEY CONSUMERS

	COUNTRY	ANNUAL CONSUMPTION PER CAPITA		
		KG	LB	OZ
1	Central African Republic	3.0	6	10
2	Turkmenistan	2.3	5	1
3	Angola	1.8	3	15
4 =	Greece	1.6	3	8
=	New Zealand	1.6	3	8
6	Switzerland	1.4	3	1
7 =	Germany	1.2	2	10
=	Ukraine	1.2	2	10
9 =	Austria	1.1	2	0
=	Canada	1.1	2	0
=	Slovenia	1.1	2	0
	UK	0.5	1	1
	World	0.2	0	7

Source: *Food and Agriculture Organization of the United Nations*

TOP 10 SWEET BRANDS IN THE UK*

1 Polo Mints **2** Maynard's Wine Gums **3** Rowntree Fruit Pastilles **4** Trebor Softmints **5** Trebor Extra Strong Mints **6** Starburst **7** Werther's Original **8** Bassett's Liquorice Allsorts **9** Chewits **10** Bassett's Jelly Babies

Excluding chocolate, for year to 25 March 2001
Source: *Cadbury Trebor Bassett*

TOP 10 ⭐
OLDEST-ESTABLISHED BRITISH CHOCOLATE PRODUCTS

	PRODUCT	YEAR INTRODUCED
1	Fry's Chocolate Cream	1853
2	Fry's Easter Egg	1873
3	Cadbury's Easter Egg	1875
4	Cadbury's Chocolate Drops*	1904
5	Cadbury's Dairy Milk	1905
6	Cadbury's Bournville	1908
7	Fry's Turkish Delight	1915
8=	Cadbury's Milk Tray	1920
=	Cadbury's Milk Chocolate Flake	1920
10	Cadbury's Creme Egg#	1923

* Now Chocolate Buttons
# Original version

TOP 10 ⭐
ICE CREAM CONSUMERS

	COUNTRY	ANNUAL CONSUMPTION PER CAPITA LITRES	PINTS
1	Australia	16.6	29.2
2	Italy	14.2	25.0
3	USA	13.9	24.5
4	New Zealand	13.2	23.2
5	Sweden	12.2	21.5
6	Ireland	10.3	18.1
7	Norway	9.2	16.2
8	Canada	9.1	16.0
9	Israel	9.0	15.8
10	Finland	8.8	15.5
	UK	7.9	13.9

Source: *Euromonitor*

TOP 10 ⭐
CHOCOLATE CONSUMERS

	COUNTRY	ANNUAL CONSUMPTION PER CAPITA KG	LB	OZ
1	Switzerland	11.8	26	0
2	UK	9.8	21	10
3	Belgium	8.5	18	12
4	Ireland	7.8	17	3
5	Norway	7.7	17	0
6	Germany	7.3	16	1
7	Austria	6.3	13	14
8	Australia	5.8	12	13
9	USA	5.7	12	9
10	Sweden	4.8	10	9

Source: *Euromonitor*

TOP 10 ⭐
DATE CONSUMERS

	COUNTRY	ANNUAL CONSUMPTION PER CAPITA KG	LB	OZ
1	United Arab Emirates	35.2	77	10
2	Saudi Arabia	30.7	67	11
3	Iraq	16.7	36	13
4	Libya	14.2	31	5
5	Algeria	12.1	26	12
6	Iran	11.7	25	12
7	Egypt	11.4	25	2
8=	Sudan	5.5	12	2
=	Tunisia	5.5	12	2
10	Kuwait	4.7	10	6
	UK	1.9	4	3
	World	0.8	1	12

Source: *Food and Agriculture Organization of the United Nations*

TOP 10 ⭐
CHOCOLATE BRANDS IN THE UK*

	BRAND
1	Cadbury's Dairy Milk
2	Mars Bar
3	KitKat
4	Maltesers
5	Celebrations
6	Snickers
7	Aero
8	Cadbury's Roses
9	Nestlé Quality Street
10	Galaxy

* For year to 25 March 2001
Source: *Cadbury Trebor Bassett*

TOP 10 ⭐
COCOA CONSUMERS

	COUNTRY	TOTAL COCOA CONSUMPTION (TONNES)
1	USA	656,200
2	Germany	284,500
3	UK	217,600
4	France	186,000
5	Japan	131,900
6	Brazil	124,600
7	Italy	97,200
8	Russia	95,600
9	Spain	67,600
10	Canada	63,500
	World	2,767,300

Cocoa is the principal ingredient of chocolate, and its consumption is therefore closely linked to the production of chocolate in each consuming country. Like coffee, the consumption of chocolate tends to occur mainly in the Western world and in more affluent countries. Europe has the highest intake of the world's regions, with a total cocoa consumption of 1,381,600 tonnes; the Americas are next with 1,021,300 (over half of which is accounted for by the US); Asia and Oceania consume 303,400 tonnes; and lastly, Africa, where 61,000 tonnes are consumed.

Did You Know? Chocolate was consumed mostly as a drink until 1879, when Swiss manufacturer Rudolphe Lindt added cocoa butter, and Daniel Peter pioneered the first milk chocolate bar.

Alcoholic & Soft Drinks

TOP 10 ★
ALCOHOL-CONSUMING COUNTRIES

COUNTRY	CONSUMPTION PER CAPITA, 1999 (100 PER CENT ALCOHOL) LITRES	PINTS
1 Luxembourg	12.2	21.5
2 Ireland	11.6	20.4
3 Portugal	11.0	19.4
4 France	10.7	18.8
5 Germany	10.6	18.7
6 Czech Republic	10.5	18.5
7 Romania	10.3	18.1
8 Spain	9.9	17.4
9 Hungary	9.7	17.1
10 Denmark	9.5	16.7
UK	8.1	14.3

Source: *Productschap voor Gedistilleerde Dranken*

After heading this list for many years – and with an annual consumption that peaked at 17.7 litres (31.2 pints) per head in 1961 – France was overtaken by Luxembourg, which is acknowledged as the world's leading alcohol consumer. While Western European countries have the highest average consumption of alcohol in the world – 8.0 litres (14.1 pints) per person per annum compared to a world average of 3.8 litres (6.7 pints) – the trend is towards lower drinking levels. Average consumption in Western Europe fell by 5.9 per cent between 1990 and 1999.

SCHWEPPES

German-born Jean Jacob Schweppe (1740–1821), an amateur scientist, moved to Geneva, Switzerland, where he became interested in the manufacture of artificial mineral waters. He moved to London in 1792 and began producing his own brand of soda water, forming Schweppe & Co. (later Schweppes Ltd.). By the 1870s, the company was also making ginger ale and "Indian Tonic Water", adding quinine to sweetened soda water after the style of the British in India, who drank it as an antidote to malaria, and thus beginning the fashion for gin and tonic.

WHO WAS • WHO WAS • WHO WAS • WHO WAS

TOP 10 COUNTRIES WITH THE BIGGEST INCREASE IN BEER PRODUCTION
(Country/percentage increase, 1980–98)

❶ China, 2,783 ❷ Argentina, 435 ❸ South Africa, 208 ❹ Brazil, 207 ❺ Turkey, 116 ❻ Mexico, 105 ❼ Chile, 94 ❽ Portugal, 91 ❾ Poland, 81 ❿ Finland, 66

UK, –13
Source: *Productschap voor Gedistilleerde Dranken*

TOP 10 ★
BEER-DRINKING COUNTRIES

COUNTRY	CONSUMPTION PER CAPITA, 1999 LITRES	PINTS
1 Czech Republic	159.4	280.5
2 Ireland	154.7	272.2
3 Germany	127.5	224.3
4 Luxembourg	109.0	191.8
5 Austria	108.9	191.6
6 Denmark	101.9	179.3
7 UK	99.0	174.2
8 Belgium	97.5	171.5
9 Australia	91.2	160.4
10 Slovak Republic	88.1	155.0

Source: *Productschap voor Gedistilleerde Dranken*

TOP 10 ★
BEER-PRODUCING COUNTRIES

COUNTRY	PRODUCTION, 1998 LITRES	PINTS
1 USA	23,770,000,000	41,829,328,810
2 China	17,300,000,000	30,443,726,900
3 Germany	11,170,000,000	19,656,441,010
4 Brazil	8,156,000,000	14,352,545,470
5 Japan	7,178,900,000	12,633,090,810
6 UK	5,665,200,000	9,969,352,696
7 Mexico	5,465,700,000	9,618,281,972
8 Russia	3,253,000,000	5,724,476,509
9 South Africa	2,563,900,000	4,511,830,717
10 Spain	2,499,100,000	4,397,798,722

Source: *Productschap voor Gedistilleerde Dranken*

TOP 10 ★
WINE-PRODUCING COUNTRIES

COUNTRY	PRODUCTION, 1998 LITRES	PINTS
1 Italy	5,418,800,000	9,535,749,556
2 France	5,267,100,000	9,268,795,026
3 Spain	3,032,000,000	5,335,571,096
4 USA	1,870,300,000	3,291,266,036
5 Argentina	1,267,300,000	2,230,134,977
6 Germany	1,080,000,000	1,900,533,240
7 South Africa	815,500,000	1,435,078,572
8 Australia	741,500,000	1,304,856,850
9 Chile	547,500,000	963,464,767
10 Romania	500,200,000	880,228,451

Source: *Productschap voor Gedistilleerde Dranken*

TOP 10 ★
WINE-DRINKING COUNTRIES

COUNTRY	CONSUMPTION PER CAPITA, 1999 LITRES	PINTS
1 Luxembourg	61.0	107.3
2 France	57.2	100.7
3 Portugal	51.7	91.0
4 Italy	51.5	90.6
5 Switzerland	43.6	76.7
6 Argentina	35.6	62.6
7 Greece	35.2	61.9
8 Spain	33.7	59.3
9 Uruguay	32.0	56.3
10 Austria	30.9	54.4
UK	14.5	25.5

Source: *Productschap voor Gedistilleerde Dranken*

COLA-DRINKING COUNTRIES

TOP 10

	COUNTRY	CONSUMPTION PER CAPITA, 1998	
		LITRES	PINTS
1	Mexico	97.9	172.3
2	United Arab Emirates	95.1	167.4
3	Bermuda	89.6	157.7
4	USA	85.3	150.1
5	St. Lucia	77.3	136.0
6	Bahrain	76.7	135.0
7	Dominica	76.6	134.8
8	Belize	73.7	129.7
9	Luxembourg	67.1	118.1
10	Grenada	66.9	117.7

Source: *Euromonitor*

TOP 10

SPARKLING WINE-DRINKING COUNTRIES

	COUNTRY	CONSUMPTION PER CAPITA, 1999	
		LITRES	PINTS
1	France	4.3	7.6
2	Germany	3.9	6.9
3 =	Hungary	2.1	3.7
=	New Zealand	2.1	3.7
5	Australia	1.6	2.8
6	Czech Republic	1.4	2.5
7	Belgium	1.3	2.3
8 =	Italy	1.2	2.1
=	Poland	1.2	2.1
10 =	Portugal	1.0	1.8
=	Romania	1.0	1.8

Source: *Euromonitor*

TOP 10

COFFEE-DRINKING COUNTRIES

	COUNTRY	ANNUAL CONSUMPTION PER HEAD			
		KG	LB	OZ	CUPS*
1	Finland	11.37	25	1	1,706
2	Norway	10.56	23	4	1,584
3	Denmark	10.09	22	4	1,514
4	Sweden	8.70	19	3	1,305
5	Austria	8.19	18	1	1,229
6	Germany	7.58	16	11	1,137
7	Switzerland	7.26	16	0	1,089
8	Netherlands	6.19	13	10	929
9	France	5.52	12	3	828
10	Belgium and Luxembourg	5.33	11	12	800

* Based on 150 cups per kg (2 lb 3 oz)

Source: *International Coffee Organization*

TOP 10

CHAMPAGNE IMPORTING COUNTRIES

	COUNTRY	BOTTLES IMPORTED, 2000
1	UK	20,433,640
2	USA	19,268,837
3	Germany	14,235,737
4	Italy	8,239,536
5	Belgium	7,320,681
6	Switzerland	6,518,658
7	Japan	3,174,914
8	Netherlands	2,122,547
9	Spain	2,035,983
10	Australia	1,434,895

Source: *Comité Interprofessionnel du Vin de Champagne (CIVC)*

TOP 10 COUNTRIES WITH THE BIGGEST INCREASE IN ALCOHOL CONSUMPTION

(Country/percentage increase, 1970–99)

❶ Brazil, 466.8 ❷ Paraguay, 275.0 ❸ Turkey, 177.8 ❹ Colombia, 166.6 ❺ Cyprus, 114.8 ❻ Ireland, 97.0 ❼ Venezuela, 96.8 ❽ Finland, 70.7 ❾ Greece, 69.6 ❿ Cuba, 69.3 *UK, 52.1*

Source: *Productschap voor Gedistilleerde Dranken*

TOP 10

SOFT DRINK-* DRINKING COUNTRIES

	COUNTRY	ANNUAL CONSUMPTION PER CAPITA	
		LITRES	PINTS
1	USA	219	385
2	Mexico	151	265
3	Iceland	140	246
4	Malta	134	236
5	Norway	126	222
6	Canada	122	215
7	Australia	120	211
8	Israel	111	195
9	Chile	110	194
10	Ireland	109	192
	UK	97	171

* Carbonated only

Source: *Zenith International*

As one might expect, affluent Western countries feature prominently in this list and, despite the spread of so-called "Coca-Cola culture", former Eastern Bloc and Third World countries rank very low – some African nations recording consumption figures of less than 1 litre (1.76 pints) per annum.

TOP 10

BEST-SELLING SOFT DRINK BRANDS IN THE UK, 2000

	BRAND	SALES (£)*
1	Coca-Cola	451,700,000
2	Robinsons	163,000,000
3	Pepsi	132,500,000
4	Ribena	121,100,000
5	Sunny Delight	108,900,000
6	Tropicana Pure Premium	82,900,000
7	Lucozade	68,200,000
8	Schweppes	61,000,000
9	Ocean Spray	54,200,000
10	Tango	52,900,000

* In 12 months to 12 August 2000

Source: *Checkout/ACNielsen MMS*

Did You Know? Champagne was invented by blind Benedictine monk Dom Pierre Pérignon (1639–1715), cellarmaster of the Abbey of Hautvilliers, France.

ON THE MOVE

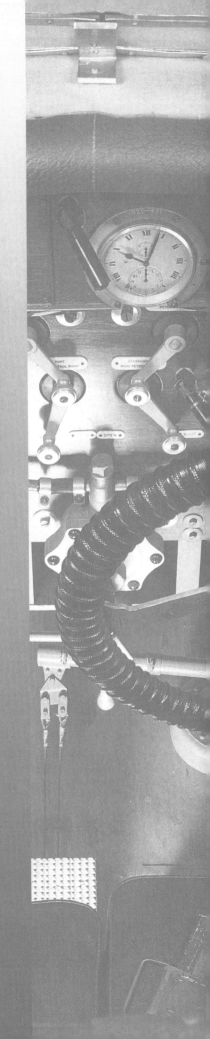

Speed Records

FIRST AMERICAN HOLDERS OF THE LAND SPEED RECORD

DRIVER*/CAR/LOCATION	DATE	KM/H	MPH
1 **William Vanderbilt**, *Mors*, Albis, France	5 Aug 1902	122.44	76.08
2 **Henry Ford**#, Ford *Arrow*, Lake St. Clair, USA	12 Jan 1904	147.05	91.37
3 **Fred Marriott**#, Stanley *Rocket*, Daytona Beach, USA	23 Jan 1906	195.65	121.57
4 **Barney Oldfield**#, Benz, Daytona Beach, USA	16 Mar 1910	211.26	131.27
5 **Bob Burman**#, Benz, Daytona Beach, USA	23 Apr 1911	227.51	141.37
6 **Ralph de Palma**#, Packard, Daytona Beach, USA	17 Feb 1919	241.19	149.87
7 **Tommy Milton**#, Duesenberg, Daytona Beach, USA	27 Apr 1920	251.11	156.03
8 **Ray Keech**, White *Triplex*, Daytona Beach, USA	22 Apr 1928	334.02	207.55
9 **Craig Breedlove**#, *Spirit of America*, Bonneville Salt Flats, USA	5 Aug 1963	655.73	407.45
10 **Tom Green**, *Wingfoot Express*, Bonneville Salt Flats, USA	2 Oct 1964	664.98	413.20

* *Excluding those who subsequently broke their own records*

Record not recognized in Europe

LATEST HOLDERS OF THE MOTORCYCLE SPEED RECORD

RIDER/MOTORCYCLE	YEAR	KM/H	MPH
1 **Dave Campos**, Twin 1,491cc Ruxton Harley-Davidson *Easyriders*	1990	518.45	322.15
2 **Donald A. Vesco**, Twin 1,016cc Kawasaki *Lightning Bolt*	1978	512.73	318.60
3 **Donald A. Vesco**, 1,496cc Yamaha *Silver Bird*	1975	487.50	302.93
4 **Calvin Rayborn**, 1,480cc Harley-Davidson	1970	426.40	264.96
5 **Calvin Rayborn**, 1,480cc Harley-Davidson	1970	410.37	254.99
6 **Donald A. Vesco**, 700cc Yamaha	1970	405.25	251.82
7 **Robert Leppan**, 1,298cc Triumph	1966	395.27	245.62
8 **William A. Johnson**, 667cc Triumph	1962	361.40	224.57
9 **Wilhelm Herz**, 499cc NSU	1956	338.08	210.08
10 **Russell Wright**, 998cc Vincent HRD	1955	297.64	184.95

All the records listed here were achieved at the Bonneville Salt Flats, USA, with the exception of No. 10 (Christchurch, New Zealand). Nos. 1 and 2 had two engines and were stretched to 6.4 m (21 ft) and 7 m (23 ft) respectively.

COOL RUNNER

In 1904 Henry Ford set the land speed record – although it was actually achieved on ice – on the frozen Lake St. Clair, near Detroit. A former employee of Thomas Edison, Ford (standing) had established the Ford Motor Company the previous year.

LATEST HOLDERS OF THE LAND SPEED RECORD

DRIVER/CAR	DATE	KM/H	MPH
1 **Andy Green**, *Thrust SSC**	15 Oct 1997	1,227.99	763.04
2 **Richard Noble**, *Thrust 2**	4 Oct 1983	1,013.47	633.47
3 **Gary Gabelich**, *The Blue Flame*	23 Oct 1970	995.85	622.41
4 **Craig Breedlove**, *Spirit of America – Sonic 1*	15 Nov 1965	960.96	600.60
5 **Art Arfons**, *Green Monster*	7 Nov 1965	922.48	576.55
6 **Craig Breedlove**, *Spirit of America – Sonic 1*	2 Nov 1965	888.76	555.48
7 **Art Arfons**, *Green Monster*	27 Oct 1964	858.73	536.71
8 **Craig Breedlove**, *Spirit of America*	15 Oct 1964	842.04	526.28
9 **Craig Breedlove**, *Spirit of America*	13 Oct 1964	749.95	468.72
10 **Art Arfons**, *Green Monster*	5 Oct 1964	694.43	434.02

* *Achieved at Black Rock Desert, USA; all other speeds were achieved at Bonneville Salt Flats, USA*

FERRARI

Enzo Ferrari (1898–1988) attended his first motor race at the age of 10, vowing to become a racing driver. He achieved his ambition while working for a car-maker, later becoming part of the Alfa Romeo team and starting his own firm in 1929. Ferrari retired from driving and began producing his first racing cars in 1940, and his first Grand Prix cars in the late 1940s. For over half a century, Ferraris have been among the most desirable – as well as the most expensive – of all cars, while the company's Formula One cars lead the constructors' table for the most wins.

TOP 10 ★
FASTEST PRODUCTION MOTORCYCLES

MAKE/MODEL	KM/H	MPH
1 Suzuki GSX1300R Hayabusa	309	192
2 =Honda CBR1100XX Blackbird	291	181
=Honda RC45(m)	291	181
4 =Harris Yamaha YZR500	289	180
=Kawasaki ZZR1100 D7	289	180
6 Bimota YB10 Biposto	283	176
7 Suzuki GSX-R1100WP (d)	280	174
8 Suzuki GSX-R750-WV	279	173
9 =Bimota Furano	278	173
=Kawasaki ZZR1100 C1	278	173

TOP 10 ★
FASTEST PRODUCTION CARS

MODEL*/ COUNTRY OF MANUFACTURE	KM/H#	MPH
1 McLaren F1, UK	386	240
2 Lamborghini Diablo 6.0, Italy	335	208
3 Lister Storm, UK	323	201
4 Marcos Mantara LM600 Coupe/Cabriolet, UK	322	200
5 Ferrari 550 Maranello, Italy	320	199
6 Renault Espace Privilege/Initiale 3.0 Auto, France	312	194
7 =Ascari Escosse, Italy	>305	>190
=Pagani Zonda, Italy	>305	>190
9 =Callaway C12, USA	305	190
Porsche 911 Turbo, Germany	305	190

* Fastest of each manufacturer
# May vary according to specification modifications to meet national legal requirements
Source: Auto Express/Top Gear Magazine

It is believed that it would be virtually impossible to build a road car capable of more than 402 km/h (250 mph), but these supercars come closest to that limit. The list includes the fastest example of each marque, but excludes "limited edition" cars.

TOP 10 ★
PRODUCTION CARS WITH THE FASTEST 0–60MPH TIMES

MODEL*/ COUNTRY OF MANUFACTURE	SECONDS TAKEN#
1 Renault Espace F1, France	2.8
2 McLaren F1, UK	3.2
3 Caterham Seven Superlight R500, UK	3.4
4 =Marcos Mantara LM600 Coupe/Cabriolet, UK	3.6
=Westfield FW400, UK	3.6
6 Lamborghini Diablo 6.0, Italy	3.9
7 Ascari Escosse, Italy	4.1
8 =AC Cobra Superblower, UK	4.2
=Callaway C12, USA	4.2
=TVR Tuscan Speed Six 4.0, UK	4.2

* Fastest of each manufacturer
# May vary according to specification modifications to meet national legal requirements
Source: Auto Express/Top Gear Magazine

SUPERCAR
Racing technology applied to a road car in the McLaren F1 set new records for speed and acceleration. It was also at one time the highest-priced production car ever built.

Cars & Road Transport

MOST COMMON TYPES OF PROPERTY LOST ON LONDON TRANSPORT

	TYPE	NO. OF ITEMS FOUND, 1999–2000
1	Books, cheque books, and credit cards	21,443
2	"Value items" (handbags, purses, wallets, etc.)	20,823
3	Clothing	19,532
4	Cases and bags	13,451
5	Umbrellas	9,279
6	Mobile telephones	8,769
7	Keys	7,634
8	Spectacles	5,981
9	Jewellery, cameras, laptop computers, etc.	5,829
10	Gloves (pairs)	2,658
	Total items in Top 10	115,399

Source: *London Transport*

COUNTRIES WITH THE LONGEST ROAD NETWORKS

	COUNTRY	LENGTH* KM	MILES
1	USA	6,348,227	3,944,605
2	India	3,319,644	2,062,731
3	Brazil	1,980,000	1,230,315
4	China	1,210,000	751,859
5	Japan	1,152,207	715,948
6	Russia	948,000	589,060
7	Australia	913,000	567,312
8	Canada	901,902	560,416
9	France	893,000	555,071
10	Germany	656,140	407,706
	UK	371,603	230,903

* Both paved and unpaved roads

The proportion of paved roads varies considerably: 1,517,077 km (942,668 miles) of India's total are paved, while only 184,140 km (114,419 miles) of Brazil's total are paved.

FIRST COUNTRIES TO MAKE SEAT BELTS COMPULSORY

	COUNTRY	INTRODUCED
1	Czechoslovakia	Jan 1969
2	Ivory Coast	Jan 1970
3	Japan	Dec 1971
4	Australia	Jan 1972
5 =	Brazil	June 1972
=	New Zealand	June 1972
7	Puerto Rico	Jan 1974
8	Spain	Oct 1974
9	Sweden	Jan 1975
10 =	Belgium	June 1975
=	Luxembourg	June 1975
=	Netherlands	June 1975

Seat belts were not designed for use in private cars until the 1950s. Ford was the first manufacturer in Europe to fit anchorage-points; belts were first fitted as standard in Swedish Volvos from 1959.

COUNTRIES WITH THE MOST SALES OF MOTOR VEHICLES

	COUNTRY	CARS	COMMERCIAL VEHICLES	TOTAL SALES, 1999
1	USA	8,698,284	8,716,444	17,414,728
2	Japan	4,154,084	1,707,132	5,861,216
3	Germany	3,802,176	318,901	4,127,077
4	Italy	2,349,200	196,298	2,545,498
5	France	2,148,423	386,983	2,535,416
6	UK	2,197,615	288,100	2,485,715
7	China	610,814	1,314,282	1,925,096
8	Spain	1,406,907	227,516	1,634,423
9	Canada	806,440	733,939	1,540,379
10	South Korea	910,725	362,304	1,273,029

Source: Ward's Motor Vehicle Data Book, *2000 edition*

FRENCH JAM

France has one of the world's highest ratios of cars to people and can claim a record traffic jam of 176 km (190 miles), which occurred between Paris and Lyons on 16 Feb 1980.

TOP 10
COUNTRIES PRODUCING THE MOST MOTOR VEHICLES

	COUNTRY	CARS	COMMERCIAL VEHICLES	TOTAL, 1999
1	USA	5,554,390	6,451,689	12,006,079
2	Japan	8,055,736	1,994,029	10,049,792
3	Germany	5,348,115	378,673	5,726,788
4	France	2,603,021	351,139	2,954,160
5	Spain	2,216,571	609,492	2,826,063
6	Canada	1,122,287	1,050,375	2,172,662
7	UK	1,748,277	232,793	1,981,070
8	South Korea	1,625,125	329,369	1,954,494
9	Italy	1,402,382	290,355	1,692,737
10	China	507,103	1,120,726	1,627,829

Source: Ward's Motor Vehicle Facts and Figures

A CAR IS BORN
Japan's car production, which places increasing reliance on advanced robotic technology, closely rivals that of world leader the USA.

TOP 10
BESTSELLING CARS OF ALL TIME

	MANUFACTURER/MODEL	YEARS IN PRODUCTION	ESTIMATED NO. MADE*
1	Toyota Corolla	1966–	23,000,000
2	Volkswagen Beetle	1937–#	21,500,000
3	Volkswagen Golf	1974–	over 20,000,000
4	Lada Riva	1972–97	19,000,000
5	Ford Model T	1908–27	16,536,075
6	Honda Civic	1972–	14,000,000
7	Nissan Sunny/Pulsar	1966–94	13,571,100
8	Ford Escort/Orion	1967–84	12,000,000
9	Honda Accord	1976–	11,500,000
10	Volkswagen Passat	1973–	10,435,700

* To 1 January 2001

Still produced in Mexico

Estimates of manufacturers' output of their bestselling models vary from the vague to the unusually precise 16,536,075 of the Model T Ford, with 15,007,033 produced in the US and the rest in Canada and the UK between 1908 and 1927.

THE CAR IN FRONT ...
The Toyota Motor Company was started in 1937, in Koromo, Japan, by Kiichiro Toyoda. Its Corolla model became the world's bestselling car.

TOP 10
BESTSELLING CARS IN THE UK, 2000

	CAR	SALES
1	Ford Focus	114,512
2	Vauxhall Astra	93,263
3	Ford Fiesta	91,783
4	Vauxhall Corsa	84,514
5	Peugeot 206	80,991
6	Vauxhall Vecta	70,704
7	Ford Mondeo	69,377
8	Renault Mégane	64,666
9	Renault Clio	61,209
10	Volkswagen Golf	57,359

Source: Ward's AutoInfoBank

Road Accidents

AGE GROUPS MOST VULNERABLE TO ROAD ACCIDENTS IN GREAT BRITAIN

	AGE GROUP	KILLED OR INJURED (1999)
1	15–19	38,771
2	20–24	38,598
3	25–29	37,818
4	30–34	35,436
5	35–39	28,187
6	40–44	21,267
7	10–14	19,132
8	45–49	16,797
9	50–54	15,892
10	5–9	13,426

The high proportion of accidents among teenagers and people in their early twenties is accounted for partly by inexperience and recklessness in controlling motor cycles and cars.

THE 10 WORST YEARS FOR ROAD FATALITIES IN GREAT BRITAIN

(Year/no. killed)

❶ 1941, 9,169 ❷ 1940, 8,609 ❸ 1939, 8,272 ❹ 1966, 7,985 ❺ 1965, 7,952 ❻ 1964, 7,820 ❼ 1972, 7,763 ❽ 1971, 7,699 ❾ 1970, 7,499 ❿ 1973, 7,406

MOST COMMON CAUSES OF FATAL CRASHES IN THE US

	CAUSE	FATALITIES (1999)
1	Failure to keep in proper lane, or running off road	16,904
2	Driving too fast for conditions, or in excess of posted speed limit	11,100
3	Failure to yield right of way	5,076
4	Inattention (talking, eating, etc.)	3,908
5	Operating vehicle in erratic, reckless, careless, or negligent manner	2,985
6	Failure to obey traffic signs, signals, or officer	2,817
7	Swerving due to wind or slippery surface, or avoiding vehicle, object, non-motorist in roadway, etc.	1,986
8	Drowsiness, sleep, fatigue, illness, or blackout	1,808
9	Overcorrecting/ oversteering	1,793
10	Making improper turn	1,323

Source: *National Highway Traffic Safety Administration*

In this list – which remains astonishingly consistent from year to year – other causes include obscured vision (1,310 fatalities) and driving on the wrong side of the road (1,256), with a further 20,552 fatalities being reported with no cause listed and 601 as "unknown". The total number of drivers involved is 56,352, with the sum of the numbers and percentages being greater because in some cases more than one factor resulted in the fatal accident.

SPEED LIMIT

Excess speed is a major cause of accidents the world over. Speed limits, increasing surveillance by speed cameras, and rigorous enforcement attempt to reduce the toll that speeding motorists take on lives.

MOST ACCIDENT-PRONE CAR COLOURS

	COLOUR	ACCIDENTS PER 10,000 CARS OF EACH COLOUR
1	Black	179
2	White	160
3	Red	157
4	Blue	149
5	Grey	147
6	Gold	145
7	Silver	142
8	Beige	137
9	Green	134
10=	Brown	133
=	Yellow	133

Figures released by the Department of Transport appear to refute the notion that white cars are safest because they are the easiest to see, especially at night. These statistics were immediately disputed by some car manufacturers, insurance companies, and psychologists, who pointed out that the type of vehicle and age and experience of drivers were equally salient factors. In the light of these comments, until further surveys are conducted it would be misleading to consider any colour "safer" than another.

OBJECTS MOST FREQUENTLY INVOLVED IN ROAD ACCIDENTS IN THE UK

	OBJECT COLLIDED WITH	ACCIDENTS (1999)
1	No object involved	52,584
2	Various permanent objects	7,216
3	Trees	3,117
4	Lamp posts	2,267
5	Crash barriers	2,197
6	Ditches	1,901
7	Roads signs and traffic signals	1,497
8	Telegraph/electricity poles	797
9	Bus stops and shelters	132
10	Submerged (rivers, canals, etc)	31

THE 10 ★ COUNTRIES WITH THE MOST DEATHS BY MOTOR ACCIDENTS

	COUNTRY	DEATH RATE PER 100,000 POPULATION*
1	South Korea	32.3
2	Latvia	27.1
3	El Salvador	24.4
4	Lithuania	23.8
5	Venezuela	22.3
6	Greece	22.1
7	Estonia	20.7
8	Portugal	19.2
9	Russia	18.5
10	Belarus	18.3
	UK	5.8

* In countries/latest year for which data available

Source: United Nations

Not all countries report accurate statistics, but the Top 10 represents countries in which visitors clearly need to take special care on the road.

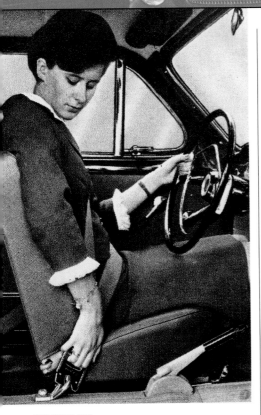

BELTING UP

Seat belts were first fitted as standard equipment in Swedish Volvos from 1959 and became compulsory in most countries from the 1970s onwards.

THE 10 ★ COUNTRIES WITH THE HIGHEST NUMBER OF ROAD DEATHS

	COUNTRY	TOTAL DEATHS*
1	USA	41,471
2	Thailand	15,176
3	Japan	10,805
4	South Korea	10,416
5	France	8,918
6	Germany	7,792
7	Poland	7,080
8	Brazil	6,759
9	Turkey	6,416
10	Italy	6,326
	UK	3,581

* In latest year for which figures available

THE 10 ★ MANOEUVRES MOST FREQUENTLY CAUSING VEHICLE ACCIDENTS IN THE UK

	MANOEUVRE	ACCIDENTS (1999)*
1	Going ahead (various)	183,947
2	Turning right, or waiting to do so	48,082
3	Held up while waiting to go ahead	35,176
4	Going ahead on a bend	31,495
5	Stopping	17,781
6	Parked	14,990
7	Turning left, or waiting to do so	13,830
8	Overtaking	13,683
9	Changing lane	6,622
10	Starting	5,636

* Vehicles other than two-wheel

THE 10 ★ WORST MOTOR VEHICLE AND ROAD DISASTERS

	LOCATION/DATE/INCIDENT	NO. KILLED
1	**Afghanistan**, 3 Nov 1982	over 2,000

Following a collision with a Soviet army truck, a petrol tanker exploded in the 2.7-km (1.7-mile) Salang Tunnel. Some authorities have put the death toll from the explosion, fire, and fumes as high as 3,000.

| 2 | **Colombia**, 7 Aug 1956 | 1,200 |

Seven army ammunition trucks exploded at night in the centre of Cali, destroying eight city blocks, including a barracks where 500 soldiers were sleeping.

| 3 | **Thailand**, 15 Feb 1990 | over 150 |

A dynamite truck exploded.

| 4 | **Nigeria**, 4 Nov 2000 | 150 |

A petrol tanker collided with a line of parked cars on the Ile-Ife-Ibadan Expressway, exploding and burning many to death. Some 96 bodies were recovered, but some estimates put the final toll as high as 200.

| 5 | **Nepal**, 23 Nov 1974 | 148 |

Hindu pilgrims were killed when a suspension bridge over the River Mahahali collapsed.

| 6 | **Egypt**, 9 Aug 1973 | 127 |

A bus drove into an irrigation canal.

| 7 | **Togo**, 6 Dec 1965 | over 125 |

Two lorries collided with dancers during a festival at Sotouboua.

| 8 | **Spain**, 11 July 1978 | over 120 |

A liquid gas tanker exploded in a camping site at San Carlos de la Rapita.

| 9 | **South Korea**, 28 Apr 1995 | 110 |

An undergound explosion destroyed vehicles and caused about 100 cars and buses to plunge into the pit it created.

| 10= | **The Gambia**, 12 Nov 1992 | c.100 |

After brake failure, a bus ferrying passengers to a dock plunged into a river.

| = | **Kenya**, early Dec 1992 | c.100 |

A bus carrying 112 skidded, hit a bridge, and plunged into a river.

The worst-ever motor racing accident occurred on 13 June 1955, at Le Mans, France, when, in attempting to avoid other cars, French driver Pierre Levegh's Mercedes-Benz 300 SLR went out of control, hit a wall, and exploded in mid-air, showering wreckage into the crowd and thereby killing a total of 82.

Which country does not appear among those with the Top 10 longest rail networks?   A Japan   B Mexico   C Argentina   *see p.233 for the answer*

Rail Transport

WORST RAIL DISASTERS

LOCATION/DATE/INCIDENT	NO. KILLED

1 Bagmati River, India, 6 June 1981   c.800
The carriages of a train travelling from Samastipur to Banmukhi in Bihar plunged off a bridge over the River Bagmati near Mansi when the driver braked, apparently to avoid hitting a sacred cow. Although the official death toll was said to have been 268, many authorities have claimed that the train was so massively overcrowded that the actual figure was in excess of 800.

2 Chelyabinsk, Russia, 3 June 1989   up to 800
Two passenger trains, laden with holidaymakers heading to and from Black Sea resorts, were destroyed when liquid gas from a nearby pipeline exploded.

3 Guadalajara, Mexico, 18 Jan 1915   over 600
A train derailed on a steep incline, but political strife in the country meant that full details of the disaster were suppressed.

4 Modane, France, 12 Dec 1917   573
A troop-carrying train ran out of control and was derailed. It has been claimed that the train was overloaded and that as many as 1,000 may have died.

5 Balvano, Italy, 2 Mar 1944   521
A heavily laden train stalled in the Armi Tunnel, and many passengers were asphyxiated. Like the disaster at Torre (No. 6), wartime secrecy prevented full details from being published.

6 Torre, Spain, 3 Jan 1944   over 500
A double collision and fire in a tunnel resulted in many deaths – some have put the total as high as 800.

7 Awash, Ethiopia, 13 Jan 1985   428
A derailment hurled a train laden with some 1,000 passengers into a ravine.

8 Cireau, Romania, 7 Jan 1917   374
An overcrowded passenger train crashed into a military train and was derailed.

9 Quipungo, Angola, 31 May 1993   355
A train was derailed by UNITA guerrilla action.

10 Sangi, Pakistan, 4 Jan 1990   306
A train was diverted on to the wrong line, resulting in a fatal collision.

Figures for rail accidents are often extremely imprecise, especially during wartime, and half of these disasters occurred during the two world wars.

FIRST COUNTRIES WITH RAILWAYS

	COUNTRY	FIRST RAILWAY ESTABLISHED
1	UK	27 Sep 1825
2	France	7 Nov 1829
3	USA	24 May 1830
4	Ireland	17 Dec 1834
5	Belgium	5 May 1835
6	Germany	7 Dec 1835
7	Canada	21 July 1836
8	Russia	30 Oct 1837
9	Austria	6 Jan 1838
10	Netherlands	24 Sep 1839

Although there were earlier horse-drawn railways, the Stockton & Darlington Railway inaugurated the world's first steam service. In their early years, some of those listed here offered only limited services over short distances, but their opening dates mark the generally accepted beginning of each country's steam railway system. By 1850, railways had also begun operating in Italy, Hungary, Denmark, and Spain.

LONGEST UNDERGROUND RAILWAY NETWORKS

	CITY/COUNTRY	OPENED	STATIONS	TOTAL TRACK LENGTH KM	MILES
1	London, UK	1863	267	392	244
2	New York, USA	1904	468	371	231
3	Moscow, Russia	1935	150	262	163
4	Paris, France*	1900	297	201	125
5	Copenhagen, Denmark#	1934	79	192	119
6	Seoul, South Korea	1974	114	183	113
7	Mexico City, Mexico	1969	154	178	112
8	Chicago, USA	1943	145	173	108
9	Tokyo, Japan+	1927	150	172	107
10	Berlin, Germany	1902	135	143	89

* Metro + RER   # Only partly underground   + Through-running extensions raise total to 683 km (391 miles), with 502 stations

Source: *Tony Pattison, Centre for Environmental Initiatives Researcher*

GOING UNDERGROUND
Now over 100 years old, the Paris Metro – with its distinctive Art Deco entrances – is among the world's longest and most used underground railway systems.

RAILROAD
Although the USA still has the longest rail network in the world, US rail mileage has declined considerably since its 1916 peak of 408,773 km (254,000 miles).

TOP 10 ★
LONGEST RAIL NETWORKS

	LOCATION	TOTAL RAIL LENGTH KM	MILES
1	USA	240,000	149,129
2	Russia	150,000	93,205
3	China	65,650	40,793
4	India	62,915	39,093
5	Germany	40,826	25,368
6	Argentina	38,326	23,815
7	Canada	36,114	22,440
8	Australia	33,819	21,014
9	France	31,939	19,846
10	Mexico	31,048	19,292
	UK	16,878	10,488

The world total is reckoned to be 1,201,337 km (746,476 miles), of which 239,430 km (148,775 miles) are narrow gauge and some 190–195,000 km (118,061–121,167 miles) are electrified.

TOP 10 ★
FASTEST RAIL JOURNEYS*

	JOURNEY	COUNTRY	TRAIN	DISTANCE KM	MILES	SPEED KM/H	MPH
1	Hiroshima–Kokura	Japan	Nozomi 500	192.0	119.3	261.8	162.7
2	Massy–St. Pierre des Corps	France	7 TGV	206.9	128.5	253.3	157.4
3	Brussels–Paris	International	Thalys 9342	313.4	194.7	226.5	140.7
4	Madrid–Seville	Spain	5 AVE	470.5	292.4	209.1	129.9
5	Karlsruhe–Mannheim	Germany	2 trains	71.0	44.1	193.8	120.4
6	London–York	UK	1 IC225	303.4	188.5	180.2	112.0
7	Skövde–Södertälje	Sweden	3 X2000	277.0	172.1	171.3	106.4
8	Piacenza–Parma	Italy	ES 9325	57.0	35.4	171.0	106.2
9	North Philadelphia–Newark Penn	USA	1 NE Direct	122.4	76.0	153.0	95.0
10	Salo–Karjaa	Finland	S220 132	53.1	33.0	151.7	94.3

* Fastest journey for each country; all those in the Top 10 have other similarly or equally fast services

Source: Railway Gazette International

Japan is the leader not only for scheduled train journeys: its MLX01 Maglev train holds the world speed record for an experimental vehicle, travelling at over 550 km/h (341.7 mph). At the other end of the scale, Albania has achieved a 47 per cent increase from 34.2 km/h (21.3 mph) to 50.5 km/h (31.3 mph).

Did You Know? Before they were adopted nationally, the American Railway Association introduced Standard Time Zones in 1883 to overcome the timetable confusion resulting from some 100 different local times.

Water Transport

TOP 10 ★
LONGEST CRUISE SHIPS

SHIP/COUNTRY/YEAR BUILT	LENGTH M	FT	IN
1 *Norway* (former *France*), France, 1961	315.53	1,035	2
2 =*Voyager of the Seas*, Finland, 1999	311.12	1,020	9
=*Explorer of the Seas*, Finland, 2000	311.12	1,020	9
4 *Disney Magic*, Italy, 1998	294.06	964	8
5 =*Disney Wonder*, Italy, 1999	294.00	964	7
=*Millennium*, France, 2000	294.00	964	7
7 *Queen Elizabeth 2*, UK, 1969	293.53	963	0
8 *Costa Atlantica*, Finland, 2000	291.70	957	0
9 *Grand Princess*, Italy, 1998	289.51	949	10
10 *Enchantment of the Seas*, Finland, 1997	279.60	917	4

Source: *Lloyd's Register, MIPG/PPMS*

For comparison, the *Great Eastern* (launched in 1858) measured 211 m (692 ft) long. The *Titanic*, which sank dramatically on its maiden voyage in 1912, was 269 m (882 ft) long and, until the influx of new vessels in 1998, would have ranked 8th in this Top 10. Former entrant in this list the *Queen Mary* (311 m/1,019 ft) is now a floating museum at Long Beach, California.

PORT OF CALL
Its substantial and well-protected harbour has contributed to Singapore's becoming the most important commercial centre in Southeast Asia.

TOP 10 BUSIEST PORTS*
(Port/location)

1 **Singapore**   **2** **Hong Kong**, China
3 **Kaohsiung**, Taiwan   **4** **Rotterdam**, Netherlands   **5** **Pusan**, South Korea
6 **Long Beach**, USA   **7** **Hamburg**, Germany   **8** **Antwerp**, Belgium
9 **Los Angeles**, USA   **10** **Shanghai**, China

* Ports handling the most TEUs (Twenty-foot Equivalent Units)
Source: *International Association of Ports & Harbors*

TOP 10 ★
COUNTRIES WITH THE LONGEST INLAND WATERWAY NETWORKS*

COUNTRY	LENGTH KM	MILES
1 China	110,000	68,351
2 Russia	101,000	62,758
3 Brazil	50,000	31,069
4 USA#	41,009	25,482
5 Indonesia	21,579	13,409
6 Colombia	18,140	11,272
7 Vietnam	17,702	11,000
8 India	16,180	10,054
9 Dem. Rep. of Congo	15,000	9,321
10 France	14,932	9,278
UK	3,200	1,988

* Canals and navigable rivers
# Excluding Great Lakes
Source: *Central Intelligence Agency*

The navigability of the world's waterways varies greatly: only 3,631 km (2,256 miles) of those of India, for example, are navigable by large vessels.

THE *UNITED STATES* GAINS THE BLUE RIBAND

From the 19th century onwards, ocean liners vied for the prize for the fastest transatlantic crossing by a passenger ship. The record, popularly known as the "Blue Riband", and the Hales Trophy, awarded since 1935, go to the vessel with the fastest crossing, which is based on average speed rather than shortest time because the route lengths vary. In 1838 the record stood at 7.3 knots over an 18-day voyage. This was steadily improved upon until, in 1938, the *Queen Mary* established the westbound record crossing at a speed of 30.99 knots. It took until 15 July 1952 for the *United States* to establish a new record of 3 days 10 hours 40 minutes at an average speed of 34.51 knots. A new eastbound record of 2 days 20 hours 9 minutes (41.28 knots) was set in 1998, but the *United States'* westbound record has remained unbeaten for half a century.

50 YEARS AGO · YEARS AGO · YEARS AGO ·

THE 10 ★
WORST MARINE DISASTERS

LOCATION/DATE/INCIDENT	APPROX. NO. KILLED
1 Off Gdansk, Poland, 30 January 1945	up to 7,800

The German liner Wilhelm Gustloff, *laden with refugees, was torpedoed by a Soviet submarine, S-13. The precise death toll remains uncertain, but is in the range of 5,348 to 7,800.*

2 Off Cape Rixhöft (Rozeewie), Poland, 16 April 1945	6,800

A German ship, Goya, *carrying evacuees from Gdansk, was torpedoed in the Baltic.*

3 Off Yingkow, China, 3 December 1948	over 6,000

The boilers of an unidentified Chinese troopship carrying Nationalist soldiers from Manchuria exploded, detonating ammunition.

4 Lübeck, Germany, 3 May 1945	5,000

The German ship Cap Arcona, *carrying concentration camp survivors, was bombed and sunk by British aircraft.*

5 Off St. Nazaire, France, 17 June 1940	3,050

The British troop ship Lancastria *sank.*

6 Off Stolpmünde (Ustka), Poland, 9 February 1945	3,000

German war-wounded and refugees were lost when the Steuben *was torpedoed by the same Russian submarine that had sunk the* Wilhelm Gustloff.

7 Tabias Strait, Philippines, 20 December 1987	up to 3,000

The ferry Dona Paz *was struck by oil tanker* MV Victor.

8 Woosung, China, 3 December 1948	over 2,750

The overloaded steamship Kiangya, *carrying refugees, struck a Japanese mine.*

9 Lübeck, Germany, 3 May 1945	2,750

The refugee ship Thielbeck *sank during the British bombardment of Lübeck harbour in the closing weeks of World War II.*

10 South Atlantic, 12 September 1942	2,279

The British passenger vessel Laconia, *carrying Italian prisoners-of-war, was sunk by German U-boat U-156.*

Recent re-assessments of the death tolls in some of the World War II marine disasters mean that the most famous marine disaster of all, the sinking of the *Titanic*, the British liner that struck an iceberg in the North Atlantic and sank on 15 April 1912 with the loss of 1,517 lives, no longer ranks in this list. However, the *Titanic* tragedy remains one of the worst-ever peacetime disasters, along with such notable incidents as that involving the *General Slocum*, an excursion liner that caught fire in the port of New York on 15 June 1904 with the loss of 1,021 lives.

THE 10 ★
WORST OIL TANKER SPILLS

TANKER/LOCATION/DATE	APPROX. SPILLAGE (TONNES)
1 *Atlantic Empress* and *Aegean Captain*, Trinidad, 19 July 1979	273,875
2 *Castillio de Bellver*, Cape Town, South Africa, 6 Aug 1983	255,125
3 *Olympic Bravery*, Ushant, France, 24 Jan 1976	250,000
4 *Amoco Cadiz*, Finistère, France, 16 Mar 1978	223,275
5 *Odyssey*, Atlantic, off Canada, 10 Nov 1988	140,075
6 *Haven*, off Genoa, Italy, 11 Apr 1991	136,500
7 *Torrey Canyon*, Scilly Isles, UK, 18 Mar 1967	124,150
8 *Sea Star*, Gulf of Oman, 19 Dec 1972	123,175
9 *Irenes Serenade*, Pilos, Greece, 23 Feb 1980	118,950
10 *Texaco Denmark*, North Sea, off Belgium, 7 Dec 1971	102,375

Source: *Environmental Technology Center,* Oil Spill Intelligence Report

ENVIRONMENTAL DISASTER
The 1979 collision of the Atlantic Empress *and the* Aegean Captain *off Trinidad resulted in the worst oil spill of all time.*

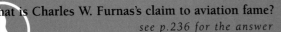

What is Charles W. Furnas's claim to aviation fame?
see p.236 for the answer

A The first aeroplane passenger in the US
B The first to use a parachute
C The first to land an aircraft on water

235

Air Records

THE 10 ★
FIRST TRANSATLANTIC FLIGHTS

	AIRCRAFT/CREW/COUNTRY	CROSSING	DATE*
1	**US Navy/Curtiss flying boat** *NC-4*, Lt.-Cdr. Albert Cushing Read and crew of five, USA	Trepassy Harbor, Newfoundland, to Lisbon, Portugal	16–27 May 1919
2	**Twin Rolls-Royce-engined converted Vickers Vimy bomber#**, Capt. John Alcock and Lt. Arthur Whitten Brown, UK	St. John's, Newfoundland, to Galway, Ireland	14–15 June 1919
3	**British airship** *R-34*+, Maj. George Herbert Scott and crew of 30, UK	East Fortune, Scotland, to Roosevelt Field, New York	2–6 July 1919
4	**Fairey IIID seaplane** *Santa Cruz*, Adm. Gago Coutinho and Cdr. Sacadura Cabral, Portugal	Lisbon, Portugal, to Recife, Brazil	30 Mar–5 June 1922
5	**Two Douglas seaplanes,** *Chicago* **and** *New Orleans*, Lt. Lowell H. Smith and Leslie P. Arnold/Erik Nelson and John Harding, USA	Orkneys, Scotland, to Labrador, Canada	2–31 Aug 1924
6	**Renamed German-built** *ZR 3* **airship** *Los Angeles*, Dr. Hugo Eckener with 31 passengers and crew, Germany	Friedrichshafen, Germany, to Lakehurst, New Jersey	12–15 Oct 1924
7	**Dornier Wal twin-engined flying boat** *Plus Ultra*, Capt. Julio Ruiz de Alda and crew, Spain	Huelva, Spain, to Recife, Brazil	22 Jan–10 Feb 1926
8	**Savoia-Marchetti S.55 flying boat** *Santa Maria*, Francesco Marquis de Pinedo, Capt. Carlo del Prete, and Lt. Vitale Zacchetti, Italy	Cagliari, Sardinia, to Recife, Brazil	8–24 Feb 1927
9	**Dornier Wal flying boat**, Sarmento de Beires and Jorge de Castilho, Portugal	Lisbon, Portugal, to Natal, Brazil	16–17 Mar 1927
10	**Savoia-Marchetti flying boat**, João De Barros and crew, Brazil	Genoa, Italy, to Natal, Brazil	28 Apr–14 May 1927

* All dates refer to the actual Atlantic legs of the journeys; some started earlier and ended beyond their first transatlantic landfalls

 # First non-stop flight

+ First east–west flight

ATLANTIC FLIER

Alcock and Brown made the first non-stop Atlantic crossing in 16 hours 28 minutes in a converted Vickers Vimy bomber.

THE 10 ★
FIRST PEOPLE TO FLY IN HEAVIER-THAN-AIR AIRCRAFT

	PILOT/NATIONALITY/AIRCRAFT	DATE
1	**Orville Wright**, USA, *Wright Flyer I*	17 Dec 1903
2	**Wilbur Wright**, USA, *Wright Flyer I*	17 Dec 1903
3	**Alberto Santos-Dumont**, Brazil, *No. 14-bis*	23 Oct 1906
4	**Charles Voisin**, France, *Voisin-Delagrange I*	30 Mar 1907
5	**Henri Farman**, UK, later France, *Voisin-Farman I-bis*	7 Oct 1907
6	**Léon Delagrange**, France, *Voisin-Delagrange I*	5 Nov 1907
7	**Robert Esnault-Pelterie**, France, *REP No. 1*	16 Nov 1907
8	**Charles W. Furnas***, USA, *Wright Flyer III*	14 May 1908
9	**Louis Blériot**, France *Blériot VIII*	29 June 1908
10	**Glenn Hammond Curtiss**, USA, *AEA June Bug*	4 July 1908

* As a passenger in a plane piloted by Wilbur Wright, Furnas was the first aeroplane passenger in the US.

THE 10 ★
FIRST ROCKET AND JET AIRCRAFT

	AIRCRAFT/COUNTRY	FIRST FLIGHT
1	**Heinkel He 176***, Germany	20 June 1939
2	**Heinkel He 178**, Germany	27 Aug 1939
3	**DFS 194***, Germany	Aug 1940#
4	**Caproni-Campini N-1**, Italy	28 Aug 1940
5	**Heinkel He 280V-1**, Germany	2 Apr 1941
6	**Gloster E.28/39**, UK	15 May 1941
7	**Messerschmitt Me 163 Komet***, Germany	13 Aug 1941
8	**Messerschmitt Me 262V-3**, Germany	18 July 1942
9	**Bell XP-59A Airacomet**, USA	1 Oct 1942
10	**Gloster Meteor F Mk 1**, UK	5 Mar 1943

* Rocket-powered # Precise date unknown

ROCKET PILOT
X-15 pilot Joseph A. Walker held the world record seven times in 1960–62, before finally losing the mantle to William J. Knight.

THE 10 ★
FIRST FLIGHTS OF MORE THAN ONE HOUR

	PILOT	HR:MIN:SEC	DATE
1	Orville Wright	1:02:15	9 Sep 1908
2	Orville Wright	1:05:52	10 Sep 1908
3	Orville Wright	1:10:00	11 Sep 1908
4	Orville Wright	1:15:20	12 Sep 1908
5	Wilbur Wright	1:31:25	21 Sep 1908
6	Wilbur Wright	1:07:24	28 Sep 1908
7	Wilbur Wright*	1:04:26	6 Oct 1908
8	Wilbur Wright	1:09:45	10 Oct 1908
9	Wilbur Wright	1:54:53	18 Dec 1908
10	Wilbur Wright	2:20:23	31 Dec 1908

* First ever flight of more than one hour with a passenger (M. A. Fordyce)

TOP 10 ★
FASTEST X-15 FLIGHTS

	PILOT/DATE	MACH*	FLIGHT KM/H	MPH
1	William J. Knight, 3 Oct 1967	6.70	7,274	4,520
2	William J. Knight, 18 Nov 1966	6.33	6,857	4,261
3	Joseph A. Walker, 27 June 1962	5.92	6,606	4,105
4	Robert M. White, 9 Nov 1961	6.04	6,589	4,094
5	Robert A. Rushworth, 5 Dec 1963	6.06	6,466	4,018
6	Neil A. Armstrong, 26 July 1962	5.74	6,420	3,989
7	John B. McKay, 22 June 1965	5.64	6,388	3,938
8	Robert A. Rushworth, 18 July 1963	5.63	6,317	3,925
9	Joseph A. Walker, 25 June 1963	5.51	6,294	3,911
10	William H. Dan, 4 Oct 1967	5.53	6,293	3,910

* Mach no. varies with altitude – the list is ranked on actual speed

Although achieved more than 33 years ago, the speeds attained by the rocket-powered X-15 and X-15A-2 aircraft are the greatest ever attained by piloted vehicles in the Earth's atmosphere.

TOP 10 ★
BIGGEST AIRSHIPS EVER BUILT

	AIRSHIP	COUNTRY	YEAR	VOLUME CU M	CU FT	LENGTH M	FT
1 =	Hindenburg	Germany	1936	200,000	7,062,934	245	804
=	Graf Zeppelin II	Germany	1938	200,000	7,062,934	245	804
3 =	Akron	USA	1931	184,060	6,500,000	239	785
=	Macon	USA	1933	184,060	6,500,000	239	785
5	R101	UK	1930	155,744	5,500,000	237	777
6	Graf Zeppelin	Germany	1928	105,000	3,708,040	237	776
7	L72	Germany	1920	68,500	2,419,055	226	743
8	R100	UK	1929	155,744	5,500,000	216	709
9	R38	UK*	1921	77,136	2,724,000	213	699
10 =	L70	Germany	1918	62,200	2,418,700	212	694
=	L71	Germany	1918	62,200	2,418,700	212	694

* UK-built, but sold to US Navy

THE FIRST JET AIRLINER

The jet airliner began life only 50 years ago, with the launch on 3 May 1952 of the scheduled BOAC de Havilland Comet service between London and Johannesburg, a distance of 10,821 km (6,724 miles) flown in stages in a journey time of 23 hours 34 minutes. The 36-seat aircraft *Yoke Peter* inaugurated the route, following exhaustive tests on freight-only flights to destinations such as Beirut, New Delhi, Jakarta, and Singapore. By August 1952, a weekly Comet service to Colombo, Ceylon (Sri Lanka), had also been established. Soon after, several crashes involving Comets cast doubts over the safety of passenger jets, but these were overcome as the world's airline routes became established.

50 YEARS AGO · YEARS AGO · YEARS AGO · YEARS

Did You Know? Following a feud with the Smithsonian Institution in Washington, DC, the Wright Brothers' *Flyer*, the first aircraft to fly, was kept in the Science Museum, London, from 1928 until 1948.

237

Air Transport

THE 10 ★
WORST AIRSHIP DISASTERS

LOCATION/DATE/INCIDENT	NO. KILLED
1 Off the New Jersey coast, USA, 4 Apr 1933 *US Navy airship Akron crashed into the sea in a storm, leaving only three survivors.*	73
2 Over the Mediterranean, 21 Dec 1923 *French airship Dixmude is assumed to have been struck by lightning when it broke up and crashed into the sea.*	52
3 Near Beauvais, France, 5 Oct 1930 *British airship R101 crashed into a hillside leaving 48 dead, with two dying later, and six survivors.*	50
4 Off the coast near Hull, UK, 24 Aug 1921 *Airship R38 broke in two on a training and test flight.*	44
5 Lakehurst, New Jersey, USA, 6 May 1937 *German Zeppelin Hindenburg caught fire when mooring.*	36
6 Hampton Roads, Virginia, USA, 21 Feb 1922 *Roma, an Italian airship bought by the US Army, crashed, killing all but 11 men on board.*	34
7 Berlin, Germany, 17 Oct 1913 *German airship LZ18 crashed after engine failure during a test flight at Berlin-Johannisthal.*	28
8 Baltic Sea, 30 Mar 1917 *German airship SL9 was struck by lightning on a flight from Seerappen to Seddin, and crashed into the sea.*	23
9 Mouth of the River Elbe, Germany, 3 Sep 1915 *German airship L10 was struck by lightning and plunged into the sea.*	19
10=Off Heligoland, 9 Sep 1913 *German Navy airship L1 crashed into the sea, leaving six survivors.*	14
=Caldwell, Ohio, USA, 3 Sep 1925 *US dirigible Shenandoah broke up in a storm, scattering sections over many miles of the Ohio countryside.*	14

Fatalities occurred from the earliest days of airships: the *Pax* crashed in Paris on 12 May 1902 killing its Brazilian inventor and pilot Augusto Severo and his assistant, and on 13 October of the same year Ottokar de Bradsky and his mechanic were killed in an airship crash, also in Paris.

TOP 10 AIRLINERS IN SERVICE
(Aircraft/no. in service)

1 Boeing B-737-300, 1,076 **2** Boeing B-757-200, 913 **3** Airbus A-320, 839 **4** Boeing B-727-200, 771 **5** Boeing B-737-200, 752 **6** Boeing B-767-300, 560 **7** Boeing B-747-400, 524 **8** Boeing B-737-400, 460 **9** Raytheon Beech 1900, 408 **10** Saab 340, 407

Source: Air Transport Intelligence at www.rati.com

THE 10 ★
WORST AIR DISASTERS

LOCATION/DATE/INCIDENT	NO. KILLED
1 Tenerife, Canary Islands, 27 March 1977 *Two Boeing 747s (Pan Am and KLM, carrying 364 passengers and 16 crew and 230 passengers and 11 crew respectively) collided and caught fire on the runway of Los Rodeos airport after the pilots received incorrect control-tower instructions.*	583
2 Mt. Ogura, Japan, 12 August 1985 *A JAL Boeing 747 on an internal flight from Tokyo to Osaka crashed, killing all but four on board in the worst-ever disaster involving a single aircraft.*	520
3 Charkhi Dadri, India, 12 November 1996 *Soon after taking off from New Delhi's Indira Gandhi International Airport, a Saudi Airways Boeing 747 collided with a Kazakh Airlines Ilyushin IL-76 cargo aircraft on its descent and exploded, killing all 312 on the Boeing and 37 on the Ilyushin, in the world's worst mid-air crash.*	349
4 Paris, France, 3 Mar 1974 *A Turkish Airlines DC-10 crashed at Ermenonville, north of Paris, just after take-off for London, with many English rugby fans among the dead.*	346
5 Off the Irish coast, 23 June 1985 *An Air India Boeing 747 on a flight from Vancouver to Delhi exploded in mid-air, perhaps as a result of a terrorist bomb.*	329
6 Riyadh, Saudi Arabia, 19 Aug 1980 *A Saudia (Saudi Arabian) Airlines Lockheed Tristar caught fire during an emergency landing.*	301
7 Kinshasa, Zaïre, 8 Jan 1996 *A Zaïrean Antonov-32 cargo plane crashed shortly after takeoff, killing shoppers in a city centre market.*	298
8 Off the Iranian coast, 3 July 1988 *An Iran Air A300 airbus was shot down in error by a missile fired by the USS Vincennes.*	290
9 Chicago, USA, 25 May 1979 *The worst air disaster in the US occurred when an engine fell off an American Airlines DC-10 as it took off from Chicago O'Hare airport and the plane plunged out of control, killing all 271 on board and two on the ground.*	273
10 Lockerbie, Scotland, 21 Dec 1988 *Pan Am Flight 103 from London Heathrow to New York exploded in mid-air as a result of a terrorist bomb, killing 243 passengers, 16 crew, and 11 on the ground, in the UK's worst-ever air disaster.*	270

FIERY FINALE

Astonishingly, 61 of the 97 people on board the Hindenburg survived its explosion, but the awesome images of the catastrophe heralded the end of the airship era.

FLYING HIGH
First flown in 1982, and now costing upwards of $70 million each, the Boeing B-757-200 has a maximum range of 7,240 km (4,520 miles) and is extensively used on both short- and long-haul routes.

TOP 10 ★
BUSIEST INTERNATIONAL AIRPORTS

AIRPORT/LOCATION	INTERNATIONAL PASSENGERS PER ANNUM
1 London Heathrow, London, UK	50,612,000
2 Frankfurt, Frankfurt, Germany	32,333,000
3 Charles de Gaulle, Paris, France	31,549,000
4 Schiphol, Amsterdam, Netherlands	30,832,000
5 Hong Kong, Hong Kong, China	28,316,000
6 London Gatwick, Gatwick, UK	24,385,000
7 Singapore International, Singapore	23,799,000
8 New Tokyo International (Narita), Tokyo, Japan	22,941,000
9 J.F. Kennedy International, New York, USA	17,378,000
10 Zurich, Zurich, Switzerland	16,747,000

Source: *International Civil Aviation Organization*

TOP 10 AIRLINES WITH THE MOST AIRCRAFT
(Airline/country/fleet size)*

❶ American Airlines, 714 **❷ United Airlines**, 603 **❸ Delta Airlines**, 600
❹ Northwest Airlines, 424 **❺ US Airways**, 384 **❻ Continental Airlines**, 364
❼ Southwest Airlines, 327 **❽ British Airways**, UK, 268
❾ American Eagle Airlines, 245 **❿ Lufthansa German Airlines**, Germany, 233

All from the US unless otherwise stated
Source: Airline Business/*Air Transport Intelligence at www.rati.com*

TOP 10 ★
AIRLINES CARRYING THE MOST PASSENGERS

AIRLINE/COUNTRY	PASSENGERS, 1999
1 Delta Airlines, USA	105,500,000
2 United Airlines, USA	87,100,000
3 American Airlines, USA	84,700,000
4 US Airways, USA	58,800,000
5 Southwest Airlines, USA	57,700,000
6 Northwest Airlines, USA	56,100,000
7 Continental Airlines, USA	45,500,000
8 All Nippon Airways, Japan	42,700,000
9 Air France, France	39,800,000
10 Lufthansa, Germany	38,900,000

Source: Airline Business/*Air Transport Intelligence at www.rati.com*

BOEING
The name of William Edward Boeing (1881–1956) is known the world over from the aircraft made by his company – the world's largest. Detroit-born Boeing made a fortune in the timber industry and, having become passionate about aviation, set up an aircraft manufacturing company in 1916. The firm prospered, and in 1927 set up an airline, Boeing Air Transport. Boeing retired from the business in 1934, when US Government anti-trust legislation made it illegal for a company to both build aircraft and operate an airline. The airline was sold off and became United – one of the world's largest – while the Boeing Company continued to supply the world's airlines with its aircraft.

On what unusual surface did Henry Ford set the land speed record in 1904?
see p.226 for the answer
A Ice
B Salt
C Volcanic lava

239

World Tourism

TOP 10

TOURIST DESTINATIONS IN ASIA AND THE PACIFIC

	COUNTRY	TOTAL VISITORS (2000)
1	China	31,236,000
2	Hong Kong	13,059,000
3	Malaysia	10,000,000
4	Thailand	9,574,000
5	Singapore	7,003,000
6	Macau	6,682,000
7	South Korea	5,336,000
8	Indonesia	5,012,000
9	Australia	4,882,000
10	Japan	4,758,000

Source: *World Tourism Organization*

TOP 10

TOURIST DESTINATIONS IN THE AMERICAS

	COUNTRY	TOTAL VISITORS (2000)
1	USA	52,690,000
2	Canada	20,423,000
3	Mexico	20,000,000
4	Brazil	5,190,000
5	Puerto Rico	3,094,000
6	Argentina	2,988,000
7	Dominican Republic	2,977,000
8	Uruguay	1,968,000
9	Chile	1,719,000
10	Cuba	1,700,000

Source: *World Tourism Organization*

TOP 10

COUNTRIES OF ORIGIN OF VISITORS TO THE UK

	COUNTRY	UK VISITORS (1999)
1	USA	3,939,000
2	France	3,223,000
3	Germany	2,794,000
4	Ireland	2,075,000
5	Netherlands	1,617,000
6	Belgium and Luxemburg	1,130,000
7	Italy	1,076,000
8	Spain	829,000
9	Australia	728,000
10	Canada	660,000

Source: *IPS/BTA/LTB*

TOP 10

TOURIST DESTINATIONS IN EUROPE

	COUNTRY	TOTAL VISITORS (2000)		COUNTRY	TOTAL VISITORS (2000)
1	France	74,500,000	6	Germany	18,916,000
2	Spain	48,500,000	7	Poland	18,183,000
3	Italy	41,182,000	8	Austria	17,818,000
4	UK	24,900,000	9	Hungary	15,571,000
5	Russia	22,783,000	10	Greece	12,500,000

Source: *World Tourism Organization*

TOP 10

OLDEST AMUSEMENT PARKS

	PARK/LOCATION	YEAR FOUNDED
1	**Bakken**, Klampenborg, Denmark	1583
2	**The Prater**, Vienna, Austria	1766
3	**Blackgang Chine Cliff Top Theme Park**, Ventnor, Isle of Wight, UK	1842
4	**Tivoli Gardens**, Copenhagen, Denmark	1843
5	**Lake Compounce Amusement Park**, Bristol, Connecticut, USA	1846
6	**Hanayashiki**, Tokyo, Japan	1853
7	**Grand Pier**, Teignmouth, UK	1865
8	**Blackpool Central Pier**, Blackpool, UK	1868
9	**Cedar Point**, Sandusky, Ohio, USA	1870
10	**Clacton Pier**, Clacton, UK	1871

IT JUST KEEPS ROLLING ALONG

In operation since 1914, the Rutschbanen in Copenhagen's Tivoli Gardens is Europe's oldest working roller coaster. The oldest one in the US predates this by 12 years.

TOP 10 ★
WORLDWIDE AMUSEMENT AND THEME PARKS, 2000

PARK/LOCATION	ATTENDANCE
1 Tokyo Disneyland, Tokyo, Japan	16,507,000
2 The Magic Kingdom at Walt Disney World, Lake Buena Vista, Florida, USA	15,400,000
3 Disneyland, Anaheim, California, USA	13,900,000
4 Disneyland Paris, Marne-La-Vallée, France	12,000,000
5 Epcot at Walt Disney World, Lake Buena Vista, Florida, USA	10,600,000
6 Everland, Kyonggi-Do, South Korea	9,153,000
7 Disney–MGM Studios at Walt Disney World, Lake Buena Vista, Florida, USA	8,900,000
8 Disney's Animal Kingdom at Walt Disney World, Lake Buena Vista, Florida, USA	8,300,000
9 Universal Studios Florida, Orlando, Florida, USA	8,100,000
10 Lotte World, Seoul, South Korea	7,200,000

Source: *Amusement Business*

TOP 10 ★
MOST VISITED LONDON ATTRACTIONS

ATTRACTION	APPROX NO. OF VISITORS (2000)
1 Millennium Dome	6,000,000
2 British Museum	5,700,000
3 National Gallery	5,000,000
4 Tate Modern	3,600,000
5 London Eye	3,500,000
6 Madame Tussaud's	2,600,000
7 Tower of London	2,400,000
8 Chessington World of Adventures	1,600,000
9 Natural History Museum	1,528,729
10 Westminster Abbey	1,250,000

TOP 10 ★
OLDEST ROLLER COASTERS*

ROLLER COASTER/LOCATION	YEAR FOUNDED
1 Leap-the-Dips, Lakemont Park, Altoona, Pennsylvania, USA	1902
2 Scenic Railway, Luna Park, Melbourne, Australia	1912
3 Rutschbanen, Tivoli Gardens, Copenhagen, Denmark	1914
4 Jack Rabbit, Clementon Amusement Park, Clementon, New Jersey, USA	1919
5= Jack Rabbit, Sea Breeze Park, Rochester, New York, USA	1920
= Scenic Railway, Dreamland, Margate, UK	1920
7= Jack Rabbit, Kennywood, West Mifflin, Pennsylvania, USA	1921
= Roller Coaster, Lagoon, Farmington, Utah, USA	1921
9= Big Dipper, Blackpool Pleasure Beach, Blackpool, UK	1923
= Thunderhawk, Dorney Park, Allentown, Pennsylvania, USA	1923
= Zippin Pippin, Libertyland, Memphis, Tennessee, USA	1923

In operation at same location since founded

Leap-the-Dips at Lakemont Park, Altoona, Pennsylvania, the world's oldest roller coaster, was out of operation from 1985, but was restored and reopened in 1999.

TOP 10 ★
FASTEST ROLLER COASTERS

ROLLER COASTER/LOCATION*/YEAR OPENED	KM/H	MPH
1= Superman The Escape, Six Flags Magic Mountain, Valencia, California, 1997	161	100
= Tower of Terror, Dreamworld, Gold Coast, Australia, 1997	161	100
3 Millennium Force, Cedar Point, Sandusky, Ohio, 2000	148	92
4= Goliath, Six Flags Magic Mountain, Valencia, California, 2000	137	85
= Titan, Six Flags Over Texas, Arlington, Texas, 2001#	137	85
6= Desperado, Buffalo Bill's Resort and Casino, Primm, Nevada, 1994	129	80
= HyperSonic XLC, Paramount's Kings Dominion, Doswell, Virginia, 2001#	129	80
= Nitro, Six Flags Great Adventure, Jackson, New Jersey, 2001#	129	80
= Phantom's Revenge, Kennywood Park, West Mifflin, Pennsylvania, 2001#	129	80
= Superman The Ride of Steel, Six Flags, Darien Lake, New York, 2000	129	80

In the US unless otherwise stated
#*Under construction at time of going to press*

THE OLDEST ROLLER COASTER

The first simple roller coasters were built in 1884 at Coney Island, New York, by Lemarcus Adna Thompson, but the world's oldest surviving example is Leap-the-Dips at Lakemont Park, Altoona, Pennsylvania, USA. Invented and built in 1902 by the Edward Joy Morris Company to a design Morris had patented in 1894, it is small and slow by modern standards, measuring only 443 m (1,452 ft) long and standing 12 m (41 ft) at its highest point, with a maximum speed of 16 km/h (10 mph). A figure-of-eight design, it operates on a principle known as side friction. One of the few remaining examples of the type, it was placed in the National Register of Historical Places in 1991 and attained National Landmark status in 1996. Leap-the-Dips was recently restored and re-opened in advance of its 100th anniversary.

Did You Know? The world's oldest surviving Ferris wheel, dating from 1895, is in Asbury Park, New Jersey, USA. Europe's oldest has stood in the Prater, Vienna, Austria, since 1897.

THE SPORTING WORLD

Summer Olympics

MOST SUCCESSFUL COUNTRIES AT ONE SUMMER OLYMPICS

	COUNTRY	VENUE	YEAR	GOLD	MEDALS SILVER	BRONZE	TOTAL
1	USA	St. Louis	1904	80	86	72	238
2	USSR	Moscow	1980	80	69	46	195
3	USA	Los Angeles	1984	83	61	30	174
4	Great Britain	London	1908	56	50	39	145
5	USSR	Seoul	1988	55	31	46	132
6	East Germany	Moscow	1980	47	37	42	126
7	USSR	Montreal	1976	49	41	35	125
8	EUN*	Barcelona	1992	45	38	29	112
9	USA	Barcelona	1992	37	34	37	108
10	USA	Mexico City	1968	45	28	34	107

* Unified Team representing the Commonwealth of Independent States (former Soviet republics), formed in 1991

OLYMPIC MEDAL-WINNING COUNTRIES THAT HAVE NEVER WON A GOLD MEDAL

	COUNTRY	SILVER	MEDALS BRONZE	TOTAL
1	Mongolia	5	9	14
2	Taipai	4	6	10
3 =	Chile	6	3	9
=	Philippines	2	7	9
5	Georgia	0	8	8
6 =	Latvia	5	2	7
=	Slovenia	2	5	7
8	Puerto Rico	1	5	6
9 =	Ghana	1	3	4
=	Israel	1	3	4
=	Lebanon	2	2	4
=	Moldovia	2	2	4
=	Namibia	4	0	4
=	Nigeria	1	3	4

SUMMER OLYMPICS ATTENDED BY THE MOST COMPETITORS, 1896–2000

	LOCATION	YEAR	COUNTRIES REPRESENTED	COMPETITORS
1	Atlanta	1996	197	10,310
2	Sydney	2000	199	10,000*
3	Barcelona	1992	169	9,364
4	Seoul	1988	159	8,465
5	Munich	1972	121	7,123
6	Los Angeles	1984	140	6,797
7	Montreal	1976	92	6,028
8	Mexico City	1968	112	5,530
9	Rome	1960	83	5,346
10	Moscow	1980	80	5,217

* Estimated

OLYMPIAN OPENING

Widely regarded as one of the most successful Olympics of modern times, the 2000 Sydney Games were launched by the arrival of the Olympic flame borne by 400-m champion Cathy Freeman.

British rower Steve Redgrave, here with team members Matthew Pinsent, Tim Foster, and James Cracknell, won his fifth consecutive gold at the 2000 Olympics.

TOP 10 ★
SPORTS WITH THE MOST OLYMPICS MEDALS FOR THE UK

SPORT	GOLD	SILVER	BRONZE	TOTAL
1 Athletics	49	83	59	191
2 Swimming*	14	22	26	62
3 Cycling	10	22	18	50
4 Shooting	14	15	18	47
5 Tennis	16	14	16	46
6 =Boxing	13	10	21	44
=Rowing	21	16	7	44
8 Yachting	17	14	9	40
9 Equestrianism	5	8	9	22
10 Wrestling	3	4	10	17

* Not including diving, water polo, or synchronized swimming

TOP 10 ★
COUNTRIES WITH THE MOST SUMMER OLYMPICS MEDALS, 1896–2000

COUNTRY	GOLD	SILVER	BRONZE	TOTAL
1 USA	872	659	581	2,112
2 USSR*	485	395	354	1,234
3 Great Britain	188	245	232	665
4 France	189	195	217	601
5 Germany#	165	198	210	573
6 Italy	179	144	155	478
7 Sweden	138	157	176	471
8 Hungary	150	134	158	442
9 East Germany	153	130	127	410
10 Australia	103	110	139	352

* Includes Unified Team of 1992; excludes Russia since then

 # Not including West/East Germany 1968–88

TOP 10 ★
MEDAL WINNERS IN A SUMMER OLYMPICS CAREER

WINNER	NATIONALITY	SPORT	YEARS	GOLD	SILVER	BRONZE	TOTAL
1 Larissa Latynina	USSR	Gymnastics	1956–64	9	5	4	18
2 Nikolay Andrianov	USSR	Gymnastics	1972–80	7	5	3	15
3 =Edoardo Mangiarotti	Italy	Fencing	1936–60	6	5	2	13
=Takashi Ono	Japan	Gymnastics	1952–64	5	4	4	13
=Boris Shakhlin	USSR	Gymnastics	1956–64	7	4	2	13
6 =Sawao Kato	Japan	Gymnastics	1968–76	8	3	1	12
=Paavo Nurmi	Finland	Athletics	1920–28	9	3	0	12
8 =Matt Biondi	USA	Swimming	1984–92	8	2	1	11
=Vera Cáslavská	Czechoslovakia	Gymnastics	1964–68	7	4	0	11
=Viktor Chukarin	USSR	Gymnastics	1952–56	7	3	1	11
=Carl Osburn	USA	Shooting	1912–24	5	4	2	11
=Mark Spitz	USA	Swimming	1968–72	9	1	1	11

Larissa Latynina won six medals at each of three Games between 1956 and 1964. The only discipline at which she did not win a medal was on the beam in 1956, when she came fourth. The only Winter Games competitor who would be eligible for this list is Björn Dählie of Norway, who won a total of 12 medals (8 gold and 4 silver) for Nordic Skiing in the Olympics of 1992–98.

TOP 10 COUNTRIES AT THE SYDNEY OLYMPICS WITH THE HIGHEST RATIO OF MEDALS
(Country/medals per million population)

1 Bahamas, 6.80 **2** Barbados, 3.76 **3** Iceland, 3.65 **4** Australia, 3.09
5 Jamaica, 2.72 **6** Cuba, 2.61 **7** Norway, 2.26 **8** Estonia, 2.07
9 Hungary, 1.68 **10** Belarus, 1.66

Great Britain, 0.47   Source: eCountries

The Bahamas, with a population of 294,000, tops this list of Olympic medal winners with one silver and one gold won by their female sprinters. Barbados came 2nd, having won just one bronze in the men's 100 m.

What sport was introduced in the 1998 Winter Olympics?
see p.247 for the answer

A Snowmobile racing
B Women's ski-jumping
C Snowboarding

Winter Olympics

COMPETITOR-ATTENDED WINTER OLYMPICS

	HOST CITY	COUNTRY	YEAR	COMPETITORS
1	Nagano	Japan	1998	2,177
2	Albertville	France	1992	1,801
3	Lillehammer	Norway	1994	1,736
4	Calgary	Canada	1988	1,425
5	Sarajevo	Yugoslavia	1984	1,274
6	Grenoble	France	1968	1,158
7	Innsbruck	Austria	1976	1,123
8	Innsbruck	Austria	1964	1,091
9	Lake Placid	USA	1980	1,072
10	Sapporo	Japan	1972	1,006

The first Winter Games at Chamonix, France, in 1924 were attended by 258 competitors representing 16 countries. Subsequent Games have seen the numbers of both competitors and countries generally increase: a total of 72 countries took part at the XVIII Games at Nagano.

TOP 10 ⭐

WINTER OLYMPIC MEDAL-WINNING COUNTRIES, 1908–98

	COUNTRY	GOLD	SILVER	BRONZE	TOTAL
1	Norway	83	87	69	239
2	Soviet Union*	87	63	67	217
3	USA	59	59	41	159
4	Austria	39	52	53	144
5	Finland	38	49	48	135
6	Germany#	46	38	32	116
7	East Germany	39	36	35	110
8	Sweden	39	28	35	102
9	Switzerland	29	32	32	93
10	Canada	25	25	29	79
	Great Britain	7	4	13	24

* *Includes Unified Team of 1992; excludes Russia since then*

\# *Not including East/West Germany 1968–88*

Figure skating was first featured at the 1908 Summer Olympics held in London, and ice hockey as part of the 1920 Summer Olympics at Antwerp.

FINNISH FIRST

At the 1998 Nagano Games, Finland added two gold, four silver, and six bronze medals to its tally, with Jani Soininen winning gold in the ski jumping event.

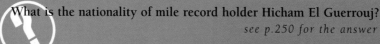

What is the nationality of mile record holder Hicham El Guerrouj?

see p.250 for the answer

A Moroccan
B Dutch
C Egyptian

INDIVIDUAL GOLD MEDALLISTS AT THE WINTER OLYMPICS

MEDALLIST/COUNTRY/SPORT	GOLD MEDALS
1 Bjørn Dählie, Nor, Nordic skiing	8
2 =Lydia Skoblikova, USSR, Speed skating	6
=Lyubov Yegorova, EUN*/Rus, Nordic skiing	6
4 =Bonnie Blair, USA, Speed skating	5
=Eric Heiden, USA, Speed skating	5
=Larissa Lazurtina, EUN*/Rus, Nordic skiing	5
=Clas Thunberg, Nor, Speed skating	5
8 =Ivar Ballangrud, Nor, Speed skating	4
=Yevgeni Grishin, USSR, Speed skating	4
=Sixten Jernberg, Swe, Nordic skiing	4
=Johan-Olav Koss, Nor, Speed skating	4
=Galina Kulakova, USSR, Nordic skiing	4
=Chun Lee-kyung, Kor, Short track speed skating	4
=Matti Nykänen, Fin, Ski jumping	4
=Nikolai Simyatov, USSR, Nordic skiing	4
=Raisa Smetanina, USSR, Nordic skiing	4
=Alexander Tikhonov, USSR, Biathlon	4

* EUN = Unified Team (Commonwealth of Independent States 1992)

WINTER OLYMPIC MEDAL-WINNING COUNTRIES, 1908–98 (MEN'S EVENTS)*

	COUNTRY	GOLD	SILVER	BRONZE	TOTAL
1	Norway	76	79	56	211
2	Soviet Union#	52	35	35	122
3	Finland	29	38	35	102
4	Austria	26	33	37	96
5	Sweden	32	23	31	86
6	USA	33	32	20	85
7	Switzerland	19	24	25	68
8	East Germany	24	19	23	66
9	Germany+	27	14	15	56
10	Italy	17	22	15	54

* In figure skating, men's singles and pairs have been counted together

Includes Unified Team of 1992; excludes Russia since then

+ Not including East/West Germany 1968–88

The only person to win gold medals at both the Summer and Winter Games is Eddie Eagan of the US. After winning the 1920 light-heavyweight boxing title, he then went on to win a gold medal as a member of the American four-man bobsleigh team in 1932.

SNOW FALL

Seen here in an uncharacteristic pose, Nordic skier Bjørn Dählie has won a record eight gold medals at three Winter Olympics, 1992–98.

ON BOARD

Introduced at the 1998 Games, the snowboarding halfpipe event was won by Nicola Thost, adding to the tally of German medal winners.

WINTER OLYMPIC MEDAL-WINNING COUNTRIES, 1908–98 (WOMEN'S EVENTS)*

	COUNTRY	GOLD	SILVER	BRONZE	TOTAL
1	Soviet Union#	35	28	32	95
2	USA	26	27	21	74
3	Germany+	19	24	17	60
4	Austria	13	19	16	48
5	East Germany	15	17	12	44
6	Finland	9	11	13	33
7	=Canada	11	9	8	28
	=Norway	7	8	13	28
9	Switzerland	10	8	7	25
10	Italy	7	8	9	24

* In figure skating, women's singles and ice dance have been counted together

Includes Unified Team of 1992; excludes Russia since then

+ Not including East/West Germany 1968–88

American Football

TOP 10 ★
PLAYERS WITH THE MOST CAREER POINTS

	PLAYER	POINTS
1	Gary Anderson*	2,059
2	George Blanda	2,002
3	Morten Andersen*	1,934
4	Norm Johnson	1,736
5	Nick Lowery	1,711
6	Jan Stenerud	1,699
7	Eddie Murray*	1,591
8	Al Del Greco*	1,568
9	Pat Leahy	1,470
10	Jim Turner	1,439

Still active 2000 season

Source: *National Football League*

TOP 10 ★
RUSHERS IN AN NFL CAREER

	PLAYER	TOTAL YARDS GAINED RUSHING
1	Walter Payton	16,726
2	Barry Sanders	15,269
3	Emmitt Smith*	15,146
4	Eric Dickerson	13,259
5	Tony Dorsett	12,739
6	Jim Brown	12,312
7	Marcus Allen	12,243
8	Franco Harris	12,120
9	Thurman Thomas*	12,072
10	John Riggins	11,352

Still active 2000 season

Source: *National Football League*

TOP 10 ★
LONGEST CAREERS OF CURRENT NFL PLAYERS

	PLAYER/TEAM	YEARS
1=	Gary Anderson, Minnesota Vikings	19
=	Morten Andersen, Atlanta Falcons	19
=	Eddie Murray, Washington Redskins	19
4=	Darrell Green, Washington Redskins	18
=	Trey Junkin, Arizona Cardinals	18
=	Bruce Matthews, Tennessee Titans	18
7=	Irving Fryar, Washington Redskins	17
=	Al Del Greco, Tennessee Titans	17
=	Mike Horan, St. Louis Rams	17
=	Warren Moon, Kansas City Chiefs	17

Source: *National Football League*

TOP 10 ★
BIGGEST WINNING MARGINS IN THE SUPER BOWL

	GAME*	YEAR	MARGIN
1	San Francisco 49ers v Denver Broncos	1990	45
2	Chicago Bears v New England	1986	36
3	Dallas Cowboys v Buffalo Bills	1993	35
4	Washington Redskins v Denver Broncos	1988	32
5	Los Angeles Raiders v Washington Redskins	1984	29
6	Baltimore Ravens v New York Giants	2001	27
7	Green Bay Packers v Kansas City Chiefs	1967	25
8	San Francisco 49ers v San Diego Chargers	1995	23
9	San Francisco 49ers v Miami Dolphins	1985	22
10	Dallas Cowboys v Miami Dolphins	1972	21

Winners listed first

Source: *National Football League*

TOP 10 ★
POINT SCORERS IN AN NFL SEASON

	PLAYER/TEAM	YEAR	POINTS
1	Paul Hornung, Green Bay Packers	1960	176
2	Gary Anderson, Minnesota Vikings	1998	164
3	Mark Moseley, Washington Redskins	1983	161
4	Marshall Faulk, St. Louis Rams	2000	160
5	Gino Cappelletti, Boston Patriots	1964	155*
6	Emmitt Smith, Dallas Cowboys	1995	150
7	Chip Lohmiller, Washington Redskins	1991	149
8	Gino Cappelletti, Boston Patriots	1961	147
9	Paul Hornung, Green Bay Packers	1961	146
10=	Jim Turner, New York Jets	1968	145
=	John Kasay, Carolina Panthers	1996	145
=	Mike Vanderjagt, Indianapolis Colts	1999	145

Including a two-point conversion

Source: *National Football League*

TOP 10 ★
PLAYERS WITH THE MOST PASSING YARDS IN AN NFL CAREER

	PLAYER	PASSING YARDS
1	Dan Marino	61,361
2	John Elway	51,475
3	Warren Moon	49,247
4	Fran Tarkenton	47,003
5	Dan Fouts	43,040
6	Joe Montana	40,551
7	Johnny Unitas	40,239
8	Dave Krieg	38,151
9	Boomer Esiason	37,920
10	Vinny Testaverde	36,296

Source: *National Football League*

Did You Know? Until improvements in the rules and equipment were introduced, American college football was one of the most dangerous of all team sports, the 1905 season resulting in 18 deaths and 159 other serious injuries.

TOP 10

HEAVIEST PLAYERS IN THE NFL

PLAYER/TEAM	WEIGHT KG	LB
1 **Aaron Gibson**, Detroit Lions	172	380
2 **Willie Jones**, Kansas City Chiefs	169	372
3 **L. J. Shelton**, Arizona Cardinals	163	360
4 **David Dixon**, Minnesota Vikings	162	358
5 **Anthony Clement**, Arizona Cardinals	159	351
6 =**Derrick Fletcher**, Washington Redskins	159	350
=**Stockar McDougle**, Detroit Lions	159	350
8 **Tra Thomas**, Philadelphia Eagles	158	349
9 **Yusuf Scott**, Arizona Cardinals	158	348
10 =**Jon Clark**, Arizona Cardinals	157	346
=**Korey Stringer**, Minnesota Vikings	157	346

Source: *National Football League*

TOP 10

MOST SUCCESSFUL TEAMS

TEAM	SUPER BOWL GAMES WINS	LOSSES	PTS*
1 **Dallas Cowboys**	5	3	13
2 **San Francisco 49ers**	5	0	10
3 **Pittsburgh Steelers**	4	1	9
4 **Washington Redskins**	3	2	8
5 **Denver Broncos**	2	4	8
6 =**Green Bay Packers**	3	1	7
=**Oakland/ Los Angeles Raiders**	3	1	7
8 **Miami Dolphins**	2	3	7
9 **New York Giants**	2	1	5
10 =**Buffalo Bills**	0	4	4
=**Minnesota Vikings**	0	4	4

* *Based on two points for a Super Bowl win, and one for runner-up; wins take precedence over runners-up in determining ranking*

Source: *National Football League*

TOP 10

LARGEST NFL STADIUMS

STADIUM/HOME TEAM	CAPACITY
1 **Pontiac Silverdome**, Detroit Lions	80,311
2 **FedEx Field**, Washington Redskins	80,116
3 **Giants Stadium**, New York Giants/Jets	79,469
4 **Arrowhead Stadium**, Kansas City Chiefs	79,409
5 **Ralph Wilson Stadium**, Buffalo Bills	75,339
6 **Pro Player Stadium**, Miami Dolphins	75,192
7 **Sun Devil Stadium**, Arizona Cardinals	73,273
8 **Ericsson Stadium**, Carolina Panthers	73,250
9 **Cleveland Browns Stadium**, Cleveland Browns	73,200
10 **Alltel Stadium**, Jacksonville Jaguars	73,000

Source: *National Football League*

TOP 10

COLLEGES WITH THE MOST BOWL WINS

COLLEGE	WINS
1 Alabama	28
2 University of Southern California (USC)	25
3 Penn State	23
4 Tennessee	22
5 Oklahoma	21
6 Nebraska	20
7 Georgia Tech	19
8 =Georgia	18
=Texas	18
10 =Florida State	17
=Michigan	17
=Mississippi	17

Bowl games are end-of-season college championship games, played at the end of December or beginning of January each year. The "Big Four" Bowl games, and members of the Bowl Championship Series, are the Rose Bowl (Pasadena), Orange Bowl (Miami), Sugar Bowl (New Orleans), and Cotton Bowl (Dallas).

TOP 10 MOST SUCCESSFUL COACHES IN AN NFL CAREER

(Coach/games won)

1 **Don Shula**, 347 2 **George Halas**, 324 3 **Tom Landry**, 270 4 **Curly Lambeau**, 229
5 **Chuck Noll**, 209 6 **Chuck Knox**, 193 7 **Dan Reeves***, 179 8 **Paul Brown**, 170
9 **Bud Grant**, 168 10 **Marv Levy**, 154

* *Still active 2000 season* Source: *National Football League*

THE FIRST ROSE BOWL

The Valley Hunt Club in Pasadena, California, first staged its Tournament of Roses in 1890. A celebration of California's mild winter weather, it grew in popularity and, following the event's famed parade, it was decided to stage a college football game. At the first-ever Rose Tournament game, held on New Year's Day 1902 at Tournament Park, the University of Michigan beat Stanford University with a score of 49–0 before a crowd of 8,000. So great was the defeat that the organizers decided not to stage the event again, the following year replacing it with a Roman-style chariot race. It was not until 1916 that football returned to the festivities, but as the crowd outgrew the seating capacity at Tournament Park, a new 57,000-seat stadium was constructed; the first game was held there on 1 January 1923. The stadium, and the annual game played there, were named the "Rose Bowl" by Harlan "Dusty" Hall, the Rose Tournament's press agent.

100 YEARS AGO · YEARS AGO · YEARS AGO

Athletic Achievements

LONGEST LONG JUMPS*

	ATHLETE/COUNTRY	YEAR	DISTANCE METRES
1	Mike Powell, USA	1991	8.95
2	Bob Beamon, USA	1968	8.90
3	Carl Lewis, USA	1991	8.87
4	Robert Emmiyan, USSR	1987	8.86
5 =	Larry Myricks, USA	1988	8.74
=	Erick Walder, USA	1994	8.74
7	Ivan Pedroso, Cuba	1995	8.71
8	Kareem Streete-Thompson, USA	1994	8.63
9	James Beckford, Jamaica	1997	8.62
10	Yago Lamela, Spain#	1999	8.56

* Longest by each athlete only   # Indoor

HIGHEST POLE VAULTS*

	ATHLETE/COUNTRY	YEAR	HEIGHT METRES
1	Sergei Bubka, Ukraine#	1993	6.15
2	Maxim Tarasov, Russia	1999	6.05
3 =	Okkert Brits, South Africa	1995	6.03
=	Jeff Hartwig, USA	2000	6.03
5	Rodion Gataullin, USSR#	1989	6.02
6	Igor Trandenkov, Russia	1996	6.01
7 =	Jeane Galfione, France	1999	6.00
=	Tim Lobinger, Germany	1997	6.00
=	Dmitri Markov, Belarus	1998	6.00
10	Lawrence Johnson, USA	1996	5.98

* Highest by each athlete only   # Indoor

FASTEST MILES EVER RUN

	ATHLETE/COUNTRY	YEAR	TIME
1	Hicham El Guerrouj, Morocco	1999	3:43.13
2	Noah Ngeny, Kenya	1999	3:43.40
3	Novreddine Morceli, Algeria	1993	3:44.39
4	Hicham El Guerrouj	1998	3:44.60
5	Hicham El Guerrouj	1997	3:44.90
6	Novreddine Morceli	1995	3:45.19
7	Hicham El Guerrouj	1997	3:45.64
8	Hicham El Guerrouj	2000	3:45.96
9	Hicham El Guerrouj	2000	3:46.24
10	Steve Cram, UK	1985	3:46.32

The current world record is almost 13 per cent faster than Roger Bannister's breakthrough first sub-four-minute mile of 1954, and over 20 per cent faster than the unofficial record set by British runner Walter Chinnery in 1868.

THE 10 LATEST WINNERS OF THE JESSE OWENS INTERNATIONAL TROPHY

(Year/athlete/sport)

1 2001 Marion Jones, athletics **2** 2000 Lance Armstrong, cycling **3** 1999 Marion Jones, athletics **4** 1998 Haile Gebrselassie, athletics **5** 1997 Michael Johnson, athletics **6** 1996 Michael Johnson, athletics **7** 1995 Johann Olav Koss, speed skating **8** 1994 Wang Junxia, athletics **9** 1993 Vitaly Scherbo, gymnastics **10** 1992 Mike Powell, athletics

The Jesse Owens International Trophy has been presented by the International Amateur Athletic Association since 1981. It is named in honour of American athlete Jesse Owens (1913–80).

HIGHEST HIGH JUMPS*

	ATHLETE/COUNTRY	YEAR	HEIGHT METRES
1	Javier Sotomayor, Cuba	1993	2.45
2 =	Patrik Sjöberg, Sweden	1987	2.42
=	Carlo Thränhardt, West Germany#	1988	2.42
4	Igor Paklin, USSR	1985	2.41
5 =	Charles Austin, USA	1991	2.40
=	Hollis Conway, USA#	1991	2.40
=	Sorin Matei, Romania	1990	2.40
=	Rudolf Povarnitsyn, USSR	1985	2.40
=	Vyochaslav Voronin, Russia	2000	2.40
10 =	Hollis Conway, USA	1989	2.39
=	Zhu Jianhua, China	1984	2.39
=	Dietmar Mögenburg, West Germany#	1985	2.39
=	Ralph Sonn, Germany#	1991	2.39

* Highest by each athlete only

Indoor

FASTEST TIMES IN THE LONDON MARATHON

MEN

	RUNNER/COUNTRY	YEAR	HR:MIN:SEC
1	Antonio Pinto, Portugal	2000	2:06:36
2	Abdelkhader El Mouaziz, Morocco	2001	2:07:11
3	Antonio Pinto	1997	2:07:55
4 =	Abel Anton, Spain	1998	2:07:57
=	Abdelkhader El Mouaziz	1999	2:07:57
6	Steve Jones, UK	1985	2:08:16
7	Dionicio Ceron, Mexico	1995	2:08:30
8	Dionicio Ceron	1994	2:08:53
9	Douglas Wakiihuri, Kenya	1989	2:09:03
10	Yakov Tolstikov, USSR	1991	2:09:17

WOMEN

	RUNNER/COUNTRY	YEAR	HR:MIN:SEC
1	Ingrid Kristiansen, Norway	1985	2:21:06
2	Ingrid Kristiansen	1987	2:22:48
3	Joyce Chepchumba, Kenya	1999	2:23:22
4	Derartu Tulu, Ethiopia	2001	2:23:57
5	Ingrid Kristiansen	1984	2:24:26
6	Tegla Loroupe, Kenya	2000	2:24:33
7	Grete Waitz, Norway	1986	2:24:54
8	Grete Waitz	1983	2:25:29
9	Ingrid Kristiansen	1988	2:25:41
10	Veronique Marot, UK	1989	2:25:56

TOP 10 ⭐
FASTEST WOMEN EVER*

ATHLETE/COUNTRY	YEAR	SECONDS
1 Florence Griffith Joyner, USA	1988	10.49
2 Marion Jones, USA	1998	10.65
3 Christine Arron, France	1998	10.73
4 Merlene Ottey, Jamaica	1996	10.74
5 Evelyn Ashford, USA	1984	10.76
6 Irina Privalova, Russia	1994	10.77
7 Dawn Sowell, USA	1989	10.78
8 Inger Miller, USA	1999	10.79
9 Marlies Göhr, East Germany	1983	10.81
10 =Gail Devers, USA	1992	10.82
=Gwen Torrence, USA	1994	10.82

* Based on fastest time for the 100 metres

TOP 10 ⭐
FASTEST MEN EVER*

ATHLETE/COUNTRY	YEAR	SECONDS
1 Maurice Greene, USA	1999	9.79
2 =Donovan Bailey, Canada	1996	9.84
=Bruny Surin, Canada	1999	9.84
4 Leroy Burrell, USA	1994	9.85
5 =Ato Boldon, Trinidad	1998	9.86
=Frank Fredericks, Namibia	1996	9.86
=Carl Lewis, USA	1991	9.86
8 =Linford Christie, UK	1993	9.87
=Obadele Thompson, Barbados	1998	9.87
10 Dennis Mitchell, USA	1991	9.91

* Based on fastest time for the 100 metres

Many would argue that Michael Johnson (USA) should be in this category with his remarkable 200-metre record of 19.32 seconds (equivalent to a 100-metre time of 9.66 seconds), but his best 100-metre time is only 10.09 seconds.

KEEPING UP WITH THE JONES

Marion Jones' personal best of 10.65 seconds for the 100 metres makes her the fastest living female athlete. The record-holder at 10.49 was Florence Griffith Joyner, who died in 1998.

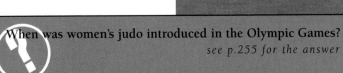

When was women's judo introduced in the Olympic Games?   A 1896
see p.255 for the answer   B 1936
C 1992

251

Basketball Bests

TOP 10 ★
DIVISION 1 NCAA TEAMS

	COLLEGE	DIVISION 1 WINS
1	Kentucky	1,765
2	North Carolina	1,753
3	Kansas	1,708
4	Duke	1,606
5	St. John's	1,602
6	Temple	1,542
7	Syracuse	1,522
8	Pennsylvania	1,495
9	Oregon State	1,481
10	Indiana	1,472

Source: *NCAA*

NCAA basketball was launched on 17 March 1939. Ironically, James Naismith, basketball's inventor, died on 28 November of the same year.

TOP 10 ★
POINT SCORERS IN AN NBA CAREER

	PLAYER	TOTAL POINTS*
1	Kareem Abdul-Jabbar	38,387
2	Karl Malone#	32,919
3	Wilt Chamberlain	31,419
4	Michael Jordan	29,277
5	Moses Malone	27,409
6	Elvin Hayes	27,313
7	Oscar Robertson	26,710
8	Dominique Wilkins	26,668
9	Hakeem Olajuwon#	26,511
10	John Havlicek	25,395

* *Regular season games only*
\# *Still active at end of 2000–2001 season*

Source: *NBA*

TOP 10 ★
COACHES IN THE NBA

	COACH	GAMES WON*
1	Lenny Wilkens#	1,226
2	Pat Riley#	1,049
3	Don Nelson#	979
4	Bill Fitch	944
5	Red Auerbach	938
6	Dick Motta	935
7	Jack Ramsay	864
8	Cotton Fitzsimmons	832
9	=Gene Shue	784
	=Jerry Sloan#	784

* *Regular season games only*
\# *Still active 2000–2001 season*

Source: *NBA*

Lenny Wilkens reached his 1,000th win on 1 March 1996, when the Atlanta Hawks beat the Cleveland Cavaliers 74–68 at The Omni. Pat Riley, as coach of the LA Lakers, the New York Knicks, and the Miami Heat, acquired the best percentage record, with 1,049 wins from 1,515 games, representing a 0.692 per cent success rate.

TOP 10 COACHES IN THE NCAA
(Coach/wins)

1 Dean Smith, 879 **2** Adolph Rupp, 876 **3** Jim Phelan*, 816 **4** Henry Iba, 767 **5** Bob Knight*, 764 **6** Lefty Driesell*, 762 **7** = Jerry Tarkanian*, 759; = Ed Diddle, 759 **9** Phog Allen, 746 **10** Lou Henson*, 740

* *Still active 2000–2001 season*   Source: *NCAA*

TOP 10 ★
BIGGEST ARENAS IN THE NBA

	ARENA/LOCATION	HOME TEAM	CAPACITY
1	**The Palace of Auburn Hills**, Auburn Hills, Michigan	Detroit Pistons	22,076
2	**United Center**, Chicago, Illinois	Chicago Bulls	21,711
3	**MCI Center**, Washington, DC	Washington Wizards	20,674
4	**Gund Arena**, Cleveland, Ohio	Cleveland Cavaliers	20,562
5	**Alamodome**, San Antonio, Texas	San Antonio Spurs	20,557
6	**First Union Center**, Philadelphia, Pennsylvania	Philadelphia 76ers	20,444
7	**Charlotte Coliseum**, Charlotte, North Carolina	Charlotte Hornets	20,085
8	**Continental Airlines Arena**, East Rutherford, New Jersey	New Jersey Nets	20,049
9	**The Rose Garden**, Portland, Oregon	Portland Trailblazers	19,980
10	**Delta Center**, Salt Lake City, Utah	Utah Jazz	19,911

The smallest arena is the 15,200-capacity Miami Arena, home of the Miami Heat. The largest-ever NBA stadium was the Louisiana Superdome, used by Utah Jazz from 1975 to 1979, which was capable of holding crowds of up to 47,284.

Source: *NBA*

TOP 10 ★
PLAYERS WITH THE HIGHEST POINTS AVERAGES

	PLAYER	POINTS SCORED	POINTS AVERAGE
1	Michael Jordan	29,277	31.5
2	Wilt Chamberlain	31,419	30.1
3	Shaquille O'Neal*	16,812	27.7
4	Elgin Baylor	23,149	27.4
5	Jerry West	25,192	27.0
6	Bob Pettit	20,880	26.4
7	George Gervin	20,708	26.2
8	Karl Malone*	32,919	25.9
9	Oscar Robertson,	26,710	25.7
10	Dominique Wilkins	26,668	24.8

* *Still active 2000–2001 season*

Source: *NBA*

In how many Olympic Games did Hungarian fencer Aladár Gerevich win seven golds?   *see p.255 for the answer*   A Three   B Five   C Six

TOP 10 TEAMS WITH THE MOST NCAA CHAMPIONSHIP WINS

(College/wins)

❶ UCLA, 11 **❷** Kentucky, 7 **❸** Indiana, 5 **❹** = North Carolina, 3; = Duke, 3 **❻** = Cincinnati, 2; = Kansas, 2; = Louisville, 2; = Michigan State, 2; = North Carolina State, 2; = Oklahoma A & M*, 2; = San Francisco, 2

* Now known as Oklahoma State

TOP 10 PLAYERS WITH THE MOST CAREER ASSISTS

(Player/assists)

❶ John Stockton*, 14,501 **❷** Magic Johnson, 10,141 **❸** Oscar Robertson, 9,887 **❹** Mark Jackson*, 9,235 **❺** Isiah Thomas, 9,061 **❻** Maurice Cheeks, 7,392 **❼** Lenny Wilkens, 7,211 **❽** Rod Strickland*, 7,026 **❾** Bob Cousy, 6,995 **❿** Guy Rodgers, 6,917

* Still active at end of 2000–2001 season
Source: NBA

TOP 10 ★
POINTS SCORED IN THE WNBA

PLAYER/GAME		DATE	PTS
1	**Cynthia Cooper**, Houston v Sacramento	25 July 1997	44
2	**Cynthia Cooper**, Houston v Utah	16 Aug 1999	42
3	**Cynthia Cooper**, Houston v Charlotte	11 Aug 1997	39
4	**Jennifer Gillom**, Phoenix v Cleveland	10 Aug 1998	36
5	=**Cynthia Cooper**, Houston v Los Angeles	1 Aug 1997	34
	=**Cynthia Cooper**, Houston v Phoenix	7 Aug 1997	34
	=**Ruthie Bolton-Holifield**, Sacramento v Utah	8 Aug 1997	34
	=**Ruthie Bolton-Holifield**, Sacramento v Cleveland	12 Aug 1997	34
	=**Cynthia Cooper**, Houston v Sacramento	3 July 1998	34
	=**Cynthia Cooper**, Houston v Detroit	7 Aug 1998	34

Source: WNBA

MAGIC TOUCH

Magic (Earvin) Johnson turned professional in 1979, becoming one of the NBA's most legendary players.

TOP 10 ★
FREE THROW PERCENTAGES

	PLAYER	ATTEMPTS	MADE	PERCENTAGE
1	Mark Price	2,362	2,135	90.4
2	Rick Barry	4,243	3,818	90.0
3	Calvin Murphy	3,864	3,445	89.2
4	Scott Skiles	1,741	1,548	88.9
5	Larry Bird	4,471	3,960	88.6
6	Reggie Miller*	6,038	5,338	88.4
7	Bill Sharman	3,559	3,143	88.3
8	Ricky Pierce	3,871	3,389	87.5
9	Kiki Vandeweghe	3,997	3,484	87.2
10	Jeff Malone	3,383	2,947	87.1

* Still active 2000–2001 season

Source: NBA

TOP 10 ★
PLAYERS TO HAVE PLAYED MOST GAMES IN THE NBA AND ABA

	PLAYER	GAMES PLAYED*
1	Robert Parish	1,611
2	Kareem Abdul-Jabbar	1,560
3	Moses Malone	1,455
4	Buck Williams	1,348
5	John Stockton#	1,339
6	Artis Gilmore	1,329
7	Elvin Hayes	1,303
8	Caldwell Jones	1,299
9	Sam Perkins#	1,286
10	Karl Malone#	1,273

* Regular season only

 # Still active at end of 2000–2001 season

Source: NBA

Combat Sports

BOXING CHAMPIONS WITH THE MOST CONSECUTIVE SUCCESSFUL DEFENCES*

FIGHTER/DIVISION/REIGN YEARS	DEFENCES
1 Joe Louis#, Heavyweight, 1937–49	25
2 Ricardo Lopez, Strawweight (WBC), 1990–	22
3 =Henry Armstrong#, Welterweight, 1938–40	19
=Khaosai Galaxy, Junior bantamweight (WBA), 1984–91	19
=Eusebio Pedroza, Featherweight (WBA), 1978–85	19
6 =Wilfredo Gomez, Junior featherweight (WBC), 1977–83	17
=Myung Woo Yuh, Junior flyweight (WBA), 1985–91	17
8 Orlando Canizales, Bantamweight (IBF), 1988–94	16
9 =Miguel Canto, Flyweight (WBC), 1975–79	14
=Bob Foster#, Light heavyweight, 1968–74	14
=Carlos Monzon#, Middleweight, 1970–77	14

* One champion per division listed
\# Undisputed champion

BOXERS WITH THE MOST KNOCKOUTS IN A CAREER

BOXER/COUNTRY*	CAREER	KNOCKOUTS
1 Archie Moore	1936–63	129
2 Young Stribling	1921–63	126
3 Billy Bird	1920–48	125
4 Sam Langford, Canada	1902–26	116
5 George Odwell	1930–45	114
6 Sugar Ray Robinson	1940–65	110
7 Sandy Saddler	1944–65	103
8 Henry Armstrong	1931–45	100
9 Jimmy Wilde, UK	1911–23	99
10 Len Wickwar	1928–47	93

* All from the US unless otherwise stated

Although this is the most generally accepted Top 10, boxing historians disagree considerably on this subject. Some, for example, include exhibition matches as well as the professional bouts on which this list is based. As the dates suggest, careers of this length, and the numbers of contests implied by knockout figures in the hundreds, are things of the past.

HEAVYWEIGHT CHAMP

Evander Holyfield enjoyed a brief reign as undisputed World Heavyweight Champion, defeating Buster Douglas for the WBC, WBA, and IBF titles in October 1990, before losing two years later to Riddick Bowe.

BOXERS WHO HAVE FOUGHT THE MOST BOUTS*

BOXER/COUNTRY#	YEARS	BOUTS
1 Len Wickwar	1928–47	466
2 Wildcat Monte	1923–37	406
3 Jack Britton	1904–30	357
4 Johnny Dundee, Italy	1910–32	340
5 Billy Bird	1920–48	318
6 George Marsden	1928–46	311
7 Duke Tramel	1922–36	305
8 Maxie Rosenbloom	1923–39	300
9 Harry Greb	1913–26	299
10 Sam Langford, Canada	1902–26	298

* Excluding exhibition bouts
\# All from the US unless otherwise stated

LATEST UNDISPUTED WORLD HEAVYWEIGHT CHAMPIONS

YEAR	FIGHTER/COUNTRY*
2001	Hasim Rahman
1999	Lennox Lewis, UK
1992	Riddick Bowe
1990	Evander Holyfield
1990	James Buster Douglas
1987	Mike Tyson
1978	Leon Spinks
1974	Muhammed Ali
1973	George Foreman
1970	Joe Frazier

* All from the US unless otherwise stated

"Undisputed" champions are those who are recognized by the four main governing bodies: World Boxing Council (WBC), World Boxing Association (WBA), International Boxing Federation (IBF), and World Boxing Organization (WBO).

JUDO CHAMPIONS
Brazil gained two silver medals for judo at the 2000 Olympics, one of them won by Tiago Camilo, seen here defeating Gil Offer of Israel in the Lightweight class.

TOP 10 ★
OLYMPIC FREESTYLE WRESTLING COUNTRIES

	COUNTRY	MEDALS			
		GOLD	SILVER	BRONZE	TOTAL
1	USA	44	35	24	103
2	USSR*	31	17	15	63
3	=Bulgaria	7	17	9	33
	=Japan	16	9	8	33
	=Turkey	16	11	6	33
6	=Iran	5	9	12	26
	=Sweden	8	10	8	26
8	Finland	8	7	10	25
9	Korea	4	7	8	19
10	Great Britain	3	4	10	17

* Includes Unified Team of 1992; excludes Russia since then

Great Britain's three gold medals in the freestyle event all date from the 1908 Games.

TOP 10 ★
OLYMPIC GRECO-ROMAN WRESTLING COUNTRIES

	COUNTRY	MEDALS			
		GOLD	SILVER	BRONZE	TOTAL
1	USSR*	37	19	13	69
2	Finland	19	21	19	59
3	Sweden	20	16	19	55
4	Hungary	15	10	11	36
5	Bulgaria	9	14	7	30
6	Romania	6	8	13	27
7	Germany#	4	13	8	25
8	Poland	5	8	6	19
9	=Italy	5	4	9	18
	=Turkey	11	4	3	18

* Includes Unified Team of 1992; excludes Russia since then

 # Not including West/East Germany 1968–88

The principal difference between freestyle and Greco-Roman wrestling is that in the latter competitors may not seize their opponents below the hips or grip using their legs.

TOP 10 ★
OLYMPIC JUDO COUNTRIES

	COUNTRY	MEDALS			
		GOLD	SILVER	BRONZE	TOTAL
1	Japan	23	12	13	48
2	France	10	5	17	32
3	Korea	7	10	13	30
4	USSR*	7	5	15	27
5	Cuba	5	7	8	20
6	Great Britain	–	7	9	16
7	Netherlands	4	–	7	11
8	=Brazil	2	3	5	10
	=China	4	1	5	10
	=Germany#	1	1	8	10
	=Italy	2	3	5	10

* Includes Unified Team of 1992; excludes Russia since then

 # Not including West/East Germany 1968–88

Judo made its debut at the 1964 Tokyo Olympics, but for men only. Women's judo was not introduced until the 1992 Barcelona Games. Judo was not included in the 1968 Mexico City Games.

TOP 10 ★
OLYMPIC FENCING COUNTRIES

	COUNTRY	MEDALS			
		GOLD	SILVER	BRONZE	TOTAL
1	France	39	38	33	110
2	Italy	40	36	26	102
3	Hungary	33	20	26	79
4	USSR*	19	17	18	54
5	Germany#	6	8	9	23
6	Poland	4	8	8	20
7	USA	2	6	11	19
8	West Germany	7	8	1	16
9	Belgium	5	3	5	13
10	Romania	3	3	6	12
	Great Britain	1	9	0	10

* Includes Unified Team of 1992; excludes Russia since then

 # Not including West/East Germany 1968–88

Hungarian competitor Aladár Gerevich (1910–91) achieved the unique feat of winning seven gold medals at six consecutive Games, spanning the 28 years from 1932 to 1960.

THE 10 WRESTLING WEIGHT DIVISIONS
(Weight/limit in kg/lb)

❶ **Heavyweight plus**, over 100/over 220 ❷ **Heavyweight**, 100/220
❸ **Light-heavyweight**, 90/198 ❹ **Middleweight**, 82/181 ❺ **Welterweight**, 74/163
❻ **Lightweight**, 68/150 ❼ **Featherweight**, 62/137 ❽ **Bantamweight**, 57/126
❾ **Flyweight**, 52/115 ❿ **Light-flyweight**, 48/106

Did You Know? Italian-born Angelo Parsi won four Olympic medals in judo for two different countries, competing for Great Britain in 1972, when he won a bronze, and for France in 1980 and 1984, winning a gold and two silvers.

Test Cricket

TOP 10 ★
HIGHEST INDIVIDUAL TEST INNINGS

	BATSMAN	MATCH/VENUE	YEAR	RUNS
1	Brian Lara	West Indies v England, St. John's	1993–94	375
2	Gary Sobers	West Indies v Pakistan, Kingston	1957–58	365*
3	Len Hutton	England v Australia, The Oval	1938	364
4	Sanath Jayasuriya	Sri Lanka v India, Colombo	1997–98	340
5	Hanif Mohammad	Pakistan v West Indies, Bridgetown	1957–58	337
6	Walter Hammond	England v New Zealand, Auckland	1932–33	336*
7 =	Don Bradman	Australia v England, Leeds	1930	334
=	Mark Taylor	Australia v Pakistan, Peshawar	1998–99	334*
9	Graham Gooch	England v India, Lord's	1990	333
10	Andrew Sandham	England v West Indies, Kingston	1929–30	325

* Not out

Gary Sobers' achievement was all the more remarkable since he was aged only 21 years 216 days, making him the youngest batsman to score a triple century. Sanath Jayasuriya is a new entry not only to this list, but also to that of Top 10 Partnerships in Test Cricket, where he shares No. 1 status, by a 109-run margin over the former record-holders.

TOP 10 ★
HIGHEST TEAM TOTALS IN TEST CRICKET

	MATCH	VENUE	YEAR	SCORE
1	Sri Lanka v India	Colombo	1997–98	952–6 dec
2	England v Australia	The Oval	1938	903–7 dec
3	England v West Indies	Kingston	1929–30	849
4	West Indies v Pakistan	Kingston	1957–58	790–3 dec
5	Australia v West Indies	Kingston	1954–55	758–8 dec
6	Australia v England	Lord's	1930	729–6 dec
7	Pakistan v England	The Oval	1987	708
8	Australia v England	The Oval	1934	701
9	Pakistan v India	Lahore	1989–90	699–5
10	Australia v England	The Oval	1930	695

India's highest total is 676–7, v Sri Lanka at Kanpur in 1986–87.

TOP 10 ★
LOWEST COMPLETED INNINGS IN TEST CRICKET

	MATCH	VENUE	YEAR	TOTAL
1	New Zealand v England	Auckland	1954–55	26
2 =	South Africa v England	Port Elizabeth	1895–96	30
=	South Africa v England	Birmingham	1924	30
4	South Africa v England	Cape Town	1898–99	35
5 =	Australia v England	Birmingham	1902	36
=	South Africa v Australia	Melbourne	1931–32	36
7 =	Australia v England	Sydney	1887–88	42
=	New Zealand v Australia	Wellington	1945–46	42
=	India* v England	Lord's	1974	42
10	South Africa v England	Cape Town	1888–89	43

* India batted one man short

The record low occurred at Eden Park, Auckland, on 28 March 1955, when the home side was dismissed in a total of 27 overs by the England team led by Len Hutton, playing his last Test. England's lowest total is 45, when dismissed by Australia at Sydney in 1886–87.

TOP 10 ★
PARTNERSHIPS IN TEST CRICKET

	BATSMEN	MATCH	YEAR	RUNS
1	Sanath Jayasuriya/ Roshan Mahanama	Sri Lanka v India	1997–98	576
2	Andrew Jones/ Martin Crowe	New Zealand v Sri Lanka	1990–91	467
3 =	Bill Ponsford/ Don Bradman	Australia v England	1934	451
=	Mudassar Nazar/ Javed Miandad	Pakistan v India	1982–83	451
5	Conrad Hunte/ Gary Sobers	West Indies v Pakistan	1957–58	446
6	Vinoo Mankad/ Pankaj Roy	India v New Zealand	1955–56	413
7	Peter May/ Colin Cowdrey	England v West Indies	1957	411
8	Sidney Barnes/ Don Bradman	Australia v England	1946–47	405
9	Gary Sobers/ Frank Worrell	West Indies v England	1959–60	399
10	Qasim Omar/ Javed Miandad	Pakistan v Sri Lanka	1985–86	397

Gundappa Viswanath, Yashpal Sharma, and Dilip Vengsarkar put on 415 runs for India's third wicket against England at Madras in 1981–82; Vengsarkar retired hurt when the partnership was on 99.

RUN MAKERS OF ALL TIME IN TEST CRICKET

PLAYER/COUNTRY	YEARS	TESTS	RUNS
1 **Allan Border**, Australia	1978–94	156	11,174
2 **Sunil Gavaskar**, India	1971–87	125	10,122
3 **Steve Waugh***, Australia	1985–	135	8,965
4 **Graham Gooch**, England	1975–95	118	8,900
5 **Javed Miandad**, Pakistan	1976–94	124	8,832
6 **Viv Richards**, West Indies	1974–91	121	8,540
7 **David Gower**, England	1978–92	117	8,231
8 **Geoff Boycott**, England	1964–82	108	8,114
9 **Gary Sobers**, West Indies	1954–74	93	8,032
10 **Colin Cowdrey**, England	1954–75	114	7,624

* *Still active in 2001*

WICKET TAKERS OF ALL TIME IN TEST CRICKET

PLAYER/COUNTRY	YEARS	TESTS	WICKETS
1 **Courtney Walsh**, West Indies	1984–2001	131	513
2 **Kapil Dev**, India	1978–94	131	434
3 **Richard Hadlee**, New Zealand	1973–90	86	431
4 **Wasim Akram***, Pakistan	1985–	100	409
5 **Curtly Ambrose**, West Indies	1988–2000	98	405
6 **Ian Botham**, England	1977–92	102	383
7 =**Malcolm Marshall**, West Indies	1978–91	81	376
=**Shane Warne***, Australia	1992–	87	376
9 **Imran Khan**, Pakistan	1971–92	88	362
10 **Dennis Lillee**, Australia	1971–84	70	355

* *Still active in 2001*

TOP 10 OUTFIELDERS WITH THE MOST CATCHES IN A TEST CAREER

(Fielder/country/years/catches)

❶ **Mark Taylor**, Australia, 1988–99, 157 ❷ **Allan Border**, Australia, 1978–94, 156 ❸ **Mark Waugh***, Australia, 1990–, 152 ❹ = **Greg Chappell**, Australia, 1970–84, 122; = **Viv Richards**, West Indies, 1974–91, 122 ❻ = **Ian Botham**, England, 1977–92, 120; = **Colin Cowdrey**, England, 1954–75, 120 ❽ = **Walter Hammond**, England, 1927–47, 110; = **Bobby Simpson**, Australia, 1957–78, 110 ❿ **Gary Sobers**, West Indies, 1954–74, 109

* *Still active in 2001*

RUN MAKERS IN A TEST SERIES

	BATSMAN	SERIES/TESTS	YEAR	RUNS
1	**Don Bradman**	Australia v England (5)	1930	974
2	**Walter Hammond**	England v Australia (5)	1928–29	905
3	**Mark Taylor**	Australia v England (6)	1989	839
4	**Neil Harvey**	Australia v South Africa (5)	1952–53	834
5	**Viv Richards**	West Indies v England (4)	1976	829
6	**Clyde Walcott**	West Indies v Australia (5)	1954–55	827
7	**Gary Sobers**	West Indies v Pakistan (5)	1957–58	824
8	**Don Bradman**	Australia v England (5)	1936–37	810
9	**Don Bradman**	Australia v South Africa (5)	1931–32	806
10	**Brian Lara**	West Indies v England (5)	1993–94	798

Don Bradman's remarkable tally against England in 1930 came when he was making his debut on English soil. He scored his runs in just seven innings, at an average of 139. He scored just eight runs in the first innings of the opening test, but then went on to score 131 in the second innings.

BEST BATTING AVERAGES IN A TEST CAREER*

	BATSMAN/COUNTRY	YEARS	INNINGS	NOT OUT	RUNS	AVERAGE
1	**Don Bradman**, Australia	1928–48	80	10	6,996	99.94
2	**Graeme Pollock**, South Africa	1963–70	41	4	2,256	60.97
3	**George Headley**, West Indies	1930–54	40	4	2,190	60.83
4	**Herbert Sutcliffe**, England	1924–35	84	9	4,555	60.73
5	**Eddie Paynter**, England	1931–39	31	5	1,540	59.23
6	**Ken Barrington**, England	1955–68	131	15	6,806	58.67
7	**Everton Weekes**, West Indies	1948–58	81	5	4,455	58.61
8	**Walter Hammond**, England	1927–47	140	16	7,249	58.45
9	**Gary Sobers**, West Indies	1954–74	160	21	8,032	57.78
10	=**Jack Hobbs**, England	1907–28	102	7	5,410	56.95
	=**Sachin Ramesh Tendulkar**#, India	1989–	131	13	6,720	56.95

* *Minimum qualification: 20 innings*   # *Still active in 2001*

What was James Moore's 1868 cycling first?
see p.263 for the answer

A First to ride a one-wheeled cycle
B First to win a cycling race
C First to cycle round the world

Football Stars

TRANSFER FEES BETWEEN ENGLISH CLUBS

	PLAYER	FROM	TO	YEAR	FEE (£)
1	Rio Ferdinand	West Ham United	Leeds United	2000	18,000,000
2	Alan Shearer	Blackburn Rovers	Newcastle United	1996	15,000,000
3	Dwight Yorke	Aston Villa	Manchester United	1998	12,600,000
4	Emile Heskey	Leicester City	Liverpool	2000	11,000,000
5	Chris Sutton	Blackburn Rovers	Chelsea	1999	10,000,000
6	Stan Collymore	Nottingham Forest	Liverpool	1995	8,500,000
7	Dietar Hammann	Newcastle United	Liverpool	1999	8,000,000
8=	Kevin Davies	Southampton	Blackburn Rovers	1998	7,500,000
=	John Hartson	West Ham United	Wimbledon	1999	7,500,000
10=	Stan Collymore	Liverpool	Aston Villa	1997	7,000,000
=	Duncan Ferguson	Everton	Newcastle United	1998	7,000,000

Transfer fees appear to have spiralled in recent years, but it was a similar story in 1979, when Trevor Francis became Britain's first million-pound footballer. In 1962, Manchester United made Denis Law Britain's first £100,000 player when they bought him from Italian club Torino. The first four-figure transfer fee came in 1905, when Middlesborough paid Sunderland £1,000 for Alf Common, and the first £100 deal was clinched way back in 1892, when Aston Villa bought Willie Grives from West Bromwich.

SIGNINGS TO MANCHESTER UNITED

	PLAYER/SIGNED FROM	YEAR	FEE (£)
1	Ruud van Nistelrooy, PSV Eindhoven (Holland)	2001	19,000,000
2	Dwight Yorke, Aston Villa	1998	12,600,000
3	Jaap Stam, PSV Eindhoven (Holland)	1998	10,750,000
4	Fabien Barthez, Monaco	2000	7,900,000
5	Andy Cole, Newcastle United	1995	6,250,000
6	Henning Berg, Blackburn Rovers	1997	5,000,000
7	Massimi Taibi, Venezia (Italy)	1999	4,500,000
8	Jesper Blomqvist, Palma (Italy)	1998	4,400,000
9	Roy Keane, Nottingham Forest	1993	3,750,000
10	Teddy Sheringham, Tottenham Hotspur	1997	3,500,000

GOAL SCORERS AT WEMBLEY*

	PLAYER#	GOALS
1	Bobby Charlton	27
2	Gary Lineker	25
3	Jimmy Greaves	20
4	Alan Shearer	18
5	Geoff Hurst	17
6=	Kevin Keegan	16
=	Nat Lofthouse	16
=	David Platt	16
=	Bryan Robson	16
=	Ian Rush	16

* As at the closure of the original stadium in October 2000

All England Internationals except Ian Rush, who played for Wales

England's first international at Wembley was a 1–1 draw with Scotland on 12 April 1924. Billy Walker, scorer of England's first goal, went on to become manager of FA Cup-winning teams Sheffield Wednesday (1935) and Nottingham Forest (1959).

LATEST ENGLAND PLAYERS TO SCORE A HAT-TRICK

	PLAYER	SCORED AGAINST	VENUE	YEAR
1	Alan Shearer	Luxemburg	Wembley	1999
2	Paul Scholes	Poland	Wembley	1999
3	Ian Wright*	San Marino	Bologna	1993
4	David Platt*	San Marino	Wembley	1993
5	Gary Lineker*	Malaysia	Kuala Lumpur	1991
6	Gary Lineker*	Spain	Madrid	1987
7	Gary Lineker	Turkey	Wembley	1987
8	Gary Lineker	Poland	Monterrey	1986
9	Gary Lineker	Turkey	Wembley	1985
10	Bryan Robson	Turkey	Istanbul	1985

* Scored four goals

The first players to score hat-tricks were Oliver Vaughton and Arthur Brown, in the same match against Ireland on 18 February 1882, won by England with a record 13–0 scoreline. The last player to score five goals for England was Malcolm Macdonald (against Cyprus at Wembley in 1975).

ENGLAND GOAL SCORERS IN FULL INTERNATIONALS*

	PLAYER	GOALS
1	Bobby Charlton	49
2	Gary Lineker	48
3	Jimmy Greaves	44
4=	Tom Finney	30
=	Nat Lofthouse	30
=	Alan Shearer	30
7	Vivian Woodward	29
8	Steve Bloomer	28
9	David Platt	27
10	Bryan Robson	26

* As at 18 December 2000

Had Gary Lineker not been substituted in his final game, against Sweden in 1992, he may well have gone on to equal or beat Bobby Charlton's record.

THE 10 ★
FIRST PENALTY KICKS IN AN FA CUP FINAL

PLAYER/MATCH	YEAR	PLAYER/MATCH	YEAR
1 Albert Shepherd, Newcastle United v Barnsley*	1910	**6 Ronnie Allen,** West Bromwich Albion v Preston North End	1954
2 Charlie Wallace#, Aston Villa v Sunderland	1913	**7 Danny Blanchflower,** Tottenham Hotspur v Burnley	1962
3 Billy Smith, Huddersfield Town v Preston North End	1922	**8 Kevin Reeves,** Manchester City v Tottenham Hotspur*	1981
4 George Mutch, Preston North End v Huddersfield Town	1938	**9 Glenn Hoddle,** Tottenham Hotspur v Queen's Park Rangers*	1982
5 Eddie Shimwell, Blackpool v Manchester United	1948	**10 Arnold Muhren,** Manchester United v Brighton and Hove Albion*	1983

* Replay   # Penalty kick missed

THE 10 ★
LATEST FOOTBALLERS OF THE YEAR

YEAR	PLAYER/TEAM
2000	Roy Keane, Manchester United
1999	David Ginola, Tottenham Hotspur
1998	Dennis Bergkamp, Arsenal
1997	Gianfranco Zola, Chelsea
1996	Eric Cantona, Manchester United
1995	Jürgen Klinsman, Tottenham Hotspur
1994	Alan Shearer, Blackburn Rovers
1993	Chris Waddle, Sheffield Wednesday
1992	Gary Lineker, Tottenham Hotspur
1991	Gordon Strachan, Leeds United

The Footballer of the Year award is presented by the Football Writers' Association. All players in the English League, irrespective of country of origin, are eligible. In 2000 the trophy was named The Sir Stanley Matthews Trophy.

TOP 10 ★
MOST CAPPED ENGLAND PLAYERS

	PLAYER	YEARS	INTERNATIONAL GOALS	CAPS
1	Peter Shilton	1970–90	0	125
2	Bobby Moore	1962–73	2	108
3	Bobby Charlton	1958–70	49	106
4	Billy Wright	1946–59	3	105
5	Bryan Robson	1980–91	26	90
6	Kenny Sansom	1979–88	1	86
7	Ray Wilkins	1976–86	3	84
8	Gary Lineker	1984–92	48	80
9	John Barnes	1983–95	11	79
10	Terry Butcher	1980–90	3	77

Bobby Charlton's 49 goals scored in international matches stand as the all-time record, with Gary Lineker's 48 just behind. Outside the Top 10, Jimmy Greaves scored 44 goals in just 57 matches.

TOP 10 ★
MOST CAPPED ENGLAND GOALKEEPERS*

	PLAYER	YEARS	CAPS
1	Peter Shilton	1970–90	125
2	Gordon Banks	1963–72	73
3	David Seaman	1980–2001#	62
4	Ray Clemence	1972–83	61
5	Chris Woods	1985–93	43
6	Ron Springett	1959–65	33
7	Harry Hibbs	1929–36	25
8	Bert Williams	1949–55	24
9	Gil Merrick	1951–54	23
10	Sam Hardy	1907–20	21

* As at 23 February 2001
 # Still active

During Peter Shilton's international career, he conceded only 80 goals and managed to keep a clean sheet in 65 of his 125 games. Only one man, Marco van Basten of Holland, scored a hat-trick past him. Had Shilton been selected for every England game played between his first and last appearances, he would have won 216 caps; as it was, he missed 91 games in that period.

TOP 10 ★
OLDEST ENGLAND INTERNATIONALS

	PLAYER	YEAR OF LAST MATCH	AGE YRS	DAYS
1	Stanley Matthews	1957	42	103
2	Peter Shilton	1990	40	292
3	Leslie Compton	1950	38	71
4	David Seaman	2001*	37	186
5	Sam Hardy	1920	36	227
6	Tom Finney	1958	36	200
7	Dave Watson	1982	35	240
8	Jesse Pennington	1920	35	230
9	Frank Hudspeth	1925	35	207#
10	Ian Callaghan	1977	35	185

* Still active
 # Hudspeth was born in April 1892, the day unknown. He was thus 35 years and 177–207 days old

THE 10 FIRST INDUCTEES INTO THE FIFA HALL OF CHAMPIONS

(Player*/country)

1 Franz Beckenbauer, Germany **2** Sir Bobby Charlton, England **3** Johan Cruyff, Holland **4** Eusebio, Portugal **5** Stanley Matthews, England **6** Pelé, Brazil **7** Michel Platini, France **8** Ferenc Puskas, Hungary **9** Alfredo di Stefano, Argentina **10** Lev Yashin, Soviet Union

* In alphabetical order

FIFA launched its first Hall of Champions on 12 January 1998. These were the first 10 retired players inducted into the Hall "for sporting success that contributed to the positive image of the game".

What innovation did motorcycle makers Harley Davidson introduce in 1909?
see p.264 for the answer

A The twist-grip throttle
B The kick-starter
C The crash helmet

International Football

MOST WATCHED WORLD CUP FINALS

	HOST NATION	YEAR	MATCHES	SPECTATORS	AVERAGE
1	USA	1994	52	3,587,538	68,991
2	Brazil	1950	22	1,337,000	60,773
3	Mexico	1970	32	1,673,975	52,312
4	England	1966	32	1,614,677	50,459
5	Italy	1990	52	2,515,168	48,369
6	West Germany	1974	38	1,774,022	46,685
7	France	1998	64	2,775,400	43,366
8	Argentina	1978	38	1,610,215	42,374
9	Mexico	1986	52	2,184,522	42,010
10	Switzerland	1954	26	943,000	36,269

Since the World Cup's launch in 1930, a total of 24,814,267 people have watched the 580 final-stage matches, at an average of 42,783 per game. The worst-attended finals were in Italy in 1934, when the 17 matches were watched by 395,000, at an average of 23,235 per game.

COUNTRIES IN THE WORLD CUP

	COUNTRY	WIN	R/U	3RD	4TH	TOTAL PTS*
1	Brazil	4	2	2	1	27
2	Germany/West Germany	3	3	2	1	26
3	Italy	3	2	1	1	21
4	Argentina	2	2	–	–	14
5	Uruguay	2	–	–	2	10
6	France	1	–	2	1	9
7	Sweden	–	1	2	1	8
8	Holland	–	2	–	1	7
9 =	Czechoslovakia	–	2	–	–	6
=	Hungary	–	2	–	–	6
	England	1	–	–	1	5

* Based on 4 points for winning the tournament, 3 points for runner-up, 2 points for 3rd place, and 1 point for 4th; up to and including the 1998 World Cup

LEAST SUCCESSFUL WORLD CUP COUNTRIES

	COUNTRY	TOURNAMENTS	MATCHES PLAYED	WON
1	South Korea	5	14	0
2 =	El Salvador	2	6	0
=	Bolivia	3	6	0
4	Republic of Ireland	1	5	0
5	Egypt	2	4	0
6 =	Canada	1	3	0
=	Greece	1	3	0
=	Haiti	1	3	0
=	Iraq	1	3	0
=	Japan	1	3	0
=	New Zealand	1	3	0
=	South Africa	1	3	0
=	United Arab Emirates	1	3	0
=	Zaïre	1	3	0

HIGHEST-SCORING WORLD CUP FINALS

	YEAR	GAMES	GOALS	AVERAGE PER GAME
1	1954	26	140	5.38
2	1938	18	84	4.66
3	1934	17	70	4.11
4	1950	22	88	4.00
5	1930	18	70	3.88

	YEAR	GAMES	GOALS	AVERAGE PER GAME
6	1958	35	126	3.60
7	1970	32	95	2.96
8	1982	52	146	2.81
9 =	1962	32	89	2.78
=	1966	32	89	2.78

FRANCE WINS WORLD CUP

Host nation France celebrates its win against Brazil in the 1998 World Cup, one of only seven different victorious countries since the first Cup in 1930.

TOP 10 ⭐
GOALSCORERS IN FULL INTERNATIONALS

	PLAYER	COUNTRY	YEARS	GOALS
1	Ferenc Puskás	Hungary/Spain	1945–56	83
2	Pelé	Brazil	1957–91	77
3	Sándor Kocsis	Hungary	1947–56	75
4	Hossam Hassan*	Egypt	1985–2000	73
5	Gerd Müller	West Germany	1966–74	68
6	Imre Schlosser	Hungary	1906–27	60
7	Kazuyoshi Miura*	Japan	1990–2000	55
8=	Gabriel Batistuta*	Argentina	1991–2000	54
=	Ali Daei*	Iran	1993–2000	54
10	Joachim Streich	East Germany	1969–84	53

* Still active in 2001

TOP 10 RICHEST FOOTBALL CLUBS
(Club/country/income in £)

1 **Manchester United**, England, 110,900,000 **2** **Bayern Munich**, Germany, 83,500,000 **3** **Real Madrid**, Spain, 76,100,000 **4** **Chelsea**, England, 59,100,000 **5** **Juventus**, Italy, 58,500,000 **6** **Barcelona**, Spain, 55,700,000 **7** **Milan**, Italy, 54,100,000 **8** **Lazio**, Italy, 50,000,000 **9** **Internazionale**, Italy, 49,100,000 **10** **Arsenal**, England, 48,600,000

TOP 10 ⭐
MOST EXPENSIVE TRANSFERS

	PLAYER	FROM	TO	YEAR	FEE (£)
1	Luis Figo	Barcelona	Real Madrid	2000	38,700,000
2	Herman Crespi	Parma	Lazio	2000	35,700,000
3	Christian Vieri	Lazio	Inter Milan	1999	34,000,000
4	Marc Overmars	Arsenal	Barcelona	2000	25,000,000
5	Nicolas Anelka	Arsenal	Real Madrid	1999	24,500,000
6	Denilson	Sao Paulo	Real Betis	1998	24,000,000
7	Marcio Amoruso	Udinese	Parma	1999	22,700,000
8	Gabriel Batistuta	Fiorentina	Roma	2000	22,500,000
9	Nicolas Anelka	Real Madrid	Paris St. Germain	2000	22,000,000
10=	Rivaldo	Deportivo	Barcelona	1997	19,000,000
=	Ruud van Nistelrooy	PSV Eindhoven	Manchester United	2001	19,000,000

RAVELLI'S REIGN
Swedish goalkeeper Thomas Ravelli's record number of appearances for his country was unchallenged until Germany's Lothar Matthäus played his 143rd game in February 2000.

TOP 10 ⭐
MOST CAPPED INTERNATIONAL PLAYERS

	PLAYER	COUNTRY	YEARS	CAPS
1	Lothar Matthäus*	West Germany/Germany	1980–2000	150
2=	Claudio Suarez*	Mexico	1992–2000	147
=	Hossam Hassan*	Egypt	1985–2000	147
4	Thomas Ravelli	Sweden	1981–97	143
5=	Majed Abdullah	Saudi Arabia	1978–94	140
=	Mohamed Al-Deayea*	Saudi Arabia	1990–2000	140
7	Cobi Jones*	USA	1992–2000	134
8	Marcelo Balboa*	USA	1988–2000	128
9=	Mohammed Al-Khilaiwi*	South Korea	1992–2000	127
=	Peter Schmeichel*	Denmark	1987–2000	127

* Still active in 2001

TOP 10 EUROPEAN CLUB SIDES WITH THE MOST DOMESTIC LEAGUE TITLES
(Club/country/titles)

1 **Glasgow Rangers**, Scotland, 49 **2** **Linfield**, Northern Ireland, 43 **3** **Glasgow Celtic**, Scotland, 36 **4** **Rapid Vienna**, Austria, 31* **5** **Benfica**, Portugal, 30 **6** **Olympiakos**, Greece, 29 **7** **CSKA Sofia**, Bulgaria, 28 **8** = **Ajax**, Holland, 27; = **Real Madrid**, Spain, 27 **10** = **Ferencvaros**, Hungary, 26; = **Jeunesse Esch**, Luxembourg, 26

* Rapid Vienna also won one German League title, in 1941

In what sport has Park Joo-bong won the most world titles?
see p.273 for the answer

A Badminton
B Trampolining
C Judo

Free Wheelers

STREET SKATEBOARDERS

	SKATEBOARDER/COUNTRY*	POINTS#
1	**Carlos de Andrade**, Brazil	490
2	**Kerry Getz**	470
3	= **Kyle Berard**	445
	= **Eric Koston**	445
5	**Chris Senn**	440
6	**Pat Channita**	406
7	**Rick McCrank**, Canada	377
8	**Ryan Johnson**	340
9	**Chad Fernandez**	320
10	**Andy Macdonald**	310

* All from the US unless otherwise stated

 # Based on skateboarder's best four US events and best two from Europe/Brazil in the World Cup Skateboarding Tour

These skateboarders are ranked by World Cup Skateboarding (WCS), the organization recognized worldwide as the sanctioning body for skateboarding. The World Cup Skateboarding Tour has been held since 1994 and already includes 18 events in nine countries. Despite its name, street skateboarders rarely skate on the actual street itself, but prefer kerbs, benches, handrails, and other elements of urban landscapes.

VERT. SKATEBOARDERS

	SKATEBOARDER/COUNTRY	POINTS*
1	**Bob Burnquist**, Brazil	600
2	**Andy Macdonald**, USA	570
3	**Pierre-Luc Gagnon**, Canada	535
4	**Rune Glifberg**, Denmark	480
5	**Sandro Dias**, Brazil	425
6	**Lincoln Ueda**, Brazil	410
7	**Anthony Furlong**, USA	370
8	**Max Schaaf**, USA	350
9	**Buster Halterman**, USA	325
10	**Cristiano Mateus**, Brazil	320

* Based on skateboarder's best four US events and best two from Europe/Brazil in the World Cup Skateboarding Tour

Vert. skateboarding is skateboarding on the vertical rather than the horizontal plane, which usually involves skateboarding on ramps and other vertical structures specifically designed for skateboarding. Skateboarding first became popular with surfers as a means of keeping in shape when there were no waves to surf, but over the past 40 years the sport has gained worldwide recognition in its own right, with a world ranking system since 1995.

DOWNHILL RIDERS IN THE UCI MOUNTAIN BIKE WORLD CUP, 2000 (MEN)

	RIDER/COUNTRY	POINTS*
1	**Nicolas Vouilloz**, France	1,256
2	**Steve Peat**, Great Britain	1,184
3	**David Vazquez**, Spain	1,166
4	**Mickael Pascal**, France	966
5	**Cedric Gracia**, France	944
6	**Gerwin Peters**, Netherlands	942
7	**Bas De Bever**, Netherlands	919
8	**Eric Carter**, USA	895
9	**Fabien Barel**, France	890
10	**Oscar Saiz**, Spain	854

* Total points scored over a series of eight competitions

DOWNHILL RIDERS IN THE UCI MOUNTAIN BIKE WORLD CUP, 2000 (WOMEN)

	RIDER/COUNTRY	POINTS*
1	**Anne Caroline Chausson**, France	1,340
2	**Missy Giove**, USA	1,203
3	**Katja Repo**, Finland	1,117
4	**Sari Jorgensen**, Switzerland	952
5	**Leigh Donovan**, USA	935
6	**Sabrina Jonnier**, France	934
7	**Marla Streb**, USA	905
8	**Nolvenn Le Caer**, France	897
9	**Tara Llanes**, USA	895
10	**Sarah Stieger**, Switzerland	891

* Total points scored over a series of eight competitions

FINNISH THIRD

Born in Helsinki, Finland, in 1973, Katja Repo has competed in professional cycling events since 1993, and finished third in the 2000 World Cup.

INTERNATIONAL ROLLER HOCKEY COUNTRIES, 2000

	COUNTRY	POINTS*
1	Argentina	2,615
2	Spain	2,585
3	Portugal	2,560
4	Italy	2,485
5	Brazil	2,235
6	France	2,210
7	Switzerland	2,160
8	Angola	2,025
9	Chile	1,980
10	Germany	1,955

* Ranked by the ELO system, which employs a statistical formula to calculate the probability of winning future games based on the results so far attained

LONGEST TOURS DE FRANCE

	WINNER/ COUNTRY/YEAR	STAGES	DISTANCE KM	MILES
1	Lucien Buysse, Belgium, 1926	17	5,745	3,570
2	Firmin Lambot, Belgium, 1919	15	5,560	3,455
3	Gustave Garrigou, France, 1911	15	5,544	3,445
4	Philippe Thys, Belgium, 1920	15	5,503	3,419
5	Léon Scieur, Belgium, 1921	15	5,484	3,408
6	Ottavio Bottecchia, Italy, 1925	18	5,430	3,374
7	Ottavio Bottecchia, 1924	15	5,427	3,372
8	Philippe Thys, 1914	15	5,414	3,364
9	Philippe Thys, 1913	15	5,387	3,347
10	Henri Pélissier, France, 1923	15	5,386	3,347

USA IN TOUR DE FRANCE
After triumphing over illness, Lance Armstrong won the 2000 Tour de France, thereby elevating the USA to fifth place among nationalities competing in the world's most prestigious cycle race.

COUNTRIES WITH THE MOST TOUR DE FRANCE WINNERS

	COUNTRY	WINNERS
1	France	36
2	Belgium	18
3	Italy	9
4	Spain	8
5	USA	5
6	Luxembourg	4
7=	Holland	2
=	Switzerland	2
9=	Denmark	1
=	Germany	1
=	Ireland	1

The Tour de France is the toughest, longest, and most popular cycling race in the world.

OLYMPIC CYCLING COUNTRIES

	COUNTRY	MEDALS GOLD	SILVER	BRONZE	TOTAL
1	France	37	21	23	81
2	Italy	34	15	7	56
3	Great Britain	10	22	18	50
4	USA	12	14	17	43
5	Germany*	11	13	12	36
6	Netherlands	13	15	7	35
7	Australia	7	13	11	31
8=	Belgium	6	8	10	24
=	Soviet Union#	11	4	9	24
10	Denmark	6	7	8	21

* Not including West/East Germany 1968–88

\# Includes Unified Team of 1992; excludes Russia since then

TOP 10 OLDEST CLASSIC CYCLING RACES

(Race/first held)

1 Bordeaux–Paris, 1891 **2** Liège Bastogne–Liège, 1892 **3** Paris–Brussels, 1893 **4** Paris–Roubaix, 1896 **5** Tour de France, 1903 **6** Tour of Lombardy, 1905 **7** Giro d'Italia (Tour of Italy), 1906 **8** Milan–San Remo, 1907 **9** Tour of Flanders, 1913 **10** Grand Prix des Nations, 1932

Did You Know? The first recorded cycle race, held at the Parc de St. Cloud, Paris, on 31 May 1868, over a 2-km (1.24-mile) distance, was won by British doctor James Moore (1847–1935).

Motor Racing

DRIVERS WITH THE MOST GRAND PRIX WINS

DRIVER/COUNTRY		CAREER	WINS*
1	Alain Prost, France	1980–93	51
2	Michael Schumacher, Germany	1991–	44
3	Ayrton Senna, Brazil	1984–94	41
4	Nigel Mansell, UK	1980–95	31
5	Jackie Stewart, UK	1965–73	27
6	=Jim Clark, UK	1960–68	25
	=Niki Lauda, Austria	1971–85	25
8	Juan Manual Fangio, Argentina	1950–58	24
9	Nelson Piquet, Brazil	1978–91	23
10	Damon Hill, UK	1992–99	22

* As at January 2001

FORMULA ONE DRIVERS WHO HAVE RACED THE MOST KMS

DRIVER/COUNTRY		CAREER	KMS RACED*
1	Riccardo Patrese, Italy	1977–93	52,114
2	Alain Prost, France	1980–93	48,971
3	Gerhard Berger, Austria	1984–97	45,655
4	Nelson Piquet, Brazil	1978–91	45,451
5	Graham Hill, UK	1958–75	44,245
6	Jean Alesi, France	1989–	40,565
7	Nigel Mansell, UK	1980–95	39,926
8	Michele Alboreto, Italy	1981–94	39,863
9	Ayrton Senna, Brazil	1984–94	37,940
10	Niki Lauda, Austria	1971–85	37,498

* As at January 2001

TOP 10 DRIVERS WITH THE MOST FORMULA ONE WORLD CHAMPIONSHIP TITLES

(Driver/country/titles)

1 Juan Manuel Fangio, Argentina, 5 **2** Alain Prost, France, 4
3 = Jack Brabham, Australia, 3; = Niki Lauda, Austria, 3; = Nelson Piquet, Brazil, 3;
= Michael Schumacher, Germany, 3; = Ayrton Senna, Brazil, 3; = Jackie Stewart, UK, 3;
9 = Alberto Ascari, Italy, 2; = Jim Clark, UK, 2; = Emerson Fittipaldi, Brazil, 2;
= Mika Hakkinen, Finland, 2; = Graham Hill, UK, 2

FORMULA ONE WORLD CHAMPION DRIVERS AND CONSTRUCTORS OF THE LAST DECADE

DRIVER/COUNTRY	POINTS	YEAR	POINTS	CONSTRUCTOR/COUNTRY
Michael Schumacher, Germany	108	2000	170	Ferrari, Italy
Mika Hakkinen, Finland	76	1999	128	Ferrari
Mika Hakkinen	100	1998	156	McLaren/Mercedes, UK/Germany
Jacques Villeneuve, Canada	81	1997	123	Williams/Renault, UK/France
Damon Hill, UK	97	1996	175	Williams/Renault
Michael Schumacher	102	1995	137	Benetton/Renault, Italy/France
Michael Schumacher	92	1994	118	Williams/Renault
Alain Prost, France	99	1993	168	Williams/Renault
Nigel Mansell, UK	108	1992	164	Williams/Renault
Ayrton Senna, Brazil	96	1991	139	McLaren/Honda, UK/Japan

LATEST WORLD CHAMPION ENDURANCE MOTORBIKE RIDERS

YEAR	RIDER(S)/COUNTRY	BIKE
2000	Peter Linden, Sweden/ Warwick Nowland, UK	Suzuki
1999	Terry Rymer, UK/ Jéhan d'Orgeix, France	Suzuki
1998	Doug Polen, USA/ Christian Lavielle, France	Honda
1997	Peter Goddard, Australia/ Doug Polen, USA	Suzuki
1996	Brian Morrison, UK	Kawasaki
1995	Stephene Mertens, Belgium/ Jean Michel Mattioli, France	Honda
1994	Adrien Morillas, France	Kawasaki
1993	Doug Toland, USA	Kawasaki
1992	Terry Rymer, UK/ Carl Fogarty, UK	Kawasaki
1991	Alex Vieira, Portugal	Kawasaki

The World Endurance Championship includes four 24-hour races, at Le Mans (France), Spa Francorchamps (Belgium), Oschersleben (Germany), and Bol d'Or (France), and two 8-hour races at Estoril (Portugal) and Suzuka (Japan).

HARLEY AND DAVIDSON

In Milwaukee, Wisconsin, in 1901, childhood friends William Harley (1880–1943) and Arthur Davidson (1881–1950) began their first motorcycle-building experiments, based on a bicycle with an engine they built themselves. Davidson's two brothers joined the firm, which steadily increased production and introduced such innovations as the twist-grip throttle (1909). The Harley-Davidson soon became sufficiently established that 20,000 were supplied to the US army in World War I, and 90,000 in World War II. The firm remains the oldest-established and one of the largest motorcycle companies in the world.

WHO WAS · WHO WAS · WHO WAS · WHO WAS ·

TOP 10 ★

MOTORBIKE RIDERS WITH THE MOST GRAND PRIX WINS

	RIDER/COUNTRY	YEARS	RACE WINS
1	Giacomo Agostini, Italy	1965–76	122
2	Angel Nieto, Spain	1969–85	90
3	Mike Hailwood, UK	1959–67	76
4	Rolf Biland, Switzerland	1975–90	56
5	Mick Doohan, Australia	1990–98	54
6	Phil Read, UK	1961–75	52
7	Jim Redman, Southern Rhodesia	1961–66	45
8	Anton Mang, West Germany	1976–88	42
9	Carlo Ubbiali, Italy	1950–60	39
10	John Surtees, UK	1955–60	38

All except Biland were solo machine riders. Britain's Barry Sheene won 23 races during his career and is the only man to win Grands Prix at 50cc and 500cc.

TOP 10 ★

MOTORBIKE RIDERS WITH THE MOST SUPERBIKE WORLD CHAMPIONSHIP WINS

	RIDER/COUNTRY	WINS
1	Carl Fogarty, UK	56
2	Doug Polen, USA	27
3	Raymand Roche, France	23
4	Troy Corser, Australia	19
5 =	Colin Edwards, USA	15
=	John Kocinski, USA	15
7 =	Pier Francesco Chili, Italy	14
=	Scott Russell, USA	14
9	Giancarlo Falappa, Italy	12
10	Aalon Slight, New Zealand	11

Since the race series began in 1988, the World Superbike Championship has become one of the most popular of all motorcycle events, enhanced by the riders' use of familiar road machines with which fans can identify.

TOP 10 ★

DRIVERS IN THE WORLD RALLY CHAMPIONSHIPS

	DRIVER/COUNTRY	WINS*
1 =	Juha Kankkunen, Finland	23
=	Carlos Sainz, Spain	23
3 =	Tommi Mäkinen, Finland	20
=	Colin McRae, UK	20
5 =	Markku Alen, Finland	19
=	Didier Auriol, France	19
7	Hannu Mikkola, Finland	18
8	Massimo Biasion, Italy	17
9	Bjorn Waldegaard, Sweden	16
10	Walter Röhrl, Denmark	14

* As at 1 January 2001

Launched in 1973 under the aegis of the Féderation Internationale de l'Automobile (FIA), the World Rally Championship begins each year in January with the Monte Carlo Rally, after which a further 13 rallies are held across the world.

THE 10 ★

LATEST MANUFACTURERS TO WIN THE WORLD RALLY CHAMPIONSHIPS

YEAR	MANUFACTURER/MODEL
2000	Peugeot, 206 WRC
1999	Toyota, Corolla WRC
1998	Mitsubishi, Lancer Evolution V
1997	Subaru, Impreza WRC
1996	Subaru, Impreza
1995	Subaru, Impreza
1994	Toyota, Celica GT4
1993	Toyota, Celica GT4
1992	Lancia, Integrale Evoluzione
1991	Lancia, Integrale 16V

The first World Rally Championship was won by an Alpine Renault, since when the event has been dominated by Lancias, which have won 10 times.

THE 10 ★

LATEST WINNERS OF THE WORLD RALLY DRIVERS CHAMPIONSHIP

YEAR	DRIVER/COUNTRY
2000	Marcus Grönholm, Finland
1999	Tommi Mäkinen, Finland
1998	Tommi Mäkinen
1997	Tommi Mäkinen
1996	Tommi Mäkinen
1995	Colin McRae, UK
1994	Didier Auriol, France
1993	Juha Kankkunen, Finland
1992	Carlos Sainz, Spain
1991	Juha Kankkunen

TOP 10 ★

MONTE CARLO RALLY-WINNING CARS

	CAR	WINS*
1	Lancia	12
2 =	Hotchkiss	6
=	Renault	6
4	Ford	5
5	Porsche	4
6 =	Mini-Cooper	3
=	Mitsubishi	3
=	Subaru	3
=	Toyota	3
10 =	Citroën	2
=	Delahaye	2
=	Fiat	2
=	Opel	2
=	Saab	2

* Up to and including 2001

The Monte Carlo Rally has been run since 1911 (with breaks in 1913–23, 1940–48, 1957, and 1974). The appearance of Hotchkiss in 2nd place is perhaps surprising, but it won the Rally six times between 1932 and 1950.

After whom or what are Derby races named? **A** Edward Stanley, 12th Earl of Derby
see p.268 for the answer **B** The city of Derby
C From the French *d'arbre*

Golfing Greats

TOP 10 ★
YOUNGEST WINNERS OF THE BRITISH OPEN

	PLAYER/COUNTRY	AGE YRS	AGE MTHS
1	Tom Morris Jr., UK	17	5
2	Willie Auchterlonie, UK	21	1
3	Severiano Ballesteros, Spain	22	3
4	John H. Taylor, UK	23	3
5	Gary Player, South Africa	23	8
6	Bobby Jones, USA	24	3
7	Tiger Woods, USA	24	6
8	Peter Thomson, Australia	24	11
9 =	Arthur Havers, UK	25	0
=	Tony Jacklin, UK	25	0

The dates of birth for Tom Kidd and Jack Simpson, the 1873 and 1884 winners, have never been established. Hugh Kirkaldy, the 1891 winner, was born in 1865 and could have been either 25 or 26 when he won the title, but, again, his exact date of birth has never been confirmed.

TOP 10 ★
BRITISH AND EUROPEAN PLAYERS WITH THE MOST WINS IN THE RYDER CUP

	PLAYER/COUNTRY	WINS
1	Nick Faldo, UK	23
2	Severiano Ballesteros, Spain	20
3	Bernhard Langer, Germany	18
4	José Maria Olazabal, Spain	15
5 =	Peter Oosterhuis, UK	14
=	Ian Woosnam, UK	14
7 =	Bernard Gallacher, UK	13
=	Tony Jacklin, UK	13
9	Neil Coles, UK	12
10 =	Brian Barnes, UK	11
=	Colin Montgomerie, UK	11
=	Christy O'Connor, UK	11

The Ryder Cup was launched in 1927 by Samuel Ryder. Held every two years, the venues alternate between the US and Great Britain.

TOP 10 ★
LOWEST WINNING SCORES IN THE US MASTERS

	PLAYER*	YEAR	SCORE
1	Tiger Woods	1997	270
2 =	Jack Nicklaus	1965	271
=	Raymond Floyd	1976	271
4 =	Ben Hogan	1953	274
=	Ben Crenshaw	1995	274
6 =	Severiano Ballesteros, Spain	1980	275
=	Fred Couples	1992	275
8 =	Arnold Palmer	1964	276
=	Jack Nicklaus	1975	276
=	Tom Watson	1977	276
=	Nick Faldo, UK	1996	276

* All from the US unless otherwise stated

The US Masters, the brainchild of American amateur golfer Robert Tyre "Bobby" Jones, is the only major played on the same course each year, at Augusta, Georgia. The course was built on the site of an old nursery, and the abundance of flowers, shrubs, and plants is a reminder of its former days, with each of the 18 holes named after the plants growing adjacent to it.

TOP 10 ★
WINNERS OF WOMEN'S MAJORS

	PLAYER*	TITLES
1	Patty Berg	16
2 =	Louise Suggs	13
=	Mickey Wright	13
4	Babe Zaharias	12
5 =	Julie Inkster	8
=	Betsy Rawls	8
7	JoAnne Carner	7
8 =	Pat Bradley	6
=	Glenna Collett Vare	6
=	Betsy King	6
=	Patty Sheehan	6
=	Kathy Whitworth	6

* All from the US

BEST OF THE REST

Swedish golfer Annika Sorenstam (b. 1970) won more LPGA tournaments (18) than any other player in the 1990s, and is the highest earning non-American woman golfer of all time.

TOP 10 ★
CAREER EARNINGS BY WOMEN GOLFERS

	PLAYER*/YEARS	WINNINGS# ($)
1	Betsy King, 1977–2000	6,828,688
2	Annika Sorenstam, Sweden, 1992–2000	6,200,596
3	Karrie Webb, Australia, 1995–2000	6,162,895
4	Julie Inkster, 1983–2000	6,057,400
5	Beth Daniel, 1979–2000	6,022,461
6	Dottie Pepper, 1987–2000	5,882,131
7	Pat Bradley, 1974–2000	5,743,605
8	Patty Sheehan, 1980–2000	5,500,983
9	Meg Mallon, 1987–2000	5,466,338
10	Nancy Lopez, 1977–2000	5,297,955

* All from the US unless otherwise stated
# As at 20 November 2000

TOP 10 ⭐
WINS IN A US SEASON

	PLAYER	YEAR	WINS
1	Byron Nelson	1945	18
2	Ben Hogan	1946	13
3	Sam Snead	1950	11
4	Ben Hogan	1948	10
5	Paul Runyan	1933	9
=	Tiger Woods	2000	9*
7 =	Horton Smith	1929	8
=	Gene Sarazen	1930	8
=	Harry Cooper	1937	8
=	Sam Snead	1938	8
=	Henry Picard	1939	8
=	Byron Nelson	1944	8
=	Arnold Palmer	1960	8
=	Johnny Miller	1974	8
=	Tiger Woods	1999	8

* *Woods' total in 2000 includes his British Open win which, since 1995, has been included as an Official US PGA Tour event*

Source: *PGA*

Having won eight Tour events in 1944, Byron Nelson went on to shatter the US record the following year with a stunning 18 wins.

TOP 10 MONEY-WINNING GOLFERS, 2000

(Player*/winnings in 2000#, $)

1 **Tiger Woods**, 9,501,387 **2** **Phil Mickelson**, 4,791,743
3 **Ernie Els**, South Africa, 3,855,829 **4** **Hal Sutton**, 3,061,444 **5** **Lee Westwood**, UK,
2,966,066 **6** **Vijay Singh**, Fiji, 2,702,858 **7** **Darren Clarke**, UK, 2,671,040 **8** **Mike Weir**,
2,547,829 **9** **Jesper Parnevik**, Sweden, 2,499,079 **10** **David Duval**, 2,471,244

* *All from the US unless otherwise stated*
# *As at 18 December 2000*

This list is based on winnings on the world's five top Tours: US PGA Tour, European PGA Tour, PGA Tour of Japan, Australasian PGA Tour, and FNB Tour of South Africa.

TOP 10 ⭐
PLAYERS TO WIN THE MOST MAJORS IN A CAREER

	PLAYER*	BRITISH OPEN	US OPEN	US MASTERS	PGA	TOTAL
1	Jack Nicklaus	3	4	6	5	18
2	Walter Hagen	4	2	0	5	11
3 =	Ben Hogan	1	4	2	2	9
=	Gary Player, South Africa	3	1	3	2	9
5	Tom Watson	5	1	2	0	8
6 =	Bobby Jones	3	4	0	0	7
=	Arnold Palmer	2	1	4	0	7
=	Gene Sarazen	1	2	1	3	7
=	Sam Snead	1	0	3	3	7
=	Harry Vardon, UK	6	1	0	0	7

* *All from the US unless otherwise stated*

GOOD AS GOLD

In a career spanning over 30 years, Jack Nicklaus, nicknamed the Golden Bear, won more majors than any other player in golfing history.

Horse Racing

JOCKEYS IN THE GRAND NATIONAL

	JOCKEY*	YEARS	WINS
1	George Stevens	1856–70	5
2	Tom Oliver	1838–53	4
3 =	Mr. Tommy Pickernell	1860–75	3
=	Mr. Tommy Beasley	1880–89	3
=	Arthur Nightingall	1890–1901	3
=	Ernie Piggott	1912–19	3
=	Mr. Jack Anthony	1911–20	3
=	Brian Fletcher	1968–74	3
9 =	Mr. Alec Goodman	1852–66	2
=	John Page	1867–72	2
=	Mr. Maunsell Richardson	1873–74	2
=	Mr. Ted Wilson	1884–85	2
=	Percy Woodland	1903–13	2
=	Arthur Thompson	1948–52	2
=	Bryan Marshall	1953–54	2
=	Pat Taaffe	1955–70	2
=	Fred Winter	1957–62	2
=	Richard Dunwoody	1986–94	2
=	Carl Llewellyn	1992–98	2

Amateur riders are traditionally indicated by the prefix "Mr."

DERBY

The man who gave his name to horse races in the UK, US, and elsewhere was Edward Stanley, 12th Earl of Derby (1752–1834). He offered a prize for a race for 3-year-old fillies, which was named after The Oaks, the house he lived in near the Epsom racecourse in Surrey, UK, and in 1780 he introduced a race for 3-year-old fillies or colts, which was named the Derby. Further Derbies followed – the Hong Kong Derby was first run in 1873, and the Kentucky Derby followed shortly after in 1875 – while the name came to be used in a more general way to describe other sporting events.

JOCKEYS IN THE ENGLISH CLASSICS

	JOCKEY	YEARS	1,000 GUINEAS	2,000 GUINEAS	DERBY	OAKS	ST. LEGER	WINS
1	Lester Piggott	1954–92	2	5	9	6	8	30
2	Frank Buckle	1792–1827	6	5	5	9	2	27
3	Jem Robinson	1817–48	5	9	6	2	2	24
4	Fred Archer	1874–86	2	4	5	4	6	21
5 =	Bill Scott	1821–46	0	3	4	3	9	19
=	Jack Watts	1883–97	4	2	4	4	5	19
7	Willie Carson	1972–94	2	4	4	4	3	17
8 =	John Day	1826–41	5	4	0	5	2	16
=	George Fordham	1859–83	7	3	1	5	0	16
10	Joe Childs	1912–33	2	2	3	4	4	15

TOP 10 JOCKEYS IN THE PRIX DE L'ARC DE TRIOMPHE

(Jockey/wins)

1 = Jacko Doyasbère, 4; = Pat Eddery, 4; = Freddy Head, 4; = Yves Saint-Martin, 4

5 = Enrico Camici, 3; = Charlie Elliott, 3; = Olivier Peslier, 3; = Lester Piggot, 3; = Roger Poincelet, 3; = Charles Semblat, 3

JOCKEYS OF ALL TIME IN THE UK

	JOCKEY	CAREER	CAREER FLAT WINNERS
1	Gordon Richards	1921–54	4,870
2	Lester Piggott	1948–95	4,513
3	Pat Eddery	1969–2000	4,232
4	Willie Carson	1962–96	3,828
5	Doug Smith	1931–67	3,111
6	Joe Mercer	1950–85	2,810
7	Fred Archer	1870–86	2,748
8	Edward Hide	1951–85	2,591
9	George Fordham	1850–84	2,587
10	Eph Smith	1930–65	2,313

When Pat Eddery rode Silver Partriarch to victory in the St. Leger at Doncaster on 13 September 1997, he became only the third member of the elite "4,000 club" – jockeys who had won more than 4,000 races.

MONEY-WINNING JOCKEYS, 2000

	JOCKEY	WINS	PRIZE MONEY (£)*
1	Richard Quinn	140	2,410,519
2	Kevin Darley	155	2,308,043
3	Pat Eddery	127	1,914,121
4	Richard Hills	81	1,616,370
5	Richard Hughes	102	1,441,774
6	Kieren Fallon	59	1,383,116
7	John Reid	71	1,365,981
8	Frankie Dettori	47	1,324,141
9	Jimmy Fortune	93	1,162,768
10	Michael Hills	73	1,049,495

Total, including money won for coming 2nd or 3rd

Source: Racing Post

Prize monies are shared between various interested parties, including the horse owner, trainer, and yard staff. Jockeys will generally receive around five per cent of the total prize money.

TOP 10 ★
JOCKEYS IN THE 1,000 GUINEAS

	JOCKEY	YEARS	WINS
1	George Fordham	1859–83	7
2	Frank Buckle	1818–27	6
3=	Jem Robinson	1824–44	5
=	John Day	1826–40	5
5=	Jack Watts	1886–97	4
=	Fred Rickaby Jr	1913–17	4
=	Charlie Elliott	1924–44	4
8=	Bill Arnull	1817–32	3
=	Nat Flatman	1835–57	3
=	Tom Cannon	1866–84	3
=	Charlie Wood	1880–87	3
=	Dick Perryman	1926–41	3
=	Harry Wragg	1934–45	3
=	Rae Johnstone	1935–50	3
=	Gordon Richards	1942–51	3
=	Walter Swinburn	1989–93	3

Raced at Newmarket, the 1,000 Guineas, for three-year-old fillies, was first run in 1814. In addition to his wins in this race, jockey George "The Demon" Fordham (1837–87) achieved a further 2,580 victories in his career.

TOP 10 ★
JOCKEYS IN THE 2,000 GUINEAS

	JOCKEY	YEARS	WINS
1	Jem Robinson	1825–48	9
2	John Osborne	1857–88	6
3=	Frank Buckle	1810–27	5
=	Charlie Elliott	1923–49	5
=	Lester Piggott	1957–92	5
6=	John Day	1826–41	4
=	Fred Archer	1874–85	4
=	Tom Cannon	1878–89	4
=	Herbert Jones	1900–09	4
=	Willie Carson	1972–89	4

In 1824, Jem Robinson (1793–1865) won a wager that he would win the Derby and the Oaks, and marry within the same week.

TOP 10 ★
NATIONAL HUNT JOCKEYS, 2000

	JOCKEY	PERCENTAGE WON	RUNS	WINS
1	Tony McCoy	27	531	144
2	Richard Johnson	19	623	122
3	Tony Dobbin	23	264	61
4	Adrian Maguire	18	277	51
5	Norman Williamson	18	276	50
6	Mick Fitzgerald	20	227	47
7=	Noel Fehily	24	150	36
=	Carl Llewellyn	11	302	36
9	Timmy Murphy	13	256	34
10	Andrew Thornton	11	300	33

Source: Racing Post

TOP 10 ★
TRAINERS WITH THE MOST FLAT RACE WINS, 2000

	TRAINER	TOTAL PRIZE MONEY (£)*	WINS
1	Richard Hannon	1,738,073	135
2	Mark Johnston	1,661,440	130
3	John Dunlop	1,702,587	97
4	Sir Michael Stoute	2,966,712	91
5	Mick Channon	1,183,629	90
6	John Gosden	1,550,983	82
7=	Alan Berry	566,386	73
=	David Nicholls	763,121	73
9	Barry Hills	936,916	72
10	Henry Cecil	1,154,697	62

* Including money won for coming 2nd or 3rd
Source: Racing Post

TOP 10 ★
FASTEST WINNING TIMES OF THE EPSOM DERBY

	HORSE	YEAR	TIME MIN	SEC
1	Lammtarra	1995	2	32.31
2	Mahmoud	1936	2	33.80
3	Kahyasi	1988	2	33.84
4	High-Rise	1998	2	33.88
5	Reference Point	1987	2	33.90
6=	Hyperion	1933	2	34.00
=	Windsor Lad	1934	2	34.00
=	Generous	1991	2	34.00
9	Erhaab	1994	2	34.16
10	Golden Fleece	1982	2	34.27

TOP 10 ★
MONEY-WINNING STALLIONS IN THE UK, 2000

	STALLION	WINS	TOTAL PRIZE MONEY (£)*
1	Sadler's Wells	77	2,571,043
2	Grand Lodge	40	1,486,179
3	Indian Ridge	74	887,576
4	Rainbow Quest	41	671,612
5	Fairy King	28	664,226
6	Machiavellian	39	642,832
7	Danehill	37	642,173
8	Common Grounds	61	629,990
9	Caerleon	44	629,894
10	Diesis	31	624,823

* Including money won for coming 2nd or 3rd
Source: Racing Post

TOP 10 JOCKEYS IN A FLAT RACING SEASON
(Jockey/year/wins)

❶ Gordon Richards, 1947, 269 ❷ Gordon Richards, 1949, 261
❸ Gordon Richards, 1933, 259 ❹ Fred Archer, 1885, 246 ❺ Fred Archer, 1884, 241
❻ Fred Archer, 1883, 232 ❼ Gordon Richards, 1952, 231 ❽ Fred Archer, 1878, 229
❾ Gordon Richards, 1951, 227 ❿ Gordon Richards, 1948, 224

Did You Know? The first ever sporting event to be televised live in the UK was the Derby on 3 June 1931. Only employees of the television company and journalists were able to view the broadcast.

Rugby Records

TOP 10 ★
POINT SCORERS IN A RUGBY LEAGUE MATCH

	PLAYER	MATCH/YEAR	POINTS
1	George West	Hull Kingston Rovers v Brookland Rovers, 1905	53
2	Jim Sullivan	Wigan v Flimby & Fothergill, 1925	44
3	Sammy Lloyd	Castleford v Millom, 1973	43
4 =	Dean Marwood	Workington Town v Highfield, 1992	42
=	Darren Carter	Barrow v Nottingham City, 1994	42
=	Dean Marwood	Workington Town v Leigh, 1995	42
=	Iestyn Harris	Leeds Rhions v Huddersfield Giants, 1999	42
8 =	Paul Loughlin	St. Helens v Carlisle, 1986	40
=	Shaun Edwards	Wigan v Swinton, 1992	40
=	Martin Offiah	Wigan v Leeds, 1992	40
=	Martin Pearson	Featherstone Rovers v Whitehaven, 1995	40
=	Lee Briars	Warrington Wolves v York, 2000	40

TOP 10 ★
HIGHEST-SCORING VARSITY MATCHES*

	WINNERS	SEASON	SCORE
1	Oxford	1909–10	35–3
2	Cambridge	1975–76	34–12
3	Cambridge	1935–36	33–3
4	Cambridge	1984–85	32–6
5	Cambridge	1926–27	30–5
6	Cambridge	1934–35	29–4
7	Oxford	1988–89	27–7
8	Cambridge	1978–79	25–7
9	Oxford	1910–11	23–18
10 =	Cambridge	1989–90	22–13
=	Cambridge	1927–28	22–14

* Based on score of winning team

TOP 10 AUSTRALIAN RUGBY LEAGUE TEAMS
(Team/Grand Final wins)

❶ South Sydney, 20 ❷ St. George, 15 ❸ = Balmain, 11; = Eastern Suburbs, 11 ❺ = Canterbury-Bankstown, 6; = Manly-Warringah, 6 ❼ = Brisbane Broncos, 4; = Parramatta, 4; = Western Suburbs, 4 ❿ Canberra, 3

TOP 10 ★
TRY SCORERS IN THE 2000 SUPER LEAGUE*

	PLAYER/CLUB	TRIES
1 =	Sean Long, St. Helen's	20
=	Tommy Martyn, St. Helen's	20
=	Darren Rogers, Castleford Tigers	20
4 =	Steve Renouf, Wigan Warriors	18
=	Jason Robinson, Wigan Warriors	18
6 =	Steve Collins, Hull FC	17
=	Kevin Iro, St. Helen's	17
=	Kris Radlinski, Wigan Warriors	17
9 =	Brett Dallas, Wigan Warriors	16
=	Alan Hunte, Warrington Wolves	16
=	Martin Moana, Halifax Blue Sox	16
=	Robbie Paul, Bradford Bulls	16
=	Keith Senior, Leeds Rhinos	16

* League matches only; excluding play-offs

TOP 10 ★
SCORING TEAMS IN CHALLENGE CUP FINALS*

	TEAM	POINTS
1	Wigan Warriors	414
2	Leeds Rhinos	309
3	St. Helens	211
4	Widnes Vikings	158
5	Bradford Bulls	137
6	Huddersfield Giants	130
7	Warrington Wolves	129
8	Hull FC	128
9	Wakefield Trinity Wildcats	118
10	Halifax Blue Sox	110

* Including the two-stage finals during World War II

TOP 10 ★
WINNERS OF THE CHALLENGE CUP

	CLUB	YEARS	WINS
1	Wigan Warriors	1924–95	16
2	Leeds Rhinos	1910–99	11
3 =	Widnes Vikings	1930–84	7
=	St. Helens	1956–97	7
5	Huddersfield Giants	1913–53	6
6 =	Bradford Bulls	1906–2000	5
=	Halifax Blue Sox	1903–87	5
=	Wakefield Trinity Wildcats	1909–63	5
=	Warrington Wolves	1905–74	5
10 =	Castleford Tigers	1935–86	4

The first Challenge Cup final, then known as the Northern Union Cup, was held at Headingley, Leeds, on 24 April 1897. When Wigan was eliminated by Salford in 1996, it ended Wigan's eight-year run without defeat in the Challenge Cup.

TOP 10 ★
POINT SCORERS IN THE SUPER LEAGUE*

	CLUB	TOTAL POINTS
1	St. Helens	4,237
2	Wigan Warriors	4,184
3	Bradford Bulls	3,935
4	Leeds Rhinos	3,363
5	Halifax Blue Sox	3,086
6	Warrington Wolves	2,852
7	London Broncos	2,742
8	Castleford Tigers	2,625
9	Sheffield Eagles	2,027
10	Salford City Reds	1,815

* Over the five seasons up to and including 2000

TOP 10 ★
HIGHEST-SCORING INTERNATIONAL RUGBY UNION MATCHES*

	MATCH (WINNERS FIRST)	DATE	SCORE
1	Hong Kong v Singapore	27 Oct 1994	164–13
2	New Zealand v Japan	4 June 1995	145–17
3	Japan v Thailand	4 Nov 1996	141–10
4	Hong Kong v Taiwan	9 Nov 1996	114–12
5	South Korea v Malaysia	5 Nov 1996	112–5
6	England v Holland	14 Nov 1998	110–0
7	Italy v Poland	26 May 1996	107–19
8	Italy v Czech Republic	18 May 1994	104–8
9=	Argentina v Paraguay	24 Sep 1995	103–9
=	Hong Kong v Malaysia	3 Nov 1996	103–5
=	Japan v Malaysia	26 Oct 1994	103–9

* 1 March 1993 to 1 January 2001, ranked by winner's score

TOP 10 ★
INDIVIDUAL POINT SCORERS IN ONE WORLD CUP TOURNAMENT

	PLAYER/COUNTRY	YEAR	PTS
1	Grant Fox, New Zealand	1987	126
2	Gavin Hastings, Scotland	1995	104
3	Thierry Lacroix, France	1995	103
4	Gozalo Quesada, Argentina	1999	102
5	Andrew Mehrtens, New Zealand	1995	84
6	Michael Lynagh, Australia	1987	82
7	Rob Andrew, England	1995	70
8	Ralph Keyes, Ireland	1991	68
9	Michael Lynagh, Australia	1991	66
10	Gavin Hastings, Scotland	1987	62

TOP 10 ★
POINT SCORERS IN MAJOR INTERNATIONALS*

	PLAYER/COUNTRY	YEARS	PTS
1	Neil Jenkins, Wales	1991–2000	939
2	Michael Lynagh, Australia	1984–95	911
3	Diego Dominguez, Italy	1991–2000	787
4	Gavin Hastings, Scotland	1986–95	733
5	Grant Fox, New Zealand	1985–93	645
6	Andrew Mehrtens, New Zealand	1995–99	594
7	Matthew Burke, Australia	1993–99	509
8	Gareth Rees, Canada	1986–99	492
9	Stefano Bettarello, Italy	1979–88	483
10	Hugo Porta, Argentina	1973–80	408

* Full International Board countries and British Lions

TOP 10 ★
CLUBS PROVIDING THE MOST PLAYERS FOR BRITISH LIONS' TOURS

	CLUB	PLAYERS
1	Cardiff	25
2	Newport	19
3	Swansea	14
4	Llanelli	13
5=	Oxford University	10
=	Queen's University, Belfast	10
7	Blackheath	9
8=	Cambridge University	8
=	Harlequins	8
=	Leicester	8
=	London Scottish	8
=	London Welsh	8

TOP 10 ★
MOST CAPPED RUGBY UNION PLAYERS

	PLAYER/COUNTRY	YEARS	CAPS
1	Philippe Sella, France	1982–95	111
2	David Campese, Australia	1982–96	101
3	Serge Blanco, France	1980–91	93
4	Shaun Fitzpatrick, New Zealand	1987–97	92
5	Rory Underwood, England/British Lions	1984–96	91
6	Jason Leonard*, England/British Lions	1990–2000	90
7	Mike Gibson, Ireland/British Lions	1964–79	81
8	Willie John McBride, Ireland/British Lions	1962–75	80
9	Ieuan Evans, Wales/British Lions	1985–97	79
10	Rob Andrew, England/British Lions	1985–97	76

* Still active 2001

TOP 10 ★
BRITISH LIONS' BIGGEST TEST WINS

	OPPONENTS	TEST/YEAR	SCORE
1	Australia	2nd Test, 1966	31–0
2	South Africa	2nd Test, 1974	28–9
3=	South Africa	3rd Test, 1974	26–9
=	South Africa	1st Test, 1997	26–16
5=	Australia	2nd Test, 1950	24–3
=	Australia	2nd Test, 1959	24–3
7	South Africa	1st Test, 1955	23–22
8	South Africa	3rd Test, 1938	21–16
9	New Zealand	2nd Test, 1993	20–7
10=	Australia	2nd Test, 1989	19–12
=	Australia	3rd Test, 1989	19–18

This list is based on the greatest number of points scored by the Lions, not the greatest margin.

TOP 10 RANKED RUGBY UNION COUNTRIES*

❶ New Zealand ❷ England ❸ Australia ❹ South Africa ❺ France ❻ Wales ❼ Argentina ❽ Scotland ❾ Ireland ❿ Western Samoa

* As at 29 December 2000

In what Olympic sport has the USA won more than three times as many medals as the next country?
A Cycling
B Swimming
C Figure skating

see p.275 for the answer

What a Racquet

WINNERS OF THE TABLE TENNIS WORLD CHAMPIONSHIP

	COUNTRY	MEN'S	WOMEN'S	TOTAL
1	China	13	13	26
2	Japan	7	8	15
3	Hungary	12	–	12
4	Czechoslovakia	6	3	9
5	Romania	–	5	5
6	Sweden	4	–	4
7=	England	1	2	3
=	USA	1	2	3
9	Germany	–	2	2
10=	Austria	1	–	1
=	North Korea	–	1	1
=	South Korea	–	1	1
=	USSR	–	1	1

Originally a European event, table tennis was later extended to a world championship. This Top 10 takes account of men's wins since 1926 and women's since 1934. Winning men's teams receive the Swaythling Cup, and women the Marcel Corbillon Cup. The championship has been held biennially since 1959.

WINNERS OF WOMEN'S GRAND SLAM SINGLES TITLES

	PLAYER/NATIONALITY	A	F	W	US	TOTAL
1	Margaret Court (née Smith), Aus	11	5	3	5	24
2	Steffi Graf, Ger	4	5	7	5	21
3	Helen Wills-Moody, USA	0	4	8	7	19
4=	Chris Evert-Lloyd, USA	2	7	3	6	18
=	Martina Navratilova, Cze/USA	3	2	9	4	18
6=	Billie Jean King (née Moffitt), USA	1	1	6	4	12
=	Suzanne Lenglen, Fra	0	6	6	0	12
8=	Maureen Connolly, USA	1	2	3	3	9
=	Monica Seles, Yug/USA	4	3	0	2	9
10	Molla Mallory (née Bjurstedt), USA	0	0	0	8	8

A – Australian Open; F – French Open; W – Wimbledon; US – US Open

WINNERS OF INDIVIDUAL OLYMPIC TENNIS MEDALS

	PLAYER/COUNTRY/YEARS	GOLD	TOTAL
1	Max Decugis, France, 1900–20	4	6
2	Kitty McKane, GB, 1920–24	1	5
3=	Reginald Doherty, GB, 1900–08	3	4
=	Gunnar Setterwall, Sweden, 1908–12	0	4
5=	Charles Dixon, GB, 1908–12	0	3
=	Mary Joe Fernandez, USA, 1992–96	2	3
=	Suzanne Lenglen, France, 1920	2	3
=	Harold Mahony, Ireland, 1900	0	3
=	Jana Novotna, Czech Republic, 1988–96	0	3
=	Vince Richards, USA, 1924	2	3
=	Josiah Ritchie, GB, 1908	1	3
=	Arantxa Sanchez-Vicario, Spain, 1992–96	0	3
=	Charles Winslow, South Africa, 1912–20	2	3

TOP 10 MALE TENNIS PLAYERS*

(Player/weeks at No. 1)

❶ Pete Sampras, USA, 276 ❷ Ivan Lendl, Czechoslovakia, 270 ❸ Jimmy Connors, USA, 268 ❹ John McEnroe, USA, 170 ❺ Bjorn Borg, Sweden, 109 ❻ Stefan Edberg, Sweden, 72 ❼ Jim Courier, USA, 58 ❽ Andre Agassi, USA, 51 ❾ Ilie Nastase, Romania, 40 ❿ Mats Wilander, Sweden, 20

* Based on weeks at No. 1 in ATP rankings (1973 to 2000)

BRILLIANT CAREER

In 1995, Andre Agassi was the 12th player to be ranked world No. 1. In 1999, he became only the fifth male player to complete a Grand Slam.

THE 10 ★
LATEST WINNERS OF THE SQUASH WORLD OPEN (FEMALE)

YEAR*	PLAYER/COUNTRY
1999	Cassandra Campion, England
1998	Sarah Fitz-Gerald, Australia
1997	Sarah Fitz-Gerald
1996	Sarah Fitz-Gerald
1995	Michelle Martin, Australia
1994	Michelle Martin
1993	Michelle Martin
1992	Susan Devoy, New Zealand
1991	Susan Devoy
1990	Martine le Moignan, Guernsey

* No championship in 2000

Source: *Women's International Squash Players Assoc.*

THE 10 ★
LATEST WINNERS OF THE SQUASH WORLD OPEN (MALE)

YEAR*	PLAYER/COUNTRY
1999	Peter Nichol, Scotland
1998	Jonathon Power, Canada
1997	Rodney Eyles, Australia
1996	Jansher Khan, Pakistan
1995	Jansher Khan
1994	Jansher Khan
1993	Jansher Khan
1992	Jansher Khan
1991	Rodney Martin, Australia
1990	Jansher Khan

* No championship in 2000

Source: *Professional Squash Association*

TOP 10 ★
PLAYERS WITH THE MOST BADMINTON WORLD TITLES

	PLAYER/COUNTRY	MALE/FEMALE	TITLES
1	Park Joo-bong, South Korea	M	5
2 =	Han Aiping, China	F	3
=	Li Lingwei, China	F	3
=	Guan Weizhan, China	F	3
=	Lin Ying, China	F	3
6 =	Tian Bingyi, China	M	2
=	Christian Hadinata, Indonesia	M	2
=	Lene Köppen, Denmark	F	2
=	Kim Moon-soo, South Korea	M	2
=	Chung Myung-hee, South Korea	F	2
=	Nora Perry, England	F	2
=	Yang Yang, China	M	2
=	Li Yongbo, China	M	2

TOP 10 ★
DAVIS CUP-WINNING TEAMS

	COUNTRY	WINS
1	USA	31
2	Australia	21
3	France	8
4	Sweden	7
5	Australasia	6
6	British Isles	5
7	Great Britain	4
8	West Germany	2
9 =	Czechoslovakia	1
=	Germany	1
=	Italy	1
=	South Africa	1

The UK has been represented by the British Isles from 1900 to 1921, England from 1922 to 1928, and Great Britain since 1929. The combined Australia/New Zealand team took part as Australasia between 1905 and 1922. Australia first entered a separate team in 1923 and New Zealand in 1924. South Africa's sole win was gained when, for political reasons, India refused to meet them in the 1974 final.

TOP 10 ★
CAREER MONEY WINNING WOMEN TENNIS PLAYERS

	PLAYER/COUNTRY	WINNINGS ($)*
1	Steffi Graf, Germany	21,895,277
2	Martina Navratilova, USA	20,396,399
3	Arantxa Sanchez-Vicario, Spain	15,747,252
4	Martina Hingis, Switzerland	15,080,325
5	Monica Seles, USA	12,891,708
6	Lindsay Davenport, USA	11,934,628
7	Jana Novotna, Czech Republic	11,249,134
8	Conchita Martinez, Spain	9,335,263
9	Chris Evert-Lloyd, USA	8,896,195
10	Gabriela Sabatini, Argentina	8,785,850

* To end of 2000 season

GOLDEN GIRL

In 1995 the first player ever to win all four Grand Slam titles four times each, Steffi Graf is also the sport's highest-earning female player of all time.

Water Sports

POWERING AHEAD

American powerboat racer Bill Seebold retired in 1997 after 46 years in the sport, during which he won 912 races and some 60 championships.

TOP 10 ★
FASTEST WINNING TIMES OF THE OXFORD AND CAMBRIDGE BOAT RACE

	YEAR	WINNER	MIN:SEC
1	1998	Cambridge	16.19
2	1999	Cambridge	16.41
3	1984	Oxford	16.45
4	1996	Cambridge	16.58
5	1991	Oxford	16.59
6	1993	Cambridge	17.00
7	1985	Oxford	17.11
8	1990	Oxford	17.15
9=	1974	Oxford	17.35
=	1988	Oxford	17.35

The Boat Race was first rowed at Henley in 1829 and was won by Oxford. The course from Putney to Mortlake (6.78 km/4 miles 374 yards) has been used since 1843, although the race was rowed in the opposite direction in 1846, 1856, and 1863. The race has been rowed annually since 1856, except during the two World Wars.

TOP 10 ★
POWERBOAT DRIVERS WITH THE MOST RACE WINS

	DRIVER	COUNTRY	WINS
1	Bill Seebold	USA	912
2	Jimbo McConnell	USA	217
3	Chip Hanuer	USA	203
4	Steve Curtis	UK	185
5	Mikeal Frode	Sweden	152
6	Neil Holmes	UK	147

	DRIVER	COUNTRY	WINS
7	Peter Bloomfield	UK	126
8	Renato Molinari	Italy	113
9	Cees Van der Valden	Netherlands	98
10	Bill Muncey	USA	96

Source: Raceboat International

TOP 10 ★
WINNERS OF THE MOST SURFING WORLD CHAMPIONSHIPS

	SURFER/COUNTRY	WINS
1	Kelly Slater, USA	6
2	Mark Richards, Australia	4
3	Tom Curren, USA	3
4=	Tom Carroll, Australia	2
=	Damien Hardman, Australia	2
6=	Wayne Bartholemew, Australia	1
=	Sunny Garcia, USA	1
=	Derek Ho, USA	1
=	Barton Lynch, Australia	1
=	Martin Potter, UK	1
=	Shaun Tomson, South Africa	1
=	Peter Townend, Australia	1
=	Mark Occhilupo, Australia	1

TOP 10 ★
WATERSKIERS WITH THE MOST WORLD CUP WINS

	SKIER/COUNTRY	MALE/FEMALE	SLALOM	JUMP	TOTAL
1	Andy Mapple, UK	M	29	-	29
2	Emma Sheers, Australia	F	2	15	17
3	Jaret Llewellyn, Canada	M	-	16	16
4	Toni Neville, Australia	F	4	7	11
5	Wade Cox, USA	M	10	-	10
6=	Bruce Neville, Australia	M	-	9	9
=	Kristi Overton-Johnson (née Overton), USA	F	9	-	9
8	Freddy Krueger, USA	M	-	8	8
9	Scot Ellis, USA	M	-	7	7
10=	Susi Graham, Canada	F	6	-	6
=	Carl Roberge, USA	M	1	5	6

Waterskiing was invented in 1922 by 18-year-old Ralph W. Samuelson of Lake City, Minnesota, USA, using two 2.4-m (8-ft) planks and 30 m (100 ft) of sash cord. It grew in popularity, and the first international governing body, the World Water Ski Union, was established in 1946 in Geneva, Switzerland. Its successor, the International Water Ski Federation, organized the Water Ski World Cup, which by the year 2000 had expanded to include the Moomba World Cup, the US Masters, the US Open, the French Masters, the Recetto World Cup, the Austrian Masters, the Italian Masters, and the British Masters.

What sort of vehicles are used in the Iditarod Race?
see p.277 for the answer
A Dog sleds
B Hovercraft
C Land yachts

TOP 10 ⭐
OLYMPIC ROWING COUNTRIES

COUNTRY	GOLD	MEDALS SILVER	BRONZE	TOTAL
1 USA	29	29	21	79
2 =East Germany	33	7	8	48
=Germany*	21	13	14	48
4 Great Britain	21	16	7	44
5 USSR#	12	20	11	43
6 Italy	14	13	10	37
7 =Canada	8	12	13	33
=France	6	14	13	33
9 Romania	15	10	7	32
10 Australia	7	8	10	25

* Not including West/East Germany 1968–88

\# Includes Unified Team of 1992; excludes Russia since then

TOP 10 ⭐
FASTEST MEN'S 100-M FREESTYLE TIMES IN THE SUMMER OLYMPICS

SWIMMER/COUNTRY	YEAR	TIME (SECONDS)
1 Pieter van den Hoogenband, Netherlands	2000	47.84
2 Pieter van den Hoogenband	2000	48.30
3 Matt Biondi, USA	1988	48.63
4 Pieter van den Hoogenband	2000	48.64
5 Alexander Popov, Russia	2000	48.69
6 Gary Hall Jr., USA	2000	48.73
7 =Alexander Popov	1996	48.74
=Michael Klim, USA	2000	48.74
9 Michael Klim	2000	48.80
10 Gary Hall Jr.	1996	48.81

Gary Hall Jr., who makes two appearances in this list, in two Olympics, is a member of a family of swimmers. His grandfather, Charles Keating, was an All-America swimmer at the University of Cincinnati, his uncle was a member of the 1976 US Olympics team, and his father, Gary Hall Sr., won silver medals at the 1968 and 1972 Olympics and a bronze in 1976.

TOP 10 ⭐
OLYMPIC SWIMMING COUNTRIES

COUNTRY	GOLD	MEDALS* SILVER	BRONZE	TOTAL
1 USA	192	138	104	434
2 Australia	45	46	51	142
3 East Germany	38	32	22	92
4 USSR#	18	24	27	69
5 Germany+	12	23	30	65
6 Great Britain	14	22	26	62
7 Hungary	24	20	16	60
8 Japan	15	20	14	49
9 Netherlands	14	14	16	44
10 Canada	7	13	19	39

* Excluding diving, water polo, and synchronized swimming

\# Includes Unified Team of 1992; excludes Russia since then

\+ Not including West/East Germany 1968–88

WATER BOY

At the 2000 Sydney Olympics, Australia's teenage swimming sensation, Ian Thorpe, added three gold and two silver medals to his country's impressive tally.

SWISS ROLL

The bobsleigh event has been part of the Winter Olympics since 1924. Switzerland has won more medals than any other country.

TOP 10 OLYMPIC BOBSLEIGHING COUNTRIES

(Country/medals)

① Switzerland, 26 **②** USA, 14 **③** East Germany, 13 **④** = Germany*, 11; = Italy, 11
⑥ West Germany, 6 **⑦** Great Britain, 4 **⑧** = Austria, 3; = Soviet Union#, 3
⑩ = Canada, 2; = Belgium, 2

* Not including East/West Germany 1968–88   # Includes Unified Team of 1992; excludes Russia since then

---

TOP 10 ★
SKIERS IN THE 2000/01 ALPINE WORLD CUP (FEMALE)

	SKIER/COUNTRY	OVERALL POINTS*
1	Martina Ertl, Germany	346
2	Janica Kostelic, Croatia	239
3	Michaela Dorfmeister, Austria	186
4	Sonja Nef, Switzerland	166
5	Anja Paerson, Sweden	165
6	Regine Cavagnoud, France	144
7	Christel Saioni, France	135
8	Brigitte Obermoser, Austria	131
9	Andrine Flemmen, Norway	109
10	Karen Putzer, Italy	101

* Awarded for performances in slalom, giant slalom, super giant, downhill, and combination disciplines; as at 30 November 2000

Source: *International Ski Federation*

TOP 10 ★
SKIERS IN THE 2000/01 ALPINE WORLD CUP (MALE)

	SKIER/COUNTRY	OVERALL POINTS*
1	Hermann Maier, Austria	276
2	Lasse Kjus, Norway	246
3	Stephan Eberharter, Austria	240
4	Michael Gruenigen, Switzerland	168
5	Heinz Schilchegger, Austria	152
6	Andreas Schifferer, Austria	140
7	Fredrik Nyberg, Sweden	135
8	Kjetil Andre Aamodt, Norway	131
9	Josef Strobl, Austria	114
10	Didier Cuche, Switzerland	101

* Awarded for performances in slalom, giant slalom, super giant, downhill, and combination disciplines; as at 30 November 2000

Source: *International Ski Federation*

TOP 10 ★
MEN'S WORLD AND OLYMPIC FIGURE SKATING TITLES

	SKATER/COUNTRY	YEARS	TITLES
1	Ulrich Salchow, Sweden	1901–11	11
2	Karl Schäfer, Austria	1930–36	9
3	Richard Button, USA	1948–52	7
4	Gillis Grafstrom, Sweden	1920–29	6
5	=Hayes Alan Jenkins, USA	1953–56	5
	=Scott Hamilton, USA	1981–84	5
7	=Willy Bockl, Austria	1925–28	4
	=Kurt Browning, Canada	1989–93	4
	=David Jenkins, USA	1957–60	4
	=Ondrej Nepela, Czechoslovakia	1971–73	4

TOP 10 ★
FASTEST SPEED SKATERS*

	SKATER/COUNTRY/DATE	TIME IN SECONDS OVER 500 M
1	Jeremy Wotherspoon, Canada, 29 Jan 2000	34.63
2	Michael Ireland, Canada, 18 Mar 2000	34.66
3	Hiroyasu Shimizu, Japan, 20 Feb 1999	34.79
4	Jan Bos, Netherlands, 21 Feb 1999	34.87
5	Minetaka Sasabuchi, Japan, 29 Jan 2000	35.08
6	= Syoji Kato, Japan, 18 Mar 2000	35.10
	=Toyoki Takeda, Japan, 29 Jan 2000	35.10
8	Junichi Inoue, Japan, 19 Mar 2000	35.13
9	Patrick Bouchard, Canada, 29 Jan 2000	35.18
10	Sylvain Bouchard, Canada, 28 Mar 1998	35.21

* All speeds attained at Calgary

Source: *International Skating Union*

Did You Know? British ski enthusiast Sir Arnold Lunn (1888–1974), credited with introducing the slalom event in 1923, was knighted in 1953 "for services to skiing".

TOP 10 ★
WOMEN'S WORLD AND OLYMPIC FIGURE SKATING TITLES

	SKATER/COUNTRY	YEARS	TITLES
1	**Sonja Henie**, Norway	1927–36	13*
2=	**Carol Heiss**, USA	1956–60	6
=	**Herma Plank-Szabo**, Austria	1922–26	6#
=	**Katarina Witt**, East Germany	1984–88	6
5=	**Sjoukje Dijkstra**, Holland	1962–64	4
=	**Peggy Fleming**, USA	1966–68	4
=	**Lily Kronberger**, Hungary	1908–11	4
=	**Michelle Kwan**, USA	1996–2001	3
9=	**Tenley Albright**, USA	1953–56	3
=	**Meray Horvath**, Hungary	1912–14	3
=	**Anett Potzsch**, East Gemany	1978–80	3
=	**Beatrix Schuba**, Austria	1971–72	3
=	**Barbara Ann Scott**, Canada	1947–48	3
=	**Madge Syers**, GB	1906–08	3
=	**Kristi Yamaguchi**, USA	1991–92	3

* *Irina Rodnina (USSR) also won 13 titles, but in pairs competitions, 1969–80*

\# *Plus three further titles in pairs competitions*

TOP 10 ★
OLYMPIC FIGURE-SKATING COUNTRIES

	COUNTRY	GOLD	SILVER	BRONZE	TOTAL
1	USA	12	13	14	39
2	Soviet Union*	13	10	6	29
3	Austria	7	9	4	20
4	Canada	2	7	9	18
5	GB	5	3	7	15
6	France	2	2	7	11
7=	Sweden	5	3	2	10
=	East Germany	3	3	4	10
9	Germany#	4	4	1	9
10=	Hungary	0	2	4	6
=	Norway	3	2	1	6

* *Includes Unified Team of 1992; excludes Russia since then*

\# *Not including East/West Germany 1968–88*

Figure skating was part of the Summer Olympics in 1908 and 1920, becoming part of the Winter programme in 1924.

TOP 10 ★
FASTEST WINNING TIMES OF THE IDITAROD DOG SLED RACE

	WINNER	YEAR	DAY	HR	MIN	SEC
1	**Doug Swingley**	2000	9	0	58	6
2	**Doug Swingley**	1995	9	2	42	19
3	**Jeff King**	1996	9	5	43	19
4	**Jeff King**	1998	9	5	52	26
5	**Martin Buser**	1997	9	8	30	45
6	**Doug Swingley**	1999	9	14	31	7
7	**Doug Swingley**	2001	9	19	55	50
8	**Martin Buser**	1994	10	13	2	39
9	**Jeff King**	1993	10	15	38	15
10	**Martin Buser**	1992	10	19	17	15

Source: *Iditarod Trail Committee*

The race, which has been held annually since 1973, stretches from Anchorage to Nome, Alaska, the course following an old river mail route and covering 1,864 km (1,158 miles).

TOP DOUG

Doug Swingley from Simms, Montana, is one of only two non-Alaskans (the other is Martin Buser) to win the gruelling 1,864-km (1,158-mile) Anchorage-to-Nome Iditarod dog sled race.

Sporting Miscellany

FASTEST WINNING TIMES FOR THE HAWAII IRONMAN

	WINNER/COUNTRY	YEAR	TIME HR:MIN:SEC
1	Luc Van Lierde, Belgium	1996	8:04:08
2	Mark Allen, USA	1993	8:07:45
3	Mark Allen	1992	8:09:08
4	Mark Allen	1989	8:09:16
5	Luc Van Lierde	1999	8:17:17
6	Mark Allen	1991	8:18:32
7	Greg Welch, Australia	1994	8:20:27
8	Mark Allen	1995	8:20:34
9	Peter Reid, Canada	2000	8:21:01
10	Peter Reid	1998	8:24:20

This is perhaps one of the most gruelling of all sporting contests, in which competitors engage in a 3.86-km (2.4-mile) swim, followed by a 180-km (112-mile) cycle race, ending with a full Marathon (42.195 km/26 miles 385 yards). The first Hawaii Ironman was held at Waikiki Beach in 1978, but since 1981 it has been at Kailua-Kona.

OLYMPIC SPORTS WITH THE MOST LOTTERY FUNDING IN GREAT BRITAIN

	SPORT	LOTTERY FUNDING* (£)
1	Hockey	10,900,000
2	Rowing	9,598,048
3	Athletics	9,204,886
4	Swimming	6,035,015
5	Sailing	5,136,765
6	Cycling	4,999,420
7	Gymnastics	4,871,522
8	Badminton	4,800,000
9	Canoeing	4,507,093
10	Judo	3,749,628

Total received 1997–2000

In the period from 1997 up to the 2000 Sydney Olympics, British Olympic sports received some £80 million in lottery funding. Rowing and cycling were notably successful recipients, whereas hockey and swimming failed to win a medal.

MOST DANGEROUS SPORTS IN THE UK

	ACTIVITY	DEATHS OVER FIVE-YEAR PERIOD	RISK OF DEATH PER 100 MILLION PARTICIPANTS
1	Air sports	51	1,000
2	Mountaineering	51	100–200
3	Motor sports	65	120
4	Boating and sailing	69	60
5 =	Fishing	50	30
=	Horse riding	62	30
7	Swimming and diving	191	10
8	Hockey	2	4
9	Rugby	2	3
10	Soccer	14	2

Source: *Professor David Ball,* Sports Exercise and Injury

ALL-AROUND CHAMPION COWBOYS

	COWBOY	YEARS	WINS
1	Ty Murray	1989–98	7
2 =	Tom Ferguson	1974–79	6
=	Larry Mahan	1966–73	6
4	Jim Shoulders	1949–59	5
5 =	Joe Beaver	1995–2000	3
=	Lewis Feild	1985–87	3
=	Dean Oliver	1963–65	3
8 =	Everett Bowman	1935–37	2
=	Louis Brooks	1943–44	2
=	Clay Carr	1930–33	2
=	Bill Linderman	1950–53	2
=	Phil Lyne	1971–72	2
=	Gerald Roberts	1942–48	2
=	Casey Tibbs	1951–55	2
=	Harry Tompkins	1952–60	2

ROUGH RIDE

Recognized as the "ultimate cowboy championship", the title of PRCA World Champion All-Around Cowboy is the most prestigious title in professional rodeo.

THE 10 LATEST WINNERS OF THE BBC "SPORTS PERSONALITY OF THE YEAR" AWARD

(Year/winner/sport)

1 2000 Steve Redgrave, Rowing **2** 1999 Lennox Lewis, Boxing **3** 1998 Michael Owen, Football **4** 1997 Greg Rusedski, Tennis **5** 1996 Damon Hill, Motor racing **6** 1995 Jonathan Edwards, Athletics **7** 1994 Damon Hill, Motor racing **8** 1993 Linford Christie, Athletics **9** 1992 Nigel Mansell, Motor racing **10** 1991 Liz McColgan, Athletics

First presented in 1954, when it was won by athlete Chris Chataway, the annual award is based on a poll of BBC television viewers. At the end of the 20th century, Muhammed Ali was voted the "Sports Personality of the Century".

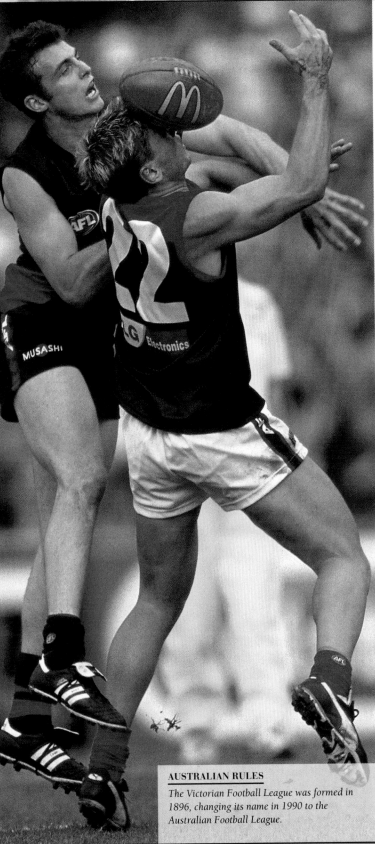

AUSTRALIAN RULES

The Victorian Football League was formed in 1896, changing its name in 1990 to the Australian Football League.

TOP 10 ★
HIGHEST-EARNING SPORTSMEN

	SPORTSMAN	SPORT/TEAM	2000 INCOME ($)
1	Michael Schumacher, Ger.	Motor racing, Ferrari	59,000,000
2	Tiger Woods, USA	Golf	53,000,000
3	Mike Tyson, USA	Boxing	48,000,000
4	Michael Jordan, USA	Basketball, Chicago Bulls	37,000,000
5	Dale Earnhardt*, USA	Stock car racing	26,500,000
6	Grant Hill, USA	Basketball, Detroit Pistons	26,000,000
7	Shaquille O'Neal, USA	Basketball, LA Lakers	24,000,000
8=	Oscar De La Hoya, USA	Boxing	23,000,000
=	Lennox Lewis, UK	Boxing	23,000,000
10	Kevin Garnett, USA	Basketball, Minnesota Timberwolves	21,000,000

* Killed February 18, 2001 during Daytona 500

Used by permission of Forbes *magazine*

TOP 10 ★
SPORTING EVENTS WITH THE LARGEST TV AUDIENCES IN THE UK, 2000*

	PROGRAMME	DATE	CHANNEL	AV. AUDIENCE
1	Euro 2000: England v Romania	12 June	ITV	14,944,000
2	2000 Grand National	8 Apr	BBC1	8,942,000
3	Brazilian Grand Prix	24 Mar	ITV	7,368,000
4	*Sports Personality of the Century*	12 Dec	BBC1	7,200,000
5	Wimbledon 2000: Men's Final Day	9 July	BBC1	6,714,000
6	*The Day Down Under*: Olympic Round-up	27 Sep	BBC1	6,482,000
7	The Boat Race	25 Mar	BBC1	6,055,000
8	World Championship Snooker	1 May	BBC2	5,759,000
9	The Six Nations Cup: France v Italy and Ireland v Wales	1 Apr	BBC1	5,213,000
10	British Open golf tournament	23 July	BBC1	4,055,000

* Top-rated event per type of sport   Source:

TOP 10 AUSTRALIAN FOOTBALL LEAGUE TEAMS
(Team/Grand Final wins)

1 = Carlton Blues, 16; = Essendon Bombers, 16
3 Collingwood Magpies, 14 **4** Melbourne Demons, 12
5 Richmond Tigers, 10 **6** Hawthorn Hawks, 9
7 Fitzroy Lions, 8 **8** Geelong Cats, 6 **9** Kangaroos (North Melbourne), 4 **10** South Melbourne, 3

Did You Know? The first ever rodeo organized as a competition was held at Prescott, Arizona, on 4 July 1888. It was won by Juan Leivas, who won a silver trophy and the title "Best Cowboy".

279

Index

Acknowledgments

UK research assistants:
Laurence Hill, Manuela Mackenzie

Special US research:
Dafydd Rees with help from Bonnie Fantasia, Linda Rees, and Christiaan Rees

Thanks to the individuals, organizations, and publications listed below who kindly supplied information to enable me to prepare many of the lists.

Caroline Ash, Professor David Ball, Javier Beltram, Richard Braddish, Henry Button, Tina Cardy, Pete Compton, Kaylee Coxall, Luke Crampton, Sidney S. Culbert, François Curiel, Steve van Dulken, Philip Eden, Steve Fielding, Raymond Fletcher, Christopher Forbes, Russell E. Gough, Monica Grady, Stan Greenberg, Andrew Hemming, Duncan Hislop, Heidi Gyani, Doug Hopper, Andreas Hörstemeier, Tony Hutson, Alan Jeffreys, Tony Jupp, Larry Kilman, Rex King, Robert Lamb, Jo Littmoden, Dr Benjamin Lucas, John Malam, Chris Mead, Ian Morrison, William Nicholson, Sarah Owen, Tony Pattison, Adrian Room, Leslie Roskind, Bill Rudman, Jacob Schwartz, Robert Senior, Lisa E. Smith, Mitchell Symons, Thomas Tranter, Lucy T. Verma, Tony Waltham, Peter Wynne-Thomas

Academy of Motion Picture Arts and Sciences, ACNielsen MMS, Adherents.com, *Airline Business,* Air Transport Intelligence, American Jewish Year Book Vol.100, Amnesty International, *Amusement Business, Annual Abstract of Statistics, Art Newspaper,* Art Sales Index, Associated Examining Board, Association of British Insurers, Association of Tennis Professionals (ATP), Audit Bureau of Circulations Ltd, Australian Department of Immigration and Multicultural Affairs, Australian Football League (AFL), *Auto Express,* BAFTA, Bank of England, BARB/SPC, *Billboard,* Booker Prize, *The Bookseller, BP Amoco Statistical Review of World Energy 2000,* BPI, BRIT Awards, British Academy of Composers & Songwriters, British Association of Toy Retailers, British Bankers' Association, British Broadcasting Corporation (BBC), British Cave Research Association, British Columbia Vital Statistics Agency, *British Crime Survey 2000,* British Library, British Museum (Natural History), British Small Animal Veterinary Association, British Video Association, BRMB/Mintel, *Cadbury's Confectionery Review,* Cameron Mackintosh Ltd, Cannes Film Festival, Carbon Dioxide Information Analysis Center, Central Intelligence Agency, Central Statistics Office/An Príomh-Oifig Staidrimh, Ireland, Centre for information on Language Teaching and Research, Certification

Office, Channel Swimming Association, *Checkout,* Christian Research, Christie's, CIN, CIVC, *Classical Music,* Columbia University (Pulitzer Prizes), Computer Industry Almanac, Inc, Corporate Intelligence on Retailing Ltd, Countryside Agency, *Criminal Statistics England & Wales,* Cyngor Cefn Gwlad Cymru/Countryside Council for Wales, Davis Cup, Death Penalty Information Center, De Beers, Deloitte & Touche, Department of Trade and Industry, Department of Transport, *The Economist,* Electoral Reform Society, Energy Information Administration, English Nature, English Tourist Board, Environmental Technology Center, Ernst & Young, Euromonitor, Eurotoys, Eurovision Song Contest, *FBI Uniform Crime Reports,* Film Council, *Financial Times,* Fleetwood-Owen, *Flight International,* Food and Agriculture Organization of the United Nations, Football Writers' Association, *Forbes,* Forestry Commission, Formula One, *Fortune,* Global Reach, Gold Fields Mineral Services Ltd, Golden Rose of Montreux Awards, Governing Council of the Cat Fancy, Harley Medical Group, Hawaii Ironman, Health and Safety Executive, HM Treasury, Home Accident Surveillance System (HASS), Home Office, Honda UK, House of Commons Reference Library, Iditarod Trail Committee, Interbrand, International Amateur Athletic Association, International Associatiion of Ports and Harbors, International Atomic Energy Agency, International Civil Aviation Organization, International Cocoa Organization, International Coffee Organization, International Commission on Large Dams, International Federation of Red Cross and Red Cross Societies, International Game Fish Association, International Skating Union, International Ski Federation, International Table Tennis Federation, International Telecommunication Union, International Union for the Conservation of Nature, International Water Ski Federation, Inter-Parliamentary Union, IPS/BTA/LTB, Kennel Club, Library Association, Lloyds Register of Shipping/MIPG/PPMS, London Theatre Record, London Transport Lost Property, Mazda UK, Meat and Livestock Commission, *Melody Maker,* Ministry of Agriculture, MRIB, Museum of Rugby, NASA, National Academy of Recording Arts and Sciences (NARAS), National Basketball Association (NBA), National Collegiate Athletic Association (NCAA), National Football League (NFL), National Highway Traffic Safety Administration, National Hurricane Center, National Retail Federation, *New Musical Express,* New South Wales Registry of Births, Deaths and Marriages, Niagara Falls Museum, Nielsen Media Research, Nobel Foundation, Norwich Union, NPD Group Worldwide, Office for National Statistics, Office of Fair Trading, Oxford University Press, Patent

Office, PC Data Online, Pet Food Manufacturers' Association, PetPlan Pet Insurance, Phillips Group, Phobics Society, Popular Music Database, Produktschap voor Gedistilleerde Dranken, Professional Golfers' Association (PGA), Professional Rodeo Cowboys Association (PRCA), Professional Squash Association, Public Lending Right, *Publishers Weekly, Q Magazine, Raceboat International, Racing Post, Railway Gazette International,* RAJAR, Really Useful Group, Recording Industry Association of America (RIAA), *Regional Trends, Road Accidents Great Britain 1999,* Royal Academy, Royal Aeronautical Society, Royal Mint, Royal Opera House, Covent Garden, Royal Society of Arts, Royal Television Society, Ryder Cup, Salt Institute, Scott Polar Research Institute, Scottish Natural Heritage, Scottish Office, *Screen Digest,* showbizdata, Siemens AG, W.H. Smith Ltd, *Social Trends,* Society of Motor Manufacturers and Traders Ltd, Society of West End Theatre (SWET) Awards, Sony Radio Awards, Sotheby's, *Spaceflight,* Stanford Institute for the Quantatitive Study of Society, *Statistical Abstract of the United States,* Stockholm International Peace Research Institute, Stores/Ernst & Young, *The Sunday Times, Television Business International, Time, Top Gear,* Tour de France, Toyota UK, Tree Register of the British Isles, UCI Mountain Bike World Cup, UNESCO, UNICEF, United Nations, Universal Postal Union, University of Westminster, US Bureau of Economic Analysis, US Census Bureau, US Committee for Refugees, US Geological Survey, US Immigration and Naturalization Service, US National Park Service, US National Science Foundation, US Patent and Trademark Office, *Variety,* Victoria and Albert Museum, Volkswagen UK, Ward's Automotive, *Wavelength,* Whitaker BookTrack General Retail Market, Whitbread Literary Awards, Women's International Squash Players Association, Women's National Basketball Association (WNBA), World Association of Newspapers, World Bank, World Cup Skateboarding, World Health Organization, World Intellectual Property Organization, World Motorbike Endurance Championship, World Rally Championship, World Resources Institute, World Superbike Championship, World Tourism Organization, Zenith International.

Index
Patrica Coward

DK Picture Librarians
Melanie Simmonds

Packager's acknowledgments:
Cooling Brown would like to thank Carolyn MacKenzie for proof reading and Peter Cooling for technical support.

Picture Credits

The publisher would like to thank the following for their kind permission to reproduce their photographs:

(Abbreviations key: t=top, b=bottom, r=right, l=left, c=centre)

Advertising Archives: 199tl.

AKG London: Marion Kalter 121; Tony Vaccaro 122tl.

Allsport: 279; Andrew Redington 266tr; Ben Radford 243l, 260; Clive Brunskill 242l, 245, 273; David Cannon 242c, 267; Doug Pensinger 242r, 263tr; Gary M Prior 246l; Jamie Squire 244; Michael Steele 262bl; Mike Powell 243r, 247bl, 251; Nathan Silow 247tr; Nick Wilson 275; Scott Barbour 255; Shaun Botterill 261, 276tl; Simon Bruty 5bc, 254; Stephen Dunn 253; Stu Forster 272; Tom Herbert 268-269.

Apple Computer: 212.

Aviation Images: Mark Wagner 239.

Bite Communications Ltd: 202tr.

The Booker Prize for Fiction: 99r, 111.

Breitling SA: 46c, 63b.

Capital Pictures: Phil Loftus 145.

China Photo Library: 96b.

Christie's Images Ltd: 99l, 108bl, 118tr, 119br, 123br, 176bl.

Bruce Coleman Ltd: Jeff Foott 34bl.

Corbis: 73tr; Bettmann 158br, 226; Bob Rowan/Progressive Image 195tr, 206bl; C Moore 93r; Daniel Lane 79l, 88tl; Earl Kowall 30r, 44l, 97br; Jack Fields 3, 77br; James Marshall 8l, 18l; Jay Dickman 215t; Jean-Pierre Lescourret 224l, 228; Jim Richardson 26bl; Kevin Fleming 45tl; Michael S Yamashita 155br, 229tl; Natalie Fobes 214bl; Paul A Souders 207tr; Peter Turnley 72l; Phililp James Corwin 71; Richard T Nowitz 22t; Robert Holmes 104tl; Sheldan Collins 103t, 194bl; Stephen Frink 35br; Trisha Rafferty/Eye Ubiquitous 198; Wayne Lawler/Ecoscene 21t.

Brian Cosgrove: 9r, 24-25.

Eyewire: 210l.

Gables: 52bl.

Galaxy Picture Library: D. Roddy/LPI 13tl; Gordan Garradd 10tr.

Gettyimages Stone: Antonia Reeve 102tl; Ron Sherman 98l, 105br; Will and Deni McIntyre 19tc; Yann Layma 78l, 85t.

Ronald Grant Archive: 181tr; "1992 Warner Bros/DC Comics 170br; "1998 Warner Bros/Brian Hamill 170tl; "1998 Universal/Dreamworks, photo Bruce Talamon 180bl; "1996 20th Century Fox 158-159; "1985 Amblin/Universal 161tl; "2000 Chan Kam Chuen/Columbia/Sony 163; "1996 Hollywood Pictures/Buena Vista 168tr; "2000 Jaap Buitendijk/Dreamworks/Universal 153r, 157br; "1999 K Wright/New Line 152c, 157tl; "1997 Keith Hamshire/Eon Productions, photo Keith Hamshire 168bl; "1961 Paramount 152r, 179; "1999 Warner Bros, photo Jason Boland 189; "1999 Ralph Nelson/Castle Rock/Warner Bros 153l, 173; "1998 Ron Phillips/Hollywood Pictures 152l, 175tr; "1975 United Artists/Fantasy Films 164; "1997 Wallace Merie/20th Century Fox/Paramount 156bl; "1996 Warner Bros/Universal/Amblin 174; "1996 Working Title/Polygram 165.

Hulton Getty: 60tr.

Kobal Collection: ©1975 Universal (UIP) 159br; "1989 Columbia 160bl; "1993 Sam Goldwyn/Renaissance Films/BBC 154; "1995 New Line Cinema/Entertainment Film 169tr; ©1997 Columbia Tristar 171; ©2000 Arte France/Blind Spot/Dinovi 166; ©2000Bob Marshak/Universal 167; ©1994 Paramount UIP 161br.

London Features International: Jen Lowery 2.

Mclaren Cars Limited (www.mclarencars.com): 227.

The Museum of the Moving Image: 177.

NASA: 10bl, 16; Finley Holiday Films 11t.

Nordfoto: Liselotte Sabroe 240.

Panos Pictures: Caroline Penn 104br.

Amit Pashricha: 211br.

PetExcellence: 277br.

Photodisc: 3, 47l, 51tr, 77l, 192; - 218-219, 220-221, 256-25 258-259.

Popperfoto: 238bl; Reuter 217l.

Redferns: 132tr; Amanda Edwards 147; David Redfern 130br, 138bl; Ebet Roberts 134; Fin Costello 126c, 133br; Graham Salter 150; Harry Herd 131tl; JM International 136tr, 140; Michel Linssen 178; Mick Hutson 5c, 126l, 127r, 139r, 141, 148bl; Nicky J Sims 146; Paul Bergen 126r, 127l, 137r, 142, 149t; Richie Asron 151; Tom Hanley 143tr.

Rex Features: Bill Zygmant 125.

Science Photo Library: 48l; Frank Zullo 12bl; GJLP 49br; Hank Morgan 48tr; Hans-Ulrich Osterwalder 28tl; Laguna Design 27tr; Peter Thorne, Johnson Matthey 203br.

Bill Seebold's Bud Light Racing Team: Rick Stoff 274.

Frank Spooner Pictures: G Mingasson-Liaison 278; Regan/Liaison 172.

Steiff Teddy Bears: Paul & Rosemary Volpp 98l, 114.

Still Pictures: Fritz Polking 33cr.

Swift Imagery, Swift Media: 107.

Sygma: Corbis 235br.

Kim Taylor: 41br.

Topham Picturepoint: 57tc; Associated Press 237tl; Max Nash/SEF 56b; Tony Arruza 29t; Young Joon 65tr.

Toyota (GB) PLC: 229br.

Jerry Young: 37tr.

All other images © Dorling Kindersley.
For further information see: www.dkimages.com

Hereward College

LEARNING RESOURCES
CENTRE

INTRODUCTION TO

VICTORIAN
STYLE

INTRODUCTION TO

VICTORIAN STYLE

DAVID CROWLEY

**MALLARD
PRESS**

A QUINTET BOOK

Mallard Press
An imprint of BDD Promotional Book
Company, Inc.
666 Fifth Avenue
New York, N.Y. 10103

Mallard Press and its accompanying design and logo
are trademarks of BDD Promotional Book
Company, Inc.

Copyright © 1990 Quintet Publishing Limited
First published in the United States of America
in 1990 by the Mallard Press.

ISBN 0 792 4535 0

All rights reserved.
This book was designed and produced by
Quintet Publishing Limited
6 Blundell Street
London N7 9BH

Creative Director: Peter Bridgewater
Art Director: Ian Hunt
Designer: Sally McKay
Artwork: Danny McBride
Editor: Shaun Barrington
Picture Researcher: Liz Eddison

Typeset in Great Britain by
Central Southern Typesetters, Eastbourne
Manufactured in Hong Kong by
Regent Publishing Services Limited
Printed in Hong Kong by
Lee Fung Asco Printers Ltd

CONTENTS

INTRODUCTION

ABOVE *The gulf between the prosperous and the destitute in Victorian England
concerned many artists and writers of the period. Ford Madox Brown's* The Last of
England *of 1863 depicts the plight of those forced to emigrate to escape poverty.*

or H. Stannus and other contemporary eulogists for late 19th-century British culture the word 'Victorian' was synonymous with progress. In his 1891 study of the life and work of the artist Alfred Stevens, Stannus revealingly wrote '. . . our peculiarly modern or VICTORIAN style'. Yet Matthew Arnold, in his book *Culture and Anarchy* of 1869, equated the upper reaches of Victorian society with barbarism, and the middle classes with philistinism. The meaning of what it was to be a Victorian was as complex then as it is now. Today it does not simply describe a period in history, the 64-year reign of a queen from 1837 to 1901. For while 'Tudor' and 'Georgian' are evocative of phases in British history, 'Victorian' has entered the English language as a rich adjective that describes more than the past. It has become a term which is frequently used to describe attitudes today. 'Victorian' now rings of strict morality, prudery, solemnity, Christian ethics, ideas about individual industry coupled with responsibility to the community, and above all conventionality.

Prominent Victorians displayed these characteristics in ready measure: Prince Albert, the Prince Consort, who was once described as the most 'Victorian of Victorians'; the arch-moralist Samuel Smiles, author of *Self-Help*, the Victorian manual; John Ruskin, champion of the Gothic and Christianity in art and design; Florence Nightingale, the 'lady with lamp' in the Crimean War; General Charles Booth, the founder of the Salvation Army who combined two Victorian passions, religion and the military; Octavia Hill, the philanthropist who attempted to combine charity and profitability in housing schemes for London's working classes.

The collection of values associated with these people can be traced through to the artifacts with which millions of ordinary Victorians surrounded themselves. Paintings like Richard Redgrave's *The Outcast* of 1851 showing a women cast out into the night clutching her illegitimate child, Ford Maddox Brown's *Work*, which celebrates labour and criticizes idleness, and innumerable paintings of biblical scenes found their way into many Victorian homes as popular engravings.

Even ordinary day-to-day items found in Victorian homes echoed the values found in greater society. The rise of the Gothic style in mid-19th century Britain, which penetrated the homes of all classes, was for its proponents a highly moral style reflecting hard work and craftsmanship.

Domestic goods reflected the greater Victorian world in other ways. The British Empire and developments in international communications brought to Victorian homes new goods and materials, and exotic styles. Fashions swept across England in the wake of colonial and international exhibitions. Liberty's, a shop selling furnishings, fabrics and decorative art in London's Regent Street built its reputation by selling Japanese style goods from the mid 1870s.

In fact, Victorians had particular relationships and fascination with the objects that surrounded them. As the middle classes grew, and the standard of living improved for the majority of the population (despite occasional trade depressions), people could increasingly afford the products of manufacturing industry. This was not lost on contemporary observers. John Hollingshead wrote in 1862:

> We may not be more moral, more imaginative, nor better educated than our ancestors, but we have steam, gas, railways and power-looms, while there are more of us, and we have more money to spend.

In a new age of mass consumption, advertising and retailing were becoming increasingly sophisticated in order to capture ever-growing markets. The late 19th century saw a series of innovations including department stores and national advertising campaigns in the press and on the streets.

To consume was to assert taste and social position. A home and its contents was the primary site of status in all levels of society. Methods of mass production were developed to make art for the common man, such as neo-Classical 'Parian' figures. In the middle years of the century, mantelpieces in Liverpool's terraced houses could display that which had previously been available only to the private collector in Mayfair.

In earlier centuries, the major problem facing people concerning the objects in their lives was how to secure them. In the Victorian period, it appears that the newly affluent lacked confidence in their new found ability to buy the products of manufacturing industry. This is revealed by the success of books like Charles Eastlake's *Hints on Household Taste,* which aimed to educate the middle classes on the appropriate ways to furnish and decorate their homes.

Victorian society was fascinated by inventive achievement and technological novelty. Popular journals, such as the *MacMillan Magazine,* chronicled new developments in science and art. Over six million people, in just six months, flocked to The Great Exhibition of the works of industry of all nations in 1851, to view the achievements of industry and handicraft.

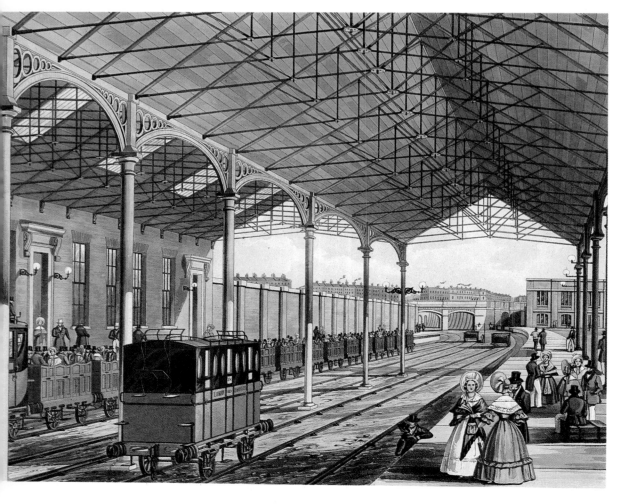

LEFT *The railway system rapidly became a key element in the infrastructure of industrial Victorian Britain boasting 6,800 miles of operational track by 1851. This coloured engraving of 1837, the year of the first publication of Bradshaw and Blacklocks railway timetable, shows the London terminus of the London and Birmingham Railway at Euston Square.*

TASTE AND HISTORY

Despite the receptivity of popular taste to the new, the novel and the exotic, the Victorian period has frequently been maligned as a low point in the history of style. The story of art and design in much of the 20th century has been written by men and women inspired by the values of Modernism. Nikolaus Pevsner's *Pioneers of Modern Design* is a good example of the Modernist anti-Victorian viewpoint. Pevsner dismissed 19th-century preferences for extravagant ornament, narrative devices, *trompe l'oeil*, sentimentality and decorative novelty as 'bad taste'. Another art historian recalled attitudes to Victorian culture in the 1960s with these words:

> I was taught only to revile the memory of Edwin Landseer, painter of *The Monarch of the Glen* . . . Similarly, Edwin Lutyens, extravagantly expressive architect to an Edwardian imperial class, was always held to me as what was wrong in architecture until Modernism cleared it up. As for William Burges, High Victorian designer, well in my youth, he was just *unspeakable*.

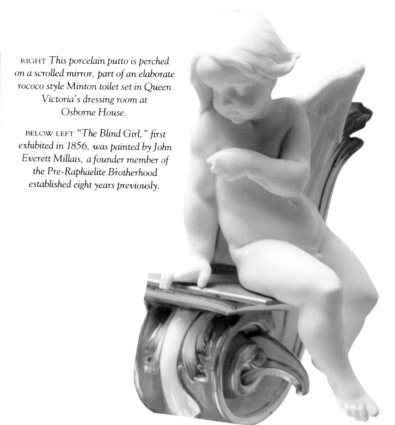

RIGHT *This porcelain putto is perched on a scrolled mirror, part of an elaborate rococo style Minton toilet set in Queen Victoria's dressing room at Osborne House.*

BELOW LEFT *"The Blind Girl," first exhibited in 1856, was painted by John Everett Millais, a founder member of the Pre-Raphaelite Brotherhood established eight years previously.*

But it is interesting to note that as the dominance of Modernism in culture has withered away, Victorian art and design has become the subject of increasing attention. In art galleries throughout the world Victorian paintings have been taken out of store and put back on display. There have been major exhibitions of Pre-Raphaelite art and the Gothic architecture and design of William Burges. One of the most successful exhibitions at the Royal Academy in London in the 1970s was 'Great Victorian Paintings'. In auction rooms, works by artists such as Ford Maddox Brown and Lawrence Alma-Tadema have reached prices that would have been inconceivable just a few years earlier.

The values in art and design that the Victorians held so dear correspond with those that Post Modernists prize today. Just as Owen Jones sought eclecticism in his survey of the styles of all periods and places, *The Grammar of Ornament* in 1856, a designer like Ettore Sottsass, founder of the Memphis design group in 1981, is celebrated for very similar enthusiasms.

During the reign of Modernist architectural thought, a building such as Charles Barry's Houses of Parliament, a 19th-century edifice decorated in the architectural style of the Middle Ages, the Gothic, was considered the height of irrationality. With the rise of Post Modernism, this building is now regarded as an important part of Britain's architectural heritage.

Of course it is an exaggeration to say that all artists and designers of the Victorian period have been relegated to minor positions of importance by cultural historians of the 20th century. Certain figures such as the designer Christopher Dresser and the architect Lewis Cubitt, have been ascribed roles of great importance. Typically, these Victorian artists and designers have been championed by people in the 20th century who find echoes of their own ideas in the 19th century. Art Nouveau style posters, for example, became popular in the 1960s when flowing organic forms and sensual depictions of women became fashionable in graphic design.

Occasionally this has led to a misrepresentation of the intentions of a particular artist or designer. Christopher Dresser, for example, is often hailed as a proto-Modernist for his designs of electro-plated metalwork in the 1870s, produced by such firms as Elkington and Company. These highly geometric and 'functional' vessels appear to prefigure designs produced at the Bauhaus in Germany in the 1920s. Accordingly, Dresser's designs have been regarded as major stepping stones to the taste for highly abstract, geometric design in the 20th century. A closer inspection of Dresser's interests show him to have been far more a Victorian – particularly in his eclecticism – than a prophet of Modernism. The pluralism of his interests can be gauged by the fact that around the year 1880, he was still designing these 'modernist' electro-plated manufactures, at the same time working for the Linthorpe pottery designing expressive forms based on primitive art from Fiji, and promoting very restrained and sophisticated Japanese furniture.

ABOVE *An electroplated tureen designed in 1880 by Christopher Dresser for Hukin & Heath of Birmingham. Author of "Principles of Domestic Design," Dr Dresser's fresh uncluttered approach to domestic metalwork anticipated modernist design criteria.*

BELOW LEFT *A pottery cigar tray designed by Dresser for the short-lived Linthorpe pottery in Yorkshire (1879–81).*

BELOW *Dresser's Clutha glass of the 1880s and 90s, produced by the Glasgow firm of James Couper & Sons, were remarkable for their flowing organic form, subtle colouration and great delicacy.*

RIGHT *This recently restored tricycle rocking horse, still in perfect working condition, was manufactured in Paris during the 1880s.*

Alongside these academic debates among art historians about the merits and demerits of Victorian culture, another kind of historian has quietly but systematically contributed to our knowledge of Victorian style: the amateur collector. While museums have concentrated on the most celebrated artistic and commercial achievements of the period, all kinds of everyday ephemera have been collected. Our understanding of Victorian life would be incomplete without these collections of song sheets, stamps, advertisements, penny dreadfuls, lace, matchboxes, children's toys, *cartes de visites*, packaging and countless other day-to-day mass-produced items. WP Frith's painting *The Railway Station*, exhibited at the Royal Academy in 1858, is just as much a product of its age as a tinplate clockwork toy train made by the firm of Marklin in the 1870s. Futhermore, that child's toy would bear fruitful examination alongside a full scale steam locomotive running on the London to Birmingham line operated by the Great Midland Railway of the same period. The marks of Victorian style and the Victorian mind are to be found in all three objects.

THE VICTORIAN AGE

Victorian values did not come into being with the accession of Victoria to the throne in 1837, nor did they end in 1901 on her death. Just as they were displayed in the activities of figures such as Hannah Moore, the evangelizing philanthropist in the first years of the 19th century, the early decades of the 20th century saw the continuity of the same concerns.

Victorian values, however, were not firmly entrenched until the late 1840s and were already breaking down by the 1870s. This is the age that has come to be known as the 'High Victorian period'. These years saw the height of British economic dominance, intense innovative activity in industry and communications and the untrammelled growth of the British Empire. In the 1870s Victorian Britain went through the first of a series of crises of confidence; social investigators told of the extent of deprivation in her cities, while the scramble for colonies in Africa by her European rivals disturbed the nation's confidence in the British Empire, and the economies of those same countries were clearly developing at a faster rate than Britain's. A new generation, who did not share the beliefs of their parents, came to regard the term 'Victorian' with scorn.

The same trends can be recognized in Victorian art and design. The most significant works of art, craft and industry of the High Victorian period were, in essence, celebrations of Victorian culture. The decades after 1870 saw the ascendancy of designers and artists who used their work to issue a challenge to Victorian morality, propriety and taste. These figures will be dealt with in the concluding chapter; this book's primary concern is with style in the High Victorian period.

EARLY VICTORIAN STYLE

The strain of Classicism which had dominated taste in the first quarter of the century, the 'Regency' style, slowly went out of fashion. This style was typified by the highly regimented and restrained 'Greek' terraces surrounding Regent's Park in London, designed by John Nash. The Victorian mind, seeking novelty and exoticism, was not satisfied with this neo-Georgian Classicism: terraces of uniform white facades, and rooms tastefully decorated with pale freezes depicting tales of Greek mythology and furnished with Chippendale chaises longues, Wedgwood vases and Hepplewhite cabinets. Even Nash, the leading architect of the Regency period, bowed to this restlessness with 'good taste' by extending and improving William Porden's Royal Pavilion in Brighton, in the style of an Indian palace during the second decade of the century. This amazing building pre-figured Victorian fashions in architecture and design in its Chinese and Gothic details, and the use of structural cast iron. (But it should be remembered that the taste for Classical art and design never completely disappeared in the Victorian period.)

Under the influence of Paris and *Le Style Empire*, French fashions dominated British style in the 1830s and 1840s. This can be seen most directly in the Rococo Revival, which men like Benjamin Dean Wyatt, the architect and son of James Wyatt, promoted as a grand style, befitting the increasingly grand British Empire.

ABOVE *This Victorian Coalport pot-pourri with its complex florid design is expressive of the Victorian enthusiasm for decoration, often regardless of overall aesthetic effect.*

LEFT *The chamber of the House of Lords designed by Augustus Pugin (1815–52), architect responsible for the interior and exterior decoration of the Houses of Parliament in Medieval Gothic style.*

RIGHT *The elaborately carved neo-rococo furniture by Henry Belter featured in this American 19th century interior echoes the mid-18th century fashion for chinoiserie.*

The Rococo style originated in France in the 1730s, and by the second half of the 18th century was used as a term to describe the European fashion for rich ornament, often in the form of marine and floral motifs, scrolling and curvilinear designs. Widely regarded as a frivolous style, Rococo broke all the rules of Classical good taste; symmetry, balance, geometric order and architectonic decoration. In all areas of the decorative arts, it was characterized by flights of fancy, *trompe l'oeil*, illusionary construction and, above all, ostentatious decoration.

The sources of the mid 19th-century Rococo Revival in Britain are to be found in the popularity of floral ornament in the 1820s promoted by firms such as Gillows of London and Lancaster. The firm decorated its furniture with rich acanthus ornament and lavish scrolled carving. The fashion for Rococo design had been stimulated by the availability in London of items of furniture displaying the very high standards of French craftsmanship after the Revolution. Collectors such as King George IV were able to profit from the misfortunes of the French aristocracy, and acquired the best Rococo designs of the 18th century.

The origins of the Rococo Revival in Britain were aristocratic. In 1824 the Duchess of Rutland, for example, employed Benjamin Dean Wyatt to redesign Belvoir Castle, in Leicestershire, in the Louis XIV style. Here, Wyatt and his younger brother Matthew Coates Wyatt, employed motifs and decorative forms taken directly from Rococo sources. An example of this can be found in one room at Belvoir, in which they utilized wainscoting from a late 18th-century chateau owned by Louis XIV's second wife, Madame de Maintenon. Benjamin Dean Wyatt was also employed by the Duke of Wellington to design and furnish Apsley House, and to furnish the homes of the Duke of York and the Marquis of Stafford.

But the Rococo Revival at its height – in the 1840s – was a solidly bourgeois affair. Numerous manufacturers used the Rococo style to give their products the air of expensive elegance. These goods were not historical re-creations of 18th-century designs, but generalizations of Rococo characteristics; C and S scrolls, naturalistic ornament, cabriole legs, balloon backs, deep upholstery and curvilinear forms. The kind of furniture regarded today as typically 'Victorian', originates from this mid 19th-century Rococo Revival. A button-backed, deeply upholstered armchair in a richly coloured velvet and with curved walnut legs, is as much a symbol of the Victorian era as the Albert Memorial.

Although no longer in the vanguard of style by the mid 1850s, Rococo continued to be a popular decorative style. It was an excellent vehicle for the bourgeoisie to display their wealth and taste, and consequently has been identified as the worst example of Victorian excess by historians of applied art.

LEFT *The topheavy, elaborately scrolled handles and overlarge cartouches of this Minton neo-rococo pot pourri point to its 19th century rather than 18th century manufacture.*

RIGHT *Once again ornament triumphs over design in this Minton pot pourri. Similar handles, a stylistic element derived from the 18th century vogue for chinoiserie, are occasionally seen on Georgian ceramic teapots.*

BELOW *One of a set of carved mahogany chairs produced at the end of the Victorian era. Though the basic shape is Georgian, the complex scrolls on the chair back would find no prototype in any 18th century design directory.*

It was not popular with contemporary foreign observers who described the fashion in terms of distaste. One German aristo-crat visiting the country, wrote:

 Everything is in the now revived taste of the time of Louis the Fourteenth; decorated with the tasteless excrescences, excess of gilding, confused mixture of stucco painting etc.

The apparent luxury and excess of Rococo became available to the poorer classes with developments in furniture making and decorative techniques. The firm of George Jackson and Sons produced a kind of putty which could be modelled, painted and then gilded on site to give the appearance of skilfully carved wood at one quarter of the cost. In 1833 Benjamin Dean Wyatt used this method to decorate the gallery in Apsley House, for Wellington, saving almost £1,600. Similar-ly, the development of papier-mâché furniture encouraged highly moulded Rococo forms such as cabriole legs, previously the products of costly craftsmen.

Both at the time and in later years, the Rococo Revival came under attack. Pevsner, reviewing Rococo style objects from the Great Exhibition wrote:

 You see an extremely elaborate pattern, the charm of which, during the Rococo period, would have been based on the craftman's imagination and unfailing skill. It is now done by machine and looks like it.

The Great Exhibition was dominated by the Victorian Rococo Revival. Ralph N. Wornum's highly critical essay *The Exhibition as a Lesson in Taste* acknowledged this highly influential style, stating rather clumsily: 'The Louis Quatorze varieties perhaps prevail in quantity, the Louis Quinze, and the Rococo'. Despite this, however, The Great Exhibition marked the first major Victorian attempt to break free from the dominance of French trends in taste and the search for a truly Victorian Style.

THE CRYSTAL PALACE AND POPULAR TASTE

The end of the century marked the rise of the great department stores, such as Harrods, Whiteleys and Selfridges whose marble halls, filled with the manufacturing wealth of the British Empire, were in fact essentially inspired by the example of the great Crystal Palace exhibition of four decades previously.

y the middle of the 19th century Victorian Britain had proved itself to be the most successful industrial nation on earth. Thanks to the efforts of Britain's inventors, merchants and manufacturers, propped up by the markets and raw materials of the Empire, British industry dominated the world. One could buy Manchester's cottons in Delhi, and Sheffield's metalwork in Sydney; the epithet 'workshop of the world' rang true. Prince Albert said in 1851: 'No-one who has paid any attention to the particular features of the present era will doubt for a moment that we are living in a period of most wonderful transition'. Victorians felt themselves to be living in an age of unprecedented change and invention; science was redefining the world, railway travel had become commonplace, daily newspapers, printed by machine, were at their cheapest, and the homes of the middle class displayed the dramatic developments in manufacturing industry in their most basic contents; cutlery, dinner services and furnishings.

Yet questions of style perplexed Victorian designers and intellectuals. British art and design was widely regarded to be second rate when compared to French decorative arts of the period. Styles originating in Paris were held up in London, to be the zenith of artistic achievement. Writers, intellectuals, designers and manufacturers argued that Britain, with its commercial superiority and Christian moral leadership, ought to produce art and design worthy of its achievements in commerce and industry, rather than plagiarizing those of her rivals. Goods manufactured in Britain were inexpensive and dominated international markets, but the goods produced by her immediate rivals, Germany and France, were considered to be superior in terms of design and style, or in contemporary parlance 'art'. London watched as these pretenders to her commercial crown, rapidly industrialized to challenge British markets. In 1835 the Select Committee of Arts and Manufactures, formed under Robert Peel's government to investigate this very problem, reported:

To us, a peculiarly manufacturing nation, the connection between art and manufactures is most important – and for this merely economical reason (were there no higher motive), it equally imports us to encourage art in its loftier attributes.

The Committee noted that despite the rapid industrialisation of the previous 60 years, artists and designers had not been incorporated into manufacturing industry, and that artists had distanced themselves from commerce. The Committee came to the conclusion that state-sponsored schools of design should be established so that their graduates could be employed by industry to improve the standards of design and ornamental decoration. The first of these schools was founded in 1837 in Somerset House in London, and was given a small budget to purchase books, plaster casts of classic art and specimens of manufactured items. During the mid 1840s part of this collection toured the country by train to eleven new provincial branches of the School of Design. In the 1850s the Schools of Design secured the private collection of decorative art owned by Ralph Bernal MP and that of a French lawyer Jules Soulages, which included majolica, iron work, and goldsmiths' pieces.

During these years, Henry Cole, a senior civil servant, was addressing the same problem of raising the standards of design. Cole was a man of unbridled enthusiasm for improving the public good. During his career he reorganized the Public Records Office, helped Roland Hill to introduce penny postage, built Grimsby Docks, was the first director of the South Kensington Museum (later London's Victoria and Albert Museum) and standardized the gauge for railways. After meeting Herbert Minton of Minton and Company, the most successful ceramic manufacturer of the period, Cole designed a bone china tea service which Minton produced. Cole rigorously researched the design and style sources for this service, including going to the British Museum to study Greek earthenware 'for authority for handles'. He also went to Minton's factory to observe the manufacturing process. In 1846 these white, simple ceramic forms, hardly decorated by the standards of the day, aroused much critical acclaim, winning a silver medal from the Royal Society of Arts and receiving the admiration of the Prince Consort.

LEFT *Inkstand and pen tray designed by the Royal Academician John Bell for Minton & Co. Artist and manufacturer collaborated on several projects through the medium of Henry Cole's influential design company, Felix Summerley's Art Manufactures.*

ABOVE RIGHT *The production of the Penny Black, the world's first adhesive postage stamp, issued on 6 May 1840, was one of a multitude of projects which involved the creative talents of Henry Cole, designer, writer, entrepreneur and reformer.*

Henry Cole believed that the best way to improve Victorian design and public taste would be to persuade industry to employ fine artists. Cole looked back to the successes of Josiah Wedgwood almost a century earlier, who had employed figures like George Adams, the King's architect, to design his pottery. In much the same spirit he commissioned a painter, William Wyron, in 1839 to design the Penny Black, the first postage stamp. Similarly, in 1845 he invented a Christmas tradition by asking a painter specializing in domestic scenes, John Callcott Horsley, to illustrate a greeting card. Cole himself had some experience of art, for he had studied under the watercolourist David Cox and shown at the Royal Academy in his youth. To bring art to manufacturing industry, in 1847 he launched a company which he called Felix Summerley's Art Manufactures. Cole (under the pseudonym of Felix Summerley) acted as an entrepreneur, commissioning designs from renowned artists and persuading manufacturers to use them.

Under the Summerly scheme, the royal academician, John Bell, designed the Sabrina Urn, the Sugar Cane treacle pot, and a salt cellar decorated with a boy and a dolphin which was produced by Minton and Co. Bell's designs were frequently highly commended in the *Journal of Design and Manufactures*, although the *Art Union Journal*, a rival publication, found itself 'unable to appreciate' his 1848 matchbox in the shape of a crusader's tomb.

Richard Redgrave RA, had been appointed botanical lecturer to the Government School of Design in 1847. He also

ABOVE *This naturalistically painted jug and matching glass was produced by Richardson of Stourbridge, one of the more progressive glassmakers of the mid 19th century and frequent collaborator with Felix Summerley, alias Henry Cole.*

produced a number of projects for Summerly's Art Manufacturers. This included a superb painted glass water carafe, produced by JF Christy, which is reminiscent of the very best Arts and Crafts glass at the end of the century, and a striking papier-mâché tray inlaid with mother of pearl and ivory produced by Jennens and Betteridge. Although he had trained as a painter, Redgrave increasingly became known as a designer and a respected critic of Victorian taste. In 1849 he became the editor of the *Journal of Design and Manufactures* and in 1855 he was a member of the executive committee of the British Section at the Paris *Exposition Universelle* .

Summerly's Art Manufactures employed some of the most able and popular artistic talent in Britain at that date, including William Dyce and Daniel Maclise, who had both been commissioned to paint frescoes for the Palace of Westminster, the former painting *The Baptism of Ethelbert* and the latter *The Meeting of Wellington and Blucher*. Summerly's Art Manufactures persuaded Britain's leading manufacturers to produce the designs of some of Britain's leading artists. Their products were as diverse as christening cups and letter boxes. Although, Summerley's Manufactures aimed at the reform of Victorian taste, its creations were 'conventional' in many respects: the designers did not refute historicism and encouraged the use of ornament. Henry Cole closed down the 'Art Manufactury' in 1848, not because it was commercially unsuccessful, for it appears that some of the items produced were very popular, but because his attention had moved on to other fields.

Through the Schools of Design and Summerly's Art Manufactures there emerged a core of artists, designers and intellectuals linked to Cole. The key figures in this – 'the Cole Group' – apart from those already mentioned, were Matthew Digby Wyatt, Ralph Nicholson Wornum, Gottfried Semper, Owen Jones and George Wallis. Matthew Digby Wyatt was author of *The Industrial Arts of the Nineteenth Century* and designer of ceramics and interiors. Ralph Nicholson Wornum trained as a painter, but became a writer and was, in fact, a vigorous critic of Henry Cole until offered the postion of librarian and keeper of casts at the Schools of Design in 1852. Gottfried Semper, a German refugee from the failed 1848 Revolution, was employed as a teacher by the School of Design in its new home at Marlborough House in 1852, and was noted for the ornamental details of the funeral car of the Duke of Wellington, but is most famous for his classic text, *Der Stil*, an investigation of the origin of style. Owen Jones was a prolific writer and theorist on ornament, famed for his book *The Grammar of Ornament* and a practitioner in all fields of design. George Wallis, was an artist who had studied under Dyce and was the principal at the Birmingham School of Design. The Cole Group became the

Claret jug with pear shaped glass body on three legs by Christopher Dresser, c. 1879.

design establishment of mid 19th-century Britain. They wished to bring a rational influence to bear upon Victorian style, arguing through their mouthpiece, the *Journal of Design and Manufactures*, for simplicity over complexity. Carpets and fabrics, for example, were not to be 'suggestive of anything but a level or a plain'. Considering a trowel covered with amorini decoration, the Journal was to the point: 'we think it ought to be unmistakably a trowel'. In contrast, describing a chintz by Owen Jones, the *Journal* stated in 1852:

The design is, as it ought to be, of perfectly flat unshadowed character. Secondly, the qualities and lines are equally distributed, so as to produce at a distance the appearance of levelness. Thirdly, the colours produce a neutral tint. And lastly . . . it is quite unobtrusive, which a covering of handsomer stuffs ought to be. The lines and forms are graceful too, when examined closely.

LEFT *Between 1872–6 William Morris produced 17 wallpaper designs using naturalistic motifs. "Larkspur" illustrated here was also produced as a printed cotton during this period with the help of dye-works owner Thomas Wardle of Leek in Staffordshire.*

RIGHT *This drawing, published by the illustrated London News in June 1850, gives some idea of the vastness of Thomas Paxton's great 1,848 foot long building situated between Rotten Row and the Carriage Road in London's Hyde Park.*

THE GREAT EXHIBITION OF 1851

The most eminent of Cole's collaborators was the Prince Albert of Saxe-Coburg-Gotha, husband of Queen Victoria. In his capacity as President of the Royal Society of Arts, of which Cole had been a member since 1846, the Prince Consort attempted to promote the application of art to industry. In 1847, the Prince and Cole planned a number of annual didactic exhibitions to display 'select specimens of British Manufactures and Decorative Art' to the public and industry with the specific intention of raising standards of taste. The 1848 exhibition at the Society of Arts' small house showed over 700 items. This scheme proved successful with attendance increasing five-fold in 1849, although Cole was criticized for the heavy represent-ation of Summerly's Art Manufactures in the exhibitions.

These smaller displays led the way to an immense one; London's Great Exhibition of the works of industry of all nations in 1851. It has never been fully established whether the Great Exhibition was Cole's or Prince Albert's idea, for Cole is recorded as proposing a national industrial design exhibition in 1848, but the credit is frequently given to the Prince, whose contribution was considerable.

Cole and Digby Wyatt visited the French *Exposition Nationale* in 1849 to prepare a report for the Royal Society of Arts. Since the 1790s the French had organized a series of national indus-trial exhibitions, but the one in 1849 was the largest. Cole discussed with the Prince Consort the possibility of holding such an exhibition in London. The Prince's enthusiastic re-sponse included the exhortation that 'It must embrace foreign productions'.

At the first planning meeting at Buckingham Palace in June 1849, the character of the exhibition was quickly established. Its scope was to be international and orientated to industry. Awards were to be given for the best objects and machines to encourage exhibitors. It was to be housed in a temporary building in Hyde Park between Rotten Row and Kensington Drive. The organization of the exhibition was to come under the auspices of a royal commission led by the Prince Consort.

Initially financial support was slow in coming. To set the scheme in motion, the Queen gave £1,000 and Prince Albert donated £500, and in a nationalistic gesture some workmen are reported to have made small donations from their wages. In true Victorian spirit, the exhibition was financed by two speculators, James and George Munday who undertook re-sponsibility for the building and deposited a £20,000 prize fund in return for five per cent interest on the amount advanced and a percentage of the profits. In October of that year Cole also outlined the scheme to the financial community in London, and engendered the support of 5,000 'influential persons'. Potential financial difficulties during the course of the organization and building of the exhibition site were avoided by a guarantee fund of £250,000.

With the financial arrangements secured, the Royal Com-mission was issued on 3rd January 1850 and Prince Albert was made its chairman. Albert was not a symbolic figurehead in these arrangements, but an energetic agent. Philip Cobden MP wrote of the Prince:

> I would not flatter anybody, but I would say, that having sat at the same board as His Royal Highness, I can speak of his efforts not as a prince, but as a working man. There is not one in the numbers of the Commissioners . . . that has done half the labour towards carrying out this exhibition'.

A GREENHOUSE LARGER THAN A GREENHOUSE EVER BUILT BEFORE

The design of the building housing the Great Exhibition was open to competition and entries were invited from 'competitors of all nations'. Although 245 entries were received, the Building Committee decided to amalgamate the best ideas in a number of designs into a single building made of brick, topped with an enormous sheet-metal dome, looking something like a railway station. Abuse was hurled at this scheme by such as *The Times* newspaper which had already protested at the use of Hyde Park, and in particular, the destruction of the trees on site. *The Times* leader fulminated: 'The first and main reason, why we protest against the erection of such a huge structure on such a site is that it is equivalent to the permanent mutilation of Hyde Park . . . Once more we entreat the Prince and his advisors to pause ere it be too late'.

The story of how this problem was resolved, and how the Great Exhibition came to be housed in the temporary building which *Punch* magazine affectionately dubbed the 'Crystal Palace', is quite remarkable. Joseph Paxton, a gardener and landscape architect at Chatsworth, home of the Duke of Devonshire, aware of the problems facing the Building Committee, began 'doodling' at a committee meeting in Derby in June 1850. He scribbled out a basic design and structural plan for a large glass-paned building. This design extended the structural ideas he had employed in the greenhouse he had designed at Chatsworth, which in turn had been derived from the skeletal form of the leaf of the *Victoria Regia* water lily

(which Paxton had introduced to Britain in the year of Victoria's coronation). On his return home, he continued working on this sketch and wrote to the Society of Arts in London, offering to show his plans to them within eight days. These days were spent furiously working with William Henry Barlow, a railway engineer, to resolve the technical problems of design.

By coincidence, on the train to London to show his plans, Paxton met Robert Stephenson, the renowned engineer, who was a member of the Building Committee. Paxton spent the journey discussing the design with Stephenson, who appeared to be enthusiastic. In contrast, the Committee were more hesitant, and Paxton's designs toured the offices of the Society of Arts, the Board of Trade and Buckingham Palace. Frustrated, Paxton decided to go public in an attempt to win support for his design and arranged for it to be published in the most popular paper of the day, *The Illustrated London News*.

It appears that Paxton had judged the public mood correctly, for opinion swung behind his elegant design. Paxton was told that his 'Crystal Palace' would be considered if he submitted a firm tender within four days. This Paxton did, and with estimated costs that compared favourably with the price of the official building, the Committee had little choice but to accept his design, with the proviso that the height of the Palace be extended to allow the building to be constructed around the elm trees on the site, thus mollifying public opinion. This resulted in the arched transept which became the striking feature of the building.

Somewhat inevitably, as soon as Paxton's design was accepted a contrary wave of public opinion washed over London, foretelling the collapse of the glass building onto visitors to the exhibition. Even more hysterically, others suggested that London would be starved by the volume of visitors to the exhibition or that the crowds would trigger an epidemic of bubonic plague.

In August, as the foundations were being laid, another controversy welled up. It became known that Paxton was unqualified in any profession despite the successes of his career. The voices of gloom rang across London again, fortelling the imminent collapse of the Crystal Palace. Yet this criticism and alarm in no way deterred building, which steadily continued. The first column was raised at the end of September. Six months later the building was complete.

Paxton's design for the Crystal Palace stands in the history of architecture as a masterpiece of mass-produced, standardized, prefabricated parts; a precursor of the Modern Movement of the 20th century. Contemporary observers were not blind to the implications of the Crystal Palace. The architect Thomas Harris wrote: 'iron and glass have succeeded in giving a distinct and marked character to the future practice of archi-

LEFT *Paxton's great design was novel not only by virtue of its sheer compass but also in the method of its construction, a modular one based on steel which prefigured modern architecture.*

RIGHT *The Palm House at Kew Gardens was constructed some five years previous to the Great Exhibition from a design by Richard Turner, an entrant for the 1851 competition.*

tecture'. It was an outstanding achievement in iron and glass, the materials of Victorian engineering, but what distinguished it from suspension bridges, railway stations and market halls of the period, is the speed with which it was constructed and its sheer scale. Intended to be the symbolic length of 1,851 feet (in fact, it appears that the building fell three feet short of the original plans), it was bigger than the palace at Versailles and was three times longer than St Paul's Cathedral in London.

The building was based on a 24-foot grid and was ingeniously constructed from an enormous number of prefabricated parts, the heaviest of which were the 24-four foot girders at one ton each. The amount of material employed was phenomenal; 300,000 panes of glass (of a size that had never before been

manufactured), iron weighing about 4,500 tons, 34 miles of guttering, and over one million feet of sash-bars. In the six months before the opening of the exhibition on the 1st of May, 1851, an average of two thousand men were employed on site at any one time.

Paxton's design incorporated a number of novel inventions. The guttering was an ingenious system which prevented condensation. He also designed a trolley which could be moved across the site in all weather, carrying the glazier's equipment. As a consquence of the scale and novelty of the Palace, a number of unorthodox building and testing methods were employed. Soldiers marching in step were used to test the strength of the galleries before they were secured into place.

RIGHT *Minton, whose display of plant pots and jardiniere's are featured here, was just one of 7,351 British exhibitors. An additional 6,556 stands were occupied by exhibitors from overseas.*

While the building work was under way, members of the Cole Group were planning and prophesying. Swept up in the spirit of new opportunity, they foretold a brighter future in which art and industry would meet in a new alliance. A Cole spokesman stated: 'Since the period of the Reformation we believe that the prospects of Design have never been so good as at the present time in England'. Digby Wyatt and Henry Cole himself had been on the central selection committee, emphasizing the exhibition's professional aims.

Half of the exhibition space was to be given over to exhibits from Britain, and the rest to foreign entries. Each country was allocated space, and the responsibility to fill it. British competitors had to pass through a regional and then a national committee. The entries had to fall into a three-tiered classification system devised by Prince Albert; 'the raw materials of industry, the manufactures made from them, and the art used to adorn them'. In true Victorian spirit, Dr Lyon Playfair, a member of the central selection commitee, subdivided these into a further 30 divisions, such as 'Machines for direct use, including Carriages, and Railway and Naval Mechanisms' and 'Woollen and Worsted Manufactures'. Although Fine art was excluded, for theoretically the exhibition was concerned with the 'Works of Industry', it was represented in a final category entitled 'Sculpture, Models (in Architecture, Topography and Anatomy) and Plastic Art'. Each division was overseen by a panel of specialists in that area.

ABOVE *Queen Victoria and Prince Albert visiting the Indian pavilion. The Queen a frequent visitor, was fascinated by the "ingenious" inventions on show as she delighted in viewing the Aubusson tapestries, Turkish silks and Swiss watches.*

The appearance of the Crystal Palace was not due to Paxton alone. Owen Jones, a member of the Cole Group and superintendent to the exhibition, and with the responsibility for the decoration of the building, used primary colours, red, yellow and blue, to decorate the iron frame of the building. Jones believed that this would make the Crystal Palace 'appear higher, longer and more solid'. Charles Barry, the architect of the new Palace of Westminster after the fire in 1835, suggested placing the flags of all nations along the profile of the roof.

BELOW *The Agricultural section of the Crystal Palace exhibition featured new farming machinery that still required horse power.*

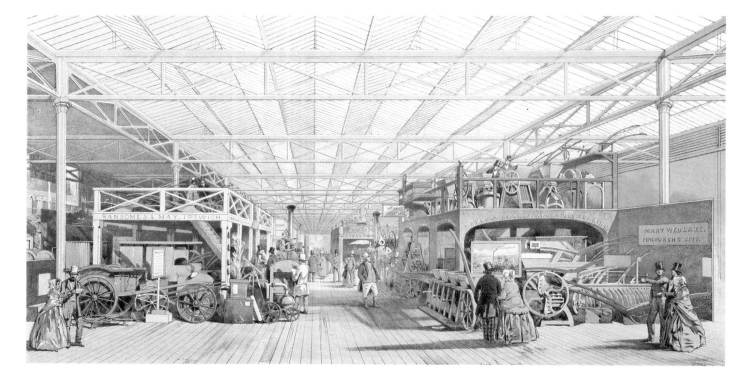

THE EXHIBITION OPENED

The world's first international exhibition of industry was opened on the 1st of May 1851 by Her Majesty Queen Victoria. It was originally planned that this inauguration would be a private ceremony because the Queen had been attacked in June of the previous year by Robert Pate, and was wary of public attention. But again *The Times* thundered, its leader column stating:

> What an unworthy part would these nervous advisers cause the Queen of England to play! Surely Queen Victoria is not Tiberius or Louis XI, that she should be smuggled out of a glass carriage into a great glass building under the cover of the truncheons of the police and the broadswords of the Life Guards. Where most Englishmen are gathered together, there the Queen of England is most secure!

And so again public opinion swayed officialdom, and the Great Exhibition was opened to a crowd of 25,000 observers. The Police estimated that as many as 700,000 people filled Hyde Park that day.

The opening ceremony was full of the pomp and circumstance that characterized Victoria's reign; the Archbishop of Canterbury offered prayers, guns saluted, dignitaries and royalty read addresses, soldiers marched and a choir of 600 sang Handel's *Hallelujah Chorus*.

On the 11th of October the exhibition closed to the public. In the course of the five and half months that it was open over six million visitors attended. The busiest day, during the last week, saw 109,915 people pass through its doors.

The Crystal Palace was a superb exhibition space. All contemporary comment described the galleries and transept bathed in brilliant light. Charles Barry, even though a Gothic architect, paid great compliment by writing that it 'flashed on the eye more like the fabled palace of Vathek than a structure reared in six months'. Another observer described the central court thus:

> In the midst is seen the Fountain of Glass; behind it, and also in groups near the south entrance, are beautiful tropical plants, sheltered by the elm-trees which rise above them; and above all springs the light and elegant arch of the wonderful Transept. The glitter of the falling waters in the gleaming light which pours down unobscured in this part of the building, and the artistic arrangement of the groups of the objects of art and industry in the immense vicinity of the Transept, renders this a peculiarly attractive part of this immense structure.

TOP *Queen Victoria, accompanied by Prince Albert, the Prince of Wales and the Princess Royal, inaugurated the Great Exhibition with impressive pomp and ceremony. The great day was declared a public holiday, thereby attracting at least half-a-million visitors to Hyde Park.*

The main avenues of the building were filled with large free-standing exhibits and decorated with colourful flags and red banners stating the name of the exhibitor in white letters. The galleries overlooking the central avenues housed hundreds of cabinets containing smaller items, and hanging tapestries. Despite being dubbed somewhat icily, 'the Crystal Palace' the splendid pomp of the exhibits and Owen Jones' primary colour scheme, made the experience of visiting the Great Exhibition a colourful, and exciting one. In trying to assess the impact of the exhibition on its visitors, it ought to be remembered that many had never travelled outside their own towns and villages, let alone to London and an international event of such a scale. The Queen recorded in her journal meeting a Cornish woman, aged 80, who 'had walked up several 100 miles to see the exhibition'. On special 'shilling' days the lower middle classes flocked in their thousands. Thomas Cook made his fortune by taking over 160,000 people on excursions which included travel and the price of entry to the exhibition. Even *The Times*, initially very critical of the exhibition plans, wrote of the first day: 'There were many there who were familiar with the sight of great spectacles . . . but they had not seen anything to compare with this'.

An event as fantastic as the Great Exhibition inevitably generates an accompanying mythology. Two weeks before the opening ceremony, for example, an unforeseen problem arose, when Crystal Palace became home to flocks of sparrows who threatened to redecorate the building and its visitors in somewhat less pleasant hues than those intended by Owen Jones. The Commissioner's solution to this problem, after much

LEFT *The Machinery Court of the Exhibition, situated in the central aisle, included the "Great Hydraulic Press" used in 1849 for the construction of the Britannia tubular bridge over the Menai straits.*

deliberation, was to employ two sparrow hawks. A letter to the *Morning Chronicle* stated that the 'most universal complaint' about the Great Exhibition was that the refreshment staff serving there were unwashed, and that 'their hands and faces would be greatly improved by a moderate use of soap'. An Admiral at Portsmouth dockyard offered to place a vessel at the disposal of the workmen, so that they would be able to visit the exhibition in the capital. Henry Cole retold the story of when the Duke of Wellington, a national hero, attended the Great Exhibition:

When at its fullest, 93 thousand present, the Duke of Wellington came, and although cautioned by the police, he would walk up the nave in the midst of the crowd. He was soon recognized and cheered. The distant crowds were alarmed and raised the cry that 'the building was falling'. There was a rush.

Fortunately, the building did not collapse, although it appears as if the Duke of Wellington did, for Cole proceeds to describe him being carried out of the palace looking 'pale and indignant'.

THE EXHIBITS

There's taypots there,
And cannons rare;
There's coffins filled with roses;
There's canvas tints,
Teeth insthrumints,
And shuits of clothes by Moses,
There's lashins more
Of things in store,
But tim I don't remimber;
Nor could disclose
Did I compose
From May time to Novimber.

ABOVE *Punch, whose editorials dubbed the exhibition building the "Crystal Palace,"
here gently mock the vanity of a crowd of female visitors.*

William Makepeace Thakeray's humerous ode *Maloney's Account of the Crystal Palace*, written in the style of the satirical magazine *Punch*, acknowledged the vast scale of the Great Exhibition. More precisely, there were 13,937 exhibitors, a large number of whom, according to the *Official Catalogue*, arrived after the opening on the 1st of May, 1851. Over half of the exhibits were from British competitors, who used this opportunity to produce and display their best, most extravagent, and beautifully finished manufactures. These British objects were placed in the western end of the building.

Exhibits were arranged along the categories established by the Prince Consort and Dr Lyon Playfair. There was a stained glass gallery, a Mediaeval Court, a Hall of Furs, Feathers and Hair, a moving machinery section and so on. Every Victorian enthusiasm was represented in some shape or form. The Queen, for example, thougt that a collection of stuffed animals in comical poses such as 'The Kittens at Tea' was 'really marvellous'. The cutting, drilling, riveting, wire-drawing machinery of the moving machinery section were as frequently dressed in historical architectural styles such as Gothic and Egyptian, as the lamps and furnishings in other sections. *The Exhibition Anthem* was composed by Martin Tupper and translated into 30 languages.

Every conceivable style of decorative art was there on view: bookbindings in ecclesiastical Gothic; elegant urns in Grecian styles; Italianate tea services; silverware in Renaissance styles illustrated with cupids and arcadian scenes; innumerable chairs, escritoires and side-tables in the fashionable Louis XIV style; Japanese lacquered boxes, and thick piled carpets and richly decorated cloths of floral motifs. Tuberville Smith produced a richly coloured floral fabric, which the official catalogue described as a 'flower garden (which) seems to have been rifled of its gayest and choicest flowers . . . it almost requires one well instructed in botany to make out a list of its contents'.

ABOVE *John Dickinson's two volumes of
colour lithographs entitled
"Comprehensive Pictures of the Great
Exhibition" (1854) bring to life the
extraordinary variety and quantity of
products on show, estimated at
approximately 112,000 items.*

A number of novel decorative techniques were developed by craftsmen and manufacturers to produce strikingly innovative objects. A Mr Kidd, for example, developed a technique by which he laid jewels and precious ornaments under glass and flooded them with silver creating what he called 'Illuminated Glass'. British craftsmen adopted techniques from all over the world to display their skills. Messers. Hewett and Co., for example, exhibited an ivory basket which the official catalogue compared to the best Chinese craftsmanship.

Semi-scientific objects such as clocks and telescopes received just as much attention from the stylists and ornamentalists. Gray and Keen of Liverpool showed a number of barometers in a range of styles, including a Gothic form with an elaborate dial plate and another in the shape of a patent anchor. Multifunction furniture was a further preoccupation of the Great Exhibition. The firm of Taylor and Sons produced a sofa for a steamship and the company of RW Laurie, manufactured a portmanteau, both of which could be turned into life rafts.

Machinery and raw materials filled much of the exhibition space. Outside the west end of the building visitors could survey the engine room housing two Armstrong boilers which supplied the power to the machinery inside. Here too the public could marvel at a 24-ton block of coal, symbolic of Britain's industrial achievement, which had been hewn at the Staveley mine owned by the Duke of Devonshire. Alongside this were placed slabs of concrete, granite obelisks and massive iron anchors. Inside the Crystal Palace, the public's attention was demanded by the triumphs of Victorian inventive genius, confirming Albert's belief in a 'period of most wonderful transformation'. The Victorians could wonder at working telegraph machines, Crampton's *Liverpool*, the fastest express locomotive in the world, the De La Rue envelope-making machine, much admired by Queen Victoria, which could fold 2,700 an hour. A whole section was given over to agricultural implements. Commentators were greatly impressed by their mechanization.

The exhibition also contained many bizarre items, which were frequently great achievements of their kind. To design reformers like Henry Cole and the Prince Consort, they were curiosities that distracted from the concern of the Great Exhibition to improve public taste. From Prussia came an iron stove designed by Edward Baum in the shape of a full suit of armour, and a garden seat made from coal for Osborne House was on display in the British section. There were a number of *tour de force* items intended to show the skill of the maker or the versatility of a particular material, such as J Rodger and Sons' sportsman's knife which had eighty blades, or the Daydreamer chair, which became a major topic of discussion. This chair was made from papier-mâché, a material associated with small domestic, ornamental items such as trays, and inlaid with mother-of-pearl in the forms of snowdrops, poppies and angels, and covered with buttoned upholstery. It was decorated with 'two winged thoughts:' one 'troubled', in the form of bat-like wings, and one 'joyous', illustrated by a crown of roses, both divided by a symbol of hope, the rising sun. The centrepiece of the entire exhibition was a 27 feet high crystal fountain which was made from four tons of glass by F and C Osler.

The international sections generated enormous interest from the British public, and large numbers of visitors travelled from all over the world to see this unique event. For the first time under one roof it was possible to see the products of industry and handicraft from all over the globe. To walk through the eastern avenues of the Great Exhibition was to observe the industrial achievements of North America, the British Empire, the Near and Far East and Europe. One visitor from Nottingham was overwhelmed at what faced him:

 I was astonished at the outside of the building, but when I entered at the door of the south of the transept I beheld a site which absolutely bewildered me. The best productions of art and science of almost all lands lay before me. I gazed with astonishment. I knew not what direction to take.

The Indian section was a British cause célèbre, as the jewel in the crown of the her Empire. Victoria praised it very strongly and a French writer claimed that it took viewers back to a 'heroic age'. It was assembled by the East India Company and contained, among other items, shawls and fabrics, particularly beautiful silks, a stuffed elephant (which they were unable to find in India, but secured in a museum less than fifty miles from London) draped with hangings and a covered and cantilevered howdah, ornamental swords and shields in precious metals. The Koh-i-noor or Mountain of Light diamond was specially transported from Bombay by *H.M.S. Medea* and presented to the Queen at a ceremony two months after the exhibition had opened.

The substantial French section appears to have been widely regarded as the height of fashionable style. With the rivalry characteristic to both nations, one English writer discussing French silks, argued:

> As yet France triumphs; a highly cultivated taste both in the combination of colours and the beauty of design in all its detail excercises a powerful influence over the demand and supply; but when once England has succeeded in educating her workmen, so that they will produce designs which will carry off the prestige which now attatches itself to the productions of the loom of Lyons, the superiority of France will be at an end.

With about 1,750 exhibitors, the French display was as diverse as that figure suggests; from highly carved Rococo cabinets made from exotic woods such as pear and ebony, highly naturalistic floral ornamentation on decorative boxes, and book-covers in carved ivory, to more prosaic objects such as a sewing machine 'adapted for coarse cloth'. Despite examples of French technical and scientific ingenuity, such as a prototype submarine which had traversed the English Channel, and a calculating machine, English comment concentrated on the achievements of French applied art.

The American display deserves special mention, for apart from the stuffed black-eyed squirrels and over 6,000 fossils

were some objects that received much enthusiastic attention at the time and have subsequently come to be seen as key designs of the 19th century. In American industry lay the seeds of the future, for her McCormick Reaper, Hobbs lock, and Colt revolver displayed characteristics that came to be highly valued in 20th century design; a simplicity of form, restrained ornament and an emphasis on functionality. In marked contrast to countries like France, ornamented decorative design was very rare in the American section. This was widely attributed at the time to the new country's lack of traditions and a market for expensive applied art.

American art also turned a few heads: August Kiss's *Amazon* was a novelty made from zinc, and Hiram Power's famous *Greek Slave* proved to be very popular. The latter, a classically posed nude chained, and leaning against a tree-stump was the centrepiece of the American section, set against a background of red plush and under a special canopy. One critic wrote of this piece: 'The Greek Slave is one of the "Lions" of the exhibition and most deservedly so'.

Among the other nations represented, China aroused great curiosity with the peculiar eastern workmanship of its exhibits. There was colonial produce from the Bahamas, Trinidad and the Eastern Archipelago. Tunisia recognized the trade opportunities that would result from showing her unique handicrafts and raw materials to the rest of the world. Russia concentrated on jewellery from St Petersburg, and items made in malachite. Switzerland's goods generated respect, if not enthusiasm. Canada's national display was judged to have similar qualities to American design. The display from Turkey was very popular for the exoticism and quality of the arabic patterns found there. Arranged without the formal rigidity of some of the European states, this section was frequently described as a 'Turkish

Bazaar', a phrase with evocative power in conservative mid-Victorian Britain.

Juries were established by the commissioners of the Great Exhibition to search out in every category 'the best of their kind'. Constituted by an equal number of foreigners and British subjects, the 34 juries were able to bestow bronze Council Medals for 'some important novelty of invention or appreciation, either in material or process of manufacture, or originality combined with great beauty of design', or a lesser Prize Medal to those who had shown 'a certain standard of excellence in production or workmanship'. Out of a total of 13,937 exhibitors, 170 Council Medals were awarded. Britain, not unexpectedly, received the greatest number of prizes, followed by France. In the categories of applied art, such as the class entitled 'Furniture, Upholstery, Paper Hangings, Papier Mâché and Japanned Goods', the French were dominant. France won 54 medals in all categories. Britain won 52 of her 78 medals in the categories that related to machinery.

When the exhibition closed, it was declared a triumph. It made a phenomenal profit of £186,437. Much debate centred on what to do with this money; Paxton was awarded £5,000 for his contribution to the success of the venture and most of the rest was spent on educational purposes. An 87-acre plot of land was purchased in South Kensington, in London. On this site today stands the Victoria and Albert Museum (which contains many of the best examples of decorative art and design on display at the Great Exhibition), the

Science and Geological Museums, the Royal Albert Hall, the Imperial College of Science and Technology, and the Royal College of Music.

The Crystal Palace was dismantled, despite calls for it to remain on its Hyde Park site to be used as a winter garden. It was reconstructed in Sydenham in South London and was re-opened by the Queen on the 10th of June, 1854. It became a much loved place for Londoners to spend their leisure time, visiting the new Renaissance Court, designed by the Cole Group member, Matthew Digby Wyatt, or wandering through the grounds laid out by Thomas Paxton. It was used as an exhibition space again in 1911, the year of the coronation of George V, for a festival of Empire. In November, 1936, its central transept caught fire and the building was destroyed. The closing hours of the Crystal Palace were as spectacular as the opening ones, for the flames which engulfed it could be seen in eight counties.

The Great Exhibition set in motion a number of enormous international exhibitions. Each subsequent show tried to be larger, grander and more exotic than the preceding one. They were given hyperbolic names like the *Exposition Universelle* and the *Weltausstellung* and were symbolized by amazing icons championing industrial inventiveness. The World's Colombian Exposition in Chicago in 1893 displayed an enormous ferris wheel with 36 cars each carrying 40 people. At the 1889 Paris *Exposition Universelle*, Gustave Eiffel built his famous Eiffel Tower, then the tallest building in the world.

RIGHT *A painted and gilded lacquer box decorated with an inset view of Paxton's Crystal Palace. Some of the glass windows are ingeniously embellished with mother-of-pearl inlay.*

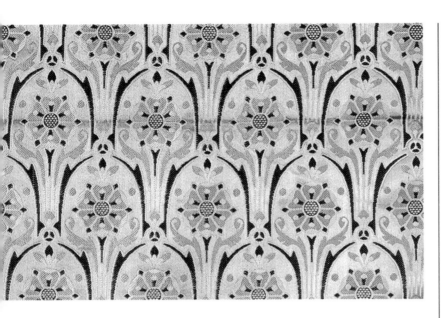

LEFT *"Sutherland," an Arts and Crafts textile design by Oen Jones originally produced as silk tissue by the London firm of Warner, Sillet & Ramm.*

RIGHT *This painted rosewood cabinet of 1871 by T.E. Collcutt has been described by a recent critic as "one of the most original, attractive and influential pieces of furniture ever designed by a Victorian architect."*

BELOW *This drawing room is typical of the eclecticism of late Victorian taste. Elaborate papier-mache furniture decorated with painted flowers and mother of pearl inlay vies with a Japanese style cabinet and "Chrysanthemum" wallpaper designed by William Morris.*

POPULAR VICTORIAN TASTE

To Henry Cole the exhibition was a disappointment, for his hopes of finding a union between art and industry had not been met. The critics lashed out at the use of excessive orna-ment, the out-and-out historicism and the absurdity of the majority of the exhibits. *The Times* stated: 'The absence of any fixed principles in ornamental design is apparent in the Exhi-bition – it seems to us that the art manufactures of the whole of Europe are thoroughly demoralized'. Cole and his colleagues could only extend their support to a few of the objects displayed. Of the exhibits, Gottfried Semper wrote that only 'objects in which the seriousness of their use does not allow for anything unnecessary, e.g. coaches, weapons, musical instruments and the like, sometimes showed a higher degree of soundness in decoration and in the methods by which the value of func-tionally defined forms is enhanced'.

But the comments of design theorists should be contrasted with those of mid-century enthusiasts for Victorian culture. Dr W Whewell was inspired by the Great Exhibition to write: 'we perceive that in advancing (from earlier ages of history) to our form of civilization we advance also to a more skilful, power-ful, comprehensive and progressive form of art'. The flocks of visitors that travelled to the Great Exhibition, and particularly those who returned again and again (for it was possible to buy a season pass), were more likely to agree with Whewell than Cole. The most popular exhibits and frequently those that incurred the critics' wrath, were the ones that displayed the most ostentatious ornament, and that were the most historicist, and in the terms of their critics the most 'dishonest'.

The same values and qualities so prized by visitors at the Great Exhibition were echoed in the furnishing and decorative predilections of middle class Victorians. They liked their furniture to be ostentatious and conspicuous, emphasizing surface over structure, and display rather than rational construction. The middle decades of the 19th century saw the dominance of veneering, graining, ormolu, gilt, embossing and chasing and many other forms of decorative treatment. Even wheel chairs were given scrolled, carved legs.

Although widely associated with Victorian architecture, historicism also dominated the decorative arts. Greek, Roman, Gothic, Egyptian and other historical styles provided sources which manufacturers could plunder at will. They were able to purchase 'grammars' of decorative and ornamental patterns which could be imitated, often without due respect for the nature or the overall form of the artifact. The manufacturers of the 'Daydreamer' papier-mâché chair, exhibited at the Crystal Palace (see above), could not be specific about the hybrid style in which they had cloaked this novelty, so they described it as simply 'Italian'. History sometimes provided inappropriate models for the demands of Victorian life. George Angell's silver flagon in the Gothic style was wholly impractical, awkward to handle and difficult to clean. But to many, ownership of this object would confer prestige outweighing its impracticalities.

ABOVE RIGHT *The Hope vase (1855), designed for Henry Thomas Hope by Louis Constant Sevin and carved by J.V. Morel, depicts the rescue of Andromeda from the dragon by Perseus. A blend of rococo fantasy and renaissance ornament, this centrepiece's decorative complexity nevertheless bears the stamp of the 19th century.*

Although highly decorated, this sideboard (below right) by Philip Webb (c.1862), a founder member of the Morris firm, reveals a growing concern of the burgeoning Arts and Crafts Movement with plain forms, in radical opposition to the High Victorian yen for profuse plastic ornamentation (below left).

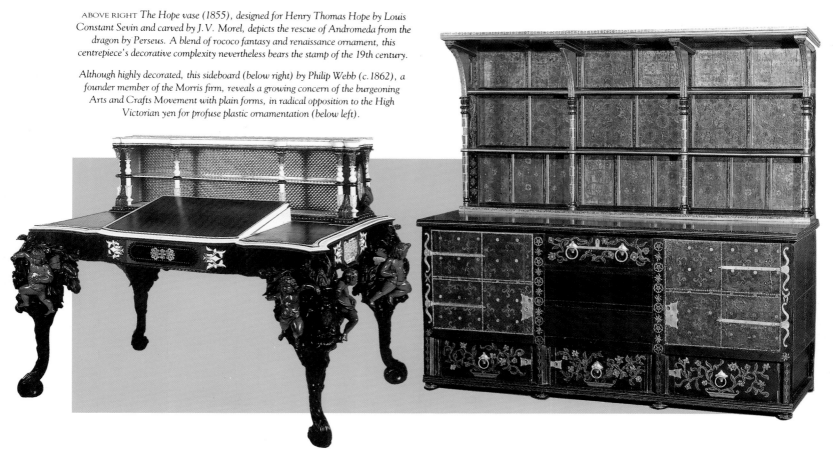

ABOVE *Medieval style oak cabinet designed by J.P. Seddon with decorative panels painted by Madox Brown, Morris, Burne-Jones and Rossetti illustrating the honeymoon of King Rene of Anjou.*

RIGHT *Ormulu and gilt decorated desk in the French style, typical of the ponderous furniture so eagerly amassed by wealthy Victorian families.*

ABOVE RIGHT *An Emile Gallé vase, with engraved and enamelled moths, 1885–90. Gallé drew his inspiration from many sources, including Venetian and Islamic glass. This design reveals the popular Japanese influence.*

BELOW RIGHT *A Minton ewer (1865) with relief neo-rococo syle modelling by H. Protat, decorated with majolica glazes.*

FAR RIGHT *This steel vase, damascened in gold and silver and inlaid with emerald and ruby settings by French silversmith Frederic-Jules Rudolphi incorporates an eclectic mix of Gothic and Islamic design motifs.*

ABOVE *This Arts and Crafts ebonised wooden corner cabinet with painted panels dates from c. 1880.*

The Victorians were also fond of *trompe l'oeil* effects, particularly if they simulated expensive materials. Glass was painted to look like marble, and zinc was electro-plated to make it indistinguishable from sterling silver to the untrained eye. This was not just the province of British Victorians: in America, Alexander Jackson Davis was commended for his painted illusionary canvas walls at Lyndhurst, the country home of Jay Gould in Tarrytown, which resembled ashlar stonework.

Victorians liked their objects to contain narrative devices. Mottoes, pithy sayings and psalms were engraved into metalwork, stitched into fire screens and cushions and carved into chair backs. Sets of cutlery, engraved with coats of arms were most prestigious domestic items, rifles would have hunting scenes engraved on their gunstocks, fishknives would be illustrated with views of fishermen, and clocks with Old Father Time. A Rococo-style chair from Dublin shown at the Great

FAR RIGHT AND BELOW *G. P. Wetmore's Chateau sur Mer in Newport, Rhode Island. The new American millionaire class aped European styles, particularly the neo-rococo, in an effort to invest social position based on money with grandeur and cultural respectability.*

Exhibition, with carved dogs for arms, had carved across its back the legend: 'Gentle when stroked, angry when provoked'.

The rising middle classes, prosperous on the incomes from commerce and industry, were keen to display their wealth. Drawing rooms were brimming with armchairs, sofas, chaises longues, rich drapes and curtains, thick pile carpets and so on. Their concern was usually not with the patronage of craftmanship or art, or the cultivation of a knowledge of the antique, but the overt display of fashionable taste. Manufacturers responded by developing techniques for mass producing furniture, ceramics and metal ware, and even fine art. In 1844 Benjamin Cheverton patented a 'three dimensional pantograph' which allowed scaled down copies of busts of 19th-century heros such as the Duke of Wellington, to be made cheaply in alabaster or wax, and machine-carving, anathema to the purist, enabled the furniture industry to create pieces with the scrolling and turned balusters of handcrafted masterpieces.

ROYAL INFLUENCE

Queen Victoria, painted by Franz Xavier Winterhalter in 1859.
Described by his royal patron as "excellent, delightful Wintherhalter," the German
artist was commissioned to produce a large number of pictures, of which over a
hundred still form part of the Royal Collection.

 ueen Victoria was crowned in 1837 at the age of 18. By the end of her long rule in 1901, the country over which she reigned had been transformed in every aspect. When she came to the throne, after George IV, the popular support for the monarchy as an institution was uncertain. When her son Edward became King, he inherited the high esteem in which the sovereign was held by her subjects, and the monarchy was widely regarded as a fundamental institution in British society. But the transition from what could be described as mass indifference to the new Queen in 1837 to a sense of national loss when she died, was not an even one. Her reign was marked by a number of low points in support for the crown at the time of the death of her husband, Prince Albert, in 1861, and her ensuing period of widowhood during which she was reluctant to play out her public role. But this was retrieved in later years when there was widespread public recognition of her hard work and concern with the Empire. At the end of the century, text books and children's primers embroidered a cult of regal glorification:

'Beautiful England – on her island throne –
Grandly she rules, with half the world her own.
From the vast empire the sun ne'er departs:
She reigns a Queen – Victoria, Queen of Hearts.'

Made Empress in 1876, the Queen was not just a figurehead for the *realpolitik* of statesmen like William Gladstone and Benjamin Disraeli, but played an active role in international affairs. Although the relationship between the monarchy and parliamentary politicians slowly diminished after the death of Albert, who had exerted a discreet influence on the affairs of state, on occasion she challenged the positions of her ministers, such as Gladstone's support for Irish Home Rule. Yet Victoria's devotion to duty was not maintained without doubts and tribulations. She wrote in her journal on New Year's Day 1881:

I feel how sadly deficient I am, and how oversensitive and irritable, and how uncontrollable my temper is when annoyed and hurt. But I am so overdone, so vexed, and in such distress about my country, that that must be my excuse. I will pray daily for God's help to improve.

Although obviously not a typical Victorian, for as a woman her life was not circumscribed by the demure, domestic roles that most women were forced to play, she held the beliefs and attitudes so characteristic of Victorian Britain. As a devoted Christian, her actions were guided by faith, and the moral codes of the day. Her preferences in art, decorative art and

ABOVE *Prince Albert's election to the Presidency of the Society for the encouragement of the Arts, Manufactures and Commerce in 1849, nine years after his marriage to Queen Victoria (below) was official recognition of his enthusiastic involvement in many aspects of his adopted country.*

design were as conservative and middle brow as those of the majority of most of her subjects. In this sphere, as in many aspects of her life, Victoria followed the lead of her husband, to whom she was devoted. She exclaimed in her journal after the opening of the Great Exhibition: 'This day is one of the greatest and most glorious days of our lives, with which to my pride and joy, the name of my dear Albert is for ever associated!'

The Queen and Prince Albert had married in 1840, three years after her succession to the throne. He was born in Rosenau, Coburg in 1819 and was the son of the Ernest, Duke of Saxe-Coberg-Gotha. As a youth he was a great lover of nature and country sports. In his late teens he went with his brother to Brussels to study history, science and European languages. Here, a friend wrote:

> Albert was distinguished by his knowledge, his diligence, and his amiable bearing in society. He liked above all things to discuss questions of public law and metaphysics, and constantly, during our many weeks, juridical principles or philosophical doctrines were thoroughly discussed'.

His marriage to Victoria was considered by statesmen throughout Europe to be politically advantageous. But it must be

noted that their love for one another was genuinely felt. The young Princess wrote to her uncle after first meeting with him; 'Albert's beauty is most striking, and he is most amiable and unaffected – in short fascinating'.

Albert's position as the Prince Consort, after Victoria's accession to the throne in 1837, was difficult. He was unable to play a public role in national political affairs and in fact he was expected to be no more than a discreet advisor to the Queen. Frustrated by these restrictions, he ploughed his energy into good works and cultural patronage.

It must be remembered that the royal preferences in fine and applied art exerted a major influence on the fashionable taste of the day. The Prince Consort acknowledged this, saying:

> There are two great auxillaries in this country which seldom fail to promote the success of any scheme, – fashion and a high example. Fashion, we know, is all in all in England, and if the Court – I mean the Queen and myself – set the example hereafter . . . the same taste will extend itself to wealthy individuals.

The royal couple were expected to be more than interested consumers of paintings and furniture. As patrons of the arts, they were to set an example for less cultivated minds. Prince Albert is known to history as a great promoter of industry and the economy (not least for his part in organizing the Great Exhibition), but Queen Victoria and the Prince Consort were

ABOVE *"Dignity and Impudence" by Sir Edwin Landseer (1802–73), favourite painter of the Queen. A specialist in depicting animal subjects his popularity was based on his ability to blend Victorian sentimentality with high moral tone.*

BELOW *Balmoral Castle, bought in 1852, rapidly became a popular and idyllic retreat for the Royal pair. The mania for all things Scottish provoked a national and international boom in tweed and tartan manufacturing.*

fully conscious of their roles as a tastemakers in the fine arts. Characteristically, Prince Albert enacted this role with the vigorous and rational enthusiasm that is found in all his other interests be they model farms or the decoration of the Palace of Westminster.

ROYAL PATRONAGE OF THE FINE ARTS

Fine art described every event in the lives of Victoria and Albert. The Queen kept albums of watercolours by artists such as Eugene Lami and John Nash with which to recall royal trips to foreign countries, their houses, and official events. Other painters were engaged to paint specific subject matter. Sydney Cooper, for example, was brought to Osborne House, the Royal home on the Isle of White, to paint a favourite Guernsey cow. He recorded in his autobiography Albert's great interest in the progress of the painting and their conversations about art. The painter Wilhelm Keyl went to Windsor Castle to record the Queen's pets and the farm animals.

Another popular Victorian painter, Sir Edwin Landseer, was a regular visitor to the royal households at Balmoral, Osborne and Windsor. This brilliant Romantic painter of animals prided himself in being able to capture animals in movement, such as in his painting *The Hunted Stag* which

LEFT *Landseer, thought by Queen Victoria as early as 1837 to be "certainly the cleverest artist there is," four years later painted "Eos," a portrait of the Prince Consort's favourite greyhound.*

hangs in London's Tate Gallery. From 1839 onwards, Landseer was engaged by the Queen to record the royal family's pets and sporting animals, including the very beautiful portrait of a greyhound *Eos*. In this classically composed canvas, the dog stands in profile against a tiled floor and a table, and a charmingly painted top hat and white kid gloves are at its feet. Landseer was one of the Royal couple's favourite artists, and was rewarded by the Queen with a knighthood for his services in 1850.

In 1840 he started work on a portrait of Victoria and Albert and their daughter, the Princess Royal, Victoria, which is now in the Royal Collection. This portrait is far more elaborately finished than his paintings of subjects from nature, probably respecting Albert's preferences, and in accordance with the tastes of the time for glossy varnishes and a studied informality of pose. The conversation piece illustrates the Queen meeting the Prince, who in the German aristocratic tradition was a keen hunter, in the Green Drawing Room at Windsor after his return from a day's sport. At his feet lie a brace of ducks, and the royal dogs frolic on the floor giving Landseer the opportunity to display his virtuoso talents as a painter of animals. The Queen is reported to have been very pleased with the painting, which portrays her husband as a handsome, affectionate man. She wrote in her diary that the effect was 'altogether very cheerful and pleasing'.

Landseer also gave the Queen and the Prince Consort lessons in drawing and etching in 1842, for both were keen

amateurs. At the begining of their marriage they spent many hours drawing, and in later life they produced together a delightful portrait of their children. Under the influence and the teaching of Landseer, the Queen drew and the Prince etched a portrait of their pet dog Islay (a dog much despised by many of Victoria's courtiers).

But neither the Queen nor the Prince laid any claim to being an artist. Explaining his philosphy of royal support for the arts to Lady Bloomfield over dinner at Windsor, Albert is reported to have said:

I consider that persons in our position of life can never be distinguished artists . . . Our business is not so much to create, as to learn to appreciate and understand the works of others, and we never do this till we have realized the difficulties to be overcome. Acting on this principle myself, I have always tried to learn the rudiments of art as much as possible'.

Prince Albert was well known as a connoisseur of art. The illustrator of Dicken's novels, Phiz (Hablot Knight Browne), produced an affectionate pen drawing of the Prince as a life model posing for a group of young artists entitled *The Hero of a Hundred Portraits*, such was Albert's reputation as a patron to the arts. W P Frith, the painter of such popular paintings as *Derby Day*, a great success at the Royal Academy of 1858, paid tribute to the Prince by describing how, in response to suggestions from Albert, he modified the engraving of his painting. He wrote: 'I put many of the Prince's suggestions to the proof after the close of the exhibition, and I improved my picture in every instance'.

It would appear that the Prince Consort was more advanced in his tastes than his Queen, for when he brought John Everett Millais' *Christ in the House of his Parents* to show her in 1850, she appears to have declined the opportunity to buy it. This painting, now hanging in the Tate Gallery, was originally displayed at the Academy's exhibition of 1850, and was a key painting of the avant-garde of the period, the Pre-Raphaelite Brotherhood. This and four other Pre-Raphaelite canvases hung there, came under heavy attack from the art establishment of the day. William Rossetti, Millais' colleague, wrote in his diary: 'Millais' picture has been the signal for a perfect crusade against the PRB ... in all the papers – *The Times*, the *Examiner*, *The Daily News*' even Dickens' *Household Words*, where a leader was devoted to the PRB and devoted them to the infernal gods – the attack has been most virulent and audacious'. It is interesting to note that, despite the scorn heaped upon these artists the Prince's artistic curiosity was sufficiently raised to ignore these cries of artistic perversity.

As well as encouraging contemporary artists, the Prince Consort was renowned as a collector of early German and early Italian paintings. It is widely recognized that Albert's activities as a collector made major contributions to the Royal Collection and the National Gallery. He employed a German painter and engraver, Ludwig Gruner as an advisor on art. Gruner acquired a number of major works of art on the Prince's behalf in the 1840s and 1850s, including Lucas Cranach's *Apollo and Diana* . The Prince also acquired a Duccio *Crucifixion* in 1846, and Fra Angelico's *St Peter Martyr*, which the Queen bought for him.

The Prince's activities were not only restricted to collecting works of fine art. He began work on a study of the entire *œuvre* of Raphael, the Italian Renaissance painter. In the true Victorian spirit of classification, he began collecting reproductions (prints, engravings and photographs) of works, both attributed to Raphael and those of established provenance. Over 1,500 items were catalogued and now reside in the British Library. Raphael, was for the Prince, the pinnacle of artistic achievement. Buckingham Palace and the Frogmore Mausoleum were decorated with reproductions of Raphael masterpieces.

LEFT *This miniature by Richard Thorburn presents Prince Albert and his brother Ernest II of Saxe-Gotha in 17th century costume, an affectation reflective of the historical revivalism of the day.*

THE ROYAL HOMES

The two great royal homes of Buckingham Palace and Windsor Castle were not greatly modified by their new inhabitants in the years after Victoria's 1837 Coronation. Windsor had received much attention from George IV who had employed the architect Jeffrey Wyattville to redesign much of the interior, and Victoria and Albert concerned themselves with the grounds and its lesser buildings. Civil servants had plans to demolish the Royal Lodge and the small fishing cottage near Viginia Water, but the Prince orchestrated their restoration. New stables were built and the grounds near the Park were relandscaped to give more privacy to the royal family. The estate itself was the focus of the Prince's attention at Windsor, with its twin functions of a sporting park for deerhunting and agricultural land. However, the Prince's fondness for hunting fuelled controversy, with *Punch*, the satirical magazine, leading the pack of critics.

Similarly, Buckingham Palace was not greatly changed by the Queen during her long reign. Improvement and extensions were hampered by problems of finance. As a building owned by the British people in which to house their monarch, any work on it could not be financed from the private purse of the Queen or the Prince Consort, but had to be approved by parliament by due proceedure. George IV's architect, John Nash, had started a series of very costly alterations to the building in the 1820s, and had incurred the displeasure of parliament for it. Despite these alterations, the Palace's new occupants found that it did not meet their requirements, for it was barely habitable and incomplete. The Palace was unhygienic, with strange smells rising out of the sewers, and kitchens that shocked Dr Lyon Playfair, who had been called in to survey the building. The ever growing royal family, with its servants and perpetual guests, felt cramped by the building. In February 1845, Robert Peel, the Prime Minister, replying to pleas from the Queen for money to extend and improve the building, had to state that it was not a judicious moment. These were the 'hungry forties', a period of terrible economic hardship in Britain.

In the following year, after a commission had investigated the problems at the Palace, the Government allocated a sum of £150,000 for improvements. A number of changes were made to the exterior of the building, of which the most significant was the architect Edward Blore's redesign of the facade, done with the Prince's encouragement. According to one recent history of the building, this facade was influenced by Caserta, a Bourbon Palace which the Prince had seen in 1839 on a visit to Italy. Unfortunately, this new architectural aspect did not last long, for it was built in poor quality stone which

ABOVE AND BELOW *Osborne House, like Balmoral, was bought from the savings that resulted from Prince Albert's reform of Royal Household expenditure. Situated near Cowes on the Isle of Wight, this seaside house was purchased in 1845 and redesigned in the Palladian style by Thomas Cubitt, following the specifications of the Prince Consort.*

began falling before the building was completed. Despite contemporary architectural thought, which then preferred unstuccoed stone, the building had to be plastered white to prevent further damage to its frontage.

Royal influence can be seen to a greater degree in the interiors of Buckingham Palace. The Queen owned Brighton Pavilion, Nash's marvellous Indian-style regency residence in the heart of the town, but thought that it was an inappropriate setting in which to bring up her family. The building offered no privacy from the crowds that were flocking to the seaside town in increasing numbers. In 1847 the interiors of the Pavilion were dismantled and many of their fittings removed to Buckingham Palace. Despite Blore's suggestion that Buckingham

BELOW LEFT *The nurseries at Osborne are typical of the relaxed informality that characterised this Royal retreat.*

RIGHT *This horn stool and chair at Osborne House illustrate the often bizarre nature of Victorian taste.*

Palace ought to have new modern interiors, the Prince insisted that the superb fittings from Brighton be used for the new reception rooms. The small dining room has a number of items, notably a magnificent mantelpiece, from Brighton. A number of rooms were added to the south side of the Palace in the early 1850s, including a ballroom and a supper ballroom. The Prince's preference for Italianate art and design is reflected in this ballroom, with its copies of Raphael's series of paintings, *The Hours*. The Queen described the opening ball in 1856 in her diary: 'everyone could rest and every one could see. It was most truly a successful fête, and everyone was in great admiration of the rooms'.

But it is Osborne House, built in the late 1840s for the royal family, and Balmoral Castle purchased in the autumn of 1852, that give a greater indication of royal taste, and a much better picture of the day-to-day lives of the royal family.

Osborne House on the Isle of Wight was first seen by the the Queen and the Prince Consort in 1844, and they immediately fell in love with it. They purchased it in the following year, the Queen writing:

We have succeeded in purchasing Osborne on the Isle of Wight . . . It sounds so snug and nice to have a place of one's own, quiet and retired, and free from all woods and forests, and other charming departments who really are the plague of one's life.

The royal couple liked Osborne, for unlike Brighton Pavilion, it offered a quiet retreat near the sea, allowing the Queen to use her new steam-powered yacht. The Prince could excercise his ideas about running an estate with complete freedom. Although the initial plans were to improve the existing 16-room building, Thomas Cubitt's survey of the mansion suggested that it would be less expensive to build afresh. Cubitt submitted his plans for the new building in April 1845 which offered a private pavilion for the use of the royal family and a number of rooms for her guests. These did not meet all their social and political commitments, and so a number of smaller houses were built. A Swiss-style cottage stands in the grounds, brought over from Germany, which the royal children used to play in. It contained a scaled down shop and a kitchen. The inspiration for the Italianate style of Osborne House is assumed to be the Prince Consort's, for its views reminded him of the Bay of Naples. He is reported to have altered Cubitt's original classical designs, to make them 'more academically correct'.

Osborne was a far more familial, domestic home than any of the Queen's other residences. It contained a number of up-to-date features including ventilation and bright nurseries for Victoria and Albert's nine children. The theme of the family was continued in the works of art decorating the house, including a family portrait by FX Winterhalter, and a number of statues of the children by Mary Thornycroft. While Buckingham Palace housed a grand organ, Osborne heard the sounds of Albert playing the piano and harpsichord. It seems as if Osborne marked a very happy period in the lives of the Queen and her Prince. In her long widowhood she often recalled their time there fondly.

Both Victoria and Albert were keen on the Scottish Highlands making a number of trips in the early 1840s. It appears that Albert was much taken with Scottish life, and the Highlands may have reminded him of the mountains of Thungria and time spent there in his youth. They first saw Balmoral Castle, in the Deeside region, in 1848 and fell under its spell. It had been rebuilt in the 1830s in the then fashionable Scottish Baronial style; a heavy, Scottish Gothic, characterized by a

ABOVE, LEFT AND OPPOSITE
Osborne House,
like Balmoral, was bought from the
savings that resulted from Prince
Albert's reform of Royal Household
expenditure. Situated near Cowes on
the Isle of Wight, this seaside house was
purchased in 1845 and redesigned in the
Palladian style by Thomas Cubitt,
following the specifications of the
Prince Consort.

light coloured granite and historicist detailing such as tiled turrets and archer's slits.

The Prince Consort took possession of Balmoral four years after first seeing the castle, because complications in Scottish law demanded an Act of Parliament to allow its purchase. The Prince again planned to improve and enlarge the building. A new ballroom was built. In decorating the interiors the Prince was swept up in an passion for all things Scottish, to the distaste of one visitor:

> The curtains, the furniture, the carpets, the furniture (coverings) are all of different plaids, and the thistles are in such abundance that they would rejoice the heart of a donkey if they happened to look like his favourite repast which they don't.

John Philip painted a portrait of the Prince, in full highland dress with Balmoral Castle in the background, and both the Prince and the Queen had lessons in traditional Scottish dancing. Albert, never at home in London, loved the Highlands with its opportunities for hunting and drawing nature. Royal parties made expeditionary trips into the wilder parts of the countryside which were recorded by the artist Carl Haag, and the Queen in her book *Leaves from the Journal of Our life in the Scottish Highlands,* in 1868.

GOOD WORKS

The Victorian period was an age of great social changes and reforms. Many of the key institutions of British society today were initiated in the second half of the 19th century. These included the education system which was extended to all sections of society by the 1870 Butler Education Act, and public libraries, initiated by an Act in 1850 which empowered local authorities to offer their services for free. Growing concern was felt over public health, and in particular the threat of cholera which claimed the lives of many early Victorians. This led to the development of municipally run sewage systems and clean water distribution. Increasingly, the upper and middle classes felt obliged to improve the standards of living of the poor. Many individuals excercised their philanthropic concerns by starting or joining charities. A number of charitable schemes were begun in the last decades of the century to provide sanitary housing for the poor, such as the Peabody Trust, or to provide pensions for domestic servants, or to encourage temperance. Characteristically, Victorian social improvement was generally felt to be an area for voluntary effort; the work of the individual rather than parliamentary legislation and public funding.

The Prince Consort was no less Victorian in this aspect than any other member of society. In 1844 Albert was made the president for the 'Society for Improving the Condition of the Working Classes', which set itself the task of designing cheap sanitary housing for the poor. Employing the architect, Henry Roberts, the Society displayed some of their houses at the Great Exhibition, near the Hyde Park Barracks. These homes were technically far superior to any of the speculative buildings then being erected in Britain's cities. They included

a number of novel features such as hollow bricks to prevent dampness and better insulation. Interestingly, they were not simply plain, utilitarian shells for their poor occupants to inhabit, but contained some pretty brick detailing, and had a pleasant 'Elizabethan' character. After the exhibition these buildings were taken down and re-erected in South London, where they still stand at the entrance to Kennington Park.

It seems that the Prince Consort was a much greater enthusiast for reform than the Queen and he took on many engagements as her deputy. These included the laying of innumerable foundation stones and the opening of hospitals, colleges and homes for retired sailors and soldiers. He was also a great educationalist and was inaugurated as the Chancellor of Cambridge University in March, 1847. His activities there, perhaps to the dismay of some of those around him, were not those of a figurehead and he achieved considerable changes in the curriculum. His greatest educational legacy was the complex of scientific and educational institutions in South Kensington, which was dubbed 'Albertopolis' in his honour. As has already been noted in Chapter Two, the Great Exhibition was a considerable financial success. Albert dictated that its profits should be spent in the spirit of the exhibition, suggesting:

an establishment in which by the application of Science and Art to industrial pursuits the Industry of all nations may be raised in the scale of human employment, and where by the constant interchange of Ideas, Experience and its results each nation may gain and contribute something.

ABOVE *French engraver Gustave Dore, already celebrated for his illustrations to Dante's Inferno and the Bible, produced during 1869–71 a telling series descriptive of the endemic squalor and poverty of Victorian London. Prince Albert's model lodging house (below) erected in Hyde Park for the 1851 Exhibition, was one of many high-minded attempts to ameliorate the problem.*

The government matched the profits of the exhibition, and an 87 acre plot of land in South Kensington was purchased. The site on which the Albert Hall now stands was originally intended to house the National Gallery, which the Prince wanted moved from its busy spot overlooking Trafalgar Square.

The keystone to the development was the South Kensington Museum, which was built by Captain F Fowke of the Royal Engineers. This museum, then surrounded by fields, and opened to the public in 1857, was in the Italian Renaissance style, with earthy red brick, and detailed terracotta mouldings. The interiors of the South Kensington Museum mark the progression of Victorian style through the 1860s and 1870s. Most of the initial interiors were decorated by School of Design pupils, such as Godfrey Sykes and James Gamble who designed the first refreshment room. The enamelled iron ceiling of this room was a technique revived by the French Sèvres Factory in the 1840s and highly lauded at the Great Exhibition of 1851. This room was a stunning *tour de force* in cream, red and ochre tiles successfully combining industrial design and decoration.

The firm of Morris, Marshall, Faulkner and Co., the leading edge of mid-Victorian design, was commissioned to decorate the West Dining Room, next to Sykes and Gamble's room. This second space marks a great contrast with the first, for it is replete with mediaevalist touches, including stained glass windows and painted wall panels representing the seasons of the year. The Museum's exhibits were of both scientific and artistic interest and included the Sheepshank collection of paintings, and objects on loan from the patent office, drawing great crowds to the Museum.

The Prince Consort died in 1861, before much of the South Kensington complex was begun. But the Science Museum, the Royal College of Music and the other educational institutions commenced after his death, stand as tributes to his reformist and educationalist zeal.

Another of the Prince's notable activities was his chairmanship of the commission which selected the works of art to decorate the Houses of Parliament. Three years before Victoria came to the throne, the Palace of Westminster was destroyed by a fire so great that it could be seen on the South Downs. A competition was launched in 1835 to design a new building in either Elizabethan or Gothic style, which Charles Barry, a Gothicist won. Building work began in 1840, and in 1841 the commission, led by the Prince, was instituted. The commission was constituted by, in the words of Richard Redgrave RA, 'the most eminent statesmen of all parties, with some representatives of literature and dilettantism of the country: art was strangely omitted'. With Barry's plans complete, it was clear to the commission that large, decorative paintings and major works of sculpture were demanded. Seeking advice on their preference for frescoes, the commission turned to Germany where Ludwig I was employing leading members of the Nazarene school to decorate his Munich home. This led to some concern that the Prince, as a German, would wish to employ German artists to decorate the home of British democracy. But in April 1842, the commission announced a competition for cartoon drawings depicting scenes from British history or literature. One year later, 140 cartoons were displayed to the public at Westminster Hall. The winning entry was Edward Armitage's *Caesar's Invasion of Britain*, with GF Watts' *Caractacus Led in Triumph Through the Streets of Rome* and CW Cope's *Trial by Jury* coming second and third.

It was decided that the commission needed to test the ability of these, and a number of other favoured painters as fresco artists, for the technique was not practised or taught in Britain at the time. Consequently, the first commission was not awarded until 1845, to William Dyce for his *The Baptism of Ethelbert*. This work shows Ethelbert, the 7th century King of Kent, being christened by St Augustine in Canterbury. Appropriately for the technique, this fresco has some of the character of early Renaissance art in its treatment of space and triangular composition. Dyce had spent some time in Italy studying fresco painting, and was heavily influenced by the Nazarene school, who were a group of artists working in the early years of the century in Germany. Johann Overbeck and Franz Pforr formed this quasi-religious brotherhood in 1809 and began painting in the deserted monastry of St Isadoro in Rome. Heavily influenced by Durer, Raphael and Perugino, they aimed to regenerate German religious art. A further three artists, Cope, Daniel Maclise and J C Horsley, were commissioned a year later and all four frescoes were unveiled to the public in 1848.

Despite the authority of the commission and the talent of the artists who worked on them, the frescoes at the Palaces of Westminster have not been highly regarded by historians of art. The high aspirations behind the project were not met: the technique of fresco was not revived, as had been hoped by the Prince. Others have noted that these works lack the maturity and richness found in the oil paintings by these artists. It also appears that the commission's concern with technique was not rigorous enough, for within a few years the frescoes were visibly deteriorating.

RIGHT *One of the reading rooms in the Library of the House of Lords designed by Augustus Pugin. Converted to Catholicism in 1835, Pugin believed that a Medieval Gothic revival would encourage a return to pre-Reformation spiritual values.*

The image of royalty during the Victorian era was disseminated throughout England and the colonies on a mass scale. Public works, like the coat-of-arms embroidered on the Coronation chair in the House of Lords (above right) and the royal cypher blazoned on this marble drinking fountain (below right) were matched by commercial production. Ceramic portraits of the Queen and her family, such as this 1837 Goss ware likeness (above), were found in most middle class homes.

Allegory played a large part in royal iconography. Thomas Brock's Queen Victoria Memorial in front of Buckingham Palace (below) presents the Queen surrounded by eight symbolic marble and bronze groups. Similarly Gibson's sculpture in the Prince's Chamber, House of Lords, (above) has Victoria flanked by Justice and Mercy.

THE CULT OF MONARCHY

During the course of her long reign Queen Victoria was transformed into a national and imperial icon. In tribute, her name was given to areas of the world: new stretches of Empire such as the Victoria Falls; the State of Victoria; and hundreds of towns across the globe. With less pomp, the products of manufacturing and commerce adopted her regal name for even the most prosaic of products, such as the 'Victoria' fountain pen and the 'Victoria' chiming clock. The lives of the royal couple were enveloped by a personality cult, so that even their own property was graced by their names. In 1844, for example, her new steam yacht was named *Victoria and Albert*.

Another Victoria and Albert, the museum, is an interesting case in point. The Museum of Manufactures was renamed as

the Victoria and Albert Museum in May 1899, the date of the Queen's last public engagement. She was in South Kensington to lay the foundation stone of a new facade designed by Aston Webb. As she made her short speech under the cover of a pavilion, she may have looked back to the building and seen the original facade, above the lecture theatre. On the pediment, designed by Reuben Townroe, she would have seen herself portrayed as Hera giving laurels to industry, art and other virtues, with her name, V I C T O R I A, radiating above her head like a halo. This mosaic in gold and terracotta tiles made by Minton and Company, a memorial to the Great Exhibition, payed greater tribute to the Queen. Similarly in the refreshment room thousands of ornamental tiles simply stated 'Victoria'.

The name Victoria and her image were associated with a number of objects emblematic of their age. The Penny Black, as an example, the first postage stamp, introduced by Roland Hill and Henry Cole, depicted the Queen's head in profile.

COMMEMORATIVE
MEMORABILIA

*Victoria's accession in 1837 marked the beginning of the royal souvenir industry.
Objects such as this jug (below left) commemorating her proclamation are
comparatively rare, a situation which changed radically in the years that followed.
The Diamond Jubilee of 1897 inspired objects as diverse as these four lace and gilt
framed royal photographs (bottom right), a porcelain mug decorated with the royal
coat-of-arms (below right), stitched ribbons (right, opposite right), and this
embroidered commemorative picture (left) Ephemera such as this dinner menu
(opposite bottom centre) and reception programme (opposite bottom right)
celebrating the Golden Jubilee of a decade before, were treasured as much as this
emphatically imperial commemorative plate (top right).*

Hill's national postage system was a triumph of the Victorian Age, and it was appropriate that it was symbolized by the Queen. In June 1857, the first Victoria Cross medals were awarded in Hyde Park to heroes of the Crimean War. The Queen gave her name to the greatest symbol of military valour, an iron maltese cross made from guns captured at the battle of Sebastopol in 1855.

Royal jubilees and anniversaries presented manufacturers with the opportunity to produce popular items to celebrate these occasions. Although the Silver Jubilee of her coronation

LEFT AND BELOW *The Albert Memorial is a complex construction based around a 15ft high gilt-bronze figure of the Prince enshrined beneath a richly decorated Gothic revival canopy. Designed by George Gilbert Scott, the memorial was erected during 1863–76 at a cost of £120,000, raised by public subscription.*

was overshadowed by the death of the Prince Consort in the previous year, the Golden Jubilee of 1887 saw floods of jubilee medals, ceramics and popular prints all depicting the Queen. The marriages of her children to the aristocracy and nobility of Europe also provided opportunities for commemorative objects.

When Victoria came to the throne in 1837, a number of fashions were triggered that appear slightly odd today. The Victorian doll was the essential toy for children of the middle classes. It was the subject of fashion changes that mimicked life and technical innovations, such as the development of talking dolls in the 1830s. On Victoria's accession blue eyes became fashionable, superseding the taste for brown.

But the fashionability of the living Queen was little compared to the veritable cult of the Prince Consort after his death in December, 1861. This was fuelled by the Queen's protracted period of mourning. She demanded that his rooms at Windsor, Balmoral and Osborne remain as he had left them. Every night his clothes were laid out by his bed as if he was to wear them the following day. In her own bedroom was a photograph of the dead Prince and casts of his face and hands, which had been taken by the sculptor William Threed. She sent to their children relics of his life and locks of his hair.

Despite the Prince Consort's request that she would not 'raise even a single marble image to his name', the Queen commissioned a number of memorial projects, including scale statues and busts for the royal homes and as gifts to friends and servants. Key royal portraits from the early 1860s depicting the Queen alone or with her children, feature busts of Albert as the focal point. Both Albert Graefle and Joseph Noel Paton were commissioned to produce such paintings in 1863.

Following the Queen's example, a number of commemorative projects were set in motion throughout the country. The most famous of these was the 'The National Memorial to His Royal Highness the Prince Consort', which is better known as the Albert Memorial and stands in Hyde Park. The design was by the Gothic architect, George Gilbert Scott, selected from among several projects by seven prominent architects who worked as the advisory panel to the memorial committee. He regarded it as a chance:

> to erect a ciborium to protect a statue of the Prince . . . designed in some degree on the principles of the ancient shrines. These shrines were models of imaginary buildings, such as had never in reality been erected, and my idea was to realise one of these imaginary structures with its precious materials, its inlaying, its enamelling etc. etc.

It appears that Scott's scheme was selected because he placed great emphasis on the Gothic being Albert's preferred architectural style, and the English tradition of Gothic memorials, artists were carved in a running frieze around the podium supporting the memorial.

John Clayton designed glass mosaics which were made in Venice and placed in the gables of the canopy, on the themes of art and virtue. A running mosaic, below the gable, relates the inscription: 'Queen Victoria and Her People – To the Memory of Albert Prince Consort – As a Tribute of their Gratitude – For a Life Devoted to the Public Good'. Smaller white sculpted figures decorate the heights of the towering structure, which is topped with a cross.

Critics noted that the statue of the Prince was dwarfed by the magnificence of the structure designed to house it. *The Times* argued that it was inappropriate to commemorate the Prince's life of 'purity' with wealth and luxury. But the format of Albert memorials had been set, and in the following years other cities, like Manchester, erected Gothic memorials to the Prince.

Stained glass windows, appropriate symbols of illumination and piety, were commonly chosen as memorials to the Prince. These often alluded to the Prince's life and good works through biblical scenes and parables. St Mary's in Nottingham, for example, chose New Testament stories that were 'emblematical of the Reformatories, Schools, Hospitals, Asylums, and other institutions, which H.R.H. patronized; and of the

ABOVE *Prince Albert, Queen Victoria's "dear angel" died suddenly of typhoid in 1861, to her immense grief. His study (right) was preserved after his death.*

citing the example of the Eleanor Crosses erected by Edward I after the death of his wife in the late-13th century. All the other proposed designs were derived from Classical architectural forms. Scott's design was not without its critics, including Henry Cole, who challenged the historical veracity and plausibility of Scott's scheme. Despite this, the memorial was begun in May 1864 and was opened to the public in July 1872.

The memorial consists of a 175 feet high, richly ornate architectural canopy, which protects a bronze statue by J H Foley, of the Prince, who sits looking south to where the Albert Hall stands. The canopy rests on a base which has groups of figures at each corner representing Manufactures, Agriculture, Commerce and Engineering; the cornerstones of Victorian wealth. At the bottom of the steps which lead up to the memorial stand a further four groups symbolizing Europe, Asia, Africa and America. These eight groups were commissioned from the major sculptors of the day – John Bell, William Theed and William Calder Marshall. Characters from history, placed in thematic groups such as poets and musicians and

general benevolence which he practised'. The most important stained glass window dedicated to the Prince's life was installed in Saint George's Chapel at Windsor in 1863. This Gothic window made reference to the Prince through biblical symbolism and was intended 'to stir up one deeper feeling of love, and thankfulness for an example so noble'.

A number of institutions commissioned paintings as memorial tributes to the dead Prince. The Royal Society of Arts, of which the Prince had been the President, raised a sum of £700 by subscription. It decided to spend part of this sum on portraits for the Society's Great Room. This room had been decorated by James Barry in the 1790s with a series of history paintings, supplementing the portraits of Lord Romney by Joshua Reynolds and Lord Folkstone by Thomas Gainsborough that were already hanging there. In 1863 the Society proposed to replace these two portraits with contemporary ones of the Prince and the Queen. CW Cope was commissioned to paint the portrait of the Prince. The Prince stands, in garter robes, staring directly out at the viewer. By his left hand lies the Charter of Incorporation of the 1851 Great Exhibition, his greatest achievement. A weeping cherub and the hourglass in the painting refer to the fact of the Prince's death, and the overall effect of this painting is of sombre tranquillity. Appropriately, J C Horsley's portrait of the Queen has more verve. She is

shown with their children, in a composition formed by a twisting plan of the Crystal Palace held by the young Prince Edward and his sisters.

Many popular portraits of the Prince were produced in different media. A number of firms made woven silk portraits of the dead Prince, shown with his family, his coat of arms or with edifying epithets such as 'The Earth is the Lord's and the fulness thereof'. The demand for photographs of the late Prince was very great, with 70,000 postcard images being sold during the first week of national mourning. The writer Alfred Mumby noted:

> Crowds round the photograph shops, looking at the the few portraits of the Prince which are still unsold. I went to Meclin's to buy one: every one in the shop was doing the same. They had none left: would put my name down, but could not promise even then. Afterwards I succeeded in getting one – the last the seller had – of the Queen and Prince: giving four shillings for what would have cost but eighteen pence a week ago.

All kinds of ceramic wares were produced in Albert's memory. At the Great Exhibition of 1862, a number of manufacturers displayed such items, including Copeland with their famous 'Albert Tazza'. This large porcelain ornamental plate depicts

LEFT *"Queen Victoria presenting colours to the 79th Cameron Highlanders" painted by Sidney Hall in 1873.*

RIGHT *This small drinking fountain, surmounted by a sculpture of the Empress of India, still stands today on the Island of Mahe in the Seychelles.*

BELOW *Victoria, as yet uncrowned, is pictured here being driven in state through cheering crowds on 4 October 1837 on her first visit to Brighton after the death of William IV. The entrance to the Royal Pavilion can be seen through the triumphal arch and floral amphitheatre festooned with flags.*

Albert's successes as 'promoter of the arts', 'president of societies for science' and 'chancellor of an university'. The same company also issued a small statuette of a relaxed Prince, dressed in a morning coat and seated in an armchair. This figure, designed by George Abbott was made in Parian ware, an unglazed porcelain developed in the 1840s.

A range of more utilitarian memorial goods found their way on to the Victorian marketplace including buckles and belt clasps and a tape measure decorated with a photographic portrait of the Prince. Amateur artists could hand colour prints of such subjects as the Union Jack at half mast, musicians could buy sheet music for hundreds of ballads and hymns dedicated to their Prince, and others could spend their leisure hours reading numerous pen portraits of his life in penny editions.

Despite the fact that the Queen was not amused by many of the popular commemorative items produced by opportunist manufacturers, the popularity of memorial items across all price ranges and contemporary comment testify to the genuine sense of loss at the death of the Prince.

Her Majesty QUEEN VICTORIA passing under the TRIUMPHAL ARCH through the AMPHITHEATRE (designed by M'Fabian) erected in Honor of HER MAJESTY'S first visit to BRIGHTON Oct 4th 1837. Dedicated by permission to the QUEEN by Her Majesty's Most Obed' Humble Servant.

W. H. MASON.

THE BATTLE OF STYLES

"Isabella and the Pot of Basil" (1866–8) by the Pre-Raphaelite artist William Holman Hunt. Based on a scene from the Keats' poem, the painting brings together an extraordinary amalgam of cultural styles, ranging from a Turkish hanging lamp to a majolica pot reminiscent of contemporary "Art Pottery," that seem far removed from the original medieval Italian setting.

id 19th-century architecture and design was trapped in a paradox. The Victorians lived in an age of amazing inventiveness and imagination. They were as aware of the progresses made in their time as any historian today. The triumphs of their age and the leading figures behind these success were proclaimed, although without mention of the ill-effects of many of their achievements, by writers like Samuel Smiles in books such as *Invention and Industry* and in journals like the *MacMillan Magazine*. But while engineers, entrepreneurs and scientists were building the future, 'the mother of the arts', architecture, appeared to be sinking into ever greater retrospection. Historicism dominated architecture, and architecture exerted great influence over the applied arts. It is hard to distinguish separate developments in these two areas of design until the end of Victoria's reign because the leading decorative artists were usually, first and foremost, architects. Futhermore, it is hard to talk of design as a separate profession until the last decade of the 19th century, when the Arts and Crafts Movement, under the influence of ideas drawn from traditional handicrafts, came to prominence.

THE DUNGEON OF ARCHAEOLOGY

Historicism was widely regarded as a problem, even by those architects whose practice was most firmly entrenched in one of the many historical styles of the day. George Gilbert Scott, the Gothicist, wrote in 1850:

I am no mediaevalist, I do not advocate the styles of the Middle Ages as such. If we had a distinctive architecture of our own day, worthy of the greatness of the age, I should be content to follow it; but we have not.

The proponents of each divergent style believed that it had the most to offer modern man. Scott, as he implied in the quote above, chose the Gothic because he believed that it combined the spiritual in its 'Christian' forms and the rational in that it provided building solutions for every kind of architectural problem, from his great St Pancras railway station to the humblest of cottages. Conversely, the Classicists, men like Sir Robert Smirke, the architect of the British Museum, believed that their chosen architectural language embodied the great transcending values of art, democracy and civilization.

Futhermore, beyond the very general architectural classifications of Classical and Gothic, a series of sub-divisions can be drawn up, whose proponents were pitched against each other. Until the Enlightenment of the 18th century, architecture had followed a set of conventions that established a hierarchy of appropriate forms. The monumental Doric order, for example, was considered suitable for buildings such as prisons, whereas the more decorative Corinthian, was used in buildings such as clubs. With the rise of notions of the picturesque in the late 18th century, these Classical rules of design broke down. Architects began to search for novelty and variety. Great architecture came to be seen as less the successful application of established rules and more the source of delight and surprise.

The earliest Gothic Revival buildings of the mid 18th century paid little heed to historical accuracy. They were the projects of romantics and enthusiasts rather than pedants. Horace Walpole's home Strawberry Hill, begun in 1749, originally contained a number of Classical elements such as a Palladian chimneypiece in the style of William Kent. He augmented these details with a diverse range of Gothic forms: the staircase wallpaper was derived from ornament found in Worcester Cathedral; St Alban's Abbey provided the inspiration for the doors to the gallery, and Richard Bentley designed a set of chairs to match some 16th-century stained glass Walpole had installed there.

During the 19th century British architects began to be concerned with greater veracity and historical styles were divided into periods and sub-styles. Thomas Rickman's book *Attempt to Discriminate the Styles in English Architecture* of 1819 established the three categories still used to describe the Gothic

ABOVE *Built in 1867–74 by George Gilbert Scott, St Pancras Station, one of the two great termini of the London Midland Region, incorporates design elements from both French and Italian Gothic architecture. W. H. Barlow's great glass and steel 690 ft trainshed (below) runs behind this imposing frontage.*

RIGHT *Coe & Hofland's design for the new Foreign Office building, to be located near Downing Street, was one of many submitted in the classical style.*

today: Early English, Decorated, and Perpendicular. By the middle years of the 19th century, each of these styles had its supporters. As an example, although most Victorian Gothic buildings were typically in the Perpendicular style, the great architectural theorist, August Welby Northmore Pugin, was a dedicated proponent of the Decorated (preferring to call it 'English Middle Pointed'). Similarly, Classical architecture was subdivided into a number of styles; neo-Classical or Palladian and so on. The architect and archaeologist, Charles Cockerill, in his support for a variant called 'Classical Antiquity', was just as concerned with historical veracity as his Gothic counterparts.

Victorian architectural practice hit a crisis in the middle of the century because of this highly self-conscious and academic approach to historical style. Victorian thinking was widely based on a belief in the evolutionary nature of progress, but in their new found concern with accurately recreating the achievements of the past, architects hit a dead end. Scott acknowledged this, writing: 'The peculiar characteristic of the present day, as compared with all former periods, is this – that we are acquainted with the history of art'.

The crisis in Victorian architecture, and in particular, its fixation with historical styles, is neatly encapsulated in the story of the competition for the Foreign Office building in Whitehall in 1856. This episode not only reveals the extent to which architects were bound by historicism, but also the meaning that was attached to particular styles within Victorian society.

THE FOREIGN OFFICE COMPETITION

By the mid 1850s, due to Britain's growing role in international affairs, the Foreign Office had outgrown its headquarters. Lord Palmerston's Liberal government announced a competition to build new offices on a site near Downing Street. Most of the projects submitted were in Classical style and the winning design by H B Garling was heavily influenced by the new Louvre building in Paris. Palmerston did not like this design, and set Sir James Pennethorne, architect to the Board of Works, the task of designing the building.

George Gilbert Scott was one of the small number of Gothic architects who had submitted a design in the original competition and had been awarded third place. On hearing that the winning design was to be rejected and a non-competitor commissioned, Scott lobbied strongly to have his project reconsidered, or in his words; 'I thought myself at liberty to stir'. He described this design in his autobiography of 1879, thus:

> I did not aim in making my style 'Italian Gothic', my ideas ran much more towards the French, to which for some years I have devoted my chief study. I did, however, aim at gathering a few hints from Italy . . . I mean a certain squareness and horizontality of design. . . . I combined this . . . with gables, high pitched roofs and dormers. My details were excellent and well suited to the purpose.

LEFT *Despite its prosaic function, the first letter box, set up at Ludgate Circus in 1855, was ornamented and surmounted by a ball finial.*

There were many in parliament who supported Scott, for it was felt that the Gothic was the most appropriate architectural style for a major state commission. This architectural language was argued by its proponents to be a singularly national style echoing the nearby Westminster Hall, the Henry VII Chapel of Westminster Abbey and the still incomplete new Houses of Parliament by Charles Barry. The Gothic style, particularly in its Perpendicular form, was also associated with Anglicanism, ie the High Church, and nationalist and royalist politics, ie High Tory. In February 1858, a new Tory Government came into power, bringing a number of Scott's supporters in with it. One of these, Lord John Manners, was made First Commissioner of Works with the responsibility for the Foreign Office project. He appointed Scott as architect to the scheme.

However, another political swing occurred and in June 1859 the Liberal Party was brought back into power. Scott attempted to persuade Palmerston of the merit of his design. But when Palmerston suggested that another architect might be able to meet his demands, Scott capitulated and produced further designs in a 'Byzantine' style. These too did not meet with the Prime Minister's approval, who called it a 'neither one thing nor t'other – a regular mongrel-affair'. Scott was only able to secure Palmerston's necessary consent with an

Italian Renaissance-style design. The great claims made for the new Foreign Office, at its opening in 1873, seem somewhat reduced by Scott's admission that he 'bought some costly books on Italian architecture and set vigorously to work'.

The conflict between Scott and Palmerston had little to do with the fitness of the design; it came about because of their divergent stylistic preferences. When the building was complete, in plan, it differed little to Scott's original design. The building, in Portland stone and coloured granite, is dominated by an Italianate tower, that could just as easily have been erected in polychromatic bands of brick and carved masonry underneath a tower mimicking the Venetian Early Renaissance.

But what the episode does illustrate is the importance placed on style in the this period. Victorian edifices and artifacts were seen to be made attractive, fashionable and meaningful by being cloaked in historical decoration and ornament. Even the most functional things were disguised in this manner; water works were dressed up as Greek temples, and sewing machines as painted *objets d'art.*

VICTORIAN NEO-CLASSICISM

The story of neo-Classicism in the 19th century can be traced back to the Palladianism of William Kent in the early 18th century. Its development was also influenced by James 'Athenian' Stuart in the 1760s, notable for his Spencer House and his book *Antiquities of Athens* of 1762. In the 1760s, Stuart was succeeded in his position of eminence by Robert Adam, whose calm elegant variant of Classicism, inspired by Pompeii, led fashionable taste until the 1780s. He in turn was superseded by James Wyatt, whose allegiance to Classical idioms was erratic, and who produced his most famous buildings in the Gothic style such as Lee Priory in Kent.

Around the turn of the century the interest in Classicism, which had until that point been diverse in character, took on a particularly Greek aspect with men like Thomas Hope arguing for Greek over Roman orders. The installation of the Parthenon Sculptures in the British Museum in 1816, brought back from Athens by Lord Elgin in 1806, fuelled the interest in neo-Classicism. This was reinforced by manufacturers such as Wedgwood, who had been producing highly Classical ranges of ceramics in their black basalt since the 1760s.

Neo-Classicism peaked in the first decades of the century when a number of prestigious architectural commissions such as the new Covent Garden Theatre, University College in London and the British Museum were assigned to Classicists. At that point, this Classical heritage in Britain was particularly vigorous; some observers believed it had become the national style. They felt that British art and design, derived from Greek models, outshone the rest of Europe. 'At the present moment', wrote Thomas Kebble Hervey in 1834, 'no school of sculpture can claim to take the lead of England'.

The taste for neo-Classicism, or 'the Greek' as contemporaries referred to it, had declined by Victoria's accession to the throne in 1837. This is usually characterized as a revolt against

LEFT *The British neo-classical sculptor John Gibson (1760–1866) studied under both Flaxman and Canova. His "Tinted Venus" (1851) is the best known of his attempts to revive the classical practice of colouring statues.*

RIGHT *This ornamental Minton vase of tinted Parian ware overlaid with exquisitely fashioned passion flowers and foliage in decorative relief, was manufactured in 1854.*

FAR RIGHT *The Elgin Vase with its delicately etched classical motifs and running frieze was completed by John Northwood.*

James Bunning's Coal Exchange, for example, which was finished in 1849, in its exterior form recalls the Tower of the Winds in Athens.

In Scotland and the industrial cities of the north of England the neo-Classical style continued to be popular. Perhaps the greatest of these buildings is J A Hansom's Birmingham Town Hall which was opened in 1849. Hansom's classical design had been chosen in preference to Gothic designs by Charles Barry and Thomas Rickman. It was based on the the form of the Temple of Castor and Pollux in Rome, and stands on an open site in the centre of the city. Although not a large building, an impression of massiveness was achieved by beautiful, fluted Corinthian columns supported by a rusticated podium. In Scotland a number of late Classical buildings were erected in the 1850s. These included W H Playfair's National Gallery of Scotland in Edinburgh of 1850–4 and Alexander Thomson's Caledonia Road Free Church in Glasgow in 1856–7, which

the 'good taste' of Chippendale furniture and Nash terraces, and a desire for novelty and 'flights of fancy' exemplified by the bizarre tastes on display at the Great Exhibition. It was specified in the competition to design the new Houses of Parliament in 1835 that the only acceptable styles were to be the Gothic or Elizabethan. But neo-Classicism continued to exert an influence on Victorian art and design until the 1860s when many of its leading proponents died, including the sculptor, John Gibson in 1866, and Sir Robert Smirke, the architect, in the following year. Although other architectural styles, such as the Gothic, won many of the prestigious commissions of the day and had more vigorous advocates, 'the Greek' continued to be popular in certain fields of design, such as municipal building and memorial sculpture.

Although Sir Robert Smirke's British Museum, the most prominent Victorian neo-Classical building in London, was completed in 1847, it was designed in the 1820s and so belongs to an early period of architectural taste. Other buildings in London of the Victorian period displayed neo-Classical traits.

are both conspicuous examples of the Grecian style in Scotland. Thomson was in fact the last great polemicist of the neo-Classical style. In the 1860s, as the Goths took the high ground with their concern with Christianity and morality, he retaliated with his *Enquiry into the Appropriateness of the Gothic Style for the Proposed Buildings for the Univeristy of Glasgow*. But the battle was lost and the university was built in the architectural language of the Middle Ages.

Futhermore, railway companies continued to commission neo-Classical buildings in the 1840s and the 1850s. This association with railway architecture was established by Philip Hardwick's monumental Doric arch at Euston Station in London in 1835–7. The affluence of mid-century railway companies can be seen in the quality of some of the classical buildings which they commissioned. The railway station in Ashby-de-la-Zouch, designed by Robert Chaplin in the late 1840s, contains many superb details. Despite the relative anonymity of this minor architect, this building is a work of great scholarship in its precise detailing, with crisp guttae and laurel wreaths running around the metope.

Despite its apparent decline, neo-Classicism continued to dominate mid-Victorian sculpture. John Gibson RA, who achieved great notoriety for his polychromatic *Tinted Venus* at the Great Exhibition, was the most successful sculptor of the period. But it must be noted that, as he had lived in Italy since 1817, he was somewhat outside debates about style in Victorian Britain. His best known commission was his statue of the Queen in the House of Lords of 1854.

Novel techniques in the manufacture of *objets d'art*, such as Parian ware, also stimulated the taste for neo-Classical sculpture. Parian is a kind of near-porcelain developed by the firm of Copeland and Garrett in 1842, quickly followed by other ceramic manufacturers such as Minton and Company. It was used as an inexpensive substitute for marble in the production of busts and figurines, and because of this was suited to neo-Classical forms. By using a pantograph, manufacturers were able to produce accurately scaled-down versions of well-known works of sculpture for the mass market. A number of well known neo-Classical sculptures were reproduced by firms like WT Copeland in this fashion. The *Bust of Clytie* in the collection of the British Museum, for example, was reproduced by Copeland in 1855 at the request of the Art Union of London and displayed in the firm's Bond Street shop four years later. Copeland also commissioned contemporary Classicists, including Edgar George Papworth RA, to produce works which they reproduced as 'Parian Statuary'.

If the death of neo-Classicism appeared obvious to contemporary commentators, Victorian manufacturers paid more heed to their customers. There was always room in the market-

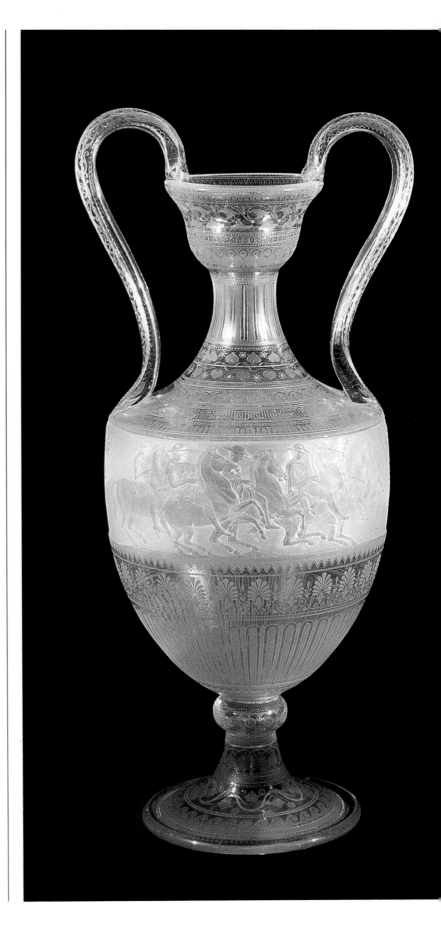

The vaulting and walls of the choir of St Pauls Cathedral are resplendent with glass mosaic work of Byzantine richness designed by Sir William Richmond. The ceiling with its saucer domes illustrating the Benedicite canticle from the Morning Prayer, pictured here was completed during 1892–5.

place in decorative objects for a small number of neo-Classical items. All the major firms producing decorative art and furnishings continued to produce neo-Classical goods, including the cabinetmakers, Holland and Sons; Minton and Company, the ceramic manufacturer, and Elkington, Mason and Co., a firm famous for their electro-plated metal ware.

In the years of the presidency of the 'frontier candidate', Andrew Jackson, from 1829 to 37, neo-Classicism fared in America in much the same way as it did in Britain. Many prominent commissions were given to neo-Classicists, including Thomas U Walter who built Andalusia, the imposing Pennsylvania home of the banker, Nicholas Biddle, in 1833. In the south, many Greek-style mansions were built along the banks of the Mississippi. It is also worth noting that a number of architects attempted to compose in this style, generally associated with brick and masonry, in wood, occasionally with great aplomb and success.

At the Great Exhibition, the American sculptor Hiram Powers' *Greek Slave* was the subject of much attention. This statue, created eight years earlier, was only allowed to be shown in public after it received the assent of a committee of prominent clergymen, who were persuaded by its author that her nudity was a consequence of her slavery.

But by the 1840s the Gothic Revival came to dominate American design led by two architects, Richard Upjohn and Alexander Jackson Davis. Similarly, in the fine arts the fashion for classical subjects, notable in the early years of the 19th century, gave way to a taste for Romantic scenes, typified by the work of the Hudson School.

THE VICTORIAN RENAISSANCE REVIVAL

British artists and designers, since the age of the Grand Tours, looked to Italy for inspiration. Just as the English miniaturist Samuel Cooper travelled to Rome in the 1640s, William Dyce followed him there in the 1820s. Accordingly the Victorian period was not exempt from the influence of the Italian Renaissance, and many of the best late 19th-century paintings

show it. In fact, it is difficult to distinguish a particular revival for the Italian Renaissance proved to be a perpetual influence on Victorian artists and designers.

MID VICTORIAN RENAISSANCE REVIVAL

At the beginning of the 19th century, 15th- and 16th-century paintings were barely represented in the National Gallery; by the end of Victoria's reign it had the greatest collection of these works outside Italy. Interest was stimulated in the Italian Renaissance by some of the greatest works of art history scholarship, among them John Ruskin's *Stones of Venice* of 1849, and Walter Pater's *The Renaissance* of 1873. And no doubt the Victorians enjoyed the idea of associating their own *risorgimento* in the arts with the glories of that period.

Beyond a minor vogue for picturesque Italianate villas in the first few decades of the early 19th century, such as Charles Parker's Villa Rustica built in the 1830s, it is possible to discern two groups of artists and designers who were considerably influenced by the Italian Renaissance.

THE RENAISSANCE STYLE AND ESTABLISHMENT TASTE

The first of these groups were the circle of designers and theorists around Prince Albert and Henry Cole. The Prince Consort was a major influence on the revived use of Renaissance style in the Victorian period. His 'Island Palace Home', Osborne House on the Isle of White, is in the form of an Italianate villa. In addition to this he was also instrumental in the decoration of a garden pavilion in the the grounds of Buckingham Palace in 1844. The central room in this picturesque summer house was decorated with a fresco depicting Comus, the Greek god of mirth, and two others were decorated with classical themes derived from Pompeii, and romantic episodes from the novels of Walter Scott. Here the Prince employed eight eminent royal academicians, including Charles Eastlake and Daniel Maclise, to direct the project. It is not too fanciful to compare the Prince Consort's patronage of these artists with the princely patronage of Raphael at the Villa Farnesina in the early 16th century.

Henry Cole, through Felix Summerly's Art Manufactures, encouraged a number of Renaissance revivalists, including the sculptor John Bell who designed for Minton a salt cellar in the form of a boy with a dolphin and a shell. This figure in Parian ware is straight from Botticelli.

Cole was also instrumental in the appointment of the most important revivalist, Alfred Stevens, to the School of Design in 1845, where he was employed to teach 'drawing and painting, ornament and geometrical drawing and modelling'. Stevens, born in 1817, was the son of a decorator from Dorset. Although a precocious talent in his youth, he had been unable to afford the apprenticeship premiums to study under Edwin Landseer, and was sent to Naples in 1833, presumably to study. But

ABOVE *William Holman Hunt's painting "The Light of the World," was by the end of the century to achieve the status of a Protestant icon as a result of its wide dissemination in photographic and engraved reproductions.*

Stevens was no 'grand tourist', for when he arrived he knew no Italian and no arrangements had been made for his stay.

During his eventful 18 months in Naples, he was involved in a number of political intrigues and moved in the criminal circles of that city. He made his living from producing paintings and portraits. In 1835, he walked to Rome, which he found in political chaos, and so moved on to Florence where he spent four years working in the Uffizi Gallery. Here, he produced near copies of masterpieces, which dealers would sell to wealthy tourists as original works of art, a number of which found their way back to England. Consequently, on his return in 1842, he had a better grounding in Italian Renaissance art than any other English artist bar William Dyce.

In England, Stevens used his broad range of talents, and proved to be an astute self-publicist. Working as a painter, he entered the competition for the decoration of Westminster Palace. As a decorative designer he worked for a number of British manufacturers. In 1850 he left London and the Schools of Design, and moved to Sheffield, where he was employed by the iron-founders, Henry E Hoole and Company. They exhibited his designs at the Great Exhibitions of the middle years of the century. He designed an andiron to match Hoole and Company's Pluto Dog stove shown at the 1862 International Exhibition in London, which was decorated with classical scrolling and two symmetrical muse-like figures. He was also employed by Minton and Company, the ceramic manufacturers, to produce a series of vases and plates. When these were exhibited in 1862, Stevens was awarded a Certificate of Honourable Mention.

His first major success was as a sculptor when he produced the winning entry in a competition to design the memorial to the Duke of Wellington for St Paul's Cathedral in 1856. (This was actually only a partial success, for it was not erected until 1920, 45 years after Stevens' death.) The shrine was inspired by Matteo Carmero's early 16th-century high altar in the church of St John and St Paul in Venice. It is constructed in contrasting light stone and inky bronze, and depicts Wellington on horseback on a superb neo-Classical base. Underneath this architectural canopy lies a sepulchral Wellington. Set against the architectural order of the canopy, Stevens sculpted contorted allegorical figures of valour and cowardice.

At St Paul's in 1864, he also executed some beautiful mosaics which ornament the spandrel panels between the main arches. They depict three old testament figures: Isaiah, who is shown scanning a message from God; Jeremiah, who dictates a warning against cruel leaders; and Daniel receiving guidance from God through the intercession of angels. These mosaics echo the style of fresco work in the Sistine Chapel, and Stevens was regarded a 'mere copyist of Michelangelo'.

From 1851, Stevens was employed to design the interiors and furnishings of a number of rooms in Dorchester House in London's Park Lane by its owner, Robert Stainer Holford. The dining room is in a High Renaissance style with beautifully sculpted caryatids crouching around the fireplace. In Carrara marble, they support the classical entablature-shelf, which is made from Bardiglio marble. The border around the grate is superbly decorated with inlay work. This fireplace and a number of other details in the house, including some very fine furniture, mirrors and doors, are exceptional examples of the Renaissance Revival in Victorian Britain. Unfortunately Stevens never completed his work at Dorchester House. He appears, for all his considerable talents, to have been unable to see his schemes through to their conclusion.

Stevens' influence as a teacher, inspired by the glories of the Italian Renaissance, can be seen in many projects of the 1860s and 1870s by his pupils from the School of Design. The most prominent of these was Godfrey Sykes, a key figure behind the decoration of the Victoria and Albert Museum. Here, Sykes designed the ceramic and terracotta ornament that characterizes the western wing of the building. Terracotta decoration received a timely revival in the 1860s, prompted by Ludwig Gruner's *The Terracotta Architecture of Northern Italy* of 1867. Sykes also designed an influential alphabet in earthenware tiles, for the refreshment room in the Victoria and Albert Museum, which revived a Venetian 16th-century tradition of letters decorated with figures symbolizing each initial.

Another member of the Cole Group was the German emigré Gottfried Semper. With his encyclopedic knowledge of the history of architectural and ornamental style, Semper was a key supporter of the Renaissance Revival. While practising as an architect in Germany in the 1840s, he designed the Dresden Gallery and Opera House in a neo-Renaissance style. In Britain, Semper designed a cabinet for the London firm Holland and Sons which was shown at the Paris *Exposition Universelle* in 1855. This cabinet in ebony is ornamented with a centrally set porcelain panel, a copy of William Mulready's *Crossing* painted by George Grey, and a number of Wedgwood plaques. The most striking details of this piece of furniture are the carved legs which are decorated with lion heads and shields.

It should be noted that the Renaissance style was chosen by the mid-Victorian design establishment; the Prince Consort and the Cole Group. As the experience of the Foreign Office competition showed, it was also the architectural preference of the political establishment of the day. A number of prestigious schemes resulted in Renaissance-style buildings. The Gothic architect William Burges, under pressure from his client, produced a Renaissance Worcester College in Oxford, 1864.

HIGH RENAISSANCE REVIVAL ART

The harbingers of the second wave of the Victorian Renaissance Revival, in contrast to the first, were regarded at the time as a *nouveau arrivé* movement in art. A writer in the *Art Journal*, reviewing an exhibition of the work of some of the key figures, in 1871, wrote:

> Since Pre-Raphaelitism has gone out of fashion, a new, select, and also small school has been formed by a few choice spirits . . . The brotherhood cherish in common, reverence for the antique, affection for Italy; they affect southern climes, costumes, sunshine also a certain *dolce far niete* style . . . Taken as a whole, it may be accepted as a timely protest against the vulgar naturalism, the common realism, which is applauded by the uneducated multititudes who throng our exhibitions.

This author may have overstressed the extent to which these Renaissance revivalists constituted a 'brotherhood', but he was correct in his characterization of their works.

A core of four Renaissance revivalists can be identified in the painters; Albert Moore, George Frederick Watts, Frederic Leighton and the sculptor, Alfred Gilbert. From 1877 to 1891, the painters lived and worked near each other in Kensington. Watts and Leighton were close, although Moore is reported to have been a more withdrawn character. Leighton, who also worked a sculptor, was a great supporter of youthful Gilbert.

Like their Renaissance heroes Titian and Cellini, all four artists drew inspiration from the antique, clothing their allegorical characters in flowing classical costume like figures from the Elgin Marbles. More direct inspiration came from the 16th century masters. Leighton's bronze *Athlete Struggling with a Python*, for example, bore a strong resemblance to Michelangelo's David. This *tour de force* of anatomical detail, de-

scribes a muscular athlete straining to hold a snake at arm's length. It was exhibited at the Royal Academy in 1877, to much critical acclaim. Ten years later, Carl Jacobsen a Danish brewing magnate, commissioned Leighton to make a replica of this piece in marble for his museum in Copenhagen. Leighton's sculpture, regarded by Jacobsen as one of the best classical works of the 19th century, was acquired to complement his great collection of classical art.

These artists drew their Renaissance inspirations in a characteristically Victorian fashion. In the 18th century, classical subjects would be widely understood as symbolic social or political comments on the society of the day. Jacques Louis David, for example, used classical allegories in such paintings as *The*

RIGHT *Erected in 1893 to the memory of the seventh Earl of Shaftesbury, Alfred Gilbert's Angel of Christian Charity, popularly known as Eros, still dominates Piccadilly Circus. The extraordinary delicacy and poise of the figure was achieved by casting in light-weight aluminium rather than the traditional but less malleable medium of bronze.*

Oath of the Horatii, to great political effect in late 18th century France. The Republican sympathies of this painting of 1785, were an important pre-signifier of the impending French Revolution. In contrast, the political stability of late Victorian Britain – or perhaps more accurately the complacency of the ruling classes – led some artists to find their Renaissance inspiration in the luxury and beauty of Mediterranean civilization. These Renaissance revivalists shared little of the social moralism and documentary concerns of realist artists in Britain during the same period, such as Luke Fildes and Frank Holl.

George Frederick Watts, Frederic Leighton and Albert Moore painted canvases of luxuriating beauty and sumptuous colour. Typically, their art depicted leisurely scenes of figures in repose or children playing in arcadian landscapes. Only Watts appears to have allowed worldly troubles to enter his Renaissance Revival dreams of perfected civilization. His *The Denunciation of Cain* of 1872 was exhibited at the Royal Academy under the title *My punishment is greater than I can bear*. It is a masterly canvas depicting a contorted Cain overcome with guilt after murdering his brother. Overhead, six angels plummet earthbound to witness the scene. The figure of Cain was widely thought to have represented a London slumlord, racked with guilt for his actions. In the mid-years of his career, Watts was fascinated with grand theatre and tragic myths, painting canvases with titles like *Love and Death* and *Chaos*. But throughout his life he painted beautifully calm poetic works on the themes of love and hope as found in classical mythology. His late work of 1900, *Peace and Goodwill*, shows a mother and child, an outcast Queen and her son, calmly sitting and looking toward a glowing light at the edge of the picture.

Albert Moore's work from the 1860s onward was populated with carefully modelled figures, adopting poses of great restraint and serenity. He is best known for his paintings of women in dream-like states, such as *Beads* of 1875 and *A Workbasket* of 1879. Draped in transparent silks, they lie on beige sofas in rooms bordered by screens and drapery and littered with classical artifacts; ewers, urns and so on. His considered use of colour tended to the pale and the pastel, and his brushstrokes were thin and flattened. Although Moore painted Greek maidens, he achieved a transcendental, timeless sense of place, and his work was not that of an historian but an aesthete.

Frederick Leighton, later Lord Leighton of Stretton, was a painter of quite exraordinary ability. Like Moore, his paintings frequently depict sleeping women in classical dress and poses. In works like *Flaming June* of 1895, he displayed his virtuoso talent by exquisitely portraying every fold of a dreaming woman's transparent dress veiling her beautiful body. The colour scheme is dominated by this flaming orange dress. She lies, folded within herself; a difficult pose to render in correct perspective but one which the artist successfully mastered.

Alfred Gilbert, born in 1854, was 24 years younger than his ardent supporter and fellow Renaissance revivalist, Frederick Leighton. In the early 1880s he travelled to Florence and was inspired there to produce his first statue in bronze. This piece, *Perseus Arming* of 1882, was cast by the almost forgotten method of *cire-perdue*. It bears a strong similarity to Donatello's *David*, although Gilbert said that he intended it as a challenge to Cellini's *Perseus with Head of Medusa*. When it was exhibited at the Grovesnor Gallery in 1882, it was a great success, drawing comment for its novel colouring and surface texture. When it was shown at the Paris Salon of 1883, it was given an honourable mention, an honour which was rarely extended to an English artist.

This bronze was seen by Leighton who was so impressed that he commissioned a statue from Gilbert on the theme of Icarus. After the showing at the Royal Academy in 1884, Gilbert became overnight the most famous sculptor in England, and Leighton persuaded him to return to his native country. In the 1880s he was commissioned to produce major sculptural works celebrating Queen Victoria in Winchester Castle, Henry Fawcett in Westminster Abbey and the Earl of Shaftesbury in Piccadilly Circus.

This memorial to Shaftesbury, commonly known as *Eros*, has become one of the best known works of sculpture in Britain. Anthony Ashley Cooper, Seventh Earl of Shaftesbury, had been a leading Victorian philanthropist and the Lord Mayor of London. In 1886 he commissioned Gilbert to create a statue in his memory. The memorial is a fountain topped by a bronze statue of Eros firing his bow. Gilbert felt that both these elements appropriately embodied Shaftesbury's selfless love. Gilbert's relationship with the committee overseeing the project was fraught and when he looked back on these years at the end of his life he regretted ever leaving Italy.

To Victorian Britain the Renaissance Revival, a variant of historicism in the fine arts, was strikingly new. These artists were British equivalents of such continental *fin de siècle* masters as Gustave Klimt in Vienna, and Puvis de Chavannes and Gustave Moreau in Paris.

HIGH VICTORIAN GOTHIC

The mid Victorian period saw the culmination of the Gothic Revival which had been progressing in a rather sporadic fashion since the 1750s. In the 18th century, interest in the Gothic was the dilettante hobby of aristocrats and the rich. Under the influence of romantic novels by writers like Hugh Walpole, who owned an early Gothic Revival home, and Sir Walter Scott, men like William Beckford at Fonthill Abbey and Sir Roger Newdigate at Arbury Hall planned homes in the Gothic style. For these patrons, this style was a picturesque diversion rather than an exercise in historical veracity. Like Scott's *Waverley* novels, these buildings were to their owners places where they could escape the realities of business and politics and dream of a chivalrous time of mediaeval knights and pageants. Edward Blore published a rhapsodic book called *Monumental Ruins* in 1826 which became an important source book for early 19th-century designers and patrons fantasizing about a picturesque past. At Goodrich House in Herefordshire, Sir Samuel Rush Meyrick employed Blore to create his 'Hastilude Chamber' in which to house his famous collection of armour.

Related to the rise of the Gothic was the increasing popularity of antiquaria. Led by academic and literary taste in the late 18th century, in the early part of the 19th century it became highly fashionable to collect and decorate one's home with antiques and authentic architectural details. The Gothic encouraged the taste for mediaevalist objects; suits of armour, heraldic motifs, stained glass and carved masonry. The market in old Flemish architectural carvings grew to such an extent that there was a flourishing trade in fakes emanating from Belgium.

Many writers have characterized this phase of the interest in the Gothic as merely pastiche when compared with the mid-Victorian's highly moral and clerical attitude to it. But it must be noted that this romantic and picturesque phase of the Gothic was underpinned by some serious scholarship such as E J Wilson's *Specimens of Gothic Architecture* of 1821–3. Furthermore, the later phase of the Gothic, although inspired by the writings of theorists like John Ruskin and A W N Pugin, was for the many people who bought mediaevalist objects and lived in Gothic style homes just another turn of fashion. Many manufacturers who borrowed this style for their products saw it as just another language in the repertoire of style.

LEFT *Wall paper designed by A. W. Pugin for the Houses of Parliament. Incorporating the Tudor Rose and the portcullis intertwined with the royal cipher, it was produced by S. Scott, J. G. Crace*

RIGHT *The chromolithographed frontispiece to Pugin's "Glossary of Ecclesiastical Ornament and Costume, Compiled and Illustrated from Ancient Authorities and Examples" (1844), one of several major works of research on Medieval Gothic styles.*

THE ARCHITECTURE OF TRUTH

The Gothic Revival shifted into a new phase and intensity under the influence of a young designer, and more significantly, a theoretician, called August Welby Northmore Pugin. In the year of his death, 1851, he wrote, although without humility, but quite correctly:

> My writings, much more than what I have been able to do, have revolutionized the taste of England.

He was led into his chosen career by his father, August Charles Pugin, who was renowned as a draughtsman and the author of a number of seminal books on mediaeval architecture. Pugin's short life was punctuated by many dramatic events: at the age of 15 in 1827 he was employed as a furniture designer by the firm of Morrel and Seddon at Windsor Castle; three years later he was shipwrecked in Scotland while captain of a schooner; at 19, he was the director of a firm of stonemasons on the verge of bankruptcy; in 1835 he was employed as a designer on the new Houses of Parliament; in his twenties he converted to Catholicism, a major turning point in his life; and in his thirties he worked for a number of firms as a designer of ecclesiastical items. He married three times and had eight

children. His death in 1851 was reputedly due to a nervous breakdown and overwork. He was a prolific designer of furnishings, stained glass, ceramics and metalwork.

Pugin's most important designs were for furniture and fittings for the Houses of Parliament under the architect Charles Barry. This commission, secured by Barry in 1835, was a major milestone in the story of the Gothic Revival in the 19th century, Parliament having decided that it was the appropriate style for this most important of national buildings. The project was on such a scale that it came to dominate the rest of the lives of both designers. Charles Eastlake wrote in 1872, in his book *A History of the Gothic Revival*:

> It would be impossible to overrate the influence brought to bear upon decorative sculpture, upon ceramic decoration, ornamental metal-work, and glass-staining, by the encouragement given to those arts during the progress of the works at Westminster. In the design of such details Pugin's aid was, at the time, invaluable. It was frankly sought and freely rendered. Harman's painted windows and brass fittings, Minton's encaustic tiles, and Crace's mural decoration bear the evidence of his skill and industry.

Despite achieving his place in the history of art for these designs, Pugin regarded himself as first and foremost an architect, although he received only a small number of commissions. His first major project was to remodel Scarisbrick Hall for Charles Scarisbrick, a wealthy Catholic aristocrat. Here, between 1837 and 1845, Pugin tested out his ideas about the Gothic as a style suitable in every aspect. His intention was to build an authentic mediaeval manor house. He wrote:

> As regards the hall I have nailed my colours to the mast – a bay window, high open roof, two good fireplaces, a great sideboard, screen, minstrel gallery – *all or none*. I will not sell myself to the wretched thing.

This uncompromising concern with every aspect and detail of a design can be seen in all his buildings, from his own small house, St Marie's Grange, for his family in Wiltshire, to larger commissions such as St Wilfred's at Hulme in Manchester, built between 1839 and 1842.

But Pugin's historical significance lies in his activities as a propagandist for the Gothic style. As a keen student of architectural history, Pugin brought to the Gothic Revival a moral and ideological urgency which his predecessors had lacked. Through his books and to a lesser degree, his designs, he harangued Victorian Britain on the themes of spirituality, and honesty. In his book of 1836, *Contrasts, or, A parallel between the Noble Edifices of the Fourteenth and Fifteenth Centuries, and Similar buildings of the Present Day; Shewing the Present Decay of*

THE HOUSES OF PARLIAMENT

Under Barry's supervision Pugin produced designs in metalwork, such as the great brass gates that lead into the Lords Chamber (right), furniture, stained glass, encaustic tiles, decorative painting and woodcarving. His work can be admired in the Lord's library (opposite lower left) and more particularly in the Chamber itself. Here the magnificent painted and gilded throne canopy (below left) bears the royal coat-of-arms (left), surmounted by effigies of St George and four knights holding the badges of the four main orders of chivalry (far left).

LEFT *Strawberry Hill, Twickenham, a unique building in the "Gothick" style commissioned by Horace Walpole, Earl of Orford (1717–97), a suitably eccentric abode for the author whose "Castle of Otranto" (1864) initiated the Gothic horror genre.*

RIGHT *The central hall of the Natural History Museum, London. The inclusion of Medieval italianate features reflects the celebrated critic John Ruskin's broader approach to Gothic revivalism.*

Taste, Pugin rhetorically made the case for Gothic architecture by contrasting an idealized mediaeval Britain with contemporary society. A typical example is the section entitled 'Contrasted Residences for the Poor', which compares the daily lives of the poor in both societies. According to Pugin a typical diet of a poorhouse in the Middle Ages was; 'beef mutton bacon/ale and cider/milk porridge/wheat bread/cheese', signifying wholesomeness and a traditional, national diet. In the mid 19th century, a poorhouse menu read '2oz of bread 1 pint of gruel/2oz of bread 1 pint of gruel 1oz of bread ½ pint of gruel/oatmeal potatoes', a far more restricted and dull diet. The conclusion to be drawn was obvious: Victorian society lacked the variety and goodness that characterized the mediaeval period. Pugin saw in the Middle Ages a sense of social order and Christian values lacking in his own era. Victorian architecture must therefore also be deficient.

Pugin developed a philosophy of architecture which centred around the model of English Gothic of the 14th century. For Pugin, firstly, it was the national architecture and as such correct for Victorian Britain, just as the Renaissance Revival was correct for Italy; secondly, it was a Christian architecture in its concern with 'upwardness', in contrast to variants of Classicism which was symbolic of mammon; and thirdly, it was an architecture fit for the purposes to which it was put.

This philosophy was augmented with ideas about honesty in architecture. Pugin believed that historical details should not be copied unless they had a useful function. For example, he rejected castellated forms and battlements as inappropriate in the Victorian world. But conversely, to prove that the Gothic

was a flexible and evolving architectural language, Pugin set about designing two railway bridges, that highly charged symbol of the industrial age.

Pugin stated that: 'There should be no features about a building which are not necessary for convenience, construction or propriety'. Ornament was to be avoided unless it 'enriched the essential construction of the building'. This was not an out and out rejection of ornament in architecture but a concern with 'propriety'. In Pugin's thought, a clear architectural hierarchy existed which equated decoration with decorum. He felt that it was entirely suitable for the area around the altar, to be treated with the richest ornamental detail, but areas like the naves should be left plain. Pugin's concern with truth meant that these functional parts of buildings were not to be disguised, but to be revealed honestly.

Pugin's ideas about 'fitness' translated to furniture design. In a pattern book published by Ackermann in 1836 entitled *Gothic Furniture in the Style of the 15th Century*, he showed a heavy X-framed chair and stool. These items of furniture were highly unusual for their day, as Pugin made no attempt to hide their simple constructional elements with marquetry or hidden joints. His theories of design rejected contemporary preferences for disguised construction and applied decoration as dishonest. In much the same way, Pugin believed that architects should not hide or distort the functional aspects of a building such as the flues to achieve a symmetrical facade, as was the practice in Classicism. In his own house, St Marie's Grange in Alderbury, built in 1835–6, he self-consciously broke the roofline with irregularly placed chimneys.

Pugin's influence on his contemporaries was muted by his Roman Catholicism, which restricted his contact with other influential promoters of the Gothic. John Ruskin was another major theorist of the style who distanced himself from Pugin because of his religion, although many of the latter's ideas surface in Ruskin's key writings; *The Seven Lamps of Architecture* published in 1849 and his *The Stones of Venice* of 1851–3. In these texts we find the same concerns with craftsmanship, honesty, Godliness and national style, although with different emphases. Ruskin's main lines of attack were against what he called 'dishonest' and machine-made ornament. He believed that; 'all noble ornamentation is the expression of man's delight at God's work'.

Accordingly, Ruskin was highly critical of the Crystal Palace and its contents, and the design theories of the Henry Cole group, describing the teachings of the latter as 'a state of distortion and falsehood'. He believed that the best example for young British designers could be found in the craft traditions established in the Middle Ages. Here, like Pugin, he found a model of a happy society which produced beautiful things and concluded that these two facts were not unrelated. In his books he developed a social theory of doing, encapsulated in the rhetorical question: 'Was it done with enjoyment – was the carver happy while he was about it?' But Ruskin himself

was never a designer, artist or craftsman, and has been much ridiculed by historians for a failed attempt at bricklaying during the building of the Natural History Museum in Oxford in the late 1850s.

Ruskin travelled widely through Europe in the 1840s, and, as revealed in his book *The Stones of Venice*, was greatly influenced by Italian mediaeval art and architecture. His preferences in art were the Italian 'primitives', artists such as Fra Angelico and Massacio, rather than the celebrated heroes of the Renaissance, Raphael and Titian. From these sources, he developed a strong sense of colour and a taste for smooth surfaces, and throughout his life argued the merits of constructional simplicity and massive composition over fussy detail and complex ornament.

The Natural History Musuem in Oxford of 1855–60 is the realization of a number of Ruskinian ideas. The building also marked the end of the dominance of the English Perpendicular style, used to such strong effect by Barry and Pugin in the new Houses of Parliament, and the beginning of the High Gothic Revival. Many small Perpendicular churches had been built over the country in the 1830s and 1840s including Benjamin Ferrey's Christ Church, in Endell Street, London of 1842–44 and St Giles by George Gilbert Scott and W B Moffat in Camberwell Church Street, London in the same period. But

LEFT *The Royal Courts of Justice in the Strand, desribed as Victorian "perpendicular", were begun in 1874 by G. E. Street and completed in 1882, a year after his death. The Central Hall (right), 238 ft long by 80 ft high, gives access to the various courts.*

as Gothic architects began entering competitions for grander buildings and a younger generation began to practice, the Gothic became a more eclectic style. In true Victorian fashion, and under Ruskin's influence architects began to include French, German and Italian Gothic elements in their buildings. In addition to a larger variety of styles, the proponents of the High Victorian Gothic advocated a wider range of materials than their predecessors, including marble and coloured brick. Through Ruskin's influence two supporters of the High Victorian Gothic style, Thomas Deane and Benjamin Woodward, were commissioned to design the Natural History Museum. This beautiful building displays a broad range of architectural devices: constructional polychromy borrowed from Venetian Gothic of the 14th century; a sharp roof topped with a metal finial that echoes Flemish Gothic, and attendant buildings, housing laboratories, inspired by the 14th-century Abbott's Kitchen, Glastonbury. Here, the thrusting verticality of the 'English Pointed' style gave way to an Italian horizontality. Ruskin's influence can be seen in the capitals above each window, for each was to be carved differently with motifs indicating the function of the building. Highly skilled stone masons, the O'Shea brothers were brought from Ireland to carve these features depicting flora and fauna. The heart of the museum is a tiled courtyard, under a canopy of glass and Gothic ironwork. Around this airy room run two raised cloisters supported by columns. Each column is made from a different stone, with an individual carved capital.

The Gothic (despite Pugin's Roman Catholicism) was strongly identified as an Anglican style. The Cambridge Camden Society, for example, was established in 1836 to promote Anglicanism and Gothic architecture of the 14th century. This group, renamed the Ecclesiological Society in 1846, exerted an influence on such projects as Anthony Salvin's restoration of the Holy Sepulchre Church in Cambridge and Sydney Smirke's improvements to the Temple Church in London in the early 1840s. The Society also produced a book entitled *Instumenta Ecclesiastica* which was a kind of pattern book of church fittings and decorations. They employed well-known Gothic architects such as William Butterfield who designed an alphabet 'intended for use where a most legible character, and yet one in harmony with Pointed work is required' and other items such as church plate.

Butterfield was a key architect in the development of High Victorian Gothic. His first major building project was All Saints Church, in London, commissioned by the Ecclesiological Society in 1849. Butterfield had been strongly under the influence of Pugin's ideas until this scheme which marked a new stage in his thought. Built on a restricted site in Westminster, the church was reported to have been the tallest spire in London – 222 feet at that date. It is rather simply decorated, with bands of coloured brick. In the higher parts of the spire and the clergy residence, this simple ornamental effect is enriched by diagonal patterning. This accords with John Betjeman's observation that: 'A general Victorian principle was that Gothic is more elaborate the nearer it reaches heaven'. This is reinforced by narrow tall windows set above each other so that the general effect of Butterfield's design is of a thrusting verticality.

The interior of All Saints is as significant as the exterior. It is very brightly decorated in geometrical patterns in rich colours; reds, black, different hues of white, striking green and yellow. Butterfield also employed a number of different decorative techniques. Following Pugin, the chancel and other significant parts of the church are more highly decorated; the east end of the church, for example, is superbly frescoed. Pugin's influence can be seen in the concern to reveal the structural features of the building through different materials and treatment; the piers are of unornamented polished red granite and the pulpit incorporated pink granite, red Languedoc and brown, grey and green marbles, composed with great geometric clarity.

George Edmund Street followed Butterfield's example at All Saints in using brick polychromy in many of his buildings. This decorative device, intended to reveal the structural simplicity of Gothic architecture, became a characteristic aspect of High Victorian Gothic design. In his books, such as *Brick and Marble in the Middle Ages* (1855), he helped stimulate the taste for rich banded brickwork in architecture. His competition design for Lille Cathedral in France of the same year showed his ability to compose in coloured brick on a massive scale. In later buildings such as the St James the Less near the Thames (1859–61) and St Mary Magdalene in central London (1867–78), Street was able to realize his talents as an artist in brick. In the latter, the dramatic rocket-like spire is set off by tight horizontal bands of red and cream brick. Through relatively minor projects like these, Street acquired a reputation for absolute thoroughness. He relished attention to detail, writing of the 12 years it had taken to complete St Mary Magdalene: 'happy is the architect who is allowed to work in this way. Most of our churches in these days are built in a hurry, just as if what ought to last for centuries would do appreciably less work if it were, itself, less than a 12 months coming into full existence.' His churches of this period, both inside and out, are stunning examples of High Victorian Gothic concern with detail, colour and pattern.

As a Gothicist, Street did not restrict his architectural practice to churches and designed a number of secular buildings in this style. In fact, the last major state commission to be built in the Gothic style was Street's Law Courts on the Strand in London, which he secured in a competition in 1866. Ten years earlier, most of the entrants for the Foreign Office competition were Classicists: all the designs for the Law Courts were Gothic. The dominance of the Gothic in the 1860s is clear.

The building was begun in 1874 and completed eight years later. Its facade is a complicated asymmetrical series of turrets, castellated details and irregularly placed arched windows, fronting a great hall with a high vaulted ceiling. This building which was regarded rather unfavourably by both the lawyers and judges who worked there, who disliked the complex system of corridors and narrow stairs, and architectural critics who felt that the building lacked coherence. Street's attempt to design each and every detail of the building is believed to have contributed to his early death at the age of 57 in 1881, before the building was completed.

George Gilbert Scott was another prominent architect who employed the Gothic as a secular style. After his Albert Memorial of 1862, discussed in the preceding chapter, he is most famous for the Midland Hotel at St Pancras Railway Station, in London, designed in 1865. Somewhat paradoxically, this railway station hotel, a potent symbol of Victorian progress,

was cloaked in the architectural language of the 13th century. It stands today in the centre of London, looking a rather pale shadow of its former self, clothed in red Gripper bricks from Nottingham, Leicester slates and earthy terracotta mouldings. The highly profitable Midland Railway Company were looking for a building that would outshine Lewis Cubitt's Kings Cross station nearby. Scott certainly gave them one. It fronts a dramatic train shed designed by the engineer, William Barlow, which had an unrivalled span of over 243 feet. The hotel is a marvellous curved building climaxing in a clock tower and a spire at its western end. But beyond its picturesque qualities, in this building Scott also sought to prove that the Gothic was a suitable building style for the modern world. Cantilevered iron girders arched over open spaces; and he argued contra Ruskin that; 'iron constructions are, if anything, more suited to Gothic than Classical architecture'.

Scott bore the brunt of criticism from contemporary observers who felt that he had ignored the Pugin's ethos of 'propriety'. In 1872, as the building was rising, J T Emmett wrote:

> There is here a complete travesty of noble associations, and not the slightest care to save these from sordid contact. An elaboration that might be suitable for a chapter-house of a cathedral choir, is used as an advertising medium for bagman's bedrooms and the costly discomforts of a terminus hotel.

Part of John Ruskin and A W N Pugin's intellectual bequest was to persuade Gothic architects of the 1860s and the 1870s that they were responsible for the smallest of details in their buildings. Like Pugin himself, who had been employed by ceramic manufacturers such as Minton and producers of ornamental metalware such as Harman, and William Butterfield working for the Ecclesiological Society, younger Gothic architects built reputations for their furniture and decoration designs as much as their architectural practice.

One such key architect turned designer was William Burges, who had organized the Mediaeval Court at the London Exhibition of 1862. Burges' mediaevalism and symbolism closely associates him with the Pre-Raphaelite Brotherhood. He is credited with the design of the first piece of High Victorian Gothic furniture, a cabinet designed for H G Yatman in 1858. This piece, now on display in London's Victoria and Albert Museum, was designed in the style of 13th-century French *armoires* which he had seen in Noyon in 1853. It was painted by Edward J Poynter with classical scenes, and beautiful Gothic geometric patterning in gold, dusky red, veridian and sienna. Burges was a great academic, a member of the Royal Archeological Institute, and well known for his essays in the *Gentleman's Magazine*. His designs in metalwork were renowned for their historical veracity, and on one celebrated occasion in 1875, his Dunedin Crozier, a bishop's staff, was illustrated in a French magazine as an example of a 13th century antique.

LEFT *The clock tower of St Pancras Station reaches a height of 300 ft. Architect George Gilbert Scott was also responsible for the interior of the station hotel, its grand staircase supported on iron girders decorated with fine Gothic detailing (right).*

William Burges had already won a series of prestigious architectural competitions, including the one for the design of Lille Cathedral in 1854, and the memorial of the Crimean War in Costantinople in 1857, both designs in the High Gothic style. But he is perhaps best known for his association with the wealthiest man in Britain, the Marquis of Bute. His patron shared his interest in antiquity, and continued to commission metalwork, furniture and ceramic designs from Burges long after the fashion for 13th-century French Gothic design had passed. This relationship resulted in the most amazing and opulent artifacts and buildings of the Gothic Revival, dubbed by contemporary observers 'Burgesian Gothic'.

In 1868 he was employed by Bute to restore Cardiff Castle. This project, completed in 1881, resulted in a building that is more theatre than architecture. As if to spite the unfashionability of castle building in Britain in the 1870s, Cardiff Castle stands massive and solid. The upper reaches of the castle are like a mediaeval fantasy; ornate turrets, archery slits, finials and spires. In 1875 Bute commissioned Burges to restore Castell Coch in the same spirit. On a wooded hillside, this austere

fort contained a host of mediaeval details: circular turrets and towers, rough stonework, deep eaves and even a moat.

In their opulence and luxury, the interiors of these two architectural fantasies far outstrip any castle of the Middle Ages. The drawing room at Castell Coch is a stunning vaulted chamber with richly decorated walls painted by Charles Campbell. The extraordinary Arab Room at Cardiff Castle of 1881 shows Burges at the height of his skills as a decorative designer; interestingly it is not in a Gothic style. This domed room is Arabic in inspiration, and its importance lies in Burges's ability to compose in pure form. The superb ceiling rises to a beautiful octagonal painting of eight eagles by means of jutting and scalloped cornices and niches.

Burges also designed for Lord Bute an amazing range of silver plates, vessels and cutlery, rich in ornamental detail, which were produced by the most skilled silversmiths of the day. In 1869 he designed a claret jug that is decorated with a leopard climbing a tree trunk. Two beautifully detailed characters like figures from early Christian art ornament its lid. The body of the vessel is decorated with mediaevalist forms; heraldic devices and floral motifs, a classical panel spans its neck, and a mask, in the Renaissance style, looks out below the spout. Although in its basic form this piece began with the Gothic, Burges's genius created a work of stunning eclecticism.

THE GOTHIC REVIVAL
IN AMERICA

The Gothic Revival in America was initiated by a leader of fashionable taste, Andrew Jackson Downing, and an architect, Alexander Jackson Davis. Together they steered America away from the neo-Classical tastes of the 1830s to the Gothic, by a series of books illustrated by Davis of Gothic cottages and picturesque ruins.

Wealthy clients were persuaded by Davis to build houses along the Hudson River that resulted in a style known today as 'Hudson River Gothic'. One such patron was Jay Gould who had a house called Lyndhurst built for him in Tarrytown by Davis, begun in 1838. This building contains all the fashionable picturesque Gothic Revival details of the period: an informal plan, asymmetry, turrets, battlements, tracery and arches. Other architects followed the lead of Davis and Downing, including the English born Richard Upjohn who designed New York's Trinity Church in 1840 in the Perpendicular style. America saw similar shifts of architectural taste within the Gothic during the mid years of the century as there were in Britain. In 1870 Frederick Church, for example, designed a marvellously simple chapel in Olana near the Hudson river. In its polychromatic tiling and brickwork, this building echoes William Butterfield's architecture of the 1860s.

The classical design, constructed entirely of marble, boasts corinthian pilasters and columned portico (above). Not to be outdone, his brother Cornelius commissioned Hunt to build him a Renaissance style villa, "The Breakers" (above). Meanwhile as industrial wealth flooded into the cities housing was required for a new middle class. Brownstones in New York (right) and clapboard houses in San Francisco (opposite above left) aped their peers in the ecleticism of their architectural design.

Built by Richard Morris Hunt (1889–92), William K. Vanderbilt's imposing Marble House (below right) was the grandest of the baronial summer "cottages" built in fashionable Newport, Rhode Island.

ABOVE *The late Medieval drawing room of Eastnor Castle, Herefordshire 1840.*

At the more humble end of the social spectrum the Gothic also proved to be popular with the middle classes. A number of major manufacturers commissioned architects to design Gothic furniture and decorative art. A W N Pugin led the way in the 1840s by working for firms like Minton and Company, the ceramic manufacturer. He designed a bread plate in 1849 for this firm which was displayed at the Birmingham Exhibition of that year. It is a delightful piece of glazed earthenware decorated with simple motifs based on sheaves of corn. Around the lip of the plate runs the maxim 'waste not want not'. Pugin was challenged for his use of a rich blue glaze by critics who noted that craftsmen in the Middle Ages did not have this colour available to them. Pugin responded in characteristic fashion by vigorously arguing that the Gothic was an evolving and organic language of design that developed along the grain of Victorian society rather than a fossilized style.

Following Pugin, other architects designed Gothic domestic goods. William Burges organized a mediaevalist display at the London Exhibition of 1862. John Pollard Seddon exhibited a desk inlaid with beautiful coloured woods in geometric patterns, and Philip Webb showed mediaevalist pieces of furniture there.

The Gothic Revival found its way into the mass market through pattern books. In 1867 Charles Bevan and B J Talbert produced their *Gothic Forms Applied to Architecture*, which gave manufacturers excellent models with which to fuel the Gothic Revival.

THE PRE-RAPHAELITE INFLUENCE

PRE-RAPHAELITE BROTHERHOOD

The influence of the Gothic was not restricted to architecture and the applied arts. Through the inspired pen of John Ruskin, the Middle Ages called the most radical of mid Victorian artists to take up their brushes and crusade both morally and aesthetically.

The enigmatic initials PRB first appeared on Dante Gabriel Rossetti's small canvas *The Girlhood of the Virgin Mary* exhibited in 1849. The Brotherhood was the outcome of discussions between William Holman Hunt, Dante Gabriel Rossetti and John Everett Millais in the summer of 1848. Their debates about the nature and role of art, concentrating on its edifying and spiritual potential, brought them close to the ideas of the Nazarenes, German artists working in Rome in the first decades of the century. Led by Franz Pforr and Freidrich Overbeck, the Nazarenes were a community of artists dedicated to the church and the regeneration of German religious art.

This trio of English painters, all in their early twenties, decided to challenge the 'old gang', the entrenched art establishment of the day, and to revitalize English art. Rossetti and his fellow iconoclasts regarded English art as technically poor, morally bereft and intellectually barren. They were not entirely mistaken or alone in this opinion; *Punch*, a barometer of Victorian attitudes, pilloried leading artists of the day for the repetition of subjects in their paintings. Regarding Pickersgill's *The Burial of King Alfred,* the satirical magazine pleaded: 'King Alfred is dead at last; and we hope that British artists will leave off finding his body any more, which they have been doing in every exhibition these fifty years'.

Whilst Millais was away from London working on a series of commissions, Rossetti gathered together a number of other artists including his brother, Walter Rossetti, Thomas Woolner, Frederick George Stevens and James Collinson. At a meeting with Millais in London a brotherhood of seven was formed. Each artist placed differing emphasis on the role of their union, for example, while Collinson sought a specifically Christian art, Woolner saw the Brotherhood as a way of promoting humanist ideals. But they collectively shared a distaste for academicism in art, believing that artists should look to Nature and the intuitive skills of mediaeval artists.

At a further meeting of the group, the name was selected. Although it appears that they knew little about Italian art before Raphael, they were united in their dislike of much art after him and in particular, Roman and Bolognese 16th-century painting. In choosing the name 'Pre-Raphaelite', they intended the more general meaning of 'Early Christian' and 'Brother-

ABOVE *Dante Gabriel Rossetti was one of the founder members of the Pre-Raphaelite Brotherhood. While others were more concerned with social themes, Rossetti was renowned for his allegorical paintings of woman, such as his Le Joli Coeur of 1867 .*

hood' called to mind a religious zeal. 50 years later, William Holman Hunt recalled the conspiratorial atmosphere of these meetings, writing:

 When we agreed to use the letters PRB as our insignia, we made each member solemnly promise to keep its meaning absolutely secret, foreseeing the danger of offending the reigning powers of the time.

Although the Pre-Raphaelites saw themselves as artistic revolutionaries, the subjects of their paintings were the classic themes of romantic art through the ages. They produced paintings on religious, historical and literary themes, and rarely on contemporary topics. Although it must be notd that some of the most successful Pre-Raphaelite works, such as *The Awakened Conscience* by Holman Hunt and Rossetti's *Found,* were sharp and highly moralizing interventions against contemporary mores.

J E Millais' 1851 painting *The Return of the Dove to the Ark* is a clear illustration of the Brotherhood's religious devotion. It is a painting of rich colour and great beauty. Through a powerfully simple composition, it depicts Noah's daughters holding the dove which has just returned with the olive branch. When this painting was displayed in the window of a frame maker's shop in Oxford it was seen by William Morris and Edward Burne-Jones and proved to be a great influence on the course of their careers.

FAR LEFT "The Bower Meadow" by
Dante Gabriel Rossetti, poet, artist and
with Holman Hunt and Millais, one of
the three important founder members of
the Pre- Raphaelite Brotherhood.
Hunt's Lady of Shalott (1886) (left),
based on Tennyson's poem, exemplifies
the Brotherhood's penchant for historical
and literary themes. The same year
Millais painted "Bubbles", a portrait of
his grandson, shortly to become famous
as an advertisement for Pears Soap
(opposite below).

Literary themes in Pre-Raphaelite art are exemplified by Holman Hunt's late work *Isabella and the Pot of Basil* which took its theme from a poem by John Keats. A number of the Gothic details in this painting are worthy of note, such as the highly painted stand. The embroidered cloth that covers this piece of mediaevalist furniture was made by Hunt's own hands. He was frequently unable to procure the studio props needed accurately to render the scenes he wished to depict and was often forced to make his own.

Pre-Raphaelite ideas about 'truth to Nature' were not fixed by theories of plein-air painting, but were more concerned with an accuracy of detail and fidelity to the appearance of things. William Holman Hunt's painting of 1851 *The Hireling Shepherd* depicts a young couple sitting in a tree-lined field full of sheep. The young man holds in his hand a wasp, so lifelike that it is possible to make out its minute legs. Every leaf, blade of grass, and sheaf of corn can be clearly discerned.

The 1850s saw the ascendancy of the Pre-Raphaelites, although not without some criticism. A journal, lasting only four issues, was published called *The Germ*, which propagandized their ideas about art. When the Brotherhood exhibited seven works at the Royal Academy in 1850, including Collinson's highly underrated *Answering the Emigrant's Letter*, they drew very sharp attack from the art establishment of the day. The journal *Athenaeum* called their work 'a perversion of talent'. The art world felt affronted that its own young artists, trained in its academies, should be attacking its dearly held values. To

the stale kinds of the Academy, this art seemed ugly and unconventional. But by 1852 the Pre-Raphaelites had moved out of the rarefied art world and achieved national acclaim. Rossetti, writing to William Scott Bell, said:

> Millais has been in Oxford as a witness in a trial regarding some estate or contested will. The judge, on hearing his name, asked if he was the painter of that exquisite painting in the Academy. This looks like fame.

Paintings by the Brotherhood began to be bought by the rising middle classes; northern industrialists and merchants. These patrons bought, with genuine pleasure, art which was directed at the emotions and experience. Today city galleries in manufacturing towns like Manchester and Birmingham have excellent collections of Pre-Raphaelite art through private bequests.

By the mid 1850s the Brotherhood started to move apart with Woolner leaving for Australia in 1852 and Holman Hunt going to Palestine in 1854. Interestingly, Millais became a member of the art establishment, despite the scorn he had poured on it as a Pre-Raphaelite. His work increasingly pandered to popular taste and depicted scenes of a sentimentality now and forever associated with the Victorian age. By the last year of his life in 1896, his career had turned full circle and he was made President of the Royal Academy of Art.

But the Pre-Raphaelite spirit was maintained by other artists who identified with their ideals. Ford Maddox Brown, for example, in 1848 impressed Rossetti with a painting called

Wycliffe Reading his Translation of the Bible to John of Gaunt. The effect of this highly mediaevalist painting on Rossetti was such that he asked to become Maddox Brown's pupil. This brought him into the Pre-Raphaelite circle. Paradoxically, the effect of the Brotherhood's thought on Maddox Brown's art was to deflect him from his mediaevalist interests. He adopted a more spiritual and moral attitude to Victorian society, as evinced by his paintings *The Last of England* and *Work*. These paintings also reflect the Pre-Raphaelite fascination with naturalism and detail. *The Last of England* was inspired by Woolner's departure to Australia and shows a couple looking from the bow of a departing ship carrying emigrants to new lives. This oval-shaped masterpiece is superbly composed. The young couple stand framed by their umbrella and the ship's netting. Maddox Brown wrote of this painting: 'The minuteness of detail which would be visible under such conditions of broad daylight, I have thought it necessary to imitate, as bringing the pathos of the subject to the beholder'.

During the late 1850s Rossetti produced some of his most beautiful work as an illustrator. From the early years of that decade, under Ruskin's influence, he had been working on a series of watercolour miniatures on literary themes from the works of Alighieri Dante and chivalric mythology. His first illustration proper was produced for William Allingham's *Day and Night Songs* in 1854. Both Morris and Burne-Jones recalled being greatly moved when they first saw it. It depicts a trio of singing women being watched intently by a handsome young man. They stand in a mysterious confined space pierced by rectangular openings through which can be seen the sea and a town at night.

Following this drawing, Rossetti was approached by Edward Moxon, who was planning to publish an illustrated edition of the poems of Alfred Tennyson. Rossetti agreed to contribute five drawings, which were to become some of the best known illustrations of the Victorian period and greatly contributed to his fame. He depicted *Sir Galahad*, *St Cecilia*, *The Lady of Shallott*, *The Weeping Queens* and *Mariana in the South*. All five are rich in mediaevalist detail appropriate to the subjects of these romantic poems, published by Moxon in 1859.

THE PRE-RAPHAELITES AND DESIGN

The Pre-Raphaelite torch was held aloft by a number of young Victorian designers. As has already been noted, in 1853 Edward Burne-Jones and William Morris came under the spell of Millais' captivating painting *The Return of the Dove to the Ark* in Oxford, when they were undergraduates. In the following year both saw Holman Hunt's *The Awakened Conscience* and *The Light of the World* at the Royal Academy. Although both had come to Oxford to study for the priesthood, they were deflected from their chosen careers by the example of the Brotherhood. They took up drawing and painting and started a journal, *The Oxford and Cambridge Magazine,* inspired by *The Germ*. Morris decided to become an architect and Burne-Jones resolved to be a painter.

In 1855 Morris, articled to George Edmund Street, the Gothic architect, and Burne-Jones, trying to make his way as a painter, moved into Rossetti's bohemian circle. Although Morris was working in Street's offices in Oxford, he spent his free time writing poetry and copying and studying early Christian art under the influence of Rossetti, whose paintings became increasingly mediaevalist as the decade passed. Morris decided to give up his apprenticeship with Street, and came to London. With Burne-Jones, he rented rooms in Red Lion

Square and unable to find furnishings to their taste, they decided to make their own. Rossetti wrote to the poet William Allingham:

> Morris is doing the rather magnificent there, and is having some intensely mediaeval furniture made – tables and chairs with incubi and succubi. He and I have painted the back of a chair with figures and inscriptions in gules and vert and azure, and we are all three going to cover a cabinet with pictures.

These solid and architectonic items of furniture, like William Burges's early pieces of the same period, were strongly influenced by French Gothic design of the 13th century. They were illustrated with Arthurian tales and stories by Dante, painted by Rossetti and Burne-Jones.

When Morris moved from Red Lion Square to his new house in Kent after his marriage to Jane Burden in April 1859, he again decided to draw upon his circle of artistic friends to design and decorate their home.

The Red House was designed by Philip Webb, who had met Morris in Street's office. In red brick and with pitched roofs, the house is a testament to the beauty of the unselfconscious tradition of English vernacular architecture that is often ignored as a major inspiration behind the Gothic Revival. Rossetti described the house as 'a most notable work in every way, and more a poem than a house such as anything else could lead you to conceive, but an admirable house to live in too'. Philip Webb also designed a solid oak table and some plain rush-seated chairs which were, in their simplicity, as far

ABOVE *Carved and painted washstand embellished with original Chinese bronzes for taps (1879–80) by William Burges, installed in the guest bedroom of his home, Tower House in Melbury Road, Holland Park.*

LEFT *The Red House, in Bexleyheath, Kent, was designed by Philip Webb for William Morris and his new wife and completed in 1860. The firm of Morris, Marshall, Faulkner & Co. was founded a year later.*

RIGHT *Gothic style wardrobe designed by Philip Webb and painted by Edward Burne-Jones with scenes from Chaucer's "Prioress' Tale" given to William and Jane Morris as a wedding present.*

from anything that could be bought in the fashionable shops of London as possible. Rossetti painted tiles which were set around Webb's beautifully sculptural fireplace and Morris designed simple floral patterns to decorate the walls.

The decoration of these rooms in London and the Red House proved to be one of the most important events in Morris's life and in the history of design. These experiences turned his career away from architecture, and led him to become the most sophisticated practitioner and thinker about design of the period. Fired by the Gothic Revival and the example of the Pre-Raphaelites, Morris and his associates developed a language of decorative art that left behind the blind historicism of their predecessors and pointed toward design in the 20th century.

At Ford Maddox Brown's suggestion Morris rallied his friends to form a 'co-operative' to produce well designed and tastefully decorated furnishings. Formed in 1861, they called themselves Morris, Marshall, Faulkner and Company, Fine Art Workmen in Painting, Carving, Furniture, and the Metals (usually simply described as 'The Firm') with Burne-Jones, Webb and Rossetti as partners and designers.

The Victorian design establishment and the furniture trade, although highly critical of these amateurs, were not untroubled by their arrival on the scene, because The Firm had the support of the leading critic and design thinker of the day, John Ruskin. Despite the obvious distance between the Cole Group and Morris and his colleagues, echoes of the former can be heard in Morris's calls for 'artists of repute' to devote their energies to the decorative arts. The Firm was able to do this most admirably and in 1862 showed a number of items at the International Exhibition in London, including a sofa and a number of hand-painted tiles by Rossetti; a sideboard and washstand by Webb; and the St George Cabinet which was designed by Webb and painted by Morris. These pieces were designed by members of The Firm and put out to skilled craftsmen to be made. Walter Crane, the graphic designer and friend of Morris described these pieces as:

> representing in the main a revival of the mediaeval spirit (though not the letter) in design; a return to simplicity, to sincerity, to good materials, and sound workmanship; to rich and suggestive surface decoration, and simple constructive forms.

11 years after Pugin's death, Morris, Marshall, Faulkner and Company had realized his dearest wishes.

Initially they were only able to secure commissions for stained glass, notably at All Saint's in Bingley in 1864, designed by Richard Norman Shaw. But by the end of the 1860s The Firm had become fashionable in artistic circles. 'Soon',

noted Walter Crane, 'no home with any claim to decorative charm was felt to be complete without its vine and fig tree so to speak – from Queen Square'. In 1865 Morris sold the Red House to move to Queen's Square in London to concentrate his energies on The Firm.

The Firm's designs in that decade were delightfully simple, usually drawing their inspiration from nature. In Morris's wallpapers and fabrics like Daisy and Fruit, both of the early 1860s, floral motifs were highly stylized and flattened, in subdued, tasteful colours. If they appear complex to modern eyes they ought to be compared to contemporary tastes for realistic representations of nature in the brightest possible hues. Philip Webb cultivated an aesthetic of the everyday, writing: 'I never begin to be satisfied until my work looks commonplace'. In fact many of The Firm's products at this time, were almost pure re-creations of vernacular forms; in about 1860 Ford Maddox Brown designed a chair that is in essence a traditional rush-seated Sussex chair.

But underneath these very beautiful designs for fabrics, wallpapers, stained glass, ceramics and furniture lay a very considered philosophy about the alienation wrought by Victorian industry and the democratic potential in art. Following Ruskin, Morris established the link between industrialization and the decline in the standards of design in manufacturing. He fulminated against 'those inexhaustible mines of bad taste, Birmingham and Sheffield'. Through its products, the members of The Firm sought to redirect the society in which they lived.

Morris defined handicraft as 'the expression by man of his pleasure in labour'. This philosophy moved him to learn all the craft techniques in which he designed. A host of tales have entered the mythology of the history of design which

WILLIAM MORRIS DESIGNS

The firm of Morris, Marshall, Faulkner and Company transpired as a result of the communal effort of Morris and his friends over the decoration of the Red House. Architect Philip Webb, designer of this wall cabinet (c.1861), painted with scenes from the life of St George by Morris (below), was to collaborate with the Firm until well into the 90's. (far left) "Daisy", inspired by a wall-hanging designed by William Morris for the Red House, was the first of his wallpapers to be printed for the Firm between 1864–6. Ford Madox Brown, one of the founder members, and Morris designed this stained glass window of St Peter and St Paul (left) for Middleton Cheney, Northamptonshire in 1865.

In 1871 Morris took on the lease of Kelmscott Manor, Oxfordshire, here depicted on the frontispiece of his Utopian novel, "News from Nowhere" (1893), published by the Kelmscott Press (below right). This exquisite Morris hanging of artichokes in crewelwork embroidered on linen (above right) was produced in 1877, two years after the designer had become sole owner of the now renamed Morris & Co.

THIS IS THE PICTURE OF THE OLD HOUSE BY THE THAMES TO WHICH THE PEOPLE OF THIS STORY WENT HEREAFTER FOLLOWS THE BOOK IT SELF WHICH IS CALLED NEWS FROM NOWHERE OR AN EPOCH OF REST & IS WRITTEN BY WILLIAM MORRIS

describe Morris arm deep in bright blue vats of boiling dye or handmaking the paper for the books published by his Kelmscott Press. Morris declared his aim to be to make 'artists craftsmen and craftsmen artists'. The irony of Morris's socialist aspirations and his desire to bring his own aesthetic within reach of the common man was that inevitably the price of his handcrafted designs was in almost all cases well beyond the means of the Victorian working classes.

By the end of the 1860s Morris's place in the history of art was guaranteed. The development of his thought and his influence on other designers makes him the most important figure in 19th-century design in Britain and, arguably, throughout the world.

THE QUEEN ANNE MOVEMENT

The 'Queen Anne Movement' was a label attached to a small group of artists and designers in the 1870s that stuck. It was a misnomer on two accounts; it had little to do with Queen Anne or the early years of the 18th century, nor did it constitute a 'movement' for those associated with it lacked the self-consciousness of a cabal like the Pre-Raphaelite Brotherhood, or the intellectual programme of the Arts and Craft Movement of the 1880s.

The Queen Anne Movement does not fit neatly in the sequence of historical revivals that make up this chapter. Its artists and designers were all of a younger generation than the figures discussed earlier, bar William Morris and Edward Burne-Jones. The leading Queen Anne architects, Richard Norman Shaw and Philip Webb, for example, were both born in the 1830s. Fierce attachment to one style over another was characteristic of an earlier generation of men like the Goth, Pugin, and the neo-Classicist Alexander Thomson, both dead by the time the Queen Anne Movement was in full swing. But it must still be acknowledged as a historicist style, albeit a pluralist one.

Queen Anne was, like all the other revivals described, led by architects, but its influence can be seen in other areas of art and design, including fashion and illustration. It was a bridge from the High Victorian period to the final decades of the century, when architects and designers shed historicism and developed genuinely new stylistic languages. The influence of the movement can be seen in a number of *fin-de-siècle* progressive trends such as the Garden City movement and dress reform. But it is its High Victorian characteristics and stylistic origins that will be described here.

The Gothic started to lose its exclusively Christian associations in the late 1850s and the 1860s. As practised by younger Gothicists, it became a highly aestheticized style. It has already been shown that the work of artists and designers like Edward Burne-Jones, Dante Gabriel Rossetti and William Burges brought to the Gothic Revival ideas that would have been anathema to figures of the 1840s such as Pugin.

Younger architects and designers following in the wake of these figures, including Philip Webb and Richard Norman Shaw, were to form the nucleus. Both had worked in George Edmund Street's architectural practice in the 1850s, and began to reject the out-and-out mediaevalism of the Gothic Revival. Others left the embrace of this style because they felt it had been corrupted by commerce. One Queen Anne architect, John James Stevenson, described his disaffection with

Massiveness and grand schemes were rejected by Queen Anne designers, who sought the domestic and the homely. In this they felt kinship with Morris and his circle, who were developing a parallel aesthetic in furniture and decoration. By the mid 1860s, Morris and his colleagues, Maddox Brown, Rossetti and Burne-Jones had moved on from their heavy mediaevalist furniture and were producing and selling in their shop in London near-copies of traditional country furniture and plain, tasteful fabric and wallpaper prints derived from Nature. Like the early buildings by Webb, such as Val Pricep's studio in Kensington (1864–5) or W E Nesfield's Kew Garden Lodge (1866), this furniture appeared to have characteristics adopted from English domestic buildings and furniture of the 17th and 18th centuries. Rush seating and ladder backs seemed the stylistic equivalents of red brick chimney stacks and oriel windows. As early as 1862, Warrington Taylor, in his correspondence, began to use the phrase 'Queen Anne' to describe this new style.

The Queen Anne Movement was not the first expression of interest in English vernacular architecture in the Victorian period. Although Stuart and Georgian styles were widely dismissed by fashionable architectural taste of the 1850s, two very interesting maverick buildings were erected under their influence. In 1855 Wellington College in Berkshire was built in the style of Sir Christopher Wren, the architectural visionary of the original Queen Anne period, by John Shaw the Younger. William Makepeace Thackeray, the Victorian

the Gothic; it had 'lent itself with fatal facility to the expression of loudness, vulgarity, obtrusiveness and sensationalism more objectionable by far than the dreariest classic of Gower or Wimpole Street'.

They came under the sway of intellectuals like Walter Pater who argued that 'all periods, types, schools of taste, are in themselves equal'. After years of studying French 13th-century cathedrals, and 14th-century Venice, young architects felt themselves at liberty to look at English domestic and vernacular traditions, such as tile hanging, weather-boarding and half timbering. The embryonic Queen Anne circle, which included Charles Swinburne, a poet, the painter Simeon Soloman and Warrington Taylor, Morris, Marshall, Faulkner and Company's business manager, developed a cult of Englishness. Warrington Taylor wrote:

 Everything English, except stockjobbing London or cotton Manchester, is essentially small, and of a homely farmhouse kind of poetry . . . Above all things nationality is the greatest social trait, English Gothic is as small as our landscape is small, it is sweet picturesque homely farmyardish . . . French is aspiring, grand, straining after the extraordinary, all very well in France but wrong here.

But true to Pater's thesis, Queen Anne was an amalgamation of a broader range of influences than merely national ones. In Queen Anne architecture, for example, traces of Dutch and Japanese styles can be found. Philip Webb's later houses, built between 1879 and 1891, even display the marked influence of Classical and Elizabethan design, for example, his country house Standen (1891–2) in Sussex.

novelist whose books were set in the 18th century, similarly built himself a house in Kensington (1860–2), which contained the most unfashionable of details: great sash windows and red brick with clumsy cream Portland stone dresswork. He proudly called it 'the reddest house in all the town'. But Queen Anne as practised by Norman Shaw and his friends was a much more sophisticated affair. It produced the most widely loved of English architectural styles which still exerts an influence today on domestic building.

QUEEN ANNE STYLE ARCHITECTURE

The Queen Anne style is epitomized by a number of houses built by Norman Shaw in Chelsea in the 1870s, described by William Morris as 'elegantly fantastic'. All of these houses combine similar details composed in ingenious ways giving each building its individual character. Old Swan House (1875–7), overlooking the Thames, has an immediate appearance of rather plain symmetry and regularity. But Shaw took great pleasure in small details such as the positioning of different window types. The first floor has small paned oriel windows with ornamental stonework decorated with swans, the oversailed second floor has slender bowed and sash windows set flush with the brickwork, and high dormer windows push out of the pitched roof. The unique character of this building comes from Shaw's ability to compose in a number of English architectural traditions.

Oriel windows were prominent in Shaw's two houses in Cadogan Square in Chelsea designed in 1877, as were other Queen Anne features: pitched roofs, red brick and ornamental

RIGHT AND BELOW *The Bedford Park housing project, described in the prospectus of 1881 as built in the "picturesque Queen Anne style," was predominantly of red brick with hanging tiles, steeply pitched and gabled roofs, and leaded windows.*

stonework. But the appearance of these buildings was quite different to the Old Swan House. They took on a Flemish character, with dominant Dutch-style gables emphasizing their verticality, and porches capped with broken pediments in the 17th-century fashion.

The peak, of the Queen Anne Movement came with the building of the Bedford Park suburb on the western edges of London. Inspired by the fashionable cult of ruralism, Jonathan T Carr, a property speculator, planned to build a 'village' for the artistic middle classes and approached E W Godwin and Norman Shaw to design its first homes in 1877. The 500 houses that they, and other architects such as E J May and J C Dollman, built here, were modest homes in ambling leafy streets with picturesque names like Queen Anne's Grove and Marlborough Crescent. The quaint Queen Anne style, employed for these houses at Bedford Park, can also be found in its church, school of art and pub, or as it was apt to be called 'the inn'. The church of Saint Michael and All Angels designed by Norman Shaw, constructed in 1879, was unusual because it lacked a spire – a notably aesthetic gesture.

The significance of this 'village', as Carr liked to call it, lay not in architectural novelty, for most of its buildings were plain domestic forms originating in Tudor or Stuart England, but in Carr's vision of an artistic community living in a semi-rural setting. It was populated by affluent and progressive middle class people. They were often exceptional Victorians: writers, actors, artists and political and cultural radicals. Accordingly, life at Bedford Park did not follow the humdrum patterns of suburbia. An afternoon spent discussing a radical topic such as women's suffrage, at the Conversazione Club, could be followed by evening at a garden party attended by Ellen Terry and other glittering figures of Victorian theatre.

The Queen Anne style was brought to greater public notice by the *Ballad of Bedford Park*, which was published in the St James Gazette in 1881:

> Here the trees are green and the bricks are red
> And clean the face of man
> We'll build our gardens here he said
> In the style of good Queen Anne
> 'Tis here a village I'll erect
> With Norman Shaw's assistance
> Where man will lead a chaste
> Correct, aesthetical existence.

THE QUEEN ANNE STYLE AND DESIGN

The Queen Anne impulse can also be found in a number of other fields of design and graphic art. Queen Anne interiors drew upon an eclectic range of styles. Fashionable artistic taste dictated that subtle, natural colours were preferable to modern ones such as mauve and magenta. Antiques were also in vogue, and 18th-century Chelsea and Worcester porcelain and Chippendale furniture were considered highly fashionable. The architect Norman Shaw was a great collector of blue and white china, and he designed a shop-front for the leading dealer in this ceramic ware, Murray Marks, in 1875. The influence of the East could often be found in Persian carpets and Japanese fans and plates. This eclecticism resulted in many cluttered and crowded rooms filled to the ceiling, or at least to the frieze, with fashionable bric-a-brac. In this respect owners of Queen Anne style homes chose to depart from the self-consciously humble origins of this style.

Modern furnishings were not banished from this aesthetic world and a number of Queen Anne architects practised as designers. One, R W Edis, produced a charming volume called *Decoration and Furniture of Town Houses* in 1881. This book not only illustrated fine designs for furniture and patterns for tiles and wallcoverings in a range of styles, but animated these sets with light-filled scenes of children at play.

The Queen Anne influence can also be seen in the work of a number of illustrators, who helped to popularize the movement internationally. Walter Crane, Kate Greenaway and Ralph Caldecott produced picture books that paralleled the enthusiasms of Queen Anne architects. Books such as Crane's *Cinderella* or Greenaway's *Under the Window* contained similar mixtures of vernacular, historicist and exotic details. These books proved to be phenomenally successful. Walter Crane's illustrated song book of 1877, *The Baby's Opera*, sold over 40,000 copies.

THE INFLUENCE OF THE QUEEN ANNE STYLE

The Queen Anne Movement had greater impact on the fabric of Britain's cities than any other revivalist architectural style of the 19th century. This may not be readily obvious to the casual observer who strolls through town and city centres up and down the country. But this style was largely a domestic affair and its importance lies in the thousands of suburban homes, and minor pubs, hotels and shops built in its wake.

All the leading Queen Anne architects produced designs for such commonplace buildings. In 1876 Ernest George designed a shop for the firm of Thomas Goode and Company, in South Audley Street in London in which they sold glass and ceramics. It is an elegant building in the Flemish style with prominent gables and chimneys. Similarly, Norman Shaw's place in the history of architecture was largely secured by his New Zealand Chambers of 1872 which was renowned for its oriel windows,

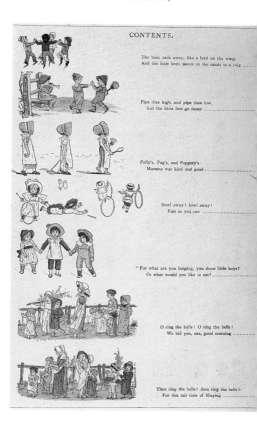

Walter Crane's 1870's Christmas card (far left) and Kate Greenaway's illustration for "The Marigold Garden" (right) echo the fashionable aesthetic emphasis on linear simplicity.

The complex, typically Victorian design of this invitation to a Colonial and Indian ball and reception at the Guildhall in London (below right), seems very different to the clarity of Randolph Caldecott's and Kate Greenaway's nursery rhyme illustration (left and below).

incorporated as much for their illuminating properties as their picturesque qualities. But beyond these architectural heroes innumerable practitioners across the country adopted the Queen Anne architectural language for their projects.

Although its major practitioners left the style in the 1880s and 1890s, with figures like Norman Shaw moving closer to forms of Classicism, characteristic Queen Anne forms proved popular with thousands of homeowners across the nation. Even today, homeowners appear most fond of architectural details revived by Queen Anne architects, such as weatherboarding, tile hanging, classical porches and so on.

During the same period, the United States witnessed a revival of domestic and vernacular architectural traditions that has become known to architectural history as the 'Colonial Revival'. Aware of debates in England, American architects, reflecting a middle-class dissatisfaction with urban life, designed buildings in the country and by the sea which borrowed heavily from national traditional architectural forms. While Norman Shaw employed the English tradition of tile hanging, American architects, such as H H Richardson at the Watts-Sherman House in Newport of 1874–5, used their American equivalent, wooden shingles.

"Where are you going, my pretty Maid?"

—The Milkmaid—

From the Original Drawing by RANDOLPH CALDECOTT

PUBLISHED BY F.WARNE & CO

In the later 1870s, the Queen Anne style provoked debate in American architectural practice. 'To those that believe in revivals,' said the architect R S Peabody in 1877, 'Queen Anne is a very fit importation to our offices'. Peabody was the architect of one of the most important vernacular revival buildings in America in the period. His 'Kragsyde' in Manchester-by-the-Sea (1882) actually owed little to Norman Shaw's own 'Cragside' of 1876. The American house, replete with dramatic gables, measured shingling, massive stonework, and erect chimneys befits its magnificent site.

But it ought not to be suggested that American architects worked in the shadow of their British Queen Anne colleagues, for they quite outshone them in the radicalism of their rejection of historicism, and their use of vernacular forms in architecture. Men like Stamford White designed homes of quite stunning innovation by 19th-century standards. His 1887 house built for William Low in Bristol, Rhode Island (unfortunately demolished) was a unique creation in wooden shinglework: a single gable sitting low and long on the brow of a hill.

THE INFLUENCE OF THE EAST

In the 19th century the West encountered the East through colonial life, wars, commercial expansion, safer and easier travel, popular journalism and scholarly works. Writers and artists romanticized the East, Rudyard Kipling's writings about India were very popular in Britain in the 1880s. Whereas the East had appeared to observers in earlier ages an exotic, alien place that was unintelligible to civilized minds, Victorian observers investigated these new worlds with vigour and enthusiasm. Some orientalists became so enamoured with their new-found world that they rejected the comforts of Victorian domesticity for a lifetime of nomadic travel in North Africa, the Far East or Asia Minor.

Although Western collectors had been acquiring the triumphs of Eastern craftsmanship for many centuries, the East was also brought to life for a broader public through international exhibitions. The Chinese section at the Great Exhibition of 1851 and the Japanese court at the London International Exhibition of 1862 were both critical and popular successes. At the latter the Victorian public were able to see beautiful hanging lanterns, delicate silks, and masterly pottery, including a superb *Satsuma* bottle which now resides in the Victoria and Albert Museum. This exhibition triggered off a fashion for all things Japanese. The firm of Liberty's founded in 1875 by Arthur Liberty was the consequence of his enthusiam for these exhibits. The leaders of fashion would visit his Regent Street shop to buy blue and white china and peacock feathers with which to decorate their homes in the highly fashionable Japanese style of the day. Fans were the pre-eminent symbol of this taste; artists such as Albert Moore and James Abbott McNeill Whistler used them as props in their canvases and in modish homes they would be positioned on mantelpieces or attached to walls.

Architects and designers led fashionable taste by incorporating Japanese characteristics in their work. The key figure in this development was Edward William Godwin, who began his career strongly under the influence of John Ruskin's ideas about the Gothic in the 1850s. He is widely credited with the design of the first item of Japanese-style furniture in Europe in a sideboard of 1867. Constructed by William Watt in dark mahogany with grey paper panels in the style of embossed leather work and silver metal details, it is a highly striking piece of furniture. Its resemblance to any known item of Japanese furniture was very slight, but its restrained and geometric qualities were widely believed to have caught the spirit of Eastern design. In fact, Godwin's knowledge of authentic Japanese craftsmanship was very thin, and he derived the style of his furniture designs from details in Hokusai prints. In 1877 he designed a house in Chelsea for the American painter, James Whistler, which was the fullest expression of the Japanese influence to date. Its interiors were very simple, with white walls, matting covering the floor, plain curtains and each room full of Chinese porcelain and Japanese prints.

The influence of the East can also be found in the fine arts. Whistler's own painting owed much to the style of Japanese woodcuts which had been arriving in Europe and America in increasing numbers since trading links were established with that nation by the United States in 1854. In fact, he was a

LEFT _Oriental pottery was influential in Europe throughout the century but it was the novelty of Japanese imports in the 1860's that made the most impact. This is reflected in James Hadley's Royal Worcester porcelain vases (1872)._

RIGHT _Pieces like this copy of a 16th century Persian bottle were displayed by Minton at the London International Exhibition of 1871._

great champion of this art, as confirmed by William Rossetti:

> It was through Whistler that my brother and I became acquainted with Japanese woodcuts and colourprints. It may have been early in 1863. He had seen and purchased some specimens of those works in Paris, and he heartily delighted in them, and showed them to us; and we then set about procuring other works of the same class.

Not only did he paint explicitly Japanese themes in such works as _The Princess from the Land of Porcelain,_ but he learned much about composition and colour from the prints for which he scoured Paris. His works of the 1870s and 1880s, such as _Nocturne in Blue and Gold, Old Battersea Bridge,_ have superb oriental scale and atmosphere.

The Near East provided more direct inspiration for other orientalist artists. For some, like Frederick Goodall, it provided a backdrop for their religious paintings. He first travelled to Eygpt in 1858 and made over 130 oil studies of domestic life and a number of these works were exhibited at the Royal Academy in 1869. Others became fascinated with the lifestyles they found on their travels and painted scenes of con-

temporary life for its own sake. John Frederick Lewis was one of the first such artists to 'go native'. He first visited Egypt in 1842 and for the following 11 years he rarely left the city of Cairo. He adopted the local style of dress and was described by William Makepeace Thackeray as living 'like a languid lotus-eater – a dreamy, hazy, lazy, tobaccofied life'. His works, such as _The Carpet Seller_ of 1860 are a documentary source for the life of the city, showing local customs, costume and trade. One of his best known works is _The Hareem_ of 1850, although the version illustrated here is only a fragment of a watercolour exhibited at the Royal Academy in 1850. In that picture the sultan on the left of the picture stares intently at a demure, semi-naked concubine who is being brought to join his hareem by a Nubian eunuch. There were several theories speculating as to why she is missing from the picture. It was thought that some Victorian 'Bowdler' took offence at her nudity and had the picture cropped. But recent evidence suggests that this is an entirely different painting, despite the remarkable similarity between it and the original work, which is known to art historians through a 1908 photograph. When Lewis's painting was first exhibited it was highly commended by both the public

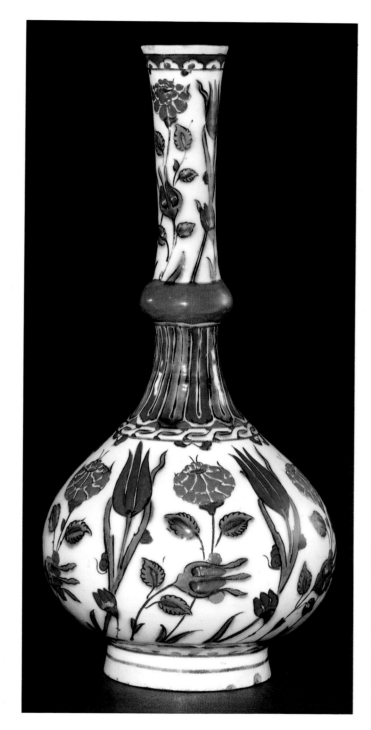

and art critics alike. The *Athenaeum,* in heaping praise on this watercolour, also anticipated public interest in the Eastern interior in the 1860s and 1870s, when it noted:

> The Appartment . . . is plain; the walls being white, with beams and supports in white wood. The only objects within it on which the riches and the taste of the owner have been lavished are the windows – one of which possesses a gorgeous enrichment of coloured glass – and the exquisitely designed lattice work.

Such praise marked the beginning of this watercolour's venerable career; it was shown at the Paris *Exposition Universelle* in 1855, and the France–British Exhibition of 1908.

RIGHT *This elegant spun glass fountain decorated with birds was made in Stourbridge c.1900. Wax fruit and stuffed animals were also popular items similarly encased within glass domes.*

LEFT *Japanned tin ware was fashionable since Regency times. This tray, edged with decorated medieval style tracery and painted with flowers and fruit dates from c.1865.*

ROMANTIC VISIONS

The Victorians built another kind of architecture, often drawn on historical models, that was outside conflicts over style. Follies, even if they were in the form of Greek temples or Gothic towers, owed less to debates over appropriate styles for empires or swings in fashionable taste than the legacy of picturesque ideas from the 18th century. These functionless buildings were like architectural ornaments for the estates of wealthy men. The motivations of the patrons of these bizarre architectural fantasies were as unique as the buildings they erected. They include monkless abbeys; illusionary castles only one wall deep; temples for dead religions; re-creations of Stonehenge; and arches for avenues that led nowhere. Furthermore, the tales which surround their flights of fancy often make it difficult to distinguish fact from fiction.

In 1840, Walter Burton May built his lovely May's Folly in Kent. Although described by some contemporary observers as a 'gimcrack with horrid stucco', it is a magnificent soaring Gothic house and tower, decorated with roman plasterwork. It is widely believed that he had it erected so that he could see the sea. It is a classic explanation of folly building, and

ABOVE RIGHT *The geometric shape of this elegant walnut cabinet by E.W. Godwin, embellished with carved Japanese boxwood plaques and ivory monkey handles, has a distinct Japanese influence.*

BELOW *No lady with aesthetic pretensions could afford not to have a fan decorated in oriental or more particularly, Japanese style.*

John Frederick Lewis (1805–76) is best remembered for his exotic depiction of Egyptian life in such works as "The Harem," painted during and after his ten year stay in Cairo in the 1840's.

typically in tales of this kind, his ambition was never realized. In May's case he failed to note that the Kent Downs stood in the way of a clear view. Another explanation was that his wife had left him for a local farmer and that he built this tower in order to lure her back.

Peterson's Tower, built in Hampshire in the late 19th century, was commissioned by Andrew Peterson. He was a retired High Court Judge who had returned from India in 1868. He built this austere tower in pre-cast concrete blocks, a novel constructional departure for the period. In fact it was a little too novel as the building had to be made safe less than fifty years later. In the local area a number of rumours concerning Peterson's motives circulated. One said he was trying to introduce Hindu burial rituals to Britain and planned to be laid to rest at the top of the tower and his wife at the base. Another suggested that the ghost of Sir Christopher Wren had visited him and wished to prove the strength of Portland cement through the agency of the good judge.

Another tower, overlooking Halifax in Yorkshire, was built by John E Wainhouse, a dye manufacturer, in the 1870s. His works issued dense smoke into the surrounding neighbourhood. He planned to build a chimney connected with his Washer Lane Dyeworks by means of an underground pipe. This was to be a tower encircled by steps, and punctuated with balconies. Unlike many folly builders who wished to make

their mark on their surroundings, Wainhouse was distressed that this chimney disturbed his view. He commissioned a second architect to redesign it as a 270 feet tall, beautiful tower topped by a cupola and a colonnade. Ironically it was never used for its original function as the dye works were bought by another owner who was less concerned about the smoke emitted from the factory. Wainhouse kept his tower, which had cost him £14,000 to construct, for use as a 'general astronomical and physical laboratory'.

McCaig's Folly, built in the 1890s in Argyll, Scotland is a breath-taking ruined amphitheatre that stands above the town of Oban which overlooks the beautiful Firth of Lorn. It was built by John Stewart McCaig, a wealthy banker, who had a passion for Graeco-Roman culture. He believed that the Colosseum in Rome was the greatest achievement of Roman culture and that such a monument would be an inspiration to the town's inhabitants. He set about building this folly as a philanthropic exercise that would provide gainful labour for the town's unemployed. Unlike the Colosseum in Rome, McCaig's building is circular rather than oval, and has a slight Gothic character in its arched windows.

Such bizarre buildings are valuable reminders of the fact that not all Victorians were dour and conscientious, that some possessed great poetic sensibility, some a great sense of humour, and others were extraordinarily eccentric.

VICTORIAN LIFE
AND DEATH

*An idealised picture of the tranquillity of a middle class Victorian home
from an 1860s children's book entitled "Pretty Tales for the Nursery."*

 lthough the 'Battle of the Styles' was fought in the houses of the aristocracy, major national architectural commissions, international exhibitions and in the salons of Victorian aesthetes, the lives of ordinary people were not untouched by Victorian style. The middle classes were receptive to changing fashions in decoration, furnishings, and everyday objects and Victorian manufacturers and retailers were happy to encourage them in this. In this respect Victorian commonplace objects are like buried artifacts to an archaeologist, for they tell us much about the lives and enthusiasms of the people who bought and used them.

To judge the tastes and lives of everyday Victorians by the most celebrated products of that culture would be a misrepresentation. Much-championed Victorian artists today such as George Frederick Watts, the author of works of great poetic sensibility such as *Hope* of 1886, did not come close to matching the mid-century popularity of a painter like William Powell Frith and his works like *Derby Day* and *Ramsgate Sands*.

THE HOME IN THE HIGH VICTORIAN PERIOD

The Victorian period was one of great domesticity. They planned, built, furnished and fitted out their homes with extraordinary vigour. Books, magazines and legislation on the subject abounded. Even at the most humble levels of society, Victorians regarded their homes as a vivid reflection of their taste and status in society. Only the very poorest, living in the harshest of cramped slum conditions, did not place great store in a gleaming doorstep or a shining door knocker, or set aside some little space in their home to display their ornaments. But it must be remembered that in Britain those very poorest constituted a large proportion of the population.

Social investigators such as Edwin Chadwick, the author of the *Report on the Sanitary Condition of the Labouring Population of Great Britain* (1842), brought to the attention of the Government and the public the extent of poor housing conditions in Britain's inner cities. As the increasingly urban population grew, the pressure on the existing housing stock became intolerable. It was typical for two families, each with children, to make their home in the dank basement of a slum house. Under these circumstances disease was rife, and the mid years

Abraham Solomon wittily
points the difference between travelling
First Class (left) and Third Class
(below) by rail during the 1850's.

OPPOSITE RIGHT Originally designed in
1891 for the billiard room at Buscot
park in Oxfordshire by William Atkin
Bury, this eight foot high ceramic
fireplace was modelled and
manufactured by the Martin Brothers of
Southall, Middlesex.

OPPOSITE BELOW Rosewood love-seat
by American designer John Belter
(fl. 1840–60) specialist in richly
upholstered neo-rococo style furniture.

of the century saw waves of cholera epidemics which killed great numbers of slum dwellers. In the 1870s politicians such as Benjamin Disraeli took up the cause of the badly housed and encouraged speculative building. Large numbers of houses were built of varying quality to be rented by the lower classes. At the same time a few municipal schemes in Liverpool, Nottingham and Huddersfield resulted in homes for the poor, and charitable institutions such as the Peabody Trust built tenements for the working classes financed by middle-class philanthropy. But the majority of these homes were erected through private enterprise. Such houses tended to be laid out in terraces, and were broadly derived from vernacular housing traditions or a much diluted form of 18th-century Classicism. They occasionally have very charming details, such as neat tiled porches and simple decorative mouldings above gound floor windows. Although much of this housing was defective in many respects, it must be noted that the small terraced house brought about a marked improvement in the quality of life for many who lived in them.

The middle classes were also courted by speculative builders who built suburban homes on the fringes of most cities. With their leafy streets and respectable gardens they appealed to those who longed to live in the country but had to work in the city. The Queen Anne style of the 1870s was the most popular architectural language employed in these schemes because of its modest, domestic feel.

Taken as a whole, the period between the 1860s and 1900 has been aptly described by social historians as a 'housing revolution'. The established nobility and gentry played their part in this enthusiasm for building. Relatively modest Georgian family homes were remodelled in 'new' fashionable styles such as the Gothic. An elevation to the peerage was often accompanied by a comparable rise in the status of the house. Charles Brudenell-Bruce, for example, spent £250,000 improving his family seat, Tottenham Park in Wiltshire, when he was made Marquis of Aylesbury.

New money earned in commerce sought old status by buying country homes and acting out the role of the squirearchy. These rich magnates would immediately mark their arrival with the construction of ostentatious wings and towers, new houses for their tenants displaying their philanthropy and prominent entrance lodges. The very rich would even have built entirely new houses in the grand style of country residences at very great cost. John Walter III, the owner of *The Times* newspaper, had Bearwood erected between 1865 and 1874 at the price of £250,000. This Tudor-style mansion with some Gothic detailing was designed by Robert Kerr, the author of *The Gentleman's House*. In 1864 Kerr, a guide to taste, offered rich patrons the opportunity to own homes in 11

different styles including Rural Italian, Revived Elizabethan and Palladian.

These grand homes of the rich led popular taste, and the correspondence of domestic values from the affluent through to the working classes in the Victorian period is striking. All classes pursued the same values of comfort and elegance. Echoes of drawing rooms in the grandest of mansions could be found in Victorian parlours throughout the nation.

A classic item of Victorian furniture was the *etageré*, sometimes known as the 'whatnot'. These pieces were screens or

LEFT *Victorian cast-iron bed with half-tester in fabric of 18th century design.*

RIGHT *Floral decorated balloon backed chair from Pennsylvania c. 1820.*

stands supporting shelves on which were placed artistic bric-a-brac, vases with flowers or stuffed animals protected by glass domes, or whatever took the owner's fancy. At their most ornate these highly decorative items of furniture would contain mirrors and all kinds of artistic motifs such as rococo carving, classical pediments and so on. But even the homes of the lower middle class had similar items of display furniture, even if of a smaller scale and poorer quality. The ornaments placed on them marked social distinction: Staffordshire figurines, for example, would not be found in a Marquis's *etageré*.

Another item of furniture widely associated with the Victorian age is the davenport, although it should be noted that this piece of furniture originated in the 18th century when a Captain Davenport charged the firm of Gillow to produce a small neat desk. In the late 19th century they had increased in popularity such that they were a characteristic feature of most middle-class homes. For the affluent these items of furniture could display the heights of Victorian cabinet-making, with ingenious hidden drawers, skilful marketry and curving cabinet lids on runners, but even the more commonplace desks made by the 'furniture factories' were highly sought after. In fact, their status lay in their decorative rather than their functional aspect, much to the annoyance of some observers. *Furniture and Decoration* commented: 'The aesthetic advantages of modern writing tables have in many instances, been obtained at the expense of convenience'.

Some items of Victorian furniture can be divided by gender, for the marked differences in lifestyle and dress of men and women dictated suitable furniture for each. The Spanish Chair, for example, was designed so that women, dressed in bulky crinolines, would be able to sit and rise gracefully. It was a kind of low, armless seat which allowed these large skirts to hang gracefully over the sides of the chair. The Grandfather, or Firesider were affectionate terms for the comfortable wing-backed, upholstered armchair in which many Victorian patriarchs would relax by the hearthside.

The name 'grandfather' also lent itself to an essential feature of middle-class drawing rooms, the grandfather clock. Long case clocks driven by pendulums, developed in England in the 17th century, were given this endearing name in 1878 by Henry C Work in a song *My Grandfather Clock*.

America made a special contribution to Victorian life with the popularization of the rocking chair. It appears to have originated in both England and the American Colonies in the 1760s, but the classic form of the rocker is known as the Boston. This simple piece of furniture, found on every porch across America, evolved from the Windsor chair with a tall comb back and a curved seat. Many people decorated their chairs with floral motifs in the style of Lambert Hitchcock, a Connecticut craftsman of the 1820s. They were imported into Britain in vast numbers and were sold as 'American Common Sense Chairs', and aids to digestion. A number of European furniture makers sought to surpass the simple excellence of the American rocker by producing upholstered chairs with spring rockers or tensioned steel frames, but only Michael Thonet, an Austrian, came close with his elegant bentwood chair exhibited at the Great Exhibition of 1851.

To modern eyes the atmosphere of mid-Victorian rooms would have appeared quite overpowering. Every possible surface was covered, decorated or draped in some way. From floor to frieze, walls were covered in richly coloured flock wallpapers, much to the distaste of figures like William Morris. He designed over 60 wallpapers between 1862 and 1896 to stem the tide of elaborate, fussy machine-made papers. Curtains made from heavy velvets or serge in the vivid colours produced by aniline dyes, and decorated with tassles and fringes, hung from massive, ostentatious frames. Mantelpieces, tables and chair backs were all copiously covered with lace and other decorative fabrics. These luxurious feasts of colour and texture were the consequence of dramatic developments and technical innovations in the cloth making industries based in the north of England. They brought these symbols of great wealth in earlier centuries down to the pocket of the lower middle classes in Victorian Britain.

In the 1870s it became increasingly fashionable to buy and furnish homes with antiques. This coincided with a general lightening of decorative taste and an interest in exotic designs. Rooms across the country began to incorporate lightly patterned wall coverings and fabrics in pale, pastel hues and were furnished with examples of Gothic, 18th-century and Japanese craftsmanship. Although both of these trends were led by fashionable taste, the extent to which this aestheticism percolated throughout society can be seen in Charles Eastlake's *Hints on Household Taste*. Here he felt it necessary to caution his readers; 'No doubt good examples of mediaeval furniture and cabinet work are occasionally to be met with in the curiosity shops of Wardour Street; but, as a rule, the 'Glastonbury' chairs and 'antique' bookcases which are sold in that venerable thoroughfare will prove on examination to be nothing but gross libels on the style of art which they are supposed to represent'. There was also a vogue for decorating different rooms of a house in differing styles. The very rich would even commission exacting reproductions of authentic period rooms. To stroll through a fashionable house of the 1880s was like touring a museum. One might leave an Adam drawing-room, pass through a hallway with Tudor-style panelling, to arrive in a Georgian dining-room.

The hearth was a particularly important place in all Victorian homes. It became a highly romanticized symbol of home, comfort and assurance and a focal point of domesticity. A number of observers remembered Prince Albert leading discussions with prominent intellectuals of the day, while warming his back in front of a roaring fire. Robert Kerr wrote in *The Gentleman's House* of 1864:

For a sitting-room, keeping in mind the English climate and habits, a fireside is of all considerations practically the most important. No such appartment can pass muster with domestic critics unless there be convenient space for a wide circle of persons around the fire, embracing indeed in some degree the table; and this without inconvenience or disturbance being created at some point by the passing out and in and to and fro of all parties.

FAR LEFT *The simplicity of this writing desk designed in 1893 by C.F.A. Voysey, the last important architect-designer of the Art and Crafts movement, is worlds apart from this Italian ebonised writing desk, virtually writhing in neo-rococo ornament.*

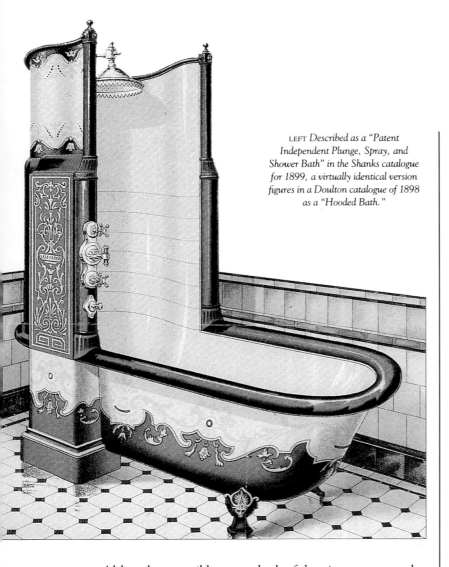

LEFT *Described as a "Patent Independent Plunge, Spray, and Shower Bath" in the Shanks catalogue for 1899, a virtually identical version figures in a Doulton catalogue of 1898 as a "Hooded Bath."*

Although ostensibly a method of heating a room, the hearth was treated in the same fashion as any other aspect of Victorian furnishing, and could be made from ostentatious materials. They were as highly ornamented as the room in which they were to be placed demanded. At their grandest they could be constructed from mahogany or any number of hard woods, lined with marble, and decorated with hand-painted tiles, classical plaques or ornate carving. The area above the entablature would receive similar decorative treatment with niches for small sculptures and shelving for fashionable *objets d'art*.

Screens were placed in front of the fire to deflect its heat. Embroidering the panels with floral motifs or sentimental sayings for these wooden frames became a popular pastime for ladies of the leisured classes. Fashionable primers such as *The Young Ladies' Treasure Book* instructed their readers on how to make a variety of screens in the shape of banners or geometric forms. Similarly, authors of these guides to domestic life suggested that less ornate mantelpieces ought to be covered in richly decorated velvets known as *mantel-valences*.

The bathroom largely escaped the ornamental excesses found in the rest of the Victorian home. Herman Muthesius, a German civil servant in Britain in the 1890s researching design and industry, was greatly impressed with the rationalism he found in this functional room. The development of the

fully plumbed bathroom was relatively speedy. In the 1860s it was unusual to find water on tap, and baths had to be laboriously filled from large matching cans. Yet by the end of the century builders proudly proclaimed their attention to sanitary detail in advertisements for new suburban homes for the lower middle classes.

SHOPPING IN THE LATE 19TH CENTURY

The nature of shopping changed dramatically in the Victorian period. As incomes and living standards rose across the nation in all classes and the population became more urban, a new generation of business men, led by figures such as William Whiteley, the department store entrepreneur, geared up the retailing industry to meet an ever increasing demand. In the early 19th century most people met their day-to-day needs in local shops such as grocers and haberdashers. Those who were less affluent relied upon the services of itinerant salesmen and travelling fairs for such simple goods as needles and cotton. Shopping was then a local affair. By the end of the century the situation had changed. Large department stores, such as Harrods and Selfridges in London, could be found in most large cities and a number of national chain stores sold their wares across the whole of the country. They encouraged sales through sophisticated advertising campaigns, fixed pricing, pre-packaged goods and product branding.

Lipton's, the grocers, was the first major chain store in Britain. It was formed in 1871 and by 1899 it ran over 500 shops. Concentrating on a small number of lines of goods sold at fixed prices, it led the way for a number of well known companies to follow its path, including Hepworth's, the made-to-measure tailor and Boot's the chemist. Stores such as these brought about marked changes in the nature of retailing. Until the 1870s advertisements and posters were usually placed by manufacturers, but then chain stores took over the function. The nature of shopping changed as well, with a new emphasis on efficient service. Stores owned by firms such as Boot's tended to be long and narrow, with a continuous working area bordered by shelves around a central aisle. These shops were made attractive through high quality fittings and decorations such as Minton tiles illustrating appropriate themes. Chairs were placed around the shopfloor should a customer feel tired and wish to rest.

The rise of Marks and Spencer, one of the most successful firms in Britain today, is worthy of comment. In 1884 Michael

Marks ran a penny stall in a Leeds bazaar under a sign which read 'Don't ask the price – it's a penny'. He sold many different kinds of small manufactures, such as cotton, needles, buttons and so on. Influenced by the experience of companies such as Woolworth's in the United States, the firm quickly expanded and by the early 1900s it owned 60 penny bazaars. These shops placed little store by lavish interior design or expensive fittings but traded under the banner of value for money.

Victorian retailing received a great boost from men such as Jessie Boot, the proprietor of the chemists Boot's. A classic Victorian entrepreneur fixated with the idea of expansion, he aimed to make his company the 'biggest and the best'. He inherited his first shop from his father in Nottingham which sold folk medicines and herbal treatments to working people. He introduced household goods to the shop's stock and employed an aggressive selling strategy undercutting his rivals. His tactics proved so successful that he was able to open a new shop in 1868, marking the beginning of a great period of expansion. Within 30 years he owned 180 shops. He believed in courting his customers, and decked out these establishments on upmarket sites with mahogany and glass fittings and electric lighting. Some shops in middle-class areas were even treated to fittings with mediaevalist touches. He was no less progres-

During the last quarter of the 19th century the great department stores such as Whiteleys, Selfridges and Harrods (above right) took on the role of "universal providers," merchandising everything from groceries to travelling cases and hat boxes (below).

sive in his advertising techniques. He quickly moved on from newspaper advertisements to hard-hitting show-business-style promotions imported from the States. In the 1890s he developed the firm's corporate image, used on all packaging and promotional material. It is still used today.

Department stores were another significant feature of Victorian retailing. Their development in Britain can be traced back to Madam Boucicaut's Bon Marché founded in Paris in 1852, and Macey's of New York founded in 1860. It was only in the 1880s that Britain saw a comparable development of large shops selling a great variety of goods in departments. Against the background of an extending transport network allowing easy access for those living in suburbs to the centre of cities, firms like Harrods in London grew from a small grocers to large retailing concerns.

Whiteley's of Bayswater was founded in 1863 by William Whitely. He had been greatly impressed by the Great Exhibition of 1851, and thought that the kind of experience evoked there could be brought to shopping. He wished to give it the character of a fashionable leisure activity. He sought to attract middle-class custom through a genteel approach to salesmanship: customers were never to be pestered by sales staff but informed and encouraged in their purchases. His empire expanded through the 1870s and 1880s: his staff grew from 15 to over 600, and he invested in four warehouses. Innumerable items were offered for sale, including drapery, jewellery, fashionable Japanese-style *objets d'art*. He offered a number of services to the public alongside the goods on display. After spending a pleasant half an hour in the refreshment room then having her hair styled, a Victorian lady could seek the advice of Whiteley's housing agency. Unfortunately, Whiteley and his store were dogged by bad luck. In the 1880s the building was badly damaged by a series of mysterious fires and in 1907 Whiteley himself was murdered in the store by a man claiming to be his son.

Department stores such as Swan and Edgar (far left) helped to democratize fashion. These 1840 summer fashions with their leg of mutton sleeves, cinched waists and wide skirts for the ladies contrast with the slimmer line of four decades later (left) though a narrow waist, achieved through the torture of whalebone corsetry, was still considered vital.

HIGH VICTORIAN FASHION

The Victorians were as involved in one 'battle of the styles' as any age before or since: the turns of fashion. Key characteristics of ornamental excess and invention, so notable in architecture and applied art, can also be seen in their clothes. Style was led by couturiers like Charles Worth, an Englishman who owned a salon in Paris patronized by Princess Eugènie and the leading figures of all the courts in Europe. As with most expressions of taste, Victorian fashion was formed in the upper levels of society and affected the most humble of working people.

Fashions changed as the Victorian world changed: in the economic revival after the 1840s, which had been a period of great hardship, women's dresses began to be made from lighter, brighter fabrics, waistlines rose, skirts became fuller and leg-o'-mutton sleeves, which had been tight at the wrist, began to fill again.

Dress also came to the attention of inventive Victorian minds. The quintessential silhouette of the mid-Victorian period was a tight bodice blossoming out from the hips into a bell-like voluminous skirt. This was achieved by the invention of a light dress frame made from steel hoops called the crinoline. Up to 35 steel springs increased in diameter as they reached the ground. The largest firm producing this fashionable accoutrement, W S and E H Thompson, became a multinational con-cern on the strength of their Crown crinoline. The crinoline replaced large numbers of stiffened petticoats lined with horse-hair which women had been wearing to achieve a fashionable form, despite their weight and discomfort. Its major disadvantage was considered to be that it occasionally tilted and revealed the ankles. Less socially gauche difficulties, such as the discomfort of sitting, were overcome with better materials and design.

The 1860s saw greater restraint in fashionable dress. The number of steel hoops was reduced to three or four at the bottom of the skirt. The bell-like shape evolved into a flat skirt front. In the later 1860s this shape, known as a half crinoline, became the bustle, a small frame attached to the lower back, which supported a pronounced mass of material often running into a long train.

As in architecture, Victorian dress was frequently historicist. In 1869 the *Englishwoman's Domestic Magazine*, a reliable index of fashionable taste, noted the comments of one fashionable couturier: 'Each lady comes to ask me not what is worn but what has not even yet been seen or worn . . . so I open an album of historic costumes and copy'.

In the 1880s, the 18th-century style of draped overskirts and tight-fitting bodices, associated with the marquises of the Pompadour period, were revived. But these were rarely pure historical re-creations, for the Victorians brought the character of their age to their costume. A full-skirted dress derived from 18th-century patterns, in a richly coloured fabric, would be decorated with machine-made embroidery and lace. Aniline dyes were discovered by Sir William Perkin in 1856 as a by-product of his researches for the new gas industry. Cloth manufacturers quickly realized their potential for producing brilliant colours such as mauve, magenta and a vivid pink.

Victorian fashions could be hazardous to women in various ways. The weight of the large number of petticoats placed a great stress on the pelvis. Numerous accounts circulated through society of women blown over cliffs in high winds. In a packed Santiago Cathedral in the 1860s, over 2,000 people died when a crinoline caught on fire, and people were unable to escape. Incredibly, narrow waistlines were considered so fashionable that some women went to extraordinary lengths to be in vogue. Tight lacing and corsetry were *de rigueur* in fashionable society. Waists of less than 20 inches were achieved at the cost of damage to internal organs. In 1895 two women are reported to have had ribs surgically removed to be able to wear narrower corsetry.

These trends in fashion dress prescribed delicate and ornamental roles for women in society. A long box-pleated train hanging from a bustle in a beautiful silk with applied decoration of floral motifs, not only indicated obvious wealth, but also leisure. Its owner always travelled by carriage, for such a train could never be allowed to drag the streets.

This ornamental vision of Victorian womanhood was reinforced by the jewellery and accessories so necessary for the maintenance of sartorial face. Elegant women would not be seen promenading without the appropriate paraphernalia: long gloves, monogrammed fans and ornate parasols made in rouched chiffon with lace flounces and ivory handles. Prestigious events in the social calendar demanded ostentatious displays of wealth. Aristocratic women were bedecked with flashing jewellery and accompanied their husbands like glittering symbols of accomplishment. For the very wealthy, even the most basic of accessories, such as hair grips, could be encrusted with diamonds or set with pearls. Such accoutrements were subject to turns in fashion, for example, at the beginning of Victoria's reign, *cannetile* jewellery was considered highly modish. It is a complex lacy goldwork, sometimes set with precious and semi-precious stones. In the 1880s taste had moved to more ostentatious, although less skilled, jewel-encrusted pieces based on simple shapes.

SUMMER FASHIONS for 1840, by B. READ & Cº 12, Hart Sʸ Bloomsbury Sqᵗ LONDON, & Broad Way, New York, AMERICA.

Much scorn was poured on working women who attempted to emulate the fashionable tastes of the leisured classes. The magazine *Punch* satirized working girls who adopted the crinoline, depicting a maid moving though a drawing room like a hurricane, her billowing skirt disturbing everything in its path. The lower classes appear not to have been inhibited by this. Cheap illustrated magazines showed what fashionable society was wearing and they sought to emulate it; skirts could be purchased, for example, with a band to hold the train up while a woman worked.

Against this background of highly impractical clothes, a number of attempts were made at dress reform. In 1851 an American, Amelia Bloomer, came to England proclaiming the merits of a sensible and not unfeminine costume known as bloomers. She proposed that women should wear a simple bodice, a wide skirt reaching just below the knee, and underneath that a pair of loose fitting trousers reaching to the ankles and tied with lace. This notion was derided by the British press and public. The greatest attempt at dress reform did not happen until the 1880s under the auspices of the Aesthetic Movement.

By the somewhat exaggerated standards of women's costume in the period, male dress in the Victorian period appears relatively practical. Although social convention wrapped masculine dress in strict social codes, where different occasions demanded particular costume, men were not greatly inhibited by the clothes they wore. The essential character of men's dress was in most respects little different from the formal dress of the 20th century. Lounge suits first worn in the 1850s, were a useful and comfortable style of dress. It is the fashionable accessories of the period that mark the characteristic Victorian differences in masculine fashion. Top hats, and silver- and ivory-topped canes have long since fallen out of use.

Victorian men appear to have allowed colourful novelty to enter their wardrobes in one respect: their waistcoats. Often known as 'fancy' waistcoats, these were fashionable until the 1870s when the three-piece-suit came to dominate taste. They were often decorated with lavish embroidery, figured silks with small patterns, or woven velvet. Under the influence of Prince Albert, tartan waistcoats became very popular in the 1850s.

VICTORIAN TOYS

Social historians have argued that children became visible in the late 18th century. In earlier ages they had simply been regarded as young adults. The Victorians created a picture of childhood as a time of innocence and wonderment that remains with us today. That they doted on their offspring is proven by the thousands of toys that they showered on them. A French observer wrote:

 They have an extraordinary regard in England for young children, always flattering, always caressing, always applauding what they do . . .

Victorian parents combined love for their children with a passion for education. The period marked the greatest development in the British educational system. By the end of the 1870s every child, however humble his or her origin, could expect to receive a rudimentary education. Similarly, homes across the country were filled with pedagogical toys such as building blocks and teaching board games imparting knowledge of the Empire or regal genealogy.

The doll was the essential Victorian toy for little girls. Producers brought to dollmaking all the characteristic Victorian inventiveness of their age. Dolls at the beginning of the young Queen's reign had wax modelled heads and rag bodies. The rich could import from Germany and France talking china manikins which exclaimed 'Mama', or 'shut-eye' dolls whose eyes would roll back when tilted. In the middle decades of the century manufacturers tried a number of different materials to bring the look of expensive china dolls to the growing middle class market, including papier-mâché. In the 1860s, they came up with an unglazed porcelain called bisque, which gave a matt surface and realistic appearance. Bisque dolls ranged from miniature princesses in ballgowns with elaborately looped hairstyles, to gardeners in green velvet jerkins with miniature tool kits. Around this time it also became fashionable to have little baby dolls with chubby faces and jointed limbs. The Victorian public were fascinated by dolls. Some of the most popular exhibits at the 1851 Great Exhibition were dolls made by a Parisian, Madam Augusta Montari.

Dolls' houses rank alongside dolls as Victorian toys of the first degree. These toys date back to the 16th century, and

LEFT *French clockwork doll (c. 1870) and English doll wearing ruched and flounced dress (c. 1840). Victorian dolls of this quality were dressed in up-to-the-minute fashions.*

LEFT *A Lutz-type, tinplate,
one horse sleigh made in Germany in the
1870's. German toys were very popular
in Britain for their skilful workmanship.
Here, a mechanism causes the horse to
dip realistically.
Girls amused themselves with dolls
(below left) and, if the family could
afford it, dolls' houses. (below) A
modern reproduction of the mid-19th
century German dolls' house used by
the Royal children at Osborne House.*

German craftsmen had built a great reputation for amazing inventiveness and attention to detail. In the 19th century, dolls' houses proved to be very popular and could be found in many Victorian nurseries. Young middle-class girls played out their future roles as mistresses of large households with them. These little homes were precise re-creations of Victorian domestic life: servants were ensconced in the attic; drawing rooms filled with scaled-down sets of Rococo chairs with tiny cabriole legs and authentic stuffed seats and in kitchens ovens would cast a glowing light over tiny sets of china neatly displayed on tall Chippendale-style dressers. These homes were populated with tiny 'poured wax' dolls dressed in authentic costumes, wearing tiny mohair wigs. English dolls' houses tended to be made in wood and followed the form of the Georgian townhouse; classical porches, painted red brick and tall facades. They opened at the rear to allow little hands to direct the lives of their inhabitants. Toward the end of the century, German dolls' house makers produced less expensive houses with paper facades that were exported throughout the world.

Just as girls' toys displayed the Victorians' domestic concerns, toys for boys displayed enthusiasm for technological

progress. The last quarter of the century saw the great rise of tinplate toys. Against the background of the massive growth in the railway system in Britain known as 'Railway Fever', young boys received tinplate locomotives as birthday and Christmas presents. These beautiful scaled-down models of the great trains and carriages of the Great Western Railway or the London, Midland and Scotland Railway, were correct in every detail, including their richly coloured liveries. Again, German skill proved far superior to that of British toymakers, and the best of these toys were made by the firm of Marklin. They produced railway masterpieces complete with miniature tracks and signals.

Toy soldiers often populated the other shelves of nursery cupboards. Originating in Germany in the 1870s, these tiny

tin armies soon invaded Britain and the rest of the world. Britain responded by producing superior cast figures authentically painted in regimental colours.

American toys became popular in Europe in the last decades of the 19th century. They often displayed a wittier character than many of their European equivalents. American ingenuity produced many wind-up and mechanical toys in tin, such as circus merry-go-rounds, walking toys, and mechanical money boxes. In return, the German toy industry exported colonial-style dolls' houses to the States, playing on American picturesque sensibilities.

FLOODS OF PRINT

If a pressman working in a small printing office at the turn of the 19th century had been transported in time to the end of Victoria's rule, he would not have recognized his trade. Encouraged by the growth of literacy, the repeal of the 'taxes on knowledge', and the demands of magazine publishers and manufacturers who wished to promote and package their products, this industry underwent a dramatic technological transformation. *The Times* newspaper, in the 1810s, was printed by skilled pressmen on two small iron-framed hand-presses, 65 years later it was produced on a gigantic steam-powered Walter Press watched over by an unskilled machine minder. The catalogue of innovations in 19th-century printing is impressive. In 1851 lithographic printing received a great boost from Georg Sigl, an Austrian engineer, who patented a machine which could print 800 to 1,000 coloured sheets an hour; in the 1870s a number of inventors developed off-set lithographic techniques which increased production rates many times. Similarly in type setting attempts were made to speed up labour intensive methods. In the 1840s, Young and Delcambre from Lille built a machine called the *Pianotyp*

ABOVE *Crandall's menagerie, a painted wood American toy of 1874. Detachable parts meant that a variety of hybrid animals could be constructed.*

RIGHT *The toy train made its first appearance in the Victorian era . . .*

FLOODS OF PRINT

Invented in 1798 by Alois Sennenfelder, lithography was further
developed to print colour to replace the expense of laborious handcolouring. From
1840, with the publication of the first colour sheet music covers, chromolithography
was employed for posters, cards, invitations and book illustrations.
The printers' skill can be seen in the variety of effects achieved. The "Louise
Quadrille" cover (below) and the "Crystal Falls Waltz," both by the celebrated
graphic artist Alfred Concanen c.1880–90, could appear hand drawn to the
untutored eye. So rapid were advances that the "British Isles March" of c.1870
(below right), cannot match the quality of this programme for Gilbert and Sullivan's
"The Gondoliers" (below left) of two decades later.

RIGHT Woodcut techniques were still used, as seen in this "Puss in Boots" pantomime poster.

LEFT Jules Cheret (1836–1932) began the French vogue for art posters in the 1860s. The glowing colours and immense verve of his lithographic work is unmistakable.

which could set over 6,000 characters an hour compared to 500 by a skilled compositor.

Newspapers and magazines were the primary beneficiaries of these radical innovations. They reduced costs, increased print runs and brought graphic images to a public hungry for vivid depictions of the dramatic news stories of the day; wars, sordid court cases and national disasters. The Victorian era saw the great days of illustrated journalism and the weekly *Illustrated London News*, founded in May 1842, was the king of them all. It specialized in visual hyperbole and sensational stories. In its first edition the leading article described 'The Great Fire of Hamburg', and was illustrated with a woodcut copied from an old print of the city augmented with clouds of smoke and raging flames. *The Illustrated London News* employed artists who recorded important events, such as royal visits and international exhibitions. Their sketches were then worked up as elaborate and careful woodcuts by highly skilled wood engravers, pre-eminently John Gilbert and Walter Wilson. An average of 1,500 graphic images were produced in this magazine every year. It was so successful that it was followed by a host of competitors including *The Graphic* which was founded in December 1869. In the 1880s both journals began to incorporate photographic images as illustrations for their news items and the highly skilled trade of wood engraving began to decline.

Another, less auspicious kind of news sheet was popular with the Victorian public, which has become known as the Penny Dreadful. In the time-old tradition of chap books, these slight reports of licentious happenings and sordid crimes satisfied voyeuristic appetites. Victorian readers, or even those who were unable to read and bought them simply for their graphic content, were able to enjoy the horrors of tales like 'The Murder of Eliza Short late of Shoreditch who was strangled by a masked man', published in 1864.

This taste for the macabre received official sanction in *The Illustrated Police News* which reported dramatic and violent crimes with graphic accounts of dastardly deeds. The attempted murder of Mrs Moratti by her husband was illustrated in the May 1865 edition of the paper with a woodcut of a naked woman, her throat gashed and bleeding, fleeing across the roof tops of Hackney pursued by her husband.

Equal inventiveness was applied to advertising material in this period. In characteristically Victorian fashion, posters and publicity material were densely laid out and typographically busy. The 'Egyptian', 'Antique' and 'fat faced' types first used in the 1810s and 1820s, came to prominence in the Victorian period. Advertisers quickly realized the advantages of these bold letterforms which grabbed the attention of potential customers. In the mid years of the century a great variety of

different display typefaces were designed. Commerce increasingly employed specially engraved wooden letters to bring novelty to their promotional material. Handbills announcing a local cattle market, for example, would be printed with types decorated with farmyard tools and animals.

Newspapers were the primary advertising media employed by manufacturers, despite the reluctance of the newspaper proprietors themselves. In the early years of the 19th century they placed strict restrictions upon these public communications. Although the whole front page of newspapers of the time were given over to public notices and advertisements, these conservative proprietors felt that illustrated notices, broken columns or the use of larger, bold typefaces would give unfair advantage to the companies that used them. Ingenious advertisers thought up eye-catching ways of getting round these restrictions such as repeating the same notice down the entire length of a column. These restrictions were slowly relaxed though the century and woodcut illustrations began to surface in the classified pages of newspapers. The most notable example of this occurred in the 1820s when the English artist, George Cruikshank, was employed by the firm producing Warren's Shoe Blacking to design an illustration of a cat with its hackles raised standing before a black riding boot. This image was printed above a 32 line verse called *Ned Capstan, or a Land-Cruise Postponed*, extolling the merits of this product in a number of newspapers of the day.

Toward the end of Victoria's reign, manufacturers found other ways to promote their products. The most important of these was branding. Some of the best known products today owe their identity to anonymous graphic designers in the late

LEFT AND RIGHT *The Valentine card, a Victorian invention, was often decorated with flowers, intended to impart volumes to the initiate of "the language of the flowers."*

BELOW LEFT *Greetings cards grew more elaborate as the century drew to a close, a testament to increasing mechanization as these pierced wedding and souvenir cards demonstrate (below right).*

19th century who produced striking packaging for everyday items. It is hard to visualize a Coca-Cola bottle now without thinking of its curvilinear bottle, or of Cadbury's chocolate or the firm of Boot's, founded by James Boot in 1850, without remembering their famous calligraphic logos. This iconography was reinforced by newspaper advertisements and posters that often simply depicted the product, little more was needed to register in the subconscious of 19th-century consumers.

Handbills were also a key advertising medium for Victorian commerce. People walking through the streets of London would have hundreds of sheets of paper pressed on them urging attendance at choral concerts or abstinence from alcohol, persuading them to see 'the miraculous giantess' or exhibitions at the Royal Academy. One late-Victorian recorded collecting over 30 such bills on a short morning stroll through Holborn. Sandwichboard men were also a characteristic feature of Victorian street life. William Smith, the manager of the New Adelphi theatre, in promoting Watts Philip's play, *The Dead Heart* in 1859, had five million handbills printed and distributed, and employed men to walk around the streets of the capital carrying heart-shaped boards.

Phineas Taylor Barnum, the greatest circus leader of the 19th century who greatly entertained the Queen when he

brought the Barnum and Bailey Circus to London in the 1880s, was a master of hyperbolic advertising. His use of trumpeting 'fat' typefaces echoed the fanfare style of his posters. 'WHAT IS IT? MAN OR MONKEY' questioned one such poster in 1861 in letters six inches high.

The shaded, florid, and three-dimensional faces for these bold advertisements were to the distaste of this traditionalist who lamented the Victorian pursuit of novelty. He wrote:

> The chaste and dignified black letter and Old Face sprouted horns and were dishonoured. They bellied out into obesity, they were eviscerated and herring-gutted; they thickened to Dorics, shrieked to hysterics, shrank to hairlines. The world of Caslon and Baskerville, Janson and Boldoni and Aldus became the world of Caliban.

Lithography was a revolutionary colour printing technique developed in the 1790s by Aloys Senefelder in Munich. It was a highly elaborate process which was slowly refined over the course of the century so that by the 1890s artists in France, such as Jules Cheret and Henri Toulouse-Lautrec were able to exploit its graphic fluidity to produce great works of poster art. But in the High Victorian period it must be noted that one field of commercial graphic art utilized this technique to great effect; the song sheet. In fact, Senefelder developed the art of lithography expressly to produce attractive song sheets. They first appeared in Britain in 1840, and by the middle of the century a number of graphic artists had built their reputations on the strength of their designs for music covers. One of the most prolific, Alfred Concanen, produced witty caricatures of Victorian characters; music hall singers such as George Leybourne known as 'Champagne Charlie', one-man-bands, dandies and fops. The letterings used for the song titles were often beautiful examples of Victorian taste; highly florid and ornamental.

The establishment of the penny postage system in the 1840s by Roland Hill enabled Victorian Britain to become the first society to celebrate anniversaries and special occasions with greeting cards. Henry Cole inaugurated this tradition when he asked the painter J C Horsley to design a Christmas card in 1843. This 'new' tradition established itself so quickly that by the 1880s the Post Office had to make its first appeal to post early for Christmas. In contrast, the tradition of sending Valentine cards was a genuinely old one. Despite being married, Samuel Pepys recorded in his diary sending gifts on 14th of February to the object of his affections, Sir William Batton's daughter. 19th-century conventions demanded not the sending of gifts but rather the despatch of written messages of love. Printers in dark back streets produced thousands of sentimental cards with glowing verses like:

> How can I want the love to grant.
> And thou so kindly pressing,
> I am thine own, my dearest one
> Scorn not this heart confessing.

In their design these cards were no less sweet, decorated with flowing floral borders, cupids and putti, doves and ribbons and lace. Churches, not surprisingly, were popular motifs, for whilst Pepys' motives may have been somewhat less than honourable, the Victorian mind was bound by a strict sense of moral propriety, (publicly at least).

VICTORIAN FUNEREAL CULTURE

The Victorian age was a highly romantic one, and there was no greater expression of this than in attitudes toward death. They created a complete funereal world in architecture, dress, and social codes. Queen Victoria herself was the main protagonist in this grand theatre, spending virtually the whole of the 1860s in mourning for her husband, Albert. She became nationally known as the 'Widow of Windsor', and spent the rest of her long life surrounded by mementoes of their two decades together.

Funerals of national figures gave the public the opportunity to participate in this grand pageantry. The extraordinary funeral of the Duke of Wellington, a national hero and a legend to the troops that had served under him, was one such affair. He died in November 1852 and was laid in state for one week before his burial. On the first day the public were admitted, three people were killed in the crush, such was the clamour to see this subject of national veneration. On the last day, 65,073 people filed past his body in the Chelsea Hospital.

The procession began in the early morning of the 18th of November, 1852 from Buckingham Palace. It was led by six battalions of infantry, followed by five squadrons of cavalry. The slow pace of the procession was marked by military bands playing death marches and dirges. The stately funeral car, designed by Prince Albert and Gottfried Semper, was majestic. Decorated with Renaissance-style forms such as dolphins, heraldic devices and ornamental militaria, it was was 27 feet long, made from bronze and weighed over ten tons. The Duke's coffin was covered with a silver pall and lay on a guilded bier. It took 12 horses to pull it through the streets of London.

In the drizzling rain, tens of thousands lined the route of the funeral cortège leading to St Paul's Cathedral. The Times

Model of the Duke of Wellington's funeral car, specially constructed
for the Great Man's state funeral, 18 November 1852. The original cost £11,000,
weighed approximately ten tons, measured 27 ft long by 10 ft broad with a height of
17 ft and was drawn by twelve black horses harnessed three abreast.

The monument to the Duke of Wellington by Alfred Stevens (1818–75) in St Pauls Cathedral. The victor of Waterloo is depicted in heroic equestrian pose atop a marble architectural conceit of sombre classicism, flanked by allegorical figures of Valour and Cowardice

newspaper reflected the pitch of feeling when it stated: 'It was impossible to convey any idea of the emotion felt by the nation, nothing like it had ever been manifested before'. As the cortège passed the thronging crowds, who had travelled from all over the country, all the men present doffed their hats as a sign of respect.

Inside St Paul's 1,800 people were packed into the naves and aisles. Here the pageantry intensified, with the Duke's coffin followed by his insignia, his spurs borne on a velvet cushion by York Herald, his sword and target by Leicester Herald, his surcoat by Chester Herald, and his coronet by Clarenceux King of Arms. The final act of this grand perform-

ance was when the Duke's Comptroller broke Wellington's staff into pieces and Garter King of Arms laid them in the grave, at which point guns fired across London.

It is interesting to note that the Queen, while approving of the pomp and ceremony of this event, disapproved of 'black' funerals, in which every element of the ceremony was covered in black crepe. Even Temple Bar, the entrance to the City, was entirely cloaked in this fashion, at Albert's behest. Her own funeral, in 1901, which she planned down to the minutest detail, was to be a cheerful event. The pall covering her coffin was white and gold, and the streets of London were bedecked in purple cashmere and white satin.

The importance attached to state funerals was almost matched by the consecration of lesser individuals. It was commonly thought necessary 'to provide silver-plate handles of the very best description, ornamented with angels' heads from the most expensive dies. To be perfectly profuse in feathers. In short, to turn out something absolutely gorgeous'.

Funerals were excellent opportunities for conspicuous displays of wealth and status. Even the lower classes placed great store in having a 'decent' ceremony. One writer estimated that nationally over £4 million was spent on funerals a year in the 1850s, a very great sum at that time.

Strict social codes were established concerning mourning. *Sylvia's Home Journal*, for example, advised its readers that a period of 21 months was the appropriate length of time for a mother to be in mourning for a dead child. A widow was expected to spend an even longer period dressed in black and wearing mourning jewellery. Although visible expressions of grief were to be found in all ages, the Victorian period took this phenomenon to new heights. It was not unheard of for a woman to be married in a black wedding dress should a period of mourning coincide with her wedding. Mourning was divided into stages so that the immediately bereaved would be expected to wear the plainest and darkest of costumes and those further into their period of mourning were able to wear greys, striped silks in black and white, and a greater range of trimmings. Bonnets, capes and shawls were considered appropriate items of mourning dress as they encouraged modesty. Whole industries sprang up to supply the accoutrements of grief. The Whitby producers of jet, a black semi-precious stone, prospered through the fashion for mourning jewellery. A 'Mourning Warehouse' owned by Peter Robinson in London's Regent Street kept 'garments in stock for every degree'.

Cemeteries and graveyards also received much Victorian attention. This was a most religious of ages and some objected to the use of classical, ie pagan, decorative forms in Christian memorials. The Gothic ideologue, Pugin, thundered: 'If we worshipped Jupiter, or more Votaries of Juggernaut, we would

Highgate cemetery boasts a mixture of funerary architectural styles, ranging from Ptolemaic Egyptian of the catacombs (below) and obelisks to the severe classicism of sculpture urns and sarcophagi.

raise a temple, or erect a pagoda. If we believed in Mahomet, we should display the crescent, and raise a mosque'.

He drew the conclusion that the only appropriate form was the cross, and advocated the revival of mediaeval forms.

All forms of mementoes were used to remember the dead. Little girls would be expected to stitch epitaphs on samplers, and memorial cards would be framed and hung above the hearth. The Victorians' fascination with death can also be seen in less venerable items. It was traditional for apprentice carpenters to make a small coffin, to be used as a tool box, as their first task. This also proved to be a popular shape for other small functional boxes, such as snuff and powder containers.

CRITICS OF VICTORIAN TASTE

ABOVE *James McNeill Whistler, an American trained in Paris, was instrumental in bringing the influence of French Impressionism to England. With its emphasis on mood and atmosphere* Nocturne: Blue and Gold *(1872–75) moves away from the anecdotal tradition of Victorian painting.*

uring the Victorian period there were many critics of society and its values. Challenges were issued to every aspect of 19th-century life. Thomas Carlyle, in his book *Past and Present* of 1843, related the development of the industrial revolution to the erosion of spirituality that he saw around him. Charles Dickens criticised many facets of Victorian society from housing to the legal system.

Artists, designers and architects played a significant role in this attack on Victorian values. It is possible to find challenges in every area of art, design and industry, issued to Victorian orthodoxy. The tight-laced corset and the bustle were met by the long, freely-flowing robes of the dress reformers. Commercial retailing derived from American selling techniques found their aesthetic equivalent in Liberty's in Regent Street which sold the fashionable and exotic. The advertising posters in bold fancy types on the streets of every city were quietly attacked by William Morris and his Kelmscott Press. The great symbol of Victorian comfort, the deeply upholstered, wing-backed 'Grandfather' armchair found its match in the great icon of the Victorian domestic revival, a Morris and Co. rush-seated, ladder-backed Sussex chair. Even colours were immediately recognizable as belonging to one side of Victorian society or another: newly invented aniline dyes which gave rich purples and green reeked too strongly of Victorian commerce and industry for their critics, who preferred natural dyes produced by traditional means or gentle pastel hues.

WILLIAM MORRIS

The seeds of dissent were sewn early in Victoria's reign with the highly moralist writings of figures such A W N Pugin and John Ruskin. As shown in earlier chapters William Morris was strongly persuaded by their anti-machine age philosophies. He proved to be a great influence both as a theorist of design and as a practising designer. Proposing an art for the people, produced by the people, he rallied against Victorian industrial production which had achieved pre-eminence in the world at the cost of great ugliness and bad taste. As a socialist he believed that in promoting vernacular craft skills, he would restore to the working man his dignity, and to everyday objects the natural ease which they had possessed in years gone by.

Morris's practice and philosophy is complex and his ambitions were rarely realized. The Firm's designs of the 1860s in

LIBERTY FURNITURE

Though fortunes of Liberty & Co. were initially based on the vogue for Japonaiserie, the company soon branched into other exotic decorative items. Moorish style oak furniture with mushrabiya fretwork of c.1880 (below opposite) was followed four years later by the "Thebes" stool (opposite left), based on Egyptian originals in the British Museum. By the end of the century the Celtic revival was inspiring designers such as Archibald Knox, responsible for this earthenware jardinière (left).

RIGHT The "Sussex" chair, a traditional rush-seated armchair of ebonized beechwood by Philip Webb, was a popular Morris design. Much of the later furniture for the Firm was designed by George Jack, Webb's former assistant, including this dining table from the 1890s (below).

In 1881, two years after Morris had set up at Merton Abbey, he patented 17 printed cotton designs including "Wey" (far left) and the still popular "Strawberry Thief." "Medway" (left) was designed and registered in 1885.

BELOW *Marquetry escritoire and stand designed by George Jack for Morris & Co. in 1889.*

fabric and stained glass were resolutely Morrisian, but in the 1870s the will appeared to falter. Under commercial pressure they produced hundreds of wallpaper and fabric designs which became increasingly florid and detailed. Chintzes such as Honeysuckle of 1875, and Wey of the early 1880s, appear to be concessions to public taste. Morris's silks were produced by mainstream producers such as the firm of Nicholson's, and his carpets by Wilton and Axminster, none of whom paid much heed to arguments against the division of labour. Similarly, Morris's pleasing embroideries of the late 1870s were not made by Morris and his friends but put out to skilled embroiderers. Despite his ideas about bringing together art and craft, only one of the craftsmen employed by the Firm progressed to becoming a designer for them. But Morris was always concerned with the nature of the work he expected his craftsmen to perform. He encouraged the hand knotting techniques of tapestry making, for example, because he believed that they allowed the worker more artistic freedom.

Morris's designs, despite his dearly held ambitions to improve the lot of the working classes by raising the standard of design in all areas of life, remained the province of the aristocratic and the rich. Morris put this much more graphically, regarding his career as 'ministering to the swinish luxury of the rich'.

After Morris took up politics in 1883, joining the Democratic Federation led by H M Hyndman, his attitude to industrial production shifted. Looking around at the soul destroying factories producing shoddy and showy products, but realizing that the benefits of good design through craftsmanship could not be afforded by the majority of society, he advocated a highly restricted use of machinery. In books like *News from*

Nowhere he painted a visionary picture of a world in which machines ran for four hours a day in factories bordered by beautiful gardens filled with sculpture. He envisaged a society free of the conspicuous consumption of Victorian materialism where the values of education and goodwill would dominate.

Although Morris's designs were only to be found in the homes of the affluent and fashionable in late 19th-century Britain, his impact on the development of art and design was enormous. Morris's thought and practice were the primary inspiration behind the avant-garde of the 1880s; the Arts and Crafts Movement. This loose alliance of artists, craftsmen and designers united around a twin asethetic and social philosophy, based on the importance of making.

RIGHT *Handmade carpets, known as "Hammersmith rugs" to distinguish them from machine-made carpets manufactured by Morris & Co., were highly labour intensive.*

BELOW *The Green Dining Room designed by Webb in 1866 for the South Kensington Museum was a tremendous success. The stained glass and wall paintings were by Burne-Jones, the polychrome raised gesso decoration by Webb, embroidered screen by Morris and his wife, and the piano was decorated by Kate Faulkner.*

THE ARTS AND CRAFTS MOVEMENT

The Arts and Crafts Movement gathered momentum with the formation of the Century Guild in 1882 by Arthur Heygate Mackmurdo and Selwyn Image. Mackmurdo had travelled through Italy in 1874 with John Ruskin as his companion and assistant, and had absorbed much of his social and aesthetic ideology. This can be seen in the development of his career, for, although trained as an architect, he had spent much time working in the East End of London with the poor. As an architect he aimed to design, build and furnish complete buildings down to the minutest of details: from the whole façade down to each key hole. He lamented the decline of the guild system of the Middle Ages which would have presented the corporate means with which to do this. He resolved to form his own guild of like-minded people who could work together to evolve a collective style. His Century Guild was constituted by Selwyn Image, a poet and designer; Herbert Horne, a designer of fabrics and wallpapers; Clement Heaton, who specialized in cloisonné enamel work; and George Heywood Sumner, who was renowned for his *sgraffito* designs, a pottery technique in which a surface glaze is scratched away to reveal bright colours.

The Century Guild aimed to turn design into art, overturning the prevailing aesthetic hierarchy. Their collective aim was 'to render all branches of art the sphere of not the tradesman but the artist'. They promoted their aesthetic philosophies through their journal *Hobby Horse* which was first published in 1884. They believed that art was too important to be hidden away in the private world of salons and the academies and wished to see it in everyday things. The Guild had its first opportunity to do this at Pownawy Hall in Chesire, when H Boddington commissioned them to design all the furnishings and fittings there.

The Century Guild aimed to develop an aesthetic that was appropriate to their own time. They rejected the historicism of Victorian art and architecture in favour of an artistic language derived from nature. This was a major departure in the late Victorian period. Although William Morris had designed simple patterns for wallpapers and fabrics in the 1860s that were derived from natural forms, his work always carried traces of historic languages. His later works, for example the books produced by the Kelmscott Press founded in 1891, maintained a Gothic character. In contrast, Mackmurdo, under the auspices of the Century Guild designed some of the most strikingly original works of the century. His title page for his *Wren's City Churches* published by G Allen in 1883, is remarkable for

its use of undulating and whiplashing floral motifs which prefigured Art Nouveau. This was not an isolated incident in Mackmurdo's design *œuvre* for in the early 1880s he designed a chair for the firm of Collison and Lock, the back of which employs brilliantly composed twisting plant forms.

A H Mackmurdo was in many respects quite unlike most of his Arts and Crafts contemporaries who were often rather serious and dour. With a flamboyant and colourful character he was somewhat closer in temperament to figures associated with the Aesthetic Movement of the 1880s and was in fact friendly with James Abbott McNeill Whistler, the painter and renowned dandy.

The conscientious core of the Arts and Crafts Movement was found in The Art Workers Guild founded in 1884 and which was later absorbed into the Arts and Crafts Exhibition Society of 1888. The Guild included some of the leading designers of the day including Lewis F Day, W R Lethaby, John D Sedding and Walter Crane. They held similar ambitions to Morris and their colleagues in Mackmurdo's Century Guild, aiming to revive the decorative arts by improving standards of design and craftsmanship. With the formation of the Arts and Crafts Exhibition Society they sought collectively to challenge the Victorian art and design establishments of the Royal Academy and the Royal Institute of British Architects. A

RIGHT *Walter Crane's "Margarete" wallpaper designed for Geoffrey & Co in 1876. Crane was later to become an influential member of the Arts and Crafts movement.*

LEFT *An oak wardrobe in the revived Queen Anne Style by Gilbert Olgilvie for the Guild of Handicraft, the co-operative group of artist-craftsmen founded by Ashbee in 1888.*

BELOW *This oak cabinet by CFA Voysey exemplifies the restraint and simplicity of much Arts and Crafts furniture.*

OPPOSITE *English Oak writing desk designed by Arthur Heygate Mackmurdo and made by the Century Guild, c. 1886.*

series of exhibitions were held in the late 1880s and 1890s, displaying works by the most able designers and artists to the public. Sharing Morris's belief in the indivisible unity of the arts, they aimed to show the fine arts alongside decorative objects, so that paintings by Walter Crane, or a youthful Roger Fry could be found hanging alongside an elegant brass teapot designed by Charles Francis Annesley Voysey.

C R Ashbee's Guild of Handicraft of 1888 was the last of the Arts and Craft guilds of the 19th century and appropriately it held the most complete vision of Arts and Crafts life. Ashbee developed his ideas as a teacher of Ruskinian philosophy in a working men's college in Whitechapel in the 1880s. He devised the idea of a pedagogical guild in which young men would be taught to design in a number of fields including cabinet-making, coppersmithing and lithography. Their designs would then be produced in workshops by craftsmen and sold to the public. The revenue from these sales would finance the organization. This system of production was to be established as a direct challenge to 'the unintelligent ocean of competitive industry'. In 1902, after 12 years based in the East End of London, Ashbee moved the Guild, the Guildsmen and their families to Chipping Camden in the heart of the Gloucestershire countryside. Here, 150 men, women and children established a communal life based on the values of hard work and wholesome living. But the scheme failed under the economic pressure to sell their lovely furniture, ceramic and metal ware to a late Victorian market that was not satisfied with such well made works of simple beauty.

THE ARTS AND CRAFTS INFLUENCE

C S Ashbee and his Guild achieved greater fame on the European continent than at home. In 1897 the Grand Duke of Hesse commissioned designs from C S Ashbee and Mackay Hugh Baillie Scott, which were made by the Guild of Handicraft. Both men stayed in his Darmstadt residence, to design two rooms. Influenced by their Arts and Crafts philosophy, the Duke then proceeded to form his own artists' colony in Darmstadt along the lines of Guild of Handicraft. He employed some of the leading artists, architects and designers of the day including Joseph Maria Olbrich and Peter Behrens.

Another group of artists and designers influenced by the philosophy of the Arts and Crafts was the *Wiener Werkstatte* (Viennese Workshops) formed by Joseph Hoffman and Koloman Moser in 1903. Their 1905 manifesto stated:

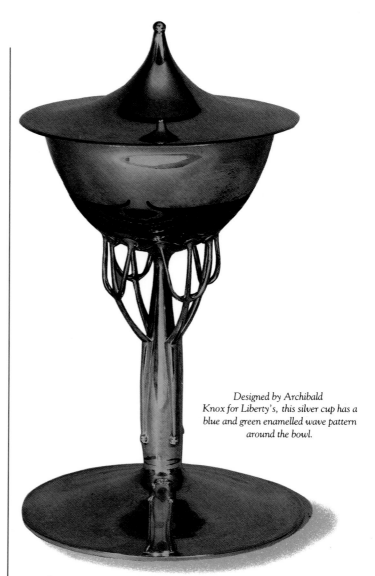

Designed by Archibald Knox for Liberty's, this silver cup has a blue and green enamelled wave pattern around the bowl.

 We have founded our own workshop. Our aim is to create an island of tranquility in our own country, which, amid the joyful hum of the arts and crafts, would be welcome to anyone who professes a faith in Ruskin and Morris.

Morris and Ruskin's influence was also to be found in America. There, figures like Frank Lloyd Wright took Arts and Crafts' themes and fixations and developed a visionary design practice that anticipated Modernist design of the 20th century. In his early buildings such as the Winslow House of 1893 and designs for furniture in the last years of the 19th century he developed a stark, undecorated design aesthetic. Despite his own home, which appears from photographs to have been rather cluttered in the Victorian style, he designed low houses with open plans and plain unornamented furnishings that are described by architectural historians as the Prairie Style. His highly abstract and geometric stained glass designs, for example, at the Dana House in Springfield, Illinois of 1902, pre-date design trends of the 1930s.

ART NOUVEAU

The English Arts and Crafts Movement was also a major inspiration behind Art Nouveau, the leading movement in art and design in the late 1890s and early years of the 20th century in continental Europe. Leading Art Nouveau figures, such as Henri van de Velde and Victor Horta in Belgium, Louis C Tiffany in America, Hector Guimard in France, Stanislaw Wyspianski in Poland, and Peter Behrens and Richard Reimerschmid in Germany, all owed debts of varying degrees to the English Arts and Crafts Movement. Stylistic precedents for Art Nouveau can be found in British design of the 1880s, for example, in the Gothic architect William Burges' own house built in Kensington between 1875 and 1880 and A H Mackmurdo's works described above. But more importantly, the Arts and Crafts Movement raised the status of applied art from that of a commercial trade to an art form.

In England Art Nouveau was widely dismissed by practitioners because it lacked the critical social philosophy, so crucial to the Arts and Crafts Movement. Walter Crane, the socialist graphic designer, spoke for many when he sneeringly described it as a 'decorative disease'.

Very few British artists and designers came close to the Art Nouveau spirit found on the continent. Those few that did were even more antithetical to the Victorian age than their sober Arts and Crafts colleagues who at least preached the values of hard work and national form. To compare the qualities found in the designs by Charles Rennie Mackintosh, a Scottish designer associated with European Art Nouveau, with those found in the work of Ernest Gimson, a figure in the mainstream of the Arts and Crafts Movement, is revealing. The Arts and Crafts Movement is beautifully summarized in Ernest Gimson's masterly furniture, simple and solid works, barely decorated and in a near functional style drawn from the materials used and the method of construction. In contrast, Mackintosh's designs are enigmatic and highly aesthetic. His sculptural pieces of furniture were decorated with symbolic motifs, mother of pearl and ivory inlays, and painted; all anathema to English Arts and Crafts thought.

Another British artist widely associated with Art Nouveau, although never part of the mainstream of the movement, and much admired by progressive tastes all over the world was Aubrey Beardsley. His reputation in the history of art was largely secured for his illustrations for Oscar Wilde's *Salome*

Beardsley's designs for the Yellow Book covers introduced a new illustrative style which featured heavy black masses, evidence, once again of the oriental influence.

LEFT AND BELOW *Mackintosh's creative employment of organic forms, in particular his imaginative use of metalwork and stained glass seen here in the doors to the Willow Tea Rooms (left), and his furniture (below) had a tremendous influence on the development of European Art Nouveau.*

OPPOSITE *Design for a dado by Walter Crane.*

and a journal entitled *The Yellow Book* in 1894. His black and white drawings, populated with strange characters and bizarre plants composed with large areas of blank space in the Japanese style, caused much indignation when first published. Their unconventional eroticism scandalized polite society. Beardsley was associated with a circle of *fin de siècle* artists and writers and his work often contained sly caricatures of them. His tailpiece for Wilde's *Salome*, for example, depicted Max Beerbohm, the author of *Zulieka Dobson*, as a foetus and Whistler, the American painter, as a faun.

Whistler was a controversial figure in Victorian society. He shocked Victorian mores with his public affairs, dashing dandyfied dress and his sardonic wit. He began his career as a navy cartographer and travelled to Paris in the 1850s. There he came under the sway of radical French painters such as Henri Fantin-Latour and Edgar Degas and joined their number by exhibiting at the *Salon des Refuses* in 1863. In his enigmatic canvases he rejected the emphasis in Victorian art on subject matter, be it sentimental, moral or patriotic, for a pure aestheticism that celebrated formal qualities. His celebrated painting, a portrait of his mother in profile, is better known by its subtitle *The Artist's Mother*, than its revealing title *Arrangement in Grey and Black*. Ruskin, who dominated orthodox art criticism by the late 1870s, described Whistler's sublime painting *Nocturne in Black and Gold* as a 'pot of paint' flung 'in the public's face'. The painter responded by issuing a writ for libel in 1878. Although Whistler won the court case, the judge summed up the public mood by awarding damages of only one farthing, the smallest possible amount. Whistler was bankrupted by the legal costs.

In the 1880s Whistler was the magnetic centre of a decadent circle in Chelsea that incurred the wrath of late Victorian morality. His friend Oscar Wilde was imprisoned for his sexual behaviour and Frank Miles, a wealthy friend and aesthete went mad and died in an asylum in 1891.

Despite the somewhat clouded picture we have of trends in art and design in the late 19th century, partly as a result of the character of its leading practitioners, the dominating concern was to find solutions to the problem of Victorian style. In turning away from historicism and conspicuous excess, these artists and designers pointed towards the 20th century. In this respect, even Walter Gropius, the founder of the radical Bauhaus school of architecture and design in Germany in the 1920s and a leading proponent of Modern Movement in design, owed a debt to William Morris and his followers.

Futhermore, these late 19th-century movements were concerned with larger issues than just style. They issued a challenge to Victorian society and its dearly held values. For Ashbee and the Guild of Handicraft, this entailed a considered retreat into communal living, and for others it took the less reasoned form of displays of decadence designed to shock middle-class morals.

To Queen Victoria and her husband Prince Albert, Victorian style, as found in the best British works at the Great Exhibition of 1851 or in the paintings by such artists as Edwin Landseer, confirmed the success of their age. They were like jewels on the crown of Victorian achievement. At the end of the century, Victoria's grandson, Ernst Ludwig, the Grand Duke of Hesse, looked to the English designers Baillie Scott and Ashbee to point towards a new world. Above the entrance to his artists' colony, intended as the cornerstone of a new utopian city, were the words:

 Let the artist show his world that which has never been nor will be.

RIGHT *Ernest Gimson, a disciple of William Morris produced furniture characteristic of the arts and crafts ideal, such as this walnut cabinet with ebony base.*

PICTURE CREDITS

KEY: **t** = top; **l** = left; **b** = bottom; **c** = center; **r** = right.

INDEX

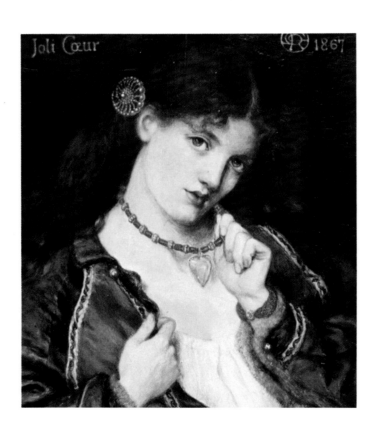